Llamas, Weavings, and Organic Chocolate

For a complete list of titles from the Helen Kellogg Institute for International Studies, see http://www.undpress.nd.edu

Llamas, Weavings, and Organic Chocolate

Multicultural Grassroots Development in the Andes and Amazon of Bolivia

Kevin Healy

UNIVERSITY OF NOTRE DAME PRESS

Notre Dame, Indiana

Manufactured in the United States of America

Library of Congress Cataloging-in-Publication Data
Healy, Kevin.
    Llamas, weavings, and organic chocolate : multicultural grassroots development
in the Andes and Amazon of Bolivia / Kevin Healy.
        p.   cm.
    "Recent titles from the Helen Kellogg Institute for International Studies."
    Includes bibliographical references and index.
    ISBN 0-268-01326-8 (pbk. : alk. paper)
    1. Rural development projects—Bolivia.   2. Cultural animation—Bolivia.
3. Indians of South America—Bolivia—Social conditions.   4. Indians of South
America—Bolivia—Economic conditions.   I. Title: Multicultural grassroots
development in the Andes and Amazon of Bolivia.   II. Helen Kellogg Institute
for International Studies.   III. Title.
HN280.Z9 C644   2001
307.1′412′0984—dc21   00-056801

∞ *This book is printed on acid-free paper.*

Contents

Preface

This book tells a story of development in Bolivia through the presentation of a range of grassroots development experiences from across the country. The stories serve as a documentary account of the sea change that is taking place in Bolivia and among large international development agencies. Bolivia, like most developing countries around the world, strove for decades to imitate Western and particularly U.S. methods of development, importing wholesale programs and the latest technologies, institutions, crops, food, and livestock from the West. Yet Bolivia's social and economic inequalities kept growing. Moreover, the imported methods took a grave toll on the environment, which contributed to the deterioration of the carrying capacity of rural farms. Finally beginning in the 1970s, faced with many striking instances of failure in the application of the Western modernization paradigm, diverse sectors of Bolivian civil society turned inward to rediscover the country's own multicultural identities and agrarian wisdom as sources of strength upon which to build development. This shift spawned a proliferation of development projects grounded in a new "indigenization" or revitalization of cultural traditions.

Bolivia's "indigenization" process began and spread through a groundswell of innovative development activities and initiatives promoted by grassroots federations and non-governmental organizations (NGOs) that ultimately changed not only the lives of thousands of Bolivia's rural people, but perspectives held by those in the capital city's corridors of power. These innovative thinkers and practitioners, excited by the new indigenization philosophy, uncovered a veritable cornucopia of formerly underutilized resources, many of which stemmed from ancient agrarian civilizations of the Andes. They also began altering prejudicial attitudes toward these resources in the business community, the government, the media, the large governmental foreign aid agencies, and the universities.

The Inter-American Foundation (IAF), OXFAM-America, Catholic Relief Services, World Neighbors, and Cultural Survival were among the U.S. aid agencies most able to respond to this call for support of indigenous resources, organizations, and technologies when it first appeared. For twenty years I have served as Bolivia Foundation Representative for the IAF, discovering, funding, and following the progress of several hundred projects in education, agriculture, artisanry, women's training, health, mining, social research, and housing. As an IAF staff member, I was privileged to follow the work of these fledgling organizations. While during this period I have served as a funnel for funds, the tide reverses now, as I act as a conduit for the communities' stories, bringing them to the wider world.

The book presents this story of Bolivian rural development and cultural change over the last half-century. The first three chapters construct a historical and contextual framework for analyzing the country's process of cultural revitalization for grassroots social and economic development in recent decades. This framework presents three main perspectives of neo-colonialism, Western-centric foreign aid programs, and the prevailing economic development models over the last half-century as contexts in which these community-based organizations strove to reverse centuries of neglect, discrimination, and exploitation. Chapter 1 begins this story with a history of rural development and underdevelopment in Bolivia both before and after the advent of Western aid. This chapter brings into focus a long neo-colonial history of anti-indigenous discrimination accompanied by assimilation policies and campaigns. The chapter also provides an overview of the socio-political context of contemporary Bolivia, including descriptions of the various ethnic groups, ecosystems, and regions of the country, to serve as background for the later chapters that take a close look at development projects in the various regions. Chapter 2 offers a history of the application of ethnocentric Western rural development models to the Bolivian countryside from its conception by North American advisors and their neo-colonial counterparts within the Bolivian government primarily during the 1950s and 1960s. Chapter 3 describes how macro-economic structures and policies over the past half-century have impacted on the socioeconomic development prospects of Bolivia's indigenous majority. This discussion follows the Bolivian history of the heavily foreign-funded economic development models of state capitalism and neo-liberalism within the national as well as global scenarios.

Chapter 4 discusses grassroots movements which mounted a challenge to the Western development models and shaped a socio-political context favorable to expressions of indigenous culture for rural development activism within a growing civil society. Chapter 5 provides an overview of the broad array of initiatives and development activities that have contributed to the recovery and revitalization of diverse indigenous cultural resources—crops, food, trees, shrubs, pastures, livestock, art, medicinal plants, organizational forms, flags, and land tenure forms—during the 1980s and 1990s. This chapter describes the activities of a minority of NGOs that have dedicated themselves to development plans based on home-grown resources and technologies from indigenous communities. These groups combined the best of the Western and non-Western worlds in their projects while favoring the latter in their advocacy work.

Chapters 6 through 14 consist of in-depth narrative histories of small-scale development projects managed by grassroots federations and NGOs that have evolved out of the new cultural revitalization-indigenization movement in different micro-regions. The project stories provide an inside view of the processes that interweave cultural recuperation and revitalization with NGO strategies for grassroots development. In each case, the highlighted organizations were able to overcome cultural barriers and institutional discrimination and carry development across new thresholds.

The nine project cases were selected from several hundred funded by the Inter-American Foundation and other donors in Bolivia between 1974 and 1994. I used two key criteria in making my selections from this large portfolio. I gave preference, first and foremost, to projects that have enjoyed some measure of success and that have demonstrated staying power. I particularly wanted to avoid those "flash in the pan" project successes that look good initially, maybe for a couple of years, but then fizzle out. All the groups selected had spiritedly managed project activities for at least a decade, although this minimum cut-off point was easily exceeded in most cases. Impressive achievements have put these projects in an "exceptional projects" category, yet their problems illustrate many of the complexities found in most, if not all, local development endeavors. Since these effective organizations were challenged by problems familiar to grassroots development practitioners the world over, the narrative histories also focus on the mistakes, setbacks, and failures that invariably crop up on the difficult, bumpy road to social and economic change.

Breadth is the other main criterion I used in selecting cases for inclusion in this book. I have included a range of projects to reflect the broad ethno-cultural, geographical, historical, and ecological diversity of Bolivia, as well as the wide variety of development activities that have taken place in the country.

The bulk of the book is divided into four sections according to project types: agro-exports, education, artisanry, and the environment. In these sections, I highlight a plethora of indigenous cultural resources taken from the country's large and diverse national patrimony. Each chapter shines the spotlight on a different indigenous resource or set of resources that has been revitalized through grassroots development project activities.

In Chapters 6 through 8, I present stories of agricultural development at the grassroots level. The three federations described in this section brought about significant social and economic gains in their communities by managing agricultural service programs for small farmers and by marketing local products both nationally and internationally. They seized economic opportunities by targeting health and environmentally conscious consumers in the United States and Western Europe willing to pay higher prices for their products. In two of the cases, farmers radically transformed their production technologies to pursue organic farming, thus contributing to better health and environmental protection in addition to raising rural income. These organizations brought social and economic breakthroughs to their respective regions and to the nation as a whole.

Chapter 6 presents the story of a multi-ethnic co-op federation that became one of the world's first and largest organic chocolate producers. For twenty years, this federation has provided agro-services to its member cacao bean farmers and steadily improved the manufacturing technology necessary for making high-quality products. Perhaps the most remarkable fact about this organization is its reliance on indigenous practices of self-management and self-governance that have been honed by native Andean communities for several hundred years.

Chapter 7 covers the history of a grassroots co-op federation of Quechua farmers from the southern altiplano who have devoted themselves to the production of a special strain of the Andean grain quinoa (*quinoa real*), once a popular food staple in the Incan diet. This organization eventually contributed in important ways to lifting this nutritious, high-protein grain from the depths of obscurity in the mid-1970s to its current "super-grain" status on the shelves of Western organic and gourmet food stores.

The third case study, Chapter 8, focuses on an Aymara herders' association of the remote central altiplano near the border with Chile, which crafted an organization around the Andean *allyu,* an indigenous form of social organization rooted in the Incan social structure that has evolved over 500 years. The centerpiece of their rural development strategy has been the revitalization of alpacas and llamas as development resources along with the recovery of native pasturelands within a participatory framework of community action. Among its achievements, AIGACAA contributed to the legalization of llama meat sales and a wider appreciation for camelid livestock as nationally important development resources.

Chapters 9 and 10 focus on two educational projects, one with mostly Aymara and Quechua altiplano Indian women and the other with urban migrant youth of mostly Aymara descent in the capital city. Both cases led to major breakthroughs benefiting these two social groups. The women's promotional agency, a tiny, self-styled, free-wheeling NGO, defied the conventions of regional society in its unflagging promotion of respect and support for indigenous women's rights and their greater participation in leadership roles through community-based training workshops. Using innovative, highly provocative methodologies from the field of popular education, they enabled Aymara and Quechua women to greatly increase their self-esteem as Indians and as women. The women's new skills and cultural consciousness enabled them to knock down barriers to female participation that had long existed in developmental and grassroots organizations.

The second case concerns an innovative educational service center for low-income youth in an urban setting. Through provision of library and counseling services, science labs, teacher training, and other programs, this after-school center extended the educational opportunities available to poor urban migrant youth. Philosophically dedicated to building a strong sense of cultural identity among its students, the center propelled the young people to participate in efforts to reform schooling. The innovative service center subsequently became a model incorporated into the national educational reform law and has been adopted by private and public entities in twelve other public school districts throughout the country.

The third section, which includes Chapters 11 and 12, highlights the groundbreaking work of indigenous artists and artisans. Here I spotlight the histories of two organizations: the first working in the Andean mountain valleys of the Chuquisaca region, the second involved with ethnically diverse craft-producing communities in the Santa Cruz region of the eastern lowlands. These arts and crafts revitalization projects enhanced appreciation for women's skills and their indigenous products, altered the traditional roles of men and women within the family economy, and generated critical sources of income for cash-strapped agricultural communities. Through the organization of museum exhibits, artisan fairs, and other promotional activities, and with the help of NGOs, the artists and artisans not only generated respect for their craft traditions, but increased their own stature as indigenous women.

The fourth and final project history section, composed of Chapters 13 and 14, focuses on projects that set out to link development activities with natural resource conservation while protecting and building upon local biodiversity. These programs both affirmed local indigenous identities and highlighted the benefits of cultural pluralism within the wider society. The first of the two case histories focuses on rural development work in the Cochabamba region's Rayqaypampa mountain communities. After several years of trial and error experimentation, a farmers' federation working closely with this NGO established a program to recover native potato seed species, reversing recent deterioration in the quality of local seed. The farmers' techniques quickly spread to other communities and enhanced both food security and potato marketability in this micro-region. The NGO simultaneously organized a bilingual (Quechua-Spanish) adult literacy program which ultimately contributed to national bilingual education reform in primary schooling.

The book's final case history highlights the work of an NGO based in the remote Beni region of northeastern Bolivia. This organization, with the most important indigenous federation in the eastern lowlands of Bolivia, organized tiny, scattered ethnic groups to defend themselves against encroaching loggers, ranchers, peasant colonists, poachers, and foreign oil interests. They helped establish the Beni's first multi-ethnic federation. For its first collective protest action, members marched across the extensive savanna of northern Bolivia and up the eastern slopes of the Andes to pressure the country's leaders into granting them legal rights to their homelands. This effort led to new laws that recognized collective land rights for the Beni indigenous and other lowland groups and expanded awareness throughout Bolivian society of the importance of cultural pluralism and of the tropical forest's biodiversity.

In putting these stories together, I have made an effort to reconstruct a chronology of events and activities that occurred as each project evolved so as to convey the ongoing struggles to improve management and member participation, to remove institutional barriers based on cultural discrimination, and to simply make the project fly. It has continuously been my purpose to give an inside view of how person-to-person development works. With this aim in mind I have occasionally used the first person in the text to illustrate the role of the project officer in the development enterprise.

The data sources for these project histories include my field notes for visits to the project sites over many years, recent interviews with members and leaders involved in each project, and project-monitoring reports and commissioned evaluations of the projects written by Bolivian professionals.

Chapter 15 attempts to identify the factors which appeared to be important in the successful outcomes in the selected grassroots development projects. Here I emphasize the enormous benefits of efforts to recuperate indigenous cultural resources in societies that have experienced colonialism and myopic Western modernization. In this final chapter, I also discuss the impact of globalization on Bolivian culture and development patterns and also a reverse-angle view with some examples of the spread of Bolivia's indigenous cultural resources within the United States.

A middle-class Anglo male from Washington, D.C., I fell in love with Bolivia long ago and felt moved to share the story of how one of Latin America's poorest and most indigenous nations is overcoming legacies of neo-colonialism and ethnocentric Western aid by blazing some home-grown development trails with its own multicultural resources of its indigenous people. The stories brought together by this book identify and describe inflection points in time where a shift occurs toward the utilization of indigenous cultural resources, often to the benefit of the communities involved. In writing the book, I also wanted to show what worthwhile foreign aid projects look like "on the ground" so that people-to-people approaches are more widely known and appreciated. And by including stories using organic production technologies, I wanted to show that consumer choices by North Americans can make a huge difference for indigenous communities thousands of miles away in the South American mountains and jungles struggling to bring improvements to their families and communities under harsh conditions.

Twice a year, as a foreign aid worker, I would spend six weeks moving about Bolivia visiting local organizations and a national network of friends and informal advisors. And when back at my home office, I remained in constant communication with the Bolivians operating and monitoring these projects and introducing new funding possibilities and fleshing out innovative grassroots development ideas. As I had opportunity to fund and follow assorted idealists, social visionaries, and innovators working for community change over many years, my admiration for these people continued to grow along with the rich material for this book.

Although Bolivia is heading in a more promising direction these days, it faces many severe challenges in a globalizing environment where the forces of rapid technological change and economic restructuring are further uprooting traditional life-ways and leaving erratic economic growth patterns and glaring social inequities in their wake. As the planet earth takes off into the new millennium with a shrinking world community, there is a critical need to harness past, present, and future indigenous contributions for humankind to the prevailing socioeconomic development strategies which hopefully will help modify and transform them as well. My book aspires to contribute in some small way to that vital goal.

Many wonderful people contributed to this work. The Bolivians include Antonio Ugarte, Rita Murillo, Hans Moeller, Mercedes Rengel, Jorge Dandler, Jorge Muñoz, Cristina Bubba, and especially Ruth Llanos.

Richard Kurin and Olivia Cadaval of the Smithsonian's Center for Folklife and Culture were important supporters and Kellogg Institute at Notre Dame provided financial support for an academic year. Ernie Bartell was especially supportive as he was years ago overseeing my first Andean sojourn. At Kellogg, Lee Tavis, Bob Pelton, Scott Mainwaring, Mary Ann Mahoney, and Erica Valenzuela were helpful friends.

I am grateful to Brooke Larson, Judith Tendler, Solon Barraclough, Susan Paulson, Karl Zimmerer, Alan Kolata, Leslie Ann Brownrigg, David Block, and Bill D'Antonio for comments and encouragement. Karen Weigert, Micheal Foley, Miguel Szekeley, and Bolivianists Sinclair Thomson and Seemin Qayum read the manuscript and provided helpful comments.

Ex-IAF editor, Ron Weber, along with my IAF colleagues David Bray, Jim Adriance, Pat Breslin, and Bob Maguire provided valued assistance along with IAF institutional support. However, the book is my independent project and does not necessarily reflect the views of the Inter-American Foundation.

I also owe debts to Caroline Brownell for the maps and Juliete Litterer, Lilian Weber, Monica Figueroa, and Farah Nazareli for other manuscript-related tasks. Special gratitude goes to attorney Joe Gebhardt for pro-bono legal assistance. My biggest debt of gratitude goes to my superb editor, Sara Taber, who helped shape the project stories and improve my prose.

Bolivian Topography

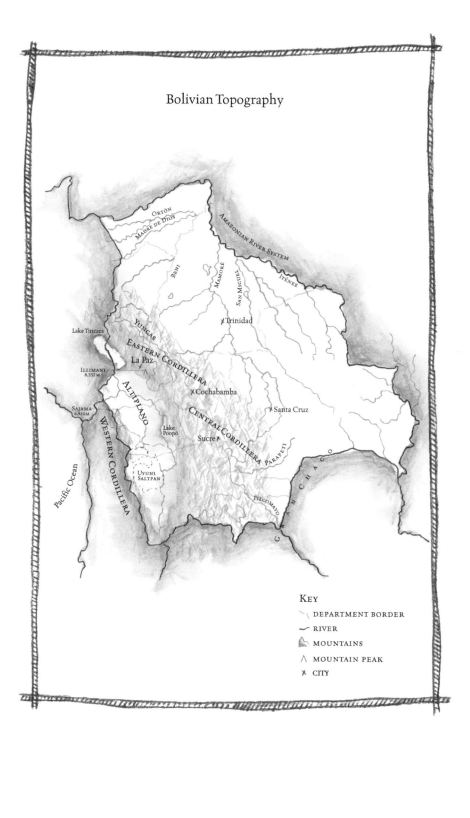

ORTÓN
MADRE DE DIOS
AMAZONIAN RIVER SYSTEM
BENI
MAMORÉ
SAN MIGUEL
ITÉNEE
Lake Titicaca
YUNGAS
EASTERN CORDILLERA
✱Trinidad
ILLIMANI
8,332 M
La Paz
ALTIPLANO
SAJAMA
6,550 M
WESTERN CORDILLERA
Pacific Ocean
Lake Poopó
✱Cochabamba
CENTRAL CORDILLERA
✱Santa Cruz
Sucre✱
PARAPETI
UYUNI
SALTPAN
PILCOMAYO
GRAN CHACO

KEY

〜 DEPARTMENT BORDER

⌒ RIVER

🖎 MOUNTAINS

∧ MOUNTAIN PEAK

✱ CITY

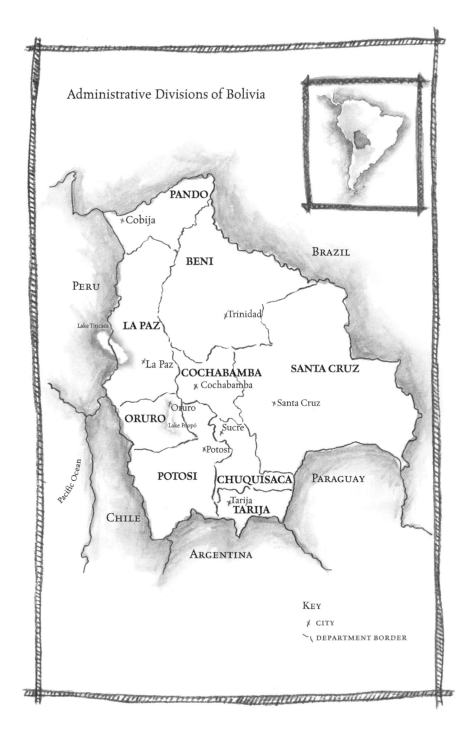

Administrative Divisions of Bolivia

BRAZIL

PERU

PANDO
✗ Cobija

BENI

LA PAZ
Lake Titicaca
✗ La Paz
✗ Trinidad

SANTA CRUZ

COCHABAMBA
✗ Cochabamba
✗ Santa Cruz

ORURO
✗ Oruro
Lake Poopó
✗ Sucre
✗ Potosí

Pacific Ocean

POTOSI
CHUQUISACA
PARAGUAY

CHILE
✗ Tarija
TARIJA

ARGENTINA

KEY
✗ CITY
〜 DEPARTMENT BORDER

CHAPTER I

National Integration within a Neo-Colonial Republic

The auctioning off of communal lands decreed during the government of Melgarejo (1864–1871) had antecedents in the dictatorial decree of Simon Bolivar, announced in the city of Trujillo, April 8, 1824, in which he abolished the indigenous community.
CARLOS B. MAMANI CONDORI (1991, 15)

A snapshot from 1968: a Peace Corps volunteer is standing with Peruvian Indian farmers on a steep mountain slope overlooking Lake Titicaca, the highest navigable lake in the world. Across the lake a beautiful vista rises: the Eastern Cordillera, the towering snow-capped peaks of Bolivia. The Peace Corps volunteer, assigned to work as an extension agent for the Ministry of Agriculture, is supervising potato planting. Under his guidance, the farmers are placing seed potatoes on top of a layer of aldrin, a chalky white pesticide, and sprinkling small quantities of chemical fertilizer in between the seeds.

The genetically improved seed variety the farmers were planting was developed by a national university at lower mountain altitudes. It was being introduced to the altiplano via extension programs. After a crash course on potatoes in Mexico, the volunteer had found himself on the front lines, inducing agricultural change in hard-pressed Andean communities. His role was to introduce the farmers to this modern technology package which would supposedly bring them both abundant yields and profits.

One frosty morning in the middle of the growing season, the Peace Corps volunteer underwent a rude awakening. From the bed in his adobe hut, he heard several farmers talking in loud, excited voices in the fields not far off. He went outside and found the farmers, by now saddled with hefty loan repayments from the agricultural credit brokered by the Peace Corps program, looking with despair into one man's palm. The man held a potato plant with black, withered leaves and miniature-size tubers that had just been dug out of the ground.

The American government, and that Peace Corps volunteer as one of its representatives, had brought the latest in scientific potato production practices to Peruvian communities. Unfortunately, the super-productive improved seed developed at lower Peruvian altitudes could not endure the lakeside frosts. The pesticide for nematodes was equally problematic for humans and subsequently banned from commercial sale. The modern technology package with its high-priced fertilizer proved itself too expensive for all but a minority of Peruvian farmers (Mayer et al. 1992). Even this variety's taste was unappetizing for sophisticated Andean potato connoisseurs.

That young American, surrounded by the clutch of despairing Peruvian farmers, was me.

In my early plunge into the world of Andean development, I had assumed that the Peruvian Indian farmers needed modern scientific approaches. At the time, I was utterly unaware of the vast storehouse of climatic and plant knowledge and remarkable agricultural skill possessed by the Indian farmers. For generations their forefathers had continually innovated and adapted their agrarian practices in this environment at 13,000 feet above sea level. It now seems obvious that farming improvement programs would benefit by consulting the framework for decision making and resource use that had been developed in this part of the world over thousands of years—and is still being developed. Farmers of these high Andean slopes and plateaus faced as many as 200 nights of frost a year, and temperatures often passed from summer to winter in the course of a single day—conditions that would humble any open-minded modern agronomist.

A National Academy of Sciences report issued in 1989 stated that agricultural mastery of the Andean mountain terrain requires minute, detailed knowledge of the wide variety of micro-climates governing the productivity of small plots up and down the steep slopes. "The region is so fragmented that rainfall, frost, sunlight, and soil type can vary over distances as short as a few meters. This complicated ecological mosaic created countless micro-climates—including some of the driest and wettest, coldest and hottest, and lowest and highest found anywhere in the world" (National Research Council 1989, 4). The International Science Council was clearly awed by the agricultural system that had been developed by Andean civilizations over some 7,000 years of discovery.[1]

Several decades earlier, the eminent ethno-historian, John Murra, had written, "Ecologically, the territory of the Andean republics seems like one of the least likely homes for man: the coast is a true desert and the highland plateaus are very high, dry and cold. And yet over many centuries the people of the region have shown their ability not only to survive in such circumstances but also to create a series of civilizations which wrung from the environment the necessary surplus to expand and flourish" (Murra 1978, 3).

Common to such mountain environments is the phenomenon of *endemism,* diverse adaptation of a single species within a specific geographical range. In the Andean environment endemism has given rise to over 3,000 potato varieties. Rob Thurston, an international agricultural expert at Cornell University, told me in a private conversation that "there are varieties and features of Andean potato species that offer effective solutions to just about any problem, whether surviving drought or controlling pests, that we have encountered in North America." One might have reasonably assumed that development planners of the 1960s would have looked more deeply into past agricultural efforts in the Andes and discovered how the genius of the diverse Andean agriculturists and the wealth of Andean potato species were still relevant concepts for solving agricultural problems in the modern era.

My initial venture at tackling development challenges in the Andes is, in retrospect, rich with irony. Near these same Lake Titicaca shores the first domesticated potato plants popped out of the soil 5,000 years earlier under the direction of the world's first potato breeders. In contrast, my own ancestors fled Cork County, Ireland, in the mid-nineteenth century because of potato blight. By over-reliance on only a few varieties of potato for national production, Ireland's system of food production collapsed. Now, as a fourth-generation Irish American and recent political science graduate from the University of Notre Dame, I had come to the birthplace of the potato with pretensions of teaching a more "advanced" technology to Andean potato sophisticates. Roughly similar tales of agricultural modernization were unfolding across the lake in the neighboring country of Bolivia and other Andean nations.

Now, as I look back at the 1968 photograph of that young Peace Corps volunteer standing with the Peruvian farmers on that precipitous mountain slope, I see, in capsule form, much that was wrong with Western approaches to development in the Americas for societies with indigenous populations. Until recently, the worldwide effort at modernization has been synonymous with the imposition of homogenization and standardization according to Western models and goals. There has been little respect for the knowledge local peoples themselves could bring to the development planning table. Five hundred years under first European and then national republican rule took a tremendous toll on the ancient agrarian civilizations of the Andes, yet as John Murra has insisted, there remain many important cultural continuities in the Andes that can serve as resources for a more realistic, ecology-conscious, and long-lasting form of rural development and modernization.[2]

Over the next two decades, traveling the Andes and Amazon as a development field officer in search of promising development projects in Bolivia, I became increasingly aware of an impressive cultural patrimony heralding from not only Andean but Amazonian cultures as well. This rich patrimony included native food, crops (tubers, cereals, fruits, vegetables), trees, pastures, technologies, medicinal plants, art, livestock, organizational practices, and also languages. These resources are deeply embedded in the social, economic, and political fabric of Bolivian society and yet have been subject to continuous discrimination. The product of creative adaptations by Andean and Amazonian peoples to ever changing historical circumstances, these resources are mutative, dynamic facets of indigenous life ready to be further adapted to a community's advantage (Larson 1995; Wolf 1982).[3] Beyond them stand complex indigenous knowledge systems which are beginning to be documented not only in Bolivia and the Andes but throughout the Third World (Warren, Slikkerveer, and Brokensha 1995). Following my growing awareness of indigenous resources and bolstered by the original congressional mandate of the Inter-American Foundation (IAF), I began to support programs that utilized native cultural elements and biological resources in a rural development strategy that moved local culture from the periphery of development planning to the center. This new perspective redefines as advantageous peoples' native resources that previously had been viewed as limitations by the development establishment.

The subject of this book is cultural revitalization and social and economic development in the Andean nation of Bolivia. Most people in the United States know Bolivia only as where Butch Cassidy, Sundance Kid, and Che Guevara fired their last shots and high-yielding coca leaf bushes furnish the key alkaloid for the illicit international cocaine industry.

Bolivia is a relatively large, landlocked country in the center of South America. Along with Guatemala, it is one of two societies in the Western Hemisphere in which the majority of the population is Native American. Bolivia conjures up comparisons to Nepal and Tibet of the Himalayas: remote, exotic nations nestled amidst the world's highest mountain ranges. Its capital, the world's highest, is set in a deep mountain canyon in the heartland of the Aymara Indians and against the dramatic backdrop of Mt. Illimani's snow-capped peaks. La Paz is an unusual Latin American capital for its continuing link to its Indian past. It is called by an indigenous name, Chukiago, by many of its poorer inhabitants, and native Aymara is the language of choice on many of its streets and in its modest residences. At the crack of dawn each day, one awakens not to the sounds of Spanish coming over the radio, but to the songs, voices, and language of the Aymara Indian world.

Indigenous culture has an equally powerful visual presence in La Paz. Beautiful primary and pastel colors seemingly float through the air, passing up and down its steep city streets on the multi-colored shawls of women with coppery faces, black braids, and jaunty derbies. Indian women in their colorful clothing are omnipresent on the curbsides, where they squat, peddling every conceivable petty commodity to urban passersby.

Demography and Geography of Bolivia

From rooftop La Paz one can look out over the rest of Bolivia—a vast land with varied topography ranging from enormous stretches of dry mountains to verdant, low-lying tropical forests—a country three times the size of California but inhabited by only seven million people. The country is divided into several cultural-geographic regions. The altiplano region, a high plateau flanked by two huge mountain ranges, the Cordillera Occidental and the Cordillera Oriental, runs 500 miles long on a north-south axis and varies from 30 to 100 miles in width. It is the largest interior drainage system in South America and home mostly to Aymara farmers, herders, and miners. Its earth-colored, treeless, rolling plains extend from southern Peru to northern Argentina. Mostly cold and dry, the Lake Titicaca basin at its northern end offers the altiplano's warmest climate and most intensive farming, herding, and fishing activities.

Running east and north of the altiplano are rugged inter-montane valleys, between 2,000 and 3,000 meters in altitude where mostly Quechua-speaking and *mestizo* (mixed Spanish-Indian blood) people manage mixed agricultural and herding activities on the flat floors of the valleys and in the deciduous forest of the mountainsides.[4] The country's third most prominent native group is Guaraní-speaking dirt farmers, hunters, agricultural workers, and small ranchers from the Andean foothills and dry low plains on the western side of the Andes in southern Bolivia. To the east of the two mountain zones are the lowland tropical rainforests stretching hundreds of miles toward the Brazilian border. Over the past fifty years, many Aymara and Quechua farmers have migrated to this region to carve out settlements and farms. Their communities often became microcosms of a larger social order of ethnic pluralism.

The native ethnic minorities of the Amazon and other parts of the tropical lowlands represent thirty distinct linguistic groups and thirty-seven ethnic groups. Once living in relative harmony with the jungle and savannas, their lifestyles have been turned upside down by rural highland migrants, ranchers, miners, and loggers, along with missionaries, NGOs, and drug traffickers.

Another migration path for the Aymara and Quechua, over the past four decades, has led to the slums of the country's rapidly growing cities as well as to Buenos Aires, Argentina. Dwindling plots, degraded soils, decreasing natural vegetation, lack of public assistance, and falling agricultural prices of the altiplano and mountain valleys have turned many Aymara and Quechua youth into economic refugees who forge new lives in the vast informal sector of petty commerce, trading, smuggling, and artisanry in Bolivian cities. Decades of anti-indigenous public policies, including a textbook application of structural adjustment measures since 1985, have led to stagnating food production, rural unemployment and underemployment, and glaring regional socioeconomic disparities. The natural environment supporting the sagging rural economy has been steadily eroding (Painter 1995); recent research indicates that 40 percent of the country's farmland is critically degraded. As if this were not enough odds stacked against them, the population is also burdened by international debt payments, absorbing close to 30 percent of the national export earnings (Dennis 1997, 37), and some of the world's worst government corruption. Trying to survive in such a context sends rural families scrambling in many directions to find work off the farm.

CURRENT STATUS OF BOLIVIA'S NEO-COLONIAL REPUBLIC

Bolivia's first indigenous vice-president, Víctor Hugo Cárdenas, has argued that behind agricultural decline and Indian poverty is an elaborate system of internal colonialism. Since the mid-1980s, Cárdenas has traveled throughout the country denouncing the many and varied ways in which Indians are made into second-class citizens and decrying the nation's refusal to accept and cherish its multicultural identity. Internal colonialism, as Cárdenas describes it, is a system in which economic discrimination toward indigenous peoples fits within a web of nationwide social and cultural discrimination. In return for the cheap labor and food which they provide to the cities and modern sector, Indian peasants receive negligible state investment in their communities. Bolivia's rural majority of mountain-dwelling Indians has been unable to stop the lion's share of national financial resources and international development aid from going to Santa Cruz commercial farmers, ranchers, and agro-businessmen (Bolivian elites who pride themselves on their pure white Spanish heritage and lack of Indian blood).

Internal colonialism in Bolivia can also be seen in terms of the unequal distribution of rights to Amazonian forests in the eastern lowlands. Bolivia has the sixth largest tropical forest in the world, yet the 40 percent of this area inhabited by diverse indigenous groups has been given out as timber concessions to several hundred non-Indian businessmen. There has been little public recognition, interest in, or knowledge about the customary rights and practices of these forest-dwelling ethnic groups.

Yet this is not to say that all Indians are poor and disadvantaged. Economic mobility has been possible for a small minority over several generations. This group includes professionals in many fields and owners of commercial and residential property in certain sections of the capital, managers of inter-provincial and downtown public transportation, and the owners of fleets of trucks used to ferry people and their products between the city and the countryside. So impressive are the amounts of capital held that sociologist and urban entreprenuer Javier Hurtado speculates that if the prominent Aymara were to withdraw their savings, the banking system in the capital city would likely collapse in short order.

Though a lucky few obtain at least economic success, the vast majority of native peoples have to endure cultural discrimination from whites and mestizos in schools, courts, businesses, public offices, and the army. Indian women, beginning in their teens, often experience humiliation as domestic servants in the homes of the middle and upper classes of Bolivian towns and cities (Gill 1994). Condescending labels such as "indio," "puro," and "t'ara" in the countryside, and "indiaco," "cholo," "cholango," and "medio pelo" in the city reflect widespread racial stereotyping (S. Rivera 1993, 68). It is not surprising within this social system that peasant migrants to the city feel compelled to change their surnames, language, dress styles, hair texture, and even their skin color.[5]

In this social hierarchy, the common goal of non-Indians is to put as much distance as possible between themselves and the Indian world despite many interactions with it in daily life.

ROOTS OF DISCRIMINATION

Sociologist Silvia Rivera traces the roots of the deep-seated discrimination toward Bolivia's indigenous peoples back to the long colonial ordeal of "exclusion and segregation" which "negated the humanity" of the country's diverse ethnic groups (1993). Anthropologist Tom Abercrombie shows the multiple ways that colonization had a profound impact on Andean religion, the reconfiguration of living spaces, and modalities of social memory (Abercrombie 1998). According to Murra, Spanish settlement subjected Andean society to some of the most relentless and harshest domination by one civilization over another in world history. Evidence for this can be seen in the loss of territory and large-scale agricultural management skills and the institution of forced labor. Scientists focused on the Bolivian Amazon have found a similar if not worse impact from disease and slavery on its indigenous inhabitants (Erickson 1995, 71).

Independence from Spain in 1825 resulted in a continuation of Indian oppression during the long period of nation building. Nineteenth-century ideologues including independence leader Simon Bolivar himself perceived nothing of value in the highland indigenous communities and created strategies to undermine them. The *ayllu,* a key kinship and territorial institution of ancient Andean society, also came under assault when its long-standing juridical status was suddenly abolished by the nineteenth-century liberal "reform" laws. In that period, liberalism was a political and economic doctrine bent on "civilizing" and "integrating" native peoples into the Spanish-criollo oligarchy's social designs of individual property rights and new land markets. This view sought to make the native peoples into industrious, market-oriented yeoman farmers (Platt 1982). Denouncing communities and ayllus as backward and obsolete institutions became a convenient way of justifying the transformation of corporate indigenous landholdings under traditional authority structures into private, individually owned landed estates or haciendas, while forcing their former residents to become an unpaid labor force. Instead of a more efficiently organized system of market capitalism, a phenomenon of "feudalization" had been set in motion. The ayllu and indigenous community lands were acquired both by force and fraud while ushering in a period of major hacienda expansion in the Bolivian highlands, mostly centered in the La Paz region of the Bolivian highlands.

These profound transformations reflected changes in the government's tax base. During its first fifty years as a republic, Bolivia's national budget derived primarily from tribute paid by the country's majority, indigenous families living within ayllus and communities. Once the state was able to support itself in 1870 through a tax on silver and subsequently tin and other minerals, the indigenous tribute became less important and the ayllus and communities expendable (Platt 1982). Indigenous lands became coveted by politically influential families bent on securing ownership rights to large holdings in the altiplano and valleys.

Historian Brooke Larson summed up these changes in the following way.

> Liberal land and tax reforms divested native Andeans of their traditional rights to communal lands, tax exemptions, and judicial privileges; free trade policies and ideologies that opened the interior highlands to cheap foreign wheat and other products which, in turn, dislodged traditional Andean traders and suppliers from regional markets; and the spread of scientific racism (in all its variants) that converted Indians into biological subjects incapable of promoting, or sharing in, Order and Progress—all converged to undercut earlier Andean modes of adaptation and struggle, livelihood and resistance. (Larson 1995, 30)

Liberal land policies also served to displace native ethnic groups from homeland areas in the frontier. One example of this frontier incursion in the lowlands of the country took place in the territory of the Chiriguanos, Tobas, and Tapietes in the southern Andes in present-day Chuquisaca,

Tarija, and Santa Cruz where economies and ecologies revolved around shifting cultivation and hunting and gathering practices. These inhabitants of the heavily forested foothills and savannas faced a flood of white settlers and their cattle. The new colonists protected themselves with newly built forts guarded by soldiers. According to historian Erick Langer the government put "vacant" public lands up for sale while ignoring ancestral rights of the occupying Indians (Langer 1989). In this way, the indigenous Chiriguanos were gradually incorporated as unpaid labor into the expanding hacienda's debt-peonage system and their tribal way of life went into rapid decline. A metaphor for the fundamental economic changes forced on the area was colonists' cattle trampling indigenous corn fields—a cattle-ranching economy replaced indigenous agriculture over a large area. The loss of control over corn not only diminished a prized staple but in some places affected community ritual and festival life. The patron—the owner or boss of a hacienda—began assuming many of the traditional functions of the *tubicha* (chief), such as the meting out of justice and the distribution of lands. This, in effect, destroyed the traditional village structure and began to severely erode the culture (Langer 1989, 154).

During the last two decades of the nineteenth century, tribal societies in the northeastern Beni region were similarly affected by white and criollo migrants interested in cattle ranching near the mission towns and the economic opportunities associated with the Amazonian rubber boom (Lehm 1999, 38). One scholar described the changing social and cultural condition in the following way: "From other sub-regions of the Oriente, especially from the mission areas to the south, natives were transported, often en masse, to work as boat-men, gatherers, and menials in forests along the lower reaches of the Beni, Mamore, and Itenez rivers. Labor was universally secured through debt peonage, an arrangement not uncommon today in parts of the Oriente. Disease, inanition, and exposure took a frightful toll" (Jones 1984, 69).

During the early twentieth century in the highlands, there were sporadic state efforts to use the primary school as a "civilizing" instrument in breaking up the kinship ties holding together the Andean ayllu. Aymara intellectual Vitaliano Soria described this policy of "hispanization." "This process of 'civilizing' the Indian was an attempt to transform Aymara or Quechua identity into a different mestizo identity, one separated from ancient ties to community or ayllu organization. The state or criollo documents treating the issue of indigenous education repeatedly use the word 'civilization' and talk of the need to transform customs considered pernicious and retrograde into life-styles associated with the notion of Western progress" (Soria 1992, 50).[6]

Anthropologist Juergen Riester has argued that evangelical and Catholic missionary groups during the twentieth century played a similar role in the eastern lowlands of the country. "The objective of the missionaries is the transformation of the presumably undignified life of the indigenous tribes, who in the eyes of the missionaries, go idly walking through the jungle without order, religion or any real work" (Riester 1976, 55).

ASSIMILATION AND AGRARIAN REFORM

Bolivia's determination to assimilate its native groups into a criollo-mestizo cultural melting pot continued unabated during the mid-twentieth century. In the aftermath of its own Chaco War and World War II, Bolivia established a national development doctrine which still viewed Indian tradition as a major obstacle holding back the nation's economic progress. Mexican sociologist Rodolfo Stavenhagen has argued that assimilationist and integrationist schemes were common throughout Latin America during this period. These development policies targeted at the indigenous populations had two principal justifications. "First, it was thought that only by means of such policies would the quality of Indian life improve. Secondly, it was felt that as long as the indigenous people lived in poverty and backwardness, isolated from the centers of modernization and growth, the country as a whole would remain backward and underdeveloped" (Stavenhagen 1992).

This official development outlook was evident in 1963 in an important speech on Latin American integration delivered by Felipe Herrera, the first president of the Inter-American Development Bank. "We must not forget that despite all the progress made by our hemisphere in the process of acculturation, in its effort to bring great groups of marginal peoples into civilized life, Latin America still has an illiteracy rate of 40 percent; that is 40 percent of the people still have not been integrated into the scale of ideas and values that determine the trends of public opinion among the more culturally advanced groups."

A deepening of this effort to integrate the Indian culturally into Bolivian society was set in motion in 1952 by Latin America's second social revolution. The Bolivian Revolution, led by the National Revolutionary

Movement (MNR), brought about a radical redistribution of land, along with suffrage and labor and education rights benefiting indigenous peoples. Bolivia's revolution abolished unpaid labor and servitude and ushered in a sweeping redistribution of land rights to the indigenous majority residing in the Andean regions.[7] At the time of independence in 1825, Indians controlled two thirds of the lands in the country. After the onslaught of the liberal reforms and by the time of the national revolution, the amount of land under ayllu and community control had dwindled to 20 percent (Cárdenas 1988). The 1953 land reform, designed to redress earlier wrongs, returned formerly usurped communal lands to individual farmers and freed communities that had been absorbed into haciendas.

Aside from land redistribution, the 1953 agrarian reform also had profound effects in restructuring relations between the countryside and the small towns and cities of the highlands. Freed from social bondage, the Indian peasants were no longer dependent on the patron for mediation with the larger society. Sociologist Andrew Pearse referred to this previous monopolistic relationship as one of "cellular confinement" (Pearse 1975). Within this quasi-apartheid, the indigenous residents were not able to leave the hacienda without permission of the patron or provincial authorities (Arrieta 1996, 200). And when in the cities, they were banned from setting foot on the central plazas. The reforms enabled former service tenants and hacienda peons to market agricultural and livestock produce for themselves, a change that triggered a proliferation of rural fairs, new marketing arrangements, and increased purchasing power for urban goods among land reform's indigenous beneficiaries (Pearse 1975). There was also increased occupational (especially petty trading) and geographic mobility for the enfranchised Indian peasantry in both the city and the countryside.

Despite the MNR's vicious persecution of its political opponents, the revolution had important effects in terms of political rights. Rapid rural unionization to implement the agrarian reform opened a niche for peasant *sindicatos* (self-governing community-based organizations dominated by male membership to serve among other things as a political constituency for the MNR) to participate in building a new political order. Organized in every village, the sindicatos opened offices in the towns, regional capitals, and in La Paz itself to give the peasantry a new political voice and representation in national interest-group politics.[8] Also for the first time in history, the indigenous masses began voting in elections for political leaders and joining national political parties.

To appreciate the magnitude of these changes for a Latin American society, one only has to compare the Bolivian situation to the decades-long socio-political violence in Guatemala over unresolved land and political participation issues or to the racism and the exclusion of indigenous peoples from important development programs and socio-political and cultural institutions until recently in Ecuador and Peru. It is also true that a higher percentage of arable land was redistributed in Bolivia than in other Latin American agrarian reforms in this century (Paige 1996, 136).

Yet the MNR had a contradictory social side to its revolution. While it was distributing land rights and opening political space for peasant participation in the highlands, its policies in the more sparsely populated tropical eastern lowlands looked quite different. The MNR created the "empresa agropecuaria" within the new laws which tended to favor the economic elites with more land, financial and technical resources, and accompanying investments in infrastructure.

The Bolivian military also interrupted the agrarian reform process in 1964, driving the country away from many of its progressive goals. Its main allies were the criollo elites from the eastern lowlands and the United States government which rebuilt and modernized the Bolivian military as part of its Latin American policy of containing communism. U.S. financial, material, and training support enabled the Bolivian army to recover from collapse in the 1950s from its military defeat at the hands of the popular militias of miners and peasants to regain the upper hand in national politics. Between 1964 and 1978, military regimes ruled the country with both a velvet glove and an iron fist, and Bolivia regained its dubious distinction as the world's most coup-prone republic (Dunkerley 1984; Malloy and Gamarra 1988). While holding power only two years, left of center military regimes antagonized Bolivia's economic elites and the U.S. Latin American policymakers with measures such as nationalizing Gulf Oil, mobilizing trade union workers into "popular" assemblies, and expelling U.S. Peace Corps volunteers. Their political tenure was short lived. Powerful conservative adversaries quickly rose up and deposed them with their own military conspiracies.

Rightist military regimes ruled the country for a total of fourteen years during the period between 1964 and 1978 and strove to subdue Bolivia's trade union movement through repression (human rights violations including arbitrary detentions, torture, and several massacres of miners and peasants) and co-optation (e.g., selective use of foreign aid)(Dunkerley 1984; Malloy and Gamarra 1988). For example, the Military-Campesino Pact structure instituted by the Barrientos regime in the mid-1960s enabled the military to co-opt the national peasant sindicato structure (a potential opposition pressure group) with its thousands of affiliates strung out across the country.[9] While de-mobilizing and neutralizing the collective power of the peasants, the military regimes made grants of huge tracts of public lands to middle- and upper-class cronies in the tropical eastern lowlands where genuine land reform was weak (Albó 1979; Urioste 1987). The ongoing reconcentration of land in the eastern lowlands in the hands of relatively few families and groups contrasts with the relatively egalitarian, "reformed" social structure of the western highlands.

Then during Bolivia's subsequent transition to democracy (1978–1982), when the United States government under the Carter White House abruptly withdrew its support for the Banzer dictatorship, the nation's political process went into "fast-forward." A national hunger strike involving 1,300 Bolivian activists further pushed open democracy's doors. Three aborted national elections and five military juntas took place before elected civilian government was established for good.

While acknowledging the positive legacies of the revolution during the 1950s, revisionist scholars such as S. Rivera and Cárdenas have called attention to yet another shortcoming of the MNR's blueprint for the nation—its strong Western-centric and anti-indigenous cultural bias. As part of its modernizing ideology and nation-building program, the MNR tried to bury the country's indigenous heritage and rapidly turn rural Indians into mestizo citizens.

When President Víctor Paz Estenssoro stepped up to the speaker's platform to outline the much-heralded land reform decrees in front of 200,000 cheering, and sometimes armed, land-hungry Indian peasants standing in the open field of a provincial town of Ucurena on August 2, 1953 (Huizer 1972, 94), he exclaimed, "From now on you will no longer be Indians ("indios") but rather peasants!" The platform of his MNR party program equated the abolishment of "Indian" identity with the destruction of the feudal order. President Estenssoro was also saying in effect that indigenous culture was a lingering blight on the nation. Bolivian sociologist Javier Hurtado, recalling those days, commented, "The MNR had an unrealistic and inappropriate image of peasants in blue overalls driving tractors within the new social and economic order they were setting out to construct. They wanted the indigenous to stop wearing ponchos and turn their backs forever on traditional agriculture."

Other Aymara observers recount how civil patrols forced Indian males off passenger trucks and cut off their braids in keeping with a modernizing society. Another demeaning practice was to spray Indians for lice with DDT, one of the new agricultural chemicals introduced through foreign aid and agricultural modernization programs. Encouragement of such "public health practices" could even be found in school textbooks. This spraying of indigenous leaders occurred when they arrived for high-level meetings to discuss the progress of agrarian reform in the chambers of government ministers during a social revolution in full swing (S. Rivera 1993; Castañeda 1997).[10]

Cárdenas, S. Rivera, and others such as prominent Bolivian anthropologist, Xavier Albó, maintain that the revolution failed to alter many aspects of the country's deeply rooted internal colonialism. Indeed, the MNR's national revolutionary policies ushered in new institutions while expanding others that had always negated and suppressed the country's multicultural identity. The rural schools' policy preference for the Spanish language and school curricula out of touch with the local cultures of the school children in native communities became another colonizing and integrating instrument.

The ideas and forms of the trade-union sindicato, the new local organization for rural political mobilization under the MNR's direction, were borrowed from twentieth-century international communists and local union organizers and were later institutionalized by the Bolivian government under the Ministry of Peasant Affairs and Agriculture. The struggles of unionized Bolivian mineworkers against the national oligarchy also provided a powerful demonstration. So the sindicatos were a far cry from an agrarian institution with indigenous roots. Genaro Flores, a famous Aymara peasant leader during the 1970s and 1980s, has boyhood memories of how the MNR cadres went from community to community replacing the local indigenous *hilacata* authorities with much younger sindicato leaders, who lacked the community trust bestowed on the elders. Yet the sheer organizational dynamism of indigenous communities led over time to reworking this recently transplanted institution, infusing it with their own traditional institutional forms, along with common leadership and ritual practices (Albó 1984b).

In some parts of the country, important aspects of the MNR's land reform laws demonstrated deep ignorance about and served to undermine time-tested Andean forms of tenure. An intricate land division system dictating the control of non-contiguous territorial, altitudinal, and climatic areas was still in operation among some Andean groups, a phenomenon poorly understood by the urban upper middle–class architects of the reform. In these cases, grants of small plots of land served to fracture these systems of resource control, sending communities headlong into heated conflicts with the government's agrarian courts. For example, east of Lake Titicaca, down in the breathtaking, steep mountain valleys of Charazani, enduring ayllu borders became annulled and replaced by the new private property configurations of these Western-minded agrarian reformers (Bastien 1978, 190).

The individual land grants wreaked complete havoc in the native management schemes in some altiplano herding communities. According to Deborah Caro, an anthropologist specializing in pastoral communities, "This change in tenancy patterns has likely undermined one of the most effective means of achieving a sustainable agro-pastoral system in the Andean highlands in several altiplano provinces" (Caro 1992, 74). In short, the MNR helped to emancipate the Indian peasants from many past abuses, political limitations, and abridged life chances, while it simultaneously replicated the same old, neo-colonial assimilationist patterns pushed since the advent of liberalism over a hundred years earlier. In some fundamental respects Bolivia would never again be the same, but in other ways a long-standing condition of neo-colonialism would continue to shape its rural development patterns.

CHAPTER 2

The Biases of Western Aid

Yankee was born on the King ranch, Kingsville, Texas. He cost $750, plus $750 plane fare when he flew to Bolivia at the age of 2 years with 11 other Santa Cruz Gertrude cows and bulls in March 1956. He now weighs 2400 pounds.

PHOTOGRAPH CAPTION, U.S. GOVERNMENT REPORT

In the 1940s, ethnocentric and enormously influential Western aid agencies began to shape an anti-indigenous national development policy which was welcomed by Bolivia's political rulers. The foreign aid entities and white, upper-class dominated government agencies operated in a kind of symbiotic relationship which reinforced a mutually shared lack of respect for Indians. To people associated with these institutions, Bolivia was a poor, struggling nation of backward rural peoples with valuable natural resources whose best chances of development depended upon a massive infusion of capital, advanced technology, and technical assistance coming from the West, especially the United States.

An influential report published by the United Nations in 1951 referred to Bolivia as "a beggar sitting on a throne of gold" for its abundance of natural resources side by side grinding poverty and human misery. It commented that the country's diversity of climates and altitudes allowed for every variety of vegetable and animal product and its Andean mountain chain contained important deposits of gold, silver, tin, antimony, lead, zinc, tungsten, copper, and iron in addition to vast timber resources (United Nations 1951, 2). Much of the rural poverty was due to the institution of the hacienda which controlled 90 percent of the arable land and exploited half the population in serf-like conditions. Another UN report stated that food consumption of important products was among the lowest per capita in the hemisphere (CEPAL-ONU 1958, 268). Two-thirds of the population were illiterate and only 11 percent of rural children attended school (Burke 1971a, 329).

The influential UN report identified cultural diversity as a major obstacle to improving these conditions. "The majority of [the people] are still living in isolation from modern civilization, speaking their ancient languages, maintaining their age-old customs and superstitions, wearing their traditional costumes, and farming their land on a subsistence scale" (United Nations 1951, 2). Bolivia was considered a likely target for the new aid approaches in health, education, industry, nutrition, and agriculture being promoted by First World countries.

The United States administrators and technicians working with the new aid programs in Bolivia had witnessed revolutionary agricultural "progress" across the North American landscape during the 1930s and 1940s—all brought about by the widespread use of mechanized farm machinery, hybrid seeds, and agricultural chemicals. These images of advanced technology and modern farming practices impressed Bolivia's political leaders and governmental administrators and led them to the conviction that this U.S. agricultural model was the answer to their underdevelopment problems.

This Western model of development also received legitimacy and support from modernization theory and neo-classical economics, both of which enjoyed prominence in the United States and were actively promoted by the U.S. State Department through its embassies in its post–World War II expansion of power (Valenzuela and Valenzuela 1978). In Bolivia itself, the first social research centers to emerge favored these and closely related development theories (Barnadas 1987, 402). The international theorists shared a view that a country's development processes could be mapped out as a lineal historical trajectory whereby developing nations would achieve economic and social progress by copying the values and institutions of Western industrial nations and importing their capital and technology. In an overview of this modernization literature, Samuel and Arturo Valenzuela found the central theoretical argument of the literature to be that

> the values, institutions and patterns of action of traditional society are both an expression and a cause of underdevelopment. Modernizing Third World elites are understood to be guided by the Western Model, adopting and adapting its technology; assimilating its values and patterns of action; importing its financial, industrial and educational institutions; and so on. Western colonialism, foreign aid, foreign educational opportunities, overseas business investments, the mass media are

important channels for transmission of modernity. The values of Catholicism, of large Indian populations, or of aristocratic rural elites have contributed to 'irrational' patterns of behavior highly detrimental to modernization. (Valenzuela and Valenzuela 1978)

In this chapter, I will discuss foreign aid's importance in shaping Bolivia's national development plans and highlight how some of the Western-centric approaches both created critical problems and sidetracked the country from fully utilizing some of its most precious indigenous resources. I will focus primarily on programs during the 1950s and 1960s that laid the tracks for the wheels of future "progress."

Foreign aid was the indispensable lubricant of the U.S. government's attempts at modernizing Bolivian agriculture. This flow of economic aid began in the 1940s and rose over the next four decades to be among the highest levels of aid in per capita terms in Latin America. On the world map, after Israel and Egypt, there are few countries that exceed the amount of U.S. taxpayer dollars on a per capita basis received by Bolivia through bilateral channels.

The amount of foreign aid allocated to Bolivia accelerated greatly during the late 1950s when, in the throes of revolutionary upheaval, Bolivia soared to the top of the State Department's list of "chosen countries" in the hemisphere. To prevent Bolivia's social revolution from turning communist and falling into the Soviet orbit, the U.S. poured lavish amounts of aid into national development under the MNR regime. This aid, by 1957, began averaging 22.8 percent of the national budget.[1]

U.S. ASSISTANCE IN AGRICULTURAL DEVELOPMENT

The Truman Administration's Point Four Program established in Bolivia the Servicio Agrícola Interaméricano (SAI), which for sixteen years was the best financed and most long-standing agricultural development program in the hemisphere. SAI's rural development strategy for Bolivia had its origins in an important technical report prepared by the State Department's Bohan Commission which engaged in a study of Bolivia during five months in 1942. Merwin Bohan, an ex-ambassador and foreign service officer, wrote the agricultural chapter which established guidelines and major policy recommendations. Influenced by the neo-colonial attitudes within his elite circle of contacts in the Bolivian government, Bohan traveled throughout the countryside, visiting both Indian free communities and haciendas to form his judgments about the natural and human resource base for modernizing the agricultural sector. In the mountains, he observed "primitive, antiquated farm practices and traditions which originated hundreds of years ago." As a Westerner, he was perplexed by the apparent "lack of motivation toward economic progress," and found that there were as yet no strong agricultural education programs imparting Western development concepts to the Indians. He found both the native "world view" and Aymara language to be inimical to the country's immediate development prospects. An exposure to the modern tractor and an opening up of the vast tropical rainforests in the eastern lowlands, he speculated, would perhaps point the Aymara to a new way of life. This vision of a "march to the east" became a blueprint for U.S. development financing of the Santa Cruz region, beginning with the construction of a road connecting Cochabamba to Santa Cruz which was completed in 1954.

For the highlands, Bohan recommended improving pasture and upgrading sheep and cattle stock through the importation of seed and purebred livestock from the United States. There was not a single mention in his report of the Andean camelid family (llamas, alpacas, vicunas) which grazed the vast rangelands of the altiplano and mountain valley landscape. According to a former U.S. aid official in Bolivia, Lawrence Heilman, the Bohan Report became a kind of in-house bible for the U.S. embassy and aid officials during the following decades (Heilman 1982).

SAI was run as a quasi-autonomous U.S. government agency from 1948 to the mid-1960s, as North American administrators and technical experts recruited and trained Bolivian field staff and operated a central office in La Paz which supervised fifty-eight branch offices in other cities and rural towns. In 1959, the combined servicios (agriculture and health) employed 500 professionals, 1,500 sub-professionals, and 2,600 unskilled workers under U.S. supervision (U.S. Congress 1960, 18). According to Heilman, the strategy of the new SAI program operated on the assumptions that "campesinos were seen as having few agricultural skills, a lack of initiative, and no financial assets enabling them to produce or increase agricultural production to any significant degree" (Heilman 1982). SAI's budget was so hefty by Bolivian standards that its program dwarfed the country's Ministry of Agriculture until the agency was brought under the latter institution's wing in 1965. Ex-Bolivian extension agents recall this era as the country's golden years of agricultural financing. As one veteran agronomist from the highland agencies remarked, "We had everything we needed to carry out high-powered agricultural modernization. We had plentiful chemical fertilizers and pesticides such as DDT and aldrin to use on our demonstration farms, modern equipment with which to vaccinate cattle and sheep, and even gas money to make frequent field visits. When the Americans left everything in the hands of the Ministry in 1966, many branch offices began closing, jeeps suddenly became scarce, and the program got too politicized for my taste."

In keeping with the Bohan Report, SAI's vision of Bolivia's future favored the seemingly limitless tropical rainforest of Santa Cruz. This warmer, lowland region offered the U.S. agricultural extension agents the kind of middle-class farm belt found back in their home states. The lowland landowners, in turn, were anxious to modernize their farms with cheap credit, modern technology, and North American–style technical assistance, both for quick profits and to escape the sweeping national land reform movement aimed at the traditional hacienda. SAI's program included land clearing, farm machinery pools, mechanized farming demonstrations, and the sale of farm machinery and supplies (Wennergren and Whitaker 1975). Figuring prominently in this influx of Western farm technology was the North American bulldozer with all its technological might to remove large swaths of the dense tropical forests.

To a country whose total farm machinery imports in its entire history added up to only 270 pieces of equipment, the United States government during the second half of the 1950s brought in 1,300 tractors and 5,000 moldboard plows to accelerate a modern farming revolution (Arrieta et al. 1990). Operations became so chaotic with the imported farm machinery that a U.S. congressional committee conducted its own investigation of the Bolivian situation. They concluded that foreign aid to Bolivia during the 1950s was often "too much too soon" in relation to these machinery pools. Road graders and tractors had remained in their original crates from months to years while others sat idle awaiting the arrival of spare parts from the United States. Outdoor storage areas in the long tropical rainy season turned to small "lakes" and "seas of mud" causing machinery to deteriorate. The report characterized the storage as a "graveyard" of trucks and deemed much agricultural equipment as "unsuited for various reasons to that locality"

(U.S. Congress 1960, 19). The report recommended reducing the machinery pools to 25 percent of inventory and temporarily halting the flow of machinery imports.

Even when the SAI program did function in Santa Cruz it helped the elites rather than Indians and created new environmental problems. Dwight Heath, professor emeritus of anthropology at Brown University who did research in Santa Cruz at that time, retrospectively summed up the picture this way:

> The region was viewed as a big green blot on the map and Bolivia's future breadbasket. The commercial sugar farmers benefited from both the grading of roads to their enterprises and agricultural credit easily repayable. The Bolivian government, partly to relieve demographic pressure in the west and partly as a buffer against Brazilian geo-political incursions to the east, was equally enthusiastic. The bulldozing of trees, the scooping of topsoil, was creating a huge dustbowl; although the American aid officials and county agents did not recognize it, local people often made bitter jokes. (personal communication 1996)

By financing forest clearing, the United States and multilateral donors expected to pave the way for the expansion of Bolivian agricultural exports and import substitution during the following decades. The dynamic economic growth, however, had a high environmental cost. A 1993 World Bank report, covering thirty years of natural resource management in Bolivia, laments the disastrous ecological consequences that have resulted from development planners' ignoring the damage being done to the fragile soils and biodiversity (World Bank 1993a). The rate of deforestation to provide land for timber, cattle raising, and various export crops such as soybeans continues today at an accelerated rate, claiming tens of thousands of hectares every year. Ironically, the World Bank report indicates that during the 1960s, World Bank documents themselves frequently identified Indian culture as an obstacle to economic growth, deploring the indigenous superstitions and "primitive customs" which actually often served as natural resource conservation practices.

In accordance with Bohan's modernization vision of eastern migration, sponsored resettlement programs enabled highland indigenous to move into the tropical jungles of the Alto Beni in northern La Paz, the Chapare in eastern Cochabamba, and Northern Santa Cruz. Under foreign aid sponsorship, the colonists learned to replace the dense polycultures of the tropical rainforest with the same Western designs deployed throughout the Third World for implanting monocultures: rectangular fields with single stands of coffee, cacao, and rice reliant upon assorted petro-chemical technologies for pest, weed, and disease control (J. Scott 1998; Henkel 1982).

Given Bolivia's internal colonialism and the nature of the Western development paradigm, there was during this period little interest in tapping the knowledge of the small native populations dwelling in the tropical forests about to be cleared. According to Heath, "In theory these lands were empty and the Indians were to be dealt with by missionaries."

Indeed, in 1954, Paz Estenssoro delegated the integration of many scattered ethnic groups of the Amazon to another U.S. organization, the Instituto de Lingüística de Verano (ILV) or Summer Institute of Linguistics from Texas.[2] Their staff which included professors in linguistics from Oklahoma and other universities established a base of operations in the remote Amazonian rainforests of the Pando at a secluded site, Tumichucua, overlooking a stunningly picturesque lake framing an island lush with emerald green forests. Here they enjoyed this view from screened-in rooms of summer cottage–like homes and set out along the back trails and rivers of the Amazon to contact and lure indigenous tribes into their self-enclosed den of Western civilization. They built a schoolhouse for reeducating ethnic groups with Spanish literacy training, evangelical religious education, and Western-type community development (Castro Mantilla 1997). Although these linguists and religious educators recuperated otherwise unknown indigenous languages for the nation's cultural patrimony, on the whole their efforts eroded many facets of indigenous culture including communal organizations and diverse spiritual cosmovisions of Amazonia. Bolivian anthropologist Rosario Leon, familiar with ILV's work, commented, "Their program used native languages to dominate the indigenous peoples, pushing them toward a Western way of life in a way that negated many strengths of their own culture and knowledge."

In addition to ignoring the lowland ethnic groups, Western-minded development planners did not consider the Indians migrating to Santa Cruz from hundreds of mountain communities capable of "developing" this region either. Heath reported, "There was a strong sense of the need for foreign migration to offset this human resource limitation. One example was the creation of Japanese colonies" (personal communication 1996). The

MNR was anxious for these traditional rice growers to share their knowledge with the Andean peoples unfamiliar with tropical agriculture.

In addition to several hundred new Japanese and Okinawan settler families that formed new colonies, the MNR's first development plan borrowed Bohan's idea to import Anglo-Saxon farm families as an important injection of human capital for speeding agricultural modernization. Their "Plan Inmediato" called for the emigration of 5,000 Southern European families to Santa Cruz, a number identical to the Aymara and Quechua expected to be settled in government-directed programs (Arrieta et al. 1990, 101). Despite these ambitious designs for gaining gringo know-how to jump-start modernization, the only immediate takers were several hundred Mennonites of Central European extraction farming in tropical Paraguay. Subsequently, small groups of Mennonites from Mexico as well as Canada trickled into Santa Cruz to join the original pioneers (Henkel 1982, 284). To lure them, the Bolivian government provided much larger landholdings and better access to bank credit than for the indigenous peasant settlers, along with easy legal residency requirements. The Japanese also began to receive continuous economic support from the foreign aid agency of their government back home. With this advantageous headstart, over the next four decades, the Japanese and Mennonites became some of Bolivia's most successful commercial farmers.

A quote from the published memoirs of George Jackson Eder, the U.S. official who negotiated the economic aid program with the MNR in 1955, reveals some of the racist thinking prevalent during this early modernization era. He wrote that, "The Asiatics and Europeans, it is true, proved far better farmers than the Indians, but I refrained from mentioning that fact at council meetings. There was simply no comparison between the intelligence, initiative, energy, and manifest prosperity of the Japanese, Okinawans, Mennonites [from Central Europe], and the equally obvious shortcomings of the Aymara colonizers. It was as though the latter had been transported bodily from a more primitive era, having little in common with modern man" (Eder 1969, 652).

The Bohan Plan recommended that commercial ranching be promoted for the Beni to integrate this region into national markets and tap the comparative advantage of its vast savanna lands for grazing (Bohan 1942). Bohan's vision for modern cattle ranching was exclusively focused on whites and mestizos with the indigenous rural communities absent from his report. Foreign aid financing and the opening of a national cattle market led to a kind of "revolution in reverse." For while a social revolution was de-molishing the hacienda system and driving the patrons off their lands in the western highlands, in the Beni commercial ranchers were gobbling up Indian lands and modernizing production by introducing cebu cattle from Brazil (Jones 1997). The Indians living in old mission towns such as San Ignacio de Moxos sought refuge from this rancher invasion of the 1950s by returning to the Chimane forest, their homeland prior to the arrival of Je-suits during the seventeenth century. Over subsequent decades, this emerg-ing cattle-ranching elite continued to consolidate its regional wealth and power with help from a variety of national and international institutions in-cluding generous loans from the World Bank (Jones 1997).

During the 1950s and 1960s, cattle and sheep improvement held center stage in the financing of livestock development with both public and pri-vate resources. Brought to the Americas by the Spaniards from the sixteenth century onward, cattle and sheep had become indispensable components of the rural household economy. More familiar to the Western eye and histori-cal experience than native llamas and alpacas, these animals were the prin-cipal focus of development plans for modernizing livestock production. Public programs to improve cattle production in Bolivia greatly favored the Santa Cruz and Beni elites (including tens of millions of dollars in uncol-lected loans) instead of indigenous peasants, and had negative ecological con-sequences in Santa Cruz as acre after acre of rainforest was transformed into low-grade pasture land. In another Santa Cruz effort, the U.S. government tried in vain for five years to consolidate an artificial insemination program for improving cattle breeds. The program floundered without the tele-phones essential for requesting the vaccine when cows were in heat. The telephone had not yet reached most of rural Bolivia. Inappropriate livestock modernization technologies were neither a U.S. nor Western monopoly. The Taiwanese set up a hog-fattening program in the southern Andean foothills with production modules of cement floors, tin roofs, glass window panes, and expensive high-nutritional feeds. Local farm families not only grumbled about the exorbitant costs of this system but about pig life-styles superior to their own. Sheep promotional programs had a more equitable design as campesinos were specified as the target "beneficiary group."

SAI and its successor, United States Agency for International Develop-ment (USAID), along with other multilateral and bilateral agencies, sup-ported the import of super-productive breeds, such as corredale, rambullet, and merino associated with sheep raising in North America. After replacing

SAI, USAID established a program overseen by Utah State University, a land grant institution in a western state with vast rangelands, to help with the modernization of sheep farming. During the 1960s this program imported 2,000 purebred sheep and 200,000 pounds of pasture seed (Heilman 1982, 244). Peace Corps volunteers trained Andean farmers in state-of-the-art sheep-shearing techniques and other practices. The World Bank also financed several large sheep-raising projects and much later even my own agency, the Inter-American Foundation, joined this bandwagon to support a small project administered by an altiplano peasant federation.

The sum total of this directed modernization, according to Carlos Salinas, the Bolivian government's national livestock director in 1995, was a glaring backward step in Bolivian rural development. During a 1994 interview in his La Paz office, the Mexican-trained veterinarian shook his head in dismay.

> Look, in just twenty years the doubling of the altiplano sheep population to 8.5 million animals has exacerbated problems of overgrazing, and caused the severe depletion and degradation of topsoil and vegetative cover in our altiplano and valley regions. We imported the best breeds from all over the world, yet we still find ourselves with only scraggly animals, weighing about 22 kilos at four years of age, and with low levels of fertility and high rates of mortality. The eating practices of these animals literally tore up the altiplano's vegetative cover by voraciously devouring the roots under the native shrubs and grasses. Our harsh climatic conditions and high altitudes are a far cry from the optimal field conditions to which these animals had been accustomed. I remember in one government agency we flew high-priced Uruguayan sheep from sea level to Sucre at 10,000 ft. and watched in horror as many of them were shrieking as though they were suffering from cardiac attacks while deboarding the aircraft.
>
> Our wool and mutton sales have also suffered from the lack of adequate markets. In our cities people prefer chicken and beef over mutton which is hard to digest. In a similar way, our prospects for competing with countries such as New Zealand, Australia or Uruguay in the export of wool have been unrealistic. It's high time we cashed in on our comparative advantage as the world's number one producer of llamas, and specialize in camelid production. By promoting sheep raising in the altiplano all this time we have been trading off more oppor-

tunities to develop improved methods for raising our native llamas, alpacas, and vicunas. Although there were some camelid programs aiming to improve marketing of alpaca fiber, our governmental agricultural institutions failed to provide the necessary resources and attention for improving the health and production conditions for this highland livestock. But, of course, foreign aid priorities greatly influenced this long-term neglect. Who is to blame for this predicament? I am not one to point a finger outside the country but rather at ourselves—the agronomists and veterinarians of my generation—for lacking the courage and common sense to question the importation of so many resources. It was only when we began listening to what the Indian herders and farmers were saying about the ecological damage caused by sheep that we began to change our views.

Salinas could have pointed a finger at the Banzer regime which in 1973 squelched a promising USAID-sponsored pilot testing of the marketing possibilities of sausage products using camelid meat (Hale 1981, 76). In addition to the project shutdown, the military rulers issued a government decree further prohibiting llama meat sales, long strangled by municipal regulations and related discriminatory practices. The military's modernization move was not only neo-colonial disdain for an indigenous cultural resource but revealed their close association with the elite cattle-ranching interests in protecting beef markets from competition in highland cities like La Paz.

Returning to the subject of sheep raising, Salinas said,

The promotion of sheep tremendously degraded our native pasture lands, the native grasses and shrubs of the altiplano, which were developed over a millennium for camelids. This pasturage, we realize now, was among Bolivia's most important resources. Bolivia received a lot of valuable foreign aid support for bringing alfalfa, barley, and oats into the country as forages for livestock. And one of the best alfalfa varieties called Ranger was a hybrid which meant that our producers would have to replenish their seeds from foreign suppliers every year. Native species on the other hand—even when Westerners recognized their value through their own research—seemed to always command far less interest from the national government and its sponsors than the imported grasses.

Salinas's reflection on native grasses were borne out by comments in technical reports in the late 1970s and 1980s about the value of this overlooked resource.

> Very little work has been performed on grassland or rangeland in Bolivia. The work that has been done in the highlands—principally measurements of productivity in caged enclosures—indicates that the highland region is potentially one of the richest, most productive grasslands in the world, rivaling and exceeding the best natural range in the United States. (Preston and Brown 1988, 54)

Native pasture grasses were only one of the many agricultural resources ignored by development planners; traditional grain and food crops were not given due consideration. Looking back over Bolivia's agricultural history in 1994, Mauricio Mamani, an Aymara anthropologist and veteran development practitioner, stated:

> Although U.S. and government programs helped to identify high-yielding native varieties of potatoes such as "Sani Imilla" for wide distribution among small farmers, in general the lack of governmental and foreign interest in promoting the native biodiversity of the potato during these decades of the modern era was a setback for rural development. All through those years, farmers were planting many valuable native varieties which the government extension agencies simply ignored. These varieties were unmatched for resisting frost in certain micro-climates, and were tastier and could be grown without expensive chemical fertilizers used for the large potatoes. Among these were the "papa amarga," or bitter potato, used for making "chuño" a freeze-dried foodstuff basic to the Andean diet. The lack of interest in maintaining potato diversity and other important aspects of traditional agriculture was also the result of the external focus of Bolivian universities, which only taught Western agricultural methods using textbooks written in the United States or England. Agronomy students found scant material about the techniques, sophistication, and potential of traditional Andean agriculture.

Mamani also lamented the indiscriminate use of chemical fertilizers. "In my home province in the altiplano, the site of a large World Bank project

[Ingavi], farmers refer to land harmed by the overuse of fertilizers as 'pacha-mama drogado'" (the drugged Pachamama, the Andean earth deity).[3] Julio Rea, another critical voice among Bolivia's agricultural scientists, has argued to me on various occasions that due to its exclusive focus on a very few native or improved varieties, the Bolivian government was blind to the fact that some valuable Bolivian seed species were disappearing from the farm-ers' fields. Agricultural development projects were not solely responsible for this disappearance; the United States food aid program contributed, too.

THE FOOD AID PROGRAM

In the throes of a disruptive social revolution, Bolivia in the mid-1950s was in dire need of massive food aid support. The emergency relief program from the United States gradually evolved into a national structural de-pendency which complicated various aspects of nutrition, native resource use, food preferences, and agricultural biodiversity over the next four decades.

The U.S. food aid program in Bolivia was put into effect in 1956 under Public Law 480, the first of its kind in the Americas.[4] This aid overshad-owed SAI's programs in monetary value (Frederick 1977, 261–62). Food aid was a public policy instrument used to dispose of large U.S. food surpluses in the Third World in order to gain foreign policy leverage, advance hu-manitarian interests, and open markets for wheat and other crops. The do-nated food, officially known as "Food for Peace," could have been more aptly dubbed "Food for Surviving the Cold War." It was sent together with other forms of aid on the condition that Bolivia resurrect from the ashes of defeat its military forces to help fight communism (Dunkerley 1984, 114).[5]

The omnipresent sacks of wheat, wheat flour, and other donated food products with their red, white, and blue handclasps and stars and stripes in-signia reached the most remote outposts of Bolivian society via a vast na-tional distribution apparatus. A primary institutional channel of this aid was through voluntary agencies such as Catholic Relief Services and its Bo-livian counterpart, Cáritas Boliviano, which worked through a wide net-work of Catholic parishes and affiliated mothers' clubs to reach poor farm families. The food aid program flowed through several channels which set different terms and conditions for its use and distribution.[6] By hooking Bolivian millers, bakers, and consumers into these wheat products, food aid also paved the way for greatly increasing regular wheat imports from the United States and Argentina.[7]

Wheat-based products (bread, macaroni, cookies, semola, flour, etc.) rose in volume and importance over the next forty years to rank among the country's most prized foodstuffs (Kietz 1992, 77; Prudencio and Velasco 1988; Prudencio and Franqueville 1995). Representing 18 percent of the calories in the diet of an urban consumer in 1960, wheat-based products grew to represent 75 percent of the calories and 70 percent of the protein by 1984. During the period 1980–1992, the consumption of wheat-based products jumped from two kilos per inhabitant to seven kilos (Prudencio and Franqueville 1995, 164). In short, the stream of wheat donations and regular sales from the U.S. and elsewhere expanded the place of wheat-based products at meals and afternoon tea time in Bolivia's low-income households. By the mid-1970s Bolivia had become the per capita world leader in food aid shipments from the United States.

The non-stop flow of this food aid became another face of an imported Western development model and cultural homogenization process influencing Bolivia's patterns of rural development. Inducing consumers to use processed white bread and other wheat-based foods like macaroni brought the decline of various home-grown and locally traded products in both the cities and the countryside.[8] First and foremost to be affected were the Quechua and Aymara producers of diverse varieties of criollo wheat in the highlands whose market conditions deteriorated (Prudencio and Franqueville 1995). Andean crop diversity as the basis of a cuisine for the moral aesthetic of a "fit livelihood" in this rugged environment (Zimmerer 1996) also suffered from these changing consumer tastes (Kietz 1992; Prudencio and Velasco 1988; Dandler et al. 1987).

Fernando Murillo, an employee of Catholic Relief Services coordinating food shipments and distribution to altiplano communities, attested to these changes.

> I personally saw how vital Andean grains in the Aymara diet disappeared from the huge influx of wheat and wheat flour and new products emerging from them such as "trigo tostado" and white bread. In the Aroma altiplano province, our wheat hand-out programs soon led Aymaras to stop consuming quinoa and in another altiplano province I observed how Andean "pito de kañiwa," a beverage made from kañiwa, became abandoned due to our food give-aways.

In Andean mountain valleys, wheat-based products reduced the use of native maize in bread, corn beer (*chicha*), and *mote,* large moist kernels served as a side dish at main meals. In several highland valleys by the late 1990s wheat macaroni had displaced local maize varieties from their traditional pedestal in prestige dishes for special occasions.

In Santa Cruz, white bread and macaroni from the national food industry began driving out of the diet more nutritious "integral maize tamales" made in the indigenous communities of Urubicha (Guarayos) and Izozog (Izoceños). Other peanut, banana, and yucca-based products made locally in Santa Cruz shared a similar fate.[9]

When wheat is milled into flour it loses 20 percent of its protein and over 60 percent of its minerals and vitamins. The mentioned Bolivian maize, quinoa, and kañiwa by contrast maintain their very high nutritional value as consumable food items. Nor were there any significant government efforts to fortify the processed wheat such as is done in the United States to restore lost minerals and vitamins.

In this way, the PL-480 food program along with regular U.S. wheat imports has served as another instance of the Western monoculture steamrolling Bolivia's cultural diversity. Over the years, many public and private, national and international agencies working in Bolivia have struggled to come up with ways such as school breakfast programs and road building and other community infrastructure programs to give food aid a positive developmental role despite the forementioned development issues. No doubt many have succeeded yet a widespread view also exists about food aid's negative psychological impact on communities in generating a welfare-like mentality among its many recipients (Kietz 1992).

THE SPREAD OF WESTERN MEDICAL ASSISTANCE

While Western-style agricultural development programs were expanding the U.S. government's role in modernizing rural Bolivian communities, parallel though more modest financing and institution building were taking place in public health. The U.S. government launched its first bilateral aid program in Bolivia under the auspices of the Inter-American Public Health Service (SCISP) in the 1940s and that was followed by the Inter-American Co-operative Education Service (SCIDE).[10] These health clinics and related education programs expanded greatly during the 1950s (Bastien 1992), when the MNR was pushing its agenda of national integration and the United States was pouring foreign aid monies into the coffers of a financially shaky, revolutionary government. Between 1942 and 1960, SCISP installed a public health care system similar to but on a much smaller scale than the SAI program in the agricultural sector. During the 1950s, the SCISP network grew to incorporate thirty-three health clinics, thirteen hospitals, and various mobile health teams giving technical assistance and training in modern health care practices and the use of synthetic drugs (Point Four 1960, 28). Meanwhile, the Bolivian Ministry established 300 health clinics throughout the country during the decade of the 1950s (Arrieta et al. 1990).

This U.S. national health care network did not become part of the Bolivian Ministry of Health until 1960. SCISP's resources served to pay the salaries of Bolivian doctors, nurses, and auxiliary nurses and to finance physical construction, medical equipment, medicines, and other supplies for the clinics and hospitals. Modern medicine was also advancing in rural Bolivia through the marketing of synthetic drugs and through programs directed by church parishes and private voluntary programs offering health care services as humanitarian aid. Vaccination campaigns reduced the incidence of critical diseases including small pox and yaws, which were among the worst in the Western hemisphere (Point Four 1960, 27). The introduction of antibiotics such as penicillin and streptomycin also made positive contributions in enhancing rural health care.

While dispensing helpful medicines and vaccinating babies, these modern health workers had views that collided with deeply held practices associated with local ethno-medicine. The gains made by Point Four were limited to certain problems and did not alter Bolivia's chronic bottom ranking among Latin America countries on important health indicators such as infant mortality, the prevalence of infectious diseases, malnutrition, and short life expectancy. Western medical facilities in the Bolivian countryside had extremely low utilization rates as could be seen in the number of empty hospital beds in the altiplano despite the serious illnesses and diseases widespread in surrounding communities.

The rural public schools, according to anthropologist Marci Stephenson, used materials that promoted personal hygiene using language in a way that suggested that there were "pre-modern" and "modern bodies," the former, of course, being associated with the dirtiness of indigenous peoples (Stephenson 1999). Western medical practitioners and traditional healers found themselves locked in a mutually suspicious, if not antagonistic, relationship that led to charges of malpractice from both sides (Bastien 1992). Families often were too poor to afford many of the modern medicines.

The operating assumption behind these programs was that native medical practices were hopelessly backward, as well as dangerous, and would soon wither in the face of scientifically based health care systems. The 1950s was the decade when bio-medicine's new drugs emerged as the universally applicable remedies for the health maladies of diverse Third World cultures (Bastien 1992, 6). Despite the promise of Western medicine, nurses and auxiliary health workers who conducted health, maternal, child care, and nutrition education programs found themselves facing radically different concepts of disease, nutrition, and medical practices. Native curing practices often entailed a highly ritualized engagement between healer and patient, included dietary and other behavioral changes, and incorporated a deep understanding of the psychosomatic base of illness—aspects usually unfamiliar to Western-trained practitioners at that time. Traditional healing practices thus remained widespread in poor indigenous communities for their low cost, convenience, and wide cultural acceptance.

The modern health practitioner often viewed native healers through a neo-colonial lens. Missing from modern medical training was any method for understanding ethno-medicine's wide-ranging role and well-established legitimacy in communities. Witchcraft and shamanism associated with ethno-medicine became convenient stigmas used by medical professionals to denigrate these cultural expressions.

Once doctors, pharmacists, and pharmaceutical firms began spreading the use of modern drugs, perceptions of traditional practitioners became even worse. Successful lobbying of the national congress led to the outlawing of ethno-medical practices in the cities and, as a result, many illiterate herbalists wound up in jail (Bastien 1992, 19).

This persecution was perhaps the most severe against the Kallawayas, Bolivia's most renowned group of traditional practitioners who had carved out an impressive role as herbal healers not only in Bolivia but throughout South America. These itinerant healers, once numbering upwards of 500 men (according to ethnographer Luis Giralt), deployed an array of medicinal and ritual objects in their healing repertoire. They attracted the sick from all over South America and were even called to the Panama Canal when canal workers contracted malaria. An 1869 photograph shows several Kallawaya wearing broad-brimmed white top hats and fine ponchos, holding in their hands the traditional coca leaf bags containing the sacred leaves used for diagnosing illnesses.

EXTENSION EDUCATION AND COMMUNITY ORGANIZATION PROGRAMS

The aid programs all included educational components and inherent designs for altering indigenous community organizations. The overriding assumption was that indigenous practices had no value in themselves and/or were detrimental to development.

The U.S. extension team experts were typically county agents transplanted from U.S. state programs or professors from vocational agricultural schools (Rice 1974). The extension service's main operating premise was that a top-down, one-way technical information flow—from the agricultural research station, via the extension agent, to the farmer—was the best way to transform agriculture. SAI began replicating a variety of North American agricultural institutions which had served so well the progress of the U.S. family farm during the nineteenth and twentieth centuries. SAI organized 4-H clubs (called 4-S in Bolivia) for stimulating such miniprojects as rabbit-raising and vegetable gardening by rural youth and offered home economics programs to teach Indian women about "model homes" and new recipes for improved cuisine and nutrition (Heilman 1982). The farmers' new rural credit system was a replica of the U.S. Farm Home Administration and SAI even tried—albeit unsuccessfully—to restructure a Bolivian university into a land grant–style college. Then the first contingent of U.S. Peace Corps volunteers arrived in 1962 to begin plugging into many of these modernizing programs.

While the 4-S clubs contributed many interesting small-scale projects, they lacked roots in rural cultural life and quickly disappeared once the SAI program terminated. Farmers and Bolivian professionals sat through many U.S.-made movies about co-operative experiences in Latin America and the United States. Some took excursions to Israel's kibbutz farms to see advanced co-op development. Yet the lack of relevance of these experiences to Bolivian rural life was evident when most co-ops disintegrated after only a few years in operation and could barely be kept afloat with outside funding. Co-operative planners and organizers failed to adapt their Western organizational system to native communal traditions of reciprocity and communal service and the co-op structures were easily manipulated for personal gain by ambitious and corrupt leaders (A. García 1970, 321).[11]

International and national community development agencies focused on the development of human resources and devoted a considerable amount of time to understanding what makes communities tick and how to mobilize them toward developmental goals. Although on one level unusually "pro-Indian," these agencies were also infected by some of the same strong biases of the Western development model.

In 1954, the International Labor Organization (ILO) of the United Nations began in Bolivia its first action program on behalf of native peoples anywhere in the world. Branches of this Andean Mission program were also set up that year in Ecuador and Peru, and subsequently spread to Argentina, Chile, and Colombia. According to the deputy director of the ILO, Jeff Rens, the objective of the program was Indian integration "by making a single people of two populations separated by origin, language and way of life" (Rens 1961). Its goal was "to awaken in them a desire for progress and a desire to help themselves." This widely publicized and well-financed program consisted of a few "bases" or centers, which offered training and technical assistance to Indian communities, initially through "international experts" from the United States, Western Europe, and other countries in Latin America. Bolivia became the site of four of these bases, more than any other country.

The Andean Mission Program, with its multiple facets, was almost a caricature of the assimilationist Western development model. According to Rens, who used "integration" as a buzzword, eucalyptus plantations were established for reforestation and soil conservation, imported sheep and cattle were introduced, schools were built to teach native youth in Spanish using an urban curriculum, industrial trades for men, and modern dress-making skills for women (Rens 1963). The Andean Mission tried to "convert Indian communities into agricultural and livestock co-operatives" and "turn thin natural pasture into sown pasture." Experimenting with over a hundred imported varieties of grasses and legumes for ten years, and ignoring the native pasture lands in front of their eyes, they declared that the altiplano was "admirably suited for large-scale stock rearing" (Rens 1961). They also unsuccessfully attempted to establish resettlement programs by uprooting entire altiplano Indian communities for relocation in Santa Cruz.

In his assessment reports, Rens drew the following conclusion. "The program has been a giant campaign of education and enlightenment of the

Indian population, as the Indians living in the influence of the bases are becoming less interested in drink or the coca leaf and are instead taking greater interest in community affairs and generally becoming less resigned and more ready to work and show initiative." As for the perceptions of the Indians themselves, Rens wrote, "In their eyes an educated Indian is no longer an Indian, he has become a man" (Rens 1961, 436). Other evaluations of the program painted a very different picture (Leonard 1966; Schwend 1962). The late Sánchez de Lozada, a former Bolivian director and father of the country's recent president, Gonzalo Sánchez de Lozada, commented, "It would be hard to imagine a bigger community development fiasco than these Andean bases."[12]

When the Andean Mission became incorporated into the Bolivian government in 1962, a strategy was designed to have its approach overhauled. The new plan called for replacing the "community improvement" approach with a "community self-help" policy. The same document, however, identified "superstition and outworn social and economic organization and traditions, low-level production methods and old fashioned farming practices, and the diversity of languages" as major obstacles to progress in rural communities.

The National Community Development Service (SNDC) which replaced the Andean Mission and emerged with funding from the United States Agency for International Development, appeared more at home promoting co-ops, 4-H, and women's clubs as forms of self-help than reinforcing and revitalizing time-honored, communal native practices. For example, rather than working with traditional authority structures, they set up parallel "community councils" and worked with the military's civic action groups. Some Bolivian observers claim the political objectives of this approach were to undermine the social and political mobilization power of the rural sindicatos. Serapio Ramos, a veteran of twenty years with SNDC, reflected glumly on the sustainability of these endeavors in a 1995 conversation. "When each public works project was completed, the 'comites' usually stopped meeting. Thus there was no follow-up to maintain the investments so today many of them have been abandoned while the communities await the return of SNDC to repair and improve them. That's because the system of self-help introduced by us no longer exists."

Anti-indigenous biases can be readily identified in the SNDC programs related to women's promotion. Evelyn Barrón, who worked with SNDC between 1971 and 1977 and rose to become its national director of women's programs, expressed embarrassment when reminiscing about SNDC's orientation.

> Much of our training was geared to help indigenous women break away from habits of some kind of imagined primitive culture. For example, we would hold classes to teach women how to hold a fork, hang curtains, enlarge their windows and raise cooking facilities off the floor in their adobe huts. Only years later did they enable us to see that the small windows were necessary to keep out the altiplano cold, and that cooking on the floor was essential for conversing with family and friends around a fire in the evenings.
> Many of our home improvement manuals were written by foreigners who never set foot in Bolivia. It was as though we in the Third World were just one big receptacle for all these community change formulas being designed and dumped down on us from up North. We often had to promote recipes for certain foods well beyond the economic reach of the rural people, or simply locally unavailable. We taught artisanry skills in crocheting and embroidery but overlooked wonderful handwoven textile traditions in dire need of recognition given the discrimination women faced wearing traditional ethnic costumes in the city. As a result of our training, women often returned to their communities with a sense of shame and cultural inferiority rather than pride and self-confidence.

A MUDDIED DEVELOPMENT PATH

Despite the financial investment backing these aid programs, the lack of success for many of them was evident. In an eleven-country study of U.S.-created extension services in Latin America, Bolivia ranked among the countries at the bottom in terms of advancing agricultural productivity (Rice 1974).

The 1960 congressional report described "white elephant" projects that typified the problems of U.S. foreign aid in Bolivia. These included an abandoned new plant for processing yucca flour that suffered from competition by U.S wheat imports and the absence of related national dietary habits; an uneconomical and poorly designed animal vaccine laboratory; and an agricultural school which was "overbuilt," with "over-equipped plants,"

"years ahead of need" and "too expensive, too elaborate for Bolivians to operate" (U.S. Congress 1960, 11–14).

A similar assessment was made by Richard Patch, a perceptive anthropologist evaluating United States aid efforts during the 1950s. He wrote "To
the campesinos' desire for seed, land, and water, the agricultural service
program too often responded by offering insecticides, sprayers, fertilizers,
and a school for training tractor mechanics. These innovations, while potentially valuable, are not adaptable to the level of agricultural technique in
Bolivia. The agricultural service has suffered from being too close a copy of
the U.S. extension service" (Patch 1960).

On the plains of Lequezana of Andean Potosi region one could see a
microcosm of how apparent successes could turn to mush under the thrust
of Western-centered development. This area became a cause celebre within
the Bolivian development community during the 1970s for its whopping
potato yields via monocropping, the use of several improved seed varieties,
petro-chemical products for fertilization and pest control and American-
made tractors. Some peasant families were able to fulfill lifelong dreams of
buying a truck. The producers had been organized into a service cooperative by SNDC and subsequently benefited from the technical assistance of a
Washington, D.C., consulting agency which flew down to provide advice.
However, by the 1980s, it was apparent that the combined misuse of tractors, pesticides, and chemical fertilizers and reliance only a few strains had
created an ecological disaster zone. In the eyes of Bolivian agronomist-
anthropologist, Antonio Ugarte, "For many development buffs and assorted
observers Lequezana's fields had moved from a widely admired grassroots
development showcase to an illustrative model about what not to do for attaining sustainable Andean development."

The Western development model did not fit the needs of many indigenous communities in Bolivia. And under strong foreign pressures, as well as
influences from its commercial interests and own colonial legacy, Bolivia
turned its back on much of its diverse base of biological and cultural resources. Symbolic of this mentality of foreign dependency was the absence
of a single monument in the capital city to an indigenous leader while numerous ones to foreign leaders such as John F. Kennedy stood tall.

From Import Substitution to Globalization: A Tale of Two Economic Development Models

The designers of the national economic priorities assume that only the large agro-businesses can truly produce wealth, and as such they waste most of the country's human potential.

TICONA, ROJAS, AND ALBÓ (1995, 154)

In addition to the problems associated with Western and neo-colonial ethnocentrism, indigenous development was held back by the macro-economic development models used widely throughout Latin America. In Bolivia, the economic development models adopted by the state shaped both the socioeconomic constraints and opportunities for Bolivia's indigenous peoples during the second half of the twentieth century. The first model, state capitalism, began with the MNR and was carried forward by a succession of military regimes and a civilian coalition government in its final phase. The second model, neo-liberalism, has dominated Bolivian economic life under freely elected civilian governments since 1985. Neo-liberalism is closely associated with globalization, which refers to the free flow of goods and services within the world economy and the increasing use of extensive information and communications technologies. Neo-liberalism's standard policies of stabilization and structural adjustment tend to reorient and liberalize the rules of the economy's operations to facilitate contemporary globalization processes. The two models offer starkly different approaches in terms of the relationship between the state and the market. In the former case, a pro-active state shapes the operations of the economy through strategic interventions while the latter model provides a hands-off approach where governments pull back, allowing market forces alone to determine the course of socioeconomic development. In practice, these economic development models are not as black and white as these abstract definitions would suggest. The Bolivian case shows that state capitalism and neo-liberalism may have overlapping similarities along with their fundamental differences.

This chapter will examine Bolivia's economic development models in terms of their main characteristics and socioeconomic and environmental consequences for different social groups, regions, and the country as a whole. It will trace the trail of the two evolving models within Bolivian national life by examining their different stages, cumulative social, environmental, and economic effects, and relationship with the global economy.

Although launched thirty-three years apart, the two models owe their origins to the same political party (the MNR), the same political leader (Paz Estenssoro), and the same principal foreign government sponsor (the United States government). In 1985, the MNR returned to power after many years and overthrew the very state-led model it had instituted in 1952, replacing it with the neo-liberal globalization strategy.

THE RISE AND EXPANSION OF THE STATE CAPITALIST MODEL

Bolivia's experience with the state capitalist model for economic development began with the national revolution of 1952. The revolution's most dramatic expression of economic nationalism was the expropriation and nationalization of the country's private tin mines, representing 70 percent of export earnings. Bolivia was the world's second leading tin producer at that time. The Bolivian state mining corporation (COMIBOL) soon was operating twenty-one mining companies, several spare parts factories, various electricity plants, farms, a railroad, and other agencies (Seyler 1989, 133), extending its control over two thirds of the diversified mining industry.

For the next three decades, the Bolivian state constructed a modern capitalist economy by enlarging its own central role to propel the country's economic growth onward and upward (Conaghan and Malloy 1994). During much of this period, the state monopolized key economic sectors of tin, petroleum, and natural gas, organized its own major enterprises, and subsidized the organization of others.[1] It played an interventionist and protectionist role through price-setting, regulating the flow of exports and imports, allocating financial credit, redistributing private and public lands, and investing in infrastructure. The MNR utilized a government entity, the Corporación Boliviano de Fomento (CBF), to stimulate diverse kinds of mostly agro-industrial production.

Two other important tenets of the Bohan-inspired MNR plan of state capitalism were economic diversification and import substitution. By 1953, mineral products, especially tin, were generating 97 percent of the economy's total export earnings (Arrieta et al. 1990). To pursue this twin strategy, Bolivia began bolstering the state petroleum company, Yacimientos Petroliferos Fiscales Bolivianos (YPFB), to reduce the oil import bill and increase potential sales in world export markets.[2] The growth of oil production and subsequently natural gas over the next two decades enabled Bolivia to attain a more diversified export portfolio as hydrocarbons began sharing center stage in the economy with mineral exports.

The MNR's strategy of economic diversification and import substitution also led to support of the expansion of a private sector for spearheading modernization and economic growth in the eastern lowlands of Santa Cruz and the Beni (Arrieta et al. 1990; Conaghan and Malloy 1994). Import substitution was very much in vogue throughout Latin America in the 1940s and 1950s thanks to the CEPAL School in Chile. The goal of import substitution was to enable Latin American countries to escape their traditional straitjacket of disadvantageous terms of trade as exporters of cheap primary goods and importers of expensive industrial products from the United States and other industrial nations. Under import substitution policies, many South American governments embarked upon an industrialization strategy to replace foreign manufactured goods with national production.

The MNR-Bolivian version of import substitution inspired by the Bohan Plan went beyond oil to target the elimination of agricultural imports such as cotton, meat, sugar, and rice, representing 25 percent of the national import bill. Bohan's view of import substitution had a contradictory twist that Bolivia would be better off spending its scarce foreign exchange earnings on importing U.S. agricultural machinery for producing food rather than on the food itself (Arrieta et al. 1990). This view, of course, was consistent with the Western ethnocentrism and "imported development" component of the national development strategy described in the previous chapter.

Thus during the decade of the 1950s, and with the helping hand of Uncle Sam, the MNR began the sizable transfer of public resources to Santa Cruz to carry out this strategy. The effort gave rise to an important new road network for national integration, which connected isolated Santa Cruz to the rest of the country. An agro-industrial sector with rice and cotton mills, oil seed, meat-processing, and textile factories along with the country's first sugar refineries also mushroomed. As described in the previous chapter, the Servicio Agrícola Interaméricano (SAI) supported numerous better-off agricultural producers involved in this modernization quest. During the decade of the 1960s, these agricultural policies attained for Bolivia national self-sufficiency in the production of these agricultural products.

Yet these policy packages for Santa Cruz and the Beni came in an elitist wrapper. Many of the initial producers welcomed into these programs had avoided expropriation of their farms and ranches under the land reform's escape clause of "empresas agropecuarias." This small power elite of commercial agricultural and ranching interests quickly gained disproportionate leverage over the state's agricultural policymakers and political leaders. The state's social exclusion was equivalent to holding state dinners with places set for the elite producers of sugar cane, rice, cotton, and cattle along with a few sugar industrialists while representatives of the indigenous majority supplying most of the country's food were conspicuously absent.[3] Their menus listed price and agricultural credit subsidies, infrastructural investments, tax breaks, protective tariffs, agricultural machinery, marketing programs, relations to the agricultural programs of the universities, and political connections. The socially closed relationships were most striking when rice producers immediately lost a place at the table because their elite leadership switched to cotton production (Grupo de Estudios 1983). The consequences of this elite policy for a group such as the Andean quinoa growers could be seen in the declining national production of quinoa during the 1960s and 1970s (Arrieta et al. 1990; Dandler et al. 1987).

THE MNR'S MODERNIZATION FOODS

The public support for rice and sugar by the MNR and successor regimes had an impact on consumption as well as production.[4] In the decade of the 1940s, the country consumed about 10,000 hectares worth of rice, half of which was imported. By the mid-1970s, rice production on Bolivian small farms had increased to 40,000 hectares and sixty medium and large rice mills were processing white rice for an ever growing national market (Arrieta et al. 1990, 228; Dandler et al. 1987, 89). Rice production and consumption also advanced through state resettlement programs where rice became the first crop planted for assuring one's subsistence under the new tropical forest conditions. Because of these efforts and changes, the availability of rice in Bolivia increased from 6.4 kilos to 36.2 kilos per capita between 1958 and 1991 (Prudencio and Franqueville 1995, 14).

The rapid growth of sugar cane production and refined white sugar followed a similar development path. In the early 1950s, Santa Cruz was producing 600 hectares of sugar cane for sale in raw form or as brown sugar for mostly regional markets. Refined white sugar had yet to reach rural Bolivia. Import substitution policies steadily increased cane production, reaching 52,000 hectares (ha.) by 1975, which was supplying an industry comprising six private and public sugar mills which in turn used advertising over radio and other means to induce rural consumption of white sugar.

The penetration of white rice and white sugar into the rural diet also resulted from increased modern truck transport over new feeder roads to widely scattered villages for the first time. Ease of conservation and relatively low prices of these mass consumption goods were other advantages. Similar to the wheat products, there was also a Western cultural status of superior "urban foods" associated with these processed and packaged products. Several case studies of grassroots development in this volume show local organizations distributing these products to their members, an indication of their wide acceptance as "artículos de primera necesidad" essential for a modernizing and monetizing rural society by the 1970s.

However, the MNR's white processed foods (including wheat flour, bread, and noodles) most likely exacerbated increased calorie and protein deficits in rural consumption between 1952 and 1970 as another blow to social development from import substitution (Morales 1984). The Centro de Estudios de la Realidad Económica y Social (CERES), a research center specializing in national agricultural and food issues, connected the arrival of these foods with the erosion of traditional, place-specific food diversity in the countryside for a doubly negative impact on both consumption and production. Rural families filled their stomachs with white rice, refined white sugar, and imported wheat products while reducing or abandoning other more nutritionally valuable food products of the Andean and

Amazonian cuisine (Dandler et al. 1987). The preference of peasant families to sell their livestock products (meat and milk) in order to purchase the processed foods needed for the "modern" low-income diet was another expression of this syndrome. Santa Cruz, the cradle of import substitution, predictably was the region with the country's worst nutritional rankings.

State capitalism's promotion of national self-sufficiency in beef also increased the status of red meat as a preferred rural modernization consumption item even though it was unaffordable for many. From public school textbooks to community education programs to radio and television ads, the superiority of beef and pork was trumpeted while nutritionally sound red meat of the llama languished in the shadows. The political and economic power of the eastern ranching establishment and enthusiastic support for beef consumption from U.S. aid agencies in the 1950s and 1960s contributed to the delay in the legalization of llama meat.

THE "ECONOMIC MIRACLE"

The state capitalist model moved along under the mostly right-of-center military regimes during the 1960s and 1970s with ever increasing amounts of foreign aid support from the United States and the multilateral banks.[5] The Bolivian economy was growing at 5.5 percent per annum during the 1970s thanks to an international commodity price boom which tripled the value of its prime exports during 1970–1974. The big ticket commodity items of Bolivia's hydrocarbons had climbed from 5.1 percent to 31.6 percent of total exports (Dunkerley 1984, 223). Simultaneously mining exports by the mid-1970s (despite almost a doubling of the price of tin) had dropped to 65 percent of national exports and was down to 27 percent of government revenues. Favorable mineral prices enabled the private mineowners to make important progress to build upon gains made during the 1960s.[6] New luxury high-rise apartment and office building construction and related job creation in the capital were signs of this economic boom while loan monies poured in from private international banks overflowing with petro-dollars. The Santa Cruz region had gone from an economic backwater of isolated ranches, farms, and indigenous communities to an economic powerhouse with a modern metropolis, densely populated new farm settlements, intricate road networks, and oil, gas, ranching, and export-oriented agro-business sectors. Some 200,000 settlers from the highlands had begun to build farms there.

These economic developments enabled the military leaders to multiply the number of state entities engaged in agricultural and other sectors of economic modernization. Bolivia with its state-owned airlines, railroads, bus stations, hotels, mines, agro-industrial factories, cement and energy companies was adding decentralized regional development corporations, agricultural marketing boards, and more agricultural institutes specializing in specific crops (World Bank 1984; Torrico 1982, 258). In several cases, state entities were created to manage projects by the World Bank and the Inter-American Development Bank. During the 1970s, this state sector grew to fifty enterprise and financial government institutions, 350 regional government agencies, and 120 organs of the central government operating as part of the national project of "modern development" (Dandler et al. 1987, 159). Meanwhile the number of public employees increased from 60,000 to 150,000 and the Bolivian state had become the major investor in the national economy (Malloy and Gamarra 1988).

Earlier import substitution policies had also paved the way for the export of sugar, cotton, and cattle (along with timber and coffee) which had increased to be 5.6 percent of national export earnings (Dunkerley 1984, 223). In step with the MNR's policies, the military regimes were "building on the best" in Santa Cruz to re-concentrate wealth and income among a small minority of producers and interlocking economic interest groups.[7] The military leader most generous with the country's public resources to bolster agricultural exports was General Hugo Banzer (1971–1978) who heaped large tracts of public lands and sizable quantities of subsidized credit from the national agricultural development bank, Banco Agrícola Boliviano (BAB), on his middle-class political associates, cronies, and fellow officers.[8] While some producers were bona fide cattle ranchers and cane growers, many others were urban professionals and businessmen interested in taking advantage of the high prices for earning short-term profits. Cotton was the agricultural money-making king in Santa Cruz and Banzer's producers were increasing its production at the rate of 45 percent per annum between 1970 and 1976.

A third economic growth phenomenon breaking into this picture of prosperity by the late 1970s was the country's rapidly expanding illicit coca-cocaine economy. Bolivian peasant farmers in the tropical Chapare region supplied coca leaves to agro-industrial and other elites from Santa Cruz for the first stages of cocaine processing for subsequent air transport to Colombian refineries. The popularity of cocaine as the recreational drug of choice in the United States by the late 1970s provided market impetus for economic growth and impressive employment generation (Healy 1986a).[9] In short, these national and international market forces, public policies, and economic changes converged to shape a narrative about Bolivia's first "Economic Miracle" under the state capitalist model.

The Social Costs of State Capitalism

While the state capitalists had greatly increased rural schooling and related literacy levels (from 31 to 67 percent between 1950 and 1976 [Klein 1982, 264]), there had been little attention paid to the quality of rural public schooling. One sign of the educational quality problem was high drop-out rate in elementary schools where 93 percent of rural schoolchildren left before the seventh grade (Carter 1971, 145). Just about every other social indicator told an equally grim story about the plight of indigenous peoples under the state capitalist model. Social and economic inequality and rural poverty were so extreme that Bolivia remained in the company of Haiti and Honduras as Latin America's most impoverished nations.

One of the most poignant demonstrations of the social contradictions contained within Bolivia's state capitalism was a 1974 peasant protest in the Cochabamba Valley. While prices for Bolivian commodities were skyrocketing on the world market, General Banzer issued decrees that doubled prices of many basic consumer goods especially the processed food staples upon which the rural poor now depended without commensurate adjustments in Andean agricultural produce. This triggered roadblockades of 100 kilometers of a main highway by 20,000 peasant protesters. Their effort represented the first rural protest mounted by the indigenous majority to defy Banzer's dictatorial rule and socially regressive economic policies (Cuadernos de Justicia 1975; Dunkerley 1984). Banzer sent the army equipped with tanks, helicopters, and machine guns to break up this non-violent protest which led to the massacre of seventy protesters and wounding of dozens of others. The tragic event became known in the annals of Bolivian grassroots peasant struggles as the "Masacre del Valle." The tragedy was documented in a publication of the National Human Rights Assembly for dissemination through grassroots and union organizations opposed to the dictatorship.

Agricultural policies geared to secure cheap food for the cities tended to lower agricultural prices for small farmers and when combined with rural population growth and environmental degradation further reduced productivity, agricultural diversity, and incomes in minifundia farming communities (Painter 1995). In a society in which indigenous peasants supplied 70 percent of the nationally produced foodstuffs, it was a cruel paradox that there were so few economic incentives, supports, or culturally appropriate and effective programs to bolster their production, technologies, and incomes. To survive under these precarious conditions, many indigenous peasant families sought off-farm sources of income and employment. Many joined a highland to lowland migrant stream as seasonal agricultural laborers earning low wages in Santa Cruz cutting sugar cane and picking cotton. The native groups of the lowlands were losing their lands, forests, and other natural resources to the elite economic groups benefiting from the military's land policies and timber concessions.

ECONOMIC DECLINE AND COLLAPSE OF THE STATE CAPITALIST MODEL

Yet by the late 1970s, when the economic boom fizzled and Banzer abandoned power in response to a nationwide hunger strike and a new United States human rights policy, lingering questions about the economic, environmental, and social viability of military-led state capitalism resurfaced. Mismanagement, corruption, and political clientelism were rife within the state bureaucracies leading to a number of public scandals including extravagant white elephant projects. The state's agricultural development bank teetered on the brink of bankruptcy from uncollected loans from cotton producers and cattle ranchers.[10] Oil production had dropped from the lack of exploration of new wells and the state tin mining industry was inefficient and unprofitable (Malloy and Gamarra 1988). Greatly increased oil, natural gas, and tin exports had been a function of higher prices rather than increased production as oil and tin declined while natural gas stagnated (Dunkerley 1984, 223). As mentioned in chapter 2, agricultural modernization in the eastern lowlands was plagued by wholesale environmental damage (World Bank 1993a) and by negative health effects from the steady spread of agrochemical residues. Topping off this grim panorama, Banzer's free-wheeling borrowing from international banks had left an international debt soaking up 30 percent of the country's annual export earnings which could have been used for social investments.

After three aborted national elections and five military juntas blocked their path to power, the Unidad Democrática y Popular (UDP), an elected coalition government, finally took office in 1982. The majority electoral support for a left-of-center program provided Bolivia with a strong mandate to begin gearing the state model toward the needs of the vast working-class majority (Lazarte and Pacheco 1992). Yet the UDP's efforts were hampered by this legacy of mismanagement, mounting international debt, falling foreign tin prices and production. Finally, the UDP responded to demands of labor and peasant movements by issuing new bills to finance development programs, in a public policy blunder that triggered one of the worst hyperinflationary spirals of the twentieth century.

Inflation reached almost farcical heights of 24,000 percent and the peso's devaluation represented a drop from 25 pesos to the dollar to 1,000,000 pesos to the dollar. One of the most absurd manifestations of this crumbling economy was having the country's third major import item as paper peso bills, printed in West Germany, Brazil, and England. Bolivian salary earners stopped depositing their currency in the national banking system to convert pesos to dollars on the black market in an attempt to protect their money from eroding in value. In mid-1985, the value of the peso could be halved within several weeks' time because of the runaway rate of currency devaluation.

An additional hardship from the hyperinflation was the cost of synthetic medicines. During 1983 and 1984, their prices increased 5,000 to 6,000 percent and one of the most important pharmaceutical firms saw its annual sales drop from $10 million to $1 million. These price rises caused many Bolivians to take renewed interest in herbal remedies for various maladies and even the Ministry of Health endorsed the use of native medicines for the first time.

The economic downturn could also be seen from the closure of 8,000 small enterprises and twenty-eight medium-size bankruptcies announced by the Ministry of Commerce in 1984. As a whole, the Bolivian economy had been registering negative annual growth rates between 1980 and 1984, while family incomes and per capita consumption had fallen by 28 and 30 percent respectively (Morales 1984). Tin production had plunged to production levels of a decade earlier and received a lethal blow from the total collapse of its international price in 1985.

As if the man-made disasters were not enough, Bolivia also suffered one of its worst droughts of the century during the 1983–84 growing season in the Western highlands. The drought continued the downward fall in rural levels of living. On a national scale the availability of the staples of the Bolivian diet such as potatoes, corn, and barley greatly declined. In many highland departments, a large part of the livestock population, especially cattle, sheep, llamas, and alpacas, died from lack of forage. Since Andean indigenous people often use a few head of cattle as a capital reserve fund for times of crisis, the massive loss of livestock pushed many poor Andean families to the edge of survival by wiping out this form of subsistence insurance.

Under pressure from the national independent peasant confederation, Confederación Sindical Única de Trabajadores Campesinos de Bolivia (CSUTCB), the UDP had produced a few albeit tenuous social gains such as greatly increased amounts of agricultural credit for the peasantry, the incorporation of the Santa Cruz cotton pickers and sugar cane cutters into the labor code, and the establishment of the government's first bilingual literacy program using native languages. Pathbreaking community-based health programs in poor urban neighborhoods also surfaced. Yet the unstable economic conditions disintegrated into chaos, ultimately compelling the UDP to make an early exit from office in 1985 (Lazarte and Pacheco 1992). As the sinking state capitalist model hit bottom, it opened the way for a radically different market-led program aggressively promoted by international financial community. By the time the Berlin Wall fell in 1989, Marx's ideas together with the political left had already been buried by an Andean avalanche of devalued pesos.

Launching Bolivia into the Globalization Era

In 1985, an MNR-led government once again played a historical role in launching the nation on a new course of economic, social, cultural, and even political change. Stabilization and structural adjustment measures instituted a radical process of dismantling the state's bloated bureaucracies and interventionist practices and setting in motion the liberalization and privatization of the national economy. These reforms would push Bolivia not only further "outward" into global markets but also "downward" into local towns and villages by decentralizing state authority and the distribution of public resources. In contrast to MNR-style modernization of national agricultural self-sufficiency, expanded state functions, national economic and cultural integration, its new neo-liberal leanings led to greater integration into global markets and use of information-based and communications technologies, reforming state agencies and forging a national identity based upon cultural pluralism.

Most of the neo-liberal reform measures and laws under the MNR coalitions took shape during two distinct intervals in time. The first set of measures, the New Economic Policy (NEP), was issued under the presidential decree no. 21060 in 1985. The NEP devalued the exchange rate, removed price controls and subsidies, and reduced the state's role in social development by slashing public budgets in the health and education fields. Tax reform measures went into effect and workers had their rights to collective bargaining reduced through measures liberalizing employer regulations for hiring and firing. The MNR's trade liberalization program also lowered tariffs to a uniform rate and replaced export taxes with enticing export incentives. The most visual symbol of neo-liberalism's arrival was the closure of the largest state-owned tin mines, the epicenter of the MNR's revolutionary dance with state capitalism.

The restructuring of the national petroleum company (YFPB) reduced its workforce by one third and led to a proliferation of oil exploration contracts with foreign firms.[11] The neo-liberal government also began methodically closing the state's decentralized corporations, agricultural marketing boards, autonomous agencies, and crop-centered institutes established by the military regimes and their foreign funders.

The second generation of neo-liberal reforms (1993–1997), the "Plan de Todos," strengthened and deepened the process of economic restructuring by focusing on institutional reforms and an array of measures to mitigate the effects of a wrenching social crisis that had deepened under the NEP (Grebe 1998). These neo-liberal reform laws aimed to redesign and shrink the state apparatus, reshape it into less of a top-down, paternalistic structure, and open channels for flows of public resources to NGOs and community-administered development programs.

New mining, environmental, land tenure, energy, electricity, banking, telecommunications, and forestry laws were incorporated into a new governmental regulatory framework suitable for a market-led economic paradigm. The "privatization" of public airlines, railways, telecommunications, and hydrocarbon enterprises gave 51 percent ownership and management control to foreign firms.[12] Out of this effort, Bolivia's innovative "capitalization program" emerged offering new pension benefits for Bolivian retirees.[13] The Plan de Todos also included educational, land, forestry, and decentralization reforms which became "indigenized" by weaving bilingual and intercultural education, indigenous territorial rights, popular participation, and other components into them. These changes and openings for indigenous cultural revitalizations promised to roll back some of globalization's powerful homogenizing effects defacing Third World cultures.

While Bolivia's reforms were the most textbook application of neo-liberalism yet to appear in the Americas, they were more than a knee-jerk response to a powerful international financial community. The Bolivian embrace of neo-liberalism grew out of an internal political consensus building and analysis among businessmen, state technocrats, MNR politicians, and their advisors anxious for the nation to exit from its profound economic crisis (Conaghan and Malloy 1994). The multilateral banks promptly stepped forward with the several hundred million dollars and technical expertise to bankroll the launching of this experiment in free market economic policy.

It was no secret that the U.S. Embassy in La Paz had been lobbying for a full-fledged neo-liberal program since the Reagan Administration's foreign policy in the early 1980s (Malloy and Gamarra 1988). By the end of the 1980s, support for this policy resided with a larger group of think-tanks, multilateral banks, and key U.S. government agencies known as the "Washington Consensus." Both generations of Bolivian reforms reflected this Washington Consensus as well as its revised thinking that occurred since the first round of adjustment programs in Bolivia and elsewhere.

THE UPS AND DOWNS OF A NEW ECONOMIC ORDER

The most immediate achievement of the NEP measures was their impact on the stabilization of prices, bringing down inflation from the stratospheric heights reached under the UDP government. Inflation first fell all the way to 66 percent in 1986, then to 11 percent the following year while averaging 12 percent per annum between 1985 and 1992. In economic growth terms, by 1987, the neo-liberal economy had reversed its downward plunge and rebounded with positive albeit low economic growth rates averaging 2.5 percent through 1990. The stabilization and adjustment program had successfully pulled back the economy from the brink of collapse and the new model appeared to be providing a new lease on life. Jeffry Sachs, a Harvard whiz kid economist who advised the MNR on the NEP through weekend consulting trips to La Paz, was subsequently invited to Poland and Russia to work some of this same policy-making magic for jump-starting their fledgling capitalist economies.

Another sign of economic revival was the spurt in export growth effectively reversing the declining levels suffered under UDP government. Tin production regained importance to represent 35 percent of the country's export earnings yet now its major producers were medium-size private mines while COMIBOL had retained only a few profitable mines. The expansion of gold mining was rapidly adding income and employment to the national economy yet its potential tax revenues evaporated from the leakage of 80 percent of this mineral through smuggling across national borders. Silver, zinc, lead, and antimony also were making incremental increases thanks to other private mining initiatives during this period (Seyler 1989, 137). Soybeans increased their export earnings fivefold with an increase from 223 metric tons to 649 metric tons, representing $8.5 million and $42 million respectively between 1985 and 1988 (Badani et al. 1990, 18).[14]

In terms of social impact, the increasing globalization of the economy by the neo-liberal reforms racked up high social costs from its inequitable patterns of economic growth resulting in the lowering of employment, wages, salaries, and production in both rural and urban areas (Avirgan et al. 1995). After many decades of state capitalism's discriminatory agricultural policies, Bolivia's small farmers were ill prepared to compete with the flood of foreign, often subsidized agricultural produce into local and regional marketplaces. These commercial spaces began to fill up with Peruvian potatoes, barley, carrots, onions, and tomatoes; Chilean fruits, jams, and dairy products; and Brazilian rice and corn. The costs of production along with increased transport costs from the removal of fuel subsidies in relation to produce market prices exacerbated the terms of trade inequities for indigenous producers.[15] This deteriorating situation was manifest in national figures showing falling food production between 1985 and 1989 (excluding soybeans, coffee, and the coca leaf) (Badani et al. 1990, 18).[16]

Yet the tremendous influx of products from the world economy into the Bolivian market was hardly a consumer paradise for the average low-income buyer. A popular refrain making the rounds in urban neighborhoods during this period was that, "Before we had enough money to buy what we needed yet due to hoarding of goods by merchants there was little to purchase. Nowadays with our markets overflowing with consumer products, we have no money to purchase them."

Indeed, Bolivian urban areas were hurting as evidenced by a rise in open unemployment from 15.5 to 21.5 percent (Iriarte 1989, 420). Yet unemployment rates appeared the less relevant social indicator in a context where most Bolivians forge economic survival practices on the streets in an ever-swelling informal economy that fills capital city curbsides with vendors peddling small quantities of every imaginable petty commodity.[17] These urban subsistence strategies multiplied from the closure of the state mines which led to dismissal of 22,000 out of 28,000 unionized mineworkers.[18] Many ex-miners also headed for the coca leaf growing areas in search of the few enticing economic opportunities in the national economy.

During this period, 130 manufacturing firms collapsed, sending an additional 4,000 workers and their families into the informal economy. Rural to urban migration resulting from the deteriorating conditions in the countryside was another source of newcomers to the informal economy for activities in petty trading, transport, commerce, and artisanry production. The numbers of women and youth swept up in this human tide of desperation also grew along with the number of street children in major cities. Black market, contraband, and coca-cocaine related activities were other pursuits enabling economic refugees to stay above water.

Alarmed by the magnitude of the national social crisis and potential political impact from the NEP's initial years, the Bolivian government established the hemisphere's first "Social Emergency Fund" (SF) crafted by World Bank's technocrats and subsequently underwritten by the Bank and other European donors geared to put unemployed people to work through investments in labor-intensive, short-term activities such as school and health clinic construction and road building. It was designed as an autonomous government unit set apart from the mainline ministries under the direction of one of Bolivia's wealthiest, honest businessmen. The SF was innovative in its demand-driven approach of responding to requests from local organizations and municipal governments as opposed to a top-down pattern of assistance. The SF channeled substantial public resources for NGO-administered development projects on a scale hitherto unknown in Bolivia. Independent researchers and World Bank's evaluations have given this experiment mixed reviews.[19] To institutionalize this entity for the long term, the "emergency" was replaced by "investment," to make it a full-fledged "Social Investment Fund."

Under World Bank guidance, the Bolivian government proceeded to set up other government "funds" modeled on this demand-driven approach, which in reality had been peddled by the Inter-American Foundation, OXFAM-America, and other small donors many years earlier. The Fondo de Desarrollo Campesino for rural credit channeled $12.8 million between 1989 and 1994 and the Fondo Nacional de Desarrollo Regional channeled $127 million between 1987 and 1994 for urban and regional investment projects covering basic sanitation to transport (World Bank 1996, 73), and a "Fondo del Medio Ambiente" was for environmental protection investments.[20] Despite the optimism about this approach to redesigning state structures as wave of the future for tackling poverty, an internal World Bank report a decade later offered a more guarded assessment.

> The two major institutions that the Bank has funded—Fondo Nacional de Desarrollo Regional (FNDR) and Fondo de Inversion Social (FIS)— have been considered successes and models for social protection for many other countries. These two social funds have contributed to capacity-building, social development, and investment in social infrastructure in the communities where they have provided resources. But the administrative structure of these and other social funds has become top-heavy, bureaucratic and duplicative. There are also some indications that the techniques used to target social fund investments have not been effective. (World Bank 1998, 7)

Perhaps a more far-reaching and financially sustainable effort at slowing the social crisis resulting from Bolivia's economic restructuring can be found in "Plan de Todos" enacted by Goni Sánchez de Lozada's coalition government.[21] This coalition government with Víctor Hugo Cárdenas, the Aymara vice-president, and his tiny indigenous political party, and with left-of-center political independents and party, the Movimiento de Bolivia Libre (MBL), used their combined political muscle to oversee the implementation of the social reforms. These and other government reformers and political elites also appeared to be hearing the drumbeats of Shining Path's guerrilla army in neighboring Peru and fearing its potential spread or emulation amid Bolivia's social crises (Van Cott 1998).

In addition to the usual timber and agro-business interests as insiders lodged within the state apparatus, the Sánchez de Lozada coalition brought into government a number of ecologists, feminists, indigenista, and other civil society activists with experience in managing community-based development programs. This progressive flair was also manifest by conferring politically correct names on new governmental units such as "Sustainable Development," "Human Development," and "Ethnicity and Gender" created under his government.[22]

Perhaps its most pathbreaking economic and political reform was welding together the interdependent laws of decentralization and popular participation. This social reform generated fanfare throughout the hemisphere and as far away as Africa where Bolivians have traveled to disseminate it. A national redistricting of political-administrative boundaries potentially empowered the rural indigenous peasantry by leaving 85 percent of the municipalities with rural majorities. This political commitment to rural residents was also advanced by transferring 20 percent (over a previous 8 percent) of the national budget allocation to municipal governments, one of the highest percentages of this type anywhere in Latin America. The related reform effort of "popular participation" was to make decentralization more democratic and community-based through local mechanisms for participatory planning, incorporation of indigenous cultural practices at submunicipal levels, and vigilance councils from civil society that oversee municipal budgets and plans. The direct elections of mayors and town council members, beginning in the late 1980s, injected democratic vitality to these changes.

The implementation of these reforms has encountered numerous obstacles including intransigent local political cultures, pervasive corruption, and a lack of national political will from a successor government. Although at first the transformation of Paz Estensorro, the patriarch of state capitalism himself, into a neo-liberal leader defied credulity, subsequently General Banzer not only refashioned himself from a state capitalist to a neo-liberal but also from a military dictator to a democratically elected president.[23] Over the long run, however, if these new structures become consolidated, they will have profound effects on the way rural communities control and develop local social services and productive infrastructure, and open spaces for a more participatory democracy.

Another important social innovation is Bolivia's progressive 1995 educational reform. To compete effectively for global markets and investments within a new global information-based economy requires a well-educated and highly skilled work force. This reform attempts to overhaul the nation's entire administrative and pedagogical school system and give primary and secondary schools a much greater share of educational resources. The educational reform involves re-training teachers and adopting an educational philosophy that values student cultural knowledge and critical analysis over common practices of learning by rote memory and copying. For the indigenous peasant majority, the commitment to bilingual and intercultural education was one of its most attractive features. This reform also bolsters indigenous participation through mechanisms of greater parental participation in rural schooling and a shift in financial, administrative, and operational responsibility over schools from the national to the regional levels (Luykx 1999, 56).

The Sánchez de Lozada government also turned its sights on reforming the country's land tenure system with its irrational land utilization practices and the vast unproductive areas that had been created by the public lands give-away under mostly military regimes. The La Ley INRA, passed by the Bolivian congress in 1996, was in essence a "reforma de la reforma," an attempt to correct the 1953 agrarian reform and the resulting chaotic tenure system and corrupted state bureaucracy that thrived on bribes from granting multiple land titles to single properties. A key set of articles spell out the mechanism of land taxes to goad large landowners into making improvements on their farms and ranches or selling them to others willing to invest in them. Another important aspect of the law for indigenous peasants was the recognition of collective land rights of diverse indigenous peoples in the county's eastern and southern lowlands. However, the implementation of these land reforms has clashed with the entrenched interests of the agro-business, timber, and ranching elite, especially under the Banzer government where such groups enjoy greater political clout. It should come as no surprise that land tax revenues outlined in the INRA reforms have barely begun to flow.

ECONOMIC GLOBALIZATION AND ITS LIMITS IN THE 1990S

What has the more open, liberalized, and privatized economy accomplished in Bolivia during the 1990s? In national aggregate terms, the share of the labor force working in services increased from 35 percent in 1985 to 69 percent in 1995. In many ways the economy has become more informalized and also feminized because of the number of women managing survival strategies within this ever expanding sector. As discussed, the major achievement was slaying hyperinflation and bringing it down to single digits after 1992 while Bolivian currency became one of the strongest in South America. Bolivia had a total of $200 million as deposits in its banking system in 1985, while in 1998 this amount had increased to $3.5 billion. Economic growth rates averaged a modest 4 percent during the 1990s and economic diversification continued apace from the growth of nontraditional exports. Bolivia is enjoying its first taste of a bona fide stock market as fourteen companies have mobilized $12 million worth of shares. And despite the problems with land taxes, Bolivia had also made significant gains in tax collection as its percentage of the GNP went from 4 to 19.6 percent between 1985 and 1998.

Soybeans remained an impressive foreign exchange earner and the leader of Santa Cruz industrial and mechanized agricultural production (which includes sugar cane and cotton) which as a whole increased at the rate of 20 percent per annum between 1989 and 1995 (Kazan 1999). Bolivian commercial farmers, Mennonite and Japanese producers, and Brazilian entrepreneurs with their "empresas agrorecuarias" to enable soybeans to generate as much as 20 percent of national export revenues during their best years.[24] However, at the end of the 1990s dark clouds were hovering above this soybean picture as the turmoil from the Asian financial crisis and Brazil's crisis in Bolivia's own backyard were taking their toll on soybean prices and Bolivia's competitiveness in these global markets.

And similar to earlier patterns of social and economic development in Santa Cruz under state capitalism, this economic boom has generated high social and environmental costs. Few indigenous peasants have access to the capital necessary to take up soybean growing. As a heavily mechanized production system using land-clearing machinery and combines, soybean production generates little seasonal employment and few if any economic benefits to the impoverished rural communities in the Eastern lowlands and Western highlands. As small peasant farmers have even less access to financial credit under neo-liberalism than under state capitalism, they have been excluded de facto from the fruits of the country's soybean boom.[25] The environmental management of the rainforest ecology associated with soybean production has taken its toll on valuable non-renewable natural resources. Soybean expansion from 50,000 to 452,000 ha. between 1984 and 1996 accelerated deforestation with the corresponding destruction of soils, wildlife, medicinal plants, and other genetic resources.

Bolivia has faithfully adopted a full-fledged neo-liberal program, yet an inability to shake its primary role as a supplier of raw materials to the global economy has placed serious limits on what is possible. Only 10 percent of total exports leave the country as finished products. The country's economic and social fate continues to rely for almost half of its export earnings on the price swings of minerals and hydrocarbons, which remain highly vulnerable to shocks from the international economy. The demise in natural gas reflected this free market vulnerability. After replacing tin as the economy's leading export in the 1980s, the value of natural gas fell from $375 million to $98 million dollars between 1985 and 1994. Whereas the mineral exports of tin and silver together with hydrocarbons represented 83 percent of the total exports in 1985, ten years later that figure had been reduced to 18 percent of total exports.

During the 1990s, the mineral export portfolio became more diversified with the rise in importance of gold and zinc while tin represented 9 percent of total exports. Yet those minerals too have been negatively affected by price cycles in world markets that led to price plunges during the 1980s and then again between 1994 and 1997, bringing an overall cumulative decline of 73 percent for Bolivia's minerals since 1980 (World Bank 1998). The struggling co-operative and small mining sectors offer vivid testimony to this pattern. Under pressures from falling prices and increased competition, at the end of the 1990s the co-operative mines had diminished from 5,000 to 842 organizations and the small mines from 6,500 to 500 enterprises (*Bolivian Times* 1998c). These combined sectors had employed upwards of 150,000 miners at the beginning of the decade. However, Bolivia's increased economic diversification also resulted from non-mineral production and sales of non-traditional exports such as flowers, leather goods, and jewelry which are a far cry from the products necessary for economic transformation of this developing nation.

Since the advent of the structural adjustment measures, Bolivia's small manufacturing sector has shown a slight increase from 15.5 to 17 percent of

GNP. The inflow of foreign products under the NEP essentially wiped out the country's large manufacturing enterprises leaving in their wake small and medium enterprise survivors that have poor access to financial credit from the private banks and inefficient technologies for competing (Larrazábal 1996). The small and micro enterprises include many artisans' activities that remain viable because of their comparative advantage of low wages and Bolivia's relatively high transport costs over expansive mountainous terrain (Buechler et al. 1998).

The modest economic growth under neo-liberal economic policies has failed to make a major dent in the nation's poverty. Since 1985, although advances have been made in reducing infant mortality and increasing life expectancy, per capita income has increased at the paltry rate of 1.7 percent per annum as two thirds of the population live on less than $400. Bolivia's social indicators remain on a par with those of sub-Saharan Africa (World Bank 1998, 1). Bolivia's structural dependency and dubious status as a major recipient of food aid shipments from the United States and elsewhere is a commentary on these societal failures. Similar to the mining industry within the global economy, the continuing terms of trade squeeze faced by the rural poor undermine many efforts at improving agricultural production and income. With the exception of hydrocarbons, the operations of the global economy require less and less of Bolivia's minerals and the national economy similarly less food from Bolivian soil. Some 81 percent of the rural population (representing 42 percent of the national total) reside below the poverty line while only 27 percent of them have access to safe water (World Bank 1998, 1). Having seven out of every ten Bolivians (both urban and rural) in poverty after trying two different economic development models over a half century suggests that prospects for the country's indigenous peoples are improving only at the margins. The concentration of economic and political power from income distribution patterns where the wealthiest 20 percent receive 56 percent of the country's aggregate labor income while the bottom 20 percent comprising indigenous social sectors receive 4 percent (World Bank 1998, 4) is both a cause and effect of this outcome. Such national figures call into question whether the current economic model is any more capable than the previous model for creating development patterns which engender greater social equity and poverty alleviation on a major national scale.

In addition to the problem of cyclical price trends for raw materials on the world market, these modest economic growth rates also result from the lowest rates of savings and investment in South America. Bolivia's investment rates averaged a coefficient of 13.8 percent of Gross Domestic Product between 1986 and 1997 even though they have tended to rise temporarily in recent years thanks to the capitalization program and foreign investments underwriting the construction of a gas pipeline to Brazil (M. Pacheco 1998, 90). Bolivia's neighbors Chile and Peru enjoy investment rates of 25 percent and have made more inviting investment climates for multinational corporations. Bolivia's 1990s' investment rates are lower than for its own much maligned state sector between 1960 and 1977. A list of factors deterring greater foreign investment include the country's tax laws for mineral exploitation, high transportation costs, chaotic judiciary and legal systems, and rampant government corruption (D. Pacheco 1992, 138; *Bolivian Times* 1998c).

Bolivia's poorly educated and low-skill workforce also dampens foreign investor interest. Having high-quality human capital is an indispensable national asset under the rules of the new information-based technologies of the global economy. The high drop-out rates, poorly trained and poorly paid teachers, substandard educational equipment, and antiquated teaching methods of the public schools present deeply rooted obstacles for competing. The national educational reform is trying to turn this situation around yet many obstacles lie in its path (Luykx 1999, 56).

The low investment rates are also a function of savings rates which at 11 percent of Gross Domestic Product are among the lowest in the world. Such low wages and earnings and precarious conditions of self-employment and farming contribute to a vicious circle where savings rates are systematically kept low. These low savings and investment rates in turn have created the need for a continuing flow of concessional loans and grants from bilateral agencies and multilateral banks to cover the country's fiscal deficit. About half of the international aid of approximately $600 million yearly are loans whose repayments have worsened an international debt which currently absorbs 28 percent of national export earnings. This debt undermines the Bolivian state's capacity to finance its own productive investments and social expenditures without having to beg and borrow from abroad. Although the state's social expenditures for the 1990s is above the levels of the first years of the NEP, they remain below the levels under state capitalism during the 1970s (Morales 1996, 133).

About one third of the foreign aid flows to Bolivia are grants to the ever-burgeoning NGO sector where hundreds of organizations manage health, education, agricultural, artisan, livestock, and other programs in the rural communities and urban neighborhoods throughout the country (J. Pérez 1996, 273). NGOs have become a kind of informal sector for shoring up middle-class employment during state lay-offs and indispensable local development actors within a neo-liberal framework of decentralization and popular participation. Yet despite such public policy favoritism toward them, many NGOs and grassroots federations enjoyed a dynamic growth prior to the advent of neo-liberalism in Bolivia and are often critics and opponents of neo-liberalism as global market forces negatively impact their community-based programs. Similar to the autonomous, decentralized, and other government agencies that multiplied during the 1960s and 1970s, the NGOs have had exponential growth during the 1980s and 1990s. Bolivian NGOs such as BANCOSOL and PRODEM have achieved deserved international prominence for their micro-finance programs for the bare-bones activities in petty artisanry, commerce, trade, and transportation within the informal economy (Buechler et al. 1998). However, they have been unable to spread these development benefits beyond 15 percent of the country's micro-enterprises (World Bank 1998, 2). The World Bank is one of Bolivia's most devoted donors (averaging almost $40 million annually since the advent of the NEP) and offers considerable technical advice in guiding Bolivia's economic and social course of action. Recently, it has redoubled its efforts for combating the country's poverty through promoting modest debt relief of $760 million via the Initiative for the Heavily Indebted Countries (HIPC) and sponsoring a consortium meeting among donors that raised an additional $980 million for new social and infrastructural investments.[26] In addition to being the first Latin American country to have a social emergency fund and gain debt relief, Bolivia is the guinea pig for the Bank's latest development planning innovation called the "Comprehensive Development Framework." Giving Bolivia preferred nation status is a recognition of its willingness to do everything asked of it to become a neo-liberal showcase on the world scene. Yet its massive poverty and socioeconomic inequality persist.

USAID is another major player in the aid game, continuing as the country's most important bilateral giver while simultaneously channeling an ever increasing share of economic and financial resources to Bolivian NGOs. USAID's relatively high economic support for Bolivia continues because the Cold War was supplanted by a Drug War in U.S. Andean policy. The ensuing combat in the coca fields goes hand in glove with economic assistance to small farmers for financing substitute crops, infrastructural investments, and various social services.

This outward leaning, neo-liberal economy has also served up the latest U.S. cultural artifacts, tastes, and institutions in Bolivia. In addition to food, fashion, and trendy brand names conveyed by the global media, Bolivians inhabit a cultural universe replete with downtown shopping malls, large supermarkets, video game parlors, ATM machines, multi-channel television, and Michael Jordan. Its cellular telephone market is booming and legal computer sales have reached 50,000 per annum while others arrive at the national market over contraband trails. Three out of twelve government ministries and most universities have opened web sites (*Bolivian Times* 1998b). Fast food signs abound in Bolivian cities of the 1990s. Bolivia has its own dynamic fast food chains and Domino's Pizza has arrived to begin the first home pizza deliveries in affluent neighborhoods in the capital (*Bolivian Times* 1999c). When Burger King opened its first franchise in the capital under the ownership of an ex-planning minister of Bolivia's second neo-liberal government, the combination of fast food with neo-liberal planning models became visually solidified. Instead of utilizing Andean cultural patrimony, Burger King distributed Dutch seed potato to peasant farmers to open a channel of local potato suppliers for its french fry production. The Westernizing cultural facets of globalization represent some of the most serious concerns among both advocates as well as critics of globalization (Friedman 1999).

An intriguing example of globalization is a phenomenon that mixes cultural with economic dimensions. Soon after the NEP opened Bolivia's borders to increased international trade, there was a growing illegal influx of secondhand American clothing on the monthly order of 3,000 tons of pants, shirts, underwear, jeans, jackets, and other clothing in 1998 for nationwide distribution. In the capital, these products are sold mostly by hundreds of street vendors operating in the informal economy (*Bolivian Times* 1999e). Bolivian wholesalers and retailers purchase them by bulk weight from U.S. distributors and then sell them to consumers from all social classes as individual items. Their extraordinary low prices and relatively high quality explain much of their popularity among the low-income populations. Urban youth are enamored with American cultural symbols and brand names such as the Nike products from sports franchises appearing on television and sweatshirts and T-shirts emblazoned with university sports icons from the likes of Notre Dame, Princeton, and Michigan.

Is this the invisible hand of the self-regulating market economy which ensures that affordable, higher quality goods reach vast numbers of low-wage consumers with few prospects for major economic improvement within the neo-liberal economy? Is this a market mechanism for ameliorating some of the excessive social inequities generated by globalization? Curiously, the major opposition to this American clothing is from the local Bolivian-owned textile sweatshops whose low-wage, labor-intensive production system cannot compete with the prices for secondhand products probably made by textile sweatshops in other parts of Latin America and Asia.

The competition among textile sweatshops, the informal sector's key marketing role, the primacy of consumers over producers, the long-distance trading networks which include smuggling activities along with the penetration of American cultural values and artifacts is a microcosm of the neo-liberal globalization paradigm operating in Latin America. Yet it is precisely this process of providing greater social equity in clothing purchases that eludes the basic health, housing, nutrition, and income needs of the majority population in Third World countries such as Bolivia. The secondhand American clothing phenomenon appears to be a measure of social equity unfamiliar to Bolivia's poor for most everything else under both state capitalism and neo-liberalism. Yet even here it is hardly a desirable model from the cultural standpoint as it represents another Westernizing cultural conquest. These macro-economic policies and structures have created difficult parameters for grassroots development even for those visionary organizations revitalizing indigenous cultural resources. This book's case studies will show the importance of these macro-micro linkages in shaping the pattern of grassroots social and economic change.

CHAPTER 4

Indigenous Challenges to the Western Modernization Models

Midway through 1781, the altiplano of La Paz and the adjacent regions were the scene of one of the longest and most significant episodes of the indigenous rebellions of 1780–82. During almost one year, the [Aymara peoples] surrounded the city of La Paz.

CÁRDENAS (1988, 502)

THE RETURN OF TUPAK KATARI AND BARTOLINA SISA

On September 15, 1973, a windy day under a cloudless, brilliant blue altiplano sky, about three dozen Aymara men and women from the Katarista movement, a key organization in the burgeoning indigenous rights struggle, hurriedly made their way past the groups of tourists at Tihuanaco, Bolivia's famous archaeological site ten miles from Lake Titicaca. They were about to hear an important speech that would become the inspirational credo of Bolivia's reinvigorated pro-indigenous movement.

Tihuanaco was the main ceremonial site of a society which, after the Incas, was South America's largest native state (300 B.C. to 700 A.D.). Its powerful agrarian economy revolved around the high-altitude herding of millions of llamas and alpacas and a flourishing agricultural system of large irrigated and solar-heated earthworks known today as raised fields (Kolata 1993; Erickson 1996). Via these two activities, these people of the high Andes were able to produce more than enough food to feed large urban and rural populations.

The winds of decolonization blowing throughout the Third World were inspiring the Aymara on this historic day to denounce the continuing internal colonialism found in their country.[1] Moving at a brisk pace, the men outfitted in ponchos with stripes and solid colors, hand-woven scarves, and knitted stocking caps and the women dressed in bowler hats and pastel-colored shawls walked past several impressive mounds and down into a sunken courtyard lined with remnants of room-size niches and ten-foot stone sculptures. Reaching the end of the courtyard, they climbed a stairway to gather in front of the Gateway to the Sun, a towering gray stone portal embellished with elaborately carved winged figures. The portal opened eastward, toward the rising sun. Its main icon was Viracocha, the Tihuanaco rain deity, and cryptic inscriptions representing an agricultural-religious calendar based upon movements in the cosmos graced the block of andestite stone.

One Aymara leader moved to the front and for the next twenty minutes or so read aloud from a document called the "Manifesto de Tihuanaco." The document began with a short quote from a speech made by the Inca ex-ruler Yupanqui to his Spanish conquerors. "'A people that oppresses another people cannot be free.' We, both Aymara and Quechua peasants, similar to other indigenous nationalities of our country, are repeating this same message today."

The Tihuanaco Manifesto recalled the importance of indigenous cultural values as a driving force throughout history and attacked the long-standing discrimination that maintained the indigenous as second-class citizens. The document's section on national development offered the following critique:

> The political leaders of the dominant minority have striven to create a development process which slavishly imitates a model taken from the context of other nations. This approach emphasizes the materialistic side of progress by equating development with the economic aspects of life. As Indian peasants, we certainly aspire to economic development in our country, yet we insist that it take place within a framework that uses our own cultural values as its point of departure. We do not want to lose our noble virtues through a process of pseudo development. Imported rural schooling, political party activity, and agricultural technical promotion have not produced significant developmental changes in the countryside. We remain convinced that true development will only occur in the countryside and the nation when we ourselves become the authors of our own progress and destiny.

Some of the Manifesto's harshest words condemned rural schooling.

It is no secret that the school system fails to reflect our values. Our government ministries have too often copied ideas and methods developed from other societies. The rural school as it now exists is totally alien to our reality, not only in the strange language it uses to impart knowledge to our rural inhabitants, but in its biased presentation of Bolivian history, social ideals, cultural values, and the human worth of social groups.

The Kataristas' Manifesto bore the signatures of representatives from four cultural institutions representing reform-minded schoolteachers, students, peasant leaders, and young Aymara professionals, among them members of MINKA, Bolivia's first indigenous NGO (Hurtado 1986). Among the young professionals were disaffected employees of SNDC, the national community development service under the control of a military government. When the reading was over, the group applauded, let out an enormous cheer for Aymara solidarity, and then hurriedly dispersed in all directions from this ancient site of indigenous power.

Genaro Flores, an Aymara sindicato leader and activist, told me later that the Manifesto was the fruit of a series of clandestine meetings of Aymara activists held in the capital city. Gregorio Iriarte, a Catholic priest and advisor to the group, said that the police state atmosphere created by the Banzer dictatorship compelled them to take the strictest precautions in preparing and reading the document. Repression had been rampant with the killing, imprisonment, and torture of many and the blacklisting and exiling of many more activists for democracy. All of the labor groups and political parties had gone underground. Despite the repression, the Manifesto had a broad effect. Iriarte commented, "Although in the current repressive political environment there was little attention to the Manifesto in the national media, little by little, and with the help of progressive church parishes, a handful of NGOs, and local sindicatos, it was disseminated to the rural population and even translated into Aymara, Quechua, and Guaraní."

By going public with this Manifesto, the Aymara Katarista activists added fuel to the fire of the indigenous resistance to cultural assimilation that had been smoldering within the Bolivian republic for over a hundred years. Bolivia's history is replete with pro-indigenous uprisings and activism designed to protect and even flaunt Bolivia's cultural patrimony. These energetic opposition efforts had included both armed ayllu rebellions and passive resistance such as sit-down strikes, court litigation with colonial titles, and blocking government land inspectors from entering communities (S. Rivera 1984). The national oligarchy's liberal nineteenth-century assault on the indigenous communities and ayllus in the name of "privatization" of the country's landholding system and replacing these social institutions with haciendas, for instance, fueled widespread campaigns led by traditional Andean authority figures (referred to in the historical literature as "the *cacique apoderado* movement"). Grassroots mobilization and resistance enabled communities there to protect both communal lands and the traditional ayllu structures of local authority (Platt 1982).

Although the many efforts at reversing the liberal assault were unsuccessful, it was not for lack of trying. One Bolivian researcher documented 1,400 minor and major uprisings between 1860 and 1950 (Antezana 1966). In 1899, when the country was engulfed in a civil war, altiplano and valley Indians led by a charismatic rebel, Zarate Willka, pragmatically joined what became the winning liberal political side to advance their agenda of land, labor, and political autonomy rights (S. Rivera 1984, 16; Condarco Morales 1965). On one occasion during this conflict, the Aymara and Quechua leaders occupied a mestizo-controlled town and reimposed their ayllu government. In another occupation, they symbolically turned the social order upside down by compelling local mestizo elites to chew coca leaves and don sandals and indigenous dress as a form of reverse assimilation to a native lifestyle (Pearse 1975). Yet after the liberal triumph, Zarate and other comrades in arms suffered betrayal and were subsequently executed by their former allies.

A newspaper editorial written by hacienda owners in 1927 shows the panic and consternation that arose among the landed elites during another period of intensified armed rebellions.

> Recent events demonstrate with evidence that the Indian civilization, if it does not modify its customs, habits, and idiosyncrasies, represents one of the biggest dangers to the future of this country. Anyone who thinks about this a little will have no doubt in agreeing if he considers that the indigenous race represents 80% of the national population. The recent actions suggest that within a few years, if nothing is done, they not only could take over our lands, but everything else as well. And instead of improving civilization, they would plunge Bolivia into a wild, barbaric condition, a veritable state of conquest. (quoted in Arze 1987, 18)

During Bolivia's Chaco War with Paraguay, when altiplano hacienda owners seized community lands while Indian conscripts were in the trenches defending the nation, another boom period in uprisings ensued. This time the same army that had trained and incorporated them as soldiers and sent them into combat with Paraguay conducted repressive operations against the activist communities who had mobilized to regain their lands (Arze 1987).

Aside from carrying out demonstrations and uprisings to maintain indigenous ways of life, the Aymara organized several schools centered upon indigenous cultural values and world views during the first forty years of the twentieth century. Although most were clandestine, Warisata's "escuela-ayllu" was established openly near the shores of Lake Titicaca. Warisata was a unique rural school district utilizing Andean ayllu mechanisms of *aynis* (forms of reciprocal exchange of goods and labor), *minkas* (communal work forms), and a *Consejo de Amauta* (elders' council) as modus operandi (Soria 1992, 57; E. Pérez 1992). The school's founders and participating families heralded it as a "new model" for rural education, but aroused hacienda owners finally succeeded in having it shut down after two successive national governments had barely tolerated it.

The Katarista movement of the 1970s and early 1980s grew out of this rebellious tradition. Its Aymara urban and rural founders drew their inspiration from two late eighteenth-century Indian rebels, Tupak Katari and Bartolina Sisa, leaders of a major anti-colonial insurrection. The rebellion spearheaded by Katari and Sisa, although ultimately put down by Spanish militia, contributed to the final stage of a long historical process which brought a new political order to the communities. Hereditary ethnic rule in hamlets across the Andes was replaced by a system of rotating leadership and communal assemblies (Thomson 1996; Rasnake 1988).[2] This egalitarian system was established before any comparable "democratization" had taken place in Spain, and at the same time that the American constitution had affirmed citizens' rights to democracy. The Spanish Crown had long relied on ethnic lords to extract tribute from local indigenous communities as linchpins in a highly exploitative system. Fearful of the ethnic mobilization that might give the indigenous peoples a military advantage in future revolts, the colonial authorities took preventive measures such as prohibiting the use of the Andean tunic as part of the daily male costume. After the rebellion, they imposed the Spanish poncho as a way to undermine ethnic unity among colonized subject populations. This measure had limited success.

In the early 1970s, Tupak Katari was only a marginal figure in the public school textbooks. To end this obscurity, the Katarista sindicato cadres put his image and revolutionary slogans on wall posters, educational pamphlets, letterheads, and sindicato banners used for protest marches and meetings, and told his story on Aymara radio shows and in speeches at peasant congresses throughout the country. Monuments went up in his name and a handful of progressive NGOs and Catholic church parishes mimeographed documents outlining the Katarista ethno-nationalist ideology for distribution in rural leadership training programs (Hurtado 1986).

Víctor Hugo Cárdenas, one of the principal behind-the-scenes authors of Katarista's public documents during this decade, told me, "There were about a dozen Aymara Kataristas in our study group reading such things as the original works of Marx and Lenin." Cárdenas clarified this position by saying contemporary theorizers and organizers had distorted Marx's views.[3] He added their ideas also became enriched by the Andean studies literature (mostly in the fields of anthropology, linguistics, and ethno-history), works by North Americans such as John Murra, various Europeans, and other scholars from places like the Institute of Peruvian Studies and the Institute de Bartolomé de las Casas in Cuzco. Cárdenas continued, "Members in our group also translated Andean historical texts from the English and French into Spanish so we could use them more easily. These works helped to sharpen and deepen our critique of the Western-centric development paradigms calling for the disappearance of Indian culture. Both groups from the left and from the right wanted us to commit cultural suicide which, as Kataristas, we vehemently opposed."

The Kataristas' founders included a core of Aymara intellectuals based in the capital city and radicalized by the ethnic discrimination faced there (Hurtado 1986; S. Rivera 1984; Albó 1984a). They were sons and daughters of the revolution of the 1950s whose parents had worked on the feudal estates until the haciendas collapsed in the face of armed peasant militias. Two NGOs in particular provided support to the Kataristas: the Instituto de Desarrollo, Investigación and Educación Popular Campesino (INDICEP) of Oruro, founded by the Oblate Order from Canada and the La Paz–based Centro de Investigación y Promoción del Campesinado (CIPCA) founded by the Jesuits. INDICEP assembled a team of sociologists and anthropologists that included the Chilean Verónica Cereceda (see chapter 11) and the influential Argentine philosopher, Rudulfo Kusch, to support them from 1968 until the military coup by General Banzer in 1971.[4] One member of INDICEP's staff was selected as the model for a widely circulated poster of Tupak Katari.

CIPCA, on the other hand, emerged under the Catholic Church's protective wing during the Banzer period. Its influence on and assistance to the Kataristas began later than that of INDICEP and its approach was more cautious. It sponsored a rural promotion and research program in the altiplano and also supported the Kataristas through informal channels with charismatic leaders such as Genaro Flores. CIPCA's inspired work with the Kataristas was led by Xavier Albó, a naturalized Bolivian from Catalonia, ordained Jesuit priest, and a recent doctorate in socio-linguistics and anthropology from Cornell University. Albó quickly threw his career into overdrive to become the country's most prolific intellectual activist in the area of indigenous issues. He was practically a one-man publishing industry at CIPCA during the 1970s, and, by the end of the 1990s, his resume listed over 270 articles and books on indigenous topics. Using the power of the pen to create evocative social science messages, Albó became a kind of late twentieth-century reincarnation of Bartolomé de las Casas, the Spanish priest whose writings to the Spanish Crown in the sixteenth century defended the Indian from the abuses of the colonial regime. Similar to the Canadian priests from Quebec working with INDICEP, Albó's Spanish roots were in the Catalonia region, known for its long political struggle for cultural and linguistic autonomy within the nation-state. Cárdenas was also a staff member at CIPCA although he was not paid by them to be a full-time Katarista advisor.

Through the 1970s, the Kataristas gained increasing acceptance in the political community as a legitimate mouthpiece for the development concerns and interests of the peasantry. At first, even sympathetic Bolivian officials snubbed the group. In 1971, for instance, under great influence from the radicalized Bolivian mineworkers, a left-of-center military government held a "popular assembly" and invited every labor and progressive political group in the country except the Kataristas.[5] Efforts such as this to marginalize the Kataristas gradually gave way to a grudging respect as politicians came to realize that they needed the Kataristas' participation in their clandestine pro-democratic activities to cultivate peasant constituents. The Kataristas even had to beat back the plan of the Banzer regime to resettle on tropical Bolivian soil thousands of white Rhodesians fleeing from the anti-colonial struggles in Mozambique. By the 1978 electoral campaign, the first democratic election in fourteen years, the major political parties were actively wooing both the Katarista-based sindicatos and tiny spin-off Indianist parties to join their political coalitions. During this period of re-building democratic institutions in Bolivia, the Kataristas replaced military-appointed bosses with elected Aymara and Quechua leaders and put into place a new democratic sindicato structure in the countryside. They also tenaciously opposed the military's concerted efforts at electoral fraud (Hurtado 1986; Alcoreza and Albó 1979). These political acts contributed to the restoration of democracy in the Bolivian countryside and gave it an unmistakable indigenous face.

During a brief period of civilian democratic rule in the late 1970s, Flores, leading the Movimento Revolucionaro Tupak Katari, rose to the top ranks of the Confederación Sindical Única de Trabajadores Campesinos de Bolivia (CSUTCB), the leading peasant trade union. The CSUTCB was a national network representing Bolivia's small farmers that had been first organized by the MNR to carry out its agrarian reform. After being coopted by the military, the structure broke free from the external control under Flores' leadership with the Kataristas. For the first time in its history, it became an autonomous social force, in the hands of its indigenous peasant members and independent of any single political party, national government, or military institution.

From this respected platform, they promoted Bolivia's pluri-cultural heritage (Aymara, Quechua, Guaraní) while opposing national economic and social policies that negatively affected the country's rural poor. To put muscle behind their demands and lodge themselves firmly into the national consciousness, they used a variety of non-violent tactics to bring about collective mobilization in different provinces as well as in the capital city. One of the most impressive non-violent protest actions occurred in 1979, when thousands of local sindicatos mobilized to build trenches and roll boulders and other debris over narrow, typically unpaved roadways to bring the sprawling country to a ten-day standstill. Through a negotiated settlement, Flores and others temporarily overturned austerity measures imposed by the International Monetary Fund. When outraged foreign tourists stranded in a cultural site near Lake Titicaca were quoted in the media complaining about losing five days of valuable vacation time, Flores responded that the indigenous people of Bolivia had been waiting 500 years for social change.

Katarista power increased when Flores rose to the top position of the national trade union confederation, the Central Obrero Boliviano (COB), which was operating underground in 1981 due to military repression. Since the 1952 revolution where it had played a key role, the COB was widely known throughout Latin America for its effective labor and political militancy including an uncanny ability to resist military repression. With its mobilization capacity via the highly politicized Syndicate Federation of Bolivian Mineworkers (FSBM), it could shut down Bolivia's state mining industry, essentially paralyzing the national government's economic lifeblood. Traditionally a stronghold of the mining working class, it was unheard of that the COB be headed by an Indian peasant rather than a mestizo Marxist miner or professional labor leader. Flores was eventually captured by the police in broad daylight on the streets of La Paz and, though unarmed himself, received a gunshot wound that permanently paralyzed him from the waist down.

Between 1982 and 1984, when efforts at democratic government resumed, local Kataristas, receiving moral and logistical support from the La Paz–based leader operating from a wheelchair, in a tiny office three blocks from the parliament and presidential palace, staged protest occupations in just about every government office and program that had anything to do with rural development (Healy 1986b). Flores' main message was:"We were protesting the way past development programs and military dictatorships had excluded our participation and wanted the new democracy to begin rural development anew. The functionaries of these official programs not only had little understanding of life in the countryside, but frequently neither spoke our language nor showed any respect for our cultural practices and traditional way of life. It is no wonder then that the programs were mostly failures" (personal interview 1995).

Katarista cadres staged occupations in the capital city offices of SNDC, the Ministry of Agriculture and Peasant Affairs, the national wool and alpaca fiber marketing board (INFOL), the Regional Public Development Corporation (CORDEPAZ), and the National Agrarian Reform Agency (INRA) to name just a few. At INRA, they called for the ouster of corrupt employees who for many years had extorted funds from peasants while processing land titles. Katarista lobbying prevented appointments of unqualified and disreputable persons to several high-level posts within the Ministry of Agriculture and Peasant Affairs. They staged an occupation to shut down the archaeological site of Tihuanaco in a push to oblige the authorities to earmark increased tourist revenues for the surrounding communities rather than the mestizo-controlled town.

Occupations of state agricultural research stations, the repositories of Western scientific knowledge that generated few benefits for communities, forced a transfer of assets from the ministry to other public and private agencies in an attempt to improve local community impact. The occupation of the public development corporation's research station in the altiplano community of Huaycullani—an action that involved over a hundred sindicato members—was held in concert with protest sit-ins in two separate government offices in La Paz. These joint actions forced shocked authorities to sign over the agricultural machinery, physical infrastructure, and research station lands to the community.

Other Katarista takeovers occurred in three Bolivian government "integrated development projects" financed by the World Bank. These high-profile multi-million dollar rural projects reflected bank president Robert MacNamara's grandiose design to rescue Third World poor by bringing them the best Western technology from the "Green Revolution" (Rich 1994). By a wide margin, these were the largest development projects ever organized to benefit Bolivian altiplano communities. As in many past cases, Aymara frustrations stemmed from the lack of participation, tangible benefits, and attention to their culture in a context of public fanfare and governmental promises of plenty. The Ulla Ulla camelid-raising project that had been organized by the World Bank for herding communities in the high Andes east of Lake Titicaca suffered a similar takeover of the facilities. Herders held its administrator, a former hacienda owner, hostage until government officials sat down and listened attentively to their grievances. Unfortunately, in all three cases, government and World Bank officials were too inflexible to accommodate Katarista demands for greater participation and redirection in planned activities, and the projects gradually ground to a halt on a disappointing note.

During the early 1980s, the "plataforma de lucha" of the trade union CSUTCB reflected the influence of its Katarista leadership. One section called for supporting a "national system of appropriate technology based upon traditional knowledge and the technology of the campesinos and utilization of local resources so as to avoid foreign dependency and the use of inappropriate agricultural inputs that negatively effect the productive capacity of the soil" (CSUTCB 1983). The document also endorsed bilingual schools and literacy programs, and the mounting of a national network of health centers combining Western and indigenous medicine. Another document a year later resulted from a grassroots congress held to rewrite and propose a new agrarian reform with the help of Albó and other advisors.

They also focused on the importance of indigenous history and cultural practices and values in establishing new collective land rights claims.

Kataristas used a variety of ethnic symbols such as displaying Andean textiles at their congresses. Indeed, a favorite image of Genaro Flores on CSUTCB pamphlets showed the leader seated behind a table draped with Aymara altiplano *awayos* (indigenous striped shawls) and flanked on either side by members of one of Bolivia's most culturally conservative ethnic groups, the Quechua-speaking Tarabuqueños in ponchos whose colorful stripes symbolized the rainbow.

While helping to make the Bolivian countryside into a democratic political environment, the Kataristas called into question rampant, negative stereotypes of indigenous society. Although Kataristas showed only moderate interest in environmental concerns, they became Bolivia's first and most powerful voice against the social and economic inequalities and the top-down ethnocentrism of various Western cultural biases in development projects so heavily promoted by the MNR and the successor military regimes. They brought to the forefront bilingual education and literacy training using native languages, the importance of historic memory for forging Andean, Native American identities (*originarios*), and claims to new rights as citizens rather than succumbing to the MNR and military designs (as well as the Bolivian political left) for being simply poor campensinos. By attaining independence from the state, any single political party, and the military and a national stage for their pronouncements, they were successful in establishing greater cultural and political autonomy for the representative voices of the rural masses. Critics have pointed to contradictions in their support of Andean organizational forms (Hahn 1996; Strobele-Gregor 1996), but it must be kept in mind that Katarismo was an influential sociocultural phenomenon that spilled over to indigenous and non-indigenous activists promoting a wide-ranging cultural revitalization agenda. Their vocal and activist presence helped pave the way for an upcoming decade of activism that would begin reshaping both the politics and design of many grassroots development activities.

INDIGENOUS ECHOES FROM THE TROPICAL LOWLANDS

While the Kataristas staged protest actions to push Aymara and Quechua cultural and socioeconomic development agendas, it was not purely coincidental that ethnic minorities in the eastern lowlands of Santa Cruz were beginning to speak out against the homogenizing forces of modernization and uneven economic growth of their region. Sixty-five representatives of the Chiquitanos, Ayoreos, Guarayos, Izoceños, and Ava-Guaraní ethnic groups from twenty-five communities sat down in October 1982 to hold the "Primer Encuentro de Pueblos Indígenas del Oriente Boliviano" in a barrio in the city of Santa Cruz. In effect, they were taking the first steps as ethnic minorities of tropical eastern Bolivia to challenge and create alternatives to the Western modernization paradigm under state capitalism. Like the Kataristas, they wanted to make the most of rights to free association guaranteed within the country's rejuvenated democracy and call the country's attention to their unresolved grievances. In several ways, though, their priorities differed from those in the highlands. For instance, the national agrarian reform legislation of 1953, which did not alter the social structure in their region, referred to them as "jungle groups in a savage condition with a primitive organization." Their farms were surrounded by powerful white and mestizo cattle ranchers, large commercial farmers, agrobusinesses, and timber enterprises whose holdings had been bolstered by government and international aid. The region's campesino sindicatos, made up of colonists from the highlands, had offered the local indigenous groups little support. With this 1982 meeting, the groups were going public with deeply felt grievances for the first time in modern history.

The delegates sat on chairs and benches in an outdoor courtyard enclosed on three sides by red brick office walls. Over the head table hung a map identifying the locations of the ethnic minorities participating in the meeting. The map was of Bolivia but if it had included Brazil, Paraguay, and Argentina it would have shown the wider spatial location of some of these same ethnic groups. At the bottom of the map were the Izoceños and Ava-Guaraníes from the family and linguistic tree of the Guaraní-speaking Chiriguanos. The Izoceños (population 6,000) grew corn along with rice, beans, and manioc, hunted wild game, fished, and raised small animals in a tiny corner of the Gran Chaco, the hot, dry plains and thorny scrub forests extending into Paraguay and northern Argentina. Although the group had lost homeland territory to the expanding white ranchers, they had never lived within the Catholic missions as the Guarayo and Chiquitano participants had. Consequently, they were the only group in this gathering that had maintained a traditional form of leadership (the *mburuvicha*).

The Ava-Guaraní, known historically as the Chiriguanos (population 40,000–50,000), subsisted on corn and other crops in the region's forested Andean foothills. Their ancestors were among the fiercest opponents to cultural, economic, and political integration during the nineteenth century. Prior to the formation of the Bolivian republic, neither the Incas nor the Europeans had been able to subdue them militarily nor annex their homelands. They were tough adversaries indeed, as proven by their frequent extractions of tribute from white settlers and soldiers, astute political alliances with foes, and a technically advanced form of guerrilla warfare (Langer 1990).

Similar to the indigenous peoples of the high valleys and altiplano, the traditional society of the Ava-Guaraní began to unravel with the advent of the liberal land policies of the late nineteenth century, which triggered an unprecedented flood of white settlers and cattle onto their homelands. Two related factors altered the then-prevailing balance of power: the construction of strategically placed army forts, and the willingness of mission Indians to fight on the side of the whites and mestizos (Langer 1990). After a string of military defeats, an *Apiaguaiqui,* a traditional Ava-Guaraní chief and shaman or "man-god," led an all-out campaign to restore their communal holdings and drive the white invaders away forever. With neither sufficient warriors nor the firepower to succeed, this audacious campaign culminated in the 1892 Battle of Kuruyuki, a bloody massacre of approximately 900 Ava-Guaraní and a few allied Izoceños. This defeat marked the beginning of the end for Ava-Guaraní hegemony in this frontier region. Survivors who attempted escape were persecuted while others were relocated to haciendas and Franciscan missions in the area (Pifarre 1989, 396). When the missions disbanded during the twentieth century, Ava-Guaraní families carved out small subsistence plots on the edges of the ranches in marginal farming areas, though some pockets of haciendas remained intact even after the 1952 land reform programs.[6]

Among the groups located in the northernmost section of the map were the Chiquitanos (population 35,000) and Guarayos (population 20,000). Hundreds of years earlier, both these tribes had been hunters and gatherers and tiny plot farmers in the dry forests of northern Santa Cruz, but their more recent experiences in Catholic missions had altered their economy (Riester 1976; Smith 1993, 52). The contemporary Chiquitanos farmed tiny plots, worked as hired hands on local ranches and commercial farms, and picked fruit and collected honey in the nearby forests and pampas (Riester 1976, 130). They resided in six widely scattered zones and most had abandoned hunting of small game under pressures from timber and cattle operations. The largest cattle rancher in one of their vicinities was a Catholic bishop, a patriarch whose large herd prompted frequent jokes that his vicariate parish resembled a "vacariato" more than a "vicariato," a play on the Spanish word "vaca" signifying cow.

The Guarayos resided in a transition belt between the humid and dry forest areas. Their original habitat—fishing and hunting land, natural pasture, and small areas for farming—had been greatly reduced first by Franciscan Missions (1840–1930) and subsequently by invading cattle ranchers and colonists from other regions (Lehm 1996). The Guarayos were reputed to be virtuoso violinists during the colonial period and expert craftspeople who produced an array of vibrant artisan wares.

The Ayoreos (population 3,000–4,000) had only four decades of experience within the structures of modern society. They had been nomadic—hunting, fishing, and gathering fruits and nuts along a wide swath in the southern Chaco plains—but were persuaded by Catholic and Evangelical missionaries to join Western society. Some Ayoreos subsequently traded in their traditional mixed economy for a sedentary existence on a property obtained by the Protestant missions. This transition to Western ways had the tragic effect of turning them into some of the poorest, most helpless, and pitied ethnic groups of Santa Cruz.

The courtyard in which the Izoceños, Ayoreos, Chiquitanos, and Guarayos held their first assembly was that of the Bolivian NGO, Ayuda Para el Campesino Indígena del Oriente Boliviano (APCOB). APCOB's staff of social scientists and engineers had been working since the late 1970s to bring about this historic meeting. Its founder, Juergen Riester, a German anthropologist, had researched and written *En Busca de la Loma Santa,* with colleague Bernardo Fischerman, on the tribes of the Amazon, Chaco, and eastern lowlands of Bolivia in the mid-1970s with the goal of enlightening Bolivians about some of their least-known ethnic groups. In addition to his comprehensive research and activism, Riester had taught anthropology in Peru and listened to stories and reports from Amazonian leaders and activist anthropologists at his apartment in Lima during an era of political ferment. Peru's Amazonian tribes were organizing themselves into modern political organizations for the first time and Riester was able to observe both their problems and important breakthroughs at close range, and to bring these lessons back to Bolivia with him.

During the mid-1970s, while living for an extended period among the Izoceños, Riester had long conversations with Bonifacio Barrientos, a chief elder, and with Víctor Vaca, a fairly well-educated younger tribesman, about a possible pan-tribal organization that would unite the indigenous minorities of eastern Bolivia into a common political front. Barrientos had proven credentials, having secured land rights for some of his communities in 1947. He had led a band of thirty "capitanes" and others across the mountain valleys and forested lowlands on foot to the city of Cochabamba where they boarded a truck and traveled the rest of the way to reach their destination: the capital of Bolivia. Although a third of the group died en route, Barrientos and the other survivors succeeded in reaching the Presidential Palace and bringing back the first collective land titles to the Izoceño communities.

Vaca, the presiding officer of the assembly, had been groomed by APCOB to play a key leadership role. In 1978, with the assistance of APCOB staff members, he initiated the first contacts among these far-flung tribes by visiting the Ayoreos. He established a genuine dialogue with them despite their long-standing animosity toward outsiders, based upon competition over the Chaco's scarce resources.

APCOB also prepared him for this historic encuentro by sending him to international conferences in Australia and Lima where in this heady international atmosphere the negative overtones that had historically been associated with the term "indígena" in Bolivia were magically transformed into instilling pride. At these meetings, indigenous representatives from across the globe vociferously advocated their long-denied cultural rights and identities. Moved by such events and discourse, Vaca returned to Bolivia and solidified his working group of Izoceño activists Abelio Arambiza, Cecilo Gomez, and Dario Nandureza to set in motion an organization-building and ethnic unification process. The "Primer Encuentro" was a most significant step in the long journey underway.

Despite previous efforts at networking, most delegates were meeting one another for the first time and had little inkling of APCOB's past and future role. Throughout the meeting, Vaca exhorted them to share reflections among themselves about what it meant to be indigenous peoples in today's world and to "value their native cultural traditions." Since "indio" or "indígena" was about the worst insult heretofore to be said about someone, for many participants the new positive spin on the words, although intriguing, was downright threatening. All through the meeting the Izoceños and APCOB staff pushed the generic term "indígena" as a way of constructing a new identity, to support modern political and developmental activism, and to rally dispersed ethnic minorities toward a common cause. The use of the terms was also a way to distinguish themselves politically from the Kataristas who preferred the term, "originarios" or "first peoples," and thus gain greater political autonomy from the highland peoples who then dominated ethnic politics in the country.[7]

Initial confusion and political inexperience caused many delegates to channel their petitions for assistance to APCOB. Oscar Castillo, a Peruvian sociologist on APCOB's staff, cleared up this difficulty. "Instead of APCOB, it's the Bolivian government that should have to satisfy the demands of your communities. Poor people have just as much right to have their interests represented by the state as rich people. Just look at the sugar cane growers and cattle ranchers who have obtained substantial benefits from the national government. The key is a representative organization and a political platform to make your specific needs known to these public officials. APCOB will help primarily to facilitate this organization building and the follow-up activities in your communities and the city of Santa Cruz."

Over the course of the three days, the delegates focused on bread and butter issues—lack of agricultural credit, the need for land titles and health services, inadequate schooling, low prices for agricultural commodities, and low agricultural wages—issues common to Indian peasant meetings such as this. Yet Vaca and other Izoceños were insistent about the importance of stressing pan-indigenous culture within their emerging agenda. He insisted on hearing representatives of the various groups speak their diverse languages, even if most in attendance did not understand them. Vaca talked about the automatic discrimination found in public offices whenever indigenous languages were spoken and how those same languages could positively transform the learning environment of public schooling in their communities. He also reiterated the value of traditional medicine and the participants' duty to reaffirm its importance while in the presence of public officials.

He spoke harshly about Izoceños' experiences with national integration.

For many years, the governmental authorities looked upon the Izoceños and other Indians as a tremendous burden on the rest of society, and held us responsible for the country's economic backwardness. That image was altered somewhat by the Chaco War when those 'useless, idle Indians' went to the trenches as soldiers and defended a fatherland at war with Paraguay. Because of our service on the battlefield, the government subsequently helped us with some of our problems in relation to abuses by local ranchers and it provided teachers for our public schools, yet private ranches continue to interfere with our lives and livelihood, and whites have run our schools over the past almost fifty years without knowing our language and culture. The educational advancement of our children has suffered greatly from the exclusive use of Spanish. (APCOB tape)

One of the most poignant statements about the cultural costs of integration was expressed in barely intelligible Spanish by an Ayoreo.

We were once a strong community with ample room for hunting and fishing in a large zone of grasslands and thorn forests. As a chief of my people, I led our move to join Western civilization by accepting plans for us worked out by evangelical missionaries. They resettled us on a small ranch-size property which cut us off from our former nomadic way of life. The missionaries promised that we'd receive more enjoyment from life and become greater than other men in the world. That promise did not turn out to be true. In the good old days, I wore the jaguar skin hat of a chief, and this gave me a great feeling of pride and self-importance, especially when clan members would walk up and place feathers of jungle birds on it as a demonstration of their respect for me. My current way of life, by contrast, has made me feel like a child again.

Despite these poignant remarks, many participants were shy about revealing humiliating experiences to a gathering of mostly unfamiliar faces. Yet everyone left determined to revitalize organizations in their communities and to form the basic building blocks of a multi-ethnic, regional organization under the name, Central de Pueblos y Communidades Indígenas del Oriente Boliviano (CIDOB).

One of the most exciting and best organized federations springing up in CIDOB's wake was the "Asamblea del Pueblo Guaraní" representing the Ava-Guaraní from the Cordillera province and forging the revival of their traditional *mburuvicha* organization. While the other ethnic-based affiliates to CIDOB had received training and support from APCOB, the Ava-Guaraní had benefited enormously from the assistance of CIPCA, more known for its work with Aymara Katarista organizations in La Paz. Xavier Albó and his colleagues applied the potent combination of action and research to enable local indigenous leadership and democratic structures to flourish in new ways (Albó 1990a; Pifarre 1989). CIPCA's efforts contributed to one of the country's best local networks of experimental bilingual schools (Guaraní-Spanish). The Asamblea subsequently grew to incorporate Guaraní communities from the regions of Chuquisaca and Tarija as well, and contributed to breaking up the hacienda system in the former.

CIDOB's affiliates also initiated numerous small-scale socioeconomic development projects under APCOB's umbrella-level supervision. Their "social-forestry" projects, for example, caught the attention of national and international environmentalists and foresters interested in halting indiscriminate logging operations. On another front, in the capital city, CIDOB members initiated the legal process to acquire land titles for communities that had yet to receive important benefits from national land reform programs.

Over the next few years, CIDOB began a quest for an entirely different concept of land rights than that advanced by the MNR. The new land rights conception was based on the "territory," a term that connoted a collective rather than an individual unit, belonging to a geographically situated ethnic group rather than to an individual family. This term did not simply refer to land, but an ethnic group's right to autonomous self-government and the inherent value of its cosmovision about and collective rights to natural resources. It implied the utilization of technologies by indigenous communities that conserved rather than destroyed natural resources. In effect, CIDOB was invigorating the highland-led indigenous social movements in Bolivia with an environmental agenda that would help create their modern political identity for making demands on the Bolivian state. The term was first adopted at a 1984 meeting of COICA, a pan-Amazonian confederation of indigenous organizations from the Amazonian river system—groups from Colombia, Ecuador, Peru, and Brazil attended along with CIDOB, representing Bolivia. These delegates deliberated long and hard over a suitable term and, according to Richard Smith, an activist from OXFAM-America who was present at the meeting, the delegates were impressed by the territorial strategies of the Iroquois nation in North America.

To advance "territorial rights" as part of an emerging indigenous identity and agenda, CIDOB and APCOB began advocating not only the acquisition of land titles for their constituents but a change in the national
laws. They began enlisting sympathetic NGOs, grassroots organizations,
and environmental organizations, along with social activists from the Catholic Church, to work together through educational seminars, workshops,
and educational events.

CIDOB carried its banner of cultural revitalization and territorial
rights to the neighboring Beni region. The Izoceños and Guarayos first
made contact with the Cabildo Indígenal in the old Jesuit mission town of
Trinidad. While impressed with the strong ethnic identity of the urban cabildo members, they soon found a different reality in the rural Beni area,
where the Mojeños and other ethnic groups were undergoing rapid acculturation to Western ways. To bring these groups aboard, the CIDOB
staffers began inviting indigenous leaders to attend their congresses in Santa
Cruz where indigenous identity was one of the main topics of discussion
and debate. After recruiting some of these leaders from the Beni, they along
with NGOs and church-based organizations assisted the emerging federations there when this region was swept up in its own ethnic movement of
cultural revitalization in the late 1980s.

Although not widely known even within Santa Cruz through most of
the 1980s and lacking the activist flair of the Kataristas, CIDOB catalyzed
tiny, ethnic minorities to work together in the lowlands. CIDOB's supervision and management of small-scale development projects had some serious difficulties due, according to anthropologist Silvia Hirsch, to its ten-
dency to operate with a top-down management style from the regional
capital. Nonetheless, CIDOB's growing influence in radio programming
and NGO-sponsored workshops and seminars was forging a new and
growing agenda in favor of indigenous rights. Other NGOs and grassroots
federations quickly followed CIDOB's example.

The Revitalizing Role of Andean Social Sciences

In tandem with the grassroots indigenous movements, radical changes
within the country's social sciences were quickly reshaping social theory in
such a way as to support the revitalization of the country's diverse cultural
patrimony as a nexus for rural development. The best place to view this se-

quence of change in intellectual focus and related grassroots social commitment is at the Universidad Nacional de San Andres, the country's major public university located in the capital city.

During the 1970s, San Andres offered the most extensive course offerings in the social sciences, including courses on theories of social and economic development within Latin America. During that decade the field of sociology had evolved from a smattering of courses in the law school curriculum to a bona fide university department (*facultad*). Lagging far behind them, however, was the facultad of anthropology which was not established until the mid-1980s—another obvious sign of neo-colonialism.

With the help of foreign scholars and Bolivian social scientists returning from centers throughout Latin America and Western Europe, especially the University of Louvain in Belgium, the number of sociology courses using Marxian and neo-Marxian theory multiplied within the university curriculum. According to historian Rene Arze, who was a student at that time,

> It was an era very much influenced by the Cuban revolution when everyone talked in orthodox Marxian terms of the "proletariat," the "national bourgeoisie," and the "theories of labor surplus," while those interested in, say, the Chaco's indigenous peoples were still seen as a bunch of weirdos, totally out of touch with mainstream intellectual and political thinking. An ethnographic museum in the capital was where these folks which included two anthropologists by the same name of Ramiro Molina usually met to organize seminars and lectures that drew only a small group of people.

The Neo-Marxian dependency school, shaped by theorists such as the German André Gunder Frank and the Brazilian sociologist and current president of the country, Fernando Enrique Cardoso, had the greatest appeal for students as a theory for explaining the socioeconomic underdevelopment of Bolivia (Barnadas 1987). By turning modernization theory inside out, "dependency theory" provided new analytic tools for understanding the growing economic linkages of trade, aid, and investment between Latin American nations and northern industrial countries. For aficionados of dependency theory, it was transplanted Western values, institutions, and technologies for transforming society along capitalist lines that were leading to deepening poverty. Bolivian students, professors, and professionals observed the low and falling national earnings for their economy from wildly fluctuating mineral prices in Western export markets throughout Bolivian history. They were also critical of the social and economic inequalities between whites, mestizos, and indigenous peoples that had widened through recent economic growth. Dependency theory helped to describe how and why this was happening. While useful corrective lenses, in some respects, neither the Marxist nor the dependency paradigm gave any importance to the positive role of indigenous culture. Gunder Frank went so far as to say that the Indians "lacked culture" (Frank 1969, 136). Anthropologist Richard Reed pointed out that social science writings often argued that Indian culture would disappear through the expansion of market systems (Reed 1995).

This national blindspot in social science began to clear up as scholarly works in Andean studies (anthropology, ethnohistory, ethnomedicine, rural sociology, socio-linguistics, etc.) proliferated in Peru, Western Europe, and the U.S. and made their way to Bolivia. By the end of the 1970s, their cumulative scholarly output was comparable in quality and quantity to the rich literature of Meso-american studies (Larson 1995).[8] For example, historian Brooke Larson pointed out a convergence in the analytical frameworks of rural sociologists, historians, and anthropologists that threw new light on the contribution made by Andean ethnic groups to the colonial market system. Whereas historians previously had depicted the Andean peoples to be passive, helpless victims of destructive European invasion, this new genre of research depicted dynamic indigenous peoples who had rebuilt societal institutions through myriad grassroots initiatives in different sectors.

One impressive example was the control exercised by Aymara herders in the overland transport by llama caravan of silver bullion and other commodities from Potosí, back and forth across the Andean chain, to the Spanish colony's two main southern export cities (Larson and Harris 1995). In her description of the indigenous peoples' influential, adaptive, but self-respecting attitude toward their cultures, Larson wrote, "Their native political structures and kin-based and barter reciprocities were used to 'redirect' agriculture toward commercial ends; engage in trade and commerce; pursue artisanry and wage labor; mortgage, sell and purchase" (Larson 1995, 19).

The emergence of these scholarly works and research trends dovetailed with and provided more solid intellectual footing for the Kataristas' emerging agendas. Influential intellectual activists—men such as Cárdenas and

Albó—used this literature to enhance their conceptions of the role of ethnicity in social mobilization, politics, education, and Bolivian rural development.

Within the Bolivian university setting, it was the new and growing sociology faculty, with support from a handful of emerging professional historians, that began transforming the horizon of social analysis, setting into place a fundamentally different view of the role of indigenous culture and ethnicity, and conceiving new analytical frameworks for studying society and history. This intellectual movement was led by Silvia Rivera Cusicanqui, a young, independent-minded professor and brilliant analyst of national political and social issues. The daughter of a prominent medical doctor, Rivera was unusual in having a second surname that was indigenous. Cusicanqui revealed bloodlines of Aymara hereditary chieftains (*caciques*) from the La Paz–based aristocracy active during the colonial period. Rivera's growing curiosity about Katarismo and her Aymara roots led her to do field work in the remote altiplano Pacajes province, a hotbed of Katarismo. This exploration of her Andean heritage and a pursuit of scientific tools for dissecting the problems of the countryside next took her to Peru where, with the help of Bolivian anthropologist Jorge Dandler, she enrolled in a master's degree program in Andean anthropology.

Rivera's personal and professional experiences resulted in a burning commitment to bring awareness of ethnic identity and indigenous culture into the university. She formed a small group of like-minded intellectual friends such as historians Rene Arze and Roberto Choque and, together with foreigners such as Frenchman Thierry Saignes and Briton Tristan Platt, put together a new journal *AVANCES* to publish research emerging from the new school of revisionist ethno-history. By the late 1970s, Rivera realized that the students often deemed to be most reticent in the university classes—young Aymara students from urban migrant and rural community social backgrounds—would be the natural and productive allies in building an authentic indigenous focus within higher education. She was soon joined by an Aymara student activist organization named Bartolina Sisa, in honor of Tupak Katari's rebel companion, which had successfully eliminated barriers blocking Aymara students from using the university cafeteria.

Among the first to stand out in this Aymara university group was Tomás Huanca, who had been born in a mud hut near Lake Titicaca where he had lived until he was twenty. He then studied on scholarship at several private Catholic institutions, where his consistent record of educational

excellence led to teachers' college and a brief career in rural teaching—
a common path of upward social mobility among Aymara. A yearning for
greater intellectual and social challenges led Huanca to enroll in the Sociology faculty where he eventually joined Rivera's quest to bring the university community into touch with indigenous issues. One of his first
intellectual contributions was a sparkling thesis showing how MNR cadres
had steered the revolutionary process away from the indigenous values and
organizational practices in communities near Lake Titicaca.

Huanca and Rivera's joint efforts abruptly ended when a 1980 military
coup forced Rivera into exile in Mexico where she authored what was to
become an important and widely read work, *Oppressed But Not Defeated:
Peasant Struggles among the Aymara and Qhechwa in Bolivia, 1900–1980,* covering indigenous rebellions against the state. Upon her return to Bolivia with
the restoration of democracy in late 1982, she and Huanca founded the
Andean Oral History Workshop (Taller de Historia Oral Andina) (THOA)
which quickly became a magnet for Aymara students wanting to uncover
Aymara and Quechua history long shunned by the academic and political
establishment. THOA used pathbreaking oral history research methods that
enabled young researchers to tap into a rich repository of oral traditions
found in the rural altiplano communities.[9]

The oral history method was combined with research in a history
archive in La Paz which contained the judicial records of land disputes. The
first of its kind in the capital city, the archive had been set up in the early
1970s and partly administered by an Aymara history student, Roberto
Choque. Choque became Bolivia's first professionally trained Aymara historian despite the institutional barriers in his path. The biggest disadvantage
was his difficulty with spoken Spanish given his rural monolingual family
background. As historian Rene Arze points out, "Native Aymara speakers
have the same problem Germans have in speaking Spanish. The two
languages don't match well." Yet despite Choque's personal struggles he
became an actor in changing the contours of his discipline within the university and went on to publish major works. Within Bolivian universities,
history had been the domain of amateur historians together with professionals from the fields of law and politics, who were apt to confine indigenous peoples to their footnotes.[10] Choque's participation in the organization
of the first archive for students and scholars in La Paz was essential for
recovering a broader perspective. THOA was one of the first university
groups to take advantage of this resource for probing Bolivia's hidden past.

One of the most intriguing stories brought to light by THOA's innovative research was a non-violent ayllu movement of the 1920s led by an Aymara authority, Santos Marka T'ula of Pacajes province, who defended indigenous collective land rights by using colonial documents from the Spanish Crown to argue before government offices and the courts. This activism eventually got him a jail term as an "Indian Subversive." Despite this confinement, his communications continued uninterrupted, with a large ayllu network of some 400 communities maintaining a permanent state of non-violent mobilization. THOA turned this academic narrative into a dramatic story broadcast to Aymara-speaking radio listeners in hundreds of altiplano communities. Similar to the previously mentioned Tupak Katari movement story, the Santos Marka T'ula story climbed to the top of the popularity charts of rural radio programming in the altiplano towns and hamlets.

THOA's rising profile in the academic community was due not only to its unconventional Andean themes and methodologies but also to the offbeat "intercultural" events sponsored by the organization. Aymara was spoken along with Spanish for the first time at public university events and on occasion the indigenous rural social etiquette of *acullicu,* a communal sharing of coca leaves for solidarity and friendship, took place in lieu of serving wine. The likes of Víctor Hugo Cárdenas, linguist Juan de Dios Yapita, sociologists Esteban Ticona and Ramon Conde, among others, stepped into the public spotlight here as prominent members of an emerging Aymara intelligentsia.

Simultaneously, THOA's dynamic publications program was reaching out to a broader readership.[11] THOA was not only adding to the academic literature but creating bilingual texts that a decade later would be in school libraries across the country—among the first fruits of the new bilingual education reform law.

THOA and other social science activity received complementary support in 1984 from a new local publishing house called Historia Social Boliviana (HISBOL). The aim of HISBOL was to translate the work of French, English, German, United States, and Peruvian scholars of Andean affairs into inexpensive, pocket-size Spanish books for distribution in Bolivia. HISBOL's publication program kept expanding and by the end of the decade, the shelves of its La Paz bookstore adjacent to the university were crammed with books on such topics as the native organizations, crops, pastures, medicines, textile art, and technology.

HISBOL's Peruvian founder, Javier Medina, was trained as a philosopher in Europe and first learned about Andean community life while a young boy on a hacienda administered by his father. Having observed the boom in Andean studies in Peru during the 1970s, and finding little of it reaching Bolivian bookshelves, he set out to rectify this situation on his own.

HISBOL's books were devoured by a growing readership. Albó continued to churn out publication after publication on the country's new ethnopolitics and many other related topics in history, political sociology, and socio-linguistics through the publishing program of CIPCA, the Jesuit NGO that employed him. A series of multi-disciplinary congresses of "Estudios Bolivianos" began taking place during the 1980s, highlighting the work of a number of new "Andeanists" working with NGO programs in rural development and research. HISBOL and Medina offered a holistic, indigenous-based view of rural development in the Andes by emphasizing that native cultural pluralism was part of the same landscape as the biodiversity of plants and animals in both mountain and the jungle environments. Having funded a sizable number of these projects, I was delighted by the contributions of these two intellectual institutions, THOA and HISBOL, particularly since colleagues at the IAF had at first doubted the practical and social utility and the wisdom of providing them with supportive grants.

And in the eastern lowlands, an extremely important initiative using social science publications knowledge occurred in the late 1980s when independent Bolivian video producer Ruben Poma made twenty documentaries for Santa Cruz television on the region's ethnic minorities in a program called *Jenecheru*. Drawing upon the anthropological and historical knowledge of Juergen Riester and others specializing in the Amazonian and Chaco socio-cultural environments, Poma's popular narratives and images depicting peoples of dignity, sophisticated knowledge, and remarkable skill reaching a national television audience began to shatter widely held negative stereotypes about "primitive" indigenous peoples. In so doing, he helped pave the way for changes that were in the works for the country's political culture involving the indigenous peoples of the eastern lowlands.

These emerging Andean and Amazonian perspectives contrasted with the development theories of both the modernization and dependency schools (and other political economy theory as well) that had overlooked the positive role of indigenous culture, without throwing out the important concepts and insights related to political economy and social class analysis for exploring Bolivia's problems.

SHIFTING FOREIGN WINDS FAVORING INDIGENOUS CULTURAL RESOURCES

In addition to the paradigm shifts in the Bolivian social sciences, winds blowing from abroad during the last half of the 1980s and early 1990s further accelerated the process of cultural revitalization. One of these currents arose in relation to the environmentalist crisis in the Amazon region. The devastation of the rainforest focused international attention on the intermingled issues of cultural pluralism, economic justice, and the proper management of natural resources. The outcry of environmentalists brought heightened interest and respect among many NGO and grassroots organizations for indigenous knowledge and cultural practices. Bolivian environmental organizations sprouted. Also new international organizations enthusiastically stepped into this context with funds for activities for conservation of biodiversity, wildlife, and soil. The environmental emphasis also had effects in Bolivian universities where courses such as rangeland ecology and agro-ecology eventually gained a legitimate place. Some institutions working on environmental issues related to bio-reserves and national parks began consulting with the native peoples. Suddenly many international environmental organizations with money to spend on technical assistance, studies, and training for small as well as large projects began setting up programs in Bolivia and exploring ways, both successful and unsuccessful, to work with Indians and save the environment.

The spreading environmental consciousness led to public appreciation for Bolivians who had long celebrated the country's many contributions to the world's biodiversity yet had received only minimal government financing, recognition, and other support. This group included a deceased botanist by the name of Martin Cárdenas and scientists such as Armando Cardozo, often referred to as the "lonely llama herder" for his single-minded devotion to his country's camelids; Gilberto Hinojosa, who championed the cause of tarhui; and Humberto Gandarillas, who emphasized a greater appreciation for the livestock, crops, and other resources native to the Andes.

Perhaps the best example of a lonely crusader bucking the establishment was Humberto Alzérreca, whose pioneering work led to greater recognition for the altiplano's native pastures. During four years of agronomy studies in Cochabamba in the early 1970s, he remembered hearing only once about a native pasture from the altiplano—a reference to *ichu,* a kind of bunch grass with little nutritional value. He told me:

> Upon graduation, my first job was at an altiplano research station, yet I quickly discovered that the modern technological package I had learned in my department was useless under these conditions. My boss sent me to conduct field trials with North American alfalfa grasses at 4,000 meters above sea level near the Andean ranges close to the Pacajes province near the Chilean border. I watched in horror as one variety after another failed to survive the climate and then my boss blamed the results on my field research skills. I finally began inquiring among the resident herders about what they used and learned the names of different grasses of this locality in Aymara.

Alzérreca received encouragement in his inquiry from an unusual scientist by the name of Carl Parker, an authority on native pastures from the Great Basin area of the American West who was with the Utah State University program in Bolivia. Alzérreca was thrilled to find a distinguished scientist as kindred spirit and told me,

> Suddenly, my eyes were seeing a totally different world and I was realizing how little I knew about the natural resources, traditional technologies, and agrarian history of my own country. I found some literature in Peru about Andean native grasses and related historical and anthropological topics on agriculture and pastoralism as little had been published on the former in Bolivia. It then dawned on me that it was none other than these native pastures that provided middle-class Bolivians like myself living at high altitudes with our daily requirements of meat, cheese, and milk, and that such natural resources dated back thousands of years in contrast to the alfalfa varieties being brought to Bolivia which had only a century or so of history.

Alzérreca proceeded to select native altiplano grasses as a thesis topic, making his academic committee most unhappy. Parker certainly helped in giving this first Bolivian study of native grasses some much needed academic legitimacy. Then at Utah State University Alzérreca avidly pursued this academic interest in rangeland ecology. Upon returning to a job at the Patacamaya research station in Bolivia, he assembled over the next few years the country's first herbarium of this kind, amounting to 3,000 species of native grasses. His supervisor and other foreign aid and national government technicians were vociferous in their complaints about this conservation work at the experiment station. Fortunately, Germans organizing similar collections at a recently founded Institute of Ecology in La Paz gave these plants a permanent home.

Battling such institutional obstacles only increased his determination. He subsequently added a doctoral degree in the same field and became Bolivia's leading authority and advocate on this topic during the decade of the 1980s. He spread this ecological consciousness to a new generation of university students through twenty-four thesis projects under his supervision. Many of these students were of rural Aymara descent attending the new agronomy faculty in La Paz, and went on to carry this specialized knowledge about the altiplano into many non-governmental as well as public development programs and agencies. During the 1990s, the Red de Pastizales (a network of native pasture advocates among public and NGO agencies) signaled a new degree of appreciation for these long-overlooked cultural resources.

Revisionist Perceptions of Indigenous Peoples

Media fanfare over the Columbus Quincentenary in the late 1980s and early 1990s created a tremendous reservoir of sympathy for native peoples and respect for their many contributions to the modern world. This change in public opinion helped to discredit "assimilationist" policies.

The several year build-up to the year of the quincentenary inspired UNITAS, Bolivia's largest and most prestigious NGO network, to sponsor three seminars on "Multicultural Reality and Its Challenge to NGOs" to share this emerging indigenous perspective. UNITAS was an umbrella organization representing dozens of organizations from different regions of the country. Many of the UNITAS member organizations were led by persons who had heavily identified with the mineworkers as the main force for radical social and political change only to watch this initiative evaporate with the dismissal of 22,000 mineworkers (out of a total of 25,000) from their jobs under the 1985 structural adjustment plan. UNITAS was now looking to the countryside for new labor movement leadership and finding it in the indigenous causes. The document produced at the conclusion of the seminar stated:

> Rural development activities undertaken in Bolivia often operate within a framework that is out of sync with the logic and traditions of the local population. This frequently leads to numerous barriers and conflicts blocking community participation and producing questionable social and economic development results in projects. This situation gives rise to a kind of "pact of minimal common interests" between development practitioners and the community for transplanting an inappropriate Western model to a specific rural locality. This prevailing approach to development negates building close ties between the two projects groups and making adjustments in plans and institutional methods to fit the goals, logic, institutions, and traditions of the native inhabitants. (UNITAS 1991, 14)

Aymara and Quechua representatives together with Izoceños, Guarayos, and Tupi-Guaraníes from CIDOB voiced their concerns in these interchanges between the NGO representatives. Evelio Arambiza, an Izoceño, made a memorable remark when he said,

> By speaking of "pueblos indígenas" and "territory," political parties and even some NGOs said we were out of the political game, outside Bolivian reality, that we were trying to hold back the march of history. We would spend much time criticizing these intellectuals because they're great copiers: we import noodles, we import wheat flour, and we also import ideology, because we don't analyze the contributions of our organized indigenous peoples, with their own models of development, organization, nation-state, economy, education and health. (UNITAS 1991, 76)

Many others also spoke in the same spirit and advocated moving beyond ethnicity to the more empowering and politically charged term of "nationalities." The legal recognition of traditional indigenous authorities and their organizations of ayllus, cabildos, and communidades became more deeply appreciated in these events for their long history in action, much longer than the Bolivian state itself.

Outside of Bolivia, indigenous issues were becoming hot subjects in multilateral and bilateral financial agencies which had begun bringing indigenous representatives and their pressing development issues to their plush boardrooms. During the 1990s, the Inter-American Development Bank eschewed its earlier integrationist outlook to oversee the creation of a "Indigenous Peoples Fund," spearheaded by a Bolivian president and headquartered in La Paz, for brokering international financial resources for projects administered by indigenous organizations throughout the hemisphere.[12]

The World Bank also joined other multilaterals in this pro-indigenous chorus. During the 1980s, it hired several anthropologists, one of whom was Shelton Davis, founder of the Anthropology Resource Center, one of the most prominent activist organizations in the United States working on South American indigenous issues. The World Bank inaugurated a small program aiming to benefit indigenous federations. As a result of this new focus, Bolivian indigenous leaders began jetting back and forth to World Bank headquarters for consultations and participating in special World Bank management training workshops held in Latin America.[13] In the late 1990s the World Bank launched a kind of "affirmative action" program in Ecuador, Peru, and Bolivia by targeting "indigenous peoples" in their loan documents which also referred to ethnic discrimination toward indigenous peoples as a key barrier to indigenous development. This later analysis was also a major reversal from the earlier 1960s' proposition which viewed indigenous culture as the main development problem. In Bolivia, the preliminary planning document of the World Bank loan dubbed the program "development with identity," endorsing the "values, norms, and technologies that the indigenous peoples themselves have been constructing through their own civilizations" (World Bank 1998).

USAID is another major donor agency that switched gears during the 1990s to take a more explicit indigenous-resource stance in financing of some agricultural development and environmental projects in Bolivia. By the mid-1990s, USAID had financed the largest ecological park ever established in Bolivia, a park stretching across the Chaco. The Izoceños, who were given major responsibilities in this environmental protection scheme, were to govern the project through their traditional community institutions, the *mburuvicha,* together with a new local development foundation. Meanwhile back in the Western highlands, USAID was busy funding the expansion of quinoa exports and the repopulation of prairies with llamas.

In 1993 the *Washington Post* announced that the U.N.'s Food and Agriculture Organization would launch a program to enhance worldwide food production by supporting the thousands of obscure edible plant species and animals that had been ignored in earlier programs and in 1989 the U.S. National Science Council released a new publication celebrating the importance of Andean native crops.

The International Labor Organization (ILO) also had long ago abandoned its 1950s "integrationist" approach. Much earlier than the World Bank, the Inter-American Development Bank, or USAID in embracing this focus, it had become a worldwide advocate for the constitutional rights of tribal and native peoples (Brysk 1994, 34). In 1989 the ILO replaced the 1959 Convention 107 emphasizing cultural integrationism with the "Revised Convention 169," obtaining signatures from eighty national governments, including Bolivia. All signatories agreed "to recognize the aspirations of indigenous peoples to assume control of their own institutions, way of life and economic development and to maintain and fortify their identities, languages, and religions within the nation states in which they live" (OIT 1989, 5).

This Convention also called for the adoption of special measures to protect the persons, institutions, property, work, culture, and environments enabling peoples so that they would benefit fully from their human rights and fundamental liberties without obstacles or discrimination. It obligated the national governments to protect their collective rights and integrity as "peoples." One of its main movers and shakers was Bolivian anthropologist Jorge Dandler who in his official capacity enthusiastically carried these concepts to indigenous peoples as well as national governments throughout the hemisphere. In 1993 the U.N. General Assembly declared the official "U.N. Year of Indigenous Peoples," and then in 1995 made this into a "Decade of Culture" to be celebrated. And in 1992, the Nobel Peace Prize went to a Guatemalan indigenous woman, Rigoberta Menchú—another important sign of the growing worldwide respect for indigenous peoples.

While none of the aforementioned agencies apologized for their past oversights, ignorance, and prejudices toward indigenous peoples, Pope John Paul II in 1993 conducted such moral hand-wringing in a speech at Santa Domingo and in 1998 a Canadian minister of education apologized to his country's native peoples for earlier compulsory re-education programs aiming to suppress their cultural identities. Clearly on many fronts a new day was dawning, bringing some newfound respect to indigenous peoples in Bolivia and throughout the Americas.

CHAPTER 5

Dethroning Monocultures and Revitalizing Diversity

After 500 years of colonial silence and 168 years of republican exclusion, we begin speaking our own truth.

VÍCTOR HUGO CÁRDENAS (INAUGURAL ADDRESS 1993)

Indigenous social movements, activist social scientists and environmentalists, anti-quincentenary's festivities, and new perspectives of international environmentalists and funders converged to create a context where forgotten or de-emphasized indigenous cultural resources were rediscovered by development institutions in Bolivia. This more favorable context might not have led to significant change in development politics and programs, however, without the proliferation of NGOs and grassroots federations that occurred during the 1980s and 1990s. Civil society grew by leaps and bounds during those decades and spawned a minority of NGOs and grassroots federations willing to break away from the pack of Western modernizers and redirect society's attention to underutilized indigenous resources. The recovery and revitalization of cultural resources now became the heart of the "people-centered development" in Bolivia, an orientation that was gaining momentum throughout the Third World (Verhelst 1990; Warren, Slikkerveer, and Brokensha 1995; Healy 1996).

The indigenization or cultural renaissance was gaining ground in several corners of mainstream society as well. A sector of progressive Catholic priests began preaching "inculturation" as an evangelization strategy after years of using an exclusively Western model of Christianity and, beginning in the mid-1980s, Bolivia's major political parties for the first time began making frequent positive references to ethnic diversity and cultural identity in their speeches and party platforms.[1]

On the multilateral financial front, there were more foreign donors wishing to support small-scale projects focused on ethnic identity and indigenous cultural resources. The Inter-American Foundation, OXFAM-America, and a host of other European and Canadian funders were eager to fund the new people-centered, indigenously grounded projects. This enthusiasm dated back as early as the mid-1970s in some cases.

I myself began funding projects in January 1978, just after a major hunger strike began bringing down some of the military barriers to the restoration of a liberal democracy. By this time the Kataristas had spread democratic practices among the altiplano's rural syndicates, and the indigenous people were primed for action. I could see in the proud faces and words of the Aymara, Quechua, Izoceños, and others coming to discuss proposals for funding the strong linkage between indigenous culture and development for them. Early on, Dan Chi, a high-ranking official at USAID, encouraged me to listen to these leaders. "The IAF has a mandate to be different from the rest of us. You have the contacts and are able to reach out to groups previously inaccessible to the United States government for various bureaucratic and political reasons. You can work with groups such as the Kataristas." The U.S. ambassador in the early 1980s, Edwin Corr, offered encouragement as well, "We have to begin unlearning many of the technologies and practices of our Westernized approach and begin relearning how to carry out rural development from the Aymara and Quechua people in these communities themselves. The IAF is ahead of the game in doing this by being able to respond to what is going on at the grassroots in this country."

In retrospect, I view my grassroots development agency's outlook and practices as ahead of its time during the 1970s and 1980s. It was remarkable that a U.S. government development agency in Latin America would have independence from short-term U.S. foreign policy and shed its traditional paternalism to place its entire program budget behind the plans, local leadership, and management control of Latin American community-based organizations. Rather than acting as designers of Western-style project proposals, adopting the latest foreign aid fads from comfortable, impersonal bureaucracies in Washington or La Paz, we were set up as "people to people" and "responsive" to the myriad local voices themselves. Our first president, Bill Dyal, even insisted the IAF work without in-country offices in Latin America, a preventive measure to avoid imposing our own "Made-in-the-U.S.A." development designs and agendas.

To add to this distinctiveness, the IAF also eschewed the State Department and USAID practices of rapid rotation of its personnel from country to country. Instead it encouraged staff to acquire a deep country knowledge and social and cultural empathy for its peoples by working on a long-term basis in a single nation. My own twenty-year career in Bolivia is perhaps an extreme example of this idea, yet such longevity was not unique. Among the many fruits flowing from such an approach was having an in-house institutional memory of lessons learned about social change over time, in their national context, an all too infrequent practice within the international development field.

When indigenous leaders dropped by to discuss their proposals at my modest hotel in a commercial district set amidst the pulsating informal economy of La Paz, they felt much more at ease than in the luxurious downtown hotels where indigenous peasants were an unwelcomed presence for management and employees. Although the project documents were not technical masterpieces, they were full of enthusiastic assertions and consensus-based plans. The indigenous leaders also offered local resources (often in kind, e.g., land and labor) to complement what outside funders provided. By adopting organizational names like the "Consejo Cultural de Promoteres Campesinos," "El Centro Nacional de Defensa de la Cultura Quechua-Aymara," and "Ayllus," they were highlighting how Katarismo had become contagious in rural communities. Their leaders were activists whose ethnic pride shone throughout their plans for socioeconomic change.

These project discussions increased my awareness of democratic values within highland cultures, an attractive asset for soliciting financial support and carrying out projects with a host of grassroots funders. The project proposals invariably carried numerous signatures and thumb prints revealing broad-based support and interest. The Aymaras and Quechuas who often waited patiently, cramped in a small hotel lobby with proposals in hand, would always insist that I sign a copy to confirm our meeting for the folks back home. Such encounters between donor representatives and development practitioners enabled a community-responsive, innovative, and culturally based paradigm to take off during the 1980s.

The fact that Bolivians began these programs in a very self-conscious manner is evident from the number of projects launching themselves as "firsts." Bolivia's story of grassroots development is replete with declarations of *primeros* congresos, seminarios, encuentros, festivales, etc., each aimed at the renaissance of one or more indigenous cultural resources. Of course, none of this would have been possible if the indigenous communities themselves had not persisted in keeping these resources alive and evolving in the face of centuries of discrimination. Their collaboration, guidance, ingenuity, and enthusiasm were necessary to enable many of their native crafts, livestock, plants, and communities to flourish once again, this time in a modern setting.

While recent years have bought exciting changes to Bolivia's development picture, the broader economic context for carrying out these innovative strategies has been harsh. During the first year of the neo-liberal adjustment strategy in Bolivia, the United Nations agricultural organization, FIDA, commissioned Solon Barraclough, one of the hemisphere's most prominent analysts of agricultural policy, agrarian structures, and history, to carry out the most comprehensive overview of the agriculture and livestock sectors ever conducted in Bolivia. Barraclough had directed many important research projects in Latin America over a United Nations career spanning four and a half decades. Barraclough's Bolivia team completed a two-volume study (FIDA 1985) examining the impacts of macroeconomic and developmental policies on the nation's stratified rural population. They covered a wide range of variables such as migration, the role of women, rural food security, employment opportunities, environmental deterioration, economic dependency, and the importance of political and social mobilization by the low-income producers. The report made an airtight case that agricultural credit, investment, and monetary and infrastructure policies in the modernization period had served more to undermine rural farms of the Indian peasantry than to strengthen them. Barraclough assessed the newly decreed structural adjustment policies and predicted that they would bring little respite, often generating more poverty and environmental degradation for peasant Indian farmers. From his team's analysis, it was clear that the country's unequal distribution of wealth underpinned the political power of a tiny minority that held control over the country's developmental resources and that their interests stood in the way of more far-reaching reforms and programs benefiting the rural majority. Standard indicators of human welfare, environmental change, and agricultural improvement continue to suggest that Barraclough's prognostication was on target.

In spite of these very serious difficulties, a number of persistent grassroots federations and NGOs have made significant progress in rural communities by tapping into indigenous cultural resources in their grassroots approaches. A number of these cases will be given close attention in the collection of narrative histories of development projects described in chapters 6 through 14. The rest of this chapter will introduce the broad picture of cultural revitalization that emerged during the 1980s and has accelerated during the 1990s.

Agricultural Knowledge and Technology

The effort to recover and employ indigenous agricultural knowledge in development planning emerged vividly among several NGOs in the La Paz and Cochabamba regions. A true pioneer in this cause was the PAC which began in the university under the name Agroecología Universidad de Cochabamba (AGRUCO). Initially this rural development entity brought European-styled organic agriculture and research to grassroots organizations in this Andean valley region with experiments in composting, the utilization of organic fertilizer, and the production of bio-gas. Subsequently, they adopted an "agro-biological" approach, where peasant attitudes were still conceived as backward and the land parcel as the target for externally induced agricultural innovation (Augstburger 1990, 14). Over the course of the decade, PAC's experiences with indigenous populations prompted it to move to an "Andean agro-ecological approach," which uses the cosmovision and technical knowledge of the Andean people as its point of departure for working on technological improvements.

Franz Augstburger, an ecologist, was the founder of this program. "When we succeeded in implanting our indigenous agriculture program in Cochabamba University's agronomy department, it was very exciting because this was the first time a program based on Andean agricultural principles had found a home at the university. When I first made a public presentation about this approach to the faculty, they wanted to lynch me on the spot. Only through the mobilization of students and representative leaders were the faculty forced to accept this new program. Our students from rural backgrounds, and Andean language homes in particular, were delighted to find out that Andean communities were treasure houses of knowledge, as it helped them appreciate their own parents and grandparents as 'professors.' Many of them subsequently went to work with NGOs to carry these unorthodox views into other development arenas."

In the La Paz region, SEMTA, an NGO that pioneered the recovery of native altiplano pasturelands during the 1980s, developed a university training program with the Institute of Ecology in the mid-1990s to advance higher level education on Andean native crops, soil conservation, and pasture restoration (Ruderfer 1995a, 1995b). Another SEMTA program recovered Andean knowledge of agricultural conditions, flora and fauna, and weather forecasting, then published the findings in a fascinating primer on local agriculture.

In 1991, a Bolivian government potato research program, PROINPA, known for its monocultural approach, developed a small program within its larger set of activities. Pushed in this direction by the International Potato Center (CIP) based in Peru, they introduced a "Tubers and Roots" program emphasizing indigenous knowledge. (PROINPA formed part of a longstanding government program, IBTA, that had shown little interest in any form of indigenous knowledge.) The new program spotlighted two Andean crops, a tuber "oka" and a type of potato called "papalisa," a winter crop that been overlooked in agricultural research programs despite its ongoing popularity in the warmer valleys of the region. PROINPA's recent research demonstrated in certain regions that the two crops did not require expensive fertilization, but that they boasted yields two and three times higher than the market-oriented potatoes grown in the same zones using chemical technologies. They also discovered that traditional techniques of intercropping oka and lima beans minimized frost damage.

Franz Terrazas, one of PROINPA's technicians, told me, "We're trying to go beyond our past approaches which require that the peasant farmer contribute his parcel to our research program without his own ideas and knowledge. 'Participatory research' requires a much more active engagement between the research institution and the farmer. . . . We're also giving greater attention to native varieties and not just for breeding new hybrids as in the past. For example, we noticed that in a field totally infested with nematodes there was only one species with no observable effects from the pest. This native potato species, known as 'Gendarme,' is from the Oruro region. It had fallen into disuse from modernizing pressures despite its resistance to the nematode."

Another example of the revalorization of Andean knowledge may be found in a program that has run trial experiments with altiplano farmers of raised-field agriculture (*Suka-collus*). In the late 1970s, archaeological research on both the Bolivian and Peruvian sides of Lake Titicaca revealed that ridged fields used for natural pasture grazing in recent times were part of the agricultural production system of the Tihuanaco civilization from 300 B.C. to 700 A.D. (Kolata 1993, 1996; Erickson 1995, 1996).

In the late 1980s, a group from Bolivia's Catholic University, under the supervision of the Bolivian archaeologist Osvaldo Rivera and University of Chicago archaeologist Alan Kolata, began trial experiments using the raised-field technology near the town of Tihuanaco. They employed local community organizations such as sindicatos and mothers' clubs to reconstruct the raised fields. In this ancient system, sedimented nutrients (organic muck) are recycled as they are carried from hillsides to build the causeways and canals of the raised fields. As conceptualized by the modern researchers, the raised-field method takes advantage of water and sun energy to moderate nighttime temperatures, thus allowing Andean field crops to survive frost damage and give respectable yields. If the theory proves true, the technique would provide a measure of food security which had been lost in the Titicaca basin area where the loss of crops due to frost has been a main contributor to rural poverty.

The raised-field system potentially offers a chemical-free alternative to the currently predominant potato production. Through collective work schemes, organized as a part of the Bolivian Raised Field Project, several thousand indigenous Bolivian farmers have been exposed to the technology, and some 120 put it into experimental production in small plots distributed over fifty-three communities of several provinces. As the program evolved, organizers of the project created a new NGO, Winay Marka, dedicated to the promotion of research of the physical and technological dimensions of the agricultural method, and also to the recovery of technologies associated with altiplano terrace-farming from the pre-Columbian period.

Although the jury is still out as to whether this ancient system is workable in today's world, the raised-field project triggered a wave of media fascination both in Bolivia and abroad. In the U.S. its story has appeared on the *National Geographic Explorers Series* and *Good Morning America* as well as on National Public Radio, and in *Smithsonian Magazine,* the *Chicago Tribune,* the *New York Times,* and the *Atlanta Constitution.* The international attention focused on the project and the promising results of the initial experimental trials increased Bolivians' pride in their country's cultural heritage and has brought on a groundswell of support for the technology. The president of Bolivia himself participated in a well-publicized harvest one year to call attention to the project, and the Bolivian army developed "Plan Verde" which has used conscripts to spread the raised-field technology through the experimental areas of the altiplano. Approximately twenty NGOs and public institutions recently organized a major research program on the raised-field technology, and both the Bolivian government and the World Bank's recent agricultural development plans mention this emerging altiplano technology.

Another outgrowth of the recent interest in indigenous agricultural knowledge has been community mapping. This technology has been spreading, not only in Bolivia but throughout the Third World (Chambers 1992). The whole notion of community mapping was revolutionary when it was first proposed since maps have been used throughout history by politically powerful sectors of society to impose their land-holding and territorial desires on native peoples. At best, indigenous peoples hired outside professionals to make maps for their legal use. Community mapping is a turn of the tables in that it enables indigenous and peasant groups to create their own maps and to gain social and political advantage from their intimate and long-standing knowledge of their environment. Settlements, houses, temporary structures, soils, trees, water resources, and forest types as recorded on these maps convey social and natural landscapes more accurately than official maps and undermine efforts to present territories as "uninhabited lands."

Community map making was put into use in the altiplano as a social and environmental "consciousness-raising" exercise and as an effective way to redraw and justify ayllu boundaries obliterated by Bolivia's haciendas and subsequent agrarian reformers. An interesting application of this methodology was in the plan to establish a Gran Chaco National Park and Integrated Management Area, a 3.44 million hectare tract stretching to the Paraguayan border which would be managed by the Izoceños and billed as the "largest terrestrial protected area in Tropical America" (Chapin 1997, 2). Over the course of a month, the people of the Izozog received training and then mapped the twenty-two communities and 19,000 square kilometers of their homelands. In the process, they renamed many of the physical features and tiny hamlets from Spanish back to the original Guaraní names.

NATIVE CROPS AND LIVESTOCK

The growing interest in native cultural resources is evident in long-neglected Andean crops now being viewed with more appreciation. These include such plants as amaranth, tarwi, the bitter potato (*papa amarga*), and quinoa. Social research in Bolivian and Peru has shown the important role of native crops in forming a strong cultural identity among Andean indigenous peoples (Zimmerer 1996; Arnold, Jiménez, and Yapita 1992; Arnold and Yapita 1996).

Tarwi, for example, is a legume native to the Andes which has greater protein value than soybeans and peanuts, grows in marginal soils, and fixes nitrogen in amazing quantities. In the rugged, arid terrain of the Potosí Department, the international NGO, World Neighbors, conducted experiments on small farms that were using tarwi as green manure. The practice doubled potato yields, increased food security, and eliminated the need for expensive chemical fertilizers (Ruddell 1995; Ruddell and Ainslie 1996). Bolivia's rediscovery of tarwi began in 1978 when agricultural engineers from the Regional Development Corporation of Cochabamba (CORDECO) learned of its qualities through Peru's national program of "Cultivos Andinos." CORDECO's program to support the cultivation of tarwi faltered along the way, however, and one of its employees, Gilberto Hinojosa, stepped out of the agency, forming the Centro Agrícola de Servicios de Desarrollo (CASDEC) in order to attain the political and bureaucratic freedom necessary to revitalize this valuable food crop. In 1982, CASDEC began a diverse program to promote tarwi including agricultural credit, technical assistance, seed, de-bittering, milling into flour, and customer promotion. CASDEC's work has improved nutrition in rural communities as well as in the city of Cochabamba and enabled farmers to diversify income sources.

Through conferences, publications, and the dissemination of research findings during the 1990s, NGOs called attention to the *papa amarga* or bitter potato. The freeze-dried tuber *chuño* was an important foodstuff for the Inca empire, lightweight and highly nutritional, easily transported by armies. In a reassessment of the papa amarga's attributes, Bolivian and Peruvian agricultural scientists shared research findings at a roundtable, the Primera Mesa Redonda sobre la Papa Amarga in 1991. The purpose of the event was "to understand and interpret the rationality, logic, and wisdom of the peasantry in its use of this potato" (Rea 1991). Agricultural researchers presented papers on such topics such as the number of native varieties, the size of cultivated areas, the ways the papa amarga is used in preparing Andean freeze-dried potatoes, and the potato's drought resistance. NGOs such as AGRUCO and SEMTA soon began mounting programs to support this type of potato, and state research stations in La Paz and Cochabamba subsequently collected 250 samples of papa amarga with which to conduct scientific experiments.

An equally vigorous recovery has been taking place with amaranth, an extremely valuable source of protein, adaptable to a wide range of environments. It had apparently disappeared for centuries in the Andes, primarily because of European colonization (Kietz 1992, 103; National Research Council 1989, 141). The decision among NGOs to revitalize amaranth emerged during a 1986 seminar on the role of internationally donated food aid (Kietz 1992, 157). In 1990, a seminar called the Primer Encuentro Interdepartamental del Amaranto, attended by forty Bolivian and foreign professionals, opened discussion on diverse ways to support this Andean crop (CIEP 1990), and led to the organization of the "Red Pro-Amaranto," a pro-amaranth network (CIEP-UTAB 1991).

A final example of crop recovery is quinoa. Quinoa's history was different from the others as it had received certain types of support. Even though Merwin Bohan called attention to it in his 1942 report, U.S. government aid programs were not in the forefront.[2] Instead organizations like OXFAM-England, the Instituto de Ciencias Agrícolas (I-ICA) of the OAS, and the Canadian Development Agency (CIDA) stepped forward to finance quinoa field research (personal interview with agronomist Hugo Villaroel; World Bank 1993a). Despite positive research findings, no major programs were undertaken by the Bolivian state to assist small farmers or to promote its marketing such as occurred in neighboring Peru during the 1970s.

One person who brought many of these native crops together for a big commercial push in the marketplace was Javier Hurtado, a sociologist and author of the definitive work on the Kataristas. Hurtado underwent a career switch to utilize his knowledge of Andean studies in the social sciences to become an innovative entrepreneur for introducing a line of of health food products for Bolivian middle-class consumers of quinoa, tarwi, amaranth, kañiwa, and other Andean produce for breads, granolas, cookies, etc. Hurtado earned the distinction of "businessman of the year" in the capital and led his own crusade to promote supernutritious kañiwa in international trade fairs in an effort to replicate the success story of quinoa.

In addition to the recuperation of native crops, there have been similar ventures with small animals and livestock of the Andes. The International Heifer Program, supported by the Methodist Church and U.S. civic organizations with a headquarters in Arkansas, had been shipping improved livestock such as cattle, sheep, swine, turkeys, rabbits, and chickens to Bolivian farmers since the 1950s. In subsequent decades the program increasingly relied on purchases of local improved animals for its programs. The Heifer Program was popular among farmers because of its effective grassroots methodology for multiplying the number of improved animals at a very low cost and with maximum participation of the rural poor via family to family livestock exchanges. It was not until the late 1980s, however, that their programs turned toward Bolivia's native animals.

Heifer approved a proposal from the Bolivian Methodist Church, an organization that had recently replaced foreigners with Aymara pastors, to incorporate alpacas as a supplement to its conventional program with cattle and sheep. The Methodist initiative drew part of its inspiration from the growing environmental movement. Heiffer began promoting and distributing improved alpacas with the same methodology and gusto it had practiced for conventional livestock.

Heifer's reorientation was also influenced by the experiences of an altiplano indigenous NGO, the Fundación Quechua-Aymara, which had been working with them to modernize rabbit production. The North American overseer for the Bolivian program Jim Hoey reported in an interview, "When we were approached by Fundación Quechua-Aymara's director Waskar Ari to replace the rabbits with cuyes, a small guinea pig which is native to the Andes, we had had one negative experience with non-native livestock. Our program had introduced into altiplano communities very large rabbits from abroad that were wreaking more havoc than generating development benefits.

"Ari described to us very convincingly the benefits to be gained from a program improving cuyes. The guinea pigs, raised by Andean rural families in the kitchen, were more rustic, easier to care for, and much less finicky about their food than imported rabbits. They made better use of table scraps and usually wound up being consumed at home rather than being sold, which made them an important meat supplement in the local diet. Similar to the llama, cuyes enjoyed a high status as ceremonial creatures, often used at important community rituals."

A final example of cultural revitalization pertaining to livestock is the recuperation of criollo cattle (*ganado criollos*) in early 1992. The long period of adaptation during the colonial period had given these cattle some advantages over the more prestigious imported livestock.

NATIVE TREES

Indigenous tree species have been another focus of recent development efforts. During the past four decades, public reforestation programs in mountain areas of the country overemphasized the importation of eucalyptus and pine trees. Although the eucalyptus tree provides rural families with wood for fuel and construction, it tends to siphon off soil nutrients and water from field crops while its shallow root system fails to prevent erosion. Recent research has also shown that the widespread plantations of introduced species cause negative changes in the animal ecology of the high Andes. The native tree forests of the high Andes attract up to thirty different species of birds whereas the new eucalyptus plantations are inhabited by only three or four bird species. The older native tree species are also thought to have more positive interactions with plants and grasses within a local ecosystem. In addition to their soil conservation and biodiversity value, numerous native tree species have been found to be excellent sources of forage for livestock.

In the altiplano, NGOs are adding native tree seedlings such as quishuara and qiñwa to their reforestation programs. A good example of a shift in priority can be found in the history of the Corporación de Desarrollo de Chuquisaca (CORDECH), active in the reforestation efforts in the inter-montane valleys of southern Chuquisaca. Between 1969 and 1989, CORDECH cultivated primarily imported eucalyptus and pine tree seedlings in its huge centralized nurseries and offered free donated food aid shipped from the United States to rural communities willing to transplant the seedlings into their areas, an effective enticement.

In 1990, with encouragement from an environmentally conscious donor, the Cooperación Técnica Suiza (COTESU), CORDECH began promoting native tree species for the first time. To start with, CORDECH took an inventory of traditional agro-forestry practices and the uses to which the indigenous population of Chuquisaca put their native species. The local people expressed interest in thirty-three native tree species, including the churqui, sirado, tipa, jarcka, podcarpus, algarrobo, and soto trees (CORDECH-COTESU 1992) which CORDECH then began cultivating. It also decentralized its nurseries by placing them in seven different provinces under the management of local NGOs. Local schoolteachers were hired as extension agents and the local school systems were used to expedite the reforestation plan.

Bolivian anthropologist Rosario Leon led an NGO-indigenous team to conduct studies of the tropical forestry management practices of the tiny Yuracaré ethnic group in Cochabamba. This research involving community map-making exercises revealed the Yuracarés' intimate knowledge of 87 native tree and plant species, 207 small animals, and 57 fish species. Leon and her team used this documentation to develop the first "indigenous management plan" for utilizing forestry resources within Bolivia's new and highly complicated Ley INRA.

In the semi-arid Chaco and mountainous Valle Grande province of the Department of Santa Cruz, a state agency, the Centro de Investigación Agrícola Tropical (CIAT), which had previously promoted exclusively exotic forage and legumes, together with the Misión Británica en Agricultura, has implemented research projects to regenerate the natural vegetative cover for sustainable cattle raising. CIAT has also identified four native tree species for promotion. APCOB enabled the Chiquitano ethnic group to set up one of the country's first communally owned sawmills to enable indigenous communities to attain value-added benefits from "internationally certified" methods for exploiting local timber.

MEDICINAL PLANTS AND NATIVE MEDICINE

Since the mid-1980s there has been greater success in combining Western with indigenous medicine in treating health problems of the Bolivian population (Alba and Tarifa 1993). Although during the 1970s international aid agencies continued to wear blinders with regard to traditional medicine,[3] there was an effort to make public health programs more community focused by using village health workers selected from the community and training them in primary health care skills. USAID, for example, made a worldwide declaration of support for ethno-medicine from its central offices in Washington (Bastien 1992, 41).

Yet other indicators suggested a resistance to change within the Bolivian branch of this powerful donor agency. Eloy Anelo, a freelance public health specialist commissioned by USAID in 1976 for a study of health care in forty highland communities, came face to face with this lack of interest. "Although not specifically requested to do so in our study, my wife and I used our maid to interview a range of traditional healers in the communities to better understand the importance of their health care practices.

Because of her indigenous descent, she had access to a world essentially closed to outsiders like ourselves. We were impressed with how much health care was going on, and recommended a program that would establish a bridge between these traditional healers and the Western public health world. The physicians from the public entities involved, however, were basically hostile toward the native practitioners and the high-ranking USAID officials showed scant interest in our ideas. All of it reflected a mentality at the time that culture was an obstacle rather than an asset to development. It wasn't until the activism of NGOs came along that some of this ethnocentric behavior began to wane."

When USAID shifted its funding of public health programs in the 1980s away from governmental agencies toward U.S. private voluntary agencies and subsequently Bolivian NGOs as well, a new path opened up using alternative approaches beyond the controls of a neo-colonialist state. Its support for Project Concern International is a case in point. The director of the project in the early 1980s was a medical anthropologist, Greg Rake. Rake contracted Joe Bastien, an ethnographer who worked with the Kallawayas, to help design and implement a public health strategy combining ethno- and bio-medicine. They proceeded to redesign the village health worker's role to make it compatible with traditional practices. They also provided training to over seventy community health workers and organized numerous workshops for doctors, nurses, health workers, and midwives as well as for anthropologists, shamans, diviners, and agronomists in both bio- and ethno-medicine (Bastien 1992, 120, 175). The workshops demonstrated curing rituals and involved participants in socio-dramas to encourage Western-trained physicians to respect and work more closely with indigenous healers. By 1989, as a result of Project Concern's change in emphasis, there were a handful of doctors and nurses actively promoting ethno-medicine, and numerous community health workers had incorporated ethno-medicine into the orientation of their village-based health posts (Bastien 1992, 188). While most of the doctors did not engage in active promotion they did display greater tolerance for those practicing ethno-medicine.

During the late 1980s and 1990s, an increasing number of those working within the USAID-supported child survival network of NGOs and PVOs began using traditional midwives (*parteras nativas*) in their primary health care programs and ethnographic knowledge in their analyses of the causes of indigenous health practices. These represented two major breakthroughs. There were also a handful of U.S. PVOs that had become convinced that medicinal plants were of value and were trying to utilize some within their health care programs. In the Chaco region, one spectacular example of this was a plant for controlling diarrhea, a major health problem in Bolivia and a cause of the country's high level of infant mortality.

PVOs also turned to traditional practitioners for the pragmatic reason of attaining community coverage. By the 1990s, Project Concern had abandoned its dual focus, yet in 1996 it began reconsidering the wisdom of this change. Having made great progress with vaccination campaigns and other preventive measures, the project faced an impasse in reaching its target population with respect to other health care activities. The Bolivian doctor in charge reported, "Our project team of two doctors and two assistants were responsible for a zone comprising seventy-one communities, each of which we found out had five traditional healers with different specializations. So despite our reservations about the medical competence of some of these people, we have been exploring ways to work together and build mutual respect for one another's approaches in reaching out to these large populations. We are sponsoring a series of workshops designed to promote collaboration between traditional practitioners and our Western trained personnel. Other Bolivian NGOs in the child survival program network as well as officials at the Ministry of Health are watching carefully to see how this works out."

A much deeper commitment to indigenous medicine began several decades earlier through the passionate pioneering work of Jimmy Salles, then a Jesuit priest in the parish of Tihuanaco. Salles had been assigned to a parish of 100,000 people scattered mostly in small communities. There was only one physician servicing these communities, so Salles began making inquiries about practitioners of native medicine and met a well-known healer, Rufino Paxsi, and his herbal repertoire. "Paxsi and I became close friends and in the late 1970s we set up training programs on the uses of medicinal plants. We also founded an association, the Sociedad Boliviana de Medicina Tradicional (SOBOMETRA), of practitioners and supporters from the cities as well as rural communities."

Salles had spent some time in political exile in Mexico due to his previous work with the National Human Rights Assembly. While in Mexico, he was gratified to find 4,000 medicinal plants officially registered with the Mexican government. He brought this to the attention of another fellow refugee, Dr. Torres Goytía, a man who would become the Minister of Health for the next democratically elected Bolivian government. With Salles' urging and SOBOMETRA's pressure from below, Torres Goytía signed a law in 1984 that gave legal recognition for the practice of traditional medicine. The law was a milestone, not only for Bolivia, but for Latin America.

While a law favoring traditional medicine was now in place, inertia and opposition within the public health establishment have been continuing obstacles to implementation. Torres Goytía had little time, given other pressing concerns, so it was left up to NGOs to promote the recuperation of this form of indigenous knowledge. Their work was made easier by the hyperinflationary prices of 1982–84 that sent citizens searching for practical alternatives to the prohibitively expensive drugs. The change in outlook was also bolstered by the environmental movement in Bolivia as people began to see the deforestation in the tropics as synonymous with the destruction of medicinal plants and by new policies put out by the World Health Organization and other international bodies. Despite the continuing lack of interest in traditional medicine on the part of university medical faculties, university biochemistry professors and students began to focus on studies of medicinal plants. This led in the mid-1990s, to the institution of a full-fledged master's degree program in traditional medicine.

Other examples from around the country demonstrate this growing interest and commitment. The Izoceños from the Chaco with the help of the Swiss Red Cross established a joint Western-ethno medical hospital and sustained it for more than a decade. They discovered among their local herbs an excellent treatment for athlete's foot. The NGO Promenat has been a leader in conducting agricultural research on medicinal plants within diverse environmental and climatic zones and has experimented with its own packaging and marketing program to distribute its products on a small scale. In the late 1980s and 1990s, there has also been a boom on the part of NGOs in research on the use of medicinal plants in their respective microregions. There was also a proliferation of scientific books, popular publications, training manuals, radio programs, newspaper columns, pamphlets, and workshops providing information on medicinal plants and their uses.

There was also an effective citizen effort by Oscar Lanza, M.D., to counter corporate dumping of nonessential medicines into Bolivian pharmacies. Lanza organized a volunteer consumer movement with branches in several regions that helped educate the Bolivian public about these drugs and successfully lobbied for national legislation regulating their importation and distribution.

And how did the famous Kallawayas fare within this new attention and positive outlook toward traditional medicine? According to ethnographer Joe Bastien, who has been in contact with them since the late 1960s, decades of systematic repression had reduced both their numbers and medical knowledge as well as the geographic radius of influence. Acculturated Kallawayas engaged in the more lucrative business of making and selling jewelry. Bastien laments a greater commercial focus on medicinal plants as "commodities" and the disappearance of the elaborate rituals of touching and spiritual prayers which provided so many comforting psychosomatic benefits to the sick. "These psychological elements were as essential as the herbs in the curing process," he insisted, "and therefore another tragic loss to society."

A number of NGOs dedicated themselves to protecting the Kallawaya home regions by creating support programs. SEMTA and other NGOs organized urban clinics to tap Kallawaya services in Aymara neighborhoods and constructed rural training centers for apprenticing younger community members in this healing tradition. SEMTA also published biographies and plant manuals and sponsored Kallawaya conferences to give them a platform for sharing experiences and ideas for future work in traditional medicine (Ranaboldo 1987). These efforts served to increase acceptance in some quarters for the remaining Kallawayas and gave them a greater public profile, status, and related self-esteem.[4]

NATIVE LANGUAGES

For decades, native languages were seen as a major obstacle by development planners and educators. During the 1950s and 1960s, students were often beaten for their inability to pronounce Spanish words or for speaking their native tongue in the classroom (Luykx 1999, 48). Yet since the early 1980s, there has been a growing movement in Bolivia to recover native languages for the purposes of "inter-cultural" development. Proponents believe that the reinstatement of native languages and their promotion through educational reform are critical to the strengthening of native cultural identity and organizational solidarity. Critics of the old system have charged that the exclusive use of Spanish in the classroom eroded cultural identity and impeded school performance and educational advancement for rural youth. As Cárdenas has pointed out, even the reading and writing of Spanish itself was learned poorly due to the policy of excluding native languages.

Bilingual educational reforms had been tried earlier with some counterproductive results. During the 1970s, USAID and the Summer Institute of Linguistics supported experimental bilingual education programs that used native language in the classroom. The programs were less than successful because they wrenched those native languages completely out of their cultural and social contexts. The texts and curricula suppressed the cultural values and lifestyles of the rural children they were trying to teach, offering little in the way of images, experiences, history, and emotional content familiar to these low-income children. As a consequence, the programs did not augment their scholastic accomplishments.

More recently, NGOs and professional linguists have been trying to reverse the past negative outcomes of bilingual education. The Catholic Bishops' Commission, for instance, sponsored bilingual educational experiments on a small scale in rural primary schools. Their educators and administrators had been greatly influenced by the writings of Xavier Albó and Juan de Dios Yapita, an Aymara linguist. In the Cordillera province of the Santa Cruz region, due to the pioneering work of CIPCA and one of the first Guaraní NGOs (Teko-Guaraní), 100 teachers and 1,000 schoolchildren in twenty-five elementary schools use Guaraní for the first two grades, then combine this language with Spanish for the remainder of primary school. The program draws from local history, culture, and ecology for its school texts to ground the curriculum in the life of the people of the area. The new bilingual educational movement has focused on the concept "educación intercultural" which replaces domination by the Spanish-based urban culture with mutual respect between the Spanish-speaking and indigenous worlds and a revalorization of the indigenous cultural system in particular.

Native languages have also moved to the front and center of literacy training in the country. Prior to the 1980s, the Bolivian government conducted its only national adult literacy campaign in the Spanish language. The Unidad Democrática y Popular (1982–1985) was the first Bolivian government to use native languages in a national literacy campaign. SENALEP, the agency set up to carry out this program, immediately organized commissions of advisors from the ranks of NGOs, indigenous organizations, linguists, sociologists, educators, anthropologists, and representatives from the staff of the Bolivian Bishops' Conferences to design a new approach to adult literacy. This collaboration between the public and NGO sectors generated bilingual literacy materials and training opportunities with a strong ethnocultural focus.

The new programs helped to lay the groundwork for the educational reforms passed in 1994 which included the first national bilingual education program. These reforms were made possible by the powerful and relentless lobbying by the Bishops' Conference of the Catholic Church under the leadership of Eduardo Gonzalez. Under this program the rural schools will use indigenous languages during the first two years of schooling and then incorporate Spanish for the remaining years. The new reforms include reading materials on native cultural resources and utilize the bilingual materials produced by organizations such as THOA for the Aymara, CENDA for the Quechua, and Teko-Guaraní among the Ava-Guaraní.

Native Weavings

Another area of Bolivian cultural life undergoing a revival is the making and marketing of hand-woven native textiles. The artisanry promoted by governmental, NGO, and even grassroots organizations such as mothers' clubs over the past four decades usually emphasized Western-style needlework. There were groups that copied native textile designs for commercially made women's woven handbags, wall hangings, rugs, and knitted sweaters, especially in the Cochabamba region, but conspicuously underemphasized were efforts to promote native textiles made on the simple looms of pre-Columbian origin.

The production of hand-woven Andean cloth and its use in specific ethnic dress styles declined greatly during the second half of the twentieth century when the MNR ushered in its modernizing ideology and greater urban contact ensued. Simultaneously, increased availability in rural communities of inexpensive, machine-made articles of clothing and privately donated used clothing shipments from the United States enabled native groups to change their costume and thus reduce the discrimination they experienced in the cities. There was a minority of communities that chose to resist the pressure to conform to Western urban dress; typically, these were geographically isolated communities in the central and southern highlands.

Although the state organizations and NGOs failed to recognize the money-earning potential of native dress as a form of decorative art, itinerant middlemen and shopkeepers in cities such as Sucre, Potosí, and La Paz perceived the commercial value of selling native textiles to tourists. These small businesses often produced huge profits for international dealers who selected out the older, higher quality pieces and resold them to a growing international market.

A 1990s development in the marketing of textile art has been the refashioning of traditional shawls (*awayos*) and overskirts (*ajsus*) into other products such as handbags, dufflebags, backpacks, shirts, bookcovers, and vests, or incorporating them into the design of leather goods such as baseball caps, shoes, and briefcases. Urban entrepreneurs and artisans cut the textile pieces into fragments and pasted them on to a range of utilitarian products for tourists and export markets, including museum shops and stores in U.S. college towns. This textile "recycling" allows the artisans to accent the exotic and ethnic, creating products with foreign tourist appeal.

Following the 500 year anniversary of the inauspicious Columbus landing on the continent, Bolivian high school and college students suddenly began buying products revalorizing the awayo. Students from major urban centers began wearing the awayo products for ethnic identification. University student imitations of ethnic dances on city streets in colorful dance processions that run for miles has also stimulated interest in the use, understanding, and display of native textile art. Despite these emerging markets for textiles, however, apparently few appreciable economic benefits trickled down to women weavers (Zorn 1997), and the market system offered few incentives for maintaining high standards in workmanship.

Local programs in the Chuquisaca and Santa Cruz regions of the country have demonstrated that the revitalization of textile arts and improved marketing bring economic benefits to rural communities, especially women (see chapters 11 and 12). These development projects have contributed to the growing national revalorization of textile art, both as a cultural treasure for the nation and as a development resource.[5] The effects of this revalorization can also be found in the frequent appearance of native textile designs on book covers, newspaper articles, television shows, graphic arts posters, art work, and even on more unconventional items such as giftwrap paper and in television spots for political candidates. The new festivals and dances, both on streets of the main cities and in provincial towns and communities, are a fashion show for traditional textiles, in all their variety of design and color.

The most spectacular recuperation effort of native weavings was led by Bolivian anthropologist Cristina Bubba, who organized a kind of commando raid on an exhibit of colonial textiles in San Francisco. Bubba arrived accompanied by indigenous leaders from the communities of Coroma that had suffered theft of this communal cultural patrimony at the hands of a North American dealer. With the support of a network of anthropologists and lawyers and threats of court action against the dealer, the Bolivian team over the next few years was able to repatriate fifty stolen colonial pieces to their home communities. Bubba's perseverance and determination led to new Bolivian laws protecting this form of cultural patrimony from transfer abroad and a cultural revitalization program in Coroma.[6] For her continual struggles to protect this Bolivian art form, she was awarded the internationally prestigious Rolex Gold Watch Award for the category of Cultural Heritage, the first South American to achieve this high honor.

ETHNIC MUSIC AND RELATED CULTURAL EXPRESSIONS

All through the 1950s, Radio San Gabriel, an altiplano radio station run by the Maryknoll missionaries, broadcast canned programs provided by the United States Embassy. These programs promoted modernization with a basic message "to fight communism and civilize the Indian." Over the past thirty years, Radio San Gabriel has made an about face. Under the influence of the progressive members of the Catholic Church, the station recruited and trained broadcasters from the surrounding altiplano communities and imbued them with the spirit of Aymara cultural revalorization. Staff of the radio station have collected and archived 3,000 folktales, 1,000 Aymara poems, and some 3,000 altiplano folk songs for broadcasts designed to promote native Aymara and Quechua culture. They have also sponsored contests for communities with the most interesting histories to encourage an interest in native history and instill community pride among Aymara and Quechua rural residents, and have been deluged with spontaneous contributions. By the early 1980s, Radio San Gabriel had become so steeped in Aymara culture and authentic voices that it was popularly dubbed the "Ministerio de Asuntos Aymaras" (the Ministry of Aymara Affairs).

Via new programming provided by the country's many radio stations, indigenous peoples have been able to savor the sounds of their once-suppressed voices, stories, and music, to listen to the words of their heroes, and to learn from the development information spread through this power-ful medium (Albó 1977b). Aymara and Quechua radio announcers wishing to promote their own cultural values and developmental agendas over the air formed the Asociación Nacional de Communicadores Nativas (ANCIN) (the National Association of Native Communicators) and began holding training programs for its members. Indigenous people have assumed previously unimaginable roles as regional broadcasters, local reporters of community news, and radio promoters of developmental agendas and grassroots struggles.

Ethnic music and dance in Bolivia, perhaps like African-American music in the United States, is the indigenous cultural form that encountered the least resistance during the 1970s movement to break down the barriers of urban ethnic discrimination. Starting in the 1970s, sparked by worldwide student rebellions, university students began wearing ponchos and using indigenous musical instruments and melodies with greater frequency, a practice that added eventually to the legitimacy and wider acceptance of these indigenous symbols among the middle and upper classes.

Centro Portales, a Swiss-supported cultural institution in Cochabamba, underwent a major shift in direction in the late 1970s. From the late 1960s to the mid-1970s, its primary method of musical promotion was to award scholarships to Bolivian students to study classical music in Europe. Gradually, Centro Portales changed its focus and began working with grassroots organizations—namely sindicatos and ayllus—to hold music festivals in rural localities. The organization has involved indigenous leaders and NGOs from selected regions in festival planning and research efforts that highlighted local music and dance history, the relationship of music to agricultural production cycles, and community elders' knowledge of festival traditions.

Examples abound of the catalyst role ethnic music and dance has played in social change in areas that once appeared impervious to powerful indigenous influences. Roberto Sahonero and his brothers, sons of a *chichera* (mom and pop type corn beer saleswoman) from Oruro, organized a dance and music school, the Centro Cultural Los Masis, in Sucre while pursuing university studies there. This cultural center soon had hundreds of school children dancing in the streets to the tunes of Andean music. Upon graduating from the Sahonero brothers' program, many students quickly formed their own *conjuntos* of Andean panpipe and flute players, filling the air with a lovely music that began softening the hard attitudes toward indigenous cultures. While promoting the music and dress of the colorful Tarabuco ethnic group, these music and dance revivalists also started one of southern Bolivia's first Quechua-Spanish bilingual, bicultural primary schools as well as a Quechua-based health center.

A different kind of cultural recovery occurred in the northern part of Potosí when a British-Aymara couple, Denise Arnold and Juan de Dios Yapita, a professional anthropologist and a linguist, rediscovered songs about the indigenous crops of quinoa, oca, potatoes, and coca that women had once sung to the seeds as part of their planting rituals. There were other songs found that were sung to female and male llamas for their mating rituals. Although this tradition had been lost, this couple was able to learn the lyrics from a yatiri (shaman) and publish them for wider appreciation and possible use in the intercultural curriculum under the educational reforms (Arnold and Yapita 1998).

Another curious combination of ethnic music and socioeconomic agenda making occurred in the barrio Villa Sebastián Pagador of Cochabamba. The residents of Villa Sebastián Pagador were urban migrants from the city of Oruro, the country's recognized folkloric capital due to its famous Carnival dance celebrations. The migrants brought with them a capacity to organize famous Carnival dances, performed in elaborate costumes representing devil deities, that drew thousands of international spectators each year. With wisdom and finesse, they used the social and cultural prestige they received as spectacular street dancers as political currency in negotiating for better city services, improved schooling for their children, and a stronger voice in city-level politics (Goldstein 1996, 15).

In addition to these initiatives, there have recently been many efforts to revive, reinvent, and re-energize traditional festivals as well as to create new ones to celebrate indigenous traditions in rural areas. These include the celebration of the Aymara new year, which has regained popularity in the altiplano in recent times. In the early 1990s, the Izoceños invented a three-day annual festival for revalorizing their traditions as indígenas in the Chaco. At the Inca Recay ruins near Cochabamba, organizations have done elaborate Inti Rymi rituals, including a llama sacrifice at dawn, for the past six years on the eve of winter solstice and the next morning.

The prominent and frequent use in public of the revitalized *wiphala,* a multi-colored indigenous flag with a checkerboard design, as a symbol of the reaffirmation of Bolivia's pluri-cultural identity and pride is another example of the rising tide of ethnic consciousness. The *wiphala* appears on pins, pamphlets, booklets, letterheads, calendars, publication covers, and posters to promote Andean cultural identity. It has become the most visible and popular symbol of the regional and national peasant sindicato movements and, as such, it is displayed during dances performed by university students in the "Entrada Folklórica Universitaria," by campesinos on labor day, and during protest marches. Local syndicates have passed formal resolutions to increase the use of *wiphalas* in meetings, assemblies, and congresses, and NGO training courses provide know-how for making the flags in a variety of sizes and forms.

NATIVE ORGANIZATIONS

Over the past few decades determined efforts have been increasing to revalorize traditional indigenous organizations and authority figures in both the highland and lowland areas of the country. Beginning in the late 1980s, a small group of NGOs began to break the pattern of disregard for native forms of organization. In most cases, the NGOs themselves shifted their thinking from endorsing Western-style organizations to supporting indigenous forms in their rural development programming. The Bolivian mission of the European Economic Community (EEC) positioned the rural ayllu as a key actor in the execution of its rural development projects in the Oruro region and hired an anthropologist consultant to produce a map identifying the location of these traditional organizations.

In the department of La Paz, three rural syndicates, with the help of NGOs, decided to return to their cultural roots by shedding their modern organizational form and replacing it with organizational forms stemming from pre-Hispanic origins. Aymara NGOs such as THOA contributed to this new approach by offering training programs enabling syndicates to convert themselves back into ayllus, which involved regaining colonial land titles and old boundaries. In the altiplano, federations of ayllus, such as ANAPQUI and AIGACAA, have been using their native styles of organization to market and export quinoa and alpaca fiber to Western Europe and the United States respectively. The growing fervor over the ayllu also sparked the organization of an ayllu federation in Chuquisaca to capture foreign tourist income. The ayllu federation of Quila Quila set up an "adventure travel" program for visiting tourists that included local tour guides, archaeological and paleontological sites, rustic lodging, nutritious Andean cusine, weaving demonstrations, and a historical lecture series. This was possible because of the revitalization of the Andean ayllu during the 1990s coincided with the globalization of eco-tourism or adventure travel where First World tourists began exploring Third World cultures and environments in unprecedented numbers.

In 1994, the country's first map was drawn up to show the distribution of the ayllus in the Potosí region (Calla 1994, 8). Another Potosí example of ayllu renewal drew upon the documentation from Roger Rasnake's doctoral dissertation on the history and symbolic structures of the Yura ethnic group. The dissertation, translated into Spanish and published as a book in Bolivia, was used by a local NGO and Yura's traditional leaders to make a case before the national government for renewed legal recognition of its original ayllu boundaries that had been eroded through colonial and neocolonial encroachments (Rasnake 1988).

This renewed national consciousness regarding the value of traditional native organizations in rural development has also spread into the lowlands of Bolivia. An example of this occurred when CIPCA, one of Bolivia's largest and most prestigious NGOs, shifted its long-established organizational focus in the Guaraní-speaking Cordillera province—at the request of the communities themselves—from syndicates to *mburuvicha,* and subsequently organized the *mburuvicha* into a federation, the Asamblea de Pueblo Guaraní, for greater political clout and a more dynamic rural development role.

Of equal vigor has been the renewed appreciation among various NGOs and grassroots organizations for traditional authority positions that had been consciously marginalized by the MNR's criollo-mestizo modernizers. Various NGOs in the highlands and the lowlands, for example, began holding workshops, seminars, and meetings which, for the first time in modern history, pulled together often elderly authorities from traditional indigenous organizations and various ethnic backgrounds. The objective was to revive the leaders' roles and influence so as to help their groups gain broader acceptance in national society. The activities by various NGOs, syndicates, and other institutions to revive traditional authority positions flourished during the quincentenary events in 1992. In the regional capitals of Potosí and Chuquisaca, congresses of traditional leaders were held in the weeks leading up to October 12th. At the Potosí meeting, "La Primera Asamblea de Autoridades Originarias"(the first assembly of Native Authorities), participants proposed to "rebaptize the names of streets, plazas, and provinces to reflect their traditional native heroes".

Another approach in the effort to support indigenous leaders has been the publication of their personal testimonies and autobiographies in various books for distribution via NGOs, radio stations, and grassroots organizational networks as part of an oral history recovery process (Tapia 1995; Huanca 1989; Condori 1988).

The lowland areas of the country have likewise witnessed an unprecedented rise in the status of indigenous leaders and a proliferation of new federations designed to promote indigenous participation in public affairs. In 1992, the Asamblea de Pueblo Guaraní sponsored Centenario de la Masacre de Kuruyuki to memorialize the final defeat of the Chiriguanos after centuries of resistance to colonial and republican rule. The two-day extravaganza of marches, rallies, and festivities brought together the largest concentration of Guaraníes within memory, attracting participants from as far away as the Argentine Chaco. The Bolivian president attended the festival and listened to petitions for land rights made by the president of the Asamblea. It was highly unusual for a Bolivian president to listen to an entire speech made in a native language. According to the organizers of the event, the anniversary of the massacre served not only to "recover and revalorize the cultural and historic memory of the Pueblo Guaraní" and its struggles, but to propel the socioeconomic development of their region.

The ferment over a revitalized political and developmental role for traditional organizations and their leaders eventually seeped into the national government when president-elect Gonzalo Sánchez de Lozada and vice president–elect Víctor Hugo Cárdenas took office in 1993. One day prior to the official inauguration these leaders presided over an indigenous ceremony, a kind of "peoples' inaugural," in the national coliseum. Hundreds of *jilaqatas, capitanes, caciques,* and other indigenous leaders from ayllus and comunidades originarios assembled to perform elaborate ritual offerings through prayers and incense burning to invoke the blessings of Andean mountain spirits. It was an unprecedented symbolic act of solidarity.

To prove that this demonstration of support was not merely for show, the national leaders one year later spearheaded congressional approval of a constitutional reform that granted official legal recognition to the country's native organizations. In the case of the ayllu, this reform restored the juridical status that had been taken away during liberal reforms of the nineteenth century. The organizations received an additional boost from the new "Ley de Participación Popular" which has multiplied the number of submunicipal districts (bringing together both ayllus and mburuvicha) eligible for municipal resources under the new laws of decentralization and popular participation. The law specifies a role for native and other grassroots organizations in the design of local development projects, and permits the receipt of funds from a pot of public resources reallocated to municipal governments. In 1995, for the first time, indigenous leaders from eastern lowland communities were elected as mayors. While the revalorization of native leaders and organizations has taken place in the name of long-overdue equality and respect, the assumption behind all the efforts has been that if indigenous forms of organization are valued and given power, they will have greater opportunity to improve the lives, development programs, and political participation of their people.

In 1994, the new government also amended the first article of the constitution to redefine Bolivia as a "multi-ethnic, pluri-cultural state." Such a change can be appreciated when placed next to the case of Peru where national governments have continued to suppress this cultural pluralism and patrimony. These are changes that Cárdenas has striven for since the 1970s, but the new ethnic consciousness of Sánchez de Lozada, a white mining magnate and criollo politician, is more intriguing. According to Cárdenas, the change in Sánchez de Lozada came about while he was living in political exile with his father in the United States. "He lived outside our neo-colonial environment and all its prejudices toward indigenous peoples for an extended period and returned with a new attitude. It often occurs that people who live outside their culture for a period of time can return to appreciate it in new ways." It also came about, of course, because it made for good politics in the 1990s, a theme that bubbled up into public life with vote-yielding power. Yet as Cárdenas himself has reiterated, these recent changes in attitude and behavior are only first steps on the road toward putting native Bolivian cultures on an equal footing with Western forms.

Through the use of indigenous resources from the promotion of native weaving to the legislation of new laws, Bolivia has begun to re-define itself. This new respect for the value of indigenous resources has led to the proliferation of grassroots development projects that take advantage of and employ indigenous resources. The following chapters present an in-depth look at nine grassroots projects that have risen out of the pro-indigenous development movement. These are stories of struggle, of many ups and downs, some more successful than others, but all are stories of people trying to reclaim their vital heritage, knowledge, and resources, and turn them to a viable means of livelihood. As program officer with the IAF, I have had the great privilege of providing support and watching these programs struggle and grow over the past twenty years. In the following chapters, I have tried to evoke the people and the places, the strategies and results of these efforts to achieve social and economic change.

CHAPTER 6

Cacao Bean Farmers Make a Chocolate-Covered Development Climb

Aymara peasants themselves brought about this re-creation of community through a process of struggle against colonial conditions of domination. . . . The community assembly acquired greater prominence as the space for political debate, elaboration, and decision-making.

SINCLAIR THOMSON (1996)

Standing in the checkout line at my local health food store, I can never resist a bar of Organic Swiss Chocolate. I buy the candy—a German product—for its smooth texture and rich flavor, but principally I buy it because the cocoa products used in its manufacture come from El Ceibo, a peasant co-operative federation in a remote zone of the Bolivian jungle that I have followed for years as part of my international aid work on behalf of the Inter-American Foundation.

El Ceibo is an unusually successful agricultural co-operative federation. A large measure of its success has been due to its employment of indigenous models of community organization. The federation relies upon the distinctively Andean practices of decision by assembly, leadership rotation, and consensus building. Its best member co-ops often have tight family groupings at their core. El Ceibo's use of these practices, along with elements of the classic, practical, business-oriented Rochdale model of co-operative organization,[1] has made it an organization that promotes constant innovation, adaptation, and growth.

Nowadays the vibrancy of El Ceibo—Central Regional de Co-operativas Agropecuarias Industriales—is on daily display in the village of Sapecho, El Ceibo's rural headquarters. In one section of the compound,

Grassroots Development Projects

Legend:

- Aymara, Quechua, Mosetén Chocolate Producers
- Quechua Quinoa Farmers
- Aymara, Quechua Herders
- Aymara, Quechua Educators
- Mestizo, Aymara Students
- Jalq'a Weavers
- Tarabuqueño Weavers
- Izoceño Weavers
- Guarayo Artisans
- Ayoreo Weavers
- Rayqaypampeño Potato Farmers
- Mojeño, Yuracaré, Chimane, Sirionó Marchers

young bookkeepers and accountants methodically thumb through recent sales and transport records. Clerks sell farm supplies and seeds from a federation-run store, while agricultural extensionists in the back room chat about a recent problem with a member's cacao trees. Across the yard, a few workers are using rakes to spread fermented cacao beans on large drying platforms, while others are shoveling dried beans into bags, which are loaded into wheelbarrows and hauled down a ramp to a warehouse where they are graded. In the president's modest office a secretary sits at her computer, finishing a letter to sales representatives in Switzerland. In the meeting hall, fifty representatives from local co-ops sit quietly in an accounting class. All the while, messengers on bicycles arrive and depart from the grounds.

While El Ceibo's progress has been steady, it has met its share of obstacles along the way. El Ceibo's is the story of an industrious, highly motivated group that uses time-honored Andean practices to pick itself up when it stumbles, reach consensus about the next step to take, and then start up the hill again.

EL CEIBO'S BEGINNINGS

In 1978, on my first field trip to Bolivia as a staff member with the IAF, I took a harrowing twelve-hour ride over mountainous and jungle terrain down the eastern slopes of the Andes to visit a new co-op organization, El Ceibo. I had first come to hear of El Ceibo from another co-operative the IAF was supporting in the Alto Beni. Now my job was to appraise the functioning of the organization and evaluate its proposal to improve the marketing of its cacao beans.

One of the co-op's few licensed drivers pulled up to my hotel in La Paz at dawn and we set out in a rickety red pick-up. The road climbed almost straight up for over an hour through a dramatic landscape of snow-capped mountaintops. Then, for the next six hours, as it descended, the road became narrower, dustier, more sinuous, and increasingly perilous as the huge green mountain walls closed in around us. On occasion I ventured a wary look over the edge. I caught glimpses of a silver river hundreds of feet below, gushing along the canyon floor. That dramatic but terrifying sight, as well as the small crosses planted at intervals along the side of the road, reminded me of perished travelers.

Several more hours of this roller coaster ride brought us to the Alto Beni, where the members of the cacao co-op live and work. The Alto Beni is a micro-region of narrow valleys and low-range mountains covered by tropical forests. The area is some seventy kilometers long and is cut in two by the Río Beni which has tributaries from the Eastern Cordillera of the Andes and eventually reaches the Amazon to the east. This narrow, slow-moving river is flanked on both sides by strips of fertile alluvial flatland and adjacent blue-green foothills. We floated across the Río Beni on a small barge and arrived on the opposite shore only minutes away from our destination, the town of Sapecho.

The dirt road dwindled into a small path leading into a grassy area resembling a soccer field: the plaza of the tiny village of Sapecho. A one-story red brick school building that stood proudly across the street from the plaza seemed a testament to the inhabitants' priorities. Nearby the co-op's name was emblazoned in green and yellow paint on the side of a small white-washed adobe building. El Ceibo is named after the majestic, native ceiba tree, known for its deep and powerful root system.

I was greeted by El Ceibo's president, Francisco Cortez. After exchanging warm *abrazos,* he proudly led us around the compound to see the co-op's service complex. In the briskness of his stride and his wide smile, I could see the co-op leader's eagerness to demonstrate that his was no fly-by-night organization in the backwaters of Bolivia. First, Cortez showed me the two-room office. Then he took me outside to view rectangular, fifteen-meter-long platforms for the drying of cacao beans, a shed full of stacked boxes for fermenting the beans, a small warehouse for storage, a row of rooms with bunk beds, and a central outhouse.

Cortez' animated features turned circumspect when he pointed over at the empty, wooden drying platforms. "The fermentation plant that you see over there has been idle for over six months. Catholic Relief Services paid for the construction, but they failed to include an operating fund for cacao purchases."

Images of unrepaired, unused electric generators, tractors, and other equipment I had seen rusting in other Latin American villages floated across my mind. I thought to myself, "Here we go again: another white elephant left by international funders."

After carefully evaluating my response, Cortez said, "As you've seen in our project proposal, we desperately need a fund for purchasing beans from the peasant farmers. We also need to build a second fermentation plant accessible to the farmers on the other side of the river, and we need a truck for hauling our beans to the capital city."

To reach the cacao-growing area later that day, Cortez, the driver, and I passed citrus groves, banana trees, rice fields, and small huts built of *motacu* palm branches draped over slatted frames. In the rural modernization era of the 1960s, resettlement programs financed first by USAID, then by the Inter-American Development Bank began transforming this rainforest into small farms. Here as elsewhere in the tropics, Western modernization programs razed large swaths of rainforest vegetation to plant rectilinear, uniform stands of single crops such as the cacao tree.[2] This shift to monoculture from forest diversity appeared to resonate with what Bohan had envisioned in the 1940s. The Aymara and Quechua Indians would be born again as yeoman farmers, transforming both this untamed natural landscape and themselves along with it. So on various fronts, they were helping to reshape Bolivia into a developed, integrated, and culturally homogenous nation. This modern farming belt in the Alto Beni was testimony to this public commitment to monocultures just as the public schoolhouse was with its curriculum of Western education in Spanish.

When we came to a stop at a co-op member's cacao bean farm, Cortez invited me to get out to view the cacao trees close up. Standing under the forest canopy I looked up into the branches of a white-barked tree about ten feet in height. At first, it seemed a quite ordinary tree, then my eyes fastened on the scarlet, yellow, and greenish pods shaped like smallish American footballs dangling from its branches. Cortez removed his machete from a sheath attached to his belt, cut a pod loose from the branch, broke it open, and then placed in my hand the white gooey pulp-like substance containing the cacao beans. I dug into the creamy pulp, extracted several beans, and stuck them in my mouth. Their fruity taste was refreshing on this hot tropical afternoon.

Next Cortez led us through the grove to the co-op member's two-room hut and showed me a pile of beans fermenting against its back wall. "The white pulp rots during fermentation, giving the bean both a dark brown color and a deeper flavor," he said. Outdoors he pointed to a straw mat used for drying the beans. His voice rose in earnestness, "You see how we need to change this home-based technology. We need to have a central fermenting and drying facility in operation so that we can turn out beans of more uniform and higher quality. A central fermentation facility would improve our negotiating position with different buyers, you see. That is why we need financing from you."

For the rest of the afternoon Cortez took me to meet different groups of farmers belonging to the co-ops. At each stop, Cortez found a spot in the shade and we sat in a circle as ten to fifteen co-op members took turns explaining their problems as farmers and their hopes for El Ceibo. The men's animated gestures, their repeated references to their belief that they could gain more economic benefits from their cacao production through organization, and their intently focused faces struck me as reflecting an exceptionally strong espirit de corps, and dogged determination. I was gaining a sense that El Ceibo rested on a bedrock of tightly knit community and family groups and that cacao beans were an effective rallying point for their aspirations.

In a development officer's mind, human factors are given considerable weight in any decision about whether or not to fund a project. During a field trip my purpose is to learn directly from the members of a community about the inner workings of their local organizations and determine the extent to which the planners of a given project have consulted with members of the larger community. We at the IAF are always on the lookout for autocratic behavior which can upset the most solid development plans and favorable market prospects. For this reason, we like to participate in small meetings to observe the behavior of community members in a group.

During the meetings under the trees, I asked the settlers standard questions. "Was cacao economically viable? What about the risks of dependency on a single crop? Were farmers putting up some of their own resources? Had community members been consulted about the proposed activities?" Unfortunately, I was not yet aware of the importance of environmental issues surrounding the Amazon rainforest so not a single question came out of my mouth on that critical topic.

As I collected observations, economic data, and other contextual facts, a case was building in favor of funding of El Ceibo. The data would form the foundation of the twenty-page document I would need to write when I returned to Washington. As I spoke with the co-op members, I was also anticipating the grueling project review sessions with my colleagues at the IAF. Through this peer review process, we approved only about one proposal in ten, but I was gaining confidence that this proposal would fly.

History and Regional Context

That night as we relaxed over plates of wheat noodles, white rice, and spicy chicken, supplemented with glasses of Kool-Aid, the co-op members told the story of the colonization of the Alto Beni and the eventual coalescing of twelve local farming co-ops into the federation.

Alejandro Paza, a tall Aymara settler with black hair that fell over his ears, offered an overview of the settlement of the region. The modern settlement of the Río Beni Valley had begun fifteen years before, although native groups, such as the Mosetenes, had been around long before that. The promised dream of rich and unlimited farmland waiting to be carved out of virgin tropical forest lured thousands of Quechua and Aymara colonists out of the mountains. The migrants had long felt squeezed in the highlands by overcrowding, land fragmentation, low prices for cash crops and livestock, and various forms of cultural discrimination. The abolition of serfdom on highland haciendas, government-organized settlement efforts, and public investments in roads had triggered many of the spontaneous peasant migrations, eventually bringing the population of the Alto Beni to about 7,000 families.

El Ceibo leaders talked about the difficulty of the move to the rainforest for settlers accustomed to wide-open spaces, cool temperatures, and traditional mountain crops. Upon arrival in the Alto Beni, they suddenly had to shed their heavy, woolen ponchos and learn to deal with heat, insects, new diseases, and a radically different agriculture using a slash and burn technology. Furthermore, starting over meant starting from scratch. Land was plentiful, but it had to be cleared by machete, a tool unfamiliar to the highlanders. Many farmers were able to clear at first only two or three hectares of the fifteen-hectare plots allotted to them by the government. In many cases, the indigenous settlers found that they had simply traded one form of poverty for another. More than half of the would-be pioneers gave up and left. Yet many others kept arriving from all over the highlands to replace them.

Cortez added, "An even bigger problem was that the best markets for our crops were far off in La Paz, 165 kilometers away by a dirt road that was frequently blocked by landslides or buried axle-deep in mud."

Co-op Take-off

As a young man, the Alto Beni settler Alejandro Paza had farmed potatoes with his parents near the altiplano's Lake Titicaca, yet the new Western agricultural technologies of monocultures with other efforts failed to improve their local economies. Facing only a future of grinding poverty, he had picked up stakes and migrated to the Alto Beni. Now, from his position as owner of a thriving cacao farm, he described the origin of the first co-ops in the Alto Beni.

"We realized during our first years as colonists that of all the crops we could grow here cacao was the most profitable and, as a tree crop, could be a stable source of income. Seedling nurseries for cacao emerged thanks to the foreign aid programs importing varieties from Ecuador, Colombia, and Brazil and plants became distributed to the farmers.

"There were several issues which caused us to join forces for economic improvement even before the organization of El Ceibo. One thing was that the government owned and managed the cacao bean fermentation plant then operating in our zone. Our own government was trying to squeeze every peso they could out of us. Their scales were rigged for cheating us on the weight of our cacao beans and to make matters worse, they would insult us with negative terms such as 'Indians.' Out of exasperation, we organized a boycott which forced the plant to shut down. We had realized that we had to avoid reliance on the government and take initiative by ourselves." I made a mental note that Paza was describing the kind of self-help qualities the IAF looks for in grassroots development projects. We often place as much weight on the activism of the community organization as on the economic viability of the proposed development activities.

Then Cortez took up the story. He described how the incipient co-ops also decided to take on the commercial middlemen. "First, we rented private trucks to haul our cacao beans to the chocolate industries in the capital city. This enabled us to earn more money from our sales and gave us a sense of the importance of working collectively toward common goals. Then one day at the door of this chocolate factory in La Paz, as we were waiting in line to receive payments for our cacao beans, we began commiserating with representatives from other Alto Beni co-ops about the low prices we were all receiving. At that moment, we realized that to have clout as peasant producers of raw materials we had to join forces in marketing our products as well as produce our own chocolate products. We then called a meeting downtown in front of the San Franciso Church and decided to create a co-op federation that would handle transport to and marketing in the capital city, and begin to establish the framework for the industrial processing of our beans."

He also disclosed that a charismatic local leader, Emilio Vilca, had led them into this promising terrain and that the incipient federation succeeded in an export venture with the help of a local chocolate industry. They were unable to duplicate this feat for another decade yet the profits earned left them with an enduring vision.

Later in my first trip, I visited the mini-chocolate industry that El Ceibo had established in La Paz. In the neighborhood of Río Seco in what was to become the city of El Alto on the altiplano above La Paz, the federation had recently built a narrow three-story red brick building on a small lot to provide office, dining, and garage space for co-op workers and members when they were in town. In front of the building under a crooked tin roof, I found two Aymara men and a woman using a large, hand-made piece of equipment to make chocolate candy. The co-op members had modified a home-made bread-making technology for use in processing cacao beans. For reducing the beans' moisture content necessary to bring out its chocolate flavor, they had improvised with another makeshift contraption that removed the bean's outer shell. One man was using a crescent-shaped rock to grind the beans into fine particles on a stone slab. A spool was used to give the candies their shape. The marble-sized candies were then set on metal sheets and placed in a small oven. After cooling and drying, the three workers wrapped each individual candy in plastic and put them in small bags with the co-op logo. "Ceibollitas, the federation's first industrial products!" my guide, a woman leader of the federation, said.

The smiling Aymara woman operating this equipment handed me one of the small round candies. Examining its light brown, gritty texture, I compared it to the smooth candy bars made by Hershey's and similar companies that I had grown up eating in the United States. With just one bite, I realized the candy was too sweet, powdery, and dry and would probably have market problems.

Sensing my uneasiness, the co-op member was quick to reassure. "Look, we are not trying to sell our candy in the downtown sectors of the city but to campesinos, poor folk like ourselves who have migrated from rural villages. They love them.

"Initially, our buyers were relatives and friends living in barrios near here," she said. "Then co-op members also began taking chocolates back home for sales in community stores in the Alto Beni. After production increased to about 150 kilos a week, Aymara wholesalers began showing up and buying in bulk. And then last week we received a visit from a representative from the state mining corporation interested in buying large quantities for their mineworkers!" There was a glow in her face as she continued. "And we are starting to find bigger clients that will enable our enterprise to grow and bring even more benefits back to the Alto Beni farming communities."

During my flight back to Washington, D.C., I thought about the many community groups and NGOs I had visited during my six-week trip. El Ceibo definitely stood out. It possessed the extra sparkle that we sought in projects. Clearly this was an organization on the move, with broad participation from the communities in the area. I subsequently described these features in documents and review committee meetings at the IAF and convinced them to make a grant for the requested $220,000. With IAF funds, El Ceibo was able to buy an additional truck to haul their beans, build a fermentation plant to give more uniform quality to their product, and establish a $100,000 fund to buy cacao beans directly from farmers. In six weeks, El Ceibo had taken off into a new phase, and I had begun the invigorating experience of following its starts and stops and ups and downs.

Stage One: Organizational Take-off — El Ceibo's Rise during the Early 1980s

When I returned to Bolivia in the early 1980s to inspect projects, I was gratified to see that the IAF's investments were making a difference in the lives of the Alto Beni peasants. The twelve member co-ops had built an effective organization for coordinating the shipment of beans between their farms and Sapecho, where the beans were processed, and La Paz, where they were marketed to private industries, and they were gaining a reputation as the most effective action agency in the Alto Beni. At this time members of the federation benefited from technical oversight provided by the first of a series of German volunteer advisors, Bernardo Edenberger, a man who had previously worked as an economist in the marketing division of the multinational cosmetics organization Avon.

At this point the federation controlled roughly two thirds of the Alto Beni's cacao production. Since the zone produced 80 percent of Bolivia's crop, this meant that more than half of the national harvest was moving through the federation's transport and marketing channels. Breaking the transport monopoly and adding value through agro-processing had allowed the federation to create a booming business. In just two years, the federation became the chief regulator of cacao prices in the Alto Beni. There was soon enough business among their members and communities to employ the full-time services of three trucks hauling cacao beans to La Paz.

In addition to using the trucks to transport the cacao beans to the market, the federation came up with a scheme for taking maximum advantage of their trucking capabilities. They loaded the returning trucks with basic consumer goods (matches, candles, wheat noodles, white sugar, cooking oil, etc.) for distribution to twenty-one co-operatives in the Alto Beni region. El Ceibo's new earnings enabled the co-ops to increase the number of products in their stores to eighteen staples, and this in turn helped to regulate their prices. The Alto Beni peasants were receiving important benefits as both consumers and producers.

El Ceibo's Unique System of Self-Management

From my first visit to the co-op federation I was struck by the vitality and high level of cooperation that characterized the group. When I visited Sapecho in the mid-1980s I was again impressed by the sense of purpose that seemed to govern the actions of the members. Everywhere I looked, people were scurrying, men were loading beans, teenagers were raking.

By this time, the federation's programs employed fifty-six persons full-time. Co-op members were constantly acquiring new skills in operating machinery and packaging products on the job. Peasant managers had become shrewd negotiators for dealing with a host of institutions, from public bureaucracies to municipal governments, private banks, and business firms.

With time I came to attribute the vitality of El Ceibo to its remarkably effective use of a key indigenous resource: its community organizational structure. The assembly system, equal wage policy, leadership rotation pattern, and the training programs seemed to derive from the community's strongly held conviction that everyone had a contribution to make, and that they could tackle and solve their problems by cooperative means and self-reliance.

El Ceibo held assemblies very frequently in comparison to other co-ops, which usually met only once a year. The frequency of the assemblies alone demonstrated their seriousness and determination, but the actual conduct of the assemblies was even more impressive. Their procedures called to mind the patient, methodical, and serious-minded consensus-building approaches long practiced in altiplano communities.

The active way in which members participated in assembly meetings impressed outside observers as well. A professional educator characterized the assemblies as a kind of mini-parliamentary process where delegates sat behind name plates for their respective co-ops and engaged in civil debate and discourse. One European volunteer working with the federation was astonished. "The meetings lasted until midnight during three days while the delegates passionately debated thorny issues. Everyone took part, even the cook, who voiced strong opinions about not only the kitchen but the whole range of services in Sapecho. Participants clearly stood on equal footing. The level of interest and patience displayed as they worked to build solutions through consensus was impressive."

One of the most unusual aspects of El Ceibo as an organization was its equal wage rule. Regardless of his or her position, skill level, or degree of responsibility, each worker (and federation managers as well) received $1.70 daily, plus a food ration or allowance for three meals a day. When I first heard of the policy I was sympathetic to the idealism, but wondered aloud whether it would continue to function with increased organizational complexity.

Luis Cruz, a leader who once herded llamas and alpacas on the treeless altiplano and had a series of adventures as a hotel waiter, truck driver's assistant, and sharecropper in Chile and Peru before migrating to the Alto Beni, convinced me that the policy was in Sapecho to stay. "The equal wage has been a pillar of our organization since its founding in 1978, and our commitment to it has never wavered. During our formative years, when we were faced with the problem of distributing our first cacao profits, there was an attempt to introduce a graduated wage structure for our workers, but it triggered strong opposition in the assembly, and eventually the equal pay position won out. We're very comfortable that the highest manager makes the same amount of money as the most unskilled manual worker at the central offices. It gives us a sense of unity to better face the many challenges which come our way."

While it had obvious advantages, El Ceibo's wage policy had not been a recipe for universal job satisfaction. One late night, after a few beers, a federation leader blurted out to me, "I have worked at the upper echelons of the federation in a variety of important jobs for a number of years, but what do I have to show for it? I am planning to leave soon so I can make money from my own cacao trees for a change." He also told me that many older farmers did not respect the younger extension agents working for the *jornal unica* (single wage) despite their extensive training. "Sometimes I think that by paying low wages the federation is guaranteeing low-quality technical assistance."

Another of El Ceibo's unusual practices, that of frequently rotating officers and co-op workers, helps to cushion the economic sacrifices associated with work for the federation. Both El Ceibo and its member co-ops rotate the occupants of their staff and leadership positions every one or two years, a practice unusual among rural co-ops in Bolivia and in the Third World development literature as a whole.

I found it fascinating that El Ceibo had come up with a solution to a problem that plagues rural co-op organizations all over the hemisphere— that of the excessive concentration of power in the hands of a few individuals. In many places co-op employees gradually become a separate vested interest group pursuing their own personal interests at the expense of the peasant producers. El Ceibo's staff rotation policy seemed a viable means to prevent such manipulations, but I wondered if there were consequences in terms of the organization's efficiency and management performance. A German volunteer close to the situation complained to me during several trips that the El Ceibo staff's literacy skills were always uneven—people with weak arithmetic skill sometimes held jobs without having the necessary minimum qualification. He insisted that the rotational practices should be re-examined. I was sure that these serious trade-offs were true, yet who was I to question the practices of an organization that, from all appearances, kept moving onward and upward and adding new co-ops? The tangible economic benefits flowing to what were now several dozen communities and the high degree of participation in decision making were as impressive as that of any other project in Bolivia.

As on other levels of the organization, a rotation system was used in the governing administrative council as well as its vigilance council. Each council member supervised a different program, division, or office (industry, transport, etc.), and half of its members changed each year, to ensure new blood. Those being replaced either moved over to other positions or returned to their farms in the Alto Beni. The centrality of leadership rotation to the co-op federation's modus operandi was evidenced by the fact that every year when I visited there was a different El Ceibo president. The only exception to this was the re-election one year of Luis Cruz. To make the transition easier for the president, El Ceibo added a six-month apprenticeship prior to taking office. This leadership rotation system, like the equal wage policy, served to block opportunities for an autocratic ruling elite to run the show.

The other striking element of El Ceibo's indigenous organizational system was its emphasis on training its workforce, using its own people as trainers. At first El Ceibo tried to use outside specialists from La Paz to supply business management and other training for its members, but the professionals were unwilling to adapt their materials to the situation in the Alto Beni.

"After long discussions in the assembly," Luis Cruz said, "we decided to use our own better educated members, some with high school degrees, to serve as trainers. This put the training programs in our own hands where it has remained.

"Our six-week course in basic accounting is the centerpiece for all local training activities," Cruz explained. "The applicants must pass an entrance exam in arithmetic to take the course and be able to complete a balance sheet from their co-ops in order to graduate. The course is taught by El Ceibo's own staff of peasant accountants and managers, and enrollments are always heavy because of the constant influx of new settlers and co-ops."

By 1985, approximately one quarter of El Ceibo's active membership of 850 campesinos had taken the course, an astonishing ratio for only thirty-five co-ops. The surplus of people with basic accounting skills enabled the co-ops to rotate bookkeeping responsibilities and avoid overburdening one or two people. I had observed member deliberations in a few co-op assemblies and had been impressed by how officers were put on the spot with tough questioning by well-prepared delegates.

In addition to the accounting course, the federation established a management training program under COOPEAGRO, using Swiss funding. This training program supplies member co-ops and federation programs with bookkeepers, treasurers, accountants, and savvy officers.

As I learned more about El Ceibo's organization, I became increasingly curious about the origins of their unorthodox institutional practices. The standard Rochdale co-op bible used in North and South America does not contain a single passage that calls for rapid turnover among managers and leaders. With a little research it became clear that the El Ceibo system of self-management was an original and quintessential Andean solution to the common co-op ailments of corrupt and entrenched leadership. This system of democratic self-management derived from the local Andean political order that had been transformed during the eighteenth century and whose final phase of widespread institutionalization resulted from the Tupak Katari rebellion. This system characterized by democratic assemblies and rotating community leadership had roots in both Spanish as well as indigenous cultural institutions. In an article (1977c), Xavier Albó described a one-year term limit in altiplano communities as reflecting an emphasis on community service and solidarity as more important goals than the acquisition of personal power.

One could also see this principle working in the internal dynamics of El Ceibo's member co-ops. Each had its own set of rotating leaders and communal assemblies. The two that I knew best, El Tropical and Litoral, were close-knit family groupings where aunts, uncles, fathers, mothers, daughters, and sons all pitched in for co-op–related activity. While the aynis and mingas that mobilized community and reciprocal family labor were disappearing here under the expansion of commercial farming and related wage labor, the co-ops were continuing to gather up some of this social capital for their own ends. The Andean cultural notion of internal organization and management appeared to have superseded the Anglo-American concepts associated with classic co-op doctrine. The Japanese had their own effective, culturally dictated patterns of internal management for a successful industrial revolution, so why not the Aymara and Quechua peoples?

Challenges on the Road to Economic Empowerment

During this early period of El Ceibo's development, into the mid-1980s, the federation met with several very difficult obstacles: opposition on the part of commercial interests in La Paz, a blight on cacao pods, and hyperinflation. Each problem threatened to bring the farmers' efforts to a halt but each was met with El Ceibo's unique, determined, and ultimately effective organizational response.

Commercial Opposition

When El Ceibo had been receiving IAF support for three years, Luis Cruz reported to me the frustrations that had accompanied the federation's attempts at price regulation. "The minute our small farmers began to have small profits, company executives in La Paz started delaying payments for our beans and blocking attempts at price regulation. Another tactic was to use their influence in the banks to block loans that might help El Ceibo ride out cyclical shortages of operating capital.

"However," Cruz said, "a taste of higher prices made our people more defiant than ever, and determined to resist the efforts by these business groups to undermine our new transport-marketing program. We met in assemblies every four months to deal with these threats and adjust our strategies and we were able to build a new warehouse in La Paz to increase our leverage in negotiations with buyers." The cool climate of the capital city retarded spoilage for up to three months, allowing El Ceibo's staff to wait for higher prices.

The Twin Curses of Witch's Broom and Blackpod

During my first check-up trip after funding, I learned something I should have found out about on my pre-funding trip. Two diseases, blackpod that attacks the fruit and reduces bean quality and witch's broom that causes the new branches of the cacao tree to wither and reduces the number of pods per tree, had become rampant throughout the Alto Beni in the late 1970s (Tendler 1983a). In 1976, the government's agricultural promotion program had unwittingly distributed imported diseased seedlings to the zone's farmers. An Ecuadorian cacao specialist who had evaluated El Ceibo quipped as we were examining a rotted pod, "It is lucky that the government did not have more public funds to spend because it would have made things even worse."

Witch's broom spread far beyond the original diseased seedlings because of the government's monocropping schemes that placed cacao farms from different families side by side. Also as one El Ceibo member pointed out to me, "When they introduced spraying of our trees for witch's broom, on many farms these poisons killed off the bugs essential for pollinating the flowers of the cacao tree!"

It would take a revolution in thinking about sustainable agriculture during the next decade for the Bolivian colonists and other interested parties throughout the world to realize that the best defense against such epidemics was through polycultures rather than monocultures and their chemical requirements. One piece of local evidence for the merits of this approach were the native criollo cacao trees on the farms of the native

Mosetenes which showed no signs of being attacked by witch's broom in their natural habitat in dense forest settings.

Unlike major producing countries such as Brazil and Ecuador, Bolivia lacked a cadre of trained professional technicians and scientists who specialized in cacao. In fact there was not one agronomist in the country at that time who was an expert on cacao, perhaps because the crop was produced by small farmers in a remote settlement area.

Witch's broom and black pod quickly became the most talked about agenda items at the federation assemblies and the federation began an all-out attack on the disease problem. Farmers had participated in a fumigation campaign in earlier years that was unsuccessful. Unable to find expertise for combating the blight effectively from national government agencies, the federation assembly took matters into their own hands and voted to petition for financial support from an organization of the Swiss government, the Co-operacion Tecnica Suiza (COTESU), with offices in La Paz. The Swiss responded favorably and began funding El Ceibo's program for agricultural extension and training called the Co-operative Education and Agricultural Extension Division (COOPEAGRO). Twenty-two peasant paraprofessionals received training in pruning techniques used throughout Latin American countries against witch's broom.

El Ceibo's election to use peasants as its agricultural extension agents was an amazingly ambitious and sophisticated approach for a group of colonists in the backlands of Bolivia. Yet after a few years of community campaigns managed by the extensionists, the blight was brought under control. According to an evaluation by Ecuadorian cacao specialists, COOPEAGRO work teams serviced 2,500 hectares, about a third of the cacao farmland in the Alto Beni, and average yields doubled from 5 to 10 quintals per hectare, generating an additional $750 in income per hectare. Yet this was still far below the 15–20 quintales that production averaged in the 1970s before the onslaught of the cacao diseases (Tendler 1983a).

After the blight was put down, a federation leader of El Ceibo confided to me an alarming notion. "If the campaign had been unsuccessful the campesinos would have turned Alto Beni into a huge coca leaf growing zone for the illicit drug industry." An unlikely expression of appreciation for El Ceibo also came from a major industrial buyer of the Bolivian business community. "Without Ceibo and its extension programs, cacao might have vanished in Bolivia."

In addition to the service they provided in fighting the blight, the COOPEAGRO program became a permanent fixture for training farmers in a variety of technical skills for the next decade.

The growing sophistication of El Ceibo's work was beginning to catch the attention of others working in rural development. In the mid-1980s a group of international development experts traveling in the zone found that El Ceibo had become a more important source of knowledge about cacao production than the government's local agricultural research program. Wherever they inquired about cacao production, they heard, "The best agricultural technicians belong to El Ceibo, so go there to get your questions answered."

Hyperinflation

During the early to mid-1980s Bolivia's hyperinflation was approaching a world record. Business enterprises without access to U.S. dollars were collapsing all over the country. Bolivian currency became so devalued that the sight of people emerging from money exchange houses with grocery bags full of bills became commonplace. Many projects supported by the IAF had been devastated, and El Ceibo's financial shakiness was no exception to the general pattern—the purchasing power of the federation's operating funds shrunk by half. Various members abandoned the organization after surveying such financial and economic wreckage. When an industrial buyer held up a large payment for three months, federation leaders helplessly watched while their customers waited for inflation to pay the major portion of the bill. El Ceibo also had to end its program of supplying the local co-op stores with basic consumer goods, as the shelves became increasingly empty. It took them years to recover this lost level of financing, but they did so by acquiring a low interest loan from the Swiss. The farmers never lost hope and continued to meet in assemblies frequently as problems cropped up.

STAGE 2: THE INDUSTRIAL LIFT-OFF

On a fact-finding mission to IAF projects in the mid-1980s, I made a visit to El Ceibo's urban installations. By this time the co-op federation had set up a bona fide industrial chocolate-processing plant; the converted bread-making contraption had been junked in a shed. Despite the difficult hurdles it faced, the federation had never lost sight of its vision of producing its own chocolate products for export. With the IAF's help, El Ceibo had purchased pieces of twenty-year-old machinery from an Italian chocolate manufacturer which enabled it to diversify and produce such products as baker's chocolate, cocoa butter, and cocoa powder. The co-op had also introduced slight improvements in the production of chocolate candies. In using a technology which had become obsolete in Europe, the federation president explained the co-operative's thinking, "We are beginning to master the skills necessary for a sophisticated industry. The factory has become a kind of on-the-job training center for acquiring the industrial skills that will eventually enable us to process all the cacao beans produced by our membership and perhaps the whole Alto Beni."

The acquisition of the discarded Italian technology moved El Ceibo light years ahead in its production goals and its ability to produce candy efficiently. I watched as one set of machines squeezed oil out of the beans to produce cocoa butter, and a six-foot upright cylinder pressed cocoa into large, round, hardened blocks. At the far end of the room, a young co-op worker stood over a table with hammer in hand breaking round blocks of cocoa into smaller chunks. After filling a bucket with this hardened cocoa, he dumped them over the top of a machine which ground them into finer particles. In another room, women co-op members in cocoa-colored uniforms weighed and bagged small quantities of this cocoa powder.

In the two-room plant with its poor ventilation, sealed windows, and dim lighting from a single bulb, six co-op workers were learning to carry out the different production roles required in its small manufacturing complex. Paint was chipping off the walls and melted cocoa oozed out of the grooves in the grinding machine, but an agreeable chocolate fragrance floated in the air. Despite the dingy appearance of the chocolate plant, the new products gave El Ceibo a sparkling image to the outside world of prospective customers and assorted admirers. And back in the Alto Beni, some seventeen new co-ops whose members had either tasted or seen the new products had joined the expanding federation. This set of new co-ops included the Moseten peoples' organization, as this ethnic group native to the Alto Beni had worked out a close modus operandi with the Aymara and Quechua colonists belonging to El Ceibo.

I saw El Ceibo products everywhere. Not only did I find El Ceibo cocoa powder and "ceibollitas" on store shelves, but they were being sold by outdoor vendors as well. Co-op leaders took pride in their accomplishments, emphasizing that their small industry was churning out a ton of cocoa powder each day, a level of production that amounted to $7,000 gross earnings by the end of each month. Gualberto Condori, an El Ceibo president who had grown up in an altiplano ayllu, studied sheep-raising in a vocational school, and worked as a local schoolteacher, remarked, "Our industry is demonstrating impressive expansion! We have moved from using 1 percent of our cacao beans to 11 percent while generating a federation record in earning 18 percent above costs after only two years in business."

AN UPHILL TRUCK SAGA

The way in which the cacao federation organized and managed itself never failed to impress me. By continually mobilizing more teams to meet new challenges, they always seemed to be empowering their communities. But in one instance, this audacity and activism led them down a path so fraught with pitfalls that the damage proved impossible to overcome, reverberating negatively throughout the organization for many years.

During the mid-1980s, El Ceibo was making great progress in the transport and marketing of its cacao beans but the sale of other local cash crops—rice, watermelon, corn, and bananas, for example—were still affected by the price-gouging practices of private truck owners. Finally, the angry and determined little federation tackled the problem and participated in a week-long road blockade that resulted in the progressive government of the Unidad Democrática y Popular (UDP) agreeing to sell the organization ten trucks. "The trucks give us the ability to regulate farm prices and freight charges. They have been very effective in keeping our produce prices up and freight charges down," reported Luis Cruz during the early phase of the federation transport operations.

Several years later, however, Luis expressed great concern about the trucking venture. The trucking program had led to one headache after another, he proclaimed. El Ceibo had racked up a debt of $80,000 from uncollected freight charges from slippery customers, and that had become a burden on the organization. In addition, the trucks were often too big for the small dirt roads in the Alto Beni, and their imported spare parts and tires prohibitively expensive. Furthermore, the organization wasn't able to just stop making the costly trips to put things in order because it was under pressure to meet the payment plan or lose the trucks to the government.

Despite repeated assembly meetings, the organization never came up with an adequate truck management scheme, and over the next seven years, I watched the transport section of El Ceibo gradually shrink in size. First ten trucks became seven, then the number dropped to five, and then to a mere two vehicles for the year 1994—just enough to run the basic cacao bean transport and marketing program. Though the organization dreams of gaining complete freedom from the middleman, this is an instance in which it faltered, and wisely picked up stakes, showing the ability to adjust necessary to any successful development program.

Stage 3: Exporting Cacao Beans and Chocolate — New Export Markets

In the late 1980s, Gualberto Condori called my hotel and told me he was most anxious to show me what the latest IAF grant had made possible at El Ceibo's La Paz office. "The federation," he said, "has accomplished one of its dreams."

With the IAF's help, El Ceibo had recently purchased a large property just outside the capital. The new quarters, including a small adobe office and a larger workshop, housed the federation's chocolate plant in far spiffier conditions. Condori gave me a tour. New chocolate-making machines had been acquired with a low-interest loan from a German aid agency. In a large storage room, dozens and dozens of boxes were stacked in piles right to the top of the high ceiling—cartons of chocolate products ready to be transported overland to a port in Chile where they would be taken by steamer to Western Europe. El Ceibo had made some modest export sales in 1985 and 1986 but now they were truly entering world markets.

Condori described the co-op federation's growing export activities. "The federation's major client is OS-3, a small Swiss firm. The firm is based in Geneva, but it distributes Third World products from community organizations to 800 stores in twelve countries throughout Western Europe and Canada. They sell to consumers willing to pay a slightly higher price for Third World products that increase employment and other benefits for small farmers like ourselves. They say it's a way to rectify some of the major social injustices in the world separating north and south, but we've learned that it is also in their economic interest to buy our products. You see, with the money we make we are able to purchase their machines for our industry and open new markets for them as well, so there is mutual interest involved in these arrangements."

By way of example, he showed me the statements on a wrapper of an Organic Swiss Chocolate bar made by Rapunzel.

Eco-trade puts your money where your beliefs are. It's economical, not political. It's not a bureaucracy. It's a bottom-up approach. Eco-trade empowers the people on the ground, literally, to protect the environment.

All Rapunzel products use ingredients purchased through the Eco-trade partners. For example, Rapunzel purchases cacao from a unique farmers co-operative in Bolivia. The El Ceibo co-op is a group of farmers that became world-class entrepreneurs to improve their quality of life.

Condori then took me to see Saturnino Mamani, the head of the all-important export division. Mamani is a good example of the way El Ceibo has educated and groomed its members to take on important roles in the organization. He first worked as a clerk in his local co-op store. As a young man, he took many of the non-formal education courses offered in the Alto Beni by NGOs on a wide range of co-op–related and other management subjects and subsequently became chief of the tiny chocolate enterprise in El Alto. Now, despite only four years of formal schooling, he was the man put in charge of El Ceibo's export expansion drive.

With a confident smile, Mamani reported, "We're doing great. El Ceibo reached $100,000 in exports in 1988 and I expect orders to keep increasing." Mamani recounted that a big boost to El Ceibo sales had come with the opening of organic markets in Western Europe. The federation was in a good position to sell organic products since Alto Beni farmers had never been able to afford much chemical fertilizer or pesticide. Their fields, streams, and crops, unlike others', had remained uncontaminated.

Like fellow professionals in my field, we had become much more aware of the fragility and importance of the Amazonian rainforest in recent years and were now anxious to fund project initiatives to remedy the critical situation. Thus I was delighted that El Ceibo was able to benefit from this eco-movement in Europe with the aid of the German volunteer professionals working with them.

While OS-3 continued to buy the federation's cocoa powder, the German firm Rapunzel was now buying the beans and using them in the manufacture of chocolate bars for sale to health food stores in the Western Europe and the United States. The German firm was paying the federation $3,200 per ton, a great price considering that the world market price had recently fallen to between $1,000 and $1,500. When I asked Mamani if the federation would have a profitable business if it were receiving normal world market prices, he said, "Everybody would have chopped down their cacao trees by now and we would have searched for another commercial product."

As I listened to Mamani, I experienced a rush of astonishment. Not only were El Ceibo's farmers pulling off this mini-economic boom with organic products when world markets were at an all-time low, but by processing their beans into chocolate powder and other products for alternative markets, these unlikely peasant upstarts were succeeding in one of the most oligopolistic markets for a world agricultural commodity. Cacao bean markets, long dominated by multinational corporations such as Hershey's, had left little room for Third World producer countries to vertically integrate their operations from farm to factory. Who would have expected that hardscrabble peasant farmers of Bolivia would be able to pull this off?

ADAPTATION IN THE FEDERATION MANAGEMENT PRACTICES

I was able to appreciate the full magnitude of the effects on El Ceibo of their expanding export sales. When I arrived in Sapecho, my reliable friend Luis Cruz ticked off a number of recent changes: the workforce had climbed to 100 full-time workers; the *jornal unica* had held up, but the federation was paying everyone $2.50 a day instead of $1.70, and they had added small bonuses for senior members and members with dependents. They had also begun to have the local co-ops buy directly from the peasant producers in lieu of the federation, to speed up the whole chain of activity from farm to market. "The big private industries have even been trying to replicate our methods but their lack of a grassroots organization has made them feeble competitors."

Transportation and marketing of cacao and other produce was made easier by the steady expansion of a graveled road network connecting the co-op communities of the Alto Beni to each other and the rest of Bolivia. The Franciscan priests managing the operation (their organizational name was OSCAR) were an unlikely crew of road-builders. Their Catholic mission combined road construction with environmental courses for adults and a one-year college preparatory program for youth brought here from all over Bolivia. The students were fulfilling their military obligation by working on the roads during the day and then by taking classes and studying at night in their rustic tent camp. They were certainly making a difference in the lives of the Alto Beni families in providing them with greatly improved travel and marketing conditions.

A New Commitment to Sustainable Development

One of the most interesting changes I found was El Ceibo's commitment to sustainable farming methods. As we stood under the forest canopy of his own cacao farm, Cruz explained this change in the federation's outlook. "The international organic buyers have become more demanding about cacao bean production practices. We used to qualify as organic simply by not using chemical fertilizers or pesticides. Now our farmers are required to grow legumes at the base of the cacao tree to choke off weeds and fix nitrogen in the soil. Fast-growing native trees are planted to provide shade and reduce the impact of heavy rainfall which caused so much leaching of good soil nutrients. These shade trees along with other plants attract insects, reptiles, and birds to facilitate the restoration of the forest's natural equilibrium and biodiversity."

He continued, "Not everyone has been able to conform to the new requirements. It involves a lot more hard work, and family members have to change the way they do their work on the farm. Because of that change in technology and a ferocious return of witch's broom which has defied control by pruning, most families within our co-ops have had to reduce their cacao acreage by half to about two hectares. We have yet to entice all our farmers into organic production techniques, but we're moving in that direction, and El Ceibo is doing everything possible to make it happen. Now many of us have come to realize that our long-term survival as farm families is dependent on such changes."

A Federation Mystique

During this visit, I was especially impressed by the devotion members seemed to feel for their organization. When the farmers spoke of El Ceibo their words glowed with reverence. A mystique had grown up around this rare and effective peasant federation.

El Ceibo's experience demonstrates that participatory development is not only about overcoming barriers and spreading tangible benefits to communities. It also involves creating a reservoir of enthusiasm that can sustain an organization over many years. El Ceibo was employing a variety of methods to cultivate the mystique so integral to its success.

During the 1980s, El Ceibo had been investing some of its profits in "cultural festivals." Luis Cruz had been influential in this native cultural orientation. Although not a self-proclaimed Katarista, his high level of cultural consciousness, revised historical reference points, and related cultural pride reflect the Katarista influence. This festival event brought together the music and dance from the co-op communities representing an array of cultural traditions brought from the highlands to their new Alto Beni home. In an El Ceibo bulletin, I found a short editorial hyping this type of investment in culture: "Similar to the root of a tree is the culture of a people, a fact which is especially important in colonization zones. For when we leave behind our homelands and become involved in our new agricultural holdings as individual farmers, the risk of overlooking our rich traditions—the music, dance, and our art forms—of our ancestors that mark us as distinct peoples becomes greater."

I was fortunate to attend one of these events during a year when co-op spirits sagged from rainfall shortages and low cacao production. The underlying objective was to boost member morale and celebrate those cultural expressions which released spiritual energies to enhance production. Some twenty El Ceibo leaders and members kicked off events with an all-night vigil in a cacao grove involving offerings to the local earth deities with libations using the sacred coca leaf and good old Bolivian beer. They also sacrificed a white llama and buried its heart in the ground as a special ceremony to elicit spiritual powers for improving their agricultural fortunes.

Festivities the next day included contests for the best cultivation techniques and wood carvings made from their prized tree as well as poetry and new songs with lyrics celebrating El Ceibo, cacao, and the Alto Beni's biodiversity. One after the other co-op flute and panpipe bands took turns playing lively background melodies while women dancers in traditional ethnic costumes bedecked with wreaths made from cacao beans and with pods draping from the exquisitely designed hand-woven Andean shawls characteristic of far-away northern Potosí spun and swirled. One male dancer impersonating a shaman made an offering to the earth deity that cleverly combined the modern "Ceibollitas" chocolate candy with the traditional coca leaves as his associated ritual objects.

The federation also sent El Ceibo calendars with colorful illustrations of the different self-managed service programs and depictions of the lush tropical setting and images of biodiversity of the Alto Beni throughout Bolivia. They distributed fancy brochures with pictures of their industrial technology, cacao trees, chocolate products, and assembly meetings far and wide. In addition, members often wore T-shirts emblazoned with the co-op name and logo. They also began referring to the vitality of their native heritage on view in the organizational practices as the glue of their social enterprise in publications and brochures. All of these were signs of an organization successfully forging its unique collective and multicultural identity. I left Bolivia soaring with a sense that small community federations could join together to make a significant impact on the lives of their families.

STAGE 4: THE GREAT INDUSTRIAL LEAP FORWARD OF 1994

In 1994, when I again visited El Ceibo's property in El Alto I saw that the federation's dream for its communities was coming true. Condori, Mamani, Cruz, and the current president, Bernardo Apaza, met me at a brand new chocolate plant set in the previously empty central area of the large lot owned by the federation. The new, red brick factory contained a huge industrial floor space with hygienic and spacious working conditions and ample florescent and natural lighting. There were also large warehouse areas and deluxe administrative offices. Pneumatically powered conveyor belts loaded the beans onto the roasting machines which ground the beans into cocoa powder. Another machine cranked out a new product, instant cocoa, for which there were already orders pouring in from Germany, Holland, and Switzerland. The "ceibollitas" were at long last approaching international standards with their creamy taste and smooth texture. Here it was at long last, the culmination of El Ceibo's developmental quest: a modern industry capable of transforming all its cacao beans into chocolate products.

Apaza and the others hastened to tell me all about the efforts that had led up to this greatly expanded industrial production.

"Several of our members just spent six months in German and Italian chocolate factories to learn to operate these modern industrial machines, and we have just installed our first four computers in our principal offices in La Paz and Sapecho.

"And have you heard about the brainstorming seminar we had last year? Twenty-four ex-federation leaders, including twelve ex-presidents, met at a fancy hotel in Coroico to review the federation's sixteen-year performance. We had excellent discussions, assessing our strong and weak points and dividing up new tasks for the future. We recommended, for example, lengthening the terms for leaders to four years. We also decided to promote sales in national markets, something that we have neglected as we have concentrated on our export strategy. Then we recommended a major advertising campaign over Aymara radio to promote El Ceibo products. We have also appointed Gualberto Condori general manager, now that he has a university degree in business administration. The federation paid for his education so now we'll get our investment back."

Yet despite all the unrestrained optimism, I later learned that it had taken two years of hard, frustrating work for El Ceibo to learn to master these new machines as the enterprise operated far below its capacity. They also used a large section of their property as a public parking lot to increase funds needed for maintaining a higher profit margin.

Earlier in the year, back in the Alto Beni, I had observed similar groundwork being laid for the big industry about to take off. Under COOPEAGRO's foreign-trained specialists, El Ceibo had converted its half-hearted, weedy little agricultural research plot into a center of agricultural experimentation for the Alto Beni.[3] High-performing varieties offering high yields as well as excellent resistance to various local blights and insects had been developed. In some cases, they had been able to reduce the initial growing period via a technique of grafting branches from older trees to new ones. I gazed in awe at the long, neat, narrow rows of tens of thousands of robust, foot-high seedlings uniformly arranged under bamboo structures and shaded by dry motacu leaves. A credit program was distributing these seedlings to members who needed to replace now unproductive trees which had been planted during the colonization programs of the 1960s and 1970s. In its emerging quest to increase support for the rainforest's biodiversity and related agro-forestry practices, El Ceibo offered new training programs and distributed instruction manuals on organic production practices to its members. It was also conducting its first forest inventory of Alto Beni tree species as data to be utilized for shaping its ecology-conscious development strategy.

At the research station, El Ceibo researchers were also investigating other commercially promising crops such as black pepper, citrus, and macadamia nuts to avoid excessive dependence on cacao and secure the economic future of both the federation and the micro-region. One exciting idea was to use the established marketing channels abroad for dried fruit which was as abundant as cacao on their Alto Beni farms. Crop as well as product diversification had become growing imperatives within the federation's plans for reducing risk and ensuring future development.

To ensure the maintenance of organic production practices among members, El Ceibo now compelled individual farmer members to sign contractual agreements stipulating the sustainable farming methods required by international buyers and had begun using some of the best farmers as local inspectors for these practices. The number of internationally certified organic farmers within their ranks had climbed from 220 in 1990 to 450 by 1997.

El Ceibo's export efforts during the 1990s had also readied the federation for their industrial leap forward. Total exports for cacao beans, cocoa powder, and cocoa butter now averaged $900,000 a year and had even earned El Ceibo the distinction, one year, of being designated Bolivia's seventh most important exporter of non-traditional products. Although the price for cacao beans to Rapunzel during this period had fallen significantly to only 30 percent above the world market price, it still provided sufficient economic incentives to continue with these marketing channels. And El Ceibo passed an important threshold during 1992 and 1993, as the export value of its manufactured chocolate products exceeded cacao beans sales for the first time.

Gualberto Condori spoke for the whole organization when he said, at the end of 1993, "We don't want to remain small-time Third World suppliers of raw material to First World countries forever. We want to sell more and more of our cacao in the form of manufactured products. Only in this way will we be able to attain the needed economic development for the Alto Beni."

Yet even with the value-added and niche market, El Ceibo was providing only modest prices to its members via its service and enterprise program. Lower international cacao earnings still allowed the 900 members along with thousands of other cacao-growing families in the Alto Beni to remain economically afloat because El Ceibo played such as effective role in price regulation and spillover benefits for farmers throughout the Alto Beni.[4]

Both leaders and technicians estimated that without the presence of their service program and industry, farmers would be receiving one half to two thirds of the current cacao income and probably would have abandoned the crop. This placed the Alto Beni farmers in a relatively better position than most Indian peasant farm communities in Bolivia reeling from the trade liberalization policies that lowered prices for Bolivian farm produce.

Future price projections worldwide for cacao also seemed to work toward El Ceibo's benefit. According to the *New York Times* in 1998, the monocropping systems of cacao production were apparently under siege all over the world from rampant problems with pests and disease. As cacao bean supplies became increasingly scarce, prices moved upwards. Under the new scenario for stable production, the future of this bean would lie with small farmers cultivating amidst the polycultures of the Third World's forests.

New Challenges of the Late 1990s

Between 1994 and 1997, despite the co-operative federation's increased production and value-added capacities, there were many other new challenges that El Ceibo had to face. A critical problem arose when El Ceibo's cocoa powder, for the first time, failed to meet the increasingly stringent environmental standards of several European countries, including those of important clients.[5] Yet its product lines of organic "liquor de cacao" and cocoa butter met the same tests, so the federation was able to keep supplying important buyers such as Rapunzel. Fortunately, by early 1998, a solution to the stringent standards was in sight, as several long-standing El Ceibo clients agreed to loan them funds to purchase the cleaning machines that could solve this problem.

The export problems, however, had given the federation impetus to expand product sales within Bolivia, which—to my great surprise—sometimes even provided higher prices. El Ceibo products were able to compete admirably with diverse Brazilian, Chilean, and Peruvian chocolate products for shelf space in the king-size supermarkets now appearing in the major cities. Total Bolivian chocolate product sales for El Ceibo in 1997 had climbed to $1,300,000, and 30 percent of this total amount went to this growing domestic market. One new product, "Quinu Coa," combining the Andean grain quinoa with cocoa, became incorporated into a national school breakfast program for improved nutrition.

El Ceibo's industrial prominence was also turning the heads of politicians, sometimes profoundly altering their perceptions about peasant economic entrepreneurship. On a televised public affairs program during Bolivia's 1997 election campaign, the left-of-center vice-presidential candidate of a small opposition political party was asked by a reporter to define the economic alternatives to the neo-liberal economic model prevailing in Bolivia. The politician blurted out that the co-op federation El Ceibo as a return to the ayllu enterprise and the triumph of popular capitalism should be replicated all over the country since its organizational principles and philosophy came from no less an authority that the Incan culture.

For many years, El Ceibo had been able to rely on the friendly, socially conscious buyers of the European fair trade movement for its principal well-paying market. Now it was swimming in the real world of big-time commercial competition. At home, the federation faced chocolate products pouring across the border in response to trade liberalization policies, and promises for more of the same from emerging regional free trade blocks like MERCOSUR (the 'common market' among Chile, Argentina, etc.). Simultaneously, the federation was striving hard to expand conventional product markets in Western Europe and the United States, as well as closer to home in Chile and Argentina.

The neo-liberal marketplace demands of higher product quality at lower cost coupled with the desire to optimize their modern chocolate factory's operations eventually led to major changes in El Ceibo's organizational structure and practices. In 1997, El Ceibo introduced greater organizational hierarchy and took oversight power from the administrative council and gave it to a group of managers. Professional specialists were to be hired at competitive salaries using fixed term contracts while El Ceibo counterparts become trained for eventually replacing them. Under pressure from several European clients seeking higher quality products, they had already hired a seasoned professional technician from a rival industrial firm to the tune of $2,000 monthly.

Also the vigilance council would no longer be the sole voice for making leadership and management accountable via internal audits and other financial controls. For the first time in the institution's history, a reputable external firm would conduct an annual audit of El Ceibo's operations. It seemed that El Ceibo was adapting once more to the changing complexities around them. They had decided to cast off rotational practices and egalitarian salary policy for some of their key enterprise personnel.

Discussed extensively in assemblies and follow-up seminars, the origin of these ideas for changes reflected the thinking of Gualberto Condori, their first college graduate. Condori was engaged in some creative thinking while completing his university thesis which focused on El Ceibo as a model Bolivian competitive enterprise combining Western and Andean organizational concepts. He and Luis Cruz were even now wearing business suits in downtown La Paz for their important meetings. They were not only exuding the organization's ever-increasing professional ethos but also asking for greater respect and less discrimination as Aymara entrepreneurs and rural community leaders.

For skeptics assuming that El Ceibo was going to jettison its cultural continuities guiding this long-term social change praxis, the remarks of current president Leoncio Tipuni are reassuring. He reiterated in a forth-right manner, "These adjustments and changes signify a modernization process of El Ceibo without forsaking our ancestral Aymara, Quechua, and Moseten cultural practices. We are simply adapting them further within the framework of globalization and market competition."

The future will no doubt bring further changes as El Ceibo continues to adjust and find its way in an ever-changing and demanding global marketplace. Yet no matter what happens in its new struggles, underneath it all, El Ceibo will continue to evolve and blaze its unique path as a multicultural social enterprise. Since its origins, the members of the co-op federation have been able to propel the organization onward and upward, with new discoveries and over never-ending obstacles in the path of their development dreams.

I was reminded of this fact in a poignant way at the event inaugurating the new factory in El Alto. I sat among federation leaders and international representatives from clients such as Rapunzel on a raised platform over-looking several hundred farmer members seated alongside the new red brick building now draped with floral wreaths and large banners bearing the Bolivian national flag and El Ceibo's emblem. Each of the thirty-seven co-ops entertained us with melodies from flutes, panpipes, and drums. The music and the costumes, ranging from purple ponchos to feathered head-dresses, reflected the diversity of cultures that had been brought together by the co-op federation.

As Luis Cruz reminisced at the mike about the numerous obstacles El Ceibo had encountered on its path to economic and social change, my mind flashed back to a scene I had observed in 1982. An Independence Day parade lit up Sapecho's darkness as town residents of all ages marched two abreast down a dirt road holding flickering candles in papier-mâché holders. Bringing up the rear was the parade's only vehicle, the El Ceibo pickup, carrying Luis Cruz and several other leaders playing lively Andean panpipe melodies. On top of the truck was mounted a miniature chocolate factory, smokestack and all. El Ceibo's peasant members had kept this kind of vision alive for over eighteen years, and it had become a reality.

CHAPTER 7

The Quinoa Trail: From South American Salt Flats to Western Health Foods Stores

Unadorned quinoa stands alone beautifully with any meal, and it may be elaborated upon in endless ways. Substitute quinoa for rice or pasta, or use quinoa in soups, salads, breads, and desserts. It enhances other foods with its flavor, texture, and superior nutritional properties.

FROM A NORTH AMERICAN COOKBOOK WITH 120 QUINOA RECIPES

In the late 1970s, a letter from a federation of co-operative farmers in the remote Bolivian province of Nor Lipez reached my desk in Washington, D.C. The envelope contained a request from a Quechua-Spanish–speaking peasant leader belonging to the Central de Co-operativas de Campesinos Agrícolas Operación Tierra (CECAOT) for funding for a project to industrialize and market an obscure Andean grain called quinoa.

I was intrigued to receive a proposal from this deeply impoverished southern altiplano region, a place often perceived as a kind of no-man's land for its harsh weather, severe terrain, and frontier-like isolation. The proposal was also of special interest because it was the first time I had found quinoa featured in a local project plan. I had first seen quinoa while in the Peace Corps and was impressed by its extraordinary nutritional value, ability to survive Andean frosts, and the sensational colors of the different plant varieties during the growing season. This high-protein grain, once the staple of the Incan diet, was used by astronauts in their voyages to the moon.

My first visit to the project site was in 1981. From La Paz, I climbed aboard a night train for the twelve-hour journey through western Bolivia. The trip spent in a dimly lit, crowded car, either sandwiched between two strangers on a hard wooden bench or seated on the aisle floor where I was constantly jostled by Indians transporting huge bundles of smuggled clothing and canned goods to Chile, was my most sleepless ever. As we hurtled through the dark, windswept mountain plains, I huddled inside my large woolen poncho, keeping one wary eye trained on my duffel bag full of the project proposals and related documents.

Exhausted and groggy as we chugged toward Uyuni at sunrise, I felt relief that my mode of transport would soon change. We passed shacks on the outer edge of the bleak and isolated altiplano town, and then as we ground slowly into its station, I spotted a large, bearish gringo with a white crew cut and a heavy overcoat among a half dozen people standing on the station platform. I knew this must be the Belgian priest cum co-op advisor waiting to drive me to the communities of Nor Lipez. A group of Catholic missionaries from Belgium had organized an active parish program in Lipez in the 1960s which had evolved into the quinoa development program that I would be visiting. After greeting me with warm *abrazos,* Padre Mario Bouvy led me to his landrover and we set out toward the project site. Padre Mario's kind, compassionate face, covered with sun blisters, hinted at his years of abiding service to Indian communities in this rugged and isolated land.

Just a few miles beyond town, we were gliding across the famous Salar de Uyuni. Over 10,000 square kilometers in size, the Salar de Uyuni is the largest salt flat deposit in South America and a source of lithium used, among other things, for jet airplanes and treating manic depression.

As we headed out over this hard-packed surface, we were suddenly all alone, with empty white plains extending into the distant white horizon. It was an odd sensation to simply drive across space without even the guidance of auto tracks. As we sped along for an hour or so in this unchanging, stark environment, I noticed that the speedometer was hovering around 120 kilometers per hour, and when I glanced down, I saw that Padre Mario had the accelerator pinned to the floor. For a few minutes Padre Mario recounted bits of local lore about people who had died on the flats. Then, to my amazement, he stopped looking out the windshield and began reading the mail he had picked up in Uyuni. For the next half hour my chauffeur looked up only occasionally to glance at his guidepost—the distant mountain on the horizon. Once I had recovered from the shock of this new way of driving, I thought to myself that this must be among the most hazardless and carefree high-speed driving in the world.

During the last twenty minutes of the ride, I finally spotted my first human being standing in the blankness—a solitary Indian woman shoveling salt from the earth into small cone-shaped mounds organized into neat rows. There was no other living creature in the white panorama. The sight of this person was a powerful image of human solitude that would stick with me for years to come. Mario explained that the salar represented a meager source of earnings for nearby villagers when other occupations such as farming failed.

When we finally put the salar behind us, we drove through a semi-desert landscape dotted with clumps of thola, a low-growing evergreen shrub. This scrubland was occasionally interrupted by small fields filled with dazzling purple, green, and red quinoa plants standing several meters high. A plant with broad leaves and bunches of seed heads concentrated toward its upper half, it appeared to be a combination of bush and stalk. Beyond the fields and rising from the edges of the pampas, there were mountain hillsides partially covered by a mixture of solid rock, cactus plants, and terraced fields of frost-resistant bitter potatoes, green beans, and more quinoa.

Mario remarked, "The farmers plant on hillsides because frost tends to wreak more havoc on the plains." He added in afterthought, "The soil of the latter is terrible though. It lacks both organic matter and clay, making the effort to grow anything other than quinoa a futile farming exercise. Farmland on the mountain slopes represents quinoa's more natural habitat and disease and insect problems are minimal there."

After another half-hour's driving stretch, we pulled at last into the village of Manica, a cluster of twenty or so single-story, two-room adobe houses, sporting flat tin roofs and small windows covered by opaque plastic. The most striking feature of the village was a complex of three smokestacks towering over several modest buildings. This imposing facility was a lime factory built by Belgian missionary priests, their grandiose 1970 development design for modernizing the province of Nor Lipez.

We drove into an enclosed parking area with tractor parts strewn in one corner, a tiny patch of colorful quinoa plants, and a pick-up parked in front of offices and dormitories. Macario Bautista, a co-op leader, and Jaime Alba, a professional agronomist, were standing in the doorway of the co-op's main office. Bautista, the peasant who had spearheaded the quinoa revitalization movement, wore blue-denim work overalls and a straw hat. He was short man with a mustache and narrow squinting eyes that closed when he smiled. Having communicated with Macario by phone and mail, it was nice to finally meet him on his own turf.

Jaime was an upbeat, ebullient professional from the city of Potosí with a long background in rural development programs. We had met several years earlier when the IAF had supported his NGO, Cáritas Boliviano, which had co-op building programs in both Nor Lipez and the Alto Beni with some of the founders of El Ceibo. His organization had given El Ceibo's affiliated co-ops some of their first Rochdale co-op lessons and had done the same for the organization I was about to visit. His ski jump nose was an unmistakable marker of his Andean mestizo identity. Over a breakfast of hot tea and biscuits baked from quinoa flour, the old co-op hand and development pro began to tell the story of development in Nor Lipez and explain the need for project financing.

QUINOA AND ITS HISTORY

Later that morning, Alba, Bautista, and I, and a few other co-op members, visited the quinoa fields in the outlying farming communities. The communities belonging to the co-op were located between ten and forty kilometers apart both in the central part of the province and at its northern edge bordering the salar. As we drove along the rough, potholed roads, I began recalling to myself the amazing facts surrounding this unusual plant. The research showed that in terms of food value, quinoa had an ideal balance of fat, starch, oil, and protein, and its high quotient of amino acids, including lysine, made it a potentially critical grain for the world's future food supply. Its protein content was higher than wheat, rice, and corn, and double that of most other grains.

Quinoa's political and cultural history was equally fascinating, and deeply rooted in the Andean mountains. It was first domesticated around 3,000 B.C. The oldest evidence of quinoa's use as a food was discovered by archaeologists on the same latitude with Nor Lipez in today's Chile. Historic research indicates that the Incas were as fanatical about quinoa as Europeans were about wheat, repeatedly imposing it on the conquered peoples under their domain. A Peruvian botanist once told me that it was the most important source of protein for the ten to twelve million people incorporated into the immense Incan empire extending from Colombia to southern Bolivia for over two hundred years. According to sixteenth-century chroniclers, quinoa was so revered by people living here that it could be found in origin myths and harvest songs. The fact that many contemporary native communities have kept growing it in recent years despite discrimination in the marketplace and government's relatively weak interest may be seen as a remnant of an age-old passion for a "culturally fit livelihood" (Zimmerer 1996).

After a twenty-minute drive through more thola-covered pampas, our little delegation finally reached the quinoa fields, several miles from the village of San Juan, where co-op members were waiting for us. As we walked into the cultivated plots, Bautista grabbed the scarlet stalk of a five-foot plant and pointed to the seeds hanging in bunches on the broad leaves suspended at its top.

"The seed heads concentrate here," he said. "Their comparatively large size, lighter white color, and superior taste make this 'quinoa real' [scientific name *Chenopodium Quinoa-wild*], of which there are eight or so varieties, the type most popular among health-conscious consumers." He also said the outer layer of the seed coat contained a bitter-tasting zaponin which is a good natural insecticide because it effectively repelled pests. Alba explained that farmers began planting in September and harvested by March in years with good rainfall, and during April and May in normal years. This variety of quinoa required twelve hours of intense sunlight each day yet only 150 millimeters of annual rainfall, he said, but yielded even more than 600 or so kilos per hectare when the rainfall was higher.

I asked how quinoa was able to thrive in such an arid and frost-prone mountain environment. Alba's face shone with pride as he explained that the quinoa real is a salar variety that is hardy and robust due to its adaptation over a millennia to the alkaline soils of the southern altiplano. At the same time, he said, there are a number of hazards for the plants. "One of these is the intense altiplano sunlight. The baby quinoa plant must be covered with branches of thola to prevent burning by those fierce rays. Then, also, predatory birds and rats threaten the fragile, young plants. Moreover, on the plains, tractor plowing leaves holes, damaging the leaves which makes it easier for worms to burrow into the membranes of the plant. Some technicians from Potosí showed us how to combat this problem with a pesticide called folilol, and prior to that DDT and aldrin were used. As far as chemical fertilizers are concerned they really are of little use here since our exceedingly dry soils won't retain them for long." He added that farmers use a compost made from llama dung for fertilization but given the dryness of the landscape it is absorbed very slowly by the plant.

Bautista explained that llama herding had been the main form of economic activity on the plains until the arrival of tractors fostered quinoa expansion. "The machines have given us a big jump in being able to plow the land more rapidly, even though the planting, harvesting, and post-harvest work are still all done by hand. Native communal work groups called *aynis* and *minkas* enable us to mobilize our labor to accomplish these tasks, including the application of the compost mixture." It was a pleasant surprise to me to learn that the introduction of tractors in this case had served to reinforce and expand the use of Andean communal practices.

A campesino co-op leader, Teodoro Veliz, gave me a brief history of land tenure in the area. "The Spanish Crown granted us a collective land title for our ayllu, which included the salar, way back in the seventeenth century. That document is the single piece of documentation that establishes our communal ownership. Families here did not receive the private land titles that were distributed in other Bolivian peasant communities in the decades following the 1952 revolution. There was no need for a land reform in Lipez. More interested in digging into our mineral-rich mountainsides, the European settlers never bothered to establish haciendas to take our lands and enslave our peoples. So communal lands have been at the base of our local society since ancient times. Since there is plenty of land on these vast pampas, families obtain rights to work them both collectively and individually from our traditional authorities."

LOCAL HISTORY AND THE ORIGINS OF THE CO-OP

Sitting around a hearth in Manica that night, I asked Bautista and Alba to tell me more about the region, particularly its geography and economy, and then to inform me about the co-op's origins and its "track record" in local development.

In a thoughtful overview, Bautista emphasized that the proximity of Nor Lipez to the Chilean border profoundly influenced the local economy and job situation. Most young people, for example, have migrated to work in Chilean mines. "The mines have been our most reliable means for remaining afloat in the modern economy, since both quinoa yields and animal production vary greatly from year to year. If our crops and pastures are not damaged by frosts, drought, and hailstorms or by pests, low prices can turn a good year into a bad one.

"My father used to talk about life before freight trucks reached our villages. Back then he made his living from the transport of goods. Every other day he would travel with his llamas to the Chilean sulfur mines up in the mountains just six miles on the other side of the border.[1] Each of his llamas would carry olive-colored mossy plants called *yareta* used for fuel up the mountainside to the mine site. Then the next day his small caravan would descend with a load of sulfur. The following day he would make the trek again. Times had changed, though, by the time I was a teenager. I can remember my very first job was to make piles of *yareta* for truckers who hauled the piles to the Chilean mining enterprises. Then when I was a little older, I migrated to Chile myself to work with pick and shovel in the open-pit sulfur mines. With only a fifth-grade education and few employment options, I stayed in this line of work for twelve years before I resettled back here in Lipez."

Alba chimed in at this point. "Bolivians are sought out by Chilean mine owners because they are the only people willing to go up to work at 4,000 meters in the mountains for such low wages. The Chileans are certainly not willing to do this kind of work. The most difficult part of the work for us has been the poor treatment, the lousy food, and the terrible housing conditions in makeshift dormitories. I think that with better treatment many more such as Macario would have remained there permanently."

Wanting to learn more from two unique perspectives, I asked Alba, the professional agronomist, and Bautista, the peasant leader, why quinoa had been the focus of their development work. Alba explained that in the 1950s and 1960s, he had worked for a variety of government programs and the U.S. Point Four Program. "I started to think about it while I was working with the Ministry of Agriculture in a USAID wheat production program. North American technicians had come to the Potosí community of Betanzos and established a training program for the introduction of chemical fertilizers, tractors, and threshers to improve wheat production. We signed up hundreds of farmers and were able to plant over 300 hectares of wheat varieties on their small plots. The rainfall that year was excellent. Everything was fine until it came time to market our wheat and, much to our dismay, we realized that the U.S. food aid program made it impossible for our farmers to compete. It was a big blow to the farmers since the prospects had been so promising up until that moment. Personally, I felt devastated by the role I had had in convincing them to sign up. After this disastrous experience, the people in that particular Potosí community lost interest in all development work and refused to even mention the word 'wheat' in my presence. This outcome got me thinking that perhaps Andean crops such as quinoa were better suited for our rural development programs. Quinoa had lodged in a special place somewhere in the back recesses of my mind, yet it was not until Padre Mario approached me years later about working in Lipez that I had a genuine opportunity to fulfill my desire. At that time I was working with Cáritas Socio-Economic Department out of La Paz and we were anxious to open programs in needy areas of the country."

I wondered whether Alba's family background (his father was director of the country's most important colonial museum, the Casa de la Moneda in Potosí) might have something to do with his fondness for native altiplano crops. Alba's wheat story reminded me of a similar analysis by the renowned Peruvian botanist, Mario Tapia, at Cornell University who attributed the decline in Peruvian quinoa production to donated U.S. wheat imports. It appeared that a parallel phenomenon had been at work in Bolivia.

A PATERNALISTIC BEGINNING

Following Alba's review of their reasons for choosing quinoa, Bautista proceeded to outline for me the process by which the co-ops and quinoa expansion got going. "Belgian missionaries from a diocesan order arrived in the late 1960s. Immediately upon their arrival, they announced their desire to do more than celebrate masses, marriages, and baptisms. They wanted to foster development activities that would raise our standard of living and better utilize our local resources. Padre Lucas was the head parish priest and very much a doer rather than an intellectual or analyst. He led the construction of the lime factory which was set up to be a big employer and generate profits for long-term financing of agricultural development in the zone.

"The factory never lived up to these ambitious expectations. Working at the parish for many years, I watched as the Belgians tried one management scheme after another using volunteers sent to shore up their shaky enterprise. One volunteer, for example, was a mining engineer but couldn't speak Spanish. His successor had studied film making in college, and most of the others had similarly dubious technical qualifications for the job. I think the priests were well intentioned but very naive. Perhaps the enterprise idea was doomed from the start by the steep energy and transportation costs in our out-of-the-way area.

"Dropping this giant industry in our provincial lap set the tone for a very paternalistic approach to agricultural development as well. The Belgians set up an agricultural mechanization program introducing the first tractors into Nor Lipez, without requesting any initiatives or resource contributions from us. This parish-run tractor rental service made it possible for us to uproot our thola shrubs and grow quinoa on the pampas. The hillside areas continued to be farmed mostly by hand for quinoa and other food crops while quinoa's expansion took place mostly on the pampas. The Belgians did not explicitly foster quinoa but since that was the only crop we could grow on the pampas, tractorization promoted the expansion of quinoa as a cash crop. So for the first time we began using some of this vast pampas for agricultural production instead of only herding llamas on thola vegetation.

"By 1975, the Belgians had grown weary of managing these programs themselves and made noises about transferring ownership of the assets and management responsibilities to the native communities themselves. With one stroke of the pen, the programs were transformed into community-based co-ops under an umbrella federation. This all looked fine on paper but the twelve participating communities remained in the dark about how agricultural co-ops actually worked. The newly crowned co-op federation even took on the same name as the Belgian program and used parish money to cover expenses for gaining legal status. We didn't have to lift a finger nor contribute a single peso for all the farm equipment, supplies, and offices handed over to us. The co-op idea was completely foreign to us at that time, something that the Belgian Church had transplanted to our altiplano province— yet the tractor services generated concrete economic benefits and we were not about to turn down an offer which handed these benefits over to us."

In the ensuing years the Belgians changed their role from acting as exclusive managers and owners of rural development programs in Nor Lipez to being advisors to those programs. This was not always an easy role change given a parish history of top-down management.

Bautista's running commentary was beginning to sow seeds of doubt in my mind about the sincerity of CECAOT's engagement in grassroots development. This was not exactly the grassroots development process that I was hoping to find in Nor Lipez. I could not help but compare them to the dynamic, self-reliant El Ceibo federation. Although an admirer of self-sacrificing church workers in remote Third World outposts, I felt that charitable hand-outs were often a development dead end and stifled community progress. The IAF sought to avoid this syndrome by requiring that communities themselves contribute something tangible, whether their land, labor, or local materials, to build a project on a solid foundation rather than paternalism. Bautista's comments made me uneasy about some of the enthusiasm that I had harbored for the project. Yet I continued listening with an open mind, hoping to find more encouraging signs of project potential.

A Promising Leadership

One great advantage CECAOT had as a development organization was the remarkable sense of commitment its advisor and leader, Alba and Bautista, had to the zone and to the project. Alba had first become involved in the quinoa revitalization effort in 1974 when Padre Mario made his first moves to change the Belgians' approach to development. Father Mario was critical of the programs established by his compatriots and determined to try other developmental approaches. His wooing of Jaime Alba to work in Nor Lipez as a development professional and bring his NGO here was a first step toward this shift. Alba had much to contribute because of his background with an NGO development organization that had refined participatory methodologies with farmers in the Alto Beni as well as in its altiplano projects. Yet I also felt that part of his strong motivation came from a determination as a nationalistic Bolivian to create viable national alternatives to the donated aid programs managed by his employer, Cáritas Boliviano, in a separate program division.

Alba was won over to the natives of Lipez during a trip throughout the zone with Padre Mario. "I was very moved by the harsh conditions of life in the villages I visited," he said. "The only connection with the outside world was the railroad and telegraph system. The geographic isolation and cold, harsh climate had long kept governments and NGOs from setting up offices and assigning professionals here. It was as far off the beaten track of Bolivian development work as one could possibly find. Like the Spaniards centuries before them, Bolivian government officials were more interested in the mineral wealth of the hillsides than in quinoa and the needs of the native inhabitants. Nor Lipez is a heavily mineralized zone with abundant quantities of copper and sulfur held in reserve by the state. The salar holds great quantities of lithium.

"When I asked young people why they were leaving for Chile and Argentina, it was usually because earnings from quinoa were so meager that it was difficult for their families to make ends meet, and the depletion of the llama herds over time had undermined the traditional pastoral and long-distance trading economy as a way of life. On one level, people recognized quinoa as a key to any future plans but the steps necessary to make it truly viable as a means of sustenance for the community remained beyond their comprehension. So as a fellow Potosino, I felt called to bring my developmental program here and try to make a difference in revitalizing quinoa."

Describing his own relationship to the quinoa revitalization effort, Bautista said that in the mid-1970s youthful urgings led him to leave his llama herds with other family members to find his fortune in the regional capital of Potosí. He wound up spending three years working in a carpentry workshop there and taking night courses in metal-mechanics.

"Then one day, out of the blue, I received this letter from Padre Mario appealing to me 'to live out the gospel by applying my talents on behalf of the communities of Lipez.' The message and wording of the letter were so strong that I began to reconsider my move to the city, wondering whether my true vocation might lie back in the countryside of the southern altiplano.

"Then something else occurred to reinforce this thinking. Shortly after the arrival of the letter, I had a dream. In this dream I was in a peasant assembly being elected to a leadership post. The image of the event was hazy in my mind, however, leaving me unclear about what path exactly to take.

"Shortly thereafter, I received a visit from Jaime. He appealed to me to help him organize a groundbreaking meeting of peasant quinoa producers from provinces of the southern altiplano. It would be the first in a series of initiatives to place quinoa at the center of a new development strategy for the area. A main objective would be to stimulate the communities to take initiative and come up with ideas rather than wait for government agencies to act. Producers would share their knowledge and experiences, openly express their frustrations, outline their problems, and generate their own ideas. He convinced me to come aboard and help plan and carry out the event. I decided to put my urban commitments on the back burner and moved with my family back to the countryside.

"I worked with Jaime and several other interested peasant leaders in organizing the 'Primer Encuentro de Productores de Quinoa del Altiplano Sur' (The First Meeting of Quinoa Producers of the Southern Altiplano). The gathering was the first of its kind, not only regionally but nationally as well. Invitations to the nearby quinoa-producing provinces brought together over 150 Aymara and Quechua male and female peasants, as well as official delegations from the government and foreign donors such as Catholic Relief Services. From there we began the struggle to find ways to organize and to process and market our quinoa."

THE SEARCH FOR A DEBITTERING MACHINE

Another piece of evidence that began to sway me in a more positive direction toward CECAOT was the story of its indefatigable quest for ways to improve the cleaning process of quinoa. The zaponins in the outer skin of quinoa real make it unpalatable unless the bitterness is removed. For centuries, peasant women had assumed the backbreaking job of debittering, the processing of a quintal (150 pounds) of quinoa required two to three days of washing and rubbing the grain in large tubs. The cleaning of quinoa by hand had been a terrible burden also for women working as servants in the city. To avoid the hard work, the women had spread rumors that quinoa had ill effects on the liver, the stomach, and the digestive system. This added to the "Indian food" stigma already attached to the grain. A better processing method was critical.

Never having received adequate support from local government agricultural stations, CECAOT formed its own committee for industrializing quinoa and began a hunt for processing machines. The fact that the Peruvians were hauling quinoa across the border for processing and earning high profits spurred them on.

Bautista was elected president of the quinoa industrialization committee. The committee developed a plan to find ways to process the grain and to sell small packages of it in various forms: a roasted version for beverages, flour for bread, cakes, and noodles, and a puffed grain cereal. The general assembly approved the plan, urging the committee to make the acquisition of a debittering machine their highest priority.

During the ensuing months, Bautista and Alba began to search for a machine that would debitter quinoa real in a fast and efficient way. The initial quest took them into small artisan workshops, vocational training centers, and food industries in Bolivian cities. The only private firm rumored to have a potentially useful debittering machine denied them access to the premises where it might be examined. Undeterred the pair next visited Peru whose large food industry was making sizable profits from quinoa due to heavy promotion of the grain by national governments during the 1970s.

Macario and Jaime traveled to the city of Cuzco, the ancient Incan capital, and found a firm, INCA BRANDS, whose manager turned out to be unsympathetic to their requests for assistance. "But on the way out of the office," Bautista said "we were able to peer into their storeroom and saw huge quantities of our variety of quinoa real.

"This revelation carried us on our way to our next stop, the city of Arequipa, where I looked up an Italian named Ganini who owned a small manufacturing workshop for agricultural machinery. By this time, we had concluded that the adaptation of agricultural machinery used for other cereals was the route of most promise. Since the zaponins are contained in the thin outer skin of the quinoa, we felt that Ganini's barley-hulling machine might be the answer to our problems.

"Ganini agreed to design a dehusking machine that could be built in a few months time. The price, $11,000, however, was beyond our means so I quickly found a phone and called a friend at Catholic Relief Services, the organization that contributed funds for the 'encuentro de quinoa' and had always shown interest in our quinoa development plans. They promised to help us with a grant for the purchase of the machine, with the proviso that we construct the facilities to house the machine ourselves."

CECAOT installed the new machine in the town of Julaca near co-op headquarters where they could take advantage of the excellent electrical system installed for the town's lime industry. Though they were delighted with the machine, it was found to remove only 60–70 percent of the zaponins and further adjustments were needed. "In Julaca, we spent hours tinkering around trying to improve the machine's performance," Alba said, "and often by noon our body and clothes were caked with zaponins. We always seemed to be wiping them from our mouths, noses, and eyes. This tedious task of trial and error, which led us to add a 15 horsepower motor for greater velocity, continued off and on for two full years until we set the official inauguration day and began regular operations."

After hearing Alba and Bautista's rendition of tracking down the debittering equipment, I could not help being impressed by their sense of mission and demonstrated perseverance. These farmers certainly deserved to have things work out, and increasingly they were proving to satisfy the IAF's project criteria.

The next day we drove over to Julaca to inspect the dehusking machine. Three co-op workers were operating the equipment. One worker, perched at the top of a ladder, poured quinoa into a tank where air pressure vibrated the grains causing them to shed their outer skin. This tank was connected by a tube to a squarish metal structure with a shoot at the bottom for funneling the processed quinoa into sacks. With a solemn expression Bautista turned to me and acknowledged that even after going through the machine, the bitter zaponin taste was still there. "As a supplement after processing the grain by machine, we have hired local Indian women in the village of Calcha some forty kilometers away to squat alongside the banks of a stream and wash and rub the remaining zaponins from the grain."

Upon hearing about this extra processing step, I asked why they had to go elsewhere to find their water. Macario explained that in Julaca the local railroad station had complete control over the village water pipeline and was only willing to ration CECAOT enough for domestic use. To me this story was sad and familiar. It was a typical kind of glitch development projects were always confronting.

At this point, Bautista made his pitch to me on behalf of CECAOT. "This extra trip and labor greatly increases our processing costs so we find ourselves once again in search of a new machine that will complete the job. We have heard that the government is successfully using a quinoa-cleaning machine in its research station near Lake Titicaca." He told me they would be requesting funds from the IAF for that technology and also for a quinoa-drying machine. The traditional methods had serious consequences for the consumer, he said, as stones, dust, and other debris were prone to collect with the quinoa during its exposure to solar drying in the open air. "You also get occasional bird droppings adding to its flavor," he winced.

A DECISION TO FUND

After this introduction to the co-op's history and technological developments in Julaca, Alba and Bautista dropped in my lap a project proposal totaling $105,000, to cover a truck (for hauling both quinoa and dry goods), additional processing equipment (a thresher, a cleaner-drier, a laminator), and to cover the organization's administrative and technical assistance requirements. As I was heading out the door after this discussion, a group of peasants passed to me, with obvious pride, several issues of their mimeographed newsletter, *El Socio.* I sat back down for a minute to read it. Immediately, I was impressed by its prose and its spirit of advocacy for quinoa. It also addressed other developmental and political issues of local and national interest. One particular passage revealed to me, in a powerful way, the strong ethnic concerns of the Lipez leaders:

> Often the ideology in our country makes us believe that the best life is in the city. This in turn stimulates the migration of youth. Yet how do they feel about life there after being there? Worse than in the campo where we have always lived? The cities tend to negate our culture and make us forget our traditions, going so far as to make us experience shame about being campesinos and impressing on us the need to change our surnames, as though by doing this we would be able to change who we truly are. This type of behavior is an expression of alienation that leads nowhere. By way of this alienation process, we are losing our precious human and cultural values. We don't have confidence in ourselves. We don't believe that we are capable human beings, or that we are as intelligent as other peoples.

During my visit several questions had formed in my mind regarding the project's social and technological feasibility, but there were other factors, such as the strong sense of cultural identity, moving me toward providing financial support. In the final analysis, it seemed to me that the needs of the inhabitants, the leadership provided by Bautista and Alba, and the way in which native producers had taken over quinoa's recovery for economic development outweighed my misgivings about Belgian paternalism. With our grant, CECAOT would join a growing group of IAF-supported peasant federations in Bolivia struggling to bring about grassroots changes in their respective micro-regions.

On my final day in Lipez, I attended a sunrise Easter celebration and church service. Huge bonfires warmed the chilly air and lit up the skies for hundreds of participants wrapped in heavy ponchos, woolen stocking caps, and warm blankets. It was a dramatic finale to my initial visit to the people of Nor Lipez and a vivid example of how they were combining Western and Andean ways to carve out a place for themselves and their rituals in the modern world.

A Major Obstacle: Drought

Unable to make a visit to the project site during the next two years, I decided to send a Bolivian agronomist to check on CECAOT's activities and write a report on his findings. The report reached me in November 1982 and I was disappointed to read that the new processing machines for diversifying products into quinoa flour and flakes were operating only in "experimental form," a clever euphemism for their minimal utility. The new machine for cleaning and drying quinoa was something of a bust, the agronomist reported, although "experimentation" continued. The upshot was that co-op workers still had to haul their quinoa forty kilometers by truck to a stream in the village at Calcha. With this lack of progress in mind, I decided to make the quinoa project a priority stop on my next trip.

An opportunity to revisit Nor Lipez finally came during a month-long stay in Bolivia in February 1983. Unfortunately, my arrival coincided with one of the worst droughts in the Andes in over fifty years. When I reached Lipez, it became apparent that only the few communities with irrigation had been spared devastating effects. CECAOT had taken a leadership role in dealing with the drought. Despite its primary concern with the fate of quinoa growers, CECAOT contributed its infrastructure and organizational skill in the province-wide emergency relief work—a sign to me of the organization's sturdiness. Sometimes grassroots organizations taken for granted in their communities are able to offer such critical organizational skill during an emergency situation.

I accompanied Padre Mario, Bautista, and the new federation peasant accountant, Juan Mamani, to a community meeting held at a schoolhouse in the village of San Juan. I was meeting Mamani, a key member of the project staff, for the first time. Mamani with his smooth bronze complexion and slanting hazel eyes was the first high school graduate to belong to CECAOT. His strong educational background had enabled him to make the most of numerous non-formal educational training programs available in Bolivia for development practitioners and he had become a masterful campo accountant.

A bleak landscape of parched earth and stunted quinoa plants came into view from the roadway while I listened to Mamani recount horrifying stories of the wholesale slaughter of llamas and sheep whose pastures had dried up. He gave estimates of animal losses reaching 14,000 llamas and 23,000 sheep. Entire communities were pulling up stakes to make a temporary mass migration to Chile, in hopes of finding employment.

In the meeting, I looked around at the tired, gaunt, despairing peasant faces in the room. There were young mothers nursing their babies and men looking elderly in middle age. I heard the grim phrase "what are we going to do to go on living?" repeated over and over again by participants. Padre Mario came up with a suggestion to intensify mothers' production of woolen sweaters for export as "every family at least has a small troop of llamas." Another suggestion was to "occupy the nearby sulfur mine held in state reserve."

At that suggestion a woman at the back of the room angrily shouted out, "Instead of creating job opportunities by developing local mineral resources, the authorities prefer to hold them in reserve. Meanwhile, we are all going to die of hunger. For whom and for what purpose is all this wealth being held this way?" Macario, leading the meeting, commented, "Perhaps we should exploit the salt deposits that have been used in emergencies in the past as an economic refuge."

Listening to the discussion, I had a sense that the assembled peasants were feeling me out as to whether the IAF could help ameliorate the situation. I finally spoke up by first reminding them that there were international and national agencies that specialized in relief operations, and that the IAF, as a development donor, was not geared up to respond quickly to emergency needs. Not wanting to add more gloom and doom to the situation, however, I left the door slightly open for funds that would both fit into CECAOT's development strategy and also help alleviate the immediate misery.

The Search for a Market: Back Roads through the Andes

Juan Mamani then brought me up to date on the federation's experiments in quinoa exportation. The previous year the federation had organized the fifth annual encuentro of quinoa growers. At the meeting, the usual issues were addressed: low prices, weak support from government agencies, and CECAOT's own organizational shortcomings. It had become increasingly apparent during the meeting that there was little follow-through between the encuentros, and that marketing had been overlooked, with all the attention focused on processing capacity. Moreover the meetings did not rally enthusiasm among the majority of members as expected; in fact some had been so bored they had fallen asleep during discussions. The leadership racked their brains for a better way to promote quinoa and then, with the suggestion of technical advisor Eugenio Jacinto, a politically committed Katarista, a new idea surfaced. Why not turn the annual long-winded meetings into a giant festival?

"We held a Fiesta de la Quinoa for the first time last year, and over 400 people from the provinces turned out. We seldom attract that many people for a single gathering around here. The topics for discussion were similar to those at the encuentros, but accompanying basketball and soccer tournaments and poetry readings enlivened the atmosphere and drew more people to participate. Displays of CECAOT's processed quinoa products were set up on tables outdoors and large posters used for advertising them hung on the co-op building walls. In addition to promoting quinoa, the festival was the first occasion in our history that brought together the folkloric dance and music groups of the province, complete with unique festival costumes and headdresses, panpipes, drums, and flutes in a single festival. Indian women reenacted Incan ceremonies which implored mountain and earth deities to protect and nurture 'mother quinoa'. There was even a province-wide competition for a Quinoa Queen. The young peasant girls selected were valued not only for their physical attributes but also for other important human qualities respected in the communities.

"The most significant result of the fiesta was the emergence of a quinoa defense committee to represent not only 250 co-op members but peasants from various provinces as well. As a result of the formation of this marketing committee, we have been able to increase sales within Bolivia and to export quinoa to Peru on three different occasions. Within the new division of labor we devised at the celebration, CECAOT has responsibility for threshing, dehusking, and washing the quinoa, and then we pass it to the quinoa defense committee for marketing, which includes exporting to Peru."

I had learned about the quinoa defense committee's first marketing venture from one of its leaders, Felix Quisbert. He described a regional quinoa market dominated by petty Peruvian smugglers clandestinely carrying off the quinoa real to buyers in the southern part of their country. "They may be small-scale operators but they are very clever and often are unscrupulous in manipulating our barter system—our traditional forms of exchange and godparenthood (compadrasco) ties. Just as our ancestors would transport salt via long-distance llama caravans to other regions and ex-change it for products such as sugar and corn, they swap wheat noodles, white sugar, and cooking oil for quinoa. Recently, they were exchanging one quintal of sugar for two and a half quintales of quinoa. That is outrageous—it's not even enough to cover our production costs.

"We decided to discover the market destination to which the Peruvian smugglers were taking our quinoa in order to go directly to those same buyers ourselves and obtain our rightful profits. Thus we set up our own un-dercover operation to trail them by train and bus back into Peru. Our tailing took us all the way to the Peruvian capital. We were amazed to find food companies in Lima willing to pay prices three times higher than in Lipez.

"After returning to Bolivia, we began organizing our defense commit-tee to make our first export venture. In order to export legally, we had to register with the Ministry of Commerce and obtain a license which, of course, required the standard bribe or *mordida* (bite) for a variety of public officials." As Quisbert related this to me, he looked at me with a cynical gleam in his eye as if to underscore the irony of having to make under-the-table payments in order to export "legally."

"On our own first exporting trip, we closed a commercial deal in Lima. I immediately changed our Peruvian money into Bolivian pesos. At that point we didn't know how to make bank deposits or how to make wire transfers of our funds to an account back home. And there was so much currency devaluation craziness at that time that people were walking around in Bolivia with large bags full of bills. We felt very self-conscious as we walked around Lima with sacks full of bills on our shoulders. At the train station, for example, many folks gathered around to watch the atten-dant weigh our money before we climbed aboard.

"Everything was okay until we attempted to cross into Bolivia at the Peruvian border town of Yunguyo. There the Peruvian customs officers on duty accused us of being narco-traffickers escaping from their country with illegal cash assets. In the next breath, they threatened to kill us and then confiscated our monies. At that point we realized that our lives were in danger and our only concern was getting out of there alive. When we re-turned to Lipez without the export earnings, CECAOT members and other grew suspicious that the story was concocted and that we had pock-eted the funds ourselves." Quisbert shook his head and laughed. "Can you imagine? After going through such an ordeal, our companeros here sus-pected that we were being dishonest with them.

"By the time we made the trip the second and third time, we had learned to use the banking system to avoid such perilous travel in Peru."

Quisbert concluded his summary with resigned but determined words: "With this year's terrible drought, there will be very little quinoa available but our committee will resume its work when production normalizes."

In response to Quisbert's report, I told the assembled CECAOT members and participants that I was very impressed by their successful outwitting of the Peruvian quinoa smugglers and their establishment of an export route because marketing was often an insurmountable bottleneck for many peasant-based development projects in Bolivia.

As I concluded my remarks a smiling Quechua woman with long braids and a black derby walked into the room with a heart-shaped cake made from quinoa flour. After sampling its delicious nutty flavor along with a cup of hot tea, the co-op leaders at the table opened up a menu of new project-funding requests. The requested items added up to $50,000, and included a fund for purchasing dry goods to help diminish the effects of the drought in communities where members from the co-ops resided. I pledged to make a presentation of their new funding needs to the IAF project review committee. I was especially interested in helping the federation to develop a program for distributing dry goods as this would strengthen the federation's pivotal relief role as well as its development work in the province.

SLUGGISH PRODUCTION

In the evening conversation the CECAOT leaders brought me up to date on the progress of their IAF-funded activities. I was disappointed that they seemed to be making only minimal use (only several hours weekly) of the processing machinery designed to churn out various salable quinoa products. They were producing only small quantities of puffed grain, quinoa flour, and flakes for the rather informal, ad hoc commercial outlets of other NGO and grassroots organizations like themselves. As a result, product turnover was slow and commercial transactions sluggish. They appeared to be without the financial capital, contacts, commercial savvy, and representation necessary for the successful marketing of their products. I learned that the $6,000 provided by the IAF as a quinoa-purchasing fund had dwindled in value, eroded by the economy's hyperinflationary gyrations. A final blow was the report that the new machine for cleaning and drying quinoa designed by an industrial workshop in the altiplano city of Oruro once again had failed to live up to expectations.

Although I was disappointed by the pessimistic assessment of CECAOT's productivity and marketing progress, I was intrigued by some hopeful news about future marketing that Juan Mamani called to my attention. Juan reminded me that David Cusack, a North American who had been in touch with CECAOT since 1982, had expressed a strong interest in quinoa and might be of help. Cusack, a social scientist from Colorado, had both written and called me during the past year about his interest in CECAOT.[2] I had never met Cusack in person but I knew that he had founded an organization known as the Quinoa Corporation to open markets for Bolivian quinoa in the United States.

Juan said he was very impressed by Cusack. "He appears to be a sort of visionary, totally committed to putting quinoa in a prominent place on the world stage. During his travels through Ecuador, Chile, Peru, and Bolivia, he met a handful of botanists and agronomists working with quinoa but he was most thrilled to discover us because we were the only grassroots organization he'd come across that actively promoted quinoa. He often remarked to us about how impressed he was with a group struggling amidst such desert-like conditions."

Cusack had asked for quinoa real seeds in order to conduct trial experiments in the Rocky Mountains of Colorado. "This Coloradan," Juan said, "had the idealistic notion that successful results in U.S. could be transferred back to Bolivia to help solve specific problems of production, genetic improvement, and marketing for the traditional farming communities of the Andes.

"I told this North American that quinoa was a gift from our ancestors and that it was not something to simply give away without receiving something in return that would benefit our quinoa cultivation efforts in Nor Lipez. Cusack then offered to acquire a machine he had seen far away on the Chilean coast, a machine, he said, that would solve all our debittering problems. So earlier this year, we made a deal to exchange some of our quinoa seed for the machine. Thus, we have renewed hopes that we may yet attain the necessary quinoa-cleaning technology."

Upon hearing all this, I wondered to myself whether North Americans might wind up benefiting from this transaction more than the communities of Nor Lipez, especially if quinoa real proved to grow well in the Rocky

Mountains. Yet I could also share in their hopes for a solution to their long-standing and perplexing technology problem.

At the conclusion of our meeting I was left wondering whether it was not just Belgian paternalism but maybe their own lack of agricultural marketing experience that was holding the organization back. After all, during modern history these folks had earned cash working in Chilean mines, not in altiplano agriculture. And before that they had engaged in llama-raising activities and in a barter economy. Perhaps Lipez, a place overrun by Peruvian smugglers, was not a good setting for honing marketing skills. I traveled back to La Paz by train, and looking out the window at the vast, empty plains of the altiplano, wondered to myself what was missing from this scenario and why the federation's program couldn't quite gel. I was perplexed.

Co-op Conflicts and Decline

I was unable to return to the zone during the next four years (1983–1987). Increasing demands on my time from dozens of other projects in our growing country portfolio made me postpone travels to Nor Lipez indefinitely. For information, I had to rely on meetings in La Paz rather than first-hand observation and discussions directly with the people in Nor Lipez. Evaluations, monitoring reports, and CECAOT's own reports and commentary in *El Socio* served to keep me abreast of the project's activities.

In 1987, just by chance, I received some news about Nor Lipez when a Bolivian friend introduced me to a Belgian development volunteer, Guillermo Roelants, who had worked with CECAOT. My somewhat cynical friend, who had a penchant for collecting gossip about troubles in development aid projects, said, "This guy has the scoop on the federation so you should go see him and find out what is really going on out there."

At our meeting, Roelants told me of his recent role as the key advisor to the quinoa defense committee. His chief collaborator in this endeavor had been Felix Quisbert. Roelants offered a negative interpretation of CECAOT's work and relayed to me his frustration as an advisor.

"I grew tired of the federation's lack of initiative in marketing quinoa. They only seemed interested in improving the processing technology. My wife, Felix, and I tried to prod them into doing more, but finally gave up and broke off from the federation to create our own quinoa-marketing organization. We have recently established a contract for selling large quantities of quinoa to the state mining corporation, and I have obtained funds from the lime factory to make large quinoa purchases from the farmers. Our system is already working better than anything the co-op has ever done in marketing."

Roelant's clenched fists and fierce tone clued me in to his anger toward CECAOT leaders. Listening to the frustrations of a disgruntled ex-project participant was not an atypical way of receiving project-related information in my line of work, yet I knew that half-truths were often mixed with considerable self-interest when such people reported on project activities. It was imperative to seek a number of viewpoints before drawing conclusions about what sounded like a messy situation. This cautionary practice was especially relevant for dealing with the Belgians who had a controversial development history in Nor Lipez.

Back in my home office, I received a copy of *El Socio,* which had a markedly downbeat tone. The federation had been called on the carpet during a regional sindicato (as distinct from the quinoa growers' association) assembly to justify many years of foreign aid–backed programs. The sindicatos, unlike CECAOT and the quinoa growers' federation, incorporated all families in the rural communities to carry out social and political tasks. I knew that development projects throughout Bolivia were being taken over by sindicatos energized by sixteen years of military rule coming to an end. In fact, I was collecting cases for a future article about this political activism to show how widespread and consequential this grassroots democratic movement had become. Up to the present most of the sindicatos' interventions had been directed toward government projects, not grassroots organizations.

The bulletin went on to say,

The persons fomenting this discord and division are a tiny group that has never been active in CECAOT. They act as though they have the right to audit our activities, and make accusations about agreements with the Belgians to which they have not even been privy. They seem to be simply interested in sticking their nose into our business, to opportunistically take advantage of the new vigor within the sindicato movement. Their behavior can only be described as infantile and capricious, and their use of slander to achieve their objectives is downright immoral. Their goal seems to be to blow up the tiny problems in order to make them into issues throughout the zone as well as in other parts of the country. They say they want to help us, yet they are damaging us by never acknowledging anything positive in our work.

The commentary went on at length to reveal the nature of the conflict and defend the co-operative's record with quinoa. The bulletin commented that the lime industry and other Belgian programs "never amounted to much, and now a sector of this foreign community is trying to destroy CECAOT, the very organization that their own compatriots once founded."

This was beginning to sound to me like those familiar prairie fires of altiplano factionalism which tend to flare up time and again in local development projects. Injections of funds can often stir up and exacerbate deep-seated jealousies, family vendettas, personal rivalries, and sheer greed. I remembered again Bolivian anthropologist Xavier Albó's publication in which he argued that the combination of factionalism and community solidarity constituted a major paradox of altiplano village life (Albó 1977c) and feared that this kind of petty factionalism was rearing its ugly head in Lipez.

During subsequent years, between 1984 and 1987, bad news about the CECAOT project continued to pour into my IAF files. Both North American and Bolivian evaluators returned with a gloomy picture of lessened productive activity in communities and member apathy. The reports suggested that members were more interested in subsidized tractor services than in any show of self-help and self-management. One evaluator questioned using quinoa as a central development strategy for Nor Lipez given its comparatively low yields and exorbitant processing costs. I felt chagrined by another observation from him that the dehusking machine was grossly underutilized. The machine was producing over the course of a year what it had the capacity to produce in a single week! It had a capacity to cover the needs of the entire southern altiplano region, incorporating three provinces, not just a small co-op federation of 250 members, he argued. The technical terminology for this rural development syndrome is referred to as "excessive production capacity." Even in *El Socio,* I found vociferous criticism of co-op members' lackadaisical behavior and declining morale.

Then in late 1984 another unexpected piece of bad news reached me by phone. David Cusack had been mysteriously murdered at an archaeological site in Tihuanaco. This was a tragic loss of an exceptionally committed and talented individual, and a blow for those hopeful about reviving quinoa.

The final blow to my faltering hopes for the project came when I received letters of resignation from both Bautista and Mamani, the two leaders who had carried the project forward with such great élan. This was definitely a leadership-heavy organization and their departure meant that probably many good things about CECAOT would vanish with them, including the lively *El Socio* bulletin, a peasant organ of communications rare among all the projects the IAF supported in Bolivia.

After the departures of Mamani and Bautista, the producers' organization and project activities did continue to function and maintain quinoa production for the market, but the level of operation was so minimal by 1987 that I decided to let the IAF grant support run out and sever ties with CECAOT. All the negative feedback about a favorite project left me depressed and searching for answers. Was the drought that wiped out not one, but two quinoa harvests responsible for this outcome? Was it the constant hemorrhaging of younger Lipez co-op members through out-migration to Chile and Argentina? Another case of a project run amuck by hyperinflation cum decapitalization? Had the Belgians' paternalistic legacy smothered any genuine self-help spirit from these peasant communities? Or had Andean community factionalism destroyed the project's initial momentum and equilibrium?

I could not resist making comparisons to El Ceibo which, despite recurrent ups and downs, had fared much better. Their effective teamwork from the top to the bottom of the organization, their ability to scale-up an industry and design self-styled, locally based training programs seemed to be qualities missing from the CECAOT situation. During the late 1980s, Jaime Alba continued to lobby me for further funding in the Hotel Oruro but after so many independent negative judgments, I decided to reject such requests. It was a painful goodbye.

Quinoa's Export Boom

During the next several years, CECAOT dropped completely off my viewing screen since the IAF had no other project grantees in Nor Lipez. Then one day in 1993, when I was walking along the narrow, busy boulevard in La Paz, I bumped into Jaime Alba. We exchanged friendly greetings and I was happy to see that, although he was now in his seventies, the twinkle in his eyes and his ebullient personality were still there. I asked him what had happened with CECAOT.

"We're doing just great," he replied. "We exported ninety tons of quinoa worth $70,000 last year."

"You what!" I exclaimed.

"Yeah, after four years of persistent and patient lobbying, we received a low-interest loan from the small projects division of the Inter-American Development Bank which enabled us to expand the co-op's quinoa production almost threefold and greatly improve our membership training. We've been able to reach United States markets which pay much better than those in Bolivia or even Peru.

"You remember David Cusack, the guy who befriended us with grandiose plans for quinoa back in 1982? He wanted to buy 200 tons from us in 1983, but because of the drought we had nothing to sell and he wound up taking only seed back to Colorado for trial planting. Well, the university there became involved and an association of quinoa growers surfaced in Colorado. It turned out that our quinoa real, unlike other quinoa varieties, does not flower in the shorter growing season of the Rocky Mountains—it can only grow in the southern altiplano, in our province and two others—but the Coloradans remained interested in us.

"Cusack's Quinoa Corporation continued to evolve after his death, and they began taking quinoa real and other varieties to health food trade shows throughout the United States. This effort introduced the U.S. consumer to Bolivian and Peruvian quinoa and now there is a chain of health food stores and small gourmet food shops, with branches in almost in every state, which sells quinoa in pasta as well as grain form. Since it's a great substitute for rice, it has caught on. This, in turn, sparked the interest of other private firms, trading companies, and brokers of agricultural commodities who began buying quinoa from here and other parts of the Andes. Our quinoa real variety is the most popular of all. We native quinoa growers from the southern altiplano have always possessed a monopoly on production of this variety. Even the Swiss have approached us recently about establishing some export deals. Meanwhile, our small-farmer membership has doubled to incorporate 500 farm families.

"Remember the quinoa defense committee that emerged in the First Fiesta de la Quinoa in Nor Lipez? Over the years, the committee grew first into a provincial organization called SOPROQUI, and then joined with other provincial organizations to become a national organization going by the name of ANAPQUI. It is not exactly a member organization like CECAOT. Rather, it has both communities and ayllus as members, is led by peasant Quechua and Aymara farmers from the southern altiplano, and provides an alternative to private buyers who gouge low prices out of native peoples. ANAPQUI is Bolivia's biggest legal quinoa exporter, and South American's largest supplier of quinoa to the Quinoa Corporation, which moved its headquarters to California. They sell a half a million dollars of organic as well as non-organic quinoa. They are also working in Western European countries where markets are beginning to expand."

"I am sure Padre Mario must be very excited by this turn of events," I said.

"He would be," Jaime replied, "but he passed away of skin cancer several years ago. What social commitment that man had! You know he's a guy who learned Quechua to be close to the people and, although a Belgian, chose to be buried with them on these pampas." My mind flashed back to the day when I first hopped off the train in Lipez and saw that sensitive face full of sun blisters—direct evidence of the rigorous character of life on the southern altiplano, which he gladly shared with the local people.

I then asked whether hard feelings continued to persist between the two organizations, the former quinoa defense committee and CECAOT. "No, time has healed our wounds, plus new people have been elected to offices in both organizations, and the people like Roelants who used to be in conflict with us left the area to take up other economic pursuits. ANAPQUI leaders even voted CECAOT's current president into the highest office on the national board of quinoa exporters."

He added, "To gear up our technical capacity and self-reliance we financed the university studies in agronomy of four youth from Lipez presently serving on our staff. Otherwise, it would be near impossible to get Bolivian agronomists to take up residence in Nor Lipez or spend long periods working with our farmers. We have learned time and again that the hardships of life there are simply too great to endure for outsiders. It is also impressive that the co-ops have doubled in membership size and strong leadership has emerged once again. The co-op members manage both communal parcels, say of eight to ten hectares each, as well as individual family production units. Both are plowed with a tractor for land preparation yet collective work brigades in Andean style take care of the other tasks such as planting and harvesting. About half the land in quinoa production is on the pampas with the remaining crops on mountain slopes where there are few disease problems.[3] We also have opened an office in downtown La Paz where our university-trained economist Freddy Ticona carries out representational duties for the organization."

I was delighted to soak up this good news, and was once again moved by Jaime's abiding commitment to Nor Lipez and the native quinoa growers there. Many years before, a CECAOT leader had mentioned to me that Jaime was the soul of the organization and now I knew more than ever what he had meant.

Ever persevering Jaime then broached the question of whether the IAF would be interested in making a grant to CECAOT now that the organization was back on its feet. I responded by saying that I would be interested in visiting the zone again and taking a look at what had happened since my last visit back in 1983.

Project Appraisal Visit of 1994: CECAOT Hailed as an Example of New Empowerment

In August 1994, Jaime, the CECAOT president, and I made the two-day trip in the co-op landrover south from La Paz across the treeless altiplano plains, past the endless miles of thola, and ultimately over the salares of Potosí, to Manica. Along the way, Jaime reported that the competition from the Peruvian smugglers continued to make life difficult for grassroots marketing despite successful exports to the United States and Western Europe.

"Much more quinoa leaves Bolivia by way of these Peruvian *contrabandistas* than via legal exports organized by ourselves and ANAPQUI. What is more, a lot of our quinoa is then exported to high-paying Western markets as a 'Peruvian product'. This *contrabanda de hormiga* [contraband by ants]—petty operations by hundreds of individual middlemen—is damaging for us. And these men boat across the river from Peru into Bolivia only three hundred yards from the official border location in Desaguadero! Their competition is tough for us because the contraband cooking oil, macaroni, sugar, and other basic goods they offer can be bought at very low prices. Meanwhile, we have to purchase our dry goods from legitimate commercial outlets in order to maintain proper receipts for the co-op bookkeepers."

That evening in Manica, different co-op representatives, mostly leaders, gathered around the dinner table sipping hot tea and discussing the latest local happenings that involved quinoa. Two Bolivian consultants hired by the European Economic Community's Bolivian development aid program coincidentally appeared that same night and attended the meeting as well. The EEC was laying the groundwork to fund a large-scale quinoa project worth upwards of eight or nine million dollars—a giant leap forward for the quinoa effort in Bolivia. The consultants were happy to discover that CECAOT as well as ANAPQUI were strong examples of the use of quinoa for the genuine empowerment of native communities. They told us, by way of contrast, that in Ecuador the Nestlé Corporation had taken control of the quinoa revitalization effort through production contracts with large commercial growers and had completely mechanized the farming as well as processing operations, thereby eliminating small-farmer participation.

The EEC consultants asked what lessons CECAOT and ANAPQUI could offer in terms of small-farmer participation in large-scale quinoa production and marketing programs. They told us that both the World Bank and the United Nations Development Fund were promoting important future investments in quinoa. Even international food aid agencies, including USAID, had started purchasing quinoa from peasant growers for distribution among women's clubs in poor communities. The recent discovery of quinoa by the giants of the international development community made me proud of CECAOT's pioneering role.

Following the discussion of the new interest in quinoa by the development community, the conversation shifted to the ecological concerns of the EEC consultants. They reported that in Ladislao Cabrera province, the use of tractors in quinoa cultivation had damaged the ecology and soil of the area. The southern altiplano winds had blown away much good topsoil to form large dunes and impoverish the farmers' fields. Their concern was that similar erosion might be taking place in Nor Lipez, and they had heard that the number of tractors was increasing. One ex-CECAOT president said that some of the local farmers had stopped using the disk plowing implement for similar ecological reasons, but that the use of tractors in new fields always brought an immediate increase in quinoa yields which lasted several years.[4] In 1983 agronomist Eugenio Jacinto had expressed his concern to me that extensive use of tractors in Nor Lipez might cause the very type of erosion the EEC consultants were worried about. The truth was, in Nor Lipez, vast expanses of new pampa lands could be misused in this way without any short- or medium-run losses to the farmer who could just move on to new areas when yields became too low.

When the consultants asked about the use of chemicals on quinoa, a factor that had implications for marketing quinoa products as organic, I remembered a conversation with Felix Quisbert, the ex-sindicato leader and founder of ANAPQUI. "We were taught by agronomists who worked out here to use folilol as an insecticide to combat the worms, rats, and birds. We also used it to defend our fields from foxes. Once the fox population was eliminated, however, a type of wild rabbit from Argentina called a 'liebre' appeared and began devastating our quinoa plants to an uncontrollable degree. In hindsight, we have realized that the fox normally hunted these rabbits and prevented them from becoming a menace to our fields, for they are, indeed, a worse problem than the foxes. The liebre does more effective damage than worms as it only appears nocturnally, making it difficult for us to detect and combat it. It's an intelligent animal, with a powerful sense of smell, that will wait several weeks after chemical spraying before returning to our fields. Another problem with folilol is that some farmers who used it experienced dizziness, headaches, and stomach pains due to its toxic qualities."

"We have had our share of environmental problems and are anxious to find better alternatives," Jaime Alba said at the meeting. "But right now we use chemicals to protect our crops since otherwise our quinoa would be destroyed, leaving us without this source of income. But don't forget about all the hard washing that is done to remove the zaponins from our quinoa grains. I imagine that the process does a good job of removing the pesticides as well."

CERTIFIED ORGANIC QUINOA EXPORTS, 1995–1997

Two and a half years later, I received another update from CECAOT leaders and Jaime Alba on their commercial progress. Although efforts to industrialize their product had not added up to much despite aid from an IDB-financed industrial engineer, they had figured out profitable ways to market quinoa grain. Most of their member farmers had adopted organic production techniques, in addition to their traditional collective practice of fertilization with compost made from llama dung. Some 7,000 ha. of quinoa was now being produced in the zone compared to the 500 ha. or so for subsistence when the small farmers' revitalization movement began twenty years earlier. Justo Mamani, the current CECAOT president, updated me. "We have been able to find buyers in Germany and Holland, in addition to the Quinoa Corporation in the United States, and last year the total value of our sales abroad climbed to $380,000. Sales should be pushing

$500,000 this year, as a Japanese firm is preparing to make orders. In addition to these new markets, we have instituted a new organic policy. We have ordered our members to stop using folilol on their plants and this year we will be using a non-toxic natural insecticide produced by the University in Cochabamba from the flower of the pireto plant that grows all over the highlands. Actually insects had become resistant to folilol so substitutes were needed for that reason as well. The vast majority of our 500 producers have complied with the new organic emphasis, including soil conservation practices in planting and harvesting.[5] An international firm came to inspect our farms in Nor Lipez and, after observing the recent changes and the absence of chemical fertilizer use, certified us as bona fide 'international organic producers,' precisely the guarantee needed to attract more clients from the growing world health food market."

It was no wonder that farmers were willing to make this switch in technology since prices had continued to climb since the early 1990s, and by 1997 quinoa had become the most expensive grain per pound on the world market as European and United States demand now greatly exceeded supply. The only drawback to this amazing rise was that it had become increasingly expensive for many lower income Bolivians. Yet subsidized school breakfast programs using products such as El Ceibo's "Quinu Coa" were designed to offset this problem for consumers, especially the most vulnerable.

CHALLENGES AHEAD

Quinoa's incursion into the organic food stores of the First World has not been an entirely gold-plated affair for ANAPQUI's and CECAOT's Quechua and Aymara farmers. Low yields which are related in part to the periodic low rainfall of Nor Lipez and adjacent altiplano provinces conspire to keep peasant earnings from skyrocketing with the new world prices. And in 1996 and 1997, no doubt because of quinoa's impressive international price and its promise as a super source of nutrition for the twenty-first century, a new U.S. quinoa variety based on a Bolivian variety from near Lake Titicaca became patented in the United States under the Plant Variety Patent Act. The seed was patented under the names of two Colorado State University agricultural scientists who had worked for over ten years on the altiplano with Bolivian government researchers.

The public disclosure of the quinoa patent triggered a storm of nationalistic protest from the Bolivian government, the two quinoa growers' associations CECAOT and ANAPQUI, the Bolivian media, and from the U.S. activist organization RAFI (Rural Advancement Foundation International) opposing the application of intellectual property rights law to food crops such as quinoa. Although the Bolivian government moved to require official authorization for removing quinoa seed from Bolivia, most was already leaving the country for Peru and Chile over contraband trails—a problem still to be tackled. Nevertheless, the government measure had significant symbolic value for its official expression of nationalistic sentiment for the value of the country's biological and cultural resources, and allying the state with small-scale Aymara and Quechua altiplano producers.

It was a rude awakening for Jaime Alba and CECAOT's current president, Juan Copa Lupa, to find that Western patent law failed to recognize indigenous communities involved in the genetic manipulation of quinoa seeds over thousands of years, while protecting individual innovators and private corporations. With anxiety levels rising, Lupa quickly fired off a plea to Colorado State's patent holders stating, "The producers of quinoa real would like to manifest our profound concern of the unfair appropriation of the quinoa (apelawa variety), the millenarian grain cultivated for more than 1,500 years. We consider this patent to be a theft of our national patrimony, and as a result we producers are alarmed and aware of what is going on."

Then in a second letter co-signed with the ANAPQUI federation they made their appeal again. "In the name of thousands of small poor Bolivian Andean farmers who survive as quinoa growers and exporters, we ask you to drop and withdraw the Apelewa quinoa patent claim as utility patent because it ignores the 'prior art' of traditional quinoa breeders in the Bolivian Andean region." A year later, under pressure from the U.S. Department of Agriculture financing their quinoa research, the Colorado owners did just that—they failed to refinance their patent claim. The quinoa grower federations were overjoyed and RAFI declared a precedent-setting triumph for the small farmers of the world in protecting their basic collective rights to agricultural seed. The key to this decision by the U.S. Department of Agriculture appeared to be the world publicity campaign generated by RAFI and the indigenous allies over the Internet about the injustices of the patent. The Internet uproar included a back and forth exchange between RAFI activists and the Colorado State researchers and reported on a tribunal on indigenous rights organized in New York to judge the ethical implications of the patenting by these scientists.

Although the new U.S. patented quinoa variety was not suitable for commercial marketing, it just might serve as a powerful precedent spurring other scientists and corporations to do the same.

Yet the two producer associations will have to remain ever vigilant. As one of the former patent-holders, Dwayne Johnson of Colorado State, told me by phone, Canadians have eyed vast prairies in Ottawa and Alberta provinces for future large-scale quinoa production. Yet Johnson is the first to admit that U.S. and Canadian conditions lack the short daylight conditions of Nor Lipez and thus the experiments with the quinoa real varieties have produced quinoa only half the size of what can be produced in the southern altiplano. Thus it is not surprising that the U.S. quinoa production covers only about 2 to 3 percent of the growing national consumption in the United States.

The Inauguration of a New Debittering Plant

In November 1997, CECAOT brought together several hundred members with government officials and foreign dignitaries to inaugurate a new technology for debittering its quinoa. The new machine, which used dryers as opposed to the old rinsing machines, *promised* once and for all to remove 100 percent of the zaponins. This locally designed technology, commissioned by CECAOT, had the same design of looping metallic tubes and attached chambers, but on a much greater scale. CECAOT president, Juan Lupa, happily announced in his speech that the quinoa-debittering process that used to take fifteen to twenty days to fill a container for shipment, because of the hand labor involved, now could be done in a week. Not only would the machine drastically cut processing costs, but it would enable them to market much larger quantities of quinoa and enhance their global competitiveness. He reiterated that this technology was the answer to their prayers and represented many years of single-minded pursuit of a coveted machine.

At the event, the co-operative also distributed a special edition of *El Socio,* the first issue of the newsletter in over ten years. Once simply a mimeographed newsletter run off in a back room at the local parish, its current glossy magazine format was eye-catching, with handsome color photos, illustrations, and smartly designed maps and charts. The special edition was dedicated to Jaime for his many years of selfless service to the Nor Lipez communities. Two large, close-up photo images of quinoa plants with yellow seedheads stood out on the cover along with the following poem highlighted in large, bold letters.

> Quinoa Real, the Golden Grain,
> I am the genuine Queen of the quinoas
> and the envy of other Queens,
> as I am truly unique, organic, and Bolivian.

And, by the way, I am also the highest priced grain on the world market!

CHAPTER 8

Grassroots Development Trekking with Alpacas, Llamas, and Ayllus

The 16th century Spanish chronicler repeatedly referred to the Aymara llama herders
as the wealthiest and most numerous of Andean highlanders.

JOHN MURRA

Two Tours of Pacajes

Pacajes province, hugging the mountainous Bolivia-Chile border, is a remote region of dry, earth-colored rangelands interspersed with small extensions of the precious wetlands called *bofedales*. On rides through its immense, intermittent grassland, a traveler passes scattered flocks of sheep and camelids, but only occasionally comes abreast an adobe hut or a woman with black braids, striped shawl, and bowler hat. The area is sprinkled with herding people who raise two kinds of camelid livestock suited to the two kinds of terrain: llama for the dry pampas and alpaca for the moist bofedales, habitat found in this locale and only a few others such as a high-altitude area east of Lake Titicaca called Ulla Ulla.

When I first visited Wariscata in 1979, the tiny village of mud and straw huts located in the heart of the region, the herding communities of Pacajes were in a desperate state and the IAF had been funding some start-up activities to begin turning things around.

At the high altitudes of the region, the land is too frost-prone for agriculture, so the local Aymara people have long pursued a way of life centered around the alpacas they raise for fleece and the llamas they raise for meat, some fiber, hides, and for their service as beasts of burden. These hardy animals have the virtue of being able to carry heavy loads and travel long distances on little water and scanty meals of the scrub vegetation.

At the time I visited, however, the herders were eking out a meager annual income of about $800 (Hale 1981), gained by selling some of their camelid products through commercial middlemen at nearby rural fairs and consuming the rest. In recent years, the herders had adopted the practice of shearing their livestock only every other year because they benefited so little from doing so, and men from local families were spending up to three quarters of the year on the road in search of jobs to supplement their extremely low incomes. The herders had no political representation for their camelid interests in the capital city and were plagued by marketing problems, animal diseases, and overgrazing.

A History of Camelid Herding

Camelid herding has a long history, related to me by Max Paredes, a balding, round-faced man in his forties, one of the advisors to the camelid herders' organization applying to the IAF for funding. During the time of the Incas, local alpaca fiber was used to make super-fine textiles to outfit Inca royalty. The llama, too, was invaluable. Llamas kept Incan soldiers fed with a high-protein diet combining dried llama meat called *charqui* (jerky) with quinoa and chuño, and llamas were indispensable for transporting goods along the Incan road system that stretched from Colombia to southern Bolivia. Their dung was essential as fertilizer for farming potatoes, quinoa, and other crops. In addition, the llama had important ritual functions, llama sacrifice being a central part of ceremonies to secure good harvests or success on the battlefield. Like the Aymara of today, the Incan rulers preferred white llamas for ritual sacrifices.

"An example of llama ritual still practiced around here is the *enfloramiento* of the llama," Max said. "This fertility rite takes place in December and January, when the first offspring are born. During the night, the llamas are led into a specially constructed corral. One of them is killed and its blood is sprinkled around for the mountain spirits in places where llamas are abundant. One by one, community members attach flowers and other decorations to the ears of the female llamas and proceed to honor them by throwing confetti and colorful streamers into the air around them. The new offspring are feted through libations throughout the day to bring plentiful reproduction. In many mountain communities in Bolivia, llama fetuses continue to be used symbolically in earth shrines, and intestines are used by shamans to diagnose illness.

"Discrimination against camelids began with the Spanish conquest of the Andes. The Catholic Church often prohibited the sale of llama meat in the markets in order to reduce its availability for Andean religious practices. The Spanish authorities, on the other hand, placed restrictions on its sale as a way to protect sales of livestock imported to the Andes from Europe. This European discrimination against llamas and alpacas and their herders has left a damaging legacy for today's native peoples and displaced this livestock with sheep and cattle over vast grazing areas, especially at lower mountain altitudes.

"But just how do you think those Spaniards got their ore from the world's biggest silver mine on the high Andean slopes to the coastal ports of South America for shipment to Spain? And how were the basic goods transported to the growing Andean cities revolving around the mining economy?"

In spite of the discrimination spawned by Europeans, Max said, the people of Pacajes had maintained a struggling but continuous herding economy until the middle of the twentieth century. Llamas were used for meat and the transport of goods across the mountains for bartering, and alpaca wool was spun for family use and for low-paying markets, including contraband and some export.

Then in the 1960s, the llama's economic value began to fall precipitously again with the opening of roads as trucks began hauling to other regions what llamas had traditionally transported. This had occurred previously in the nineteenth century when railroads replaced ancient llama routes. At the time of my 1979 visit, the herders' way of life was under threat and migration to the cities was growing.

The Four Main Obstacles

Four main problems prevented the herders from turning their animals into a decent livelihood: legal restrictions on the sale of llama meat, marketing problems with respect to alpaca fiber, widespread sickness in the livestock, and a vast problem of overgrazing. In 1979, long-standing governmental prohibitions on the sale of llama meat were a major problem for the people of Pacajes. Although a taste for llama meat was spreading as more indigenous people moved to the cities taking their food habits with them, governmental officials refused to legally permit its sale. Maintaining the prejudices of their colonial forebears, the middle classes of Bolivia deemed llama meat "cheap poor man's food," or even worse, "Indian food more suitable for dogs than humans." They had also spread the notion that the consumption of llama meat was a public health risk since the meat sometimes contained cystercercosis. At the same time they failed to sound the same alarm bells when sheep or swine were found to carry the disease. These governmental policies foreclosed an appreciation of the llama's high protein content and contributed to very low prices and declining herder incomes.

The marketing of the herders' alpaca fiber was also problematic. Much of the fiber trade took place at rural fairs using currencies from three different countries. A government marketing board, INFOL, financed by USAID in the 1970s ostensibly to help channel alpaca fiber to the market, had failed in supporting the herders' interests.[1] The government built the country's first alpaca fiber processing plant in Pucalpa, Potosí, using machinery from the early 1900s. The location was peculiar because it was 400 kilometers south over unpaved roads from the two principal production areas of Cochabamba and La Paz and the main artisan markets. And through the outlet of the local fairs, most alpaca fiber produced in the region (often secretively mixed with the more abundant Bolivian llama hair) crossed the border as contraband for Peru's large alpaca export industries. Peru had been exporting alpaca fiber since the middle of the nineteenth century, thereby providing a large market for Bolivian production as well. Yet leaving the country as contraband and as unprocessed raw material meant that the herders were receiving only a pittance. It was very similar to the way quinoa leaked out of the Bolivian altiplano economy to benefit Peruvian private sector interests.

In addition to the meat and fiber-marketing challenges, the herders of Pacajes had to contend with an enormous overgrazing problem. The whole Pacajes region had been overpopulated with sheep as well as llamas and alpacas. The key to Incan management of large camelid herds had been the maintenance and conservation of vast rangelands of tall native pastures. According to Dr. Armando Cardozo, an animal scientist and our chief authority on the subject, when these pastures had been tended by the Incas, they supported a population of 23 million camelids across the Andean empire, an area that can support only 3 million head of the same species today.

Phil Blair, an American anthropologist and the International Volunteer Services (IVS) director in Bolivia working with the herders' organization AIGACAA, railed to me about the devastating impact sheep had had on the Pacajes prairies. "It was a huge mistake to ever multiply the size of sheep herds and attempt to improve livestock quality through introducing breeds with such voracious appetites and trying to cross-breed them with criollo stock in the altiplano. It's true that sheep reproduce at a much faster rate than camelids and offer practical benefits of homespun clothing, animal dung, and meat, but in environmental terms, the North Americans have done a great disservice to the Andean ecosystem by thinking they could replicate sheep raising from the American West. The hooves of sheep dig into the soil much like a bunch of nails would. Sheep tend to forage by digging down into the plant's roots and the bigger and better imported stock did this more destructively than the adapted criollo animals. This loosens the topsoil, readying it for wind erosion and eventual desertification. Camelids, by contrast, are easier on the plant life here. They're browsers, rather than grazers, and have hooves with a soft sponge-like surface."

The fourth big problem the Pacajes herders faced was that of disease. The llamas and alpacas suffered from worms, fleas, ticks, alpaca fever, diarrhea, and hoof and mouth disease. A tick called *sarna* brought by sheep had infested the herds. By burrowing under skin layers, this tick seriously debilitates animals, stunting their growth. For a while, the herders had an effective remedy against the tick. They used smoke to penetrate the llamas' skin and kill the parasite. The treatment took place in a highly ritualized ceremony where llamas would walk in circles to flute music inside a corral filled with smoke. Sadly, there is some evidence that the spread of Protestant evangelical religious structures succeeded in rooting out this important ritual practice. At the time I visited in 1979, camelid offspring were dying from parasites and diseases at the rate of 40 percent a year, according to some sources.

In addition to the four particular challenges, there was no coherent national public policy or significant foreign aid program aimed at promoting camelid production and health. For example, as recently as the early 1970s, it was hard to find any Bolivian veterinarians who specialized in camelids.

On a 1995 trip, the plains of Pacajes presented a different picture. On that trip I toured a camelid genetic improvement center, the only one in the country under the control of farmers' organizations themselves. I observed a veterinarian from a local community as he vaccinated scores of alpacas in a campaign to improve the health of local stock. I looked out over newly fenced bofedales filled with grazing alpacas—enclosures that maintained normal carrying capacity, enabled natural vegetation to grow back, and protected the precious wetland from overgrazing. Herders were receiving technical assistance from their community members who had taken specialized training in Peruvian universities. I visited the first Bolivian llama meat slaughterhouse and toured a factory owned by the herders that produced processed fiber from Pacajes alpacas for export to Italy. Most important, a Bolivian university and an NGO had initiated a publicity campaign to promote the consumption of llama meat and favorable local policies had been established with regard to meat inspection and sales. In tandem with these feats, a recent project evaluation indicated that due to the services provided by AIGACAA the gross monthly incomes of the herders had climbed from $83 to $146 per family, a figure that meant more and better food, medicine, clothing, and school supplies for needy herder families.

This flourishing scene of camelid development took root back in the mid-1970s with the work of Max Paredes and Luis Ticona, Aymara Kataristas, from El Centro de Coordinación Campesino MINKA, the country's first indigenous NGO. MINKA had emerged in 1971 as an independent cultural institution bent on giving an indigenous cultural focus to rural development programs and bolstering the cultural pride and self-esteem of Aymara now living in the capital. It was among the three parties signing the Manifesto de Tihuanaco in 1973. To conceptualize and outline its strategy, these social activists joined forces with Phil Blair, an anthropologist steeped in Andean studies literature from Cornell University and subsequently his assistant at IVS, Charles Hale, an anthropology student from Harvard. None of them could have imagined how long it would take.

The story of the herders of Pacajes is one of tenacity, struggle, determination, and burgeoning political awareness, as well as of the gradual strengthening of a grassroots organization. None of the dramatic changes could have been accomplished without the energetic actions of the local altiplano Aymara herders who formed Asociación Integral de Ganaderos de Camélidos de los Andes Altos (AIGACAA) (the Integral Association of Camelid Herders of the High Andes).

AYLLUS

I learned about the local ayllu organization from Charles Hale, the young anthropologist. The Andean ayllu is an extended kinship and political structure made up of endogamous groups of families whose members choose their marriage partners among themselves. Each ayllu here has a central hamlet, a collection of buildings where gatherings, schooling, and organizational meetings occur and where the regular market takes place. While no one lives permanently in the hamlet dwellings themselves, each herder has another hut on his *estancia,* near the land owned and inhabited by extended family members. The members of an ayllu rotate their leadership and share an active ritual life together engaging in ancestor worship, despite increasing influences from evangelical sects.[2] Other Andeanists, too, have pointed out how the whole structure, symbolism, and practices revolving around the ayllu inculcate a collective sense of ethnic identity and closely associated territoriality. (Also see Rasnake 1988; Larson 1998.)

Yet across the southern Andes region, this indigenous organizational form has been reshaped in its practices as well as reduced in size during the past five hundred years. During recent decades, the pressure to modernize had weakened Pacajes ayllus. These Katarista activists hoped to rebuild and revitalize the Pacajes ayllus through creating a federated structure and giving them an important rural development role within the province. This was the first time I had ever seen or heard of a rural development organization placing the ayllu at the core of its management scheme and I was fascinated by this innovative strategy.

When Luis Ticona and Max Paredes, the MINKA advisors to AIGA-CAA, began to promote the idea of a camelid improvement project they traveled to all the ayllus within a forty-mile radius of Wariscata and put together programs on Aymara language radio stations for a rural and urban audience celebrating the multiple cultural, social, and economic values of these native Andean resources. The IAF had supported them in this through a three-year project grant in 1974 worth $100,000, one of its three first grants in Bolivia. Community organizing and credit programs for other altiplano project zones were covered by the grant as well. In these scattered communities, they convened small group sessions among the herding families to analyze local development problems and explore together possibilities for applying some innovative strategies for socioeconomic change. They emphasized that if the herders united as a federation of ayllus, they could forward petitions directly to the highest levels of government. This had never been done in relation to herders' interests before in the altiplano, but the white and mestizo cattle ranchers from the eastern lowlands had united in this way with great success.

Many years later, Bill Gschwend, a North American from the Washington, D.C., development agency Appropriate Technology Incorporated (ATI), described for me the assembly system of decision making employed by the ayllu-based herders' federation. "The assembly I visited was made up of about 120 male and female delegates from communities of the two regions [by this time herders from a second region had joined the association]. My immediate impression of the assembly was of an open, democratic organization that genuinely represented the affiliated ayllus and communities. The fact that the organization rotated its board of directors on an annual basis meant they had a broad-based cadre, with leadership experience in many communities. The elected delegates participated in deliberations into the evening, and then they slept, shoulder to shoulder, in the room where they had debated all day. I was especially pleased to see that there were women delegates in attendance, and that members were comfortable airing criticisms of their leaders—both, in my mind, signs of a healthy organization. Having been given complete access to their financial records, I found every single penny accounted for, albeit by a very rudimentary, hand-written, accounting system.

"A change in leadership took place right after the assembly I observed so that I was able to watch the transfer of the inventory to the new leadership as it took place over the course of an entire day. They're really bean counters. I stood by watching them count all the yarn in stock, itemize it, and then proceed to do the same for the number of animal syringes. At the end of the process, the new president signed for it all."

TWO ALTIPLANO VISIONARIES

Both Max and Luis, the two advisors to the herders' organization, grew up in Aymara farming and herding communities. Max, a man with a receding hairline and a gruff, authoritative voice, was raised in the herding community of Charana. "At no point when I was young did I consider devoting my life to herding. I was looking for a way to escape the poverty of my parents, and I saw school as a gateway to a different kind of future. I was the first in my family to receive an education, when I completed junior high.

"When I left home I first joined relatives and friends who were clearing land and building farms and homesteads in the Alto Beni where the community was growing cacao trees. After a while the tropical temperatures and insects proved unbearable for me. I was used to a mountain climate and wide open spaces. For several years, I traveled back and forth between my altiplano home and the Alto Beni until one time, on my return from a lengthy altiplano visit, I found new settlers squatting on my Alto Beni lands. That was the final frustration, so I decided to return to the highlands and find a career there, hopefully working with rural communities.

"My university became the numerous training courses and rural development experiences I had as part of my work with SNDC, whose staff I joined in 1960. At first, I chose not to work in herding communities, as 'no one can be a prophet in his own homeland,' and between 1965 and 1975, I held a variety of assignments as community development trainer and zonal director within SNDC. Then, by the time MINKA received IAF support in 1975 to conduct developmental activities in the countryside, I had become anxious to return to herding communities like those in which I had grown up, so I landed the assignment in Pacajes."

Max's partner, Luis Ticona, served initially as the accountant and bookkeeper of the herders' project being established in Pacajes. A younger man with thick black hair combed neatly to one side, he described, with quiet conviction, his devotion to the development of rural communities.

"I grew up in the province of Ingavi only forty minutes' drive from the Bolivian capital. For the first six years of my life, I observed how my parents worked like dogs for their land-owning patron from sunup to sundown. Sometimes I would accompany my mother or aunt to the patron's family in the big hacienda house where Indians waited on them hand and foot. This struck me as totally unfair. Also, from the time I was about six years old, I remember being conscious of secret nightly meetings held in the outbuildings of the hacienda. These, I later learned, were clandestine organizations preparing Bolivia's social revolution. I have a vague recollection, too, of the excitement that spread through our community when we received the news of the defeat of the army by miners and Indian peasant militias, and of the exodus of the landlords from their haciendas. Everyone began seizing control of the rich families' lands.

"Thanks to those changes, a new school was built in our village and I became the first in my family to learn to read and write in Spanish. I received my first three years of schooling in my community and the remainder in the nearby town of Viacha. Though we received a basic education, the school inculcated little pride and understanding of our own cultural heritage and history as Aymara peoples. Pictures of llamas would appear in our schoolbooks without acknowledging their many contributions to national life.

"I was recruited right out of junior high in Viacha by SNDC for a job as a community promoter. Apparently an SNDC regional chief knew somebody in my home community who recommended me. After holding several supervisory positions there in rural community work, I moved to the capital city to finish high school in a special weekend program, while simultaneously working as the coordinator of a rural youth program right out of the Presidential Palace. During this time, I took some accounting courses and meetings and while in La Paz discovered MINKA which helped to shape my strong convictions about our Aymara cultural values and the importance of our ethnic identity."

As staff members at MINKA and as Pacajes natives well acquainted with the plight of the herding communities, Max and Luis put forth the idea of starting a program to help the Aymara herders rescue the country's undervalued llamas and alpacas. Specifically, their goals, and those of the herders, were to confront legal barriers to the sale of llama meat; to add value to raw alpaca fiber by obtaining their own industrial machines that would enable the herders to spin wool and knit sweaters and other products that could be sold for good prices; to start a program of rangeland conservation; to attack the problem of disease by bringing in experienced Peruvian veterinarians; and to promote a national agenda that would support the raising of camelid livestock and boost the altiplano herding economy. Yet at the same time they had to proceed cautiously in view of the military's hostility toward grassroots organizations aiming to shake up the status quo.

As Max said, "MINKA has given us hope that we can work more effectively being independent of the government and that the future holds some solutions to our problems, and has given us a sense that our Aymara culture is worth something. The name of our project is 'Projecto Anallachi', after a high mountain peak in the project zone. By naming it this we hope at last to call attention to the strength of our people, native organizations, and camelid-raising technologies."

AIGACAA'S proposal to revitalize llama and alpaca herding through management by the democratic Andean ayllu system quickly impressed me as an innovative and viable altiplano development strategy. Also, I had seen ample evidence that the herders were hard-working people committed to improving their economic lot. I had determined to write up a proposal to support funding for the group until I learned that MINKA had already submitted a proposal to the Small Projects Fund of the Inter-American Development Bank for a highly subsidized loan worth $500,000. They were requesting another $300,000 from the IAF for equipment, salaries, vehicles, and training materials to help expand their service program even further. Hearing this, my "overfunding" radar immediately went up. The project seemed too new to make good use of $800,000 at this time. Negative experiences with other projects in the IAF's early years in Bolivia made me wary of the hazards of overfunding. Wasteful expenditures, corruption of managers, organizational splits, and petty jealousies often were the results when large amounts of capital suddenly poured into the hands of inexperienced administrators and organizations in poor communities. A strategy to scale up in an accelerated fashion just when the new federation was getting on its feet seemed to me unwise and premature.

After my visit in 1979, I shared my enthusiasm for the project with Max and Luis. I told them I admired what they were doing on behalf of camelids and ayllus, but I brought up my concerns about overfunding to give them fair warning that the IAF might not be able to fund the proposal. This kind of situation—being crazy about the group and its goals but not its plan of action—was not unusual for a development funder. Normally, one could recommend scaling back to more manageable project tasks, but in this case the IDB interest appeared to have already set the financial parameters and its related scale of activities. When I returned to my home office, I sadly had to write a letter to Max rejecting this innovative project on the basis of its unrealistic pace and scale. I wished the herders luck with their start-up activities and with the application for IDB support and expressed a sincere interest in staying in touch.

AIGACCA meanwhile was able to move along with some support from PACT and the International Volunteer Services (IVS) which employed

Blair. Even without additional funding from the IAF, AIGACAA should have been on its way.

A Struggle for Survival

Two years later, in 1981, I received a copy of an evaluation of the AIGA-CAA project from Deborah Caro, an American anthropologist friend who specialized in altiplano herding communities.[3] There had been impressive organizational growth in AIGACAA over the past two years. The membership of the federation had grown from four to fourteen ayllus in just two years' time, but the well-heeled IDB-funded camelid project I had expected to find was nowhere to be seen. The project was having only minimal impact on a handful of herders in terms of infrastructure, veterinary services, and training. Critical, unsolved problems included the prolonged absences of the Peruvian vet and the huge size of the project zone, which now stretched over 1,000 square miles. But the primary reason for the minimal progress was a change in the Bolivian political context. The IDB loan had been held up because of a military coup and most Western foreign aid to the country had been frozen because of the government's brutality and involvement in drug trafficking. AIGACAA also had to keep a low profile because independent indigenous organizations were suspect in this repressive political climate.

Over the past two years, AIGACAA had found itself in the throes of a struggle for its own existence. Between 1982 and late 1984, AIGACAA's foreign aid support vanished. IVS, MINKA, and PACT had withdrawn to attend to their own institutional problems and decisions. Max had found a job with another Bolivian NGO, while Luis had taken a staff position with an international indigenous rights organization based in Peru that offered him a broader perspective on indigenous activism in the hemisphere.

During this period, AIGACAA's sole source of income was the small profit earned through the wholesaling of some of its members' raw alpaca fiber. Also in operation was a consumer products fund that enabled members to acquire dry goods at lower prices when they made bulk purchases.

Over those bleak years, there had been an alarming degree of decapitalization in the organization. In 1981 AIGACAA's treasury had had the equivalent value of 600 llamas. By 1983 the capital stock had been reduced to 100 llamas. Similarly, the consumer fund, based on the cash earned from fiber sales, could no longer cover the amounts of rice, sugar, and noodles needed in the communities. The organization was in such disarray that even the small public education campaign and the lobbying for municipal llama markets had ceased.

In this bedraggled, bare-bones condition, AIGACAA was hit by two additional major calamities. A searing drought decimated pasture lands and the herds that depended on them, and then an unprecedented level of hyperinflation was reached in the national economy. At this juncture, the existence of the fledgling herders' organization was sorely tested.

During this period, the organization did do what it could to address the herders' problems on almost nonexistent funding. While the delay in funding did, on the one hand, curtail the organization's immediate progress on a number of fronts, on the other, it allowed the herders' federation to pull itself together and clarify its goals before the funds actually hit the coffers. I have found that sometimes a delay in funding can actually strengthen a grassroots organization, forcing it to rely on its own resources and to bring its strengths to the fore. In this case, AIGACAA floundered for a while, yet made considerable progress: addressing legal barriers to its products, providing practical training to its members, and taking its future into its own hands.

At the height of the national economic chaos of 1983, Luis Ticona returned to Bolivia and was approached by AIGACAA's leaders to resume his work with them. An IDB loan looked more likely as Bolivia had returned to civilian democratic rule. Luis reported on this phase in AIGACAA'S efforts.

"I hate to think what might have happened to the organization without the hope and eventual reality of the IDB loan. This possibility kept us persevering in the hope that we really could recover from all these crises. At the time, I thought to myself, 'too much has been invested in building up AIGACAA and providing the communities with important services to let it all go down the drain.'"

When the funders first pulled out of the zone, PACT, AIGACAA's donor agency, reprogrammed its remaining funds and sent a dozen herders for practical training in livestock management practices, animal health, and fiber shearing, and three others with high school backgrounds for academic training in veterinary medicine to the Universidad del Altiplano in Puno, Peru, located on the other side of Lake Titicaca. The dean of this veterinary school, Dr. Victor Bustinza, was one of the most widely published scholars on camelids in the world and immediately took a liking to

AIGACAA, facilitating its breakthroughs for many years to come. As one leader remarked, "Disillusioned by the Peruvian vet's lack of commitment to our zone, we had to take the bull by the horns and get our own Aymara herders trained so that our fortunes did not hang on professionals with a city mentality."

BOLIVIA'S FIRST LLAMA LOBBY

During these very precarious years, the herders' federation made remarkable inroads. In effect, it created a new Bolivian interest group. Several AIGA-CAA leaders decided that the moment had come to begin acting as a pressure group in the capital city in order to place the interests and needs of the herders on the public agenda. Luis reported, "It might have seemed an inappropriate political moment to press our agenda in view of the conservative outlook of the current military government. But when the military leaders announced a policy to push national products, and gave the example of using homespun cloth for outfitting soldiers, we decided that this was our opening to press for legal llama meat markets in the city. Our badgering of the under-secretary in the Ministry of Agriculture and Peasant Affairs (MACA) led to the creation of a commission composed of officials from MACA, the Ministry of Health, and the National Meat Commission, as well as AIGACAA leaders, to conduct a study of the viability of llama meat markets. During the next year, our group systematically examined meat inspection standards and practices and conducted several experiments using llama meat. This study led to the production of an official document, 'Reglamento de Inspección Sanitaria e Higiene de La Carne de Camélidos Sudaméricanos' (Regulations for Sanitary and Hygiene Inspection of South American Camelid Meat) which spelled out the details and feasibility of a new law legalizing llama meat sales.

"The government officials cavalierly filed the report away, showing little interest in following up with the ratification of the new law that we recommended, and the Minister informed us of his concern that the llama might quickly become extinct if everyone in the cities began eating it. This was a real put down of the Aymara entrepreneurial spirit so I argued that the herders, like good capitalists everywhere, were not so foolish as to destroy an important income source.

"Despite the government's lack of commitment, at least we now had in our possession a technical document that outlined the way to open municipal markets while ensuring the maintenance of meat inspection and sanitary standards. It was advantageous to have a document we could use to publicly promote the opening of these markets."

In addition to the training and llama meat legislation efforts, the herders took action four years later, in 1987, to protect Bolivian llama markets from international competition. One day in El Alto they discovered that several hundred high-quality llamas were being moved into a large lot by a private firm readying them for export. After making inquiries at the Ministry of Hacienda, the herders learned that the firm had received a license to export live llamas to New Zealand and the United States. This was a break with the long-standing state policy of protecting the country's comparative advantage of holding llama germplasm from the extraordinary genetic diversity of its livestock. The herders' worry was that advanced technological societies could quickly surpass the Bolivians' level of camelid development by acquiring their best breeding animals. This concern could not be dismissed as mere paranoia on the part of the herders as Bolivia had lost its chinchilla to more powerful nations by just this route.

The herders immediately took action on several fronts. They publicly denounced the bribes to government officials that had lubricated these transactions and urged the new free market government carrying out the New Economic Policy (NEP) to support legal llama meat marketing within the country and, simultaneously, protect the diversity of altiplano livestock. The organization got good media coverage and influential people attended their consciousness-raising seminars. On another front, members of the federation made visits to other herding communities in the altiplano and enlisted their support. They also arranged for the country's top camelid scientist, Dr. Armando Cardozo, to hold a press conference and make the following statement, "The government's current policy will ultimately lead to the liquidation of a precious national treasure. Bolivia should be repopulating prairies instead of exporting our finest camelids. New Zealand, a country that also has extensive grasslands, is trying to become a world class llama producer, and it would be inadvisable for us to lose our competitive advantage" (*Presencia* 1991b).

Embarrassed by the negative press and fearful of additional repercussions in public opinion, the government now felt it had to do something for llamas. As the export deal was too lucrative and too far along to suspend, the government did not reverse the new export policy, but it did respond to the herders' demand that legal llama markets be opened up. Using the earlier document obtained by AIGACAA, the government ratified a resolution that legalized, for the first time in modern history, the sale of llama meat in Bolivian municipal markets. The new law stated, "Development and economic reactivation of the national economy must have as its priority the growth and diversification of rational uses for camelid meat. It is indispensable that conditions be established to promote camelid meat as a food resource, given its high level of protein in comparison to other meats used in the domestic economy."

"Despite this significant gain," Luis reported to me, "once again, when we pressed the high-level authorities to tell us when regulations would be established to operationalize the law, we were met with stony silence. Again, the government seemed unwilling to take the next logical step. While we now had a new document to carry around and read from in our public forums, we realized that legal llama marketing was still far from a reality."

Finally, toward the end of the three years of struggle, IDB funds were once more promised to the herders. Their arrival, however, continued to be delayed time and time again. I inquired about this delay years later to Ken Cole, the director of IDB's small projects division who liked offbeat projects. He explained, "In part the delays can be attributed to a large slow-moving bureaucracy, but other complications arose due to the bank's lack of experience with Indian organizations. Any mention of the word 'ayllus' during our project review meetings drew blank stares from my colleagues and doubts about AIGACAA'S capacity to manage the project."

Luis reported, "Even after the loan approval and the signing of the agreement in January 1984, we had to wait a good eight months for the first disbursement check to reach our Bolivian bank account. By this time AIGACAA was broke and unable to cover even my salary.

"To add to this institutional hardship, IDB wanted to see a full-fledged business office functioning in downtown La Paz. They needed assurances that we were more than some fly-by-night organization on the plains of Pacajes. To meet these requirements, I found a friend willing to loan us a room in a respectable office building in the middle of downtown La Paz. We kept extending the arrangement as time passed and the check had not arrived."

When I asked Luis how he had kept his staff afloat under such financially shaky circumstances, he threw his head back in laughter, "I had to do everything myself. I changed hats from chief administrator to secretary to messenger boy every few hours every day at work. My family was supported entirely from my wife's candy stand at a high school in the town of Viacha. Fortunately, we only had young children at that time."

Seizing the Reins

The long-awaited check from the IDB arrived in late 1984, yet its value eroded considerably from the continuing currency devaluation gyrations in the national economy. AIGACAA hired a veterinarian, an agronomist, and a director as project staff. The infusion of funds and the new hirings gave the project a spurt of energy, but challenges lay ahead. After only five months, complaints were surfacing in the herding communities regarding the professionals from La Paz selected by the IDB to manage the project. The professionals' long absences from the zone, the adulteration of the veterinary products offered to the herders, and the mysterious losses of large quantities of alpaca fiber were among the concerns of the herders. A consensus was growing in the assemblies that it would be better to replace this professional team with members from their own community trained in Peru.

Luis reported, "Finally, during the first months of 1986, the members asked the AIGACAA leadership to rectify this unsatisfactory situation. Our leaders made their move during a course on the use of microscopes for detecting parasites. The leaders burst into the room, confronted the members of the consultative team with a list of grievances about their job performances, and demanded their immediate resignations. The expressions on the faces of the professionals was one of complete shock. I don't think it had ever dawned on them that an Aymara herders' organization would rise up and fire them on the spot for lack of accountability. Of course, that's the way it's supposed to be when a producers' organization is truly in charge. The leaders simultaneously filed a petition in the IDB office in La Paz requesting the team's removal.

"It was only after IDB conceded to these changes in the project management team that I felt the project was finally under our own control. We could then move forward with trustworthy people accustomed to life on these rangelands."

In 1991 AIGACAA took a gigantic leap forward by signing an agreement for a 4.4 million dollar project, with the U.N. Office of Procurement Services (UNOPS) contributing $3,200,000 and the U.N. Development Program (UNDP) $700,000. It signed another for $444,000 from ATI. AIGACAA also added $83,000 of its own to the pot. These substantial funds, to be disbursed over a five-year period, were earmarked for alpaca genetic improvement, veterinary services, native pasture recovery, and machinery necessary for producing fiber TOPS—alpaca fiber that is washed, carded, and combed into cable fiber through a series of machines. The process ensures that each meter has the same weight and moisture and that the fibers are aligned and ready for industrial spinning. The fiber-processing factory alone cost $1.2 million dollars, with $300,000 for operating capital. ATI had been subcontracted by the UNDP within the loan agreement because of its experience in working with non-governmental organizations, something with which UNOPS had little experience. The first of these funds reached AIGACAA in January 1992, and at that point the leadership once again hired a staff. This time the hirings included twenty of their own member-technicians, trained through earlier project investments.

A caveat to the U.N. support was the creation of a private corporate entity parallel to AIGACAA for owning and managing the new industry. As Serapio Ramos, a Bolivian project leader reported, "At first this did not sit well with the herders, and they criticized the leaders for agreeing to a requirement that would transform them into corporate shareholders. 'Why can't AIGACAA itself assume ownership of these new assets for producing TOPS?' they asked. We explained that, according to Bolivian law, AIGACAA, as an 'association of producers', and thus, as distinct from a co-op, was prohibited from operating as a for-profit entity. Everyone agreed that a co-operative form of organization was inappropriate since nobody wanted to replace the ayllus with local co-ops, but the members had fears that open sale of stocks would risk takeover by well-heeled investors. The bylaws obliged each new herder to purchase one share worth $25, as well as a $25 initiation fee. The older members for the time being were exempt. An additional clause in the statutes required investors to match their stock purchases by adding an equal number of shares to AIGACAA's account. We explained that the enterprise would not displace AIGACAA, but work in parallel fashion and reinforce it by generating the income to sustain its multifaceted service program into the indefinite future. But convincing the members of these advantages has proved difficult. There are still many skeptics out there in the communities unenthusiastic about this wholly new type of organization."

Revisiting Pacajes in the Mid-1990s:
The Arrival of Services to Herding Communities

Through the years I heard positive reports from Luis and Max about the many changes for the herders that had occurred as a result of AIGACAA's efforts. In the mid-1990s, for instance, I received information that AIGA-CAA's membership rolls now had 1,000 members, which included Quechua-speaking peoples from other altiplano provinces. Two hundred herders from a failed World Bank project in Ulla Ulla, Bolivia's largest alpaca zone, had also joined. Also, over the past three years, the herders' gross monthly incomes had climbed from $83 to $146 per family.[4] Finally, in September 1995, I was able to visit Pacajes and see the changes for myself.

Serapio Ramos, director of the project's extension team, accompanied me on my journey from La Paz. Serapio was short and barrel-chested, with a very smooth, unlined face for someone in his fifties. Serapio's home community was in Nor Lipez, and one of his brothers belonged to CECAOT, the quinoa growers' organization with which I had worked, so I immediately felt I was with a kindred spirit. Serapio's parents had kept some 200 llamas during his childhood.

We set out from La Paz together in a landrover one early morning and found our roadway soaked and muddied from the night's rainfall. Much to my delight, the night's precipitation had left a white blanket of snow at the higher altitudes. Llama and alpaca herds were just starting their orderly, dignified march across the rangeland to winter pasture.

After three hours of driving, we made our first stop at a place misnamed "Calientes" (warm), the location of AIGACAA's genetic improvement center. The center had come to be acknowledged as the best of its kind in all of Bolivia, and its Aymara-style self-management added to its luster as a unique rural institution. The rank and file membership of AIGACAA had put strong pressure on Serapio to have the center up and running quickly, and he had acted accordingly.

We were soon greeted by the extension agent Francisco, who provided an outline of the genetic improvement program. "There are 210 female and

95 male alpacas in our program here at the center. These have been selected on the basis of color, absence of physical defects, height, and fineness of fiber. We monitor their mating and offspring carefully, and keep records on animals' birth rates, body weights, mating frequencies, coloration, and defects. By these methods, we are trying to increase the productivity of our livestock in terms of both quality and quantity of fiber per animal." Francisco was on a five-month assignment at this solitary outpost, he said, and was anxious to return to his ayllu to take advantage of the latest rise in fiber prices.

Francisco led us down the hill toward the corrals where black, white, and brown alpacas, separated into pens by color, stood staring at us. "It is the middle of the mating season," he explained, "so we rotate the male studs every fifteen days to keep them fresh. It takes about nine generations to breed in the composite traits we need. The matter is also complicated by the fact that alpacas and llamas have an eleven-month gestation period, longer than other types of livestock around here."

After our visit to the center, Serapio and I set off again across the vast rangeland. As we drove Serapio told me about a recent evaluation conducted by ATI. According to the report, the program had inserted 3,240 genetically improved animals into AIGACAA's members' herds the previous year, the total value of this increment to herding communities representing $123,000. The 450 herder credit recipients were amazed when the new alpaca offspring had so much thicker alpaca fiber, about 45 percent more. These were impressive statistics.

"Lots of other technical changes have taken place in our zone as well," Serapio continued. "We're rapidly introducing a shearing machine powered by a gasoline-operated motor to replace the use of scissors. Just ten years ago, mind you, we were coaxing the herders to use scissors as an improvement on broken glass or the sharp edge of a tin can. Using the new shearing equipment, we have recently been able to shear 4,600 additional animals, and contribute 21,000 pounds of new alpaca fiber to the regional market.

"The use of anti-parasite baths for combating sarna is also now a widespread practice among herders. Not long ago there were only four showers in the entire zone. We have also corrected our past practice of dipping our camelids before shearing. It took us a while to figure out that the benefits of anti-parasite treatments are enhanced when applied to a sheared animal. The reduced number of parasites also increases the amount of fiber per animal. The project has also added two field labs equipped for microscopic analysis of parasites which is the envy of government veterinarians."

Serapio reported that AIGACAA now had twelve extension agents working under his supervision at its credit program office. "Technical services administered by local people certainly have proven to work much better than those provided by professionals residing in the city."

On the next leg of our trip we stopped to observe alpacas grazing in one of the newly fenced-in bofedales. The midday sun had just melted the last of the snow left by the recent storm. The kelly green vegetative cover was as smooth as a carpet, with an intricate pattern of narrow water arteries trickling through it. "The native pastures here are mostly of the *festuca* strain," Serapio explained. He pointed toward a thola plant. "Look beneath that branch and you'll find another highly valued native species hidden there, shielded by nature from the cold. Protection of these pastures has been an important focus in our recent work.

"Sadly many bofedales in the project zone have been overgrazed and degraded by inadequate pasture management." He went on to explain that AIGACAA and its extension agents had given many talks about the importance of reducing the numbers of sheep in herders' flocks. It hadn't been easy, but an evaluation using a sample of 120 families belonging to AIGACAA showed that the percentage of sheep in local herds had been reduced from an average of 38 to 23 percent, a new trend pointing in the right direction.

"An equally important grazing problem has been the famous 'Law of the Commons.' The herders have few incentives not to graze common land. They think if they don't use the land others surely will. It's an irrational, competitive game in a situation of diminishing natural resources. The sound management structures of the time-tested ayllu on the Andean plains seemed to have broken down.

"Our credit system allows herders to fence in selected bofedales. This protects them from stray livestock and allows the wetlands to regain their normal carrying capacity. The fenced-in areas become a kind of reserve to be used during the dry season when good forage becomes scarce and by lactating mothers and recent offspring. Through the credit program financed by the Fondo de Desarrollo Campesino, over the past year we've been able to fence about 2,000 hectares. That is 2,000 hectares of good pasture land recovered. A main obstacle to this kind of progress is the hesitancy of some ayllu members to join the project for collective fencing. Not everyone here belongs to AIGACAA, and others simply fear credit programs for the risks involved due to the precarious weather conditions here. Indeed, three out of the last six years have brought close to drought conditions and decimated approximately 30 percent of the camelid livestock.

"On the whole, though, things are progressing well. Via loans that allow members to purchase breeding animals and erect fences, we have been able to increase the quantity of fiber per animal without overgrazing," Serapio said. "Also, according to a recent evaluation, the work of the veterinary extensionists has resulted in a reduction of camelid infant mortality from 40 to 28 percent [Olívares, Budinich, and Hyman 1996]. This is a significant income increase for our herding families."

We headed to our final destination for the day, the village of Wariscata, the center of project activities in Pacajes since the 1970s. On our way back across this vast rolling rangeland, Mt. Sajama, Bolivia's highest peak at 19,710 feet, was emerging slowly from behind a curtain of clouds. After another hour or so of driving, it stood before us in all its majesty and splendor like a giant mound of vanilla ice cream. Looking behind us for a final gaze at the immense pampascape, I could imagine no more spectacular setting.

Wariscata's appearance was little changed from the scattering of buildings I recalled from my first trip there sixteen years before. Once inside the project offices, though, I realized the once-bare rooms were now hives of activity. Piles of brown alpaca wool and cartons of microscopes and syringes for vaccination campaigns were crammed into the small space. Serapio asked a group of the extensionists gathered in the offices to join us for a brief conversation. The role of the extensionists was to maintain effective communication between the project team and the herders of AIGACAA. This was something I had had my doubts about in earlier incarnations of the project.

The scaling-up of membership in the herders' organization had seemed too fast to me at first and the challenges of maintaining communication among herders strung out over 1,000 square miles simply boggled the mind. At the same time, the ability to provide periodic training to herders, to implant a sense of ownership, and to instill a sense of commitment among herders to the larger interests of the AIGACAA membership were critical goals.

I now found that the extensionists, who zipped around the mountain ranges on motorbikes instead of bicycles and on foot, were able to meet with even remote herders on a regular basis. Somehow they were able to accomplish this even while tending to herds of their own and tapping into the credit financing to become "model herders." The commitment of these young extensionists was truly impressive.

Curious about how improved animals translated into hard cash for a poor herding family, I presented this question to the extensionists. They explained that family incomes had almost doubled, and since healthier camelids translated into less financial outlays for animal medicines, the net income gains were even higher.

One of the younger extensionists, Felix Chambi, said that most herders owned approximately sixty alpacas in addition to llamas and sheep, but that the determining factor in their ability to maintain a large herd was access to good quality bofedales. Roughly 10 percent had large herds with up to 300 alpacas. These better-off families fell into a group of local "elites," earning enough to own a second-hand truck and an urban lot in El Alto, the city on the plains above La Paz. The latter were assets toward which many herding families aspired, given the large amount of time they spent in the city and the higher status of city life. The project apparently had not yet enhanced economic income sufficiently to provide such luxuries to the majority nor to stem the temporary migration by men for employment outside the zone.

I was, once again, impressed by the enormous difference it makes for a grassroots development project when the local people themselves, both as members and mainline technicians, become the backbone of the project. It was precisely the project's commitment to training earlier in its history that had enabled AIGACAA to replace outside professionals with local herders and take control of the project. And it was probably the resilience and adaptability of the ayllus themselves that had prevented the organization from going under during its most stress-filled times.

LLAMA MEAT'S FRESH START

On this 1995 visit I asked Serapio to take a roundabout route to La Paz so that we could pass through the town of Turco and the city of Oruro, where a great deal of progress had been made toward the legal sale of llama meat.

Luis had explained the events that had led up to the change in the status of llama meat. In the early 1990s Chileans began smuggling large numbers of llamas out of the Bolivian altiplano to supply their recently built slaughterhouse in the coastal city of Arica. The Chilean government had begun fostering llama consumption in the northern part of the country due to shortages in supplies of Argentine beef. The effect of this policy was to create a market shortage in Bolivia and turn some heads about this under-appreciated "Indian food" so in demand by Chileans. I had learned from a Peruvian friend that in some retail outlets the Aymara Chileans who had taken over this business had to use whites as sales agents in order to "de-indigenize" their market transactions in this deeply racist society. At any rate, the event had so impressed an NGO based in Oruro, CONPAC, that it took up AIGACAA's twelve-year-old banner by initiating a llama meat consumption campaign and building a slaughterhouse in the rural town of Turco.

Turco, a town of no more than 200, was a jumble of walled adobe houses lined up along muddy pot-holed streets. We stopped in front of a pink, single-story building with a flat roof and large windows, Bolivia's very first slaughterhouse for llamas. This installation was probably the first of its kind in all of rural South America as until now the only llama slaughterhouses in existence were in urban areas of Chile.

Luciano Tapia, the plant manager, gave us a guided tour. Next to an office door, I noticed photographs illustrating the sequence of steps for slaughtering a llama. In the photos, the workers were wearing long, hooded coats and gloves while handling the carcasses—a testament to sanitary con-ditions rare in rural Bolivian towns. After a brief tour of the empty but spotless, white-tiled building, Luciano explained that the slaughterhouse operation was shut down because it was the off-season. The herders would not resume selling their animals for another two months. At this point, the operation's only charge was $.50 per animal slaughtered—a very low fee designed to promote the service. Herders could either sell to the slaughter-house directly or receive a cleaned carcass wrapped in plastic with the plant's inspection seal. In either case, the meat could be sent to Oruro for butcher-ing and legal sale.

"The reason we can sell the meat legally now," Luciano said, "is that we've received a temporary permit from the government. We have done everything to comply with its regulations: we put in a permanent water supply, we set the slaughterhouse physically apart from the town, and we are providing extensive documentation of our work. The total cost of the operation has been approximately $40,000. It works well because the own-ership resides jointly with the town and a herders' association to which many AIGACAA members belong.

"We have also been promoting our meat," Luciano said, pointing to a poster of a white llama under a big caption stating "La Carne de Mejor Calidad." Information underneath the photograph detailed the superiority of llama meat compared to other types of meat in terms of protein, fat, and other factors. At the very bottom, other big blue letters read, "Let's Learn To Consume Quality Over Quantity, Valuing The Best That We Have To Offer." Claims for the ability of llama meat to alleviate arthritis, high blood pressure, goiter, arteriosclerosis, rheumatism, and lung problems were listed below. "You'll see such posters all over Oruro," Luciano said. "Agronomy students at the university have taken the lead in our llama revalorization campaign. They have plastered them everywhere."

Luciano reported that the AIGACAA resolution engineered back in 1987, together with the work of CONPAC, were responsible for the fact that herders could now sell meat legally and have it slaughtered under safe, hygienic conditions. Prior to these changes, market women in Oruro hid their llama meat under outdoor stalls until nightfall when it could be clandestinely sold.[5]

Luciano then added, "Many urban people avoided llama because of the way it was slaughtered. Just picture llamas being slaughtered in corrals full of dung. And totally un-hygienic methods were used for bleeding the carcasses and conserving the meat. Then the carcasses had a long truck ride to Oruro during which they collected dust. Sometimes the meat would even decompose before arrival. Authorities should have upgraded these practices long ago.

"It is amazing, though, how fast people in Oruro are responding to the new publicity," Luciano said. "Before, the middle classes saw the llama at best simply as a beast of burden similar to the mule, with little to offer our diet. At worst, they wrongly saw it as a carrier of cysticercosis. There's a big confusion in the public mind between sarcoystiosis and cysticercosis. Sarcoystiosis is a llama meat parasite that is almost identical in appearance to cysticercosis, but harmless for humans."

We peered inside a small plastic drying shed for llama meat. "Charqui [jerky] is an incredible 56 percent protein and is one of the most popular dishes in Oruro," Luciano said. "Aside from giving the meat a wonderful taste, the sun drying also serves to kill any disease-producing parasites present in the meat. This was also one of the Incas' favorite ways to consume llama meat."

After this brief visit to the slaughterhouse, Serapio and I headed for Oruro two hours away. Oruro is a regional capital that grew up in tandem with the regional mining economy of the nineteenth century. During the last decade, however, tumbling mineral prices and the neo-liberal development model had caused the closure of state-owned mines. The combination of its economic deterioration, location in the center of herding country, absence of a large upper-class strata of whites, and perhaps less formidable prejudices toward lower-class Indians, made Oruro an easier target than the capital for an urban llama meat–marketing breakthrough.

During our drive, Serapio briefed me on other details regarding the llama's situation. "The transformation has been startling," he said. "Lately the price of llama meat has gone up because people now associate camelid raising with vets, health care programs, and low cholesterol. Prices have jumped from $30 to $100 for a llama weighing 60 kilos. Earlier, the lower classes consumed llama instead of beef because it was more affordable. Now it has become expensive for them, but other people have become llama meat consumers, and the herders are benefiting.

"There are also various amusing stories about clandestine sales of llama meat in Oruro. One small sausage factory was caught a few years ago sticking llama meat into its sausages. People had found odd its great success in undercutting competitors from regions with more pork than Oruro, and the municipal meat inspectors conducted a surprise investigation and discovered llama carcasses and cuts strewn all over the premises. They immediately ordered the place closed. Supposedly people had been eating llama meat for years without knowing it. Sometimes, I have my doubts about this assumption, though, and wonder if everybody did know and they were all participating in a big game."

After passing through the southern poorer section of Oruro where recent migrants lived in dilapidated houses amidst unpaved avenues, broken sidewalks, and open sewers, we started looking for Bolivia's first *frial* (butcher shop) for the sale of llama. It was hard to miss: a two-story cinder block building emblazoned with big pink letters saying "FRIAL SAN PEDRO, Carne de Camelids."

Inside, Serapio introduced me to Nicolas Mamani, a man probably in his mid-thirties, who stood behind a counter busily chopping up a llama carcass. Nicolas had a dark crew cut and was outfitted in the traditional white butcher's smock.

After shaking hands, I asked Nicolas when he came up with the idea to open the country's first butcher shop for llamas in the modern era. The notion had come to him about fourteen years ago, he said, while he was working in Buenos Aires. He was an undocumented worker at the time and used to hang around the market watching the butchers at work. It occurred to him that the work of a butcher was not that difficult, so he determined to become a butcher himself. He did so and worked in regular butcher shops for a long time, but he always had this idea in his head about llamas. He had just never felt the time was right to start up a llama butchery until recently. There had been just too much discrimination going on—and of course no slaughterhouse and no vets caring for the health of the animals. Passing the meat inspectors was also a big hurdle. Finally, COMPAC brought over a butcher from a Chilean llama slaughterhouse to train Nicholas, and an AIGACAA leader convinced him to open the business.

I asked how sales were doing. "On a good day, we're able to sell the equivalent of two llama carcasses," he said. "Filet of llama is our most deluxe, expensive item. I've been getting publicity through radio spots, and the middle class and poor alike have shown up, some to buy, others just to gawk. Some tell me they suspected the ads would turn out to be some kind of joke."

The cattle ranchers in eastern Bolivia had been spreading negative propaganda against the altiplano camelids for years, Nicholas said, in order to protect their markets. "It's amazing how effective they've been, and how strong the prejudices toward llama in the city have become. Take the case of my aunt, a migrant from the countryside living in a nearby barrio. When she returned to Turco's village fiestas after only a few years of living in Oruro, she would turn her nose up at plates of llama meat on the pretext of it 'making her sick.' I would take issue with her, insisting 'come on now, you grew up eating llama and enjoyed it all your life and now you've turned against it after only a short time in the city.'"

Nicolas reported that there were now ten llama meat saleswomen in the central enclosed marketplace. They had all shifted from mutton to llama meat because there was less competition. "Unlike us, however, they do not have any refrigeration facilities and cannot offer the fancy cuts you see here in our frial."

When Serapio and I resumed our bumpy journey to La Paz, I had a chance to examine an impressive undergraduate thesis written by Clare

Sammells about llama marketing in La Paz. The following passage perhaps described the past problems in Oruro as well.

> Disease has been one of the main structural supports to the symbolic edifice of the taboo against llama meat. In modern La Paz the belief that poor and indigenous people are dirty and unsanitary complements the perception that the foods most closely associated with them, such as llama meat, carry disease. Real parasites give concrete and visible grounds for upper-class white Paceños to avoid eating llama. (Sammells 1995, 28)

She went on to explain how these prejudices in the capital city led to wild exaggerations about meat diseases and health risks such as leprosy, syphilis, and tuberculosis for the consumer. These observations helped me to appreciate the very real progress being made in changing perceptions in Oruro.

BUILDING ALPACA FIBER MARKETS

In 1985, when funding finally got underway, the herders' organization was able to take action toward its goal of developing markets for alpaca fiber. During the next two years, AIGACAA gradually built up its alpaca fiber marketing fund through a series of disbursement checks from the IDB. Luis recounted, "Although the checks arrived devaluated from currency fluctuations, we were able to buy up an appreciable quantity of fiber for the first time. Even the giant export companies in Peru had to take notice of our expanded wholesaling and marketing role. By 1987, we were purchasing 67 percent of the alpaca fiber produced in the project zone, and our membership was experiencing a new sense of optimism. In addition, our barter-exchange system enabled us to make available low-priced sugar, salt, and cooking oil for wide distribution in member ayllus and communities.

"The marketing fund also injected new life into the lackluster wholesale centers we had previously set up in Wariscata and Oruro, by channeling much more fiber through them. Out on the pampas, our members mastered the skill of grading fiber according to its color, quality, fleece type, cleanness, and other details. Of course, there were always a few members who exploited this opportunity to embezzle funds or charge higher prices than allowed for personal profit, but AIGACAA's structures enabled us to be vigilant about these practices and make the necessary changes in personnel when required.

"We also strengthened our marketing in the capital city by constructing a wholesale warehouse center and office in an El Alto neighborhood. There, the fiber was graded once again, in a more refined fashion, and about half of it was shipped off to Cochabamba for washing and spinning by contract on rented industrial machines. The final processed fiber was then ready to be sold to artisan enterprises for clothing items and handicrafts for tourist markets.

"Yet no sooner had we begun to feel proud about this breakthrough, than we experienced, first-hand, the precarious nature of the Bolivian economy. We knew that Bolivia's fortunes with alpaca basically turned on the gyrations of the Peruvian economy next door, but it was brought home to us when alpaca fiber prices took a nose dive in 1988, the third year of the marketing fund's existence. Peru slid into a major economic crisis, sending huge quantities of alpaca fiber across the border as smuggled goods for private Bolivian export firms. The fall in prices took a great toll on the pocketbooks of our membership, as well as on those of herders from other altiplano regions. That year we were forced to withhold some ten tons of fiber from the market to cut our economic losses. The severity of the economic losses was discussed at length in AIGACAA's assemblies and the leadership arrived at a consensus to begin exploring export markets in Europe. At the same time, we acknowledged our lack of leverage and the power of the Peruvian export firms to monopolize these export relations. We were really at a loss for how the limitations might be overcome."

As though these were not enough woes, AIGACAA also had to sell off its two trucks, which were both losing money. In addition a Bolivian consultant hired by USAID to evaluate the organization for possible institutional grant support was so hostile and biased toward Aymara peoples that he concluded that the indigenous organization had little future and that Luis Ticona was an entrenched autocrat blocking its future development.

The answer to AIGACAA's difficulties appeared with the arrival of a North American development expert, Bill Gschwend. Bill was from a Midwest banking family and had a long career in international development. He was then representing ATI, which had a wealth of experiences in small-scale economic development and the use of innovative technology from a worldwide network.

Bill told me about his early contact with the herders. "Although I was very impressed with the ayllu-based organizational and assembly system, I found the project itself at a low point. The price of alpaca fiber was suffering and the government officials and foreign aid officers whom I interviewed had never heard of ATI, and had kind of soured on camelid projects, given what happened with the World Bank's camelid project fiasco in Ulla Ulla." In Ulla Ulla, $17 million had been invested in such items as a plant for spinning alpaca fiber, technical assistance, research centers, vehicles, and many other activities, and six or seven years later there was nothing to show for it in the participating herding communities. Many political interests and bureaucratic ambitions had interfered with the operations of this project.

"Luis and his cohorts became very interested in ATI's help," Bill went on. "It was obvious that, having broken the grip of the commercial middlemen on their communities, something had to be done now about the international middlemen. I told them that Ian Frazier, an ATI consultant who had worked for years at the international wool board in London, had advised me that there was a growing European market for alpaca TOPS. When I left Bolivia, I sensed that the leadership was on board, but that the rank and file Aymara could not quite believe that any of this would happen."

Luis and Bill made a trip to Italy to inspect used machinery for the plant and to begin nailing down the specific buyers and price agreements. Later Bill recounted to me how the experience had unfolded. "I've always said that to have a successful project you need a good project design and a good organization." He then beamed, "And of course, lots of luck." Fortunately for AIGACAA, all of those elements were present.

In late 1992, Luis and Bill contacted a German woman, Eva Scherney, to conduct an in-depth marketing study for the organization. Eva was a respected stylist in the fashion industry and in frequent contact with the Yves Laurents, Ferragamos, and Gucchis of the world. They were amazed by Eva's ability to give them chapter and verse about every respectable textile company in Europe.

"The comeback of the alpaca yarn market was one of the most interesting revelations," Bill said. "Twenty years earlier, Eva told us, acrylics had totally wiped out the alpaca fiber market for the fashion industry, but during the past eight years, the industries had begun using a range of fiber mixes in their products, uniting the warmth and the richness of animal fibers with the washability and durability of acrylics.

"Eva also gave us another wonderful piece of news. She showed us a textile magazine which revealed the emerging 'ecological trends' and said, 'you really ought to think twice about going for all white colors à la Peru.' This contradicted everything the Peruvians had told us about the commercial advisability of whitening our herds, the modernizing methodology in force since the 1930s. Fortunately, her words came in the nick of time as we were just about to close a deal to import 100 white alpaca breeding animals from Peru with our new project funds. Eva told us there was a market for other natural colors—blacks, browns, grays—which Peru had moved itself out of through its long-established whitening strategy. Another remarkable discovery was that Bolivian alpaca's fleece was of finer quality than that of the Peruvian alpaca, oddly because of their superior 'rusticity' from being raised in extremely harsh conditions."

Luis and Bill subsequently found themselves lunching with millionaire owners of some of the biggest spinning industries in Northern Italy. One such lunch companion had annual sales of alpaca, angora, and cashmere products worth more than the entire national budget of the Bolivian government. Disappointed with Peruvian exporters and attracted by high-quality fiber in natural colors from AIGACAA, the Italian buyers were soon in Bolivia inspecting the El Alto plant and its products.

These international negotiations led to a change in AIGACAA's TOPS prices from $7.10 a kilo to $15 within a year's time (and $18 for the highly prized baby fleece). Such prices represented a twofold increase in herders' income. A promising market for herders of the high Andes appeared to be the new reality.

In 1995, on my return to the Bolivian capital, I visited AIGACAA's headquarters and factory in the El Alto section of the city. The complex of buildings was enclosed by a large rust-colored gate decorated with paintings of white and black alpacas. Luis led me on a tour of the machinery that produced the processed TOPS that I had heard so much about. I watched interconnected processing machines stretching, carding, and washing alpaca fiber. Aymara women, wearing uniforms and plastic visors, were weighing bundles of gray, beige, and black fiber and stacking it in bales with plastic covers. At the very end of the line, tube-like strips resembling cotton candy wound automatically into round metal containers. Luis picked up a ball of fiber and had me feel the soft, uniform texture that had led to Italian sales worth $600,000 over the past year.

Back in Luis's office, I told him how impressed I was with the progress.

"Yes, it is wonderful. We're not only benefiting the herders in Pacajes, but herders from other areas are calling us and asking to join our organization. We've recently been approached by indigenous representatives of hundreds of llama herders in Potosí who raise the *tampuyi* llama, a very hairy animal capable of producing a kilo of fiber annually. Its fur has the fineness of alpaca fiber, but is not yet well known abroad. We have two million llamas in this country, and this type of llama may number as high as half that. We've examined de-hairing machinery for cashmere in Europe priced at a half a million dollars and think it could be adapted for de-hairing these llamas. We've also sent samples to Italy and England. Wouldn't it be spectacular to be able to develop markets for this llama fiber as well? Peru's worldwide image is associated with the 'Alpaca Look' marketing slogan on its product tags. We want Bolivia to do the same with llamas, cornering the world market and enjoying an international profile for our 'Llama Look'. That's one direction AIGACAA is heading these days.

"We're also planning to place a bid on the World Bank–financed fiber-spinning machinery which has been sitting for over a decade in dry dock. It's slated to be put on auction under the government's privatization campaign." Clearly, AIGACAA's dream of value–added alpaca products had come true.

Concluding Reflections from La Paz

"Yes, it has been a long haul," Luis said, leaning back in his executive chair at the end of my 1995 trip. "But a truly self-managed service enterprise is not something that can be done overnight. And, of course, the challenges and pitfalls are endless. The price of alpaca fiber has fallen once again, yet the value added from our TOPS product has enabled our members to remain solvent. Another problem is that the Peruvian smugglers are back at it again. Bankrolled by the alpaca export company, Mitchells, the Peruvians try to outbid our buyers in an effort to undercut our business. They need our fiber as Bolivia supplies roughly 20 percent of this raw material to Peru. They've blocked Peruvian herders from mounting their own spinning and TOPS factories, but we've broken into their control of the TOPS market abroad and they're trying to regain dominance. One of our ongoing tasks is to build awareness within our membership that accepting

the higher prices and other incentives offered by the Peruvians will ultimately work to the detriment of our new enterprise. Some still find this
concept puzzling. This problem is serious and might be the Achilles heel of
our whole strategy.

"Another problem we are confronting is that politically powerful private enterprises are setting up joint ventures with the World Bank Investors
Project to take advantage of the TOPS market. They can't stand to see a
bunch of herders out ahead of them exporting high-quality TOPS, and
they've begun complaining to the Minister of Finance about our so-called
unfair advantages." Luis handed me a letter from the "Camara de Exporta-
dores" (Chamber of Exporters) of La Paz addressed to the Ministry's under
secretary of public investment and international financing. It read:

> The international aid policies favoring market oriented productive pro-
> jects are causing distortions in Bolivia's foreign commerce, and contra-
> dicting the country's new GATT agreements. The same phenomenon
> taking place for the production and export of TOPS by COPROCA
> [the new corporation in lieu of AIGACAA] has occurred in relation to
> the subsectors producing quinoa and cacao. This type of competition is
> totally incompatible with the new free market agreements and progres-
> sive commercial directions underway in Bolivia. We are requesting that
> the Bolivian government redefine its foreign aid policies since they are
> conflicting with and undercutting our private sector initiatives. We
> have attached a letter from INCADEX, one of the members of our
> export group, and one of the most prominent chocolate industries in
> La Paz, indicating that the co-operative federation of El Ceibo which
> benefits from subsidized international prices recently has caused two
> private industries in La Paz to go out of business.

"Various letters of this type have been written to denounce us," Luis
said. "The guy who signed it is the head of the most influential export
group in the capital and owns Bonanzas, the largest Bolivian enterprise for
exporting crude alpaca fiber. I wrote my own letter to the minister pointing out that between 1988 and 1992 their exclusive club brought over 400
tons of Peruvian fiber into Bolivian markets to use for export and wreaked
havoc for the altiplano herders. We are lucky to have allies in the United
Nations and other branches of government. With those alliances, and our
own capacity to mobilize herders, we can offset these recriminations, but it

is frustrating to have to waste so much time in meetings defending ourselves from such complaints."

Later that week, I visited the offices of the branch of the Bolivian government that had given AIGACAA support. At the recently re-named
Ministry of Sustainable Development I located the director of the national
livestock program, Carlos Salinas, a professional veterinarian of Quechua
and Guaraní descent.

Carlos's thoughts about AIGACAA's work and the altiplano's camelids
were uniformly positive. "AIGACAA and Luis Ticona spearheaded the
movement toward change. Their efforts galvanized various leading animal
scientists, including myself, and led us to organize the 'Red Boliviana de
Producción de Camélidos' [a Bolivian network of camelid production].
The network brings together public and private entities to work toward the
promotion of camelid enterprises. We sponsor round tables, seminars, and
workshops to share information and analyze programs in relation to solving
problems and to influence government policy. All kinds of NGOs, federations, and government programs have gotten on the bandwagon with their
camelid development projects, so one of my office's important tasks is to
play a coordinating role. Environmentalists have also come aboard to support the recovery and protection of native altiplano pasture lands. I'd esti-
mate that there is approximately $20 million currently in the pipeline for
camelid development projects. We also support educational programs to
change public opinion about the exaggerated dangers of eating llama meat.
Oruro and Turko are, of course, leading the way, and hopefully we'll be
able to construct slaughterhouses in El Alto and La Paz where, reportedly,
some twenty tons of llama meat are sold daily. Some of the wealthiest families in this country have recently made investments in llama-raising farms
with an eye toward future profits.

"Our network recently sponsored the first camelid livestock fair in
Bolivia. Llamas were brought to the center of the capital city for the first
time. Gourmet dishes, such as llama lasagne, were on display, and later that
same week, the first recipe including llama meat appeared in a La Paz daily
newspaper. Llama meat dishes are now appearing in fancy La Paz restau-
rants and in television ads. Bolivian meat industries have shown interest in
exporting llama sausages, and the main nightly news broadcaster ate a dish
of llama sausage before a national viewing audience.

"I might add that we have terminated all our projects promoting sheep
raising on the altiplano and are trying to create incentives for the sheep

herders to diminish their numbers. The universities in Bolivia are also finally on this Andean bandwagon and producing thesis projects that offer much new information about camelid production."

I asked Carlos his position on the loss of invaluable germplasm by the export of live animals. "AIGACAA was right to oppose the indiscriminate export of some of our best genetic llama stock. At the same time, I think we can find a sound technical way to export high-grade animals while retaining the best genetic stock for ourselves. We have over 2,300,000 llamas in this country, which makes us, far and away, the world's leading producer. We should be able to export our llamas the way the United States exports its pedigreed Brown Swiss and Holstein cattle. By doing so we could both bring valuable foreign exchange into the country and provide the herders with another source of income. Did you know that Libya has sent delegations of businessmen here interested in purchasing llamas for building herds and supplying llama meat in Middle Eastern countries where red meat restrictions prevail?"

"As you can see from my remarks, the camelid revitalization movement is bringing big changes in our thinking about Bolivia's development path. For all too long we have taken our cues from outside the country, and believed only imported resources, technologies, and knowledge were the keys to Bolivia's national development. Big changes have taken place at the macro and micro levels to refashion that old perspective. It's as though somehow we are being born all over again."

Despite the promising picture, two and a half years later the world price for alpaca TOPS unexpectedly took a tumble, gradually falling below COPROCA's costs of production. From a high of $17, the price of alpaca TOPS fell to $6 per kilo and stayed there throughout 1998. Various Peruvian export firms went out of business and alpaca herders across the Andes began deploying their most creative survival strategies. Apparently, changing fashion tastes for lighter, non-hairy cotton and acrylics became the rage, displacing alpaca and other bulkier fibers even from the mixes.[6] This consumer trend coincided with the Asian globalization crisis which brought a collapse in the Japanese market for alpaca products. The effects of such an international price upheaval pointed to the perils of globalization for such a small export firm as CORPOCA. The assumptions behind a 1992 feasibility study which was the basis for the United Nations project proved to be too optimistic. During 1999, when the price began rising and reached $9.50 a kilo, it was hoped that it was on the rebound as part of a cyclical price trend for these products within the global economy.

COPROCA suspended its export sales and retained a large stockpile of alpaca fiber worth almost a half a million dollars during several years. Despite being knocked off balance by these international market forces, COPROCA turned its attention back to internal markets—the thousands of Bolivian artisans making sweaters, ponchos, and assorted other products for national, tourist, and export markets. With the help of a grant from the IAF and a loan from the former ATI, they purchased equipment and machinery for spinning fiber into yarn and began operations to compete for this internal market with the powerful Peruvian firms that had long dominated it.

Meanwhile AIGACCA's chief sponsor and promoter of the TOPS project, ATI, had transformed itself from a foreign aid agency into a venture capital company. It was now pledging funds and hitching its fortunes to COPROCA's work with llamas as the most viable strategy for the future. This new company held its coming out / first fund-raising party in Washington, D.C., and Luis Ticona appeared in the Style section of the *Washington Post* rubbing shoulders with none other than the vice-president of the United States, Al Gore.

All in all, though, looking back over the past twenty years, AIGACCA has made many noteworthy gains for herding communities. And although critical challenges always appear to be lurking along their grassroots development path, they have played an admirable role in helping Bolivia to bring back its alpacas, llamas, and ayllus.

CHAPTER 9

Piloting Women's Popular Education

The name of Bartolina Sisa evokes the memory of a courageous woman who fought alongside Tupak Katari. . . . Mothers, wives, and daughters have done the same for many peasant leaders.

ELIZABETH JELIN (1987)

Below the blue vastness of mountain sky, a dozen women in bowler hats and brightly striped shawls sit, fanned out in a tight semicircle, watching intently as the last in a series of illustrated posters is flipped over. Preceded by color drawings of a woman harvesting potatoes, washing clothes, cooking supper, and pasturing sheep, the final poster—labeled "Community Meeting"—depicts a woman pouring soup into bowls for a group of men huddled in conversation around a table. Standing to one side and pointing to the poster, the discussion leader asks, "What is going on here in this one? What does it mean?"

"It is our true situation," says a woman near the center of the fan. "We work, but no one sees us as we are."

"Yes, my identity papers say I am a mother, but we are all farmers, too," adds another.

"It is like the campesina we talked about in that other picture, the one pasturing animals," says a third. "It is always the mothers and their daughters who are expected to look after the sheep. Who are the real sheep here anyway?"

One after another, these women are taking their turn at the educational game known in the Bolivian altiplano as rotafolio. This particular session in the courtyard of a village church in the department of Oruro has focused on the daily hardships of peasant women, but rotafolio is a mobile civics course whose posters can open windows on myriad other subjects—from literacy to ethnic identity to the effects on small farmers of inflation and debt in the national economy. The technique is not new; its origins can be traced to the illustrations in Paolo Freire's *Education as Practice for Liberty,* the influential Brazilian educator's how-to book on adult literacy training that outlines techniques for unveiling the relationship between people and their culture, suggesting how poor people can learn to shape their own lives by "naming" and transforming their social, economic, and cultural reality. Inspired by that book and Freire's pioneering volume *Pedagogy of the Oppressed,* NGOs throughout the hemisphere during the past two decades have fashioned rotafolios, puppet shows, socio-dramas, and a multitude of other educational devices into a tool kit for grassroots organizing.[1]

Evelyn Barrón was one of those inspired by Freire's revolutionary perspectives on grassroots organizing. In 1982, she and another Bolivian educator, Rita Murillo, founded the Capacitación Integral de la Mujer Campesina (CIMCA) (Integral Training for Peasant Women). Since then CIMCA has been using refined versions of Freire's educational techniques to inspire social change in Oruro, a desolate region 13,000 feet above sea level whose treeless, windswept plains, dotted with adobe villages, stretch between two Andean cordilleras. With one of the highest infant mortality rates in the hemisphere, winters of bone-numbing cold, and periodic droughts, life for the predominantly indigenous population is not easy in the best of times. But the national economic crisis of the 1980s devastated the region, reducing sheep herds to scraggy flocks, shriveling markets for small farmers' cash crops, and throwing thousands of tin miners out of work. For the next decade, more and more Aymara and Quechua men of the area were emigrating in search of work, leaving their mothers, wives, and sisters behind to eke out a living from small family farms.

Out of these seemingly barren conditions, CIMCA has emerged as a beacon for women's rights and ethnic empowerment, inspiring the people of Oruro to uncover latent resources in their communities. As Evelyn Barrón, CIMCA's director, points out, "Women are the great untapped resource of Latin America. Things are beginning to change in Oruro because we clearly cannot afford to waste the energies of more than half the people. If women are limited to looking after kids, tending livestock, and passing out food baskets from overseas aid programs, we will never touch the roots of rural poverty. Our story is still evolving, but we are getting our chance because almost everything else has failed."

CIMCA believes that the rural poor must organize to develop, but it also believes that effective organizations require active memberships. This notion is widely held in development circles, but only partially practiced. By reaching people through popular education, CIMCA has not only planted the seeds of organizational reform throughout Oruro, it has also begun to produce the problem-solving leaders and self-confident memberships those organizations must have to attack the real needs of their communities. The journey toward this goal has been a long one and its progress has been measured in fits and starts.

The Birth of CIMCA

Barrón is the guiding spirit of CIMCA's quest to mobilize the people of Oruro. I first met Barrón when visiting El Ceibo in the Alto Beni in 1980. During my breakfast one morning, she pulled up in a landrover with two other members of an NGO team and joined our table. She spoke non-stop for about fifteen minutes on the plight of rural women and everything about her manner conveyed a tremendous passion for rectifying a situation of continual hardship. Over the next few years, I had other conversations with Barrón in La Paz and found out more about her interesting background.

She was born in the tiny village of Azurduy in the southern mountain valleys in the Chuquisaca region. Her father, a combination lawyer/ landowner, was a casualty of the Bolivian land reform and watched his property shrink in size during Evelyn's childhood. Darker in skin color than her brothers and sisters, she was dubbed the black sheep of the family, and was suspected of being the illegitimate offspring of her father and one of the women workers of this small ranch. She was the family member most apt to be hanging out with the few agricultural workers and, in fact, had been raised in the skirt of one of these humble women. Perhaps it was the childhood identification with this social group that formed her early social consciousness and lifelong solidarity with the underdog.

At fifteen, bent on attaining a decent education unavailable in Azurduy, she moved to the city of Sucre where she took a day job at a dry cleaning establishment and attended subsidized courses at night. She lost an entire year recovering from tuberculosis and shortly thereafter was dismissed from a state teachers' college for a "rebellious attitude" when she tried to resume her studies. Her next attempt at gaining an education took place in the Social Work Department at the National San Andres University in La Paz but this institution was closed for its resistance activities by the Banzer military government during the 1970s. Her first professional job was with SNDC and within a few years had climbed to the top of the ladder to become its national director for women's programs. Meanwhile, she was able to finish her social work degree. At this time, Evelyn recalls that she was steeped in modernization theory and imported development models, promoting "model homes" and white bread and wheat macaroni in SNDC's women's training programs.

While residing in La Paz, she became acquainted with some of the professionals who belonged to MINKA, the center for Aymara culture and the country's first indigenous NGO, yet she was cool to a cause framed so explicitly around indigenous cultural identity.

While working with SNDC, she eventually became fatigued by a government bureaucracy full of red tape and even began harboring suspicions about the military government's real intent behind these community development programs. So she moved on to Cáritas Boliviano, a nonprofit development agency of the Catholic Church, where she became fast friends with co-worker Rita Murillo. They worked together there for several years in an office with Jaime Alba promoting grassroots development, but she was put off by the major mission of her employer, distribution of surplus U.S. food aid through local mothers' clubs. People were not starving, but nutrition levels remained substandard, and women were not learning how to improve production to feed their families. She and Murillo had a more difficult time living with this contradiction than Alba, perhaps in part because they became acquainted with the writings and thoughts of Paolo Freire, who believed that charity undermined self-esteem and left the poor at the mercy of their benefactors. Too often it was a barter in which basic necessities were exchanged for apathetic silence.

These ideas were not well received among their colleagues, so the two women left to join Catholic Relief Services, which also funneled food aid to the poor, but was staffed by several professionals interested in starting community development projects. Believing that success depended on local participation, Barrón and Murillo took charge of a training program designed to get women more actively involved in their communities. When the agency's priorities shifted, however, the two decided to found their own organization, CIMCA, and set out to test their beliefs in Oruro, an area that had few NGOs and minimal public resources.

No More White Elephants

At the time of my first visit with Barrón, the IAF was interested in encouraging Bolivians to find new models for sparking development among rural women. One of the attractive features of CIMCA's proposal was its decision to minimize administrative overhead and maximize operational flexibility. From the beginning, Barrón and Murillo were determined to invest their energies and capital in people rather than offices or buildings. From her previous experience, Barrón knew that there were plenty of public facilities and church meeting halls that were unused or underused because they had never become integrated fully with local communities. CIMCA would put these white elephants to work rather than enlarge the size of the herd by building a centralized training center.

Anyone visiting for the first time the one-room CIMCA office in the modest two-story house in a rundown section of the city of Oruro might wonder if CIMCA was an organization only in name. Looking at the battered desk, the handful of chairs, the piles of educational pamphlets with indigenous faces on the covers, the clerk occasionally interrupting her typing to answer the phone, it would seem that nothing much was happening. But if one looks at the departmental map of Oruro hanging on the wall, studded with brightly colored tags marking the communities along the route of CIMCA's van, a different conclusion rapidly comes into focus. To find CIMCA—its leaders, its trainers, its impact—one must travel into the campo.

During the organization's early years, CIMCA's van was everywhere, pulling out of the blue into one altiplano community after another. The staff of trainers would pop out, engage curious onlookers in conversation, and persuade them to call a community meeting where interest could be sparked in women's issues and popular education. After a meeting was convened, Barrón would introduce herself and the staff and explain what they hoped to accomplish. "We all know that economic development projects are needed," she would start, "but they are not enough. We need to see the true nature of our problems. If only a handful of people get rich from a project while the rest stay poor, is that development? I have been in communities where campesinos have learned how to increase their yields and made lots of money, but turned around and bought a truck rather than put some of it aside to educate their children. Perhaps you, too, have seen families take milk out of the mouths of their children to sell at the state dairy. This is giving value to things instead of people. What kind of development is it when women learn only to sew and knit and mind their own business? Isn't the world their business, too? Shouldn't they have a say about what happens to their families, their communities, their country?"

Often the meeting never got beyond the spectacle of outsiders putting on a show. But CIMCA usually found a candidate or two eager to attend a regional training session to learn how to become an *educadora popular,* a popular educator capable of promoting community development. And if the show seemed to energize everyone, CIMCA would single out the community for more intensive training by assigning a staff member to live there for a time and hold informal classes in popular education.

This scattershot approach had its drawbacks. Recruits came from every corner of the department, making it difficult to schedule regular follow-up visits to see how new educadoras populares interacted with their communities. When follow-up did occur, the results were often discouraging. Distilling years of experience, Barrón and her colleagues had focused their training on achieving an immediate impact by improving community health and nutrition. Training sessions fed this information to trainees through the latest in popular education techniques to hold student interest. When CIMCA staff visited newly trained promoters at home, however, they discovered that few families had changed their behavior. They were still selling their best sources of protein, such as eggs and meat, and were not growing the variety of vegetables needed for a balanced diet.

More alarming still, CIMCA found that many of their newly trained educadoras populares had abandoned their work, and often their villages, to get married. In selecting trainees, Barrón and her colleagues had emphasized young, single women who could read and write. Older women were thought to be too resistant to change and less energetic and imaginative in inspiring others to change. The evidence soon suggested that perhaps the young were too changeable, unable to persevere when confronted by prospective husbands who saw popular education as an unnecessary diversion from starting and raising a family.

CIMCA was running into trouble also in the handful of pilot communities singled out for intensive promotion by core staff members. Ubaldina Salinas, CIMCA's best promoter, had been assigned for several months to the village of Querarani. Enthusiasm ran high when CIMCA's van had made its first visit, but when Salinas returned to set up a women's training workshop, no one came to the first session. Each time she rescheduled, she met the same stony silence. Finally, CIMCA recalled Salinas to reassess the assignment. She reported that the men were not letting their wives attend the sessions—not because they felt they were threatened, but because they were not included. Faced with the choice of withdrawing or adapting, CIMCA sent Salinas back and opened up the sessions to all interested members of the village. That was the beginning of Querarani's development, planting the seeds of a future harvest, whose bounty would become apparent only later.

In the meantime, the crisis left an indelible mark on CIMCA, raising questions about its grassroots development strategy. Should CIMCA trainees be promoting community organizations for women parallel to those dominated by men? Would this fracture and weaken communities that were already unable to adequately defend their interests in Bolivian national society? CIMCA decided to take a pragmatic course. It would continue to work with organizations such as mothers' clubs, but it would also try to strengthen and reform community peasant organizations by probing for initiatives that would broaden their membership base and lead to women's empowerment along this other path as well.

One such opportunity seemed to open in the province of Moza. Moza's small farmers produced native potato varieties that were renowned throughout Oruro, but lack of organization left them unable to bargain for better terms from the middlemen who trucked the crop to market and received the lion's share of the profits. CIMCA decided to work with a new association of potato growers in fifteen communities, helping them consolidate their organizations by starting a project to encourage women to take a more active leadership role. Andean women play a key role in cultivating the crop, bearing primary responsibility for sorting and selecting seed potatoes for example, so it seemed obvious that their involvement was crucial for introducing new techniques to raise yields. CIMCA also hoped the time was ripe to show that women should participate in deciding how to raise profits through direct marketing. This attempt backfired, however, when ambitious male leaders grew impatient with the popular education process and tried to seize control of project assets by pushing Barrón and CIMCA's other trainers out of the zone. Suspecting that the leadership of the association viewed women's training as a goose for laying the golden eggs of outside funding and realizing that local women were not far enough along to defend their own interests, CIMCA decided to withdraw.

The loss of young women promoters, the failure to change family diets, the temporary setback in Querarani, the withdrawal from Moza all had a common thread running through them. Barrón had long believed that development projects could not work without community participation. For women to participate fully, basic attitudes had to be changed not only in society but among women. "But," Barrón concluded, "our early efforts fell short. Not because there was no need to improve nutrition or for families to raise their incomes, but because our women trainees did not truly value themselves or have a sense of their own dignity. Realizing this forced us to get at the motivational factors, those deep-seated beliefs that form a person's self-image and place in society." For CIMCA to have an impact, it would have to begin at the level of the women it hoped to energize by first encouraging them to identify their own needs. Instead of providing answers, CIMCA would teach people how to ask questions.

CRYSTALLIZING A PEDAGOGY

Paolo Freire called the process of awakening people to the power of their own questioning *conscientizaçao*. Adopting Freire's perspective, CIMCA developed a new focus on the fostering of self-awareness among Oruro's men and women. Via the concientization method, the tiny development organization was able to move some areas of rural Oruro society from inertia to productive motion. CIMCA has also transformed itself over the past decade. From an ad hoc improvisational approach, the organization has gradually developed a structured multi-phased process that has now come full circle. With the basic first phase curriculum in place, the organization began to address the complex of issues, including health and nutrition, that for a time it was forced to put aside.

There are three stages to this training process. The first stage of training takes place at a centrally located site near participants' home communities. This has two advantages. It ensures that graduates become part of a mutual support network to sponsor local development, and it facilitates the scheduling of follow-up monitoring by CIMCA staff. By the end of the 1980s, CIMCA was holding up to nine or ten centrally located micro-regional workshops a year.

Enrollment in workshops is limited to about forty people so as to encourage optimal participation. The three trainers are drawn from CIMCA's core staff of four, and from another half-dozen professionals and previously trained paraprofessionals available on a part-time basis as needed.

The first day, trainees are divided into small groups and taken outdoors for short walks and asked to make observations on what they see in the village around them. Those who overcome their shyness usually note little that is remarkable, finding only what is to be expected. On the last day of training, they will repeat this process and report back to the whole group on how their perceptions have changed from learning to see and question the hidden constraining assumptions underlying the routines of daily life.

During the intervening two weeks, participants are exposed to a variety of situations designed, as CIMCA puts it, "to help one lose one's fear." Foremost among these fears is the fear of speaking. Cooking, eating, sleeping, dancing, singing, and working together, and looking after one another's children, creates a kind of family bonding that helps make it safe to talk freely. But it is the rotafolio that deepens the talk into dialogue.

CIMCA's rotafolios are the product of sixteen years of workshops and of distilling testimonies from the whole range of women in Oruro. They are drawn by Germán Treviño, a graduate of the school of plastic arts in Oruro who has been working with CIMCA since 1984. He emphasizes that the power of the illustrations depends on "truly conveying what the compañeras tell us about their experiences. Sometimes it requires changing the rotafolio a half-dozen times before they are satisfied. The women do not want caricatures so I have to study their faces carefully." Years of studying faces for clues to the stories he has heard the women tell, Treviño says, has changed his opinions about the situation of rural women—something which he had never thought about before—allowing him to truly see their problems for the first time and to identify their humanity with his own.

This process of identification is what makes the drawings such an effective tool for consciousness raising. Rotafolios are intended to be linked together to form a fan around a central theme such as a woman's role in the village. For example, one poster showed a classroom scene with boys focused intently on the teacher and blackboard while the girls sat to one side in a sewing circle oblivious to the teaching. Together, they provide the elements of a puzzle that workshop participants will solve as they discuss an unfolding succession of narrative situations. Gradually, participants will come to identify it as the story of their own lives. Many years of workshop experience attest to the validity of the story line contained in each set of rotafolios, but each group of participants must discover and resolve that story for themselves. To emphasize that trainees are in control of the process and to ensure maximum participation among literate and illiterate alike, drawings are often no longer labeled. The point of the story emerges from the telling, but its outcome is foreshadowed from the very beginning in the strong and resolutely human faces of the indigenous women in the drawings. As one CIMCA trainee described her experience, "Before I came here, I thought I was supposed to be poor. Now I realize that is not so, and I will not let it be so for my children."

CIMCA has developed three sets of rotafolios about altiplano women, and these form the core of the first set of workshops. Trainees are asked to analyze the condition of peasant women at all stages of the life cycle—from birth, through childhood, adolescence, and marriage, into old age. In the altiplano, it is common for people to commiserate with the parents of a newborn girl, implying that they have received a burden rather than a reward. In tracing the path of that burden as it is borne from grandmother to mother to daughter, the rotafolios eventually arouse a smoldering anger among the workshop participants at the experience of discrimination they all have in common.

There are rotafolios to show that anger. Pictures of campesinas breaking the chains binding their wrists, ripping off the bandannas covering their eyes, tearing the padlocks from their mouths, and crashing through brick walls. What is interesting about this anger is that it is not directed toward men but toward gender roles. In the rotafolio of a woman smashing a wall, a man stands beside her, urging her on. Other rotafolios suggest what a freer society might look like, showing men sharing responsibility for collecting firewood, pasturing sheep, or tending an infant. The rotafolio of a girl remaining behind to herd sheep while her brother saunters off, books in hand, to school is eventually answered by one of a husband and wife watching their son and daughter study together.

The channel for change outside the family is directed toward community organizations. Another set of rotafolios focuses on the ayllu and the sindicato. Women are usually allowed to attend sindicato meetings only when their husbands are ill or have migrated in search of work, or if they are heads of household. The only leadership position open to women is "secretary of women's affairs," which often exists in name only at the regional level.

CIMCA's rotafolios offer a platform for questioning this arrangement and suggest how it might be reformed. The rotafolio labeled "Community Meeting," which shows a woman serving soup to a group of busy men, is followed by others showing a woman nervously addressing a group of seated men, working diligently beside other villagers on a community project, and finally sitting behind the table making decisions with the other community leaders.

Before the first phase of CIMCA training is over, trainees take turns tracing copies of rotafolios that they will take back to their communities for a nine-week practicum working with a local organization. During this time, a CIMCA trainer will make a return visit to see how things are going.

Those educadoras populares who have shown special promise are invited to attend a second set of workshops, which draw together people from throughout the province. Insights about family and community problems that were learned in the first workshops are now applied on a regional and national level. Introduced to the concept of "Marginality," trainees examine how economic and ethnic discrimination helps perpetuate poverty. In small groups they analyze how indigenous people, even though they are the majority, are shunned by the national media, how they are expected to shed their traditional clothing, stop speaking Aymara and Quechua, change their surnames, and cut their braids if they want to fit into mestizo culture. While learning to make and use puppets, play a variety of educational board games, and act in socio-dramas, trainees probe the humiliations they or their friends and relatives have experienced migrating to the city to look for work.

These exercises follow the same course traced by the rotafolios, channeling anger at the recognition of systematic discrimination toward a search for effective remedial action, for examples of ethnic pride that can be a catalyst for economic and social development. Again, much of the focus falls on the sindicato, which is much more than a community presence. With elected bodies at the zonal, departmental, and national levels, sindicatos have spearheaded the movement toward land reform, rural schooling, the end of military rule, and the return to constitutional democracy. CIMCA's hopes for the sindicato as a vehicle for socioeconomic change are shared by numerous other NGOs and development practitioners in Bolivia.

But CIMCA tempers its hopes with a critical eye. Rotafolios explore the dangers of corrupt leadership practices, cooptation by political parties, and the prevalence of machismo attitudes that exclude women from active participation and positions of authority. CIMCA's workshop prepares women for the rise to positions of leadership in the sindicato movement and for the struggle to hold leaders accountable to their memberships, regardless of gender. As one recent CIMCA graduate, Flora Rufino, remarked, "First by joining, then by leading group discussions, I have learned how to talk with, not at, people. Now I can speak clearly and forcefully in public. I have the skills to keep minutes or run a meeting, and I know how to analyze issues in ways that allow the community to inform itself about national as well as local problems. CIMCA has challenged me to question, and that has taught me how to think."

Critical thinking is the basis of problem solving, and the third stage of CIMCA training concentrates on technical subjects, such as community health, nutrition, animal husbandry, and agronomy. Launched in 1988, this program brings CIMCA full circle. With a cadre of popular educators who have a firm sense of self and society and are highly motivated (one, for example, put a clause in her wedding vows obligating her spouse to support her work as an educadora popular), it was only natural that they would demand to learn the kinds of skills that CIMCA had come to the campo years before hoping to teach.

The workshop brings together men and women from throughout Oruro. Professional trainers offer seminars in a variety of disciplines, and there are field trips to ongoing rural development projects being sponsored by other NGOs. These visits are a learning opportunity for everyone: CIMCA's trainees arrive full of questions, not only about how to prepare seedling nurseries, for instance, but armed with suggestions on how local women might be included more actively in the project.

Sometimes the entire workshop is held at a site specializing in a certain skill. The Centro Agropecuario del Desarrollo Altiplano (CADEA) (the Center for Altiplano Agricultural Development), a previously underutilized agricultural and livestock research station operated by the government in Oruro, is a prime example. CADEA's agronomists and extensionists were delighted with the arrangement. "We had some problems reaching campesino groups," explained one researcher, "but CIMCA has a well-developed methodology, including the rotafolio, for getting communities to apply what they are learning. Sometimes teaching a technical course can be frustrating, like shouting into the bottom of a well, but with CIMCA you know they have the ability to draw the knowledge up so it reaches campesinos' fields."

ONE WOMAN'S ROAD TO LEADERSHIP

Eufracia Wilcarani Cari is a woman whose life was transformed by her involvement with CIMCA. Cari grew up in the remote area of Orinoco in the department of Oruro, where her family eked out a living from a small flock of animals and the money Cari's mother earned baking bread to sell in outdoor markets. Cari did not attend school because of a serious illness and because her parents saw no advantage to educating a girl.

One day that changed when the local school director insisted, "Eufracia must go to class, at least to learn how to sign her name." Quickly developing a love for learning, she whizzed through elementary and junior high school. Unable to afford a teachers' college, she returned to her community, seemingly destined to a life of herding llamas.

Cari joined a mothers' club, which channeled food aid from abroad and offered classes in weaving and crocheting. In 1983, she was selected by her community to participate in a CIMCA popular education workshop. Other workshops followed until Cari emerged as a genuine educadora popular, fulfilling her dream of becoming a teacher.

Recognizing her talent for energizing rural women, CIMCA asked Cari to travel to Peru to exchange training experiences with other women's organizations. On the return trip, her bus got stuck in the middle of the night in a muddy road winding high up the side of a mountain. The driver asked the men to get out and push, and Cari and a fellow trainer joined them. As they walked to the rear talking about how to get on with the job of freeing the bus, the earth above the road gave way, sweeping the vehicle over the side of the precipice and taking the lives of all the women left on board.

When Barrón heard the news, she presumed the worst. Cari recounts the surprise on Barrón's face when she arrived two days later, safe and sound, telling the sad story of how she had learned, once and for all, the importance of women insisting on pulling their own weight.

Cari's rise to leadership began with her taking office in several local organizations, including her village sindicato. In 1988, she was elected secretary of training programs on the executive board of the regional committee overseeing hundreds of community sindicatos in Oruro, opening the way for CIMCA's methodology to be introduced throughout the department.

Looking ahead, she said, "For my remaining time in this world, I want to continue developing myself through workshops and other experiences to gain more awareness of who we are as women, and the road we have to follow together."

CIMCA REACHES OUT

After years of tireless effort in Oruro, CIMCA has moved beyond using other people's white elephants to helping NGOs and public agencies better use their own infrastructures. Overcoming the deeply entrenched barriers to reaching and mobilizing rural women is perhaps the single hardest task in development, and word-of-mouth communication about CIMCA's effective training methods has spread quickly throughout the department, and beyond. Grassroots organizations and NGOs from as far away as La Paz and the neighboring department of Potosí have lined up to seek CIMCA's counsel. The European Economic Community, which funds a rural development program in Bolivia staffed by more than 170 employees, in the late 1980s asked CIMCA to train the campesinas in its projects. The U.N. Food and Agricultural Organization asked CIMCA to support small-scale irrigation projects. Even universities are sending their students and instructors to sit in on CIMCA workshops and observe the magic first-hand.

Perhaps the most dramatic turnaround involves Cáritas Boliviano, the agency Barrón left behind on her journey to start her own development organization. As recently as the mid-1980s, CIMCA's stinging rotafolios on the negative impact of food aid on rural communities were eliciting complaints from the agency's departmental director. Since 1988, however, the relationship with Cáritas has become increasingly cordial. Frustration with the limited impact of the Cáritas program led its local director to ask CIMCA to introduce training in popular education to the sixty mothers' clubs in the province of Totora, laying the foundation for a health education program to be jointly managed by the two agencies. A similar effort took place at the request of a local bishop to revitalize a moribund network of mothers' clubs in the province of Corocoro.

CIMCA may eventually become the primary trainer of other NGO trainers in Oruro, but it has not lost sight of its goal to help make sindicatos more democratic by catapulting campesinas into leadership positions at all levels of this multi-tiered structure. As a result of CIMCA's persistence, the walls of gender discrimination are beginning to crack. Its trainees have moved beyond attending and speaking out at local, provincial, and regional sindicato congresses to win elective posts. Dozens of them have been elected to leadership councils in the various provinces of Oruro. The crowning achievement, however, was the 1989 election of four campesinas to offices on the executive committee of the departmental federation representing several hundred thousand small farmers.

The foundation for this accomplishment was laid at a CIMCA workshop for fifty women community leaders several months prior to the congress. After the course was completed, CIMCA staff divided the region by cantons and provinces and monitored the performance of trainees at sindicato meetings. Forty of the women were then invited back to a second workshop to polish their skills and plan election strategy.

The most revealing sign that something fundamental had changed occurred after the election, when one of the winners was appointed secretary of women's affairs. Rising to address the several hundred delegates, most of them men, seated before her, she declined the job, saying, "How long do we have to make believe this is a real position? You give us a seat at the table, but you go on making decisions in the back room. We are as capable as any man of filling a responsible position."

Embarrassed, the male leaders overseeing the transition of power announced she would be the new secretary of *sindicato organización,* an office that has traditionally wielded considerable clout.

Although CIMCA's pre-election workshop set the stage for this broadening of representation, the antecedents of the story reach all the way back to the community of Querarani, the scene of one of CIMCA's early false starts. After CIMCA acceded to community demands and held training workshops that included men as well as women, villagers created the Asociación Familiar Campesina (ASFACA) (the Peasant Family Association) to start local development initiatives. ASFACA has an unusual leadership structure that fills each office with a man and a woman, who are also husband and wife. The idea is in harmony with the traditional dualism of Andean culture that predates the arrival of the conquistadors, but as an expression of power sharing it emerged directly from CIMCA's workshop. CIMCA and the local communities have learned that if women's empowerment is not to be stillborn, it is important to find roots for the concept in traditional culture so that the transformation of that culture occurs from within, rather than becoming one more alien idea imposed from the outside.

Since its emergence, Querani's Asociación Familiar Campesina has started a literacy program in Aymara, worked with an international donor CARE to install a potable water system with individual standpipes for each home, planted communal vegetable gardens to diversify family diets, and purchased a tractor families can lease to till their farms. With the income from the tractor rental, the Asociación is buying a generator to bring electricity to the village. In 1989, a man and a woman from Quthat other three women trained by CIMCA as newly elected officials on the executive committee of Oruro's departmental federation of sindicatos.

CIMCA's Cultural Retooling for the 1990s

Over the next six years from 1991 to 1996, CIMCA received diminishing support from the IAF as the group began to tap financial resources from the Bolivian government's Social Investment Fund and other international funders and was able to increase its financial base by charging NGOs for training workshops. The CIMCA team now consisted of Barrón, Treviño, Ubaldina Salinas, and Natividad Salas, an Aymara-speaking woman who replaced a popular educator from the original team. They were still without secretaries, messenger boys, or hierarchies of any kind which would cramp a hands-on operating style.

CIMCA moved part of its operations to the provincial capital of Challapata, several hours' driving time across the central altiplano from the city of Oruro. In the region's high-altitude communities, a peasant livestock-raising economy prevailed. CIMCA received Bolivian government support for the construction of a training center and also received funding to hire Peruvian veterinarians. As was the case for AIGACAA, however, the outside veterinarians created more problems than services. Taking stock of the inadequate and counterproductive situation, Barrón vowed to identify and use local paraprofessional men and women vets to provide the technical help needed to revamp the zone's animal husbandry practices and with her usual dispatch, she quickly put this plan into place, hiring several local men and women to serve as veterinarians. CIMCA's training center quickly became a beehive of community meetings and capacity-building workshops. After several years of operation, it was sending educadores populares toting veterinary medicine kits to outlying communities. There they charged a small fee for services and became a permanent group focused on the needs of livestock.

The new workshops in Challapata produced twenty new sets of rotafolios on topics related to the critical problems in the local livestock economy. Since women were the movers and shakers in this livestock economy—pasturing, caring for the animals' health, performing the proper rituals, escorting them to local fairs—CIMCA seized the opportunity to bolster the women's self-esteem and skills as well.

Challapata has the atmosphere of an old colonial market center, with rustic adobe buildings and towering native *molle* trees lining the main street. Similar to many other NGOs, CIMCA was swept up in the country's 1990s fervor over indigenous rights and cultural resources, so it was not surprising that many of the rotafolios from Challapata included cultural themes, such as one with the suggestive name of "Los 500 Años" (500 Years). Under the sway of the growing passion for Andean cultural revitalization, CIMCA adjusted its training approaches once again. Now women were encouraged to identify indigenous cultural resources rather than engaging in the heretofore conventional listing of needs and problems. The concept of indigenous cultural resources, which the women themselves seemed to have the most knowledge about, was now a core premise from which local development would flow. This conceptual change in CIMCA's program reflected the ever evolving views of its founder.

At one important 1990s Challapata workshop, the CIMCA staff gathered together some sixty elders (*ancianos*) from diverse communities which led to tapping their repository of knowledge about ninety medicinal plants for four major diseases, and other livestock health problems. Barrón recalled, "We strove to bring *ancianos* from the most remote mountain communities where indigenous knowledge had not been eroded and where there had been the least contamination from Western urban influences." CIMCA then launched a program of "ethno-veterinary medicine." Local livestock were also fortified by the better management and utilization of numerous nutritious native grasses which strengthened resistance to diseases rampant in the zone. In these ways, CIMCA combined both Andean and Western knowledge in its general livestock development program and specifically in its attack on the most serious livestock health problems.

At the Challapata workshops, the CIMCA staff learned that local women were having to work harder to hold their pastoral economy together since their husbands were spending longer periods away from home trying to find cash employment with which to support their families. CIMCA's rotafolios had helped people discern the effects of the New Economic Policy (NEP) under the neo-liberal economic doctrine as one of the current factors in the economic deterioration in herding communities. It appeared, too, that the Challapata women were casting a more critical eye than men on the ills brought by modernization such as the overgrazing of the grasslands, indiscriminate use of tractors, and the difficulties imported cattle were having adapting to the high altitudes and the flavors of the local pastures. Following the workshops, CIMCA added material that encouraged women to consider such effects.

During this period, CIMCA was also influenced by Oruro's llama revival. Through the AIGACAA, NGO, and university llama meat promotional campaigns, a llama slaughterhouse and the open sale of meat in market stalls had been established in the center of the city. There were even national television advertising blitzes promoting llama meat consumption that originated in Oruro during the annual carnival celebration. Barrón found her childhood impression of the llama as simply an overworked pack animal had been transformed. And she found the rediscovery energizing. Llama meat was now a staple in her diet and she even wound up doing research on llama raising in Oruro to present at the International Women's Conference in Bejing. She presented findings about everything from mating rituals with flute music to the variety of llama dishes found in rural cuisine. She also led CIMCA staff to produce several rotafolios focused on positive community experiences with llamas. Llamas had been in the background in many CIMCA rotafolios depicting Andean rural scenes. Now they had moved to the foreground, situated as a multifaceted development resource worthy of animated, soul-searching discussions.

CIMCA's FORAY INTO THE TROPICS

During the second half of the 1990s, CIMCA carried its portfolio of gender animation methodologies and reinvigorated cultural consciousness from the Andes into the eastern lowlands of northern Santa Cruz, the site of some of Bolivia's largest peasant resettlement projects. My article in the IAF's *Journal of Grassroots Development* about CIMCA (Healy 1991) prompted

World Concerns, an international development agency working in the rural district of Yapacané, to hire CIMCA's trainers to improve their rural development program. CIMCA felt right at home among small livestock-raising communities although the tropical rainforest ecosystem required the trainers to make major adaptations in their rotafolios and other popular education materials. Here again, CIMCA proved itself a formidable force in encouraging local people to examine long-standing gender relations, economic adjustment programs, and the effects of neo-colonialism on their communities. The most convincing testament to CIMCA's positive impact came in a letter from Susan Stewart, a North American professional who oversaw the Yapacané program for two years.

> It is my great pleasure to report to you some of the impact which your work is having in the colonies of San Julian and Berlin. First, the tools which you have provided for the people there have changed their whole approach to teaching. This was the most important result of the first and second workshops. In the past, the "popular" teaching approach had always been, "I know so I am teaching you." Seeing and doing is truly believing and in the first two workshops the local "educadores populares" saw popular education in action and began directly applying what they had learned to their communities. The responses of the people to the courses are far more lively than they were previously.
>
> Second, the reintegration of the women into the community organizations has become an important issue for the people in San Julian. It is exciting to see the change in such a short period of time. The organization, Distrito de Pequeños Ganaderos Lecheros de San Julian (Small Dairy Producers' Association of San Julian) held some mid-term elections last year in which, for the first time, they decided to include women—both allowing them to vote and to hold general offices. Even more astonishing, two women were elected to general office. Because of the enthusiasm and success of these women, in this year's general election, several women were elected to hold various offices, including that of Vice-President! This is such an immense change from the previous ways of the organization that it is exciting to see. . . .

Stewart reported that as a result of CIMCA's efforts, women now felt accepted by the organization where they once felt peripheral and they had thrown themselves into work for their communities. Some examples included planting of local tree nurseries, building a corral for livestock management, and overcoming a serious dispute caused by an outside technician.

Another example of a positive outcome comes from a dairy association engineer who changed his perspective on seeing CIMCA's work. Although he had never before favored women technicians to work in the countryside, he actually went to bat for a female agronomy applicant who applied for a position in the project. The engineer says this change in his views resulted from his observations of the positive changes in the livestock program of the district. I am convinced that this change is due in large part to the work of CIMCA in the first two workshops.

A third impact of your workshops has been the installation of a new process in meetings of many local districts. Through their CIMCA training, educadores populares learned to facilitate a group analysis of their reality and current problems and they now bring this skill to every community where they work. This means all of the community meetings have become much more effective in discussing problems and bringing them out into the open. The puppets especially have really aided in this process. People so rapidly lose their inhibitions with puppets that they express things they would never otherwise talk about openly. This is also true for the mini-dramas. And the people's thoughts, once out into the open, fuel great discussions. Because the educadores populares understand how to facilitate these discussions and help groups come to consensus, great progress is being made. It seems to us that this is a very important first step in the process in establishing a process of self-help, community organization and local resolution of problems. We are delighted to see this process happening.

I must pass on here the only negative comments I gleaned from the participants in the third workshop. Although they did enjoy much of the sessions presented in the 500 Years and Aymara culture, many commented that the sessions became boring with too much information to truly be useful. The comment was that the sessions reverted to a formal education session rather than the previously used non-formal techniques and was a return to a classroom situation. I think this disappointed some people. It seems to be an ever present danger that when we have an important subject with lots of material we try to stuff it all in and it becomes a lecture session. The animators fully understand this because they always fight the same temptation in their courses.

In her closing statement, Stewart added, "We looked in vain for almost two years for the kind of programs CIMCA offers before finding anything appropriate to our needs. We feel that the work of your organization is vitally important, and that there are many areas of Bolivia which drastically need this type of work. In the Department of Santa Cruz, we do not know of any other organization that works in this way with farmers from the countryside."

Despite the criticisms of handling the 500 Years workshops, Barrón and her tiny team followed up with improved work in reshaping cultural consciousness in the area's agricultural colonies. Many families living in these resettlement communities had come from the altiplano and Andean valleys with which Barrón had been long familiar. As she worked with them, she uncovered an alarming amount of cultural erosion, indeed much more than she had observed years before in her work with the Alto Beni populations that joined El Ceibo. This cultural erosion was what Merwin Bohan had argued for when writing his 1940s blueprint for Bolivian development. Now things looked quite different to social activists like Barrón and her team. The 1990s prisms of multiculturalism and conservation of biodiversity combined with CIMCA's participatory approach gave the group a more critical lens through which to view culture and cultural change.

In Bohan's original vision, mountain people would leave their traditions and backward agricultural practices behind when they moved from the highlands to the lowland frontier. CIMCA's trainers turned this notion of progress on its head by leading Aymara and Quechua colonists to reflect on the forgotten values of their cultural heritage and how these could be used as a resource for development. This reflection process led to discussions of Pachamama (mother earth) and the other religious beliefs that undergirded their reverence of the land in the highlands. Why, the CIMCA educators asked, couldn't those same values inspire them to conserve the tropical forest? What about the classic Andean forms of community-based mutual aid such as the aynis and minkas? The CIMCA staffers inspired these dairy farmers with stories of the ways that El Ceibo organic farmers used their Andean social capital to transform their farming technologies to protect local biodiversity while at the same time putting more income into their coffers.

In Yapacané CIMCA remained faithful to its principal methodology for sustaining and spreading its educational program. As had been its practice from the beginning, the CIMCA trainers sought to propagate their governing spiritual and institutional traditions while respecting local needs—toward the goal of fostering a distinctive home-grown entity. This local offspring came into existence as the Centro de Educación Popular de Yapacané (CEPY) (Center of Popular Education of Yapacané). By 1996, ten male and female peasant educadores populares—all graduates of CIMCA's three-tiered program—were conducting workshops throughout the twenty-two communities of the zone. CEPY's organizational brochure has an unmistakably CIMCA-like tone: it announces "women's consciousness raising to reduce gender inequalities" and "revitalizing positive aspects of our culture such as respect for the family, mother earth, communal solidarity, traditional knowledge, festivals, and religious practices connecting us to the cosmos."

Before leaving the eastern lowlands, yet shifting from Yapacané to the Alto Beni, another ripened fruit of Barrón's work came into greater prominence in 1998. One of her former trainees with Cáritas Boliviano in the Alto Beni, Ana Condori, became vice-president of El Ceibo's administrative council, the first woman to hold such a high post within the organization. The wife of Luis Cruz, Condori was a veteran NGO practitioner in the La Paz region as she honed numerous skills as a community organizer and promoter, especially among indigenous women's groups. She also added income to her family budget by operating a family business marketing agricultural produce with rented trucks which helped put her two daughters through college. In the mid-1980s, with the aid of a small IAF grant, she authored her autobiography, *Mi Despertar* (Condori 1988). This book revealed her odyssey of life experiences beginning as a young girl in a rural altiplano community followed by subsequent migration for work in the capital as a domestic servant in an upper-class household and finally resettling with relatives in a farming community of the Alto Beni. In the Alto Beni, Condori experienced her first "social awakening" in one of the workshops organized by Barrón. Her life had come full circle as following her stint as a grassroots development practitioner, she was now able to serve the cacao bean producing communities from the second highest leadership position within the federation in the capital. She was breaking down the barriers to female leadership atop the micro-regional organization as another example of CIMCA's record of empowering indigenous women in the countryside.

According to modernization theory, indigenous women even more than men were wedded to traditional values and technologies and social institutions like the ayni that held back progress. CIMCA's continuing efforts certainly put that proposition to rest. Part of the secret for this success, in my estimation, has been the continual cultivation of a free-wheeling, free-spirited, earthy, and anti-bureaucratic operating style. The workshop methodology, in the hands of such passionate activists, also lends itself to a high degree of social learning and adaptation by continually collecting insights, ideas, and lessons bobbing up from the women in these impoverished communities. In addition, by remaining small, by pinching its pennies, and by keeping a relatively high profile through its special stylistic flair, CIMCA has been able to master the difficult art of self-financing and serve as a model for other NGOs dependent on foreign grants. CIMCA currently supports itself primarily from the sale of training services to other national and international agencies anxious to energize the participation of women in rural development and local and regional politics. It easily competes against literally dozens of other specialized NGOs by keeping its overhead costs low and maintaining an eager willingness to endure hardships in remote locations. Despite their many achievements, El Ceibo, CECAOT, and AIGACAA would gain from a steady injection of CIMCA's consciouness-raising programming to galvanize the greater participation of Aymara, Quechua, and Mosten women.

CIMCA has taken its educational roadshow to low-income women in Peru, Chile, and Colombia, and even further afield. The little development group made a big splash on the National Mall during the Smithsonian's 1994 Festival of American Folklife. Hispanic and Afro-American youth from Washington, D.C., flocked to CIMCA's colorful rotafolio-making demonstrations. CIMCA also received publicity that has brought its programs to people across the globe. Public television audiences in the United States, Western Europe, Japan, and Latin America, for instance, have been treated to snapshots of CIMCA's workshops in the award-winning video, "Local Heroes, Global Change." It is against this backdrop of growing international outreach and profound local impacts that we can appreciate how far a small but feisty group of women educators can carry an important message of developmental change to the world.

Remaking Urban Public Education with an Andean Cultural Twist

Compassion means going directly to those people and places where suffering is most acute and building a home there.

FROM *COMPASSION—A REFLECTION ON THE CHRISTIAN LIFE*

In 1986 the chances of a poor child living in central La Paz receiving anything that could be called an education were close to nil. At that time, parents were pulling children from school to work on the streets, hawking toothpaste and ballpoint pens. The lucky ones trudged off to school with empty stomachs and nearly empty lunch sacks to face teachers also pinched by hard times. Families were selling off furniture and clothing—anything to put food on the table. An increasing number of abandoned youth found themselves crowding together in one-room shacks. Some schools closed, while others were so broke that parents were expected to provide chalk for the blackboards. Families who had migrated from rural villages dreaming of a better future for their children awakened in a nightmare.

For years, Bolivia's presidents had despaired at the condition of the country's schools, wondering what, if anything, could be done to bring the educational system into the twentieth century. All the while, less than three blocks from the Presidential Palace, a large part of the answer was taking shape, thanks to the efforts of a visionary educator, the gifted staff he recruited, and the young people of La Paz whom they have inspired.

Antonio Sagristá had an idea for how things might be made better for the children of central La Paz. Looking out from a window of the Colegio San Calixto, the posh private Jesuit high school where many of his colleagues taught, Sagristá saw something familiar in the poor neighborhood surrounding him, and imagined a new kind of centralized youth center going up next door. Integral to his vision was the assumption that for a youth center to be effective in the neighborhood, it would have to tap, reinforce, and base itself on the creative energy of its students' ethnic roots.

The facility Sagristá and his colleagues have built is a magnet drawing schoolchildren from all over the central city and the surrounding barrios of El Alto. Six days a week they stream in and out of the Centro de Multiservicios Educativos (CEMSE) (Center of Educational Services), a modern, six-story building ensconced between a nineteenth-century church and a whitewashed adobe house with a red tile roof. All hours of the day, the corridors and classrooms of CEMSE pulsate with the energy of youth. In a top-floor room, middle school students holding notebooks lean forward intently, "deconstructing" advertisements from a video-taped World Cup match. An earnest eleven-year-old down the hall captivates a circle of his peers, using a pointer and a collage to explain the dangers of cholera. On the floor below, outfitted in blue jeans and jerseys, bronze-skinned teenage boys with names like Condori and Chambi, swing their shoulders to and fro while blowing vigorously into Andean panpipes. Standing under a backdrop on which a disembodied smile of huge white teeth and red lipstick are painted, two sixteen-year-old girls pose questions about sex and love to an auditorium packed with high school students. Other rooms are full of students hovering over chemistry experiments, undergoing physical checkups, and poring over texts at crowded library tables. Such bustle was unimaginable until Antonio Sagristá looked out his window and began to contemplate.

A VISION OF THINGS TO COME

I first heard of Sagristá in relation to an agricultural marketing study in the rural highlands. People I respected raved about the "hard-working, brainy economist" whose sophisticated analysis had made their final report so persuasive. We met for the first time when he approached the IAF on behalf of CEMSE.

Sagristá is a Jesuit from Catalonia. The seeds of his relentless idealism were planted as a boy during the Republic and survived the ravaging of Barcelona during the Spanish Civil War. His idea for a multiservice educational center in La Paz stems from initiatives he undertook with Hispanic immigrants in the Yonkers neighborhoods of New York in the late 1960s, when he founded the Spanish Community Service Foundation. The foundation used bilingual counselors and training programs to help newly arrived residents overcome barriers to housing, jobs, credit, and health services, and eventually catapulted Hispanics into leadership positions on the local school board and led to the formation of a vigorous human rights committee. Sagristá's belief that low-income populations face multiple, interrelated demands enabled the foundation to provide comprehensive services under one roof at the lowest possible cost. The insight that "economies of scale" could be innovatively put to work for social ends became his recurrent calling.

Bald, wiry, with intense eyes, Sagristá is a man of simple tastes, unpretentious bearing, and firm convictions. Although he holds a doctorate in econometrics from Cornell University, he is more worker priest than cosmopolitan academic. He spent time at Sofia University in Japan designing one of the first computer models of that country's economy, but his yearning for social entrepreneurship and community work eventually took him to the barrios of South America's poorest nation.

Sagristá had already made his mark in Bolivia by the time he arrived at San Calixto. In starting a small, innovative export enterprise, managed by amputees, that manufactured artificial human limbs at prices affordable to the poor, he had shown his adeptness at uncovering resources in impossible situations. Now, tension within the Jesuit order over social values was fueling a new quest. He and his colleagues were increasingly concerned that many of their best teachers, administrators, and professionals were being siphoned off to educate youth in the better neighborhoods of La Paz. This pattern reinforced rather than reversed the educational inequities of a city whose wealthiest private school had a budget larger than the whole public school system.

To see the disparity, Sagristá merely had to compare two nearby schools. Colegio San Calixto occupied the colonial mansion of an ex-president. Its students followed the footsteps of parents who were lawyers, doctors, dentists, engineers, and political leaders. Its tiled corridors, elegant courtyards, well-furnished classrooms, bulging library collection, and state-of-the-art science labs invited one into an environment of serious learning. Teachers earned four times the salary paid by the public sector, and concentrated on developing analytical skills among students rather than imposing lessons by rote.

Colegio Reyes, by contrast, was a typical public school, a massive box of concrete block with layers of peeling white paint. Its students were several shades darker in skin and hair color than those of San Calixto, and came from families of street vendors, low-rung civil servants, taxicab drivers, and unskilled construction workers. A shelf of books, a television for educational videos, or even a retort for mixing chemicals were not to be found. Students had to cope with emotional problems without the aid of psychologists and plan careers without guidance counselors. Teachers earning approximately $70 monthly were more intent on moonlighting than improving the performance of their students.

Sagristá envisioned a facility to bridge the growing gap between public and private education, and he was sure the high density of neighborhood public schools made the idea economically feasible. He would create a hub to serve the 17,000 children of forty-three nearby schools. This facility would offer opportunities unusual for Bolivia: remedial tutoring, use of science labs and computers, a library to cultivate the pleasures of reading, music and dance workshops to explore cultural heritage, clinics for medical checkups, a cafeteria serving nutritious foods, and teaching methods designed to develop social and analytical skills for building a better society.

Sagristá noted an additional factor that reinforced his drive for maximum efficiency. "The high number of students in school for half-day shifts guaranteed that computer and chemistry labs would not be flooded a few hours in the afternoon and sit idle the rest of the day. We could lower the expenditure per student and spread the educational benefits across an entire school district. It looked like a cost-saving model for Third World governments, and maybe even some city governments in the First World with limited funds for satisfying growing educational needs."

Sagristá had an abiding conviction that Bolivian youth were as capable and motivated as any. He was convinced, in fact, that opening the door to the "facilities of a late twentieth-century school would enhance student pride and self-esteem, and make it possible to use the advance of science to leap ahead instead of falling behind." Yet he also sensed, as a Catalonian who had grown up in a Spain whose "official" language was different than his own native tongue, that Bolivians did not need to be remade in the image of the West in order to modernize. Yes, modern resources and technology were necessary for making social, economic, and political progress as a nation, but if they were not adapted to Bolivia's own cultural values, the edifice would rest on a weak foundation.

Building a strong foundation would not be easy. Sagristá had hoped to cut costs by persuading alumni from Colegio San Calixto, many of whom were doctors, lawyers, and dentists, to contribute their time and skill. "Each professional had to volunteer only a few hours a week for us to offer comprehensive services to the needy students and parents we hoped to reach," he explained. "Here was a relatively undemanding way for the better-off to channel knowledge and services to the poor, and create greater equality of social opportunities."

To his disappointment, Sagristá learned that alumni, despite their Jesuit education (Jesuits prided themselves on inculcating strong social values to go with rigorous scholasticism), were chiefly interested in gaining a private backdoor entrance for San Calixto students to the new center. "The idea for that door sent all the wrong messages," Sagristá insists today. "It would have given the middle- and upper-class kids from this exclusive school a private pass key into CEMSE's collection of services, elevating them above whoever walked in the main entrance. I knew CEMSE would not work unless the public school teachers and students felt it was for them, so I had to hold my ground in defending the original plan. I had seen too many development projects unravel as a result of influential community members pulling strings."

To formulate the project proposal for CEMSE, Sagristá surveyed students who attended public school in the neighborhood. He found they were coming to the district from other neighborhoods whose schools were in even worse shape, and their needs were more than educational. Health problems were rampant, and the level of family support for children was increasingly shaky. Convinced by these findings of the need for comprehensive services, the Jesuits agreed to close several parishes in the city to free up staff for the educational experiment. Soon Sagristá was off to England, Spain, the Netherlands, West Germany, and the United States in search of funds to get CEMSE off the ground. Although he eventually persuaded a half-dozen donors to sign on, the Inter-American Foundation financed 60 percent of the center's construction costs.

I was impressed by Sagristá's passion for reducing educational inequalities and by his scientific mind. Yet the decision to fund seemed less clear back in Washington, D.C., where staff review meetings failed to reach consensus. I called him to explain the difficulty. The IAF was not sure what to make of CEMSE since it did not fit into the kinds of nonformal educational projects run by NGOs that received first claim to resources. Wasn't it the state's responsibility to reform the formal school system, and what did constructing such a large facility have to do with grassroots social change.

Sagristá flew to IAF headquarters at Jesuit expense to defend his proposal face-to-face with the skeptical staff. Sagristá is not the usual prospective grantee. The committee eventually approved $198,000 to construct and equip the center.

The building opened in 1986, at a pivotal moment for the national economy. Three years of hyperinflation—which crested at 20,000 percent—had led to policies of structural adjustment that produced severe economic contraction. Incomes for barrio dwellers kept falling, tens of thousands of miners and factory workers lost their jobs, and La Paz sidewalks were more crowded than ever with indigenous women selling trinkets. Yet Sagristá found hope-filled words to offer on the day of CEMSE's dedication.

"In this time of reversal and frustration," he said, "it is difficult for us in Bolivia to envision works of size and importance. Yet this work is pioneering and ambitious in its belief that physical and human resources can be mobilized here and now to raise levels of primary health and education. It will show that these two needs are inextricably linked in ways existing institutions have not imagined. This is a work capable of disarming cynics and making fatalists wonder."

On the day CEMSE actually opened its doors, Sagristá was heard remarking to colleagues, "What will happen if no one comes to the feast after we have set the table?" The quip was not far off the mark. One CEMSE staffer remembers how "the neighborhood was papered with fliers announcing the program, but for months the place stood empty, with only an occasional teacher poking around. Frankly, we would look at one another, at the walls, down at the ground, and wonder if we had a white elephant on our hands. Finally, a few students were lured in with some classes in puppetry, painting, and music."

What those curious visitors saw whetted their appetite for more. Boris Mamani, a high school junior at the time, explained the attraction. "This place was totally different from everything else we knew." There were no grades, no attendance rolls, no teachers with backs stiff as boards, looking over your shoulder as if they were carrying a stick. Students were free to follow a curiosity until it was exhausted. Mamani concluded, "Here, in discussing topics no one had ever thought of raising at school, I felt, for the first time in my life, that adults valued my opinions and ideas."

The trickle of students became a flood. Demand for services quickly grew, leading to the creation of more than twenty-five different educational and other social programs. To meet the demand, support from international donors carried CEMSE from an annual budget of $20,000 to $230,000, while staff nearly quadrupled to forty-four employees, eight of them supported by the Bolivian government. The number of users kept climbing until it would one day reach 64 percent of area students.

In 1988, the Jesuits decided to replace Sagristá with Jorge Trías, also a Spaniard, and a former director of the order in Bolivia. CEMSE's amazing institutional growth and complexity required an able administrator, and the affable and energetic Trías, whose commanding presence and wavy silver hair gives him the demeanor of a distinguished parliamentarian, filled the bill. He mastered the sometimes onerous task of fund raising. Under his leadership, the annual budget has reached $300,000, supporting thirty-seven programs and a staff of fifty-five persons, including twenty-five professionals from the fields of psychology, social work, finance, education, medicine, and dentistry. He has also successfully mobilized local sources to cover 20 percent of CEMSE's costs.

Today, CEMSE is the impressive hub of educational services for students, teachers, and parents that Sagristá envisioned a decade ago, and as he acknowledges on his regular visits, something more. Each day 700 students walk from nearby schools to take advantage of vocational, legal, health, and psychological counseling programs, to undertake projects in science labs and the audiovisual and computer centers, and to find a quiet place to study. Some 8,000 people are regular users, spending several hours, two days a week, in one program or more. Teachers also bring their classes to CEMSE for group exercises, and come themselves for specialized instruction to improve teaching techniques, plan lessons, and upgrade their own schools.

To understand the dynamics of CEMSE and what has been accomplished, it is useful to wander its halls and explore some of its services.

What Is a Library?

When Sagristá first explained the CEMSE project proposal to me, he turned to a page in the appendix containing a social survey. He pointed to the figures and said: "You know, practically speaking, the public schools in this area are trying to educate without books. According to our findings, only eight high schools have more than twenty books in their collections.

One principal who claimed to have a library took me aside to see the two books he kept under lock and key so no one would steal them." Harried secretaries doubled as librarians during recess and faced impossible tasks, such as trying to divide a single textbook among 300 chemistry students. There were no encyclopedias, dictionaries, atlases, or other reference texts.

By opening a modern library, which quickly expanded to 5,000 volumes, CEMSE transformed these deplorable conditions almost overnight for the zone's forty-three schools. The effort was spearheaded by Costa Andrade, who received rigorous on-the-job training from a professional from La Paz's largest social science library. Andrade made sure that the library had a well-lighted reading room and that its display cases were stacked with an enticing array of up-to-date texts and periodicals.

The room seats fifty, and once card catalogues and library cards were in place, she established a program of cultural events to bring people in and make sure the seats stayed full. There were discussions about poetry and short stories, a series of book fairs and exhibits, and courses on library use and the formation of student study groups. Poetry readings by students helped them overcome shyness about public presentations. Andrade also created an innovative method of book distribution dubbed the *maleta viajera,* or traveling suitcase, which makes it possible to circulate a set of children's literature, science texts, or other supplementary reading materials within the schools themselves. The suitcase brings students to the reading room looking for more, and they can take books home over the weekend if necessary. Today the library boasts a regular readership of 23,741 persons, including over 1,000 teachers.

COUNTING ON COMPUTERS

In 1986, computers were considered "luxury" items beyond most IAF project budgets, yet Sagristá was determined to get them into the school system. Given what we now know about the computer's potential for enhancing Bolivia's role in the global economy and reducing inequality in educational opportunity, Sagristá's insistence seems prophetic.

Sagristá beams excitedly as he recalls the clamor from elementary and high school students to enroll in computer training courses. Soon the center's nineteen computers were humming nonstop. About 1,000 students signed up during the early 1990s for courses in Word Perfect and Lotus 1-2-3, and the lab is one of the few services at CEMSE that covers its own maintenance and repair costs. Even parents and teachers come in for classes on Saturdays, taking advantage of course fees that are among the lowest in the city.

It gives him special satisfaction, Sagristá said in 1993, to follow the learning curve of the sixty-eight active members in the computer club, because "they become much more than keypunchers as they learn FORTRAN and other languages in which they can think and program for themselves." The idea has caught on that computers, like books, are keys to a future in almost any professional field.

MAKING THE NATURAL SCIENCES REAL

In preparing a needs assessment for the project, Sagristá had visited the public schools in the neighborhood and asked to sit in on science classes. He could not believe that students were trying to learn biology and chemistry with only blackboard exercises and mimeographed handouts. From the outset of CEMSE, he was determined there would be science labs with state-of-the-art equipment so that students could get a feel for things with their own eyes and hands.

Santiago Bolívar, a Spanish educator working for CEMSE, says that "during the first year not a single teacher came round to use our labs on a regular basis. That number increased to ten by the second year and jumped to fifty during the third. You have to realize that not only were students unfamiliar with labs, but most teachers didn't know their way around labs either because teachers' colleges in Bolivia are also badly equipped. Teachers were intimidated by all this shiny equipment, afraid it would expose them to embarrassment. So we decided to push teacher training courses beyond the original plan."

Over the next few years, some eighteen courses were offered on subjects such as low-cost chemistry experiments, how to use a microscope and other materials, group biology projects, and methods to study ecosystems. It made all the difference. By 1993, according to Sagristá, utilization rates for the labs had reached 75 percent of capacity. And a group of instructors felt so revitalized by their new competence that they reorganized the high school science teachers' association, which had been moribund for years.

Students also come to the labs on their own after taking orientation courses and workshops. They have organized science clubs at CEMSE and at their own schools that have sponsored science fairs to demonstrate the fruits of hands-on work in the labs. A recent fair drew over 370 participants, in which public school projects held their own with competition from the best private high schools of the city. The science clubs sponsor field trips and conferences, show educational videos, and monitor results coming out of Bolivian universities and other research facilities. CEMSE recently has begun to focus on heightening awareness in the local schools about ecology, laying the groundwork for serious discussion about the fate of Bolivia's rainforest and the sources of urban pollution.

MAKING FACTS CLEAR BY BRINGING THEM TO LIFE

Because 98 percent of the Ministry of Education and Culture's budget for public schools funds teacher salaries, there is little to spare for classroom materials. CEMSE has tackled the problem in two ways. First, its audiovisual center has accumulated 480 videos that school teachers can schedule for class viewing in CEMSE's auditorium. Videos on sex education, one of those teachers explains, have been especially important, "allowing us to chip away at long-held taboos blocking discussion of teen pregnancies and sexual abuse." CEMSE's growing reputation as a venue for informed discussion has also attracted the interest of Bolivia's best film and video directors, who show their work at the center and teach courses. A new critical perspective has formed among interested students and led to seminars that analyze the impact of media, including how the soap operas so popular on La Paz television perpetuate ethnic, gender, and social stereotyping.

Second, CEMSE set up an educational resource center, the Centro de Recurses Educativos (CRE), to develop low-cost classroom materials. The center's director, Luis Sardines, believes that challenging teachers to use their imaginations is the key. The CRE's six staff members have shown how to adapt familiar games such as bingo and dominoes to teach mathematics, and how cardboard boxes, milk cartons, balloons, straws, and other items can be rescued from the trash or purchased for next to nothing and transformed into educational toys for schoolchildren. Old photographs are combined with newspaper and magazine cutouts to produce posters on dental hygiene or the condition of the rainforest.

At first, local teachers were lukewarm to this flow of ideas. The CRE distributed packets of materials that wound up at the bottom of desk drawers. One reason, says Sardines, is that Bolivia's "teachers' colleges fill graduates' heads with cloudy abstractions about pedagogy that have little to do with the dynamics of educating real students." When the teacher arrives in the classroom, innovation is not rewarded by the system, so why make waves or take on new responsibilities?

"This led us to go into the schools, especially elementary schools, and demonstrate how these materials could make teaching more rewarding for both the student and the instructor." This outreach effort is geared to training teachers to produce their own materials and to sow the idea that real education is a question of active participation rather than passive consumption. The intent is dual: to break the cycle of dependency that presumes worthwhile ideas and information must be imported and to allow the CRE to maximize its limited resources by concentrating on training rather than production.

A number of schools in the zone now make their own relief maps, wall posters, and educational games. The CRE is also booked up with requests for training sessions in the other schools and even in other cities that have heard about the program. Recently staff from the national planning office charged with developing a comprehensive educational reform plan requested briefings on the center's operations and, Sardines comments wryly, "the word has somehow reached the military's geographic institute, which recently called upon us for help."

Active Minds Need Healthy Bodies

Sagristá's original survey convinced him that basic health services had to be improved if students were to take advantage of new educational opportunities. Only 12 percent of public school students were considered to be in good health; 57 percent suffered from nutritional deficiencies; 87 percent had serious dental problems, averaging ten cavities per child; and only 8 of every 1,000 had access to health care services. To redress these conditions, Sagristá hired Dr. Virginia Roncal, an articulate Bolivian physician who had been working for six years in some of the city's poorest barrios.

Roncal began by opening a medical and dental clinic and a pharmacy at CEMSE, and starting nutrition and health education programs. Although their doors were open to the entire community, elementary schoolchildren were given priority for annual checkups. Between 1986 and 1991, the number of physicals quadrupled, eventually reaching full coverage of the zone's fourteen grade schools and their 4,655 students. The Ministry of Health, by contrast, reached only 2,287 children from the city's 147 public schools during 1991.

CEMSE's clinic has become a community fixture, providing 13,373 patient consultations between 1990 and 1991 alone. Every day, waiting areas are crowded with students in school uniforms sitting next to indigenous women in bowler hats and striped shawls who have brought their babies in for primary care and immunizations. Roncal is especially pleased at the new level of cooperation from schoolteachers. "Formerly," she says, "they felt helpless to do anything for a sick child. Now they send the student right over to us. And it isn't only the ones who are sick. They send others over to do research assignments on health topics assigned as classwork. There is a growing awareness in the schools about the need for preventive care."

The annual checkups of students have also fleshed out Sagristá's original survey, highlighting the need to correct visual deficiencies and improve nutrition levels. Nearly 35 percent of students need glasses, yet they are a rare sight in the classroom. In a system that has relied almost exclusively on the blackboard for transmitting information, these children are at serious disadvantage.

Diagnosing the problem does not resolve it. At $70 a pair, eyeglasses remain beyond the reach of most families. The need is so widespread that a television-radio personality who donated spectacles to indigenous guests appearing on his programs became so popular he was able to form his own party and run for president. Of course there are not enough slots on such a program even for the children of the San Calixto zone, so CEMSE subsidizes the eyeglasses it prescribes. Thus far, only 25 percent of those in need have been able to take advantage of the offer.

The checkups also revealed that a school breakfast program was imperative for chronically undernourished students, with follow-up monitoring to chart gains in weight and height. Each morning, some 200 children sit at long tables in CEMSE's first-floor cafeteria and are served a hearty meal of fresh fruit, milk, quinoa, tea, and bread. Most of the parents in the area have yet to take advantage of the program, however, perhaps out of pride. To reach more students, CEMSE has begun a pilot program that allows teachers to pick up breakfasts for classroom distribution.

Roncal realizes CEMSE must reach out if it is to begin solving the area's endemic health problems. That requires staffing. Fortunately, the clinic has become a magnet for students and faculty from nursing and medical schools in La Paz who want hands-on training for careers in public health. But the real key to CEMSE's effort has been the recruitment of *brigadistas de salud*. These health brigades of student volunteers, who range in age from nine to sixteen, are carrying the message of preventive care into the schools and into their neighborhoods and homes.

The idea, Roncal says, "came from examples elsewhere in Latin America, including the literacy brigades of Nicaragua, but this is the first effort of its kind in Bolivia." The brigades currently consist of twenty students in grade school, eighty in high school, and several CEMSE alumni now in universities. Working with the center's doctors, nurses, and social workers, they have designed an education program that concentrates on five areas: malnutrition, dental hygiene, cholera, skin disease, and tuberculosis. Brigadistas learn to see local health problems in the wider social context of economic privation and the lack of potable water and adequate sewerage, allowing students to think about what effective national health policies might look like. The brigades then design comic books, prepare skits, compose songs, and use puppets and dance to inform their peers. Perhaps their most effective performance was during the recent South American cholera epidemic. Forming small teams of three and four students, brigadistas wearing white smocks fanned out into the schools, alerting the whole area to the need for proper hygiene to avoid infection and about treatment during the crucial early hours of the disease to reduce mortality from dehydration and to minimize further contagion.

Students and the Energizing Power of Tradition

From the outset, the organizers and staff of CEMSE had a vision that student participation through activities such as the health brigades was essential for institutional effectiveness. Drawing upon his experience in Yonkers, Sagristá began by helping students organize an umbrella organization, the Asociación Estudiantil MINKA[1] to operate as a kind of mutual fund that would permit individual members to buy textbooks and other supplies at discount rates.

When Jorge Trías became CEMSE's director, he expanded that role. Trías understood the importance of empowering students from his experience of leading one of the country's first NGOs, which had pioneered the use of nonformal education methodologies for organizing campesinos in the valleys of southern Bolivia. Trías opened the door, and a half-dozen Bolivian educators, psychologists, and administrators stepped in to help MINKA forge an identity of its own.

José Nuñez, a son of a migrant mineworker, helped lead the way. He had worked as an organizer with several NGOs and knew the field of popular education inside out. His experience had taught him that effective programs build self-esteem through the recovery and strengthening of cultural identity. Key to this process was the use of "generative words," a technique pioneered by the Brazilian educator Paulo Freire in teaching adult literacy. Generative words embody concepts that allow communities to name, analyze, and remake their reality.[2] In thinking about MINKA, Nuñez drew upon the experience of Warisata.

Warisata is a small altiplano town that started an indigenous Aymara school in the 1930s. Its people had broken with colonial conventions for running a school district and organized public education by joining several nearby communities within the political framework of an indigenous ayllu, under the supervision of a *parlamento amauta,* or council of elders. The council tapped two forms of traditional Andean communal labor—the minka (*minga*) and the ayni—to build the school and organize an active student body to maintain it. The unusual degree of local autonomy and the fact that the curriculum was grounded in the Aymara language aroused skepticism and then hostility among national educators, who shut the school down.

Nuñez and another nonformal education specialist, Augusto Román, noted that 80 percent of the students using CEMSE spoke Aymara at home. The public schools were not only providing them with an inferior education but treating their traditional culture as a handicap. The two educators hoped to adapt the educational and cultural principles of Warisata to CEMSE by allowing MINKA to tap the creative energy of its Aymara roots.

Their first step was to help stimulate student involvement by reinforcing group identity through Andean rather than Western co-operative modalities—instead of being based on the individualistic notion of one person, one vote, MINKA would become an organization of organizations. Each of the programs within CEMSE—the computer lab, the science clubs, the library, the health brigade, and the others—would organize itself as a working community and elect a representative to a student council that would act as a kind of *parlamento amauta* for focusing student enthusiasm and helping govern CEMSE.

MINKA representatives began by participating in CEMSE's high-level planning sessions and, as they gained experience, joined community council meetings with parents and teachers. MINKA assemblies not only allowed youth of one community to learn about the activities of another, they inspired students to explore how services could be improved and new ideas introduced into the schools in which they spent the greater part of their days. They created a new awareness of traditional culture and critical analysis that challenged CEMSE to look beyond the task of supporting public schools toward revitalizing the system by making it genuinely multicultural.

Leading this effort are the *animadores juveniles* (youth social animators), twenty-five students who are trained for five months in nonformal communication techniques, workshop planning, and social research to develop opportunities for nurturing cultural pride and identity. They are supported by seventy university student volunteers, many of them former MINKA leaders and animadores, who are majoring in a variety of disciplines and also back up CEMSE's core staff in providing technical services.

Perhaps the most prominent and popular MINKA members are the cultural brigades, which work tirelessly to inject the spirit of Warisata into CEMSE's service programs. The brigades grew out of a program called Free Time that was sponsored by La Paz businessmen in 1988 to get students to say "no" to illegal drugs. The students of CEMSE discovered it was better to find something to say "yes" to, and the program became a vehicle for exploring ethnic identity through social and cultural activities. The brigades have a membership of 350 youth drawn from the three levels of public schooling. The elementary group calls itself Ayni, the junior high group is named Ayllu. The high school group has named itself after Luis Espinal, a human rights activist/journalist/film critic and Catholic priest who was gunned down by the military in the early 1980s.

The brigades confront the cultural alienation of barrio youth by recovering traditional art forms, including Andean music. "During CEMSE's early days," Nuñez says, "we tried to stir up interest in this music, but without success. All you heard was hard rock being played at local festivals. Finally, we arranged for a workshop through the brigades, and over time this grew into six bands that became quite adept at the panpipe, flute, *charango,* and guitar. They didn't stop with learning the old songs; they made a real effort to understand the culture that produced the lyrics and tunes in order to convey this knowledge to audiences at their concerts. Today, most students at CEMSE are being pulled in the same direction."

The Ayni and Ayllu brigades have also helped sponsor an orchestra of students between the ages of eight and fourteen that plays contemporary music on traditional instruments. More than 1,400 young people have taken a turn during the orchestra's history. One of its most notable concerts featured an original composition that wove together different melodic themes for each of Bolivia's fourteen main ethnic groups.

The brigades are also playing a key analytic role in helping students restore pride in their own families and develop positive self-images. One girl, for instance, noted how television promotes an image of feminine beauty that most women cannot fit. Today, she says, the important issue for her is not access to cosmetics or fashions that disguise her Andean features, but discovering whether her ancestors were Quechua or Aymara.

The process of cultural recovery is often painful when it uncovers the deep-seated shame embedded in the psyches of a colonized people. Nuñez notes how many students are embarrassed by mothers who show up in the *pollera* garb of multilayered skirts, bowler hat, and vividly colored shawl that identify them to the world as *cholitas,* urban Aymara women who maintain their traditional dress despite the mestizo/criollo values of the city's mainstream. "But we are changing this," he says, pointing to the many students who now sit beside mothers wearing polleras at community meetings without betraying the slightest discomfort.

MINKA, led by the cultural brigades, played a highly visible role in La Paz during the quincentenary year marking Columbus's arrival. *Los 500 Años* became the generative word for a series of educational events that culminated with a cultural fair held on Columbus Day itself. Conferences took place in which intellectual luminaries held forth on topics such as indigenous religions, resource management, and political systems. Students addressed poetry, short stories, and letters to the dead Columbus and the Spanish landlords who followed in his wake, and presented skits that dramatized the conquest and its aftermath up to the present. CEMSE was plastered with thematic posters such as "El Mestizaje Religioso" (mestizo religiosity), which depicted the sun, moon, and mother earth on one side and the crucifix on the other.

More than 5,000 students and their families visited the fair, which probed beneath the lingering injustice to seriously consider what it meant to be a twentieth-century Bolivian. The dominant tone was expressed in letters written to Columbus and signed with Aymara names for everyman and everywoman—Huanca and Huaynoca:

> We, the dark-skinned people of America, must cease our lamentations. We must find and value whatever good the past holds for us, and use it to transform this day into a tomorrow that welcomes us.

This is the spirit that drives the youth who have passed through CEMSE and MINKA—Betty Márquez, a former MINKA leader who still volunteers her time, described what CEMSE has meant to her and her generation. "My father is a taxi driver, and he was not happy that his young daughter was showing so much independence, spending money on bus fares downtown to CEMSE, and wasting time pursuing these strange interests. But a whole new world opened up to me, a world of responsibility and self-discipline and hope. This place offers more opportunity for self-directed learning than the university I now attend, so I come back here to keep learning and growing."

MINKA and student volunteers like Márquez are turning a bright light on Bolivia's past to see what its future might look like. They travel outward on field trips to mining towns and ancient Inca trails to see where history has been made, and they are turning sharp eyes on the present to see how they can make history.

If you ask José Nuñez what kind of history these young people will make, he will tell you about a recent national election campaign when a number of them served as *reporteros populares,* or peoples' reporters, for a local radio station. "Their observations of voter manipulation, self-aggrandizement by paternalistic politicians, and disparities in election spending among the parties gave MINKA members a lot to think about. After careful analysis, they modified a number of organizational practices they had blindly copied from political parties without considering how such mechanisms were misshaping the world they would inherit, the very same world they were committed to changing for the better."

A MODEL FOR REFORM

Sagristá is certain that CEMSE has much to offer Third World governments searching for an affordable way to provide first-class education to their rapidly growing populations and pressures to compete in the global economy. Indeed, a number of those governments, including several state and municipal jurisdictions in Brazil, are building multiple-service magnet schools on their own.

The issue, however, is not simply achieving economies of scale. CEMSE's real virtue lies in the fact that students who are not compelled to attend, do attend. Dropout rates among regular users of the center have plummeted to near zero, while the overall rate for La Paz hovers at 40 percent. Students come to CEMSE and keep coming back, even after graduation, because the facility's purpose is not to remake them but to help them find themselves.

There are indications that this message is being heard by the Bolivian government. The Fondo de Inversión Social (FIS) has proposed establishing eleven urban and small town Centros Multiservicios e Interculturales (CEMEI) through NGOs and municipal governments. Each would serve as many as fifteen schools and 10,000 students. The fact that these centers have been designated "intercultural" shows that the lessons of MINKA, and the experience of grassroots initiatives across the country, have not been lost on government planners.

The plan ran into a snag, however, when the World Bank held up funds because the per pupil cost seemed too high. FIS set out to consult Sagristá to see if the proposal could be salvaged. They found him in the tiny town of San Ignacio de Moxos, site of a former Jesuit mission in the tropical hinterlands of eastern Bolivia, where he was busy adapting the CEMSE model to a rustic setting. To overcome the lack of electricity, he had pored over manuals and installed solar panels that were soon powering computers, labs, and other facilities for indigenous students of surrounding villages.

Sagristá quickly found the error in FIS's proposal: it had not pro-rated infrastructure costs across the expected life of the plan. When the World Bank learned per pupil costs were as little as $7 annually, it approved the loan and recommended that Sagristá join the Bolivian team negotiating loans to revamp the national educational system.

The new reforms will redistribute resources from an inefficient university system to support primary and secondary schools starved of basic equipment and quality teachers. They will also include *nucleos escolares* in the low-income neighborhoods and rural communities that embody the centralized service concept pioneered at CEMSE. At the same time, the

government will decentralize administrative responsibility to local communities, promoting bilingual education and greater respect for the country's
multicultural heritage. Sagristá has long wished to see these changes, and
the inclusion of the CEMSE model in the heart of the reforms will help
bring his vision of greater educational equality within the nation's grasp.

Mt. Sajama dominates this altiplano landscape in Pacajes province.

This farmstead in Izozog of the Chaco region is representative of Bolivia's arid lowlands. (Courtesy of Lorgio Vaca)

Traditional llama caravans have declined with the gradual expansion of railways and truck transport. (Courtesy of ASUR)

Only 5.5 percent of Bolivia's roads are paved and transportation costs remain high. (Courtesy of the author)

A small-town store displays an array of highly processed foods in 1975.

A woman works shoveling salt in the Salar de Uyuni, the largest salt flat in South America.

Wall posters of the eighteenth-century Aymara rebels Tupak Katari and Bartolina Sisa were used by the Katarista movement in the 1970s and 1980s. (Poster produced by INDICEP)

This photograph of Aymara rebel Pablo Zarate Willka (*center front*) and his cohorts was taken shortly after their capture by the government in 1904. (Courtesy of Cordero Archive)

Víctor Hugo Cárdenas (*right*) discusses local development issues with Aymara peasants. He was elected as Vice-President of Bolivia in 1993, the highest office held by a leader of indigenous descent. (Courtesy of Roger Hamilton)

Posters such as this one developed by CIMCA aid in grassroots consciousness-raising and organizing. (Courtesy of Germán Treviño)

El Ceibo pioneered the production of cacao beans using organic farming methods to grow healthy cacao trees. (Courtesy of El Ceibo)

El Ceibo uses modern manufacturing technology to meet the demands of the international market for chocolate. (Courtesy of El Ceibo)

An illustration from an El Ceibo advertising calendar shows the village operation in processing cacao beans for shipment to the factory. (Courtesy of El Ceibo)

(*Insert*) A woman separates cacao beans from the pulp.

CECAOT experiments with a mobile water tank in a effort to save quinoa plants during a drought. (Courtesy of CECAOT)

Agronomist Jaime Alba stands in a field of healthy quinoa plants. (Courtesy of Jaime Alba)

Camelids were not included in livestock fairs until the mid-1990s. Better breeding is now encouraged by prizes such as this award presented to champion alpaca in La Paz. (Courtesy of Jaime Alba)

Lobbying by AIGACCA made way for the legalization of llama meat sales in 1994, resulting in sanitary slaughter and marketing practices such as this enclosed display case.

CIMCA uses rotofolio posters such as this one for consciousness-raising among Aymara and Quechua villagers. (Courtesy of Germán Treviño)

CIMCA's mobile units organize workshops in the villages, where educadores populares gather women to discuss the rotofolio presentation. (Courtesy of Fernando Soria)

ASUR organized training workshops where talented weavers could teach technique and intricate design work to peers and the younger generation.

Tarabuco weavers collectively grade their textiles, thereby creating incentives for excellence in workmanship. (Courtesy of ASUR)

Aymara members of COPROCA sort alpaca fiber by color and grade for industrial processing. (Courtesy of AIGACCA)

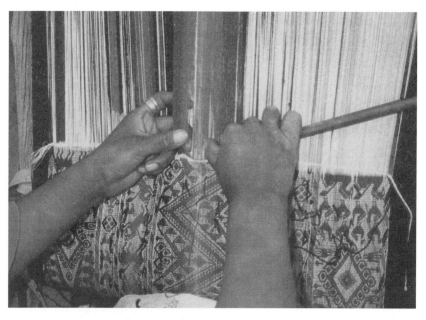

Tarabuco weavers combine unique weaving techniques with vibrant colors and complex design. (Courtesy of ASUR)

CIDAC exhibits the craftwork of the people in the Santa Cruz region in its museum-like store. (Courtesy of CIDAC)

ARTECAMPO is a federation of artisans which has built on CIDAC's educational efforts to encourage organizational skills such as bookkeeping and planning. (Courtesy of CIDAC)

CIDAC's focus is not only the revitalization of traditional crafts, but the development of artistic talent among the young. (Courtesy of CIDAC)

The recovery and promotion of Guarayo arts and crafts such as hammock weaving have led to increased appreciation of these peoples. (Courtesy of CIDAC)

Local labor is mobilized through traditional Andean practices to build a radio station needed for Rayqaypampa's Quechua radio shows. (Courtesy of CENDA)

CENDA concentrated its cultural revitalization efforts primarily around native potato production, utilizing practical demonstrations, media, and literacy programs. (Courtesy of CENDA)

Indigenous marchers from the lowlands reach the western mountains as they proceed toward the national capital of La Paz. (Courtesy of Presencia)

MARCHA INDIGENA

POR EL

TERRITORIO Y LA

DIGNIDAD

TRINIDAD
-
LA PAZ

PARTIMOS DE TRINIDAD EL 15 DE AGOST

Hermanos del Beni y de Bolivia:
Apóyennos con lo que puedan. ¡GRA

ago

Comité de Marcha · Central de Pueblos Indígeno

Indigenous marchers from the lowlands reach the western mountains as they proceed toward the national capital of La Paz. (Courtesy of Presencia)

CHAPTER 11

Recuperating a Wealth of Women's Weavings in the Valleys of Chuquisaca

Cieza summarizes prevailing 16th century opinion in admiring Inca textiles. The colors were beautiful, the scarlets, blues, yellows and blacks were better than anything in Europe.

JOHN MURRA (1978)

Few outsiders ever reach the hamlet of Qarawiri in the rugged mountains of south-central Bolivia, and those who have not come to visit a relative would, at first glance, find little reason to stop. There is no electricity and no evident source of potable water for the handful of adobe houses with thatched roofs and dirt floors. The only signs of any amenity are the weather-stained sheets of opaque plastic that cover the few small windows of each dwelling.

Between the piercing blue, midday Andean sky and the brown, barren earth is one splash of color. A woman of indeterminate age, draped in a tattered black tunic and wearing a white, bowl-shaped hat, sits before a horizontal loom braced against the wall of her house. On that loom she is opening a window into another world—weaving images of fire-red condors, dragons, foxes, llamas, and strange, nameless animals moving in every which way in a colorful yet enigmatic scene.

Finally, the woman's gnarled hands stop moving. She rises, steps back to a proper distance, cocks her head slightly, and watches the world of flux resolve into an intricately patterned world of order. Her mouth widens into a thin, toothless smile of contentment. After two months of attentive labor, she has finished weaving an *axsu*, a traditional overskirt worn by the women of the area. Although the weaver has never traveled from the place of her birth, she knows her axsus will. It will be sold at a shop that people from her community help manage in Sucre, or if its quality is as good as she believes, it might even wind up in an exhibition in Paris or Washington, D.C.

A COUPLE STRUCK BY WEAVINGS

When I said goodbye to Professor John Murra upon leaving Cornell University to take a job with the Inter-American Foundation, he offered me the names of a couple, a Spanish man and a Chilean woman, to contact regarding worthwhile Bolivian projects. For several years, Gabriel Martínez and Verónica Cereceda had promoted local theater in remote Quechua-speaking communities in the Charazani mountain valleys of Bolivia, sparking interest in the use of Quechua culture as an organizing tool. The 1971 military takeover of Bolivia had forced them to return to Chile and abandon their adopted country, but Murra reported their devotion to the Bolivian people had continued unabated.

So on one of my first trips as an IAF staff member in 1979, I tracked Martínez and Cereceda down in Lima, Peru, during a stopover en route to Bolivia. I was greeted at the front door by a slight woman with light brown hair and large sparkling eyes and a heavily bearded, loquacious man with a warm, baritone voice. The couple not only turned out to be wonderful and interesting people but Verónica and I quickly discovered a shared passion for Andean weavings.

Her interest in native weavings had flourished through her work as a curator of Andean collections in a Chilean museum and as a scholarly researcher and author of pathbreaking academic publications about the visual codes in textile art. My own interest began in 1968 as a Peace Corps volunteer when I helped the villagers on Lake Titicaca's Taquile Island organize a marketing program of some of Peru's finest and most beautiful weavings. Aquiles Lanoa, a Quechua-speaking Peruvian Peace Corps staff member and my first "maestro" on Andean development, pushed me in this direction.

Over the next ten years, I watched Taquile move from being one of Peru's poorest lakeside communities to one of its better-off through textiles and a fast-growing tourist industry controlled by the islanders (Healy and Zorn 1994c). Later in the mid-1970s, while I was doing field work for my doctoral dissertation in southern Chuquisaca, I further nourished my interest in Bolivian weaving as I learned about the traditions of the Jalq'a and Tarabucos discussed in this chapter.

Verónica and I spent several hours that first day discussing why South America's most fantastic weaving traditions received so little positive public support in the towns and cities closest to them. One glaring indication of this racism was that Bolivia had not one national museum with an exhibition representing the diverse indigenous costumes and weavings. Outside the indigenous communities themselves, the majority of the appreciation came from visiting foreign tourists, including hippies who enjoyed wearing local clothing. Some of the best weaving traditions were found among the country's poorest rural women in the isolated villages of Chuquisaca and neighboring Potosí, yet at the time, developmental organizations had little understanding of how these weaving skills could be utilized in their strategies for grassroots development.

Martínez and Cereceda, as a young married couple with two small children, had left their teaching jobs in the drama department of a Chilean university during the 1960s to form a traveling popular theater troupe. Performing in a tent to diverse audiences throughout the country, their repertory troupe of poets, singers, storytellers, and actors was inspired by the "magical realism" that Gabriel Garcia Marquez, the young Mario Vargas Llosa, and other writers were inventing to explore how indigenous, European, and African cultures had intermingled to shape a distinctively Latin American experience. The troupe stood at the forefront of a broad movement to break down barriers between performers and audiences and use theater as an interactive medium for social analysis and democratic community action. Nobel Prize winner Pablo Neruda, who composed *Alturas de Macchu Picchu,* an epic poem about the continent's Incan heritage, was among the guest artists who sometimes dropped in to perform their work.

By the early 1970s, Martínez' and Cereceda's curiosity about the roots of Latin American identity had led them to teaching jobs at a university in the Bolivian altiplano. They soon shocked their somewhat stuffy colleagues by taking theater workshops out of the classroom and into indigenous Quechua communities in the mountain valley of Charazani. Martínez and Cereceda were entranced by the area's breathtaking beauty, its rich pre-Columbian heritage, and vibrant textiles. Although the community-based theater group they organized gradually developed a repertoire that is still remembered fondly by Bolivian practitioners of popular drama, Martínez and Cereceda felt nagging doubts. The performances were given in

Quechua, but the uneasy silence or burst of unexpected laughter that the words sometimes provoked caused Martínez and Cereceda to wonder at the undiscovered depths of the language they were using, to wonder if real communication was occurring and if they were having any lasting impact.

To learn how to speak the community's language fluently, it would be necessary to become immersed in its culture. Martínez and Cereceda embarked on a new voyage of discovery to acquire the tools they needed to accomplish that task. They left the theater to study anthropology at the Catholic University in Lima. There they steeped themselves in the rich literature documenting Andean traditions, learning how to use scientific knowledge as an entryway into the dynamics of contemporary community life. Although Martínez and Cereceda had no immediate plans to return to Bolivia, I told them to keep in touch and mentioned that we could perhaps work together once they did.

After pursuing four years of doctoral studies and additional museum work in Paris, they returned to Bolivia anxious for hands-on work again and for a time took up residence in an Aymara community near Lake Titicaca. While re-establishing a life in Bolivia, they began surveying the different possibilities around the country for working with weavers, finally selecting a geographically isolated ethnic group, the Jalq'a, living in the high mountain valleys in northern Chuquisaca.

Martínez and Cereceda sent the IAF a request for financial support for a project with this indigenous group in 1985. I knew about the Jalq'a: in the mid-1970s, the mountain men and women in their distinctive white, bowl-shaped hats walking the streets of picturesque, colonial Sucre were an immediate fascination to foreigners. The axsus, the large decorative overskirts of the women, displayed stylized animals such as llamas and condors floating upside down, stretching out sideways, acrobatically swinging in a pitch-black sea. It was a kind of dream world, where eyes popped out in odd places, necks stretched and twisted with improbable elasticity, and tails become arrows shooting out between serrated rows of catlike teeth. They appeared to convey an indigenous cosmovision that celebrated biodiversity, wedding it to their ethnic identity.

I processed this small grant request of $25,000 in record time and soon thereafter Martínez and Cereceda started their explorations. Since they were two individuals rather than an NGO, the IAF had to channel its financial support through an existing NGO working in the area. A year later, in a union with other anthropologist colleagues, they formed their own organization, Antropólogos del Sur Andino (ASUR), to take full control of the weaving revival program and qualify for direct financial support from the IAF.

THE LOCAL COMMUNITIES: A HISTORY OF DEGRADATION

The project's initial activity began one crisp September morning in 1985, when the two anthropologists set out on a quest to resolve a mystery about the Jalq'a people. Joined by Bolivian anthropologist Ramiro Molina Rivera, they were determined to trace the origins of a number of weavings that years before were being passed off as antiques in tourist shops in La Paz and other Bolivian cities. Although the weavings were esteemed by collectors for their uniqueness, and their fabulist designs were reproduced on postcards, magazine covers, and posters and had inspired university-trained painters in La Paz, surprisingly little was known about their creators. Collectors and merchants referred to the weavings as "Potolo pieces," after the largest town (comprising some 600 families) in the area of their origin, fifty kilometers northeast of Sucre. No ethnographic studies of the culture or people responsible for the weavings could be found.

For several months, Martínez, Cereceda, and Molina combed the steep valleys of Chuquisaca, visiting dozens of scattered communities by jeep and on foot. Much of what they found was disturbing but unsurprising.

The area was inhabited by a group of nearly 25,000 people, all of whom called themselves Jalq'a. They were severely impoverished, with a high infant mortality rate and average family incomes of $260 per year. Their parched potato fields and small flocks of scrawny sheep and goats showed the effects of a long-standing drought. Villages lacked clean water and electric power, had few health clinics, and no tin roofs or bikes—common signs of minimal affluence among Andean campesinos—were to be found. People seemed generally dispirited and disorganized.

The three visitors were pleased to see, however, that most villagers still wore traditional ethnic dress. But the axsus worn by the women were pale reflections of the garments that had inspired the team's quest. The subtle color combinations were gone, the large decorative panels called *pallas* had shrunk in size, and the motif of exotic animals in free fall had been replaced by repetitive rows of stock figures. The adoption of geometric designs and colors used by a neighboring ethnic group was gradually erasing their tenuous connections to the past. The young women, perhaps influenced by urban values penetrating the countryside, had turned away from the exacting standards maintained by their mothers and grandmothers.

Indeed, as Martínez and Cereceda talked with villagers, they began to see that the decline in textiles was symptomatic of a deeper problem. The community's cultural structure was unraveling from changes in the regional economy. The drought had crippled subsistence production, but rising demand among the Jalq'a for macaroni, candles, cooking oil, medicines, and other consumer staples had increased the need for cash.

Beginning in the 1960s and accelerating through the mid-1970s, a ready source for that cash became available. A growing market for Andean textiles among tourists and overseas dealers had spawned a horde of itinerant traders who scoured the countryside for ponchos, shawls, axsus, belts, bags, and even grain sacks. Items with Jalq'a motifs were in heavy demand, and traders, some of them expatriates, frequented local fairs and festivals to persuade campesinos, often through badgering or trickery, to relinquish their finest textiles. The Jalq'a never learned the true market value of these items, which steadily appreciated as they grew rarer.

One day the boom was over, and the Jalq'a realized that the core of their weaving inheritance—their ritual costumes, wedding garments, and family heirlooms—were gone. Without models to inspire a new generation of weavers and the connection between weaving and ceremonial life frayed, the Jalq'a tradition seemed virtually extinct.

Whenever Martínez and Cereceda reached a new community in this depressed region, they sounded out the level of local interest. The community of Irupampa was exuberant. After several visits by the couple, a village leader confidently announced: "If you really want to start a textile workshop in Chuquisaca, put it here. Not only is the community committed to this idea, but several of our women were once highly skilled weavers and, given the chance, they will be again!"

Cereceda and Martínez learned that they were not the first outsiders to bring the idea of a crafts project to the region. Other private development agencies had sent technicians who were well versed in feasibility studies, who were optimistic about targeting markets for standardized weavings, and who were accompanied by mestizo promoters to drum up local support. None of these efforts took root; all of them withered in the atmosphere of mutual incomprehension that prevailed between project managers and potential "beneficiaries."

It helped that Martínez was fluent in Quechua, the language spoken by the Jalq'a, and that Cereceda had such an extensive background and knowledge of Andean textiles. But their greatest asset was also perhaps the most unlikely: a life of varied experience that made them more interested in the Jalq'a as a people than as artisans who could be trained to be economically productive. Cereceda knew that textiles carried many layers of meaning about their makers.

She knew textiles were essential to decoding a civilization without written texts. Textiles were more than objects of dress or adornment. Cereceda had discovered how even the selection of striped color combinations on small bags carried symbolic importance. Her work suggested that the variations in spatial relationships and figurative designs could serve as a kind of Rosetta stone for deciphering how the threads of pre-Columbian culture evolved over time and were woven into present-day life.

It was this realization that had first attracted Martínez and Cereceda to the Jalq'a weavings. The bizarre animals depicted on the axsus might be *chulpas,* creatures that, according to Andean oral traditions, "lived before the dawn of time, in dimly lit spaces, before the first sun rose over mother Earth." Chulpas were associated with creation myths that embodied the dualism in Andean thought between paired opposites of light and darkness, the spirit and the body, the world of nature and the world of man. Their power was simultaneously life-giving and menacing, capable of spreading sickness as well as reward. Here, perhaps, in the life of the people who made these weavings, was a window into the distant past of the first Andeans whose reality seemed as inscrutable as the mountain burial grounds where legend said their remains uneasily rested.

ROOTING THE PROJECT IN THE COMMUNITY

To facilitate the revival of Jalq'a weaving, Martínez and Cereceda started a grassroots support organization grounded in the belief that economic development could not be isolated from its cultural matrix. For a weaving workshop to thrive, it would have to be securely rooted in the life of the community. The project in Irupampa was therefore founded in close consultation with the local peasant organization, the communal sindicato, and would proceed at a pace determined by its participants.

The first task was not to train a few women for commercial production, but to create a space in which the entire community could explore the cultural roots that gave the Jalq'a their identity and that had inspired the master weavings of the past. Martínez, who had researched a book devoted to unraveling the meanings of a widespread Andean ritual known as "the burning of the tables," believed that little could be accomplished until the Jalq'a had made the project their own. To inaugurate the workshop, an *aysiri,* or shaman, was asked to conduct a ritual ceremony consulting traditional mountain deities called *Mallkus.*

Martínez cannot help smiling when he recalls the event. "The room was small," he says, squeezing his hands together, "and it seemed even smaller because it was packed with people from the community. A corner had been cleared, where the aysiri and his assistant carefully placed a bundle of textiles. After all the lamps were extinguished, the aysiri called upon the Mallkus to enter the pitch-dark room. You could hear people's shallow breathing, their bodies nervously shifting, as they waited for the response.

"One by one the Mallkus announced themselves through the person of the aysiri who took on the mannerisms of a condor and various other animals and spoke with the voices of several different women. These presences began to conduct a conversation among themselves and then with the audience. The shaman vanished into these personae seamlessly, in a drama of several acts that engrossed everyone for hours. At the end it was clear that the Mallkus agreed the project was good. A consensus had formed that the Jalq'a must conserve the gifts they had been given—their language and culture, textiles and traditional dress—if the world was to have meaning. People had been called to work hard and cooperate with one another and remember their common purpose on the Earth.

"About midnight, a ritual meal of meat and corn was served. The people were permitted to take what was not eaten home with them, but the bones were carefully put aside as an offering.

"At sunrise, we went to the site where the workshop would be built. Where one of the building's corners would rest, the aysiri burned the bones, and buried the heads of several sheep. The ashes were carefully read, and the signs were favorable.

"I was moved," Martínez concludes, his deep baritone voice dropping to a whisper. "The community had opened itself to us, invited us to witness their dialogue with the sacred. It was a gift of trust we were determined to keep."

During the years that would follow, ASUR would assiduously encourage the strengthening of ritual life among the Jalq'a communities. New workshops would be "blessed" in a manner similar to the one in Irupampa; offerings of coca, confetti, small candies, and libations would be made to mountain spirits to commemorate important occasions; and attention would be paid to recovering traditional songs and dances that had been fading from community life. ASUR would organize dance classes in Irupampa, encourage people to wear traditional dress at community meetings, and help people to resurrect old festival costumes that had fallen into disuse, such as the insect with huge wings that was worn by male dancers. The daughter of Martínez and Cereceda, who as a child had joined in the tent performances in Chile and the theater troupe in Charazani, would grow up to become a professional ethnomusicologist and record Jalq'a songs for a tape to be sold in Sucre and La Paz. All of these efforts built enthusiasm that would be channeled into the revival of weaving.

This auspicious start-up phase of the cultural revitalization project would also set the tone for anchoring activities of training, technical assistance, production, and marketing in methodologies of popular participation. ASUR's Quechua-speaking field workers held frequent community consultations in sindicato assemblies and leadership meetings. They established an ongoing program of skills-training workshops to prepare community members to assume a range of elementary management and technical tasks within the project's institutional structure. They created structures for overseeing the project with an Andean cultural spin dubbed *Jatun Comités* and a federation of participating communities. ASUR was well aware that the road to high-quality, marketable weavings and equitable income distribution was a social process fraught with all kinds of complexities, risks, and pitfalls. ASUR knew its long-term project would only be successful if community participation took place every step of the way.

HURDLES TO OVERCOME

Looking back, the process of that revival might seem to flow inevitably from that first benediction by the Mallkus in Irupampa, when ASUR wisely allowed the Jalq'a to place themselves at the center of the project. Verónica Cereceda remembers otherwise.

The first workshop was constructed with community labor; several experienced women weavers whom Cereceda and Martínez had met during their travels in Chuquisaca were recruited as teachers; and IAF funding was used to stockpile alpaca and sheep wool for spinning yarns. Everyone was anxious to begin, but one hurdle seemed insurmountable. The women still knew how to weave, but they did not recall the many strange animals, called *khurus,* that had been the hallmark of Jalq'a designs. Many of these were reputed to have originated in the dreams of ancestors or from cave drawings lost in antiquity. Without a stock of traditional textiles to guide them, the Jalq'a seemed unlikely to ever recreate the khurus, much less shape their world of chaotic free fall into a semblance of order.

Cereceda's solution was to contact the collectors and dealers she knew in Bolivia and overseas to get photographs of their Jalq'a weavings. Soon a photographic archive of more than 300 traditional motifs was assembled. Enlargements were printed and mounted on the workshop walls to guide teenage apprentices; others were hung in the patios of households so that mothers and their daughters could use them as models for their weaving. Eventually, photo albums and slide shows were assembled to circulate in communities outside Irupampa as word spread of the textile revival that was under way.

Cereceda still recalls the enthusiasm among the Jalq'a women when they first glimpsed the photos. She explains that it was not a question of anticipating monetary reward. Nothing had yet been woven, and there was no assurance anything would be sold. Rather it was like a lost child returning home. The photographs allowed the women to bring khurus that had been forgotten back to life and figure out how they fit together in a world of unexpectedly rich colors.

That enthusiasm was invaluable because the work itself was physically exacting. To produce the tight, thin textiles favored by the Jalq'a requires the weaver to repeatedly beat the weft with a llama bone until the threads are taut. Interlacing the warp and weft to create a free-fall motif of khurus without ordered bands requires intense concentration. Even the young women complained of back and eye strain, headaches, and sore shoulders. One apprentice spoke for many when she remarked, "Little by little we are getting accustomed to the work, but the way my shoulders ache at the loom tells me how it is to feel old." Moreover, the specific weaving techniques for producing the patterns of khurus and other trademark Jalq'a beasts had not been documented anywhere else in the world according to experts on the subject.[1]

For two years the women weavers of Irupampa practiced their art. Their textiles improved as new suppliers of wool for spinning thread were found outside the area. Indeed, in some instances, they purchased alpaca fiber from AIGACCA which had finally revved up a marketing program thanks to the IDB's financial support. This was a time-consuming but vital task since the quality of spinning had declined in the Jalq'a zone and local herds had been decimated during the years of drought.

A second deficiency was more difficult to overcome. The photographs Cereceda had collected showed how many shades had disappeared from the Jalq'a palette of colors. A handful of women were found who still remembered how to dye yarns, but transferring that knowledge and adapting it to provide weavers with ample supplies would not be easy. One elderly woman from Irupampa explained that "the generation which followed mine wove only in three colors. My grandmother told me that our ancestors used two primary colors, but in the center of each textile was a rainbow of designs in pink, green, yellow, and maroon. Preparing these colors correctly and dyeing the yarn was hard work, and messy, so it is no wonder the skill gradually died out. The men here never learned to do it, but now some of them have joined the young women to learn how."

Exposure to the World

Finally, Cereceda decided that it was time to inform the outside world of what had been accomplished. Having curated exhibits of Andean weavings in both Chile and France, she decided to do so again in Bolivia. ASUR collected the best of the new textiles and arranged in 1988 to showcase them in a public building in Sucre that had once been a Catholic church.

During the next three weeks, more than 10,000 people filed through the makeshift gallery. Javier Velasco, director of the largest NGO in the area, still remembers how people's eyes were opened by the exhibit. He explained that most middle-class residents of this city famous for its colonial architecture and Spanish legacy had probably never given any thought to the Jalq'a before, finding them indistinguishable from the horde of other rural migrants populating the poorest barrios. "Viewing this work in a museum setting was a turning point," Velasco emphasized. "It created a new respect among many city dwellers not only for the Jalq'a, but for the other ethnic groups in the region." The strange costumes that once signaled the uniform backwardness of their wearers now revealed the richness of the area's indigenous heritage.

This exhibition was followed by an even more impressive one at the Museo Nacional de Arte (National Museum of Art), located in the central plaza of La Paz across from the Presidential Palace and the National Congress. It was the first time indigenous textiles had been displayed at the Museo, and a delegation of Jalq'a men and women journeyed to the capital for the opening reception. Timoteo Mamani, one of the Irupampa workshop leaders, was well aware of the watershed importance this event held for his people when he addressed the crowd of dignitaries, including representatives of the national media. "For as long as we can remember, whenever our people have traveled to La Paz or Sucre, they have been greeted with ridicule. People we did not know would shout: 'Who are you people, where do you come from, why do you dress like Indians, why don't you go back where you belong?' Now we stand here and watch people of this great city admire our textiles. This is a great day, a day we will long remember for the great change taking place in our lives."

A great change was also taking place in their fortunes. Cereceda had used ASUR funds to buy a core of the best weavings for teaching and curatorial purposes, and the exhibitions she organized became a marketing tool to sell other work. Without knowing it, ASUR was following a path that Native American artisans in North America had adopted by using museum exhibits to familiarize the general public with Jalq'a art and museum shops to sell it.

Since 1988, the Jalq'a exhibit has been honed into perhaps the finest display of Bolivian ethnography now available. It includes superb examples of contemporary axsus, mannequins outfitted in daily dress and spectacular ritual costumes, photographs of earlier weavings, maps of the Jalq'a universe, and charts that discuss the history of the group and describe the iconography of their textiles. To provide more historical background about the Jalq'a, ASUR commissioned ethnohistorian Rossana Barragan. Although she pored over Spanish texts dating between the sixteenth and nineteenth centuries, she was unable to find mention of this mysterious group. She eventually developed a theory that bands of highland and lowland indigenous peoples joined together at the end of the nineteenth century to invent themselves as the Jalq'a (Barragan 1994).

The exhibition has also traveled to Paris, Geneva, Milan, and to the Smithsonian Institution in Washington, D.C. In La Paz, the United Nations has organized a smaller version for display in the lobby of its building to promote sales to visiting international development consultants. A credit fund has also been set up to allow Bolivian U.N. staff to purchase weavings.

But the primary marketing source is located in Sucre, at a museum and ethnic art shop set up in a renovated colonial convent. The government has made the permanent exhibition a must-see stop for foreign dignitaries visiting the colonial capital, and it attracts a steady stream of tourists and curious Bolivians. Some 4,000 people passed through its doors during the first six months of 1992.

Sales have been brisk—$60,000 worth of Jalq'a textiles in 1996 alone—and the average price keeps rising. One reason has been the steady improvement in the quality of the weaving. For example, Juana Rodriguez from the community of Maragua is now completing her eighth axsu. Each successive weaving has featured more sharply outlined khurus, softer textures, and more intricate compositions. Each has also commanded a higher price than its predecessor.

Another reason for rising prices is that the demand for better quality has become more stringent. Cereceda had to admit, "Despite the strong traditions not everyone was cut out to be a top-notch weaver. Like in any society this kind of skill was not uniformly distributed. We are trying to employ older weavers in tasks such as weaving blankets or jackets where technical skill is less demanding."

Like many weavers in the ASUR program, Rodriguez no longer relies on photographs of other weavings to inspire her own. Another weaver from Irupampa described the growing proficiency among her peers this way: "It is better that the designs come out of our heads rather than from pictures because it allows the threads to sing. We have greater freedom to create large khurus of all kinds. It is like suddenly being able to read with amazing clarity."

Cereceda welcomes this fluency because it signals that, after a lapse of nearly two decades, the Jalq'a are back in touch with the same cultural sources that inspired their ancestors to create exquisite weavings. Now the Jalq'a understand the market value of their work and can produce new textiles to meet outside demand without selling off their inheritance.

Cereceda is more circumspect when it comes to explaining the allure of Jalq'a textiles. She says that unlike the rigid patterns and symmetries which characterize most Andean textiles and make them easier to decode through comparison, the Jalq'a seem to be in touch with a primal space "that is dark, haunting, and subterranean, a region inside the earth where life is gestating, creation is ongoing, and possibility is boundless." When human figures appear, they are small and marginal, dwarfed by a universe of strange creatures. In curating the exhibit she has been careful to emphasize that the Jalq'a are our contemporaries without diminishing the mystery of the ancestral world that informs their culture.

Pressed to say more, she defers to the Jalq'a, who offer information grudgingly. Perhaps they are right to do so. The Chilean writer Ariel Dorfman once visited the Mataco people of northern Argentina and wondered why they were so reluctant to teach their language to the handful of outsiders who were interested. Dorfman finally decided that the Mataco were holding on to their last sanctuary, the core of identity that allowed them to survive the incursions of the modern world.

Elayne Zorn, a North American anthropologist and an authority on Andean textiles, thinks that outsiders' questions are often misframed, having more to do with the universalizing rationalism of Western industrial society than with a desire to understand the world view of an agrarian people with markedly different cultural roots. She says that weaving is a conceptual activity like literature or painting that communicates a way of experiencing the world, not explaining it.

STANDARDIZATION, IMPROVED INCOME,
AND EXPANDED COMMUNITY INVOLVEMENT

Martínez and Cereceda realized that the revival of Jalq'a weaving depended on the renewal of Jalq'a culture, but they also knew that the revival would not long survive unless it became economically viable. Because the goal was to revive the axsu and market it as ethnic art, it was necessary to establish a differential system of grading and pricing. Over time, the project has evolved a six-tier system, ranging from "extra" at the upper end to "D" at the lower end. By 1995, ASUR accepted the "C" and "D" categories only from teenage girls just learning their art in training courses from the ASUR's corps of twenty master weavers. Obviously disgruntled voices could be heard in the communities and there was a great deal of envy and backbiting when some women were continually earning more than others. At one point, ASUR felt compelled to slow down production that had rapidly mushroomed to include 400 weavers in their program, eliminating a fourth of them for inferior work.

The professional pride that comes from producing higher quality weavings is reinforced by the higher earnings they bring. Axsus in the Sucre store generally range in price from $100 to $200 apiece. Exceptional ones have been sold for as much as $300. After deductions for wool, dye, the communal enterprise fund, and the store's overhead, the best weavers often net as much as $100.[2]

The ability to match the area's average annual family income in two or three months makes weavers highly motivated to intensify production.[3] Yet, as one workshop leader in Irupampa indicates, the new benefits incur costs, which thus far women have willingly paid. "Our ancestors wove only to make their own clothing," she says, "not to earn money. Each year they probably produced a single axsu, in an exceptional year, two. Last year I made four. Our needs are different now, we need cash to get by. But the pace of the work can break you, and trying to fit it in between our responsibilities to our children and our other tasks, especially during planting and harvesting seasons, can leave you no time at all."

One wonders if the commercialization of weaving will eventually erode its place in the traditional culture, perhaps even introduce strains that crack Jalq'a society apart. Early signs suggest the opposite. ASUR has been careful to root quality control standards not only in technical merit, but in fidelity to the spirit of the best weavings of the past. The significant economic benefits flowing from this system reinforce the legitimacy of its dual demands. Renewed pride in Jalq'a culture has been accompanied by a boom in purchases of simple beds, chests of drawers, transistor radios, gas stoves, homespun dresses, rice and macaroni, and a house or a piece of land in the city. One woman was able to pay for emergency care for her husband after he suffered second-degree burns in an accident; another could afford to finance her daughter's wedding party.

Bolivian anthropologist Cassandra Torrico, an evaluator of the project, was impressed by the women's sense of personal advancement in becoming *superado runa* (an improved woman) and escaping the limiting conditions of subsistence agriculture for the first time (C. Torrico 1995, 30). A dependable income source brought valued material possessions into the household as well as greater control to plan future activities and make personal commitments.

Incomes do vary, depending on skill and effort, but the impulse toward individuation and social fragmentation is checked by mutual recognition that expanded future earnings depend on successful community management. The economic gains from the project have also strengthened Jalq'a family life and set in process a dynamic for expanding active community involvement. The best weavers make the most of the new opportunities by having relatives pasture the animals. Young women in several villages have stopped working as live-in domestic servants in Sucre where monthly earnings amounted to a measly $10, choosing instead to stay home with their children and weave. And their husbands are also staying home.

One man from Potolo explained that the married men there no longer migrate for several months a year to Chapare, one of the world's largest zones of coca-leaf production, in order to support their families. "Around here," he said, "men have begun to take on some of the cooking, to spend more time looking after the children and pasturing the animals.[4] Some are even spinning wool so that their wives will have more time for weaving." He acknowledged that single men must still leave to earn cash, but thought they now had more reason than ever to return home to find a wife and raise a family. "The single women here, even those without land who barely got by selling eggs or *chicha* [a corn beer], are also taking up weaving and producing some of the most beautiful work."

The changing economic role of women is also broadening their social role. A few months ago a weaver from Irupampa visited relatives in another village, which was not participating in the ASUR program. During a meeting of the sindicato, she was struck by the verbosity of the men and the silence of the women. "I saw," she said, "that my village had once been the same. But after our workshops started, the men got behind us, telling us they were not the only ones with mouths. Now we have the courage to talk about what bothers us, about our own obligations and the obligations of others. Whatever the topic, we find something to say. Yes, it seems we have learned to use our mouths for talking!"

MARKETING DECISIONS AND THE CHALLENGES OF SELF-MANAGEMENT

Thanks to financial assistance from the International Labor Organization of the United Nations and from COTESU, the development aid arm of the

Swiss government, ASUR workshops eventually spread to five additional Jalq'a communities, benefiting 400 weavers and their families. Like the woman quoted above, these women are confident that their accomplishments are not transient.

Cereceda and Martínez realize that a promising beginning may still go awry. Many other communities are clamoring to join, and a number of adept weavers have set up their own workshop in Sucre for urban migrants comprising twenty-five artisans and 110 spinners. The tourist market in Bolivia may soon become saturated, so ASUR has been exploring the possibilities overseas. Despite the neo-liberal trade openings, ASUR has discovered that its weavings at the going prices are hard to sell abroad and without the museum exhibit to frame the cultural context, it is difficult for potential buyers to appreciate them. However, the experiences of the Navajo of the southwestern United States and the Mayan Sna Jolobil of Mexico show that it is possible to maintain high aesthetic standards for textiles, promote the work through museum and gallery exhibitions, and market it through museum shops while sparking a locally based revival of indigenous culture.

Making the transition to international marketing will require a new level of sophistication, and Martínez and Cereceda have spent the past decade gearing up to help the Jalq'a acquire the tools they will need. ASUR has grown from a mom-and-pop operation, run out of the back of a jeep, to a nationally known organization with twenty employees specializing in sales, exhibitions, microenterprise development, accounting, and training. And it is on its way to having its own uniquely styled museum where marketing, curating, and business can be combined with training programs and where new weaving communities and distinct traditions can be incorporated.

The local workshops themselves have increased their functions and skill levels over this same time period. The community of Marawa is a good example of how far this decentralized management concept has been able to go. Originally relying on Irupampa for a wool supply, they later built their own workshop. It's currently governed by a leadership council headed by a Jalq'a man and a woman in keeping with the notion of an Andean dualistic social order. The sixty participating weavers hold meetings every fifteen days to discuss problems, technical flaws in the workmanship, and comment whether anyone is slacking off. Because men are more literate than women, they usually have the task of registering a weaver's raw material on standardized forms and establish individual contracts specifying dates for dyeing the wool and delivering the weaving to ASUR (C. Torrico 1995, 16). The female leader's job is the distribution of wool and dyes and follow-up supervision of both the spinning and dyeing work. Earnings from sales in the Sucre store cover the modest salaries of these leaders. In addition, training in Jalq'a weaving for teenage girls enables a fourteen year old to become a top-of-the-line weaver by the time she reaches eighteen.

ASUR is constantly working with the Jalq'a to seek ways to add value and cut costs. Microenterprises for spinning and dyeing have been established in Irupampa to guarantee ample supplies of low-cost, high-quality yarn to area weavers. Yet after six years of frustrating experimentation with locally devised, low-tech machinery to increase yarn production, they decided that a semi-industrial system is the way to go in the future. On occasion they have even purchased superior yarn from Uruguay within the new access to imported materials from globalization changes in Bolivia. The idea behind these efforts is to allow weavers to maximize the value of their labor. The time freed from using drop spindles to make their own thread can now be devoted to weaving axsus, potentially doubling artisan incomes.

Microenterprises have also experimented with using leftover material from the wool-spinning business to make hats and mattresses. In addition to axsus, the women have begun to weave smaller items—belts, handbags, purses—to diversify production. Even more significant has been the experience of product diversification and cultural revitalization for artistic textile production involving Jalq'a males. ASUR organized a workshop that currently employs twenty-four men who have developed skills originating in pre-Columbian tapestry weaving to produce pieces distinct from the women's designs yet whose mostly animal motifs in their own way are equally original and of stunning beauty. In 1997, they began to take steps to move beyond the core group to train men from a half-dozen or so communities. This was setting the stage for a vastly enlarged pool of new products and producers promising to be yet another boon to the local economy as the market appeared strong from trial sales. Thus ASUR has come up with yet another product with powerful market appeal to tourists and value comparable to women's textile earnings. The pressure on ASUR to enter this line of textile production came from Jalq'a men themselves, obviously frustrated by being upstaged by women monopolizing the "big" money-making opportunities in an otherwise male dominant society.

ASUR understands that if this complex of microenterprises in Irupampa is ever to become a hub for a thriving local rural economy, the Jalq'a must be able to manage their interests effectively. The prospects for such self-management did not look promising at first and continue to face many difficulties and challenges. The Jalq'a weavers had no formal schooling, could not add or subtract, and could barely write their own names. The men had no more than a primary school education, and most were functionally illiterate. Everyone, however, proved to have a great appetite for learning.

The literacy training ASUR inaugurated was followed by courses in accounting and management taught by specialists from La Paz. During the 1990s, night classes in Irupampa are crowded with mostly men punching the keys of their pocket calculators and practicing their penmanship. According to Martínez the women, who generally have much less formal education than the Jalq'a men, prefer the more remunerative weaving activities over administration. Male graduates of these classes are keeping project records on everything from inventories of lumber and other construction materials to the results of spinning and dyeing experiments to improve the quality of yarns. They are managing workshop funds, calculating costs, distributing wool, and refining and implementing the quality control system for textile marketing at the Sucre store. They help staff, on a rotating basis, the seven *jatun Comités* that participating Jalq'a communities have set up to oversee the workshops and microenterprises. The president of the Jatun Comité in Irupampa is the first Jalq'a to become computer literate.

Despite adding new and important skills to the community, Irupampa and ASUR have been in the throes of sorting out a juridical and functional ownership structure that will serve the seventy-seven resident families for the future. Initially, ASUR tried working directly through the local sindicatos as collective owners of the microenterprise in Irupampa. Yet there was no practice in collective ownership of assets among the current generations of adults in these communities. So in practice, this institutional design meant that ownership resided with both everyone and no one at the same time. ASUR offered Irupampa members an opportunity to purchase stock in this microenterprise in trying to forge this Western, capitalist scheme of ownership. Yet that corollary proposal also met with a weak community response. This outstanding issue remains. At a meeting in his office in 1996, Martínez said, "Together with the leadership we are trying to find a solution to the confusion and ambiguity with respect to ownership rights. We are doing our utmost to adapt this strategy to Andean concepts, yet it is not always clear to us nor among the Jalq'a how to do it."

The Irupampa experience was frustrating also in terms of the noble self-management goals. Martínez says, "We tried to turn everything over to Jalq'a management, but the leaders soon reached a moment in which they didn't know what the next step should be. So we had to reinsert ourselves again into management roles to avoid a partial collapse. It convinced us even more that we have to build a co-management model in each of the workshops as self-management remains an unrealistic working proposition at this stage of project evolution in northern Chuquisaca."

As Martínez was talking I thought to myself about the camelid herders who regrouped themselves as a corporation as an economic arm of their producers' association for managing industrial processing and export operations, and the ability of the cacao and quinoa growers to forge the basic management structures for their export enterprises. Yet it was clear to me that these altiplano peoples were better equipped to take on self-management challenges than the peoples living in the remote valleys of Chuquisaca. Indigenous peoples are heterogeneous and each group has historical and cultural specificity. The specific strategies used for empowerment and self-development must be shaped accordingly.

Cereceda and Martínez have shown that their textile revival methodology does work elsewhere within the northern Chuquisaca sub-region. When an international development agency's effort to promote a crafts program among the people of Tarabuco began floundering in the early 1990s, ASUR was asked to step in. The Tarabucos, resplendent in their black, conquistador-like helmets, long brightly striped ponchos, and richly detailed axsus, had not yet lost their native dress or weaving tradition, but the introduction of acrylic yarns, the declining quality of production, and the increased rate of seasonal migration by men in search of work showed that their way of life was under siege.

ASUR began working with more than 300 Tarabuco women from seven communities to reverse this decline. Using the methodology trailblazed among the Jalq'a, ASUR helped organize communal workshops staffed by master weavers, reinforced local ritual life, reintroduced natural yarns and streamlined the dyeing process, and mounted axsus for wall hangings that could be exhibited in museums and marketed at the Sucre store. Using a palette of some twenty-five colors, weavers compose representations of rainbows, fruits, flowers, even an Andean altar, the *Pukara,* into their axsus. The symmetrically patterned textiles with polychrome bands are very different from the Jalq'a motif of khurus in free fall. They have identical llama figures which are smaller than the stylized ones of the Jalq'a, which stand proudly upright on neat orderly rows. Today, the Tarabuco weavings match the Jalq'a in sales at the Sucre store.[5]

Now that the project has taken root, ASUR is bringing the Tarabucos and the Jalq'a together for joint meetings, training programs in self-management, and workshop inaugurations in order to build an indigenous federation to manage microregional development. They are also taking some cues from the more successful effort at building a multi-ethnic federation by ARTECAMPO of Santa Cruz discussed in the following chapter. They have sent Jalq'a and Tarabucos as consultants to other projects interested in reviving their own unique weaving traditions. Through such visits, the ASUR experience is being "scaled-out" to various parts of the country giving other groups some lessons in cultural revitalization that can be adapted to their own circumstances. They have also disseminated this revival experience through several books published about these weaving traditions (Dávalos, Cereceda, and Martínez 1992). And finally ASUR opened its own website so that the woven cosmovisions of the Jalq'a and Tarabucos can be seen across the globe.

CONTINUOUS ADAPTATIONS AND QUALITY CONTROL

Over the years, ASUR methodology has undergone constant adaptations to meet changing circumstances as community participation developed. An example of an important change in project methodology was the shift of quality control and price-setting functions from the ASUR store to the local workshops in the communities. This change transferred responsibility to the weavers themselves. Previously, ASUR's sales agent (with daily contact with buyers) would make the final determination after discussing and often negotiating the quality of a piece with its producer. This procedure worked well for a while and, as an incentive, feedback systems led to improvements in quality. Yet there were increasing suspicions among weavers of favoritism as well as confusion over standards of textile quality in relation to differential market values. These complaints were fed by envy and an atmosphere of competitiveness that at times became quite excessive.

ASUR's Mercedes Rengel, the staff member in charge of organizing the new field-based methodology for setting prices, commented that the group process has "eliminated all those tears and complaints of the weavers common to the negotiating process in the ASUR store." In her evaluation, anthropologist Torrico found much of merit in this effort at decentralization and empowerment of local groups. She acknowledged that "although the sales transaction of the local workshop could be a painful and humiliating experience of being judged stringently by one's peers, overall it was an experience of tremendous value for everyone involved. It has become an important moment for collectively discussing, arguing, and analyzing a specific piece among themselves, which greatly enhances understanding of the mechanisms and criteria for evaluating and assigning a value to their work. They expertly judge the quality and uniformity of the wool and its colors, and the harmonizing effects of the designs within a given spatial arrangement, as well as other aesthetic and technical details. This change has begun a process whereby the standards become negotiated by the people themselves rather than left solely to the marketplace to decide for them. It allows the women weavers to become the prime movers in raising community awareness about the high aesthetic standards for Jalq'a and Tarabuco ethnic art" (C. Torrico 1995). A final personal marketing touch from these changes is that each axsu on sale now has an attached ticket with the name and a color photograph of its producer.

During the summer of 1992 in Washington, D.C., the IAF brought a group of Jalq'a weavers to participate in the Smithsonian Folklife Festival's celebration of indigenous peoples five hundred years after Columbus "discovered" America. They mounted their own exhibit on the walls of a main hallway in the Sackler Museum. Martínez accompanied several Jalq'a weavers on a tour of the dinosaur exhibit at the Museum of Natural History. The Jalq'a were so taken with the exhibit that discussions arose about including dinosaurs among the khurus populating their axsus. Martínez was not surprised, because the Jalq'a have long been open to change. Indeed, the entire project has been an example of reshaping Andean culture to play a new role in the modern marketplace.

MODELS OF MULTICULTURAL DEVELOPMENT FOR THE COUNTRY

Observing the steady improvement in workmanship that has put the best of the new weavings on par with the stupendous beauty of earlier Jalq'a axsus, ponchos, and shawls, I have been impressed by the effectiveness and imagination of Martínez and Cereceda and their Bolivian colleagues such as Santiago Porcel and Mercedes Rengel. Indeed, the wave of interest in weaving traditions taking place throughout the Bolivian Andes has been influenced by ASUR's revival project.

As Bolivia takes giant strides through recent constitutional reforms to re-define itself as a pluri-cultural state, the Jalq'a and Tarabucos give added luster to this energizing national identity. For example, Sucre has been the site of a prestigious international music festival which in recent years incorporates demonstrations of Jalq'a and Tarabuco weavers as another source of cultural pride for Bolivians. When the first ladies from Latin American countries convened in La Paz in 1996 for a special meeting, they visited ASUR's textile exhibit mounted especially for them at the National Art Museum—a means to make the country's rich cultural patrimony known to prominent Latin Americans. And when the country's president, Gonzalo Sánchez de Lozada, sent a cultural program to Santiago, Chile, as a way to build good will and improve diplomatic relations, both ASUR's and CIDAC's (see the following chapter) exhibitions were front and center among a very select group of national presentations. Giant, spindly-legged khuru images hanging on banners along high office buildings in the national capital is another sign that the Jalq'as' artistic creations have gained a level of appreciation among various sectors of society.

On a more tangible rural development level, the ASUR revival has excited numerous observers committed to substituting multicultural development for eurocentric developmental approaches. Javier Medina, the founder of HISBOL, Andean social science publishing house and the author of the book *Repensar Bolivia,* believes that the Jalq'a model of ethnodevelopment can be spread throughout the country. He argues that Bolivia must reinvent its own solutions because rural models of community development imported from the industrialized West have failed to take root in the Andes.

As Cassandra Torrico has pointed out, this project also challenges gender-based theories held by Andean scholars among others that greater insertion into the market economy invariably makes women worse off (C. Torrico 1995). Jalq'a and Tarabuco women not only retain greater earnings for work than, for example, their counterparts in the maquiladora (piece workers) assembly plants, but the work has greater flexibility for fitting into the daily rhythms of the peasant family economy. The more favorable integration into tourist markets brought significant quality of life improvements.

CHAPTER 12

An Artisans' Journey from the Rural Backlands to the Regional Capital

We must accept that humanity is a beautiful multi-colored garden.

RIGOBERTA MENCHÚ (1998)

The Beginnings of a Crafts Revival

In 1981, on a street corner in downtown La Paz, I happened to bump into Judith Buechler, a North American anthropologist. In an excited voice, she told me, "Be sure to make contact with the Co-operativa Cruceño de Cultura the next time you're in Santa Cruz. They've been looking for a small development foundation to work with and I think they are the most creative bunch of people down there."

On my next visit to Santa Cruz I found myself among an unusual group of distinguished professionals and intellectuals—artists, architects, engineers, sociologists, environmentalists, and artisans—who out of an abiding loyalty to the region had become its most outspoken social conscience and most ardent promoter. They published a lively magazine, *Debate,* and sponsored frequent seminars and lectures to create public awareness about overlooked and poorly understood issues in public affairs.

The advocacy group criticized regional development policies for favoring a small minority of agro-business elites and cattle ranchers at the expense of the peasants and Indians. Successive booms in cotton, cattle, sugar cane, natural gas, oil, timber, and even illegal cocaine had made this region Bolivia's land of opportunity. The gains, however, were often ephemeral and tended to worsen, not better, social conditions for the indigenous minority. Indeed, rapid economic expansion by powerful investor and settler

CIDAC ARTECAMPO ARTISAN COMMUNITIES
DEPARTMENT OF SANTA CRUZ

AMAZONIAN RIVER SYSTEMS

BENI

BRAZIL

Urubichá
⊗
Guarayo Artisans*

R. Ichilo

R. San Pablo

COCHABAMBA

Chiquitana Artisans**

Buena Vista
Weavers

Ayoreo Weavers

Santa Cruz
⊗
Cotoca Potters

Valle Grande
Weavers

Izoceno Weavers

R. Parapeti

CHUQUISACA

GRAN CHACO

PARAGUAY

TARIJA

ARGENTINA

*Weavers, Potters,
Painters, Sculptors,
Basket Makers

**Weavers, Embroiderers

groups fueled by the military government's land grant policy often displaced them from traditional homeland areas. Indians had fewer rights here than in the Andean areas where hard-fought struggles had brought about major land redistribution. Consequently, the indigenous peoples of the eastern lowlands remained trapped in a social system of gross social inequities; Santa Cruz elites, many of pure Spanish and Italian descent, practiced some of the worst anti-Indian racism in Bolivia.

The cultural co-op's interest in approaching the IAF was a desire to go beyond public education and advocacy work to the organization of rural communities, specifically for the production of handicrafts for the market. Subsequently, they placed the program in the hands of a sub-group who formed an independent NGO specializing in crafts, called the Centro de Investigación, Diseño y Comercialización de la Artesania Cruceño (CIDAC) (Center of Research, Design, and Marketing of the Santa Cruz Artisanry). The movers and shakers behind this crafts revival were a visionary couple, Ada Sotomayer de Vaca and her husband Lorgio Vaca.

Ada and Lorgio's red-brick bungalow was situated on a tree-lined street of upper middle-class homes about a mile from the center of the city. Their small living room was a mini-gallery of paintings in rich, deep hues depicting native peoples in multi-colored striped ponchos threshing grain, feeding goats, and engaging in other activities of rural life. As Lorgio Vaca was an acclaimed painter and perhaps one of the country's most prominent muralists, I guessed the colorful canvasses must be those of my host.

After being seated at a kitchen table with tea and pastries, I asked Ada, a woman in her late thirties, about her interest in rural artisanry. She was from Peru, she said, a product of the mingling of black, Spanish, and Indian societies on the Peruvian coast. Her chosen career as a professional social worker had first plunged her into the world of Peru's fisherman where her literacy and co-op training work had an important impact.

In 1960, a few years into her work with these fishing communities, she attended an exhibition in Lima of six rising stars in the Bolivian arts community. While examining the works of this emerging group, she became mesmerized by some of the paintings. "I was standing just gazing at Lorgio's work for hours and then suddenly I felt a tap on the shoulder. It was Lorgio the artist himself, coming up to introduce himself and express his appreciation for my keen interest in his paintings. Later in the week, I took him on a tour of Lima's barrios to show him the social conditions of our capital city and my line of work. It was the start of a magical courtship which led to our marriage in Peru two years later."

In 1970, they moved with their three children back to Lorgio's hometown of Santa Cruz. When the country fell into the grip of the right-wing military dictatorship of General Banzer soon thereafter, Lorgio was blacklisted and lost state commissions for his widely popular murals. Since they had a family to support, Ada replaced him as the main breadwinner for the next six years. She started a home-furnishings business centered around the use of decorative leather and clay works that she made in a workshop and cultivated a market niche among the city's affluent upper middle class. "My shift to this work came naturally, since as a carpenter's daughter I had learned to create with my hands from a young age. I was always knitting or pressing clay into interesting shapes. The solitary nature of the work was difficult but my earnings enabled our family to stay afloat. In the course of my work, I visited many of the artisan fairs, outdoor market stalls, and downtown stores which sold arts and crafts from other regions of the country. This taught me a great deal about the world of the city's artisans, especially the leather workers, who often received some of my leftover materials.

"I opened my own store in a small colonial house only a half block from the main plaza and even sold my work in a boutique located in the city's most luxurious hotel. When democracy returned to Bolivia in 1978 and Lorgio was able to resume normal professional endeavors, I felt a need to become more socially useful, to reach out to other women less fortunate than myself. I had this gnawing sense that there was more to life than running my own successful business.

"About that time, a great opportunity to move in this direction arose when the Corporación Regional de Desarrollo de Santa Cruz (CORDE-CRUZ) (Regional Development Corporation of Santa Cruz) provided us with a small grant to research and document the artisan activities throughout our large region. My Cruceño friends had always been embarrassed about the absence of crafts from their region in our downtown artisan shops. Products from Bolivia's native cultures in the mountains filled most of the display shelves and wall space, while our 'inferior' products languished in their shadows. It was ironic that our region's rapid economic growth, the most dynamic in all of Bolivia, had forged a strong sense of regionalism with only shallow roots in our cultural heritage. We felt that a regional profile of our handicrafts would help to foster cultural awareness and concern for the region's declining native cultural patrimony and its producers.

"During the next two years [1978–1979], Laura Zanini and I traveled the back roads of our region by jeep looking for communities that had kept interesting craft traditions alive. Our exploration brought home the painful reality that in many of the communities we visited industrial products had displaced the artisanal products that had endured for many generations, some from the colonial period and others originating way back in the pre-Columbian past. Yet we were able to find pockets of artisans here and there among the widely scattered native groups of the region. We found Guarayo and Izoceño hammock weavers, Ayoreos using garabata plant fiber to make lovely handbags, and some mestizo and Chiquitaño communities weaving hats from *jipijapa* palm leaves.

"The variety and beauty of the crafts we discovered were remarkable, but all of these traditions were in decline. And all were under the pernicious influence of itinerant traders and middlemen who made unequal exchanges of consumer goods for their products. On balance, commercial dealings of this sort were contributing to the demise of artisanry traditions in these areas. We were impressed by the cultural resiliency shown by the various groups in keeping their traditions going, but it was clear that middlemen were slowly but surely undermining their work.

"At the outset of our travels, our purpose had simply been to document the existence of various artisan traditions and explore the decline in craft production and quality of workmanship in various sectors of our region. By the time our research project was winding down, however, we had reached the conclusion that it was no longer possible to remain comfortable middle-class spectators. As women, we were impressed by the artisans' tenacity in the face of numerous logistical obstacles as well as various forms of discrimination directed toward them as women and Indians. The trip had inadvertently laid the groundwork for a project to revitalize the diverse crafts traditions of our region."

After Ada's introduction, Lorgio invited me on a personal tour of his public murals scattered throughout the city. While driving along the city streets and stopping to gaze at immense colorful scenes of rural people at work, he shared his philosophy as an artist. "I am much less interested in selling paintings that will remain on walls in private residences or in private galleries than in offering my work where the masses can enjoy them and share my message. The open air public spaces where the regular people of Santa Cruz congregate to stroll and relax hold much greater value for me as settings for artistic communications. Public murals can become a kind of permanent message board available for the present and future generations inhabiting this city.

"The potential of art to address social concerns first hit me as a student in the 1950s when Bolivia was undergoing a social revolution and our entire nation's social conscience had been raised to new heights. Fired by those times of upheaval, I created my first mural working alongside other artists in Sucre."

Vaca's murals, laid out on tiles and painted in three-dimensional relief, capture historic moments as well as the daily lives of people firmly rooted in the region's rural settings. A far cry from the cardboard cutouts of military figures on horseback or independence leaders highlighted by school textbooks, Lorgio has always taken his inspiration from the region's common folk: men in straw hats plowing fields with oxen, native women carrying water jars on their heads or kneeling to thread their looms. His murals convey the swirl of life: moving oxcarts, galloping horseback riders, chanting protest marchers.

The Vacas now proposed to recuperate and revitalize the scattered arts and crafts of the Santa Cruz region. Ada's unusual combination of personal business experience, social work, and craft skills and Lorgio's inspiring visual insights into the region's rural peoples were impressive qualifications for the project they envisioned. The couple also brought to the project necessary savvy and influence to open the doors of the Santa Cruz elite who had long ignored the region's ethnic minorities. The two drawbacks were perhaps the couple's lack of anthropological expertise—a domain of professional knowledge usually sought in the leadership of IAF projects with Indians—and a lack of familiarity with the recent methods of grassroots organizing. In the development field, however, all the necessary ingredients are seldom present at the outset of a project, so one often has to make trade-offs in calculations about project success. In the final analysis, this organization seemed to have enough of the necessary ingredients—the integrity, dedication, technical skill, common sense, and imagination as well as interesting upper middle-class social connections—to make a good run at improving the declining native artisanry of the region.

A series of project review meetings at the IAF led to a two-year initial grant of $49,000 to cover three modest staff salaries, including Ada's raw material such as cotton and dyes, gas money, car repair and maintenance, and rent for the Santa Cruz office. The work would begin with the Guarayo hammock makers of Urubichá, embroiderers of Chiquitaña, mestizo hat weavers in Ichilo, and mestizo potters from the nearby tourist town of Cotoca. The work could spread to incorporate other groups in later phases of implementation.

IMPROVISING A COMMUNITY-BASED METHODOLOGY: THE EARLY YEARS

Ada set up project headquarters in a one-story, two-room adobe house about ten blocks from the center of the city. The building had a traditional facade of hitching posts holding up a red tile roof over a small porch. CIDAC staff painted decorative Cruceño motifs on the building's exterior as a sign of the crafts revitalization activity underway inside. The interior office space had the bare essentials of several desks, chairs, a small filing cabinet, a typewriter, and a slide projector, while the adjoining room, now serving as storage space, would eventually be an artisan shop.

Ada's core staff had their hands full trying to initiate and sustain support programs for the artisans of Ichilo, Urubicha, and Cotoca. Visits to the first two artisan groups required four- and twelve-hour trips respectively. Fortunately, the third group, the mestizo potters of Cotoca were a mere twenty-minute ride away on a paved road.

CIDAC's field methodology depended greatly on Ada's energy, vision, and refined aesthetic sense. She also drew, of course, upon the artistic insights of Lorgio, who was primarily occupied with his work as a painter and muralist. As a woman, Ada had an easier time than a man might have had in establishing trust with the Indian and mestizo women being recruited into the artisan revival program.

Ada described her start-up methodology in this way. "At each site, I went door to door, visiting the women in their homes, describing CIDAC's mission, and asking them about their work. I examined their materials, looms, and kilns, and offered technical advice for improving and diversifying their products while simultaneously trying to learn about their production and marketing practices. Through these visits, I added greatly to my knowledge and was able to establish some degree of rapport.

"While the recruitment process was basically successful, it certainly brought along its share of challenges. In both Ichilo and Urubicha rumors circulated that we were engaging in exploitative buying and selling techniques similar to those of the traders. Such suspicions, of course, reinforced our decision to proceed cautiously and scale back any promises of future milk and honey. Our strategy was to work with a handful of women and only add new artisans once we had achieved improvement in the products of the women already in the program.

"At each site, we appointed a coordinator who was responsible for supervising the day-to-day activities of our program. Coordinators conduct the necessary training and provide technical and organizational assistance during our long absences. Coordinators are also responsible for judging the quality of workmanship and for having the fortitude of character to establish firm product prices. Out of the small clusters of women, we then helped organize an artisan association in each place."

Ada and other CIDAC staff designed the artisan association as a way to enable artisans to compete with the middlemen who had long controlled the commercial side of their work. To accomplish this, CIDAC established "rotating" and "social" funds used to pay artisans cash up front for their labor and later pay them in kind with dry goods, their share of the profits. This system enabled CIDAC to compete fairly well although in some cases the pre-existing commercial trading relations had persisted for generations. CIDAC also made a practice of giving awards to artisans who created high-quality products to increase the artisans' incentives to remain industrious, creative, and loyal to the project.

"After several years of working toward the recovery and development of the handicrafts, we opened our own shop in the large room adjacent to our office. Thinking the store might be a key factor to encourage a market for the artisan goods, we put a lot of effort and imagination into it. Almost immediately, the shop attracted the attention of the upper middle class desiring some Cruceño artifacts for their homes. Our relatively low prices, in comparison to those in other nearby towns, also made our crafts highly attractive."

The View from Urubicha

To grasp the way this field methodology worked, visits to two distant project sites—Urubicha in northern Santa Cruz and Izozog to the south—can be helpful guides.

Some 400 Guarayo Indians live in the town of Urubicha and surrounding communities. At the time CIDAC first visited the area, most inhabitants survived by farming corn and yucca for their own consumption and small fields of peanuts for the market.

The Guarayos, who used pre-Columbian vertical looms, were skilled weavers before the Franciscan missions began the "reducción" process between 1840 and 1930. The Franciscans created central settlements (the sixty original Guarayo settlements became reduced to six) which reduced the Guarayos' access to diverse ecosystems for hunting, gathering, and fishing and made their cropping systems more sedentary (Lehm 1996, 50, 53). During the Franciscans' ninety-year stay, the Guarayos added European looms to their own for producing cotton cloth. Artisanry and animal-raising also increased as activities. Subsequently, white and mestizo cattle ranchers arrived and appropriated the Guarayos' vast savannas for their livestock. Then, with the opening of a modern road, timber companies and small farmer colonists moved into the region. This accelerated the clearing of the rainforests that had long provided the native people with the fish, fruits, and wild game. Without this environment, the Guarayos increasingly turned to precarious forms of subsistence farming combined with commercial weaving.[1]

Urubicha is typical of the older towns of Bolivia's eastern tropics. It was a charming village centered upon a grassy plaza, with a main street of red clay, and one-story row houses with porches and hitching posts. Large palm trees scattered throughout the village provided pools of shade. Some Guarayo homes had the bottom halves painted scarlet and baby blue. The only sounds in the village were those of children playing, birds chirping, and barnyard animals lowing, so that a visitor's impression was of a pervading peacefulness. Unlike other neighboring towns dominated by a tiny white minority, Urubicha was, practically speaking, under the control of the native Guarayos. A Guarayo filled the position of town mayor, and all of the schoolteachers were from the native group. Inside the doorways of their homes, Guarayo women quietly worked pulling the threads of beautiful multi-striped hammocks on looms propped up by vertical poles.

One such hammock maker was a middle-aged woman with dark hair pulled back in a bun. In a shapeless, print dress typical of the Western clothing worn by Bolivia's eastern lowland Indians, she sat in front of a half-finished hammock woven in stripes of scarlet, pink, emerald, and violet. Ada commented on the weaver's work. "This piece is a good example of the improvements in color combinations that have resulted from our technical assistance program. Before CIDAC became involved, the quality of once-beautiful Guarayo hammocks had declined greatly. The traders that had come here to buy the women's hammocks induced the weavers to make inadvisable color changes by supplying them with so many different shades of yarn. To make the hammocks more attractive, we've advocated the use of natural cotton yarn instead of acrylic, and added crocheted strips to the edges. In addition to the design work, we're helping the artisans make the association between greater skill and higher prices and interested buyers."

The weaver explained the benefits of working with CIDAC as she saw them. "Before working with Ada we sold to itinerant traders without having a clue about the worth of our hammocks in monetary terms. These guys were giving us a couple of bars of soap, a kilo of sugar, and some cooking oil for a month's work of weaving. The products they brought from Santa Cruz were lower in cost than those we could get around here so we felt we were getting a good deal.

"I combine weaving with other farm and family tasks in the course of a day's work," she explained. With pride in her eyes she held up a notebook used to record her labor costs, her material costs, and the consumer goods she received as profit reimbursement. "Dona Ada has shown us how to keep these notebooks up-to-date, and we receive help from our coordinator or a friend or family member who can write and add and subtract. The social fund returns have enabled me to acquire a set of dishes, a blanket, a blouse, and a mosquito net, all of which you see registered here. These goods are brought to us by Dona Ada once the hammocks have been sold in Santa Cruz. This arrangement has allowed our earnings to increase about three-fold above what the traders paid. Some folks around here still prefer working with the traders out of family and friendship loyalties, but I can't see the sense of that."

In addition to working on improving their weaving and record-keeping, the artisans of Urubicha had organized an association of hammock makers with the assistance of the CIDAC coordinator. The monthly meeting had begun to function as an important institution for the oversight of quality control and for setting prices that reflected the true value of the members' work. By coming together to meet with Ada, the members were able to jointly enter into agreements with CIDAC on matters such as color selection, hammock types, and quantities to be produced. The Guarayo Indians of Urubicha enjoyed such encouraging production and commercial results after only two years of CIDAC's community-based methodology.

THE VIEW FROM IZOZOG

Another perspective on the progress of CIDAC's craft revitalization program is presented by the Izozog Indian communities in the Gran Chaco, a semi-arid region with numerous ecosystems, diverse species of flora and fauna, and one of the world's remaining dry forests.

On her first exploratory trip, Ada homed in on the intricately designed ponchos, saddle bags, and cotton hammocks used by the Izoceño people living along the banks of the Río Parapeti, a river forming part of the Amazonian system that roars in the rainy season from the Andes to the northern Chaco and then peters out into the swampy marshland of Izozog. This native group joined CIDAC when the program expanded to incorporate five artisan communities beyond the initial three. A slower, troubled start in Izozog shows how varied the field response could be.

Ada knew that the people and conditions of the Chaco presented some exceptional challenges. The Izoceños have a reputation as a proud, independent-minded Indian group whose history of oppression and geographic isolation has contributed to a relatively closed society and a deep distrust of white and mestizo outsiders. "You know the Incas were never able to conquer the ancestors of these folks," Ada explained. "Just to the north of Izozog is the southern border of the empire that once spanned a good part of mountainous South America."

There were also strong racist prejudices against them in the regional capital. I will never forget the front desk clerk's reaction when I left my hotel early in one morning to make my first long trip to Izozog. When she learned where I was going, she startled me by exclaiming in a surprised tone, "Why you're going to visit those savages!" I was about to argue with her but then bit my tongue and walked out the door with a sick feeling in the pit of my stomach.

The Izoceños inhabit a tiny territory of the relatively unpopulated and inhospitable Gran Chaco, the vast, arid expanse of low, dry plains and thorn forests stretching from Bolivia into Argentina and Paraguay. This ecosystem, although larger than that of the Amazon basin, had received little attention in the media or from environmentalists at the time of our trip. From the city of Santa Cruz, the journey to the Chaco homelands of the Izozog Indians is a twelve-hour journey over dusty, potholed roads. During downpours this surface turns to squishy heaps resembling melted dark chocolate.

A straight dirt road runs through the middle of the Izoceño communities, effectively bisecting their world. There are twenty-five communities with a total of 6,000 people in an area of ten square miles. On either side of the road, hard-packed grassless earth stretches below a variety of native trees. Cactus plants stand between *algarobas* with gnarled branches and tiny leaves, and towering *taborache* trees with bulky grey trunks in the shape of giant milk bottles. The mud huts are thatched with a variety of natural grasses and plants, and homemade fences made from branches enclose the family dwellings, resulting in a harmonious blend of human effort and nature. Parades of scraggy goats and small groups of women and children gather around community wells.

Although Ada was responsible for getting the CIDAC program underway in this remote Chaco location, by this phase she had turned over this project site to fellow staff member, Hugo Pereira. Pereira, a wiry Bolivian-trained sociologist, had previously worked at an urban juvenile drug education center. Although born in one of Bolivia's few rural black communities, his family moved to an urban barrio when he was still a young boy. Ada explained, "When we interviewed Hugo for the job, it was his inveterate enthusiasm and good humor about working in the campo that made him stand out among the numerous qualified candidates. We were hiring someone to work specifically in Izozog, and thus an ability to adapt to its isolated and rugged living conditions was a prerequisite for us."

In an interview in Izozog, Pereira showed great empathy for the Izoceños. "My visits here indicate some of the worst poverty in Santa Cruz," he explained. "It is a struggle just to secure enough food to attain a minimal level of subsistence. For instance, the high temperatures have forced the Izoceños to structure their work day in a particular way. They typically rise before dawn, at 4 A.M., to get as much farm work done as possible before the excruciating heat sets in. The poor, sandy soil is much better suited to cattle raising than vegetable cultivation, but that kind of livestock is too expensive for most families. Most households have goats, chickens, and a few pigs. In a few communities there are also sheep. The rainfall also operates in weird patterns here. Often there's a big downpour, and then nothing happens for weeks or sometimes months on end. The native cattle are able to go three days without a drink of water. The Izoceños grow corn and peanuts and other subsistence crops on irrigated plots near the river banks, but even with irrigation, the Izoceño corn yields are the lowest in all of Santa Cruz. Most families must send male members elsewhere to find work. Many men migrate during the slack season to cut sugar cane and pick cotton on large commercial farms in the tropical, northern area of Santa Cruz. It is not uncommon for an entire family to pull up stakes and resettle there for several months. They return with large supplies of sugar, macaroni, and cooking oil. When picking cotton, they are able to save some money for weaving materials they can use when they return.

"We're trying hard to help them see that weaving offers a viable way to make money. Weaving has been a long-standing activity here. Women have always woven ponchos, handbags, and hammocks for family use. Luckily, the exploitative types of commercial dealings found in Urubicha are less frequent here, perhaps due to the greater isolation and general absence of any kind of commercial activity. An order of Catholic sisters once tried to start up a weaving project but made little effort to improve quality. The fineness of the weaving and lovely color schemes in older Izoceño pieces suggests that there has been a great decline from forty to fifty years ago."

When asked whether CIDAC had expanded beyond the initial circle of selected weavers, Pereira's facial muscles tightened in frustration. "The initial group of twelve weavers hasn't expanded over the past year. The lack of interest in our overtures seems to stem from slanderous attacks on us by a Santa Cruz NGO that has been running development programs here for a long time."

The hostility from the other NGO had taken Pereira by surprise since there seemed to him to be enough poverty in the zone to keep various economic development agencies busy. "I suppose it reflects jealousy on the part of that institution, and a lack of respect since we haven't worked with Indian communities as long as they have. They accuse us of being paternalistic, painting Ada as an upper-class lady with a proclivity toward charity rather than development. Yet the meager impact from their investments makes me question their motives and wonder about their insecurities. They also portray us sometimes as middlemen making huge profits by reselling weavings in Santa Cruz. The charges are outlandish. They've never even bothered to check our books or the social fund, our main profit distribution mechanism. Moreover, their influence over Izozog's native headman has added to these woes. He has been cool in response to our efforts to recruit artisans into our program. To gain his trust, I've begun a 'lineal study'—a method I learned as a sociology student—to identify weavers from his extended family. Maybe by bringing them some of the program's tangible benefits, his support may be won over.

"It may be these suspicions that have led weavers to alter the weight of their pieces. We could not believe it when we discovered weavers were padding hammocks and tapestries with extra wool to earn higher prices. They had no qualms about cheating CIDAC, the very agency subsidizing their weaving!

"As if these weren't enough obstacles in our path, we have also had to deal with community conflicts. There are four different evangelical sects waging turf battles for believers here. These influences are very divisive and confusing for the villages, and get in the way of our efforts to recruit weavers into our programs."

When I asked whether CIDAC's methodology might be inadvertently eroding Izoceño cultural values by advocating Western urban tastes, Pereira responded. "Look, we're trying to bring out the richness in their cultural expressions by taking colors from the traditional Izoceño palette and combining them in new ways for greater aesthetic and commercial appeal. Izoceños now beautifully combine black, their favorite color, with dark green, orange, and a subtle rose color. We've also discovered that the Izoceños once cultivated a native beige-colored variety of cotton and we are in the process of helping them begin to cultivate it again."

Pereira informed us that Ada makes the decisions about color combinations and technical improvements. His role is to organize the weavers, collect finished weavings from them, furnish them with cotton yarn and other materials, and bring them consumer goods purchased with sales profits. In a sense CIDAC was replicating commercial middlemen's favorite methods with, of course, the big difference of reducing raw material costs, increasing product quality, and paying much higher prices. Pereira also serves as an information channel between Izozog and Santa Cruz. There are very few weavers and a lower level of organization here than in Urubicha, so the CIDAC staff has to take more initiative in moving the revival program forward.

While finishing his summary of the project's progress, Pereira expressed frustration that the villagers had been unwilling, as yet, to let him in on the meanings of the abstract geometric motifs on the tapestries. "So far they have been unwilling to share these visual codes of their cosmovision. I take this to be another sign of the lack of trust in us. Perhaps it is due to my double disadvantage of being both a male and non-Guaraní speaker."

Later that afternoon, an Argentine anthropologist living in Izozog and doing research as an IAF Fellow for her UCLA doctoral dissertation, gave us another perspective on Izozog and the project. Silvia Hirsch was from an upper-class Buenos Aires family and had come to Izozog as part of a two-year comparative study of Guaraní political organization. Her study focused on the *Capitania,* the time-tested form of communal government.

Hirsch informed us that the Izoceños represent the merging of two distinct native groups, the Guaraní-speaking Chiriguanos, migrants from Brazil to this part of South America, and the Chanes, the original Gran Chaco inhabitants. The Izoceños lost much of their traditional homeland in the last half of the nineteenth and early twentieth centuries through a process known in colloquial terms as "cattle colonization." White ranchers turned their cattle loose on Indian communal lands and then reclaimed them as "private property."

"Izoceños practice a form of self-government, under a *capitan,* or *mburuvicha,* who presides over a governing assembly made up of the fourteen communities. This same leadership and organizational structure exists in each of the individual communities within the federated system. The top position is hereditary, yet from what I have seen, the assembly itself is a highly democratic entity which meets almost weekly to bring together viewpoints and issues from a wide range of community members. The assembly will debate issues for long periods, if necessary, in order to achieve a consensual opinion. The big gap in the system, of course, is the complete absence of women's participation either in leadership ranks or in the frequent assemblies."

In responding to questions about the disgruntled NGO, Hirsch said, "Yes, I have heard them talk about paternalism ad nauseum. But given the few options to launching such an ambitious and potentially important program, I'm not bothered by their methodology. The project has introduced important economic benefits to some very poor families. I have seen first-hand how significant the monthly income is for them. A monthly source of cash is an unheard-of luxury in this economically stagnant zone and the husbands of weavers are obviously pleased to be able to avoid cutting sugar cane. In these cases, women have replaced men as the family breadwinners. This is an incredible shift in power relations and intrigues me greatly.

"Another direct benefit for the women is the opportunity to interact with like-minded weavers and potters from other Santa Cruz ethnic groups. I saw the excitement in their faces when they returned from a regional artisan meeting organized by CIDAC. The weavers were abuzz about the outspoken, self-confident manner of the Guarayas in front of so many people. The Izoceños here are monolingual and reserved, so positive exposure to other native role models is helpful for building interest in female community activism.

"One reason the cultivation of a positive self-image and an active stance in the women is so important is that husbands have resisted their wives' attendance at artisan meetings."

Just at that moment, an Izoceña weaver, Ana Yandura, walked in the room. Over her arm she held a tapestry with red geometric designs on a solid white background. Yandura had the wide nose and cheekbones of her native group and wore an attractive pair of earrings. Her tired face spoke volumes about years of toil and drudgery in this dry and torrid climate.

She answered my inquiry about her freedom to attend the meetings of the artisan association in this way. "For a while my husband objected to my participation in the association meetings because they were at night. It bothered him that I would return home typically at 10 or 11 P.M., something I'd never done before. At one point his anger over this made me want to drop out and resign from the group. Other women have told me about similar problems. Finally the men relented, accepting that the meetings were essential for our weaving sales. Such changes in my life have made my children prouder than ever of their mother."

THE FLOWERING OF AN ARTISAN SHOP

During its first five years of activity, CIDAC excelled as a trainer of artisans, enabling them to recover old methods and designs, develop new skills, and create pleasing products for the middle-class customer. By the fifth year, CIDAC had established a network that serviced the needs of five widely scattered artisan groups in the Department of Santa Cruz, the last of which was located in Valle Grande, an Andean valley seven hours' driving time from Santa Cruz. CIDAC's framework had displaced some of the exploitative, long-established relations with middlemen. Artisans were able to take various courses in technological improvements, dyeing techniques, and methods for modifying and diversifying their traditional products to create innovative, utilitarian crafts products such as hammocks, bowls, and woven goods.

Over time, CIDAC had to increase the size of its modestly paid staff to keep up with the needs of new artisans joining the program and to expand production and marketing services. Ada believed it was important to hire professional women technicians to oversee the assorted efforts. Thus she brought in female community organizers from La Paz as well as Santa Cruz, along with financial managers, sociologists, and accountants.

The steady growth in product sales, the number of participating communities, and artisan membership over CIDAC's first five years carved out an important niche for the organization within the overall women's grassroots development of the region. Although by 1986 there were 120 artisans from five regions making products that totaled between $800 and $1,000 monthly in the CIDAC shop, fully half of the new artisans joining up were Guarayos from Urubicha. The other centers tended to grow slowly. The over-representation of crafts from Urubicha was not due just to random forces or to the different motivational levels of the other groups. It also reflected CIDAC's cautious trial and error approach in which the market was viewed as the ultimate barometer for testing products and fostering expanded production. In this CIDAC's shop played a central role.

Before I had even seen the CIDAC shop, a friend in La Paz had conveyed to me the shop's aesthetic appeal. "You have got to see it as soon as possible. It's simply marvelous," she said. When I did visit the shop in the mid-1980s, I was struck both by its beauty and its tremendous potential as a promotional showcase of Cruceño native and mestizo artisanry. The deep reds, purples, greens, and pinks in the Guarayo hammocks displayed across a wall added a brilliant luster to the entire room. Shelves and tables held an enormous array of handsome woven pieces and finely made ceramics.

Each section of the shop was devoted to the work of a particular artisan group. A selection of hand-woven bedspreads, tablecloths, placemats, belts, and handbags showed the product diversification of the free-spirited Guarayos. Their hammocks sported intricate crocheted edges and fanciful tassels. A colonial-style hammock was also displayed, as a sign of the revival of work from the distant past.

Another wall exhibited various objects woven of *jipijapa* palm leaves—another example of the product diversification fostered by CIDAC. The Ichilo straw hats had a tightly woven, yet supple texture, and an elegant feminine mystique. They were positioned next to baskets and small oval and rectangular boxes for holding jewelry, candy, cigarettes, or sewing utensils made from the same material. According to Ada, training programs with this group included the younger generation to ensure that palm-weaving skills would not be lost to the local economy.

Another section of the shop featured display alcoves set in a white-washed adobe wall. One ledge contained a neatly arranged collection of cocoa-colored birds, bowls, and other familiar animal figures of varying sizes and shapes. Ada picked up a duck-shaped flower vase and pointed out its fine proportions, smooth surface finish, and decorative wings. Different-sized urns were also placed in a corner on this side of the room, and decorative lampshades hung overhead. Ada explained that these pieces were from Cotoca. Despite a relatively weak artisan's organization, she said, the craftswomen of Cotoca demonstrated impressive technical proficiency.

Ada then led me to the display area of the newest groups belonging to the CIDAC network. I immediately recognized the hammocks from Izozog. The woolen saddle-bags and tapestries with geometric designs in bold reds, greens, and yellows next to them were less familiar to me. Although made by mountain valley peoples of Valle Grande, the work showed influence of the Aymara peoples who today populate the altiplano. Ada explained that there were not yet appreciable sales of either the hammocks or the woolen goods due to the incipient stage of organization in these two places. The Izozog weavings were not big sellers yet either—perhaps because superior weavings from the Aymara and Quechua weavers in the altiplano were sold in other shops in Santa Cruz. This is an example of the ways that market limitations have determined the direction of CIDAC's growth, and explains why artisan participation has not increased at a greater rate than it has.

In addition to displaying the products in an artful manner, each discrete exhibit space used text and photos to identify the individual artisans, their technologies, their cultural history, and geographic location. Ada explained, "We're trying to educate our customers about the lives and work of indigenous and peasant women within the region and in the nation. We want to demonstrate to them that in remote villages, talented producers of indigenous origin remain hidden and ignored. Another goal is to make our customers understand fair pricing and the declining access to raw material that some artisan communities face."

The quality of a display in another corner of the shop was so extraordinary that the exhibition of Native American life at the Smithsonian's Natural History museum flashed through my mind. Here clay sculptures of scenes from native life were perched on vertical stands of different heights. Several figurines, some six to ten inches in height on a clay base, represented native peoples both at work and at play, women weaving on their looms and grinding corn, musicians playing drums and violins. Once again this was the able work of the versatile Guarayos. Ada told me that Lorgio had helped the Guarayos build a kiln and offered a training course during a visit to Urubicha last year. "This initial training led to some fabulous sculpture by a handful of artists. The stuff sells so fast we have had to purchase several pieces for our showroom in order to maintain a permanent collection. One of the artisans, Tiburcio Mborobinchi, already has gone on the international tour circuit of Latin America."

Ada went on to tell me that the demand for CIDAC's products becomes so great at times that they have to close their doors to avoid finding themselves with a barren showroom for their customers. She said a growing group of interested buyers includes local businessmen and government leaders, and division chiefs of public development corporations who appreciate having a place to purchase deluxe gifts for important out-of-town visitors. Furthermore, Santa Cruz banks were using CIDAC's products in their window displays, which was, in essence, a form of free advertising.

"Imitation is the highest form of flattery, I guess," Ada said. "Since CIDAC has opened its shops, artisan stores featuring Cruceño crafts have proliferated both downtown and in the city's international airport. Fortunately, from our business standpoint, the products are neither well selected nor tastefully displayed, and local gossip holds that the shops are a laundering mechanism for drug dollars. Drug trafficking is so pervasive in this city that just the other day our suspicions were aroused by a shifty-looking guy who made the single largest purchase ever to occur in our store. On the spot he bought 400 Guarayo hammocks 'for Panama and Miami.' After he departed, we looked at one another and concurred that the hammocks were most likely the latest form of gift wrap for international cocaine shipments on flights heading north."

Ada spoke of CIDAC's pride in being able to open up a middle-class market during a time of economic crisis in the country. Despite the shrinking buying power wrought by hyperinflation, and a local artisans' market saturated with cheap imports from Brazil and Asia, the project had enabled the Santa Cruz women to stay ahead of most poor Bolivians. CIDAC's dazzling shop was truly casting native and mestizo women in a brilliant light.

Onward and Upward in the Late 1980s

By the late 1980s, CIDAC was exhibiting native crafts in the exhibition hall of the Casa de la Cultura (The House of Culture) which is the major public cultural center in downtown Santa Cruz. While this gave the native artisanry wonderful exposure, there were still visitors who commented, "This is beautiful stuff. Lorgio has done a great job teaching the indigenous interesting designs and uses for the raw materials available in our region. These people are finally being given some skills to raise their cultural levels closer to ours in the city." This sort of patronizing racist attitude toward the artisans, Ada said, was much too common.

In another example of such prejudice, a local artist angrily spoke out during a seminar on national art at the Casa de la Cultura. He was horrified the Casa de la Cultura was sponsoring an exhibit of native artisanry in a main gallery space typically reserved for paintings. "The leadership of the Casa has shown terrible judgment in sponsoring this show," he said, with other artists chiming in. "It's debasing the highest kinds of cultural expression by presenting this artisanry and other cheap trinkets that have nothing to do with art." I responded by suggesting that this rich source of Bolivian art has to be explored from a different perspective than that of European art criticism.

While attitudes might prove difficult to change, the continuing good news was that customers kept flowing into the CIDAC store, which now supported all eight artisan groups identified in the original project plan, plus two additional spontaneously organized groups. CIDAC's network now consisted of 350 artisans generating $60,000 in sales per year for twenty-two far-flung communities. In addition to ongoing support by the IAF, CIDAC had received $300,000 in public monies from the Social Investment Fund (formerly called the emergency fund) of the Bolivian government agency established to ameliorate the social costs of Bolivia's neo-liberal economic model. The money covered the construction of five community-based artisan centers to be scattered around the region, each to be outfitted with its own showroom, meeting hall, local office, and storage areas. CIDAC and its astonishing artisan diversity was also becoming a popular and colorful subject for local television and newspaper media.

An example of one of the newer groups were the Chiquitaña Indian families from Tajibos. Ada described this group. "Unlike most other artisans in our program, the Chiquitaños had lost all of their artisan traditions. Some were skilled seamstresses, however, so we taught them to do embroidery using cotton thread." The Chiquitañas' pillow cases and wall hangings—with their vibrant bucolic scenes, deep hues, and striking color contrasts—had quickly attained great popularity. Ada insisted that no two pieces were alike.

The most striking Tajibos piece was an image of larger than life orange and yellow bananas, pushing out from the center of a background of emerald green leaves and nocturnal blackness. A text to the side conveyed the creative inspiration of its craftswoman producer, Claudia Opimi. It read, "I am in love with my handmade embroidery craft. Now that I am doing this, I am always thinking of images I can create during my frequent walks in the campo. Everything I observe, such as nature's rich colors, the curves of its rural landscape, or its collections of plants and trees, I try to store in my memory as an image for future embroidery compositions."

Another newly organized artisan group surfaced when Guarayo youth began painting *retablos,* three eight-inch high pieces of wood hinged together for upright display. This genre of artisanry had been more common in Peru than in Bolivia. The pictures of dense, exuberant foliage, wildlife, and playful human activity depicted a stylized, idyllic view of rural life in the tropical communities near Urubicha. These images were a blend of multiculturalism and biodiversity at their best.

I learned from CIDAC staff that Ada's daughter Malena organized this project while on vacation from her studies of art history in Spain. During a month in Urubica, she encouraged the young boys to try their hand at painting and offered courses in design, the use of color, composition, and acrylic techniques. Most importantly, she kept in mind the useful advice offered by her father. "Don't try to put ideas in their heads about what to paint," he judiciously insisted. "The inspiration for this creative work must emerge from their own life experience and cultural expressions."

Her father, indeed, had been so impressed by this latest Guarayo folk art expression that it gave him frequent cause for reflection on the art history of his country. "This brings to mind the historical experience of artists in Bolivia. It was the traumatic defeat of our country in the Chaco War in the 1930s that put us on the road to reflecting about our true national identity. Until then we had remained dependent on foreign sources for our cultural inspiration. I'm referring, of course, to high brow art, not the popular art found in our highland and rural communities. Now the Guarayo retablo art has suddenly emerged out of the blue to astonish us with its authenticity, creativity, and the keen observation of environmental detail that inspires its makers. These direct and genuine images reaffirm for me that our artistic riches reside not in the cities, but in the rural communities with native peoples and peasants. This kind of art will enable Bolivia as a developing nation to shape its authentic artistic identity."

Another artisan group that unexpectedly emerged within the city of Santa Cruz is known as the Experimental Workshop. The group was housed in four single-story red-brick buildings with large windows and traditional red tile roofs. This workshop-training center was open to Chiquitaño, Guarayo, Izoceño, and other native youth, most of whom were already living in Santa Cruz and taking night classes toward their high school degrees. Originally established as a training center, this workshop was the first association to become self-financing from its sales, and in short order it became a veritable hothouse of innovative product ideas. Their latest product, small ash trays with painted relief designs of lizards and other rodents, were instant hits with buyers.

CIDAC's vitality and the various groups' ingenuity for creating new products continued unabated during these years. Ceramicists from Cotoca reshaped traditional urns into new female figures, including pregnant women; Izoceñas converted their hammocks into bedspreads for middle-class homes; and the saddle-bag weavers from Valle Grande, finding limited markets for their woolen products, began making wildly popular figurines from their corn stalks. Perhaps not surprisingly, the multicolored Guarayo hammocks were still far and away the most sought-after product in the shop.

Training courses continued year after year as CIDAC tried to keep up with the ambitious goals of project expansion. There were always new people to be trained, new product improvements to be made, and new techniques, designs, and products to be recovered and introduced. Technical training continued in the communities themselves under the guidance of the respective coordinators. In Santa Cruz, Ada and Lorgio also were able to draw from an extensive personal network of national and foreign talent as trainers to assist in the development of Cruceño artisanry.

The use of select foreign experts was part of this multi-faceted training strategy. Ada said to me during a visit to her office, "The development of our traditional handicrafts should tap knowledge and talent from outside the country as well as inside. Over the years, we have used Japanese weavers to teach new techniques with the *jipijapa* palm and potters to teach firing techniques in Cotoca. One of Argentina's most famous potters, Jorge Fernandez Chiti, has offered several courses under our sponsorship in Santa Cruz. We hired Ramon Landivar, a Bolivian-American originally from Santa Cruz and now working at a museum in the Southwestern United States, to teach different techniques for the production of pre-Columbian style pottery. Don Ramon returns to Bolivia each year to give free workshops to our potters from Cotoca and the Experimental Workshop. We also brought an Ecuadorian woman to Santa Cruz to teach the artisans from the Ichilo communities 'Panama Hat' techniques. This enabled them to open a new line of production, introduce a bleaching process into the production sequence, and innovate by using colored concentric circles in smaller objects woven from this material.

"We also utilize the city's best local talent in our training programs. Many professional potters have volunteered their time, and Lorgio and a city-based potters' group have created a specialized institution, the Centro de Investigación y Capacitación de Ceramica (CICE) (The Center for Research and Ceramics Training), to research clay and glaze types and their uses in the region. They also train native artisans in kiln technologies and ceramics-related skills such as roof tile production. Our daughter, Malena, also contributed by coordinating ceramics courses in clay preparation, the use of the potter's wheel, hand molding techniques, and kiln construction."

In addition to harnessing high-powered foreign and national talent for artisan training, CIDAC had began deploying artisans themselves as trainers. Guarayo weavers were transferring their knowledge in loom technology to the Izoceños to benefit about thirty families. A Chiquitaña woman from Tajibos had returned to her homelands in Northern Santa Cruz to teach.

CIDAC also seemed to be receiving moral support and occasional coordinated actions from CIDOB, the federation representing lowland indigenous groups which pushed the territorial rights movement (see chapter 4). CIDOB leaders expressed satisfaction about indigenous women from their communities earning cash for their families and improving their marketing and organizational skills.

THE UPHILL CLIMB TO ARTISAN PARTICIPATION

While the advances in the CIDAC story suggest a steady, sure-footed strategy of mobilizing local artisans for grassroots development, an important subtext has been the struggle to put management tasks and responsibilities directly into the hands of the women producers themselves. Ada knew, perhaps from her social work days, that the basket and hammock makers must one day manage and administer their own service program both in the city and in the hinterlands. An important milestone of participatory development would be reached when the bookkeepers, financial managers, artisan supervisors, sales agents, and planners would all come from the rural communities. Ignoring this need for self-management would mean perpetuating the artisans' dependency on a few well-intentioned professionals. Yet there was the danger, if participant management were assumed too early, of putting the grassroots organization in over its head, with far worse results for the future of the program. The experimental artisan service program was now a complex, multi-tiered system of financial and economic transactions and highly detailed documentation and information management for far-flung communities. To many observers, CIDAC began to look too much like ten different projects rolled into one. Ada and her colleagues took incremental steps in their transfer of decision-making and administrative roles to the community members. Caution and compassion helped to guide this trial and error approach.

Office and financial management skills were far more challenging to women than technical matters. The artisan skills could be practiced within the safe confines of home. The delicate art of money management for a service organization posed a more difficult and more public set of challenges. How could a typical work day referred to by the artisans as the "triple shift" (household, farm, and craft work) prepare women for roles as administrators and managers? An Ichilo hat maker commented, "Our work day consists of the following tasks and obligations: rising early, cleaning the house, making the beds, fixing breakfast, fetching water, feeding the animals, dressing children for school, washing clothes, preparing and transporting lunch to husbands in the field, making coffee for the siesta, weaving a straw hat, cooking dinner, washing the dishes, cleaning the kitchen. and then returning to weaving for the waning hours of the day."

Rural educational backgrounds were equally poor in terms of preparation for greater co-management functions. Only a handful of artisans had been to high school. In a rural society where girls were the last to be sent to elementary school and the first to be pulled out at a young age, this was not a surprising revelation. Reading, writing, and basic arithmetic were as scarce as computer management skills for native women. Even past experience in women's organizations was frequently more a hindrance than a help. The paternalistic mothers' clubs, which had reigned in the area for years, tended to stifle rather than foster self-development and women's creative energies.

Even though these disadvantages were a given, it was disappointing to learn from external project evaluators in the late 1980s that CIDAC had not gone far enough in promoting the artisan women's participation in the management of the organization. One report by Bolivian anthropologist Antonio Ugarte diagnosed the situation this way, "The artisan associations themselves were too informal and ad hoc. There was a lack of rules for member responsibilities, procedures, duties, obligations, and sanctions, making it easy for self-serving individuals to appropriate disproportionate benefits for themselves." Ugarte was suggesting that much of the power in CIDAC's program had been concentrated in the coordinators, which, if left unchecked, could lead to abuse by privileged individuals beyond the organization's control. Ugarte also mentioned complaints by artisans about having little information about sales practices in the CIDAC shop.

Ada defended CIDAC, saying that Ugarte's yardstick was taken from the political culture of the highlands, an unfair measure when applied to the different reality of the lowlands. "In the mountain provinces, native peoples have been engaged in commerce for hundreds of years and have also had a long history of participation in seasoned national grassroots organizations."

Ada also pointed to a long-standing CIDAC practice aimed at reducing the huge chasm between the world of the artisan and CIDAC operations in the big city. In this part of the program, arrangements have been made for artisans to apprentice at the shop on temporary assignments as sale clerks and bookkeepers. This experience has afforded them the opportunity to become familiar with the nuts and bolts of recordkeeping and sales, the establishment of profit margins, and with planning methods. María Jesús, an Izoceña weaver undergoing an apprenticeship in the CIDAC shop, spoke in a soft voice about her plunge into life in the big city. "Although I'm thirty-one years old, coming to work at the CIDAC shop was the first time I had ever set foot in this city. It was difficult to get around in the beginning, but now I'm an old hand at it. Before working here, I didn't have a clue about how to talk with foreigners, fill out a sales slip, compute exchange rates for different foreign currencies, cash a check, or even give change back to a customer. By working here I have learned to handle all these tasks on my own." It is Ada's belief that the experiences of María Jesús and other apprentices have helped put to rest rumors in the countryside about exploitative product sales in Santa Cruz.

Perhaps the most impressive step CIDAC has taken to build empowerment of women has been to organize a federation of artisan producers called ARTECAMPO, among the same ethnic minorities that had joined forces to form CIDOB. Now it was the women's turn to assert their distinct cultural identities and valuable skills. Ada explained, "To my knowledge, ARTECAMPO was the first multi-ethnic artisan federation of its kind in rural Bolivia. Such an initiative would have been impossible without CIDAC's organization-building efforts and the framework of support it has provided for artisans. ARTECAMPO's main event is an annual meeting where association delegates present work plans and share their experiences. These forums allow women to give each other mutual support in their artisan revival work. Women compare notes about everything from bookkeeping methods to access to vegetable fibers. The sharing among the Chiquitañas, Guarayos, and Izoceños has led, interestingly, to each group's stronger sense of its unique cultural identity and distinct cultural values. The common concerns and growing cultural pride expressed in their sessions were evident in their public petitions to government officials and follow-up newspaper accounts about their agenda and ideology. One of the biggest campaigns launched by the artisan women has been to acquire real estate in the city's center to be used for an ARTECAMPO shop. In the face of this rapidly rising public profile, governmental and development officials are no longer able to be indifferent to the country women's problems and proposals."

The ARTECAMPO women's social activism and growing reputation as a group of fine craftswomen and artists has begun to alter conventional stereotypes of native peoples here. Equally important are the changes in perceptions about women as political actors in the rural areas from which the women come. ARTECAMPO leaders are being consulted in their home villages about matters where women's opinions never counted before. "Our goal in the founding of ARTECAMPO," Ada said, "has been to build co-management structures and eventually establish full-fledged self-managed artisan programs in the various communities. By the end of the 1980s, however, outside evaluations such as Ugarte's, along with our own soul searching, led us to recognize that the management skills of the artisans lagged way behind their technical development as artisans. Thus we are now giving greater attention to this problem in order to fulfill our original pledge to establish true grassroots management."

In the early 1990s, Ada put this drive to strengthen artisan management skills and transfer responsibilities in the hands of her thirty-year-old daughter, Malena.

Malena recently spoke about CIDAC's renewed commitment to management training in the spacious facilities of the Experimental Workshop. "A number of changes have transpired during the 1990s. For one thing the federation has started holding meetings every two months instead of once a year. Clearly meeting once a year was far too infrequent to keep a widely scattered organization coherent. We now avoid having too much time elapse between identifying problems and implementing solutions. In this way we try to find short-term solutions to problems so as to avoid having them fester and contribute to new problems. For example, we recently offered a short course on report-writing for CIDAC as a solution to widespread difficulties with this task found in the associations. We also recently resolved to conduct literacy training so that women can take part in the basic accounting and administration courses. During 1992, especially, we redoubled women's training in administration, accounting, and management to speed up the transfer of service program functions and responsibilities."

When asked about her own involvement, Malena beamed. "The most gratifying aspect has been the work with the artisan women themselves. I've always had an interest in defending the rights of women, helping them to recover their creative talents, and held a general commitment to working for greater equality in Bolivian society. Despite having studied art history in Spain and taught university level courses in this country, I felt woefully unprepared to teach management and organization-building skills to poor, mostly illiterate, women. Teaching technical artisan skills has been my forte and I never expected to do this other kind of training. So, along with a handful of artisans, coordinators, and leaders, I enrolled in a popular education program sponsored by PROCESO, another IAF-financed NGO in Santa Cruz."

The three-year course, designed to prepare "popular educators" to work with peasants, youth, and indigenous women in the region, offers different three-day workshops. At first, they teach very elementary skills such as how to conduct a meeting, organize a discussion, or formulate a very simple community development project. Later there are sessions on planning program activities and the use of alternative social communications to foster animated member participation. There is an extensive use of reflection group techniques and exercises using folktales and myths from Andean and Amazonian cultural traditions. PROCESO insists on the development of analytical approaches to learning and using educational materials which enhance self-esteem and a strong sense of native cultural identity.

Malena added, "Our intensified capacity-building program in the 1990s gave us the confidence to try to decentralize several money management functions to the affiliated associations of ARTECAMPO. Several years ago, we tried to restructure these responsibilities without success. It was a real mess and everyone wound up confused and demoralized. Now, after this intensive training effort, we are trying to transfer the tasks and responsibilities once again. The coordinators and association leaders should be in better shape this time. Since we are well aware of all the pitfalls, we will proceed for a six-month trial period and then step back to evaluate the results before going any further. Under the new approach, each artisan association will manage its own rotating and social fund in a separate bank account. Our thought is that it will be easier for the artisan groups if they only have to worry about their own association."

URUBICHA REVISITED

By 1994, CIDAC and ARTECAMPO had taken impressive strides. The Guarayo hammock makers were way ahead of the other groups both in sales and in number of artisans participating in the local ARTECAMPO association. The hammock makers alone now totaled 180 artisans producing $40,000 in sales for their communities. Inspired by their economic success, nearby Guarayo traditional basket makers formed a similar association in the early 1990s.

A concrete sign of cultural revitalization in Urubicha is an A-framed white adobe building sitting in what was formerly a weed-covered lot on the main street. The spacious interior resembles the CIDAC shop in miniature. The rear of the building leads into a courtyard where Ada and I met with dozens of Guarayo women who sat facing each other on long benches placed in a square.

After some preliminary remarks, the women took turns commenting on how the revitalization of their craft work had changed their lives. A middle-aged woman, Edi Lasara, stood up and offered her testimony. "I first joined the program by taking advanced hammock-weaving classes with Ana, our coordinator. I worked hard to improve my skills in the finishing work critical to completing a hammock. This work has paid off since the sale of my hammocks has became the main source of income with which I meet the needs of my eight children. Weaving has become so time consuming that I no longer have to accompany my husband to the fields to haul firewood, jugs of water, and farm products. My son transports these products on a bicycle purchased from my earnings. I also have a fourteen-year-old daughter who does the crochet work you see on our hammocks. Girls perform this task since it requires much less arm strength than weaving on the large vertical looms."

Another woman spoke in an excited tone as though she could not wait to share her thoughts with us. "Before joining the association I was very timid and too self-conscious to speak up in a group situation," she said. "The simple act of going over to my neighbor's front porch and starting a conversation was a terrifying thought. But the association forced me to attend monthly meetings and gradually I began to feel comfortable speaking up in front of other women. In time, I became increasingly at ease in public expression and was amazed to find that my past fears were disappearing. I also was able to relearn skills in writing which I had lost from lack of practice. In our classes, we had to perform exercises preparing sales receipts and filling out information cards documenting our CIDAC transactions."

Ana Oreya, the local coordinator, then began an overview of the changes for women in Urubicha. "It is over ten years ago now that Ada first explained to us that we were losing money by marketing our hammocks through the itinerant traders. Since then, several of us have learned, through constant practice, how to calculate our costs of production and transport. That has enabled us to set prices and determine the true value of our work. We no longer rely on CIDAC staff to help us with this task. In our monthly meetings, we examine the quality of every individual piece, making sure it adheres to the high standards of craftsmanship that allow us to charge good prices. By setting prices right here in Urubicha, we force middlemen and merchant buyers to pay prices close to our own.[2] This adjustment benefits other hammock makers opting to remain independent from our organization yet participate in the market. Our association manages its own bank account in to which we deposit sales profits. By sending members on temporary assignment to CIDAC headquarters, we've also learned the ropes of marketing and other services which affect our communities.

"There is another thing to mention," Ana Oreya said. "You may notice that there are no men present at our meeting today. We generally keep them out of our meetings to avoid disclosing the amount of money earned in their presence. We are afraid they'll demand this income at home to feed their drinking habits. Men are notorious for drinking around here."

After hearing impressive testimony such as this, we walked back through the association center. Passing through the large showroom, we spotted young girls in smocks standing in a row busily stacking piles of rolled hammocks. This was a final reminder of the effort CIDAC and ARTECAMPO had made to incorporate the next generation into the weaving process so that the work would be sustained into the foreseeable future.

IZOZOG REVISITED

There have been equally impressive signs of economic and social change at the grassroots level in Izozog. By 1994, Hugo Pereira had long been re-placed in his role as CIDAC technician by Justo Yandura, one of the few Izoceños to have completed high school and taken up residence in the city of Santa Cruz. Justo was a real find for CIDAC because of his ability to move in and out of the two distinct cultural settings of the Gran Chaco and the regional capital city. Justo had also introduced CIDAC to his older brother, Angel, whose voracious reading habits made him a formidable native intellectual in the region. Angel was a self-styled folk poet, amateur song writer, and veteran field worker on several ethnographic research projects. CIDAC had hired Angel to help them penetrate the mysterious symbols and worldview embedded in the Izoceña weaving motifs. Angel had documented and clarified the two weaving design styles: the *moise* pattern style showing round figures representing floral motifs, and the geometric, rhombus *karakapepo* designs connoting the sacred within the Izoceño culture. He had also discovered that weavers had a special attachment to the symbol of the serpent which appeared in the form of elongated floral configurations on the large decorative bands of the woven hammocks and tapestries. Angel's research had brought CIDAC staff into closer touch with the secretive side of this native world. As a result, CIDAC staff and Ada had developed increased appreciation for the importance of ethnography in understanding a local project context. This change in outlook led to the subsequent hiring of a well-known specialist on the Guaraní-speaking peoples, French anthropologist Isabel Combes.

There were other interesting changes occurring in Izozog communities during the mid-1990s. The number of active weavers in the program had increased to seventy-eight persons, considerably more than the dozen or so enrolled in 1987. CIDAC and ARTECAMPO had founded a spinners' association of forty elderly women as a way of offering them a less physically demanding occupation than weaving. This new division of labor between spinning and weaving tasks gave the most productive female weavers increased time for the more remunerative occupation. By 1993, Izozog annual sales had reached $12,000, giving them the rank of third among the ten artisan associations.

There were other social changes touching the weavers' lives. Upon arriving in Izozog, we immediately ran into the *capitan,* Bonifacio Barrientos or "Boni Chico" as he is affectionately known. Despite his appearance—that of a poker-faced Indian leader who keeps distance between himself and this white outsider—he offered a warm and firm *abrazo.* Boni was in high spirits since he had just been designated Bolivia's first indigenous mayor of a newly created sub-municipal indigenous district under the new "Popular Participation Law." The dubious attitude he had held at the outset of the weaving revival had completely changed. The strongest evidence of this was his sister's recent election to the presidency of the Izozog weavers' association.

When asked about the weaving program, he asserted that the program should keep expanding to include other weavers and communities. "Weaving sales not only provide income, which is hard to come by around here, but the women's involvement in weaving has increased their political participation. The weavers now send a delegate to our formerly all-male assemblies. The women of Izozog have a role in local government for the first time ever. Anyone who generates income at the rate they do deserves to participate and have a voice in our communities."

Augusta Sanchez, a sprightly sixty-eight year old, gave a weaver's perspective on how the program was progressing. Her tiny dwelling, constructed from mud and sticks and different types of roof thatching, suggested once again that poverty was worse in Izozog than in Urubicha. Augusta described a solitary life. Her husband had passed away several years before, and her children had moved out to establish independent families. Thanks to the help of her school-age grandchildren, however, she was able to keep track of the production and sales of her weaving in her artisan's notebook. "I support myself entirely from the sale of tapestries," she said. "Being too old to work my own lands, I use my weaving income to pay young men to farm my plots of rice, corn, and peanuts." When asked how the quality of workmanship of the weavers today compared to that of her mother and grandmother, she added, "I personally believe our work surpasses the fineness and beauty of my grandmother's hammocks. Dona Ada has encouraged us to return to weaving designs that had disappeared, a change that has been for the better. It's too bad," she said, shaking her head, "but back pains prevent me from producing more than one piece each month."

When asked whether the weaving revival had changed gender roles in her community, Augusta said an important example of that phenomenon has been the change in the willingness of men to carry water from the well to the village huts. "Although exclusively a women's chore in our culture, men have agreed to do this, however reluctantly, to free up the weaver for greater time at the loom. They still try to avoid embarrassment in front of their peers by being as inconspicuous about it as possible."

Thus, in addition to bringing about increases in family income, Izozog women have also gained greater respect for themselves and established a faint, yet rising voice in community affairs. Although the initial eight years of CIDAC's artisan work in Izozog had seemed to progress in slow motion, the project was moving along briskly by 1994.

ADVANCING TO CENTER STAGE: CIDAC AND ARTECAMPO IN SANTA CRUZ IN THE MID-1990S

Back in downtown Santa Cruz, CIDAC's progress had paralleled that in the rural areas. Ada was in her mid-fifties now, her thick, close-cropped hair greying around the edges. In the CIDAC shop offices, she held up a chart showing CIDAC's progress over the last few years. "During the 1990s our artisan sales have increased about 20 percent yearly. We have begun to export products to the Alternate Trade Organizations in Western Europe and recently have sent samples to OXFAM-America in the United States. Yet we are continuing to use a cautionary strategy in order to avoid being swamped with product orders too large for our capacity. Malena is putting together our first sales catalogue to enhance our exposure abroad. This year, 1994, the total artisans in our program numbered 600 persons, with our total sales adding up to $140,000. We hope that within several years we can reach $200,000, a sum that will enable us to cover the shop's administrative costs and coordinator salaries.[3] The Dutch donor, CEBEMO, is financing us to double the number of participating artisans. The coordinators are recruiting artisans into the program with greater vigor than ever for this new phase. In addition to the 600 artisan beneficiaries, there are hundreds of other artisans living in proximity to them benefiting indirectly. Their work has improved, and they are receiving higher prices for their products as a kind of ripple effect. I might add that all these gains have been made despite severe challenges posed by the deluge of Asian-made artisan products into the Santa Cruz marketplace from globalization changes.

"Another sign of the project's impact can be found in the notebooks of the artisans where they record consumer goods acquired and social investments made from profits. Ten years ago women's notebooks contained listings of food items, clothing, or basic items for use in the campo. Increases in cumulative earnings and savings since then have made it possible for the women to invest in such things as community housing, health insurance, or the organization of a dry goods store owned by an association in a small town. The women from Ichilo devised an interesting solution to the loss of access to *jipijapa* plants that unexpectedly fell into the jurisdiction of a national park. They mobilized their savings to purchase a ten hectare plot of land for growing their own.

"Yet we also have to acknowledge the great unevenness in economic activity, and the heterogeneity in terms of organization and culture across the associations. Artisan groups with only a couple of dozen members earn only a few thousand dollars each year while others such as the Guarayos, the multi-ethnic Experimental Workshop (currently the second highest in sales), and mestizos from Ichilo are generating tens of thousands of dollars annually for their families and communities. Some groups are still struggling to find a viable market niche despite considerable effort.

"One of the groups having the most difficulty has been the Ayoreos. A number of NGO and public development programs floundered in their efforts to bring them developmental assistance. We have had similar ups and downs and have had to exercise much patience and perseverance. Recently, however, things seem to be progressing reasonably well since we installed Hugo Pereira to supervise the export to Japan of their lovely handbags made from the garabata plant. Similar to the Izoceño weavings, their designs convey a symbolic language depicting the relationship between their spiritual beliefs and local biodiversity. The Ayoreos are neither well-organized, dependable, nor very focused on their work within the association, ARTECAMPO. Many Ayoreo can be found begging on Santa Cruz street corners. Yet their poor local economy and their wonderful workmanship with grabata fiber have made us determined to help them find a viable developmental path.

"Organizational development is an ongoing concern for us among all the groups. The central problem is the one we have been struggling with for a long time—the issue of transfer. Just last week our project evaluator and national Andean textile and artisan authority, Cristina Bubba, said to us, 'People talk about self-management in the most casual terms, yet I do not know of any effective artisan associations which are truly self-managed.'[4] Our dilemma is that we have strong promoters from within the communities increasingly taking over important management functions in the community-based organizations, yet the participation of the rank and file continues to lag behind that of their leaders. The Ichilo hat makers are the only association that has been able to move management and access to information beyond the monopoly of the top people. If we fail to make major changes in this kind of participation, little fiefdoms could pop up in these isolated artisan villages, thereby undermining the service system we've spent years building up. Some artisan associations plaster office walls with charts chock full of information on prices, costs of production and consumer products, and bank balances as a way to get information out to everyone and make leaders more accountable. This should help in the effort to minimize personal self-aggrandizement at the local level, but here we're tackling a big, basic issue not only in grassroots development in Bolivia but all over Latin America."

The promotion of technical improvement is another ongoing challenge for the artisan service program. Malena, Ada's daughter, described this aspect of CIDAC's work. "All of our professional technicians are overextended. They need to have the communication skills and organizing abilities of a social worker, the cultural sensitivity of an anthropologist, and also the aesthetic sensibility of an artist. Unfortunately, such a combination of traits is difficult to find in any single person and all of our technicians struggle to meet the diverse needs of the artisans. In addition, they have so many competing tasks that tensions within our staff invariably crop up.

"My own situation illustrates this over-extension. Right in the middle of CIDAC's organizational chart, there is the Department of Design and Development. The department consists of just me, despite the fancy label. My responsibility is to examine incoming artisan products here at our central office. Given the number of associations, producers, and communities it is no longer possible for me to visit the campo. We are constantly scrambling to modify our practices to keep pace with the increasing demands on our time. Most recently, I decided to change our past practice and send written evaluations to artisans who send us their work. Previously this information was communicated to them orally."

Malena displayed a document prepared for the Chiquitañas entitled "Production Turned Over on May 4, 1994." The inside pages bore titles such as "Very Special Congratulations for Excellent Crafts," "Interesting Ideas for Improvement With Only A Little Bit of Effort," and "Enthusiasm for Good Work of the Following Embroiderers." For each artisan Malena offered individual technical advice and warm expressions of personal encouragement as well as criticism. It was clear that she had made a point to follow the progress of each artisan's work and get to know them personally.

"Constant improvement is a must because we are increasingly in the spotlight as a model of artisan promotion in Bolivia. A UN representative recently came to our offices offering to finance the replication of our project in the Beni lowlands region in eastern Bolivia. We are besieged by visits from graphic arts and interior design students who study our products, exhibits, and store displays. Clothing designers are using products such as the Tajibos embroidery on new women's garments for fashion shows in the city and our artisanry is appearing on floats for the annual carnival celebration.

"Our annual craft fair, which we have taken to other cities in Bolivia and Chile, has also become a traveling demonstration of the importance of artisanry in cultural revitalization and development of rural communities. In 1992, we mounted an exhibition in La Paz that turned into an unprecedented media celebration of Cruceño crafts. One curious sign of this successful impact was the immediate appearance of our products, albeit at much higher prices than in Santa Cruz, in downtown La Paz artisan shops. In the opening ceremony of the exhibition, the president and first lady showed and presented awards to several artisans. The government invited us, along with ASUR, to represent Bolivian popular art and handicrafts in a ten-day exhibition in Santiago, Chile. We represented the cultures of the lowlands, and ASUR the highlands, in an effort to rejuvenate Bolivian diplomacy with Chile in the long quest to recover Bolivia's route to the sea lost in a nineteenth-century war."

The most momentous event signifying CIDAC's "coming of age" was ARTECAMPO's three-day multicultural festival held on the main plaza in the center of Santa Cruz. Rolando Campen, a Dutch expatriate who had spent many years working professionally in rural development programs in

both the highlands and lowlands of Bolivia, called it a cultural transformation. "You know I have waited a long time to see such an event occur in a
city whose citizens wanted to go on replaying the conquest of our region's
native peoples rather than healing their differences. The region's elite pride
themselves on their pure Spanish heritage, the other side of which has been
raw frontier racism toward Indians, perhaps the worst of its kind in Bolivia.
Just last month a local television station transmitted an account of Santa
Cruz history with Spanish gentlemen as the harbingers of civilization for
the Amazon's primitive, barbaric native peoples. It is hard to imagine anywhere else in the country where this would happen."

The festival with 250 rural artisans was held right in front of the city's
elegant colonial buildings, financial exchange houses, eighteenth-century
cathedral, and seat of municipal government. It was as if Lorgio Vaca's
murals had suddenly come to life. Women from Cotoca stood over tables,
shaping hunks of clay into beautiful decorative birds and large urns. Older
Ayoreo women were weaving exquisite handbags from the garapata fiber
right across the street from places where, for decades, they had survived by
begging. In another area, Chiquitaña women focused on *jipijapa* palm leaf
weavings, and the Guarayos were weaving tablecloths and place mats or
hammocks with shades of green and blue stripes accented by small black
bands. Guarayo youth were sculpting scenes of native musicians and painting detailed scenes of lush tropical flora, while numerous native women
demonstrated a variety of spinning and loom technologies. At the base of a
public monument, seven women from Ichilo in yellow dresses and straw
hats stood above the crowd singing folk ballads to the resurgence of the
Santa Cruz woman artisan.

This surprising scene of celebration drew thousands of curious spectators. The festival was a spectacular metaphor for the artisans who had long
been in search of a safe, inviting place for themselves in the center of a society which had shunned them for decades.

The cultural festival ended with remarks made by the president of
ARTECAMPO and Ada. Elba Montano, the president of ARTECAMPO,
began, "We women of the campo have to undertake a 'triple shift' each day
of our lives. We have added to our full-time house and farm work, the
work of craftswomen. Yet we are not simply makers of crafts. We are also
cultural workers because, through our artisanry, we keep our cultural traditions alive, and increase our understanding of ourselves, and offer our
products for the enjoyment of others in society as well. We are a significant

part of the region's economic development, although there are many who refuse to recognize this fact."

Ada then stepped up to the mike. "In our reflections I would like to call the attention of the Bolivian public and especially our political authorities to the people here in our central plaza. . . . These people, among the most outcast members of our society, have never been given a chance to speak or to participate in their own destinies. They are typically the subjects of plans made by people in a city so far removed from their reality that the plans almost always fail.

"We are trying to help you remember our region's long-standing indebtedness to our indigenous peoples, ignored and forgotten for so many years. For in today's fiesta of color and design in our principal plaza, we are initiating a dialogue that clarifies the apparent distances that exist between art and artisanry and which recognizes that the latter is an authentic art form of the Americas. The paintbrush and oil paintings came to us from Europe when on our soil there were thriving artistic traditions in textiles, ceramics, and featherwork that today are exhibited as treasures in European and Latin American museums."

CHAPTER 13

Digging for Indigenous Potato Knowledge in the Mountains of Rayqaypampa

If genetic resources are to be retained in the South along with the rights to produce one's own food within sustainable farming systems, the case of potatoes in Bolivia is a telling example of the need for awareness to expand from below.

DANDLER AND SAGE (1985)

In 1985, when I visited Rayqaypampa, it was a scrubby mountain landscape overgrazed by sheep and goats and inhabited by struggling farmers who were at a loss in knowing how to reverse the situation of increasing poverty. The local people, outfitted in traditional, bright, embroidered leggings, complained that each year they worked harder to produce crops whose value had dropped in the past twelve months.

Rayqaypampa, situated in an isolated corner of the Mizque Province, is a traditional potato-growing microregion nestled within a set of mountain ranges of the Eastern Cordillera near Cochabamba's southern border with the Potosí region. Rayqaypampa is inhabited by small communities of 5,000 or so Quechua-speaking farmers notable for their strong sense of ethnic identity. They practice a land management system reminiscent of the ancient Andean "verticality," taking advantage of different ecologies and altitudes to grow a variety of food crops and livestock. As late as the 1960s, villagers used pack animals to transport their produce to market. In 1985, they still continued their traditional practice of bartering their potatoes and other crops at local markets, in addition to selling them for cash, all in all demonstrating a lesser degree of acculturation than most rural Cochabambinos.

In the recent past, Western technology packages for the cultivation of potatoes had been imported by NGOs and government agencies and introduced to other parts of Misque province. These technologies contributed to genetic erosion of local native potato varieties, land degradation, pest and disease problems, and increased farmer indebtedness, but what is more, the farmers had lost money in the process. Pablo Regalsky, the middle-aged man who spearheaded the effort to improve the situation in Rayqaypampa, explained, "Through encouraging the use of hybrid, sometimes imported, seed, and the indiscriminate application of chemical fertilizers and pesticides in dryland, mountainous farming areas, the NGOs have committed some of the classic mistakes documented with regard to Green Revolution technologies elsewhere in the Third World."

I first met Pablo Regalsky in 1983 when the IAF made several tiny grants to several organizations he worked with. In 1985, he founded his own organization, Centro de Comunicación y Desarrollo Andino (CENDA) (the Center of Communications and Andean Development) and applied to us for funding to study and develop a program to revitalize traditional Andean potato cultivation methods. Pablo was born and bred in a comfortable upper middle-class home in Buenos Aires. The story of his metamorphosis from a refined Argentine *porteño* to an NGO leader with an enthusiasm for home-grown rural technologies in the Bolivian backlands is an interesting one. After graduating with honors from high school, he entered the country's most prestigious university and expectations were high for his academic success. The branches of his family tree are full of writers, journalists, teachers, and health professionals, and his grandmother leads them all with the distinction of being Argentina's first female medical doctor.

Despite the high expectations of his family, Pablo found university life much less appetizing than anticipated. His interest in anthropology waned when he discovered that the university offered only a few courses in physical anthropology, a sub-field with little relevance to the social issues swirling in Buenos Aires during the time.

As Pablo described them, the 1970s were a period of political ferment. Students everywhere were excited about the potential of the labor movement to lead the country toward economic and political reforms. This movement reached a crescendo in 1973 with the return from exile of the wildly popular former president, Juan Peron. "To get more into the trenches at that point," Pablo said, he dropped out of school and took a part-time job in a metallurgy factory of 300 workers and began related studies in industrial design. This job eventually grew into full-time factory work and a union leadership post. During his many hours on the shop floor, Pablo pondered hypothetical technologies that might make life easier for the worker. His interest in technology has propelled Pablo's professional life ever since, taking him through a wide variety of forms of employment on his way to his current work in the recovery of native Andean technologies.

"I did meet my wife while at the university," Pablo said. She was one of the many Bolivians living in Buenos Aires, and she sparked his interest in the country to the north, a place given little media attention in Buenos Aires. Pablo's wife talked him into moving to Bolivia, but then, while they were still firming up their plans, she suddenly suffered a brain hemorrhage and died when just twenty-six years old. Remaining faithful to their original plan, Pablo opted to relocate to Bolivia: Argentina's military dictatorship had given him an additional incentive to leave his country. In Bolivia he met and eventually married Inge Sichra, an Austrian-born scholar of socio-linguistics of Quechua.

In Cochabamba, he landed a job with an institute developing new technologies for local industries. "I was perceived as a real catch by my employer given my industrial design studies and factory background in one of South America's major industrial centers." He joined a research team conducting technology experiments in the area of carpentry, metal works, and electricity, and eventually became chief of production. The team was operating in the black, yet the more Pablo got to know Cochabamba the more he realized that the technologies his outfit was designing had little relevance in a world of mini-family enterprises producing everything from bricks to furniture. "What intrigued me most was the fact that these tiny enterprises were out-competing industrial firms, using an entirely different logic in their business operations."

To more deeply penetrate this world of family enterprises, Pablo began volunteering his time to help a carpenters' co-operative get on its feet. Pablo also took a part-time job at the Centro Cultural Portales, a Swiss-funded foundation supporting ethnic music and school libraries, that carried him into Cochabamba's mountain farming communities, including Rayqaypampa. There he was fortunate to meet Zenobia Siles, a savvy social communications specialist and community organizer who knew most of the sindicato leaders of southern Cochabamba. By putting together a Quechua-Spanish newspaper for a barely literate peasant readership, Pablo began learning about the different agricultural technologies used in the region.

In 1983, Pablo and the foundation sponsored a workshop on socially appropriate technologies that transformed his outlook. At the workshop, he was able to exchange ideas with several Peruvians who had had interesting experiences with holistic technology approaches to farming in the Andean mountains. The Peruvians were more advanced than Bolivian NGOs in their thinking about Andean agricultural knowledge. "They helped clarify my fuzzy musings about developing alternatives to the prevailing modernization programs, and showed me that those alternatives could come right from the communities themselves. I immediately became very interested in the possibility of reinvigorating the cultivation of indigenous potatoes grown in the region for centuries, and now abandoned in deference to Western approaches."

Subsequently Pablo made a visit to Lima to delve into publications in anthropology, ethno-history, and Andean agricultural technology and botany housed in the Peruvian libraries and bookstores. Returning to Bolivia, he formed a study group in Cochabamba to analyze data comparing the potato-growing technology package of Western science with the Andean management systems. Some of the agronomy students joining this group had taken courses with AGRUCO in traditional agriculture and were working on related thesis projects.[1]

Vital to the group was the assistance received from Luz Maria Calvo. Luz Maria, a young Cochabambina fresh from graduate studies in Andean anthropology in Mexico, brought conceptual rigor and sophisticated theory to the study group's analytical framework. With the group's input, she drew up an "action-research" plan based on solid social science research methods that would enable the group to carry out a thorough exploration of local indigenous knowledge of potato farming. The study group's research made it clear that Andean peasants had developed many creative and adaptive agricultural technologies over the centuries, despite the many economic, political, and social changes working to undermine their existence as peoples. A lot had been lost, but there remained much that could be salvaged to build a better and more suitable agricultural development model in the highlands. "With our action-research plan, our intent is to discover, reinforce, and strengthen local resource management strategies used in Rayqaypampa and make recommendations for change that respect the basic premises of their ways for managing the land and other resources."

Luz Maria and Pablo reported to me the results of the study group's inquiry. They had documented numerous complaints by farmers about the genetic erosion of native potato varieties and indebtedness due to participation in the technology package programs. One student in the group had gathered data that clearly indicated that use of the package approach not only damaged the environment but caused financial loss to farmers. CENDA findings on genetic erosion in Rayqaypampa were similar to patterns in other Andean areas where many farmers also wished to keep their diverse native potatoes (Zimmerer 1996).

Luz Maria explained the group's approach. "Our assumptions and goals about agricultural development differ from those of most Cochabamba-based rural development agencies. They assume the only way to increase potato yields, peasant incomes, and market involvement is by the technology package, and that to increase soil productivity chemically based technologies are the only way to go. I argue all the time with my brother, a professional agronomist working at a top position in USAID, over this erroneous proposition. Our strategy is to work closely with the leaders of the fourteen sindicatos. We're going to push cultural mobilization around a local development program through their community base structures. I have attended some assemblies here and am impressed by how even-handedly the sub-central authorities deal with community conflicts, ranging from cattle trespassing to irresponsible drunken behavior."

Next, Pablo and Luz Maria described the goals for their project. "Our basic goal is to carry out action research; that is, to study traditional family strategies for growing potatoes and survey the array of indigenous potatoes that might be grown with the aim of developing a program to reinvigorate indigenous potato-farming practices and knowledge, to recover and grow native seed, and to develop a sales plan for regional markets.

"On the surface level," Pablo said, "our project looks like pretty conventional stuff. The difference is that our focus is on revalorizing the traditional Andean approach in each area of concern. We want to first document and then figure out how to support traditional technologies, organizational practices, and other cultural assets to make them effective not only in reinvigorating native potato production, but in dealing with local problems of genetic erosion and land degradation. The communities we've selected face incredibly critical problems, yet most of the solutions must be found within their own communities and local histories. Ours is basically a self-reliant, low-cost approach to social and economic change.

"Another key aspect of our approach is that it will feature the potato's biodiversity rather than a monoculture-type production. The national seed commission organized by the government is a disgrace as it only researches and promotes improved and exotic varieties and excludes native ones. A friend of mine in La Paz, Julio Rea, argues that these national authorities act as though Bolivia's potato-producing areas are identical to Idaho and Holland. So the recovery of potato seed will be an important part of our strategy for local development. We plan to use newspapers and radios to spread the word about our approaches, and to develop a reforestation effort with native species as integral parts of our program."

Pablo had administered two past IAF mini-project grants in a dependable and competent fashion. On hearing about the project in Cochabamba, I was immediately impressed with the focus of the project and with its leaders. At first, though, I was struck by the group members' relative youth and inexperience. With the exception of Pablo, all were young professionals in their twenties. At the same time, they were obviously smart, unusually knowledgeable about the latest thinking in development circles and the social sciences, and they had a seriousness of purpose and youthful energy that gave off a special glow. They struck me as people worth believing in.

Pablo handed over the thick project proposal prepared by CENDA which I promised to read carefully and discuss with my colleagues at the IAF. Four months later, I was back in Bolivia and my goal on this trip was to ascertain the feasibility of CENDA's project and make a final decision regarding a recommendation for funding.

There were five persons from CENDA's team with us on the eight-hour trip to the mountain hideaway of Rayqaypampa. As we got closer to the Rayqaypampa area the route narrowed to a winding, single-lane dirt road. At the summit of the hills, we looked out over a panoramic landscape of gray and olive mountain ranges, a seascape of earth-colored waves rolling in our direction. Then the road descended into parched, treeless foothills covered with the inevitable scrub grass and short, stubby bushes. The denuded landscape spoke volumes regarding the erosion of topsoil and the peeling away of the forest through overgrazing, population growth, demands for timber for fuel, and the expansion of mining enterprises. Our entrance into a zone of cone-shaped, low, sandy mountains brought us into the Rayqaypampa farming district. We were soon driving across mesas where farmers in white top hats were threshing barley with horse-driven machines next to fields full of golden stalks.

As we motored along I spotted several cylindrical structures about twelve feet in height with a radius of eight feet or so. The walls of the huts were made from branches, with roofs constructed of loose straw that draped over all sides. These structures appeared to me more African that Andean, and I was fascinated to learn that this was the Rayqaypampa natives' home-grown technology for storing potatoes.

The native people of Rayqaypampa had lived through difficult and turbulent historical periods. In the nineteenth century, many communities were broken up due to liberal land reforms and the local Indians were exploited as laborers on haciendas in a system of quasi-apartheid. Just thirty-five years before my visit the entire Rayqaypampa area was owned by a single hacienda specializing in wheat production. When the national agrarian reform began, the Rayqaypampa tenants revolted against their master and drove him from their villages. The farmers quickly redistributed among themselves the small plots they had been allowed to use as payment for the work on the hacienda, and began formally petitioning for land titles from the revolutionary government. Under the 1953 land reform, the sindicatos retained communal ownership of the lower forested slopes of *monte* at 2,000 meters for livestock grazing. Potatoes, on the other hand, were allotted the higher, better lands at the 3,200 meters range, due to their economic importance. This system, still operative at the time of my visit, means that families frequently have to walk as many as fifteen miles between the two zones in the course of a day's work.

Dusk was setting in and our day-long journey was finally coming to an end. The village of Rayqaypampa had a short main street of dilapidated adobe homes and a neglected plaza headed by a decrepit-looking chapel and bell tower. Adding to this drabness, there was an uncanny stillness about the place. The town seemed empty of any sign of life. I supposed that the Rayqaypampa people preferred living closer to their farmland rather than in a nucleated settlement pretending to be a village center.

We set out early the next day for a half-hour drive to visit a prominent local sindicato leader, Ramon Gutierrez. Don Ramon, I was told, could inform me about the current state of affairs in Rayqaypampa. Our meeting took place outdoors along the backside of his adobe dwelling on a wooden bench set up against the wall. Barnyard animals and small children scampered around us during our conversation.

Don Ramon expressed the universal frustrations shared by farmers everywhere in this age of diminishing natural resources. "It seems each year it takes more work for a smaller harvest of crops whose value keeps falling. With more and more people farming here, the land no longer rests the way it used to." During our conversation I was waiting for him to say something about CENDA's strategy of building on tradition and revitalizing cultural resources such as the native potato technology. Instead, he seemed more interested in CENDA as a source of cheap chemical fertilizers. Pablo and Luz Maria explained that CENDA was the first NGO ever to focus on Rayqaypampa and the local expectations came mostly from what community members learned in provincial and regional peasant congresses.

My growing anxiety about the gap between the NGO's and the community member's understanding of the project was allayed by Don Ramon's stylish ethnic dress. Over my years of development work, I had learned that traditional dress was a good indicator of strong cultural identity. Don Ramon was wearing a large, woolen, white hat in the shape of a church bell and a vest with bright vertical stripes over a white shirt cut from homespun cloth. It was the handsome trousers, though, that gave the outfit its unusual pizzazz, especially in a region where mestizo dress styles predominated. Three quarters of each leg of the legging-like trousers were covered with intricate, brightly colored embroidered floral and plant designs in horizontal rows. Along his calves and thighs an exhibit of the native flora in vibrant reds, yellows, greens, whites, and pinks flourished against a somber blue background. Ramon's wife's machine-made sweater and plain pleated skirt appeared rather bland next to this smashing combination of colors and stitchery. Fascinated with this interesting mixture of European and indigenous dress, I later asked Pablo about the social and cultural origins of the local people.

"It's an utter mystery," he remarked. "There are no references to Rayqaypampa in the nineteenth-century archives in Cochabamba nor in the nearby town in Aiquile." One theory suggested that people migrated to Rayqaypampa from other parts of the Cochabamba region to escape the oppressive colonial and early republican head tax in their rural communities of origin. The high number of Rayqaypampeños with fair skin made others wonder whether Spaniards may have settled in the area over time, gradually becoming assimilated by the more dominant culture of the Quechuas.

During the next several days we visited other local families and also sat in on a community assembly. Again, when I inquired about what people thought of the action-research program proposed by CENDA, I received blank stares all around. Never having seen social scientists or agricultural researchers at work, community members did not know quite what to expect. While the lack of understanding troubled me, this was common-place among other communities I knew in Bolivia. Research must first pro-vide demonstrable benefits before people formed positive opinions about it. CENDA had discussed this aspect of the project with them in numerous sindicato assemblies yet since social and agro-economic research was not the common fare of rural development projects here they had few points of reference to welcome the idea. It was especially unreasonable to expect them to understand the nature of anthropological field methods and pur-poses. Nonetheless, I remained excited about Pablo and Luz Maria's inter-est in applied research as a basis for better project planning and consensus building among the communities. It would be interesting to see how in-digenous knowledge-gathering and action could be successfully combined in a single development project.

The relatively low staff salaries in CENDA's proposal were an additional sign of the group's social commitment. I judged the emphasis on indigenous potato farming to be a solid point of focus, and by now well acquainted with the CENDA leaders' high level of competence and analytical bent, I came away with high hopes for these Rayqaypampa communities.

Six months and several project proposal revisions later, a two-year grant worth $60,000 lifted CENDA into project orbit where it would remain secure for the next ten years of IAF financing. The total amount received from the IAF over this period came to $710,000 for its core staff of anthro-pologists, economists, medical doctors, administrators, agronomists, and social communications specialists. The IAF support covered staff salaries, fuel and vehicle repair expenses, medical supplies and medicines, tree seedling purchases, and the agricultural supplies (fertilizer, native and im-proved and imported seed) necessary for conducting agricultural experi-mentation. Over time CENDA also proved to be adept at mobilizing financial and in-kind resources from local universities and church parishes, as well as several European sources.

DIGGING FOR INDIGENOUS POTATO KNOWLEDGE

When I returned to the project site several years later, it was clear CENDA had run into difficult snags. Trying to cover fourteen communities scat-tered over a 200-mile radius of rugged mountain terrain had completely overwhelmed CENDA's small, unseasoned staff. Some communities were eventually eliminated from the program while reforestation and potato experimentation activities were drastically scaled down.

Another perhaps more critical obstacle was the slow community response to CENDA's message of revitalizing local cultural resources. The negative response was especially prevalent among the younger generation. When they heard of plans for planting native trees, native medicine, or growing native potato strains, the Rayqaypampeños were often skeptical, sometimes defensive. The typical response was something like: "Native potatoes! We already have those! Why do we need your help with that? What we need are chemical fertilizers and those productive hybrids they're importing in other areas." Such attitudes were an ongoing challenge and the need to modify attitudes and educate community members became a key focus of CENDA's efforts. Nevertheless, the project had developed and expanded. A training program for community promoters and radio and newspaper programming had been developed to spread the word about the potential of indigenous potatoes. Indigenous weather forecasting was being reinvigorated as well. The core programs—the potato research, marketing planning, and studies of traditional family farming methods—were also going strong.

THE POTATO RESEARCH

Interested in the results of CENDA's potato research effort, and curious about the ways in which they were tackling the problem of doubters, I met with Carlos Espinosa. As the CENDA agronomist, Carlos, along with Luz Maria Calvo, had been studying the economic viability of different combinations of potato varieties (native versus improved) and fertilizer (organic versus chemical) on fields in ten communities. Carlos was a short and stocky man with a mustache and very much a mestizo. He had an unusual fondness for campo life, having spent his boyhood walking mountain trails with his father, a rural schoolteacher. His enthusiasm for Andean culture was also expressed by his participation in a Cochabamba panpipe band and in a small university movement reaffirming indigenous heritage.

Carlos delivered an enthusiastic report on the variety of indigenous potato species grown in the region. Local potatoes came in all shapes, sizes, and colors, he said. Some were round and elongated. Some had eyes while other varieties did not. They came in the colors of red, black, and white. The six varieties of "runa papa," "laqmu," "manzana," "punkanawi," "sayura," and "valle papa" were the most widely used in Rayqaypampa, while another twenty or so varieties were still grown by a few families in the zone. Some potatoes were appreciated for resistance to drought, others for resistance to frost, blight, or harmful pests. The "runas" and "laqmu" were amazing—valued for resistance to drought and excessive rainfall, as well as for their resistance to blight and harmful insects. The "runas" were ironically called *sonso papas* (foolish potatoes) because of their easy adaptability to a wide range of microclimates and soil types. For that reason, they had the highest commercial value in regional markets.

With regard to the research comparing native and imported varieties, Carlos had more good news. CENDA's experiments were clearly showing that local native varieties were superior to the hybrids and imported Dutch varieties with heavy and expensive fertilizer requirements, and some farmers were being convinced. The road was still uphill, though. "There has been a political, economic, cultural, and ideological onslaught in Bolivia by dominant Western society since the late 1940s which hasn't slowed. It's also partly a generational problem. The farmers who are younger and have a few years of schooling are more apt to disparage the cultural patrimony guarded proudly by the older generation. Yet when the farmers see the visible field results of our research their attitudes begin to change."

Carlos went on to say that as the CENDA staffers joined the local farmers in carrying out the potato cultivation experiments, the farmers were educating them about a panoply of other cultural resources used in Andean potato production. "Our experiments have involved some 120 plots on the widely dispersed lands of fourteen families jointly managing the research with us. The replication of plots, styles of plot management, time allotments for different tasks during the day, and many of their techniques and knowledge have become part of our working methodology. This is all part of our strategy to reinforce resource management by the local people."

In addition to their agricultural experimentation efforts, Luz Maria and Carlos were conducting dawn to dusk research on two Rayqaypampa families for greater depth of understanding of traditional farming practices. Their aim was to thoroughly document every step of the farmers' day during cropping seasons. They viewed this as the only way to attain a complete picture of the families' strategies, an important knowledge base for planning future activities. "In this way," Carlos said, "our approach will be anchored in indigenous local knowledge and the cultural continuities that have pulled these native communities through the centuries. After analyzing the performance of the different potato-growing technologies we'll draw some conclusions with the farmers about how to convert all the data into concrete action programs."

LOCAL POTATO FARMING PRACTICES

When I asked Carlos about native knowledge of potato farming, he beamed a broad smile that seemed to suggest the surrounding hills were full of treasures hidden to most outsiders such as myself. He responded, "There have been a number of things that have impressed us and have been immediately incorporated into our research methodology. For example, take the Andean practice of crop diversity. On traditional farms potatoes are grown side by side with quinoa, tarhui, lima beans, squash, and other crops on the same plot for better fertilization, optimizing one's working time in the fields and other benefits deriving from an interactive living system. Rayqaypampeños also have devised their own system for classifying soils as a basic tool in agricultural planning. This indigenous classification system certainly never appeared in any of my university texts on soils," he chuckled.

"They classify the soil according to texture, rockiness, drainage capacity, and the degree of mountain slope. In planning the year's planting, local potato varieties are matched with specific soil types and microclimates. A family will engage in making these permutations for each of some fifty to sixty different plots under their command. And then, since these families consume potatoes for breakfast, lunch, and dinner, the all-important taste factor weighs heavily in planting decisions."

Carlos went on to describe another aspect of indigenous knowledge, forecasting the weather. The practice, called the "reading of the signs," was usually carried out by members of the older generation prior to the planting season. Bird and fox calls, for instance, were used to indicate whether rainfall would permit early or late planting, and the flowering of pear trees to predict steady or fluctuating weather patterns.[2] Carlos explained that this kind of advanced knowledge about the weather helped farmers to determine which type of soil and location to put together with a specific potato variety.

The Ecological and Marketing Challenges

In addition to their studies of the viability of potato species and of local farming practices, CENDA had devoted considerable effort to the examination of the ecological status of the region and potato-marketing prospects. In CENDA's office in the city of Cochabamba, the NGO's staff showed me huge charts that depicted the different ecosystems, cropping patterns, altitudinal niches, and the numbers of livestock distributed over a cross section of several communities within the Rayqaypampa area. With its multi-disciplinary research approach, CENDA had put together a comprehensive picture of inadequate natural resource management and worsening ecological deterioration. They had assembled a mountain of data regarding genetic erosion, the deteriorating landscape, and the devastating effects of changing weather patterns on farming. I had never before seen a group take empirical research findings so seriously in the course of project planning. This conscientious attitude was also evident in CENDA's practice of holding frequent internal evaluation sessions, often including sindicato leaders from Rayqaypampa.

Teresa Hosse, the young CENDA economist, offered an overview of the group's findings regarding the marketing of Rayqaypampa's potatoes. "Unfortunately by examining records and talking to farmers, a clear negative price trend is observable. It is consistent with what is happening all over the country from structural adjustment policies. The worsening terms of trade in Rayqaypampa means that the farmers have less money available from potato sales to spend on basic household products whose prices keep climbing. Three or four years ago a sack of potatoes was worth twice as much chemical fertilizer as by today's prices. In this squeeze of falling incomes and rising production costs, farmers keep bringing new parcels into production and heap on greater and greater amounts of fertilizer to compensate for the lack of time available for thorough preparation of fields. Soil compacting results from the overuse of chemicals, and compact soil is a haven for pests and other problems. Another serious consequence of these changes has been the loss of traditional seed selection techniques. This loss in turn adversely affects potato productivity and production, and, of course, family incomes."

Teresa said she believed the worsening poverty in Rayqaypampa was a function of the interaction of such factors. The trend toward diminishing prices was hurting Rayqaypampa farmers, even though there was a surprisingly large market for the "runa papa" in southern Cochabamba. On the one hand, opportunist truckers combed the Rayqaypampa communities during the harvest period, buying up all of the "runa papa" in sight, whether disease ridden or not; on the other hand the "runa papa" was in decline from the loss of the superior traditional seed selection techniques.

Carlos and Pablo, sitting across the table from Teresa, told me about their plan for the "action" side of the NGO's strategy to improve potato production. They outlined an alternative, low-cost system for producing and supplying farmers with seed potatoes to free them from outside dependency and the complicated financial transactions of cash flows. This plan would be a real departure from the farmers' reliance on unscrupulous commercial seed suppliers and would provide a clear alternative to the Western technology package. Its goals included producing local native seeds that would be both consumable and marketable, while simultaneously reversing the decline in the potato seed quality throughout the zone.

Several years later when I was back in Bolivia, I learned that the potato seed fund had been reorganized several times as CENDA sought the most workable arrangement. Originally called the "Fund for the Recovery of Native Seed," it was now known as the "Family Improvement Units" (Unidades Familiares de Mejoramiento). Pablo enumerated the various difficulties and setbacks encountered in the course of CENDA's trial and error search for the best way to recover native potatoes.

During the first year, the Rayqaypampeños had lots of suspicions that CENDA had set the program up as a clever, manipulative way to secure local potato varieties which they would then sell in other regions for their own gain. Perhaps it was an unconscious expression of sabotage, when the farmers repaid them with rotting, infected, poor-quality seeds useless for the next planting season. The poor seed made them realize they would have to work overtime to convince the farmers that the fund was to be their very own operation and that CENDA would provide only technical assistance when necessary. They met rejection again when trying to shift the seed fund responsibilities to the sindicatos the following year. Not surprisingly, at that point, the fund was decapitalizing. Pablo had told me that it was a hard reality to swallow in that when push came to shove the sindicatos had other, more important priorities.

When the IAF had agreed to cover these losses and enable CENDA to start the whole thing over once again, I reassured Pablo that we knew they had held participatory planning sessions to work together with the sindicatos. Yet I also knew from past experience that NGO-community relations operated on many levels of complexity which could lead to false starts and problems. One is not always clear about the diverse agendas which come into play in such settings, including those of ambitious and opportunistic local leaders.

Pablo continued, "Gradually we transferred the major management responsibility to the small mutual aid groups composed of twenty to thirty families that now existed in seven communities. We hoped the families' long-established reciprocal work exchange ties would provide the glue for our seed production project as well." Networks of seed exchange ties like these have traditionally exerted a strong influence on the rich diversity of native potatoes in Bolivia as well as in the neighboring Peruvian Andes (Zimmerer 1996). Here they had disappeared, yet mutual aid groups with other purposes remained active.

The local Andean institution which mobilized the most collective labor was the *umaraga*. Roofing a family dwelling or constructing a schoolhouse are examples of this Andean practice. Rayqaypampa organizational infrastructure was based on *aynis* which served an array of purposes such as the exchange of farm labor, livestock, and farm tools among extended families and compadres. The *umaraga* and several types of *aynis* were festive occasions where the local corn beer *chicha* flows freely and numerous libations and public ritual offerings and prayers supplicate the Pachamama and other important mountain spirits.

In the collective work system reinvented by CENDA and the sindicatos, the groups plant and harvest the potato seed together on a given member's land. Each participating family borrows fifty kilos from the seed bank to be repaid in harvested potatoes of the same quality and size. While the entire group participates in planting and harvesting, the family owning the seed production plot takes care of the remaining tasks over the course of three successive growing seasons. Once harvested, this family receives half the potatoes and the rest are loaned to the individual group members. The resident family also benefits from the installation of a "demonstration corral" to keep sheep from overgrazing and provides large quantities of animal dung used for preparing organic fertilizer.

CENDA modified its three-year potato plot rotation strategy when farmers began insisting on an annual rotation of the seed production plots. The farmers questioned the prolonged flow of benefits to a single family, saying this made the chosen families potential "petty patrons" (or landlords).

The farmers wanted to spread the benefits to a larger number of households by changing the plot owners every year. Thus, during the next growing season a policy switch was made conceding to these community wishes.

CENDA's Training Program

The last topic of discussion during this second visit to CENDA was an activity that had not been contemplated in the original project plan. Training local cadres had become imperative due to the importance of popular participation and the sheer amount of work that needed doing, and to ensure the project's future after CENDA departed from the zone.

Pablo explained that CENDA's cadres were not just typical community "promoters" found in any run of the mill development program. "It's different in our case," he insisted. "We want to avoid the syndrome whereby promoters quickly become NGO employees instead of genuine community representatives and local leaders. That's why it's necessary to work closely with the sindicatos, to strengthen existing mechanisms of accountability and control used by them.

"We selected the title *Yanapakuna* for our promoters because it's a Quechua term meaning 'to help'. The Yanapakunas are on the front lines in our push toward cultural mobilization. Their work involves, among other things, changing the rapidly Westernizing attitudes of their own generation. The Yanapakunas, mostly young people in their late teens and twenties, will act as the local managers of the native seed potato funds and also oversee activities in reforestation, community health, and literacy training. They will also promote the dissemination of experiences, ideas, and materials via the newspaper and radio stations."

Use of the Media for Cultural Revitalization

After leaving Rayqaypampa, we passed through Aiquile, the nearest market town and the seat of Mizque's provincial government. There, I was able to observe CENDA's use of the radio. CENDA's goal was to promote native potato-growing technologies via a three-pronged social communications strategy: radio, newspaper, and bilingual literacy training programs. The latter activity was under the direction of Pablo's wife, Inge Sichra, an able

Quechua linguist. CENDA had been given free public service time by a station run by Italian missionary priests and the NGO's Quechua radio programs were broadcast throughout the entire three provinces of southern Cochabamba for several hours daily four times a week.

Inside the station, three Yanapakuna male communications specialists wearing white wool top hats and colorful striped vests and pants were sitting together in front of long microphones humming Andean melodies. I listened to the program as it was just beginning:

> MARIO NEGRETE: Once again our community broadcast is coming to you from the folks of Rayqaypampa, the highlands of the Mizque province. I have Teofilo with me in the booth so a big welcoming hello should go to him.
>
> TEOFILO: A big greeting for all of you in our listening audience. Here's Claudio, welcome Claudio to our show.

A recording of wayño melodies using a panpipe and charango music from Rayqaypampa then ensued.

> MARIO: This time we will speak with Pedro Sandoval who resides in Siqi, Ranchu. We will find out how he plants his potatoes.

Another interruption by a wayño song.

> TEOFILO: Bueno, Don Pedro, how did you prepare your parcel for planting potatoes?
>
> TESTIMONIO: Well, this year the rains came late and we had to begin preparing the soil just before Carnival in February so my family planted only half of our normal amount of seed. With the improved rainfall forecast now, this year's planting will begin earlier, some of us have begun, while others will do so shortly.
>
> CLAUDIO: Yes Don Pedro, tell us the type of potatoes you'll be planting.
>
> TESTIMONIO: This year I'm thinking of planting the varieties with the higher yields that include "Laqmu" and "Runa papa." We're rejecting the improved varieties such as the Dutch potato given the greater vulnerability to local diseases. Another problem with the imported varieties is their tendency to spoil quickly in our storage

bins. They have to be eaten right away or they rot. Although some agronomists say they peel faster than our potatoes, around here that's no big deal. Their lousy taste is another reason why many in Rayqaypampa are not excited about them when compared to the delicious "Laqmu" and "Runa papa." Thanks to the labors of our studious potato seed production groups these local varieties are increasingly infection free.

Here another break came, this time from Rayqaypampa carnival music using charangos.

> MARIO: Are the potatoes you mentioned from outside the region or from our own lands?
>
> TESTIMONIO: Well, these potatoes such as the "Laqmu" have been around for a long time and I really don't know how they got here and became so productive, but they're even more productive than the "Runa papa." They are resistant to diseases and spoilage, and our expectations for future production continue to climb. The potatoes brought by agricultural engineers are so fragile in the context of our Andean climate we must eat them as soon as possible after the harvest. Yet our families need potatoes to eat during the entire year.

Another music curtain break intervened.

> TEOFILO: That's our message for all our friends out there in Rayqaypampa's communities. Our local potatoes have higher yields and overall the imported seeds don't fare as well on our lands and in our mountain climate. How do you see it, Mario?
>
> MARIO: Yes, Don Pedro I agree wholeheartedly with what you're saying about these important differences.

The next show also put value on traditional practices, this time with regard to care of the soil.

> MARIO: Some out there are saying that the younger generation is no longer paying attention to Pachamama. Some of out farmers have chopped down trees to grow corn, and as a result our topsoil is

being swept down the mountainsides whenever there are heavy rainstorms. What do you think about that, Don Augustin?

AUGUSTIN: Yes, I'm afraid it's the truth, and it's certainly a sad development among our communities. We should not forget the values of our culture. It's necessary to continue *ch'allando, quowando* [offering libations to] the Pachamama. This disrespect for her is probably the reason our rainfall has been irregular and families have had to migrate more frequently to find work in the coca-growing zones of the Chapare. We cannot abandon the valuable practices taught us by our parents and grandparents. To *challar* with *l'awki* is not to suggest that we're just a bunch of drunks or vice-ridden. Rather it's a profound way of paying homage to our all important mother earth, giving her thanks for bountiful harvests. I've practiced this respect since I was a young boy. When I became married at eighteen and more recently when I reached thirty-eight years of age these practices remained important to my way of life.

After the program Pablo explained the philosophy behind the radio programs. "Personal testimony with local voices and Quechua idiomatic expressions is what appeals most to our rural listeners, so we use local people in all our broadcasts." Four Yanapakunas had been trained to produce radio scripts, conduct interviews, organize recorded materials into a program format, and carry out the actual broadcasting. They had transmitted 340 programs similar to the one we'd just heard over the past year, Pablo said.

"Farmer testimonies can also be found in our bi-monthly, bilingual [Spanish-Quechua] newspaper. The newspaper, *CONOSUR* in Spanish and *Nawpaqman,* meaning to go forward, in Quechua, is distributed among communities and towns throughout southern Cochabamba. In the newspaper, in addition to peasants throughout the region, we attempt to influence rural development planners. The newspaper has short blocks of text and excellent graphic art. Between 2,500 and 4,000 copies of each issue are printed. Each issue contains at least two articles explaining facets of traditional potato production gathered by our researchers." The issue I examined contained pronouncements in Spanish and Quechua from regional peasant sindicato congresses. The paper had a lively style and was quite appealing and informative within its agitprop tone of advocacy for the regional sindicato movement to which Rayqaypampa belonged. Pablo turned to the back page and showed me the

Rayqaypampa folk tale and Quechua crossword puzzle that close each issue.

Flipping through several back issues, I found vivid illustrations and short didactic texts that graphically conveyed Rayqaypampa's revived traditional potato seed selection techniques and two full pages devoted to outlining the mechanics of the communal seed fund. This was critical information to disseminate since the traditional selection techniques for identifying and discarding infected and other genetically inferior seed had proven to be a key factor in the seed production fund operations. In another issue, I found a didactic illustration of Rayqaypampa's traditional potato storage technology that had been improved by CENDA's agronomists and stirred up great interest among potato buffs in both governmental and NGO agencies of the region.

A third issue offered an illustrated map of the potato-marketing chain which permitted the reader to follow the route of Rayqaypampa potatoes through a series of people, places, and price changes. The large print size of the articles made them accessible to peasant readership and the black and white photos and illustrations of the Rayqaypampeños in unique ethnic outfits made for attractive copy. I had never seen a more impressive peasant newspaper although, I must add, there was not much competition.

I then asked Pablo why they had decided to publish in Quechua when so few people in Rayqaypampa could read and write in that language. He explained that they were targeting readers from other parts of the Mizque province as well as those in several neighboring provinces. At the same time, they had found that young Quechua-literate Rayqaypampeños trained by them would read the paper to their friends, or out loud in sindicato meetings. "And don't underestimate the pleasure non-readers derive from seeing their images and customs in the illustrations and photos throughout our pages. Even non-readers are attracted to the revalorization of culture they see in the images; this stimulates them to revalorize themselves and increases their self-esteem. It's impressive to them that readers appreciate not just Andean knowledge and valuable practices for potato production but the particular traditions of the Rayqaypampeños. Since a lot of the text is in Quechua, it will probably be used for post-literacy training [in Quechua] in Rayqaypampa as well as other Andean districts."

Beyond its effects on local self-esteem, Pablo went on to add, the newspaper served the purpose of sharing the Rayqaypampa development experience with other peasant populations and NGOs in southern Cochabamba.

The hope was that people in other regions might choose to emulate them and, at the very least, they hoped to stimulate exchanges of ideas and practices with other villages in different ecological zones.

I was very impressed with the Yanapakunas' efforts. Pablo was pleased as well, but expressed concern about the generational split in attitudes. He complained that modern schooling had caused young people to disparage traditional cultural expressions and knowledge. The schools had yet to be targeted for transformation, he said, because schoolteachers had so many vested interests in maintaining the status quo. Heretofore CENDA had wanted to avoid having problems with them, but it was an area for future work.

Loss of Leadership and a Boost in Morale

The year 1992 was momentous for CENDA's development program in Rayqaypampa—a year with tremendous highs, and some lows. When I traveled back to Bolivia that year, I learned that the team that had led CENDA's efforts since its inception had broken up. Experience in grassroots development had taught me that it is the talent and social commitment of the people involved that makes things happen, so the loss of Luz Maria and Carlos in this case was a great disappointment. Fundamental disagreements over whether CENDA would truly be able to identify a way out of the current ecological decline seemed to have fueled the break-up. I knew it would be difficult, if not impossible, to replace Luz Maria, given the shortage of Bolivian anthropologists, especially those of her unusually high caliber. Likewise, Carlos was a one-of-a-kind agronomist with his appreciation for Andean agriculture and the small pleasures of campo life. While CENDA's organizational upheaval was a disappointment, it did not shock me. Conflicts and splits were common within the fifty or so IAF projects operating in Bolivia. Departures and reorganizations often seemed necessary as a project evolved. Sometimes, as in this case, departing members left for career changes and other professional pursuits. Carlos was venturing into a remote province of Potosí to found his own rural development organization.

The changes in CENDA's leadership did not seem to hamper its progress. The most significant fact about 1992 was that it was the five hundredth anniversary of the Columbus-led invasion of the Americas. In the small town of Aiquile, Rayqaypampeños were part of a throng of 5,000 strong voicing collective misgivings about the historical ordeal brought about by Columbus. The radio airways in the countryside were abuzz with this controversial topic, and anti-quincentenary graffiti was popping up everywhere. The *wiphala,* the checkerboard flag symbolizing the ethnic identities and struggles of highland peoples, began appearing at every parade, march, and public occasion. While some Bolivian peasants found it a moment to rejoice in the cultural continuities and survival of native languages, medicines, ayllus, and rituals, others only wanted to express thunderous protest about colonial and republican violence.

Pablo told me during a visit to his office that the atmosphere around the quincentenary had made CENDA's work easier. "There seems to be a new spirit of cultural revitalization turned loose in the countryside," he exclaimed. "To give you some examples of how these changes have affected our program, the leaders of regional peasant sindicato congresses are writing and reading their documents in Quechua for the first time ever, often using the columns of our newspaper to do so. And then, in Rayqaypampa, the young sindicato leaders, with the Yanapakunas' help, organized a daylong assembly to honor the elders of the fourteen communities, recognizing them as *the* standard bearers of Andean culture and heritage that must not be lost. Another measure was the banning of boom boxes and foreign music at local festivals in Rayqaypampa. It was a way to encourage the playing of charangos and other native instruments in traditional melodies."

The contagious mood of cultural reaffirmation had also refueled Rayqaypampa's refusal to accept a government-sponsored program promoting Dutch potatoes. In mid-1992, I spoke with Florencio Alarcon, one of the most promising Yanapakunas to emerge from CENDA's literacy training. Florencio told me that PROSEMPA, a joint program of the Bolivian and Dutch governments, had held a public meeting to promote the use of technology package programs in Aiquile. "We showed up and challenged him with data from the comparative field experiments we've done in our communities, and insisted that the people of Rayqaypampa knew better now and had no interest in using Dutch varieties. Taken aback by these remarks, the Dutch engineer angrily shouted at me, 'What's wrong with you folks? Are you afraid of progress? What do you want anyway?' We told him our own local seed recovery program was doing just fine. He waved his fancy booklets while reiterating the merits and superiority of the technology package. Then he abruptly cut off the exchange, perhaps for fear that our

ideas would contaminate the thinking of many other community representatives present.

SCHOOLING CHANGES

The spirit of cultural revitalization that spread through the country during
1992 injected CENDA with renewed vigor and commitment. That same
year, perhaps inspired by the same spirit, the Rayqaypampa communities
began a movement to change the curriculum and structure of local schools
to mesh more effectively with their cultural values and agricultural activities. The changes in the school curricula simultaneously served to decrease
the generational cleavage that had been hampering CENDA's recovery
efforts. Pablo told me about these educational developments. "It all really
started with the Quechua literacy classes we offered in the mountain communities. The classes caught fire, and children started attending them in the
evenings along with their parents. They loved going to a classroom where,
for a change, real learning was taking place. The quality was high because
of my wife's advanced training in socio-linguistics and bilingual education
and the excellent Bolivian schoolteachers she selected to work in Rayqaypampa. Then, despite our intention to keep the local schoolteachers at arm's
length for fear of tensions that might jeopardize our other work, recent
events embroiled us in conflict with them. A few months ago in one community, several dozen families organized a private elementary school and
hired one of our Yanapakunas as the teacher. They remunerated him in the
Andean way of reciprocal exchange by working in his fields. He proceeded
to use our literacy materials and changed the dates of the school calendar to
fit the community's agricultural cycle. For the first time ever, the school vacation period would coincide with the potato harvest.

"In response to these changes and a positive learning environment,
children began abandoning nearby public schools to attend this one, and an
additional Yanapakuna joined its corps of teachers. The public schoolteachers were aghast at the trend and the school superintendent threatened to
close down the entire school district in Rayqaypampa. This triggered the
visit of a high-level commission that included leaders of the CSUTCB,
Bolivia's national peasant workers' trade union organization, the Ministry
of Education, and an official from UNICEF whose lackluster bilingual
schools operated in the area.

"The commission representatives met with Yanapakunas, local sindi-cato leaders, schoolteachers, and regional school officials in the local one-room sindicato center used for Yanapakuna training classes. At the meeting the schoolteachers in particular were visibly nervous and cautious in the presence of fifty or so Rayqaypampeños."

Pablo vividly described how sparks began to fly twenty minutes into the discussion. "During one exchange, a teacher shouted out toward the twin Rayqaypampeño leaders sitting together in identical outfits on a bench across the yard. 'You're hardly qualified to give opinions or make recom-mendations for improving our work in the classroom. Barely literate peas-ants should not be given the responsibility of teaching children in our elementary schools.'

"Another blurted out, 'We're university-trained professionals. How on earth can you expect to replace us while maintaining our high standards of teaching?'

"One Yanapakuna, Primo Caero, immediately put his hand up and said, 'Why can't the public teachers who come to work here use a school calendar that fits in with the life of the farm families in our communities? Exams are scheduled in the middle of the potato harvest season when we need our school-age children to help herd our livestock. Without this con-tribution from our children, we would not be able to harvest enough pota-toes to get our families through the year.'

"Next, Mario Caero, the Yanapakuna teacher from the Quechua school, spoke up. 'I remember many years ago as a boy sitting in the same classroom where our children now sit. I came from a household where everyone spoke only Quechua, and each day I went to class and had my hopes for learning dashed because the teacher obliged me to read Spanish words whose meanings I didn't understand. Frankly, it was a frustrating way to begin my education. Now I can see the joy on the faces of my chil-dren who are understanding the lectures and lessons spoken in Quechua.'"

Caero then said, "What all this boils down to is a fundamental lack of respect on the part of teachers for our Quechua cultural background. We would like to be afforded the same respect that teachers have been receiving from us over the past twenty years."

"Another Yanapakuna then jumped up in the back of the schoolyard. 'I've been working as a Yanapakuna literacy trainer over two years and I want to share my observations with everyone here. An important reason behind educating our children in the Quechua language and Andean culture is that we need greater pride to face the outside world. Each time we step into a government office in the city, we face immediate discrimination. When officials see that we're wearing Rayqaypampa clothing, chewing coca leaves, and speaking in Quechua, they automatically dismiss us as though we're ignorant, backward country bumpkins, and don't know anything. Compañeros, such unfair treatment should not be tolerated. It makes us experience shame and totally denigrates our dignity.'

"The Yanapakuna had more to say. 'Today we're hearing ideas that have been uttered on many occasions around here—namely that our lack of high school and university courses makes us unqualified and unprepared to teach in the schools. Missing from this attitude is any respect for the knowledge we have derived from working the land and successfully growing all kinds of food crops, knowledge that has passed from one generation to the next. Yes compañeros, I insist that high school and university degrees aren't essential for making improvements in our communities and elementary schools. There are Yanapakunas here able to teach important lessons, and without the slightest sense of shame or inferiority. They have self-confidence from the knowledge of life experiences passed down by their forefathers.' "

Pablo related the remaining moments of the meeting. "When this heated and emotional collision of opinions reached an impasse at the end of the afternoon, curious heads began turning toward the ex-national director of public schools, Severo La Fuente, to gauge his reaction and final decision. To the great surprise and chagrin of the schoolteachers, his sympathy resided with the Yanapakunas. In his concluding statement, he said, 'It is clear that CENDA has done serious literacy training in Rayqaypampa and is not manipulating this Quechua schooling movement. The representatives from Rayqaypampa communities are capable of speaking for themselves, and frankly their arguments increasingly make sense to many of us in La Paz, including our representative from UNICEF here, concerned about the future of rural education in Bolivia.'

"La Fuente then presided over and signed agreements that shocked the school teachers by tentatively recognizing the Quechua school, complete with peasant teachers, agriculturally based school calendar, and CENDA's literacy materials. Even more significant was the creation of Bolivia's first Consejo Comunal de Educación [Community Education Council]. The

Consejo would incorporate both campesinos and schoolteachers while giving the former group majority voice. The UNICEF representative undertook the final official step of having the documents rubber-stamped by the national Ministry of Education in La Paz."

Three weeks later, the Consejo held its first meeting in Rayqaypampa. A Yanapakuna was elected president, and each community was given the power to set its own school calendar on an annual basis in accordance with a local "reading of the signs" by an experienced weather forecaster.

Local teachers had immediate and strong responses to the Consejo's actions, responses that would ultimately work against them. The teachers were most furious about the peasant consejo leaders' power to evaluate their classroom performance, and even have them dismissed from their jobs. A few weeks afterwards, some 300 teachers from all over the region met to discuss this issue in Aiquile. They moved to withdraw all teachers from the school district and shut the schools down indefinitely. In their emotional diatribes, they referred to Rayqaypampeños as "campesino burros," "anarchists and rebels," and as the region's principal troublemakers. They railed that the Rayqaypampeños should be punished for insubordination to authority. The same day, a campesino leader from Rayqaypampa who happened to be in town was assaulted on the streets of Aiquile by a gang of youth connected to the town's public authorities in sympathy with the teachers.

With these events, the local conflict in Rayqaypampa was suddenly blown up into a national media issue, requiring a visit from another La Paz commission composed of top leaders of the CSUTCB such as Francisco Quisbert and Juan de la Cruz Vilca, and the National Rural Education Secretariat. After the new commission's findings came out once again in favor of Rayqaypampa, the campesinos were finally able to put their Consejo Communal de Educación into practice while teachers were compelled to return to their schools and resume teaching. It seemed that the anniversary of five hundred years of resistance had come down to this little showdown in a tiny corner of the Andes where campesinos were beginning to exercise control over local schooling. The changes in school policy not only improved the education available to Rayqaypampeños, but raised local pride. This, in turn, did much to close the attitude gap between the generations, and unify the communities behind CENDA's efforts.

Rayqaypampa's Progress with Potatoes
between 1992 and 1996

Through periodic trips to Bolivia between 1992 and 1996, I was able to observe that CENDA's potato cultivation work was becoming more and more effective and influential. An IAF-commissioned evaluation by Julio Rea, a nationally known authority on the biodiversity of the potato, praised CENDA's strategy of reinvigorating native technologies via the three-pronged social communications strategy. CENDA had created a potato cultivation model that attracted most families in Rayqaypampa and also drew seed buyers and curious NGOs working in potato programs throughout the region. The work of the development group had expanded to incorporate a flourishing seed fund, a highly effective kin-based organizational structure, and the publication of books and pamphlets. In addition, Rea, in his capacity as a Bolivian representative of the International Potato Center, was so impressed that he invited CENDA to create one of Bolivia's first germplasm banks in situ, an innovative idea that would allow farmers to play a recognized role in maintaining Andean potato biodiversity on their own farms.

The seed production efforts CENDA had started in 1989 had taken off by the time of my visit in the early 1990s. Even the periodic droughts had failed to slow the expansion of the seed groups which grew from a base of sixty-four persons in 1990 to almost 400 persons by the beginning of 1995. The seventeen autonomous groups to which they belonged were producing and distributing ten tons of seed and storing it in communally owned storage bins. The seed program also enabled farmers to make more money by selling a healthier, infection-free "runa papa" variety for the benefit of many interested peasants in southern Cochabamba. And the sindicatos, originally a reluctant and ineffectual partner, had carved out an important oversight role in relation to the seed funds. Sindicato leaders regularly inspected the storage facilities to check for possible problems and established a special "seed council" to oversee the entire production-distribution-storage operation from start to finish. Meetings held to discuss the recovery of native potato varieties were becoming so passionate and involved that all-night sessions were commonplace.

To top off their many relentless years of native seed promotion, the sindicatos, Yanapakunas, and CENDA organized the "Primer Encuentro

Regional de la Semilla de Papa Nativa de Rayqaypampa." It was a colorful festive occasion where fifty-four distinct native varieties of potato along with other Andean tubers gained prominence. The event carried the spirit of *chhalaku,* Andean reciprocal exchanges, in this instance of seed, knowledge, and experiences as well as Andean music. Aymaras from the altiplano placed native potatoes on bright red, yellow, and green *awayos* (homespun weavings) to enhance their aesthetic appeal. Farmers one after the other led discussions on the superiority of native varieties and traditional methods of farming over the Western *paquetes.* Prizes went to farmers and sindicatos planting the most native seed varieties and for the best music performers.

In addition to the recovery of indigenous seed, another exciting cultural resource was recovered through CENDA's seed program. This was the reciprocal kin-based organizational form used as the modus operandi at the base of the production system. *Aynis* and *umaraga* were being used for labor exchanges and mobilizations for particular potato-farming tasks. Anthropologist Antonio Ugarte, IAF project monitor, discovered in a CENDA evaluation meeting that the best organized and performing seed production groups typically had the strongest kinship ties among participating families.

The theoretical implications of this finding were also intriguing. Within modernization theory, kin-based relations were perceived as an anachronistic behavioral pattern to be swept away in the process of development and replaced by modern behavioral forms. Yet in contrast, the historians working in the field of Andean studies had shown that Andean kin-based relations had played an important historical role in the adaptation to a market economy and an elastic society in the Andes over four centuries (Larson 1995).

CENDA published its research results for the wider Bolivian public in two books, *Los Caminos de Rayqaypampa* and *Los Jampiris de Rayqaypampa.* The first covered findings from the research on local resource management strategies in agriculture. Its colorful cover, whose image was taken from flower motifs of men's trousers, had made it popular for window displays in airport bookstores among other places.

The second book revealed the resource management strategy widely practiced for health care in Rayqaypampa. In this book, CENDA staffer and researcher Juan José Alba noted that the ten-year-old western health clinic was used by only half the local population. Many of the 350 community members used one or more of the thirty different traditional health care specialists called *Jampiris*. The book also contained the instructions for the use of 192 different medicinal plants locally available in Rayqaypampa. CENDA's list of smaller publications wound up reaching much larger readerships. This included a short autobiography of the recently deceased "weather forecaster" and herbalist Fermin Vallejos, a series of Quechua stories used in 20,000 public school libraries by the government's bilingual educational reforms, and a booklet used in post-literacy training by CENDA and other NGOs in the region. This booklet documented traditional practices used in Rayqaypampa for biological pest management control. During the year, *Nawpaqman* kept churning out news from Rayqaypampa about the potato program's progression and delineating steps readers should take to revitalize potato varieties, traditional seed selection techniques, soil classification systems, weather forecasting techniques, reciprocal family labor, and to apply Rayqaypampa's modified storage technology for developmental purposes. The radio, though reaching a smaller local audience, continued to play an important promotional role. In truth, in all my years in the Andes I had not seen a more brilliantly conceived alternative social communications strategy for grassroots development and cultural mobilization than that employed in Rayqaypampa.

Revisiting Rayqaypampa in 1995

In late 1995, I went to visit Rayqaypampa to update my knowledge of the project. With regards to CENDA staffing, Pablo commented that two other agronomists had been hired to replace Carlos but neither of them had had his competence, adaptability to field conditions, or strong identification with Andean culture. The result had been a drop off in high-quality technical assistance. This was less problematic, he said, now that the seed production groups were increasingly autonomous.

Pablo also informed me that Luz Maria, the other former project leader and architect of CENDA's action-research strategy, had been named as the director of the ethnicity department of the government's Secretariat of Ethnic, Gender, and Generational Affairs created by the MNR and Vice-President Cárdenas to develop legislative proposals and policies for the indigenous sector of the country. Pablo had just visited her office to enlist her support in Rayqaypampa's struggle to establish Bolivia's first indigenous municipal government in the entire highland region. The country was rapidly moving down the path of increased municipalization and government decentralization due to a pathbreaking new law that was rechanneling federal funds from the regional capitals to local governments. Rayqaypampa wanted to become a full-fledged municipality as one of the first areas to take advantage of the new policy.

When I asked Pablo whether the potato program had achieved its goals, a smile of satisfaction spread slowly across his face. "The interest in imported seed has disappeared among Rayqaypampeños, and over the past five years we've been able to recover and improve five local seed varieties while the number of native varieties will increase in the future. Yet as the program is only partly meeting the potato seed needs of the individual farm families, we have to continue building local management capacity for handling much larger volumes in the future."

Pablo went on, "I recently read an article in a national magazine written by a Dutch author arguing that peasant-managed revolving loan funds for increasing potato production have been a dismal failure, decapitalizing all over the Andes. I wish he'd taken a look at how our program works without using money as the medium of exchange and how CENDA's support per participating family has declined from the 1990 level of providing 205 kilos per farm family to only 14 kilos of seed potato in 1994. This trend demonstrates indigenous autonomy, self-sufficiency, and a capacity for self-management. Over time the Yanapakunas and sindicato leaders have assumed all key supervisory responsibilities in the group's operations. The system's administrative costs remain low, and borrower delinquency minimal, both difficult aspects in most rural credit programs.

"The high-quality seed has reduced previously widespread damage to potato plants caused by harmful insects and pests. To appreciate the importance of such changes one only has to take a look at neighboring communities where farmers have suffered the consequences of infected potato seed from commercial middlemen. The soil compacting resulting from the overuse of chemical fertilizer there has caused a spread in the 'gorgoho' fungus whereas here that problem is under control."

Speaking of chemical fertilizers, I asked Pablo what had been the results of all their educational efforts. He replied that the biggest change had occurred among those young farmers with the potato seed fund who had learned to use smaller amounts of chemicals in combination with organic preparations of the soil to more effectively combat fungus attacks. Many of the young farmers had been using excessive amounts of chemical fertilizers.

Yet where the Rayqaypampa communities had made even more progress was in recuperating local knowledge about a natural insecticide made from local native plants. The Yanapakunas did the research on the dose needed from these local plant extracts and then disseminated the technology throughout the sindicato network and with the help, of course, of radio promotion. Within the last few years, the utilization of chemical insecticides on Rayqaypampa's small farms had greatly diminished.

I then asked Pablo whether the farmers continued to use other native strains independent of the fund. "Yes, certainly, they do," he replied, "but they don't benefit from the opportunities to develop those seeds to the same degree."

Driving through the arid mountain landscape, we occasionally passed old native trees with exposed, intricately sculpted root systems and I was reminded of CENDA's interest in reforesting. With only a few remnants of the old forests, CENDA had set out enthusiastically ten years ago to resurrect forests again via massive growing and replanting schemes. In past visits, I had been disappointed to find a disparity between the growth of native and exotic seedlings on the communal parcels in various communities. Sadly the imported eucalyptus and pine trees were standing tall while the native species were barely above the ground.

Pablo explained that it had proven to be almost impossible to keep the sheep out of the fenced-off parcels. "CENDA had placed too much faith in the sindicatos' ability to tackle the problem of overgrazing. Young shepherds will drop their hungry sheep over the fence with the kind of compassion reserved for a family member. Once inside they began devouring all the native seedlings in sight. The exotic species on the other hand are left alone, giving the communities many more of them to transplant." Some of the difficulty also stemmed from the loss of indigenous knowledge of seed germination and transplantation techniques.

Pablo then listed a number of measures taken by CENDA to reverse these frustrating results. "We haven't given up," he said, "and I still wake up in the middle of the night with anxiety about this problem." Among the recent measures taken, Pablo mentioned the planting of nonedible native fruit trees, model corrals that maintained sheep for longer periods, and research on the role of women in livestock management, "a grossly overlooked part of our work despite the high number of female professionals on our staff.

"We're also encouraging more individual tree ownership and the construction of high adobe walls to protect the seedlings," he added. "To motivate these and other related practices the Yanapakuna have produced and disseminated two educational slide shows on this topic and also organized an annual 'Forest Festival' where farmers compete with one another over the best native tree species. Yet we must be doing something right as many NGOs and foreign agencies send representatives here to inspect and document the self-management aspects of the seedling nurseries which are also using Andean reciprocity mechanisms albeit much less successfully than the seed funds."

Another sad note was the continuing loss of topsoil in the monte zone due to deforestation and corn expansion on the cleared plots. "We've only been able to induce about 10 percent of the young families to stop farming there," Pablo said. "Their behavior is driven both by falling potato prices due to neo-liberal economic policies and by increasing population pressures."

Finally our jeep pulled into the village of Rayqaypampa. The only apparent infrastructure change compared to my first visit ten years earlier was the antenna perched on top of one of the small adobe buildings owned by the project. CENDA was admirable for placing its priorities in human rather than physical capital. The widely distributed seedling nurseries, potato storage silos, and makeshift classrooms for Quechua literacy and other training, as well as the modest sindicato meeting halls, were a testament to this philosophy. There were twenty-four scattered groups of between ten and twenty persons each currently involved in literacy training under the direction of a Yanapakuna.

The Yanapakunas with whom I met during the next few days had learned technical and management skills critical to the coordination of the many project activities. They oversaw the radio broadcasting program, the reforestation effort, the literacy drive, and all the communal seed production activities among the thirty-five different project groups. The forty Yanapakunas operated as a kind of paraprofessional association, with monthly workshops to share experiences and coordinate activities with one another.

The success of CENDA's revitalization program and all its spin-offs was an impressive enough accomplishment for a home-grown development organization. What was even more striking was the way CENDA had, simply by responding to local needs, changed local and then influenced national educational policy, and was able to catapult the image of Rayqaypampa into the national sphere.

As I toured CENDA's programs, the significance of the changes the organization had made in national educational policy became more and more apparent to me. In a room next to the radio station, a young Rayqay-pampeño, hat pulled down over his ears, stood in front of a group of adults with a ruler in his hand. With the ruler, he was pointing to a large chart showing the local school calendar, a calendar illustrated with pictures of crops and various kinds of weather. The calendar had been prepared by the CENDA staff, along with educational authorities and the local weather forecaster. The many educational changes in Rayqaypampa had recently been given a boost by the passage of a national bilingual education reform law mandating the use of native languages and intercultural education in the early years of schooling.

Looking at the confident young teacher I flashed back to a recent interview with Vice-President Cárdenas, one of the principal architects of the new reform law. "When I heard about Rayqaypampa's educational council in the national media I immediately thought back to the days of Warisata," Cárdenas said.[3] "When the Rayqaypampa communities insisted on local control of schooling it resulted in the first instance since the 1930s of a community's being given majority control over a rural school district. And that change reversed fifty years of teacher hegemony over educational decision making. When I met with others to discuss the details of the proposed education law, the Rayqaypampa experiment was very much in my thoughts. Other community-based bilingual school experiments offered lessons with regard to curricular reform or teaching methodologies, but Rayqaypampa made a unique contribution—a model of community control of and participation in the educational policy-making process. Rayqay-pampa gave me a tangible, workable model and experience to draw upon while working with our small group of educational reformers. I even wrote a favorable opinion piece about it for a national newspaper. I seriously doubt whether the people of Rayqaypampa realize the significance of their contribution to the national educational reform effort."

Moving into a project office I sat around a table with Pablo, other staff members, and several Yanapakunas, to talk about the latest developments in reforming the school system. The personable Yanapakuna, Florencio Alarcon, commented, "A law on paper is one thing, but without pressure by farmers from below, it's unlikely that much will happen soon. For the past three years, we've had to wage a battle against the authorities in Aiquile and Rayqaypampa's local schoolteachers to get them to allow our community education council to function in an effective way. We finally had to change the jurisdiction of our school district from the town of Aiquile to Mizque to gain the necessary freedom to function properly. What is ironic is that after all is said and done, the schoolteachers are actually happier with the new calendar. They're allowed to end the school week when the truckers depart with agricultural produce for Aiquile, and this makes life easier for them as well as us."

I learned from the group that Yanapakunas were traveling to other provinces in Cochabamba to share experiences and distribute booklets on how to set up and manage community educational councils and agricultural calendars in other rural school districts. Pablo said that this outreach represented the first effort on the part of CENDA's "School of Ethno-development" to spread the Rayqaypampa model of cultural mobilization to other corners of the Andes.

While Pablo and I were driving back to Cochabamba the next day I commented that some of my friends working in education said that Rayqaypampa had become something of a household word across the nation and that a certain mystique had grown up around these people in their colorful unconventional dress. He replied that during the educational debates in the various regional and national peasant sindicato congresses, the "Rayqaypampa reforms" were often referred to with great deference.

Later when I was examining one of CENDA's many booklets, I was struck by a photo of Florencio Alarcon. The slight Rayqaypampa man was standing proudly in his beautifully embroidered trousers with floral motifs addressing an auditorium of Cochabamba university professors, students, and administrators on the issue of curricular reform in primary schooling. "What an incredible image," I laughed to Pablo. I then read an excerpt from the welcome speech made to him by the dean of the university's education faculty. It read, "This is a new experience for the university. We now recognize that the rural people of Bolivia have much to teach us. They will be drawing from their valuable knowledge of the countryside as we join together to develop curricular reform under the new national education law."

I turned to Pablo and said, "Ten years ago no one would believe that such an event would be within the realm of the possible."

CHAPTER 14

The Mouse That Roared: An Amazonian March to the Andes for Land Rights

We hope that the indigenous marchers can be heard throughout the nation without [political] intermediaries. The effectiveness by which they manage and resolve their problems one way or another will define how Bolivia will be constructed and held together during the next century.

EDITORIAL IN BOLIVIAN DAILY NEWSPAPER, SEPTEMBER 15, 1990

Ernesto Noe, a mustached Mojeño from Trinidad's indigenous cabildo assembly, spoke for all the marchers gathered this historic day—for the indigenous people from Isiboro-Sécure Park, the Chimane Forest, and the Santa Cruz region. He heralded their common purpose and their unprecedented union from the top of the church steps. "This is not a march just to secure territorial rights. By marching today we are also aspiring to gain autonomy for our indigenous authorities, and to inspire a greater appreciation for our cultures, to promote greater understanding of our educational and health needs."

A gangly, raw-boned member of the Mojeño ethnic group next took the mike. Marcial Fabricano, elected leader of the federation of indigenous communities from the Isiboro-Sécure Park in the southern Beni, spoke with simplicity and eloquence. "We are searching for a future long denied us as indigenous peoples, a future rightfully belonging to the original inhabitants of these lands. Lands that will once again return to our people's hands by the final day of this march." Marcial's words were greeted with hoots and cheers.

On the morning of August 14, 1990, 300 indigenous people from eight ethnic groups of the rain forests and savannas of the northern Beni region

361

of Bolivia gathered at the main plaza in the city of Trinidad. They were about to begin a grueling protest march that would lead to presidential decrees promising to restore their rights to their lands. The 560-kilometer march would take thirty-four days, gather 400 additional participants along the way, and traverse all the varied landscapes of Bolivia. Starting from the lowland savannas, the marchers would pass tropical rainforests, cross the Andean foothills and steep mountain river valleys, work their way up the steep faces of the Andes to the altiplano, and at last, step into the bowl-shaped capital, La Paz. The marchers would head due east from the city of Trinidad in northeastern Bolivia. Ten-minute resting periods would be declared at the end of each hour marched to help participants conserve energy for the long journey.

The Indian faces, inexpensive clothing, and rubber sandals or bare feet of the marchers revealed the humble origins of the people gathered for this momentous occasion. There were men and women of all ages. Some carried spears, others held backpacks of forest fibers or small gunny sacks. There were a few pregnant women, and many more carrying babies. Children ran almost everywhere. An old blind man, too, was standing in the middle of the crowd ready to march. Weeks of logistical planning and intense communications within the region and with La Paz had led to this moment of departure. At 8 A.M. with church bells clanging loudly behind them, the marchers took their first steps on a road that had not been, and never would be, easy.

The People of Isiboro-Sécure Park

The southern Beni is a region in northeast Bolivia where the foothills of the Andes converge with the immense emerald rainforests and olive-green savannas of the Amazon basin. Isiboro-Sécure Park is one of several areas in the southern Beni where land rights have become a critical issue for indigenous residents. Two rivers—the Isiboro and the Sécure—form borders of Bolivia's largest park, and small tributaries flow in a ribbon-like pattern in a northwesterly direction through the wild lands of the park. One third of the park is savanna land, while the remaining two thirds are composed of rainforest. The pastures of the park's savannas are flooded three months of the year, forcing the resident cattle into the intermittent clumps of forest on higher grounds. In the rainforest section of the park, narrow, canal-like tributaries cut long, looping silver paths through the dense woods. The deep green of the trees and the fresh glow of water at the base of the greenery give the place a Garden of Eden aura.

The national government created the Isiboro-Sécure Park in 1965, ostensibly to protect fragile ecosystems. Six different types of rainforest and a multitude of diverse species of flora and fauna make the park a valuable wildlife reserve.

The southeastern Beni, and the area now designated the Isiboro-Sécure Park, has been inhabited by the Mojeños and other indigenous groups (Yuracarés, Chimanes, Trinitarios, and many others whose names have been lost over time) for centuries. Until the seventeenth century, when the Jesuits arrived to conquer and convert for the Spanish crown, these indigenous peoples lived under the rule of the chieftains in clusters along the banks of the rivers. Ancestor worship, devotion to forest spirits, and jaguar cults flourished in a society closed off from the world. When the Jesuits arrived, they broke up the insular settlement pattern of the Mojeños and relocated them and the other tribal groups into mission towns under the jurisdiction of Jesuit priests. In addition to the Catholic teachings, they introduced the sixteenth-century Spanish *cabildo* system of political organization, which the tribal groups quickly absorbed and combined with their own political and religious traditions, making it their own (Jones 1980; Lehm 1999; Block 1994).[1]

During this period the groups also continued using their tribal languages while Mojeño became their *lingua franca*. Another change that occurred while the people of the southern Beni lived in the mission system was the development of a thriving cattle economy. Via this economic base, and their assimilation of the cabildo system, the indigenous people established a long-maintained practice of using the local savannas as communal grazing lands.

When the Jesuits were banished from the Spanish Americas in 1767, the cabildos and the savanna-based cattle economy remained intact. Intermittent periods of political tranquillity and economic stability followed until a regional rubber boom erupted in the mid-1800s. For the next several decades, Trinidad was overrun by white and mestizo fortune hunters who ruthlessly exploited native labor in every imaginable way. Slavery, flogging, and other abuses of Indians by whites became routine.

In 1870, the "Loma Santa" movement sprang up. This unique messianic movement, originating in the desperation of the tribal peoples to escape slavery and exploitation, exhorted indigenous people to leave Trinidad and head back to the forests in "search of a promised land." Under this strong religious ideology, many indigenous people moved into the southern gallery forests and settled at widely dispersed spots along the tributaries of what is now Isiboro-Sécure Park. On one level, the return to the woods meant an escape from the oppression of white civilization. On another, it represented an effort to recover sacred ancestral sites and live in deeper connection to traditional forest spirits (Lehm 1999). In the Loma Santa movement, it was believed, also, that those living around the "holy mount" would be rewarded with relative prosperity and tranquillity, and survive the upcoming apocalypse. Loma Santa journeys have continued to the present—at times of socioeconomic stress, the movement burgeons—and many of the scattered settlements in the park originated in such migrations.

Following the rubber boom, several other forces contributed to the extraction of lands from the indigenous population during the middle to late 1900s. According to Jim Jones, an ex-IAF fellow who lived with rural communities of the southern Beni during the late 1970s, much of the vast savanna covering half the region was in indigenous hands until as late as the 1940s. At that time the small cargo plane came into use, and entrepreneurs from the city began flying into the Beni to purchase beef and transport it to high-paying markets in urban areas. Simultaneously, white cattle ranchers began gobbling up pasturelands that had heretofore been under indigenous control (Jones 1997). This change in control over the savannas was made possible by the cheap credit available for livestock development (especially for the purchase of imported cebu cattle) and infrastructure investments through the Point Four Program of the United States government. This modernization of cattle production had been recommended as part of the Bolivian development plan written by the Bohan Commission in the 1940s.

Another factor in the dispossession of the indigenous groups in the area during the 1960s and 1970s was the practice by successive military regimes of carving up "public lands" in order to grant them to their cronies and fellow officers under the flexible national agrarian reform laws.[2] Without benefit of any strong political organization, the Mojeños and other lowland ethnic groups were defenseless in the face of this appropriation of their lands and their exclusion from the national agrarian reforms.

When, in 1965, the area was designated a park, the resident indigenous peoples at first hailed the creation of the park as a protection for their lands, but, in fact, there were no built-in protections against exploitation. A new road from Cochabamba reached the park in the early 1980s, bringing in scores of peasant colonists. Illegal poaching of wildlife that had begun in the 1940s continued unabated. More recently, small sawmills were set up within the boundaries of the park, and four cocaine labs were operating near its southern border with Cochabamba. Most astonishing of all, the requirements and rights of the Mojeños, Yuracarés, and Trinitarios who had lived in forty-three communities in the lands of the park for decades, if not centuries, prior to the Jesuit missions, were not mentioned by name in any official document establishing the park.

As colonists, sawmill operations, and ranchers grabbed more and more land of the region, the Mojeños and other groups gradually began to resist. CIDDEBENI, an NGO devoted to the retroactive inclusion of the Beni indigenous people in the agrarian reform of the 1950s, and Jorge Cortez, an IAF-funded researcher and activist for indigenous rights in the southern Beni who had linked up with CIDDEBENI, began making forays into the park in 1987. Their purpose was to help the Beni tribal peoples solidify their common indigenous identity and mobilize around the land rights issues vital to their well-being.

As Jorge Cortez put it, "What the Mojeños were saying was, 'Look, we are the ones who suffer the effects of natural resource degradation, so give us this park as a collective territory, and we'll do all we can to reverse the rampant destruction of the ecosystems.'" With CIDDEBENI's help the Mojeños devised a strategy for local development that would to take into account the fragility of the forests and incorporate relevant scientific knowledge. Their aim, which matched that of CIDDEBENI, was to change national laws to address the real needs of the Beni's indigenous people.

In August 1988, Marcial Fabricano, the leader of the federation of southern Beni indigenous people that had been formed with the help of CIDDEBENI, led me down a forest trail, passing banana groves and small gardens of rice and yucca carved out of the dense foliage. We crossed a swampy area in a dug-out canoe then came across our first Mojeño family dwelling. The walls of the hut were made of animal hide. It had an overhanging thatched roof, large open windows, and there were hand-woven baskets strewn on the ground outside its front door. A squawking macaw near the doorway strutted back and forth showing off its splendid red and orange feathers. After twenty minutes or so of walking, we reached Puerto San Lorenzo, a village situated on the narrow Isiboro River.

Marcial had only six years of schooling when he left home in the forest to join the army in 1971.[3] After a two-year stint as a conscript, he worked as a garage mechanic for the next twelve years in the city of Santa Cruz which involved him in the quasi-underground world of smuggling autos from Brazil into Bolivia. While in Santa Cruz he also became exposed to union and political organizing activities in his barrio. In 1983, after twelve years away, he returned to Isiboro-Sécure Park. He found his family impoverished and the community in disarray. Anxious to leave the seamy side of life of Santa Cruz behind him, Marcial turned to the Bible for spiritual strength and joined an evangelical sect. He also initiated a number of community projects as an informal leader. Because of Marcial's strong evangelical religious orientation, Jorge Cortez of CIDDEBENI initially had grave doubts that Marcial was the right man to lead the Mojeño people in a protracted land rights struggle.

Marcial led me to the assembly he had organized. Mojeños in baseball hats and straw hats were clustered on benches outdoors, commenting enthusiastically about the park's inaugural assembly of village cabildos held the month before. Each cabildo had sent a *corregidor* as a delegate to participate in a forum. The park-dwellers had drafted a list of grievances and demands to be sent to the authorities whose decisions determined the fate of their microregion from many miles away.

The indigenous representatives spoke of their excitement in participating in a grassroots mobilization that could lead to important changes in their lives. Over the past year, with the crucial help of Jorge and others from CIDDEBENI, they had had many local meetings that had paved the way for the formation of their new federation, a kind of intra-communal organization that would pull together the many tiny villages throughout the park and revitalize the politically dormant cabildos and corresponding traditional authorities. Jorge and the NGO had supplied critical expertise, aiding the tribal people in the planning and logistics for the forum, and in the preparation of land claim documents.

Over the next two years under Marcial's guidance, residents of the park went on to have five other such assemblies and many smaller meetings to solidify their unity and add numbers of determined people to the cause. Marcial used the outboard motorboat loaned to him by a Protestant missionary to travel up and down the small tributaries running through the park to visit settlements and exhort indigenous residents to attend the assemblies and affirm their political rights. This growing activism turned important heads as far away as La Paz, eventually bringing the Minister of Agriculture and Peasant Affairs himself to Puerto San Lorenzo in a helicopter with a proposal purporting to address their needs. The revitalized cabildos rejected it as falling short of their envisioned territory but his brief presence was a kind of moral victory—it was the first time a Bolivian cabinet member had ever set foot in the park.

Marcial's organizing zeal proved that his unorthodox evangelical beliefs were an asset rather than the liability Jorge feared. It was precisely the religious charisma and passionate faith of his leadership style that attracted participants to the movement. His use of the local Catholic chapel to conduct both Bible readings and local cabildo meetings for public prayers melted any distance between himself and the Catholic majority. While his evangelical side led him to take the unpopular measure of prohibiting drinking during the assemblies, his modern political side challenged the descendants of the Loma Santa Movement to confront their government instead of hiding in the forest. Above all, Marcial's belief that speaking out served the Lord and one does "the Lord's work" by "being of service to those in need" caught hold. Through his conviction, he inspired his brothers and sisters in the park to fight their increasing poverty and loss of control over their resources.

Now, in 1990, as they set down their bare feet on the Bolivian roads, the people of Isiboro-Sécure Park were seeing to it that their case was given attention.

THE PEOPLE OF CHIMANE FOREST

In another sector of the plaza, Carlos Navia, director of CIDDEBENI, was ushering arriving indigenous groups toward the gathering in front of the church. Many of the Chimanes, Mojeños, Movimas, Yuracarés, and Ignacianos present were tribal groups from the Chimane Forest, a 1,160,000 hectare region of southeastern Beni to the west of Isiboro-Sécure Park. These people had became involved in land rights issues after the reserve status was lifted on the rich mahogany forest they had always called home (Lehm 1999). When the status change occurred, logging companies had come in and taken large swaths of the forest. They, like the people of Isiboro-Sécure Park, had come to Trinidad to join the mobilization for indigenous land rights.

Carlos Navia, the descendent of an elite ranching and a riverboat transport family, had not always had a strong feeling for the rights of tribal people. He, personally, had spearheaded the campaign to lift the reserve status of the Chimane Forest and put it into commercial production. He had worked with local timber investors who, it turned out, had mastered environmentalist rhetoric to camouflage their interests.

"The original reasons for advocating a new forest policy were a regional crisis in the cattle economy and our desperate need for financial resources," Carlos explained. "Exploitation of the mahogany forests would generate revenues for the sagging budgets of the local municipal governments. Lumbering was attractive in a region where half the landscape was covered in forest. In addition, newly completed all-weather roads would lower the cost of transport of local products to La Paz and Santa Cruz.

"My big mistake was failing to consult the indigenous communities of some 6,000 people inhabiting the Chimane forest," Carlos said. The logging and milling operations that sprang up after the status change were so disruptive to community life that the native inhabitants immediately began denouncing him and others who had opened the forest to logging. The companies refused to replace the trees harvested with new seedlings as specified by national law. They dumped their waste materials into the nearby river and contaminated waters used for drinking and fishing. During the past two decades, they had depleted the supply of mahogany in Santa Cruz forests through selective cutting. "When we needed the government agencies to enforce the laws, it was an education for us to see how they'd been co-opted by elite groups," Carlos said. That was the turning point for him.

"Both Richard Smith, an anthropologist from OXFAM, and Zulema Lehm, a staff anthropologist at CIDDEBENI, helped open my eyes to appreciate the indigenous peoples in our regional society. Before this, I had thought of most people in the rural communities simply as campesinos and never took their ethnic identity into account. With my new awareness, I was able to go beyond applauding exotic folk dances they performed in towns several times a year to appreciate their impressive knowledge of forest ecology and their contribution as radical conservationists on a broader level. Most importantly, I came to appreciate the value of cultural pluralism in our Beni society. All of this led me to join the indigenous rights movement."

Several other forces also contributed to the activism of the Chimane forest peoples as Carlos saw it. "The Jesuits, who returned to our area in 1984 after a 200-year absence, immediately became advocates for the indigenous in conflicts with the loggers. Their strong denunciation of the abuses taking place helped build the indigenous people's awareness of their land rights, and pushed our cause along.

"Then, in 1988, the Chimane forest made history as the site of the world's first debt-for-nature swap engineered by the United States environmental organization, Conservation International (CI). In that negotiation, CI opted to work with the loggers instead of the indigenous communities. This instantly added fuel to the indigenous fire and is another reason the communities of Chimane Forest have joined the indigenous land rights movement. The confluence of all these forces gave rise to a series of local assemblies similar to those held in Isiboro-Sécure that led to demands that the authorities give attention to our grievances and consider our solutions to the land rights issue."

OTHER FORCES BEHIND THE MARCH

An Emerging Paradigm

A key reason the march was happening was due to shifts in the different paradigms of both the political left and right since the 1950s, and leaders of CIDDEBENI were steeped in the new perspectives on development and native peoples. Both Carlos Navia and Jorge Cortez formed their social consciousness as members of the Movimiento de Izquierda Revolucionario Party (MIR) (Movement of the Revolutionary Left), the party that was in the vanguard of the democratic resistance to the military dictatorships of the 1970s and early 1980s. In addition, both men had been student activists. These formative experiences predisposed them to be sensitive to the underdog, which ultimately became for them indigenous peoples. "In our work with the Beni indigenous communities," Jorge reported, "our old Marxian paradigm has flown out the window. It has been replaced by a new focus on ethnic rights and environmental conservation, and the popular term, 'sustainable development'. CIDOB had been working on this paradigm from Santa Cruz and we were also helping to bring it to the Beni. The earlier

developmental perspectives completely overlooked these two important aspects of our interconnected world. Several years ago, we were completely
ignorant of the sensitivity of fragile tropical soils, the importance of biodiversity, and the threat of global warming wrought by deforestation.
We have learned to marshal new kinds of evidence and we now present ecologically related arguments in our debates with the timber interests and their governmental allies over the rights of the Beni indigenous
communities.

"Over the past year, we have had to educate ourselves by re-examining
the agrarian reform laws in relation to forested areas, by reading numerous
international environmental publications on the tropics, and by inviting biologists and ecologists here to give talks. It's been a somewhat tense, but
stimulating and personally rewarding period in our professional lives. A new
paradigm has come into being."

Inspiration from Santa Cruz

Initiatives to organize the indigenous peoples of the Isiboro-Sécure Park
and Chimane Forest began with the work of the Confederación del Pueblos Indígenas del Oriente Boliviana (CIDOB),[4] which helped CIDAC to
work in indigenous communities in Santa Cruz. After mobilizing the
ethnic federations scattered throughout the Department of Santa Cruz,
they turned their attention to the poorly organized ethnic groups in the
rural communities of the Beni region.

In the mid-1980s, when indigenous leaders from CIDOB in Santa
Cruz went to Trinidad they found an indigenous center established by the
Jesuits when creating the mission towns several centuries earlier. The "Cabildo Indígenal de Trinidad" (the Indigenous Cabildo of Trinidad) immediately sympathized with their organizing and ethnic focus, but in the rural
communities CIDOB found people to be much less receptive and more
alienated from their cultural roots. Yet with the help of CIDDEBENI, the
Jesuits, and others, the use of the term *indígenas* in the Beni would now
take on a new meaning. Subsequently, the Mojeños, Chimanes, and others
from the Beni began traveling to Santa Cruz to taste the excitement of participation in CIDOB's multi-ethnic indigenous congresses.

After first finding receptive audiences in rural communities within
close proximity to the city's Indigenous Cabildo, CIDOB leaders along
with staff members from a government literacy program accompanied local

indigenous people such as Ernesto Noe to the Isiboro-Sécure Park and the Chimane Forest to elicit interest in the revitalization of local cabildos and ethnic identities as the basis for a new political movement. In general terms, their perspectives found fertile ground among the communities, although there were wide differences with respect to political positions and degrees of acculturation to Western values. Evangelicals, Jesuits, and many other outside influences had touched the lives of the various peoples and reshaped their communities in different ways, but they found that their common interest in securing land rights and gaining greater organizational power bound them together in a single struggle. Thus CIDOB enabled indigenous groups to come together on the basis of a pan-indigenous identity. Native languages, folk art, the cabildo method of community organization, and other cultural practices were valued elements within this strategy.

CIDOB had also earlier fused the term *indígena* with "territory" and "indigenous territorial rights" became the rallying cry. According to Richard Smith, an OXFAM anthropologist with twenty-five years of experience in this part of South America, the term "indigenous territorial rights" was adopted within the Amazon region in 1984 as part of a plank of an indigenous confederation COICA (the Coordinating Body of the Indigenous Peoples of the Amazon) that linked together federations like CIDOB from Peru, Bolivia, Ecuador, and Colombia in a pan-Amazonian strategy to protect and recover homelands of indigenous peoples.

Political Action in La Paz

In addition to the rise of land rights awareness in the indigenous peoples of the southern Beni, the birth of a new development paradigm, a new pride-instilling term, and the inspirational work of CIDOB, a long, multi-step program of direct political pressure had been necessary to forward the indigenous peoples' cause and bring the march into being.

Jorge Cortez, who did applied research on the Loma Santa movement, was a key player in the effort to influence policymakers in La Paz.

"Frustrated with our failure to interest the local authorities in the Chimane forest indigenous-logger conflicts," Jorge said, "we finally approached a friend of mine, the ex-wife of the Minister of Information. She lives in San Ignacio and has great sympathy for the Chimanes and Movimas in the Chimane forest, so she arranged for us to have a private meeting with Víctor Paz Estenssoro, the president of Bolivia, on January 12, 1988.

Personal contacts and networks are always the most useful resource for making things happen in this country," he said with a grin.

"She opened the door, and Víctor Paz showed surprisingly great interest in the situation of the native groups. He probably did so because the Bolivian government had recently been criticized in a United Nations forum in Geneva for violating the long-standing Convention 107 by failing to take action regarding the invasion by colonists of the lands of the Yuki ethnic group in lowland Bolivia which led to several deaths of the latter.

"So Carlos, anthropologist Zulema Lehm, twelve indigenous Chimanes, Mojeños, and Ignacianos from the Chimane forest, and I came together in an unprecedented opportunity for high-level dialogue. At the meeting, President Paz expressed a serious commitment to bringing about needed changes in the land tenure laws. The upshot of the meeting was his agreement to issue a presidential decree acknowledging collective rights to forest dwellers of the eastern lowlands. It was ironic to find the architect of Bolivia's thirty-five-year agrarian reform program willing and available to rectify his earlier mistakes. The earlier law had been written for agricultural peoples, and now forest-dwelling peoples would also enjoy basic rights. Jubilant with the positive reception to our story, the next surprise was to find ourselves drafting a presidential decree that was eventually signed into law. The legal framework used for the decree was based on the then-proposed ILO Convention 169 for indigenous peoples that had been discussed thoroughly in previous meetings the president held with Bolivian anthropologist Jorge Dandler and Colombian consultant Raul Arango, both of the ILO, and Oscar Arce Quintanilla, the Bolivian director of the Inter-American Indigenous Institute based in Mexico City. The executive decree included a key and important general statement:'The executive declares the national and social necessity of the recognition, allotment, and tenure of territorial areas in favor of forest groups and native community inhabitants in eastern Bolivia, as a way to guarantee their survival and socioeconomic development.'

"Unfortunately, in the real world of interest group politics there was a big caveat to this dream-like decree. When Paz Estenssoro appointed the commission to operationalize it for the Chimane Forest context, the commission's composition was stacked on the side of the logging and ranching interests, and the maps were drawn up in such a way that the timber companies maintained control of the mahogany forests.

"We struck back in response to that by making maps of our own show-ing the widespread use of forest resources by the native peoples residing in the designated logging areas. OXFAM-America financed a study that demonstrated that a wide area of the central forest was used by indigenous people for hunting, fishing, farming, and the natural harvesting of nuts and other products. We used the study to effectively rebut the commission's claims, but they were not willing to change their conclusions. Despite this setback, our efforts did help to energize the indigenous organizations for greater resolve in the territorial struggles."

As a next step, several months later in July 1989, Jorge and other CID-DEBENI members tried to take the government up on its original good faith by co-sponsoring a seminar on pertinent controversial environmental and indigenous rights issues. Timber company people, high-level govern-ment officials, NGO representatives, and knowledgeable technicians with forestry backgrounds attended the seminar. CIDDEBENI discovered kin-dred spirits among the visiting international rainforest biologists as they argued with lumber company representatives. Seventy representatives from the Chimane forest also showed up at the meeting and distributed materials advocating territorial rights for their homeland.

The next big step took place in late 1989. This was the formation of a federation linking all the ethnic groups in the Beni, the Central de Pueblos Indígenas del Beni (CEPIB) (Federation of the Indigenous People of the Beni). Zulema Lehm, the staff anthropologist at CIDDEBENI who had been trained by Silvia Rivera at THOA,[5] hailed CEPIB as a "wonderful cul-mination of the dozens perhaps hundreds of grassroots meetings we've been involved with, via the support of the IAF, OXFAM, and other NGOs." The plan was that CEPIB would join CIDOB and spread their influence over the entire Beni. The new federation consisted of ethnic groups from the Chimane Forest and Isiboro-Sécure Park, plus a new group, the people from the villages of Ibiato, only sixty-five kilometers from Trinidad. The Sirionó were engaged in a struggle with cattle ranchers, usurpers of 20,000 out of a total area of 23,000 hectares of savanna they had traditionally held.

CEPIB's program, like CIDOB's, called for revitalization on a number of fronts—native languages, crafts, the cabildo, and indigenous political au-tonomy, in addition to the centerpiece issue of indigenous territories. As a follow-up to earlier documents written by leaders in Isiboro-Sécure Park and Chimane Forest, CEPIB sent a document listing the indigenous groups' unified demands directly to the new president of the Republic, Jaime Paz Zamora. Out of this came the decision to stage a protest march ninety kilometers from San Ignacio de Moxos to Trinidad later in the month. Yet when the time came, a teachers' strike and a state of emergency declared by the government aborted these plans.

Meanwhile, there had been a confusing and unexpected change in the leadership of the land rights movement. Jorge Cortez had resigned as staff member for CIDDEBENI to take a job as advisor on environmental matters to the Ministry of Agriculture in La Paz. Jorge had worked as an assistant to Jaime Paz during his earlier vice-presidency, and Paz had sought him out when trying to fill his environmental posts now that he was president. Jorge had also been drawn to La Paz by the recently increased funding for environmental projects, by the need for expertise at the highest levels, and by the superior educational opportunities for his children in the capital. "I made sure CEPIB was on its feet before making the change," Jorge said when I spoke to him.

Marcial and other leaders were confused by Jorge's decision—to some he appeared at best co-opted, at worst a turncoat—but Zulema Lehm said, "Look at it this way. We now have an ally within the highest corridors of political power. Though, admittedly, his skills and commitment to the indigenous cause will be sorely missed." I bade Jorge farewell over the phone and expressed hope that he would find time to stay in touch.

CEPIB, meanwhile, kept its momentum in spite of the loss of an important advisor. Over the next five months of 1990 it flexed its new organizational muscle by holding two highly publicized congresses to reformulate petitions to keep pressure on the national authorities. Frustrations continued to mount, however, with each new counterproposal offered by the government through a local representative. The high-ranking ministers were increasingly hearing private-sector alarm bells in La Paz, the Beni, and Santa Cruz, and were consequently unwilling to budge in response to CEPIB's demands. Both sides manifested an unwillingness to make major compromises in their respective positions.

By July 1990, after three years of attempting to influence the government, it was clear that only a new approach could change the dynamics of the situation. The idea of the protest march resurfaced as the only way for the indigenous federations to move the national authorities. The initial proposal agreed upon at CEPIB's first meeting snowballed into a more ambitious plan—a march all the way to the capital. CEPIB's demands would be presented by the indigenous people directly to the president after having mobilized public opinion during a month of marching across Bolivia.

Marcial, now a regional leader for CEPIB, excitedly told me about the march over the phone. "We wanted to talk directly with Paz Zamora himself and make our first indigenous protest event a memorable one. We want to impress upon him our willingness to sacrifice ourselves if necessary to attain our rights.

"Threatened by our public announcement of the march," Marcial went on, "the government quickly added hundreds of thousands of hectares to the Chimanes offer but once again did little to alter the loggers' control over the central area. In response, we opted to radicalize our demands instead of modify them. From now on, we are requesting the entire Chimane Forest, the termination of forest concessions there, and the ouster of these companies from the zone.

"The government persisted in offering the park to us as an 'indigenous area,' negating our preferred term of 'indigenous territory' and the figures for the restitution of savanna lands were far below our demands. Thus it was time to march.

"In July, we issued an ultimatum to the national government: either accept our territorial demands or the march would commence on August 2nd, Bolivia's annual Day of the Indian. With the help of CIDDEBENI and the Catholic Church and with a support network of human rights activists, churches, grassroots federations, environmental, developmental, and other NGOs, we began the logistical and material preparations." Desperate to forestall this dramatic social movement from the "uninhabited forests," the Minister of Agriculture sent Jorge Cortez as his personal emissary to dissuade the CEPIB leaders from going forth with the planned march.

"Jorge showed up in this official capacity only five days prior to our departure which had been slightly delayed to August 15th. He had with him a draft proposal of a decree granting territorial rights for the park and adding more inches of indigenous territory in the other two conflictive areas. Once again the offer fell short and made clear the continuing influence of the timber interests and their allies in the private sector. I looked across the table at Jorge during our negotiations and could see in his eyes his discomfort with his new role as mediator and government representative. I doubted that his heart was fully behind his words. To us his placement in that role was a blatant attempt to divide our movement. We had been gaining strength over two years of devoted grassroots organizing and had finally crystallized into a regional federation, and we were not about to give up our fight just as we were setting off on our biggest push for indigenous land rights yet."

THE MARCH

Leading the protesters, as the march began, was a Yuracaré drummer beating out inspiring rhythms that would continue throughout the journey. He walked before a long banner whose green and red lettering read, "MARCHA POR EL TERRITORIO Y LA DIGNIDAD CENTRAL DE PUEBLOS INDÍGENAS DEL BENI" (March for Territory and Dignity of the Indigenous Peoples of the Beni) with Bolivian and Beni flags flanking its two sides. Ernesto Noe, Marcial, and Tomás Ticuasu of the Sirionó moved in step together immediately behind this banner.

During the first few kilometers, local university students accompanied the marchers. After that the only middle-class legs were those of a CID-DEBENI staff member and two dedicated journalists from La Paz filing news stories. Fortunately, my bi-annual trip to Bolivia in August coincided with the timing of the march so I was able to meet Carlos and Zulema on its sixth day to discuss their new project proposal. CIDDEBENI was already planning park-related activities to be undertaken following a successful protest event. Neither of the two were marching, however, to avoid charges of being external manipulators of Indians. On the way to Trinidad, there were posters about the march plastered everywhere. CIDDEBENI's office had the chaotic, upbeat atmosphere of a recently created command center.

Driving out to the march, we arrived at night and found the marchers asleep in a series of small ranches strung along the San Borja river. Five miles behind them was the town of San Ignacio de Moxos, a veritable hotbed of Jesuit indigenous organizing. In that town priests, sisters, seminarians, and lay people had worked tirelessly to bring about justice for the indigenous through the organization of Christian base communities (Jones 1990). Not surprisingly, local townspeople afforded the marchers a hero's welcome, while 300 or so additional indigenous people from the Chimane forest joined their ranks for the first time.

With a flashlight, we located Arnaldo Lijeron of CIDDEBENI and requested a quick update on the day's events. The biggest news had been the arrival of a governmental commission by air from La Paz with new concessions to offer. He threw his head back in laughter, saying, "Marcial insisted they march with us for five miles until we reached a place providing shade and comfort. Then the talks resumed."

The next day, I watched the three indigenous leaders examining maps in an intense discussion with the visiting authorities. Elsewhere in the riverside meadow, other march participants rested and chatted amiably in small groups. Local women stirred huge clay cooking pots while young people played the first round robin soccer tournament of the march to pass the time. On reaching the shack where the talks were taking place, I joined Carlos and Marcial, who were taking a break outside. Carlos encouraged Marcial to keep up the good fight. He said, "It's obviously a decision for CEPIB to make in assembly but it seems clear that because of growing international and national support for this undertaking, the government is becoming increasingly concerned. My advice is to continue on with the march, keep the pressure on the government, and play the situation to your advantage."

When negotiations once again led to a dead end, the government officials invited the indigenous leaders to return with them by small plane to La Paz, promising new offers from the Minister of Agriculture in the capital city. The open cabildo assembly agreed to send them to La Paz while the march would continue along its course to avoid losing time and diminishing morale.

While mingling with the marchers, I bumped into representatives of CIDOB from the Guarayo and Izoceño ethnic groups, who had just arrived. They reminded me of their relatives' participation in CIDAC's artisan revival project. CIDOB's most vital mission at the march would be to bring up the rear with bedding gear—mosquito nets and blankets for families with too much cargo—and supplemental food.

The following day Carlos, Zulema, and I left the march to participate in the educational road show CIDDEBENI was presenting in a local town. Zulema's slide presentations on indigenous management of forest areas in the Beni provided eye-opening information about indigenous knowledge and conservation practices to people oblivious to these practices and harboring strong prejudices. When a military officer present at one of these events stood up and asked Zulema what international organizations were behind the indigenous march disrupting the local status quo, she replied that the institutions were many, mostly from Western Europe and the United States, as well as from all over Bolivia.

The next evening, back in La Paz, I found Marcial slumped in a chair in his hotel lobby with a glum expression on his face. The last frustrating round of negotiations had just ended, and he would be flying back to the Beni to join the marchers the following day.

I first asked whether Jorge was present in his talks with the minister. "Jorge was nowhere to be seen," he answered, "It's just as well, though, as our trust in him has waned since he's become a government emissary, and tried to talk us out of marching." Moving on to the progress of the talks, Marcial reported, "The minister offers more Chimane forest each time but the timber extraction area remains untouched. The minister tried to sweeten the pot with offers of schools and health clinics, trivial items in the context of our struggle for territories. I'm convinced that the march will have to go all the way for us to achieve our goals."

Thanks to *Presencia,* a daily newspaper, and Radio FIDES, a lively national radio news network, it was relatively easy for me to keep track of the march while I traveled through the country visiting other IAF projects. *Presencia* belonged to the Catholic Church, Radio FIDES to the Jesuit order. Radio Fides was doubly interested in social justice concerns due to their order's earlier involvement with the Mojeño and other Beni ethnic groups. The National Bishops' Conference mandated that *Presencia* give comprehensive coverage to the march in an effort to shape public opinion in a positive direction. According to Marcial, the marchers themselves gained a morale boost each time a news broadcast about their progress came over the air via the radios some of them carried.

Hundreds of leathery feet kept moving in unison over miles and miles of savanna. At night, march participants hung their hammocks on trees along the roadway or spread their blankets on the floors of village schoolhouses. The rivers, crossed by barge, became basins for bathing and washing clothes. Each afternoon a commission of young scouts would locate an appropriate site for the day's overnight stay. The long day of marching would end about nine or ten o'clock at night. Without exception, the towns along the route embraced marchers warmly and enthusiastically. Perhaps most surprising was the town of San Borja, renowned for its powerful cattle-ranching oligarchy and drug traffickers. Here, as elsewhere, schoolchildren and other townspeople filled up the sidewalks to clap, cheer, and wave at their new heroes. At the Mass held in San Borja, the ethnic groups celebrated their cultural roots by taking turns speaking in eight different languages from the pulpit—an act that symbolized the cultural pluralism they were bringing to the consciousness of the nation.

Another giant welcoming party took place the next day in Yucumo, an area recently colonized by highland settlers. Andean colonists honored the marchers with traditional panpipe music and abundant tropical foods. The highlanders' enthusiasm softened the traditional barriers to dialogue between lowland natives and highland colonists as the two groups came together in the spirit of solidarity.

While striving to keep track of these stopovers and receptions, I found Sonia Brito, the director of a church-based NGO, La Co-ordinadora del Pueblo Indígena (the Coordinating Body of the Indigenous Peoples), who was coordinator of the material and logistical support offered by approximately fifty NGOs. "The whole support effort got off to a shaky start," she said. "The bishops threatened to withdraw assistance unless women and children were excluded. They insisted that the long-distance endurance test involved too much sacrifice. CEPIB leaders informed them that such interference was unacceptable and the march would proceed according to plan, with or without church support."

While the NGO community on the whole was very supportive of the march, I did encounter a handful of discordant voices. A professional woman revealed some doubts. "What a pity," she said. "The indigenous groups are making such sacrifices in taking on this extremely rugged trip, and in the end, given official attitudes toward them, they will most likely have nothing to show for their efforts." An anthropologist expressed concern over the radical nature of the demands. "They can't demand everything," he argued. "It's a big tactical mistake to do so. The ranchers and loggers will sway public opinion by highlighting the sheer size of the territories for relatively few people."

I was also amused by a *Presencia* interview with a Beni timber baron and ex-friend of Carlos Navia who argued that CIDDEBENI had organized the whole thing to impress foreign funders. I thought that if this were the case they were very successful with respect to this gringo.

On the fifteenth day, having crossed the flat Beni landscape and the tropical forests newly populated with highland colonists, the marchers entered the Andean foothills of the Alto Beni. There they tackled the first hilly terrain of their trip, a preparation for the upcoming ascent of the eastern slopes of the Andes. Just before a new advance was made, however, a major organizational crisis erupted among the marchers. As the marchers set foot on La Paz terrain, CIDOB announced its decision to abandon the march in a dramatic pull-out. The ostensible reason was alleged outside manipulation by various leftist interest groups. This meant CEPIB would not only lose the indispensable supply truck but also be weakened precisely as it was beginning to wedge a new awareness of indigenous rights into the national public conscience. News of lowland peoples fighting among themselves might call into question the integrity of the march and serve to discredit the movement. And the private sector loggers and ranchers would, no doubt, use the situation to their advantage. It was hard for me to fathom what had motivated this switch.

CIDOB's change of heart was a bigger surprise to me than Jorge's exit, since these activists were the very founders of Bolivia's indigenous movement in the eastern lowlands. I recalled CIDOB's preference for promoting small indigenous-run enterprise projects, like communal sawmills, in an incremental and less confrontational territorial strategy. They were different in this way from the altiplano Kataristas. Recently they had joined a mega World Bank project with the same goal in mind. Did they perhaps fear losing their favored niche with this multilateral funder? Or, alternatively, were they struck with fear about a backlash from the formidable anti-indigenous elite groups of their home region? Or was their self-image threatened by being upstaged by CEPIB, a recently created indigenous federation making dramatic entry into indigenous politics? Much of the public sympathy to the march, from the NGOs, grassroots federations in the highlands, and church organizations, experienced a mixture of shock and dismay at CIDOB's apparent betrayal. Fortunately, on the logistical front, OSCAR, an NGO run by American Franciscan priests, another IAF grantee, was able to provide a supply truck so that the march could keep moving.

Meanwhile, the march continued to make the news. Radio FIDES broadcasts made the names of many rural villages of the Alto Beni familiar to the rest of the country. El Ceibo popped up in the news as well, when the cacao farmers drove a group of native Mosetenes to the march in their co-op truck, and then helped in hauling logistical supplies. In addition, they had held a chocolate feast for the marchers when they arrived that night in Sapecho. The participation of the Mosetenes (the only lowland native inhabitants belonging to El Ceibo) led to their acquisition of territorial rights several years later. This part of the journey through the Alto Beni offered other memorable images as well. School children from the cacao farms, for example, turned out to provide foot and leg massages to weary, grateful marchers. While taking one of their extra rest stops in Sapecho the marchers played El Ceibo in several soccer matches. One of the games ended in a tie which was the first time the recently formed multi-ethnic team failed to win.

At Sapecho, having replenished many burned up calories with chocolate, the marchers were only eleven days away from the capital city, yet the most grueling part of the trip now awaited them. They walked through the small colonist towns of Bella Vista (there they were greeted by a marching high school band), Carrasco, and Caranavi, the latter a coffee trade capital overflowing with crowds waiting to see and cheer them onwards to La Paz. From Caravani, the marchers moved along a narrow road above steep, deep canyons. Below them they could hear glacial water from the high Andes gushing through the valley on its way to the Amazonian basin. Terraces planted with coca and coffee bushes began to appear on the slopes. The marchers were becoming smaller and smaller, figures dwarfed by the mountainous heights of their surroundings—the landscape a far cry from the vast savanna of earlier weeks.

The greater numbers of trucks, buses, and cars on this segment of the road meant exorbitant quantities of dust. In contrast to the increasingly rugged conditions, the people living in the small villages and towns en route showed the great spirit of Andean generosity. At each successive stop in the Yungas, food and beverage was laid out and marchers were invited to dance to Aymara panpipes, drums, and flutes. The friendliness and festivity offered by the Andean communities lent a sense of importance to the marchers' mission (Contreras 1991). As they left each hamlet, drummers and panpipe players and local sindicato leaders accompanied the marchers for a few kilometers.

Meanwhile, the marchers' appearance in the La Paz region was generating increasing excitement among organized groups sympathetic to their cause in the nation's capital. Anxious to demonstrate this solidarity, delegations of prominent human rights and trade union leaders, national peasant sindicato representatives, and active rural women's organizations began traveling to the Yungas to greet marchers and offer words of encouragement and support.

Another La Paz group unable to sit quietly still, but for different reasons, was the Confederation of Private Businessmen which was trying its best to denigrate the movement in the public eye. They took out full-page newspaper ads denouncing indigenous threats to private property and national sovereignty. The latter charge resulted from a distorted view that the indigenous were trying to create "a state within a state" by garnering political autonomy for their indigenous authorities. To counter such attacks from the government as well as the private sectors, Marcial, the leader of the march, Ernesto Noe, and Tomás Ticuasu representing the Sirionó people held press conferences upon arrival at each new village site. However, public threats from the Minister of Interior who said he was going to call out the armed forces to subdue the marchers, did strike genuine fear into their hearts, according to Marcial.

Meanwhile, contrary to Marcial's and Carlos's fears, Jorge was acting as a key advocate for the indigenous cause in the capital. I learned from him that the steady climb toward the capital city had increased the government's nervousness. Instead of getting weaker, the movement was growing, having added another one hundred or so participants while in the Yungas. "You might find it surprising," Jorge said, "that within the cabinet, the Minister of Agriculture, Mauro Bertero, has been a relatively progressive voice, with genuine sympathy for the indigenous cause. Susana Suleme, the personal secretary to the president, has been an important ally from the inner power circle as well, and finds openings here and there to facilitate the just presentation of indigenous demands." I was intrigued to hear this news of Susana. She had been a member of the Co-operativa Cruceño de Cultura (Cultural Cooperative of Santa Cruz) and had lent a hand to Ada Vaca when she was founding CIDAC. I was sure that her experience supporting indigenous women had prepared her for assisting the marchers in this way.

Jorge went on, "Bertero and Susana gained entrée for me into several important cabinet meetings when the march was becoming an important agenda item. Bertero himself kept his views close to his chest and remained very low key, several times deferring to me to make presentations on the situation. In the meetings, I tried to take the moral high road, and explain that this was a 'historic opportunity' to rewrite an antiquated agrarian reform law that had never met the needs of the Beni indigenous communities anyway.

"I had to bite my tongue when the Minister of Interior turned to me and said, 'Let's end this ridiculous adventure, Jorge. It's a lot of nonsense, and an embarrassing situation for us. It's time to send out the police equipped with billy clubs and tear gas to break up the whole thing once and for all.' The minister had already sent agent provocateurs to pose as allies of the indigenous to sow divisions among the marchers, and he was determined to take repressive actions. Luckily, Bertero's lack of endorsement prevented the proposal from going any further. After listening to these ideas and other condescending comments about Indians by ministers, I'd leave the meetings in very bad shape, feeling both depressed and even physically ill."

Jorge then related a curious turn of events. "The marchers were nearing the Yungas town of Yolosa, which is still five days of steep, uphill marching from La Paz. At that juncture, I was receiving pressure to leave the government from both sides of the conflict. Carlos and Zulema were badgering me to quit and leap over to join them. They argued such a move would undermine the government's increasingly untenable position.

"Simultaneously, several cabinet members, pressured by private sector interests, were calling for my dismissal given my connection to CID-DEBENI. So here I was caught in this cross-fire, squeezed like a piece of sandwich meat between these opposing camps. Frankly, I was confused about the next step to take in this drama.

"Then, in the midst of my bewilderment, out of the blue, I received this phone call from President Jaime Paz himself, on his personal line, requesting that I have lunch immediately with Chaca Rivera, his indigenous affairs director, and himself to talk about the march. The initiative came as a surprise as Jaime Paz had never shown the slightest interest in the march during cabinet meetings I had attended, nor had he ever consulted me about it. Rather, his attitude had been one of complete indifference. So the three of us sat down together for the longest lunch in my life. Paz insisted on hearing the whole story from start to finish, beginning with the Jesuit missions, and covering the rubber boom, the Loma Santa movement, the agrarian reform, and the revitalization of the cabildo for the focus on territorial rights. This conversation went on for about six or seven hours until Paz suddenly got up from his chair, leaned over to shake my hand, and said, 'You're right, it's a just cause. Get my secretary on the phone. Tomorrow I want the entire cabinet to make the trip to Yolosa for a meeting with the marchers.'

"Although I was not invited, I learned from friends that cabinet members were very put off by the inconveniences of the three-hour trip and the obligation to sit together with such low-status Indians. Jaime Paz, on the other hand, mingled a great deal and listened to the discussions and speeches with apparent interest and tolerance. He had to listen, for example, to a very angry, polemical speech right under his nose from Tomás

Ticuasu, about indigenous people as foreigners in their own land, deprived of rights taken for granted by other citizens.

"Despite all this, the government's negotiations again fell short of meeting the indigenous demands with regards to Chimane Forest. Even in the face of this stumbling block, however, I'm convinced that Jaime Paz, then and there, decided to recognize the indigenous territorial demands despite unrelenting pressures to the contrary from the private sector.

"I suspect two things were behind the president's change of heart. International pressure was beginning to take its toll on his psyche through a bombardment of international faxes, cables, and newspaper articles landing at the national palace. Equally important, it had probably dawned on him that there was great public relations potential in signing decrees for indigenous territorial rights under the spotlight of the media in La Paz. It promised a windfall of favorable publicity. His presidential prestige would soar if he appeared as the benevolent patriarch reaching down to aid the needy and abused indigenous peoples. He's a savvy politician and knew the palace would make a more spectacular stage set for image-making than the dusty, grubby town of Yolosa." Other observers, however, argued that it was the intransigent indigenous themselves who wanted to take the final negotiations to La Paz to continue building favorable public opinion pressure and bask in the capital's national spotlight for their efforts.

Back at the march itself, beyond Yolosa the marchers had to travel a one-lane gravel road replete with switchbacks and hairpin turns, and a continuous flow of on-coming traffic. The climb became steeper as they moved from 6,000 ft. above sea level to 8,000 and then 10,000 feet, all the while advancing up huge mountains, down into high valleys, and up steep slopes again. The cold and the oxygen shortage in the high altitudes of the Andes slowed the pace of the lowland marchers, causing people to temporarily drop out and seek assistance from a Red Cross team closely monitoring the situation. In addition to altitude-related fatigue and light-headedness, the cold temperatures, rain, sleet, and frost stymied the marchers as well. The tropical lowland peoples were once so engulfed by an eerie mountain mist that it seemed to them that they were passing into an Andean abyss. Fortunately, church teams showed up in a truck to distribute warm woolen blankets, new sandals, used winter clothing, and white pup tents suitable for sleeping outdoors in the high Andes.

Upon reaching the altiplano terrain, the marchers found a treeless land-scape with a light snow cover. Small llama herds meandered below huge faces of grey rock jutting upwards towards the imposing Cordillera Oriental. The marchers had one final victorious stop before descending en masse into the bowl-shaped capital city. The ceremonial site, known as the *cumbre* (summit), situated at 15,000 feet was the high point of the journey. A long banner with Bolivia's national colors, checkerboard wiphala flags, and bright Andean weavings with colorful striped designs had been mounted twenty feet or so above the assembled crowd. Several hundred highlanders stood waving and chanting congratulations, while others in colorful cos-tumes had already begun dancing to the lively sounds of Andean drum and panpipe melodies.

This sacred peak has long been a place where the Andean peoples made offerings to the Pachamama and other mountain deities. The sacred peak now became a symbolic "intercultural" meeting ground for the lowland and highland peoples. When the two groups came together at the cumbre they were re-writing Bolivia's national development model to embrace cultural pluralism.

At the summit ceremony, representatives of the CSUTCB (the inde-pendent national peasant union founded by Genaro Flores and the Kataristas in 1979) outfitted Marcial, Tomás, and Ernesto with *chullos* (stocking caps), *chuspas* (small hand-woven bags), and ponchos, and then covered them with confetti, streamers, and wreaths. Several shamans stepped forth to perform the classic "wilanchu ceremony" sacrificing a live llama and sprinkling its blood over the Pachamama.

Also standing on the windy mountaintop, surrounded by hundreds of joyful indigenous people, were members of several other highland develop-ment projects with which I had been involved. Luis Ticona and several AIGACAA leaders were gathered around the sacrificial llama they had just delivered by truck from the El Alto headquarters of the camelid herders' federation. Most of the visitors from AIGACAA would proceed to La Paz on foot with the marchers. In addition, standing to one side, there was a group of CIMCA "educadoras populares," another altiplano group sup-ported by the IAF anxious to march down the hill in solidarity with the people of southern Beni. It was moving to learn that the indigenous people from vastly different geographies and cultures with whom I had had the pleasure of working had come together in this way. It was also impressive to see the unification in light of the political tension that had long existed between the highland and lowland political federations. Since its birth CIDOB had wanted its confederation to be independent of a larger national confederation centered in La Paz for fear that the Aymara and Quechua agenda would dominate and marginalize their own.

After passionate speeches by leaders of different ethnic groups and regions, the highland and lowland groups fused into one solid mass of activists and headed down the mountainside shoulder to shoulder into the world's highest capital. Most of the lowlanders were about to see the capital city and reveal Amazonian peoples to its residents for the first time.

Although I was unable to stay in Bolivia for the grand finale, I received Jorge's report on this last leg. He told me what he did when the march reached the outskirts of La Paz. "Since I had not been to visit the march over the thirty-four days, I could not resist taking a long look when I heard it was close to the city. I went up by myself to Villa Fatima, the first barrio they would come to as they entered the far side of the city. I stood on a hillside, not in any official capacity but in my jeans and workshirt, watching them go by amidst dozens of cheering, admiring Aymara migrants. Don Ernesto Noe, a man of fifty-five years, was taking such heavy, deliberate steps, I realized how exhausted these marchers must be. Perhaps the flow of adrenaline from the large and joyous welcoming party sustained them during the final miles. Recognizing friends, I thought back to the long nightly meetings with elder Mojeños discussing their Loma Santa journeys, and time spent with young people reflecting that the hour had arrived for them to begin taking a collective stand on cultural and social rights. As I watched, I thought to myself how they had become a kind of 'mouse that roared' while proudly walking along this Andean mountaintop for the first time in modern history with the eyes of a nation on them."

By nightfall, the marchers had completed their cross-town trek in the capital and were making a gallant entry into the Plaza Murillo where spotlights from the Presidential Palace, National Congress building, and Cathedral illuminated the triumphal laps before yet another large crowd of jubilant well-wishers. Remaining in front, Marcial kept waving to the enthusiastic spectators on different sides of the street. Perhaps one Aymara bystander captured the sentiment of many when he turned to a friend of mine, sociologist Ruth Llanos, and exclaimed, "Why look at those clothes, they're not savages after all. They're just like us!" All day this Aymara had been hauling foodstuffs donated by market women to the marchers at various distribution points along their capital city route. Yet he had never laid eyes on them and in effect expressed a racist stereotypical image which had long pervaded in this capital city.

The final public act of the long day was a solemn high Mass celebrated by the archbishop of La Paz that included participation by one of Bolivia's popular folk singers, Luis Rico. The archbishop closed the service with the following words. "You've walked toward the Loma Santa not only today but over many years. You've shown your faces to the nation in a splendid way. You've denounced the unjust situation in which you've found yourselves, requesting urgent, effective, and concrete solutions to your demands. Your methods have avoided offending anyone, with either insults, cheating, or false statements. You have simply made a direct petition, without frills, requesting the blind of our country to open their eyes and see the injustice directed toward our indigenous peoples." Following the Mass, José Nuñez, the professional overseeing CEMSE's student volunteer program, appeared, accompanied by student leaders from MINKA, to lead a group of marchers to CEMSE for overnight accommodations just three blocks away.

The next day the capital city was buzzing over the presence of hundreds of indigenous marchers. Stories of their protest and heroism filled the newspapers and television screens. After five weeks of intensive public exposure, the indigenous groups of the Southern Beni appeared to have won the hearts and minds of the nation. Yet the marchers had to persist for two additional days of negotiations, and even threaten a hunger strike, before they finally carried the day. At this triumphant moment in the national capital, who should appear at the side of the Beni indigenous peoples but the leaders of CIDOB anxious to reunify the country's lowland indigenous movement and share in the hard-earned glory. This transparently self-serving act had the positive function of uniting the two regions of the lowlands for a common struggle that would go on and on for many years into the future.

On the 24th of September, 1990, the president and the entire Bolivian cabinet sat at the table with Marcial and other indigenous leaders to sign into law four decrees granting indigenous territorial rights and indigenous organizational autonomy: 1,100,000 hectares to the Mojeños, Trinitarios, and Yuracarés in the Territorio Indígena Parque Nacional Isiboro-Sécure (TIPNIS) (Indigenous Territory of the Isiboro-Sécure Park), 355,000 hectares and 420,000 hectares in two places to the Chimanes, Mojeños, and Ignacianos of the Chimane Forest, and finally 30,000 hectares of savanna for the Sirionó. The affected ranchers and timber companies were to be relocated to other production areas. A fourth decree called for the formulation of a law that would establish rights for all the indigenous peoples of the Bolivian lowlands.

The elation of the march infused several events occurring over the course of the week. The La Paz Prefect, an enthusiastic early convert to the cause, threw a wedding party at his private home for two young marchers from different ethnic groups who had met and fallen in love while marching together. Leaders, including Marcial, were invited to chair national university forums on indigenous rainforest conservation. Bolivia's two best professional soccer teams invited the marchers' winning indigenous team to play in a preliminary game in the national stadium before thousands of enthusiastic fans. And to cap such an arduous, self-sacrificing effort, the indigenous participants returned to the Beni on chartered Hercules aircraft, a free and once-in-a-lifetime ride. This deluxe trip was especially gratifying for many marchers expecting to make the return trip the same step by step way they had arrived.

THE LONG MARCH REVISITED

Five years after the march, in 1995, I went to interview Zulema Lehm at the CIDDEBENI office for an update on progress in the new territories. Had the indigenous territorial rights decrees created a new model for land tenure and environmental conservation in the country? Or were they just "wet pieces of paper," similar to North American treaties with Native American peoples, that would not be upheld in practice?

The IAF had been funding CIDDEBENI for a variety of training activities for the ethnic groups in the new TIPNIS with $60,000 yearly. Indeed, the march seemed to have opened the floodgates of international funding, and there were concerns about overwhelming the indigenous management capacity with so many new programs. It was another expression of the new "indigenous chic" taking hold throughout the world. The Dutch, the Danes, the Swedes, and the United Nations had become enthralled with the indigenous territories as a new legal concept in land tenure and as a grassroots management system for saving the Amazon's rainforests. CIDDEBENI itself had its hands full in managing eight different project grants from foreign donors.

As CIDDEBENI's director, and having just completed her master's thesis on the march, Zulema Lehm began by saying, "The story of the march does not end when the indigenous marchers fly off into the horizon and live happily ever after in their newly acquired territories. The march was really just the opening, obviously an important and spectacular one, to an era during which issues of territorial management and natural resource protection have become paramount. So in a sense, we're all still engaged in a long march that will continue indefinitely with the inevitable ups and downs. The private sector interest lobbies have pressured the current MNR government to have the legality of the decrees annulled since they had not been approved by congressional vote. Nonetheless, our work is proceeding as though the territories truly belonged to the indigenous groups that made the long march.

"One necessary first step, with help from the IAF and other donors, was for us to acquire comprehensive training in subjects such as community planning, environmental legislation, first aid, and techniques for demarcating boundaries and protecting natural resources. There was a tremendous dearth of management skills of all kinds, given the poor quality of schooling in the rural Beni and historic exclusion of these peoples from needed experiences.

"For example, we needed the skills to demarcate the new territories right away, as this task would be a long-term one, due to the huge tracts of terrain involved. After the government reneged on its promise to survey and demarcate the territory, the indigenous organizations had to do the job themselves, using the educational and technical programs of CIDDEBENI and other NGOs.

"The Sirionó are perhaps the farthest along in demarcating their territory. In spite of conflicts with cattle ranchers over their savanna lands, the Sirionó team has demarcated 50 percent of their territory, and finally received some technical support from the government to continue this effort.

"The Sirionós have also demonstrated an increasing facility in their negotiations with cattle ranchers and government representatives over conflicting land claims within the territory. To date, nine of the original fourteen ranches occupying savannas there have either been removed or significantly reduced in size. The other five ranches are owned by people with political clout, or people holding public office in the Bolivian congress, so they have not yet been removed. Several ranchers have legal land titles procured under the military dictatorship after dispossessing the Indian population. Also the Sirionó lands usurped by the Beni's public university have been returned to them. The Sirionó are certainly making good progress. Some of them have even become proficient in reading satellite imagery for modern map-making purposes.

"The news from TIPNIS, the former Isiboro-Sécure park, is also a mixed picture. The fact that it is the largest national park in Bolivia, with over one million hectares, partially explains why only 27 percent of its expanse has been demarcated by the indigenous team. Also, work has been suspended from time to time due to a shortage of funds earmarked for this purpose.

"One major achievement is the near completion of a management plan designating land use zones within TIPNIS. Producing such a comprehensive, technical plan is no small undertaking. It has required preliminary studies of local economies, land use (including pasturelands) patterns, and a biological inventory. New participatory map-making techniques have spurred greater participation by the Mojeños, Yucararés, and Trinitarios and served to tap their indigenous knowledge for practical ends. Presently, a study is underway to determine the sustainability of reviving the cattle economy in the natural savanna pastureland of the territories.

"TIPNIS has its own cadre of indigenous park police called territory guards. They are outfitted with police uniforms, use two-way radios, and patrol the territory's back trails. They've succeeded in stopping illegal poaching and trafficking in animal hides as well as halting the operations of the small-scale sawmills. Once the natural resource management plan is completed, their work will expand to include monitoring and conservation of the resources.

"Another important legacy of the march has been an improvement in indigenous leadership skills, especially in negotiations with outside political and economic groups. Recently, for example, the territory guards came across and detained two foreign technicians sent by a foreign private company to carry out oil prospecting in TIPNIS. The Bolivian government had issued them a permit without consulting with CEPIB. After their vocal protests, the Bolivian government agreed to meet with CEPIB and CIDOB leaders to rectify the situation. It was a clear violation of the country's new environmental codes.

"To gear up for challenges from oil companies, the groups have used technical and legal assistance provided by Ecuadorian lawyers with long track records in disputes with oil companies. As a result, the groups have been able to hammer out new agreements with the government for mechanisms such as environmental impact studies and codes of good conduct, giving leverage to CEPIB and CIDOB in negotiating future contracts with foreign firms. Indigenous representatives also went to Ecuador to examine the horrific environmental damage wrought by years of oil production activities.

"The biggest headache in TIPNIS continues to be the colonists in the south. A red line has held up for several years as the northern boundary to coca cultivation yet the colonists went to La Paz last year on their own march, and signed agreements that failed to acknowledge the existence of TIPNIS and their indigenous authorities. It really made the blood here boil to be betrayed in this way after earlier accords. The whole picture— coercive coca eradication schemes, forcible removal of peasant families, the bombing of roads [used as landing strips by traffickers], and numerous other human rights violations—complicates our work. Even a territory guard wound up in jail mistaken as a drug trafficker when operating his radio transmitter.

"The Chimane Forest was the battleground necessitating the march in the first place. Sadly, that site continues to be full of difficult problems. Five years have gone by and six of the seven timber companies in the forest are continuing to operate sawmills and export mahogany lumber to the United States. The difference is that several hundred private chain-saw operators from the town of San Borja now cut the mahogany down and sell it to the local mills owned by the firms that lost their concessions in the forest. Technically their activities are not a violation of the law, but disruptive effects on indigenous community life remain the same.

"The indigenous leaders in the Chimane Forest are not as innocent as one might hope, and thus must share in the blame. The government's own local forestry office is one of the prime wheeler dealers in these corrupt commercial dealings. There are so many entangled interests that it is beginning to resemble the illicit cocaine trade of parts of Chapare to the south.

"The people of the Chimane have not completely abandoned hope. A natural resource management plan has been developed for sustainable forestry management, and hopefully the indigenous will obtain international certification to carry out this plan. The demarcation of seventy-eight kilometers and thirty-nine kilometers respectively in the two territories is another sign of modest progress. The Chimanes and Mojeños have also shown a wonderful talent for graphically displaying the flora, fauna, rivers, settlement patterns, and small agricultural garden plots scattered throughout the forest in community map-making workshops."

A View from the Capital City

Over these five years, the lingering impact of the march outside the Beni was perhaps even more impressive than inside. I would often hear references in the media and elsewhere to the "historic march" that was a turning point in the role of the lowland indigenous group in national life. NGO professionals and the indigenous leaders continued to dwell on its significance in workshops and seminars and tell others in Latin America about it often, showing videos of the march at international conferences and workshops. President Paz Zamora himself fashioned a new political discourse on indigenous affairs following the march. A popular book, *Etapa de una Larga Marcha* (The Episode of a Long March) by journalist Alex Contreras, containing testimonies from the indigenous marchers in addition to maps and photographs, enjoyed a wide reception in the public as well.

José Pinelo, the ex-director of the largest NGO network in Bolivia, told me the first Indigenous Peoples Fund in Latin America, founded by Paz Zamora, would be included among the march's final fruits. "Paz Zamora convinced other Latin American heads of state to support the creation of this new fund, and persuaded the Inter-American Development Bank to provide preliminary institutional sponsorship. In both his speeches launching the idea in the Latin American Presidents' Conference in Guadalajara, and in the Bank's Washington, D.C., headquarters, he told the story of descending from the capital down into the dusty town of Yolosa to meet the Amazonian peoples and hear their demands. The fund will tap bilateral and multilateral agencies, and channel monies directly to the indigenous organizations themselves." Pinelo also attributed the 1994 passage of a pathbreaking constitutional reform that redefined Bolivia as a "multi-ethnic, pluri-cultural" state to the march's impact. "Just to make sure, CIDOB and CEPIB leaders were lobbying behind the scenes almost right up to the last minute."

The march's international effects were manifested in a similar march among the Amazonian peoples in Ecuador. In 1992, the members of two Ecuadorian federations copied these tested tactics for their peoples by marching for fifteen days, and camping for two additional weeks in down-town Quito, securing territorial rights for the first time in history. The whole protest endeavor also took exactly thirty-four days!

I also heard that the term "territory" was catching on at the local level in the highlands. In Rayqaypampa, for instance, sindicato leaders and Yana-pakunas, inspired by the march, had begun using this more inclusive politi-cal term to connote indigenous control and ownership of the entire physical landscape encompassing their communities.

And in 1994 Marcial Fabricano took his discourse on territorial rights to the Annual Festival of American Folklife on the National Mall in the program of "Culture and Development" jointly sponsored by the Inter-American Foundation and the Smithsonian. Marcial held workshops on the history of the indigenous march and the ongoing quest for territorial and citizenship rights in Bolivia and the Americas for an interested public during the July 4th period.

To round out my understanding of the march and its effects, I sched-uled an interview with Aymara Vice-president Cárdenas to learn about the march's importance from his vantage point within Bolivia's national power structure. He spoke passionately about the march's lasting impact.

"Prior to the march, a colonial vision of the eastern lowland's diverse indigenous peoples dominated in this country. The prevailing conventional view was that native groups using little clothing were much less human than the rest of us, and that the rainforest was practically uninhabited. This vision could be found not only among the elites but also within the middle and lower classes. The march served to transform this vision as, for the first time, these peoples not only had a human face, but demonstrated an ability to negotiate their interests with the powers that be as well as or perhaps better than experienced political actors.

"This radical change in perspective led to a more profound vision of a multicultural democracy for Bolivia. For the first time in history, Trinitar-ios, Mojeños, Guaraníes, and other lowland ethnic groups had reached the center of political power in this country. In the past, these interests received a hearing only through an occasional outspoken priest visiting the capital from the Beni, or in solitary denunciations by a human rights group of abuses to Indian workers on some cattle ranch.

"It was not only the conservative sectors of the most powerful eco-nomic elites that demonstrated a lack of interest in these people, but the intellectuals, labor, and political party leaders as well. I don't remember ever having heard of a group of political activists here in the capital concerned about, say, the problems of the Mojeños people. The Mojeños and the others were simply invisible. The march gave the eastern lowland ethnic groups a national political profile for the first time. This kind of change in access to power and perceptions of ethnic minorities is a big step forward in the construction, from the ground up, of a truly representative, multi-ethnic democracy that exists in practice as well as on paper. This democracy now ensures respect for the languages of the indigenous groups, and regards their democratic traditions as important to our national patrimony.

"The principle of multiculturalism advanced greatly by the march is also relevant to socioeconomic development in Bolivia. Under the neocolonialist paradigm, our indigenous peoples were being asked to commit suicide, to negate themselves and their cultures so that conventional development could roll along its course, remolding our country's social and economic institutions unimpeded. The march has put us on a different path, and established our country's multiple cultural, linguistic, and historic identity at the heart of a broad-based development destiny."

THE LEY INRA

Vice-president Cárdenas had taken these words to heart when several years earlier he created the subsecretariat of ethnicity, one of the few government agencies directly under his domain. They in turn were under the new Secretariat of Ethnicity, Gender, and Generation led by Ramiro Molina Barrios, whose resume included a book on llama caravans, long-term work at an ethnographic museum, and coordinating a cultural revitalization project with the Urus Muratos peoples of Oruro. This subsecretariat of ethnicity, another fruit of the 1990 march, was set up to facilitate the state's relationship with the increasingly sophisticated and determined indigenous organizations of the eastern lowlands. One of the first issues on their joint agenda was to gain collective legal titles for the indigenous peoples of the Beni along with a handful of ethnic groups from several other regions. Subsequently, in the face of the rising demands from a spreading territorial rights movement, this subsecretariat and agrarian reform functionaries had to respond to the demands of indigenous peoples in Santa Cruz, Chuquisaca, and Tarija as well.

The leader of the subsecretariat was Luz Maria Calvo, one of the architects of CENDA's cultural mobilization strategy (see chapter 13). She and her senior colleague from another office, Isabel Lavadenz, coordinated technical studies on resource management strategies to expedite legal titling that had proven to be so elusive for securing the designated territories under the previous government. Calvo deployed the same research framework for examining natural resource management strategies pioneered by CENDA in Rayqaypampa. Her office gave positive encouragement and technical guidance to the numerous lowland ethnic groups that had been galvanized into action by the historic march. Of course, there were other more powerful ministries within the Sánchez de Lozada government beholden to the agribusiness, timber, and ranching sectors adamantly opposing indigenous land rights. When the government's land rights bill neared its final version, lobbying and protests from all sides of the political spectrum greatly intensified. The agri-elite groups from Santa Cruz and the Beni, for example, were able to cut drastically the newly stipulated tax rates on their rural properties. In contrast, new political mobilizations by indigenous federations, a passionate speech to the Bolivian congress by Marcial Fabricano, and some midnight-hour dramatic politicking by Víctor Hugo Cárdenas helped to carry the day in pushing through territorial rights legislation. The Ley del Servicio Nacional de Reforma Agraria (INRA) (Ley No. 1750) was a controversial product of these negotiations, protests, and the long social process set into motion by the 1990 march. The Ley INRA granted rights to twenty-four discrete indigenous territories (legally referred to as *tierras communales de origen* to defuse the highly charged political overtones the term had attained) for numerous indigenous peoples. In subsequent years, sixteen other territorial demands became incorporated into the law to raise the sum total of affected lands to 11,744,509 hectares (de Vries 1998).[6] With the passage of this law, the cumulative effects of the 1990 march had reached a new milestone. Even organizations pursuing indigenous rights in the Western highlands such as THOA, the Aymara oral history workshop, were able to use the law's clause on tierras communales de origen in their 1990s' campaign to convert sindicatos back to ayllus. Although the Ley INRA's implementation has been slow and shaky for political, technocratic, and bureaucratic reasons, especially during the Banzer administration, the indigenous peoples across the vast lowlands of Bolivia now had a legal instrument for waging their long-term land rights struggles for greater social justice and political autonomy. For them, the long march continues.

CHAPTER 15

Blazing a Trail of Multicultural Grassroots Development for a New Millennium

The publishers of the 1900 census predicted that in a few years the indigenous race if not completely erased from national life, at least would be reduced to a minimum. They did not expect that one hundred years later we would be speaking of 'originarios' who are very much alive and now have even reformulated the Bolivian nation-state to be multi-ethnic, pluricultural, and maybe even plurinational.

ALBÓ (1999)

In the previous chapters I have told a story of grassroots development through the prism of nine Bolivian case histories. In this concluding chapter I distill from the case histories and some of the other Bolivian material key factors that contributed to their relative success. While I am trying to suggest some of the reasons that enabled the Bolivian organizations to enjoy some success, I am not offering a universal recipe for grassroots development to be applied elsewhere. My intent is a much more modest exercise in learning lessons from the Bolivian story.

It is imperative that development aid agencies and citizens, whose tax dollars finance projects in Latin America and elsewhere in the Third World, be able to recognize a good project from a developmental dead-end. The criteria I used in judging a project relatively successful, and therefore worthy of inclusion in the volume, looked at the ability of an organization to rejuvenate local cultural and biological resources and transform these resources into an ongoing flow of benefits valued by cash-poor communities. Said very simply, these projects improved the quality of local peoples' lives. They did not catapult the members of these communities into the middle class but they affected peoples' lives in tangible and meaningful ways. Examples of these improvements include increased family income levels, improved access to basic consumer goods (food, shelter, etc.), better health and nutrition, improved skills (critical analysis of society, leadership, literacy, business, and farming). The projects often profoundly changed the local peoples' self-esteem and self-confidence, and they gained respect within their wider neo-colonial society. This last improvement—in the status of the indigenous community—often helped to alter stereotypes about indigenous peoples commonly held by political and social elites and even by foreign donor representatives. Another criteria of success were projects that enabled local communities to exert greater control over their environments, including conserving local natural resources.[1]

The longitudinal perspective I was able to take made it easier to assess the lasting impact of both the crises and the breakthroughs in projects. I profiled organizations that mustered enough staying power to work through innumerable difficulties over time. Hyperinflation and currency devaluation, a sudden drop in prices for a key cash crop, or natural calamities such as crop disease and drought can unexpectedly undo the best development plans. Problems of internal factionalism, institutional splits, corruption, and management and technical inadequacies can compound project difficulties. Successful management of a development organization requires an ability to prevent these problems from either undermining the organization or overwhelming the project. The projects described in this book overcame severe challenges.

By following the organizational histories the reader can observe how successful projects first emerge, then adapt to the complexities around them, and take methodical, incremental steps to consolidate programs while steadily increasing the number of people and communities participating. Sometimes an organization took as long as eight to ten years to pace its endeavors and handle more easily the full array of ever increasing project activities and innumerable problems. The next ten years of grassroots development will most likely present comparable difficulties and institutional stresses for these organizations.

These successful developmental organizations also chipped away at institutional barriers blocking the appreciation and use of indigenous cultural resources. Sometimes this was a steady, piecemeal effort, while other times institutional barriers fell in response to one or more dramatic events. All nine projects began as obscure, fledgling organizations and wound up widely respected for their local niche. All of the projects described in the book demonstrate the art of "social learning" (Korten 1990)—another key element in successful development. Feedback mechanisms, such as community assemblies, internal evaluation meetings, or directed research, guided project leaders to make necessary adjustments in their plans and methodologies in accordance with community members' reports on project activities.

THE CULTURAL REVITALIZATION-INDIGENIZATION ELEMENTS OF A MODEL THAT PROMOTES SUCCESSFUL GRASSROOTS DEVELOPMENT

In my assessments of the Bolivian projects, I also evaluated the effectiveness with which cultural resources were utilized. During the 1990s indigenous culture became better appreciated as a bona fide, multi-faceted resource for local development. My work, and that of the IAF, adhered to this orientation more than a decade before it became fashionable. In addition to those in Bolivia, indigenous movements in Mexico, Guatemala, Ecuador, Brazil, Panama, and Colombia contributed greatly to the demise of assimilationist development policies and the passage of new laws protecting indigenous rights and resources (Albó 1990b, 1991; Yashar 1998; Van Cott 1994).

The concept of indigenous culture as used in this book resonates with that put forth by Thierry Verhelst, who believed that every aspect of life in indigenous communities should be considered as an important resource (Verhelst 1990, 17). A focus on local resources fosters greater self-awareness and self-reliance in communities and fuels the desire of local people to conserve those resources for present and future generations. Viewed from a macro-level perspective, at the level of the nation-state, emphasis on Bolivia's biological and cultural resources opened up a more self-directed and self-controlled process of socioeconomic change for the country as a whole. Taking the micro-level view, the point of view of the individual Indian, this emphasis on indigenous resources can bring material gain and can liberate local people from the shame and sense of inferiority that have gone hand in hand with being a colonized person.

The cultural-revitalization approach to development builds upon rather than squashes the complex local indigenous knowledge systems. The approach enhanced resources which already enjoyed a variety of deep-seated cultural meanings within indigenous communities. Cultural resources have typically been located at the center of indigenous cosmovision, holding together the worlds of the symbolic and the mundane, the spiritual and the natural, within a complex set of social and economic relationships. By evoking emotional attachments, indigenous cultural resources potently rally and focus the mobilization of community energies on paths toward developmental gains and indigenous rights.

At the same time, I must temper these remarks by saying that cultural resources are not a universal solution for global problems of poverty and underdevelopment. Unfortunately, there are no "magic bullets" in development anywhere, including the free market. Nor are these culturally centered approaches so pure as to exclude cultural elements, resources, and ideas of Western origin. The idea behind the cultural revitalization development strategy is not to exclude categorically contributions from other, and particularly Western, cultures, but to give a moral and material boost to indigenous resources and perspectives to compensate for decades of discrimination by neo-colonial practices and Western-minded development agencies.

In searching for an apt term to capture the kind of social change process going on in these projects, I found "multicultural development" to be more appropriate than "ethno-development," as the latter might lure development planners into an ethnocentric trap that plagued the Western modernizers at the other extreme. Bolivian anthropologist Xavier Albó refers to this peculiar cultural balancing act as "radical bilingualism," a term he borrowed from a fellow Jesuit. Albó uses the metaphor of a tree whose trunk and deep root system symbolizes indigenous cultural identity while the higher, leafy branches represent elements from other cultures deliberately grafted on in a careful, discriminating manner (Albó 1996b). With the trunk of the tree forming a positive sense of cultural identity, all cultures may interact on equal terms rather than in the classic dominant-subordinate hierarchies.

The Critics of Project-Based Cultural Revitalization

While a number of U.S. social scientists (Huntington 1996; Verhelst 1990; Kleymeyer 1994; Fischer and Brown 1996; Warren, Slikkerveer, and Brokensha 1995) have pointed to the significance of indigenous culture within

Third World development in recent years, a group of postmodern critics has parted company with them, contending that there are no real alternatives within any development framework to the problems of Western domination. Citing five decades of misguided efforts to impose a universal Western model on Third World peoples, this group of intellectuals doubts the very concept of development itself, and by implication regards with skepticism the whole notion of indigenous-led development (A. Escobar 1995; Fergusen 1990).

Arturo Escobar sums up this sweeping view:

Development was and continues to be for the most part a top-down, ethno-centric and technocratic approach, which treated people and cultures as abstract concepts, statistical figures to be moved up and down in the charts of 'progress'. Development was conceived not as cultural progress (culture was a residual variable to disappear with the advance of modernization) but instead as a system of more or less universalizing, applicable technical interventions intended to deliver some 'badly needed' goods to a 'target' population. It comes as no surprise that development became a force so destructive to Third World cultures, ironically in the name of peoples' interest. (A. Escobar 1995, 44)

Yet anti-developmentalists such as Escobar and others appear strikingly vague and ill-informed when they consider alternatives to the situation they describe. Escobar exhorts anthropologists "to study forms and processes of resistance to development intervention," apparently efforts such as the on-going work of anthropologists in the style of a Xavier Albó or Juergen Riester, who have gone far beyond Escobar's recommendation. They have studied and fostered community resistance to externally imposed development schemes, but they have also participated in alternative projects rooted in popular participation and respect for native values. The postmodern critics tend to dismiss development projects as inevitably futile exercises, regardless of their size, operating style, and focus. They label all development projects as manifestations of the conventional Western practices that have produced few benefits for the world's vast impoverished population. This thesis glosses over the impressive range of project initiatives emerging throughout the Third World that have genuinely empowered the poor and the oppressed (Verhelst 1990; Warren, Slikkerveer, and Brokensha

1995; Kleymeyer 1994; Fischer and Brown 1996; Healy 1996; Uphoff and Esman 1984; Uphoff, Esman, and Krishna 1998).

This volume, by contrast, offers a picture of small-scale projects as important crucibles in which indigenous cultural resources become rediscovered, reworked, and imbued with value for the purposes of achieving community-friendly development and broader social and economic change in a society. Local projects are the turf where multiculturalism and biodiversity meet and cross-fertilize. The projects I have described here merely hint at the resource-rich landscape of rural communities.

Escobar's critique of Western-style development projects calls into question not only the work of development anthropologists at agencies such as the World Bank and USAID but the programs of smaller aid agencies, such as the IAF, engaged in "people to people" programs.

Even in the case of seemingly progressive grassroots projects, such as those sponsored by the Inter-American Foundation and Cultural Survival, some of these [externally imposed Western] mechanisms surface despite the good intentions of the researchers. For instance, this occurs even when the donors seek to give control of a project to the community and to 'valorize' local knowledge. The fact that it is the donor who determines what is to be 'valorized,' and how, is problematic. Communities, on the other hand, have to adopt organizational forms and project designs that the donor can recognize if they are to have access to project funds, even if those forms may not respect community traditions. Since often the donors still function within the project view of development, commitment to local culture and autonomy is replaced by commitment to a project. Cultural self-definitions thus frequently remain invisible and, in some cases, are unwittingly suppressed. (A. Escobar 1991)

One wonders what Escobar would make of the "feminist" educators of CIMCA, or CIDAC's multicultural artisan revival, or of CENDA's comprehensive cultural revitalization program. All of these groups forged a developmental strategy from the praxis of community change rather than on a donor agency's proclivities. The cacao bean farmers belonging to El Ceibo designed the structures and practices of the Western Rochdale cooperative model in line with Andean communal practices of democratic management. Several Bolivian projects sprouted their self-styled cultural resistance movements and local empowerment experiences (see chapters 8 and 14) that the postmodern writers on development might find appealing if they were willing to look in the right place with an open mind.

Escobar argues that communities and ethnic groups tend to suppress their own cultural definitions when faced with Western-style rural development agencies. The Third World is obviously full of such examples, yet it is also an oversimplification to say that grassroots development organizations such as those of CENDA and ASUR have ignored local definitions of community culture. In these two projects, it was the younger generation that had turned its back on valuable Andean cultural practices. The development anthropologists, with small inputs of aid, succeeded in transforming a declining economic milieu into a font of new opportunities for cash, cultural pride, and sustainable resource use.

THE PEOPLE TO PEOPLE DEVELOPMENT APPROACH

An important characteristic of the relatively successful projects was the "people to people" approach used by the project leaders and donor agencies. When the organizers of the projects looked at the communities with which they were concerned, they saw people who were disadvantaged, downtrodden, and discriminated against. Yet, instead of defining them as "target populations," passive "beneficiaries," or dependent people in need of "help," they appreciated the people for their past and present initiatives and impressive skills. The project leaders and organizers used operating styles and organizing methodologies that met the participating communities on their own terms rather than employing the methods and terms of an outside bureaucracy or urban interest group. Nor when beginning to work with them did they assume their own ideas or technologies to be superior. They began by learning rather than teaching. Over time a mutual respect and trust grew up within these projects, enabling the different social groups to work together effectively. The people-to-people approach recognizes the dignity of the human person, communities' potential for continual self-improvement, and the need for solidarity and genuine support. It also recognizes the need to begin development projects on a small, humanly manageable scale and to take measured, incremental steps in moving forward.

SEVENTEEN KEY FACTORS FOR SUCCESSFUL
DEVELOPMENT IN BOLIVIA'S PROJECTS

1: Popular Participation

The absolutely fundamental element for successful grassroots development is popular participation. The case histories in this volume illustrate the importance of popular participation and tend to reinforce the large body of literature that has emerged during the 1980s and 1990s that documents the impressive benefits of the popular participation approach to organize developmental change in rural areas (Uphoff and Esman 1984; Uphoff, Esman, and Krishna 1998; Korten 1990; Carroll 1992; Bebbington and Thiele 1993). Over the past few decades, this insight about the key role of civil society in development has spread from organizations like the IAF and OXFAM-America to small units within the World Bank, USAID, and the Inter-American Development Bank: institutions where the top-down, centralized approach had always prevailed.

In my examination of the nine relatively successful projects, I identified six actions of popular participation that enabled successful development: community self-management, training of local people, popular education, the effective use of local paraprofessionals, educating selected grassroots participants to be professionals, and the execution of strategies for collective empowerment.

Community Self-Management. A commitment to participatory development and community self-management is a key element of all the development efforts presented in this book. The development stories presented in the indigenous agro-export sector illustrate how groups of small farmers managed their own agro-service and enterprise programs over several decades. Even in the case projects administered jointly by an NGO and a community, the NGO-created programs to prepare grassroots actors to fill as many of the leadership, technical, and management tasks as possible. To accomplish this, the NGOs either tapped and strengthened existing organizations in the communities such as the sindicatos or local mutual aid groups (aynis, umaragas, and minkas) or else created new federations. Each NGO also had to invent its own unique institutional structure without the benefit of existing organizational blueprints and models, for none existed for this kind of innovative work.

Training of Local People. When local organizations set out to build solid structures of self-management and/or co-management with an NGO, community members almost always require training in grassroots development skills. Both NGOs and grassroots federations need to have at their disposal trustworthy community members or to hire staff from elsewhere for management tasks such as obtaining raw materials, preparing budgets, and keeping accurate records.

The deplorable condition of Bolivian public schooling is a major reason why training has been a critical element in the success of the participatory development projects. The absence of solid reading, writing, and math skills in these communities became immediately evident to the NGOs and federations. Such educational gaps caused both ASUR (the Andean weavings case), and CENDA (the native potatoes case) to back up and put together literacy and numeric training programs in place for community members. Much of the success of El Ceibo, for example, arguably the best economic grassroots organization in Bolivia, can be attributed to the effectiveness and constancy of its self-managed training programs to staff its large, ever rotating labor force and leadership.

Popular Education. Popular education was another essential component. Most of the training programs described in the book used popular education methodologies and techniques growing out of Paolo Freire's pioneering work. Beginning in the 1970s, Freire's writings helped spark a movement throughout the hemisphere to reform education from the bottom up. As part of his work, Freire promoted production of materials and programs of social communications tailored to the different social classes and cultural milieus inhabited by the poor. Rotafolios, puppet and radio shows, bilingual newspapers and newsletters, and adult training and educational workshops are examples of how popular education enabled the voices, views, skills, and cultural expressions of poor indigenous men, women, and youth to find important community outlets and build social empowerment.

Employment of Paraprofessionals. Another trademark of the participatory approach was the effective use of paraprofessional workers. Paraprofessionals like "barefoot doctors" in China and "credit promoters" of the Grameen Bank in Bangladesh have played a key role, most typically in preventing development organizations from becoming too top-heavy with highly paid professionals or from becoming socially distant from their communities (Esman et al. 1980). The projects described in this book show how the employment of paraprofessionals can be a critical component of development efforts when used in a non-patronizing and imaginative way. To offer a simple definition, paraprofessionals are the better-educated, motivated, and trained community members who, in effect, mediate across the divisions of social class culture that separate urban professionals from indigenous community members. In these projects, paraprofessionals educated community members over the radio and through fairs and festivals, supervised seedling tree nurseries, agri-research and livestock genetic improvement stations, and potato seed programs, provided health, accounting, credit, and agricultural extension services, taught literary classes, and traveled to provinces to spread their belief in a grassroots development model based on cultural revitalization.

Professional Education for Selected Grassroots Participants. The self-managed federations also tried to enhance the professional credentials of their key staff members by sending them away for more advanced training in the other countries of South America and in Europe as well to Bolivian universities. This, like the other efforts, promoted local participation in grassroots development by creating and funding scholarships for members. The organizations reduced dependency on professionals with dubious social commitments to local communities.

Group Empowerment. As part of any genuine grassroots development process, group empowerment occurs when community organizations federate into larger structures to achieve favorable economies of scale and greater political clout with respect to public and private development institutions. In these cases, a shift in the local balance of power allows the indigenous peasant farmers and artisans to assert themselves both in the marketplace and in local politics. Several of the project histories reveal how changes in commercial relationships led to the regulation of local prices that favored diverse groups of small farmers, herders, and weavers through the introduction of collectively organized marketing schemes. The development organizations increased prices paid to producers for their llamas, alpaca fiber, weavings, ceramics, quinoa, cacao beans, and to a lesser extent potatoes as well. New transport and marketing arrangements broke the commercial grip of a host of local and regional middlemen whose ranks included petty smugglers, itinerant traders, truck-owners, shopkeepers, industrialists, government officials, and private exporters.

Group empowerment is also manifest when grassroots organizations "scale-up" their image, impact, and community coverage. When ideas and activities from a single small-scale project zoom "outwards," the project can influence constituencies in other geographic areas. This aspect of empowerment confronts stereotypes about the isolated, small grassroots project whose positive impact on the poor always remains local, what is sometimes called the Potemkin village syndrome.

The Bolivian government sent ASUR and CIDAC to mount exhibits in Chile and represent Bolivia's finest native art. In Santa Cruz, CIDAC/ARTECAMPO brought the region's long-hidden and suppressed cultural roots to the attention of many Cruceños. AIGACCA's lobbying efforts on behalf of the llama paved the way for altiplano-based NGOs and university programs to gain full legal recognition for llama meat. CENDA made Rayqaypampa's knowledge of mountain farming technologies available to other development organizations in Cochabamaba through their own bilingual newspaper and seminars in the regional capital. Members of Rayqaypampa's "Consejo de Educación Communal" disseminated its experiences in educational empowerment via the regional rural sindicato network and influenced the national education reform law. CEMSE's multi-educational service center scaled-up in importance when its programs and educational concepts were also incorporated into the national education reform law. El Ceibo gained control over two thirds of the nation's cacao beans and became a premiere chocolate manufacturer-exporter and the pioneer producer of organic chocolate from South American rainforests. CECAOT's vindication of quinoa contributed to the opening of markets in Western nations. The March for Territory and Dignity set in motion political forces leading to constitutional amendments, bilingual and intercultural reforms, and hemisphere-wide funding initiatives for indigenous people.

These six elements—community self-management, training of local community members, popular education, effective use of paraprofessional education, educating selected grassroots participants to be professionals, and collective empowerment efforts—are critical components of the popular participation itself essential to successful grassroots development in these nine cases.

2: Tackling of Institutional Barriers and Discrimination

The development organizations reviewed in this volume stood out for their bold efforts to remove institutional barriers and dispute discriminatory practices. The willingness and insight to challenge institutional and societal patterns was another key component to the effectiveness of the nine local development groups. Anti-discriminatory and/or cultural promotional campaigns launched by the various organizations included educational festivals, bilingual and intercultural education, fairs for native arts, museum exhibits, and publications offering historical reflections about the exclusion of native Bolivians from full citizenship and their many contributions to building the nation. The indigenous march for territorial rights was an intensive thirty-four-day cultural campaign highlighting indigenous identities and their rightful claims long hidden from the nation.

3: Energetic and Committed Leadership

Another very important ingredient in the relative success of these projects was strong, energetic leadership. Talented, committed leaders are unique individuals who combine social vision, personal drive, and an analytical, problem-solving bent of mind with excellent management skills. They used project training opportunities, advanced education, on-the-job experiences, and travel to research centers and grassroots organizations outside of Bolivia to hone their skills. Their leadership qualities and technical skills were critically important for building a bedrock of trust, respect, and commitment in the participating communities. Their busy work schedules were a non-stop stream of organizational meetings, planning sessions, federation congresses, travel, visits to communities over the back roads, and meetings with public officials. It is hard to imagine the achievements of these projects having taken place without the emergence of an inspired, persevering, and skillful leadership from the local communities.

4: Resident Skill

The classic modernization theories and practices of the 1950s and 1960s regarded indigenous peoples as blank slates on whom Western expertise and values needed to be chalked in order to begin some developmental change. Economists under the spell of neo-classical economic development theory called this key process "human capital formation." Like other agencies and advisory groups of the era, they overlooked the vital skills, knowledge, values, and organizational practices of indigenous groups, and operated on the bias of a half truth at best. Resident knowledge and skill were, in fact, a bedrock of "human capital" already in place there and available for grassroots development.

5: Community Motivation and Tenacity

The active participation of the broader community also helped to lay a groundwork for relative success. Community member support has its limits, of course. Not all community members have the disposable time or are motivated to participate in the many activities of a grassroots development effort. Yet there was sufficient community support in all of the programs to enable them to function—often flourish—rather than wither from a lack of interest and trust.

Community tenacity propelled the projects along, for example, during periods of national economic crises such as hyperinflation and currency devaluations, onslaughts from a flood of imported agricultural and artisanal products, and in the face of droughts caused by global climatic cycles, such as El Niño events. Community persistence was a necessary trait for weathering internal as well as external storms. Rifts within the quinoa grower leadership, CENDA's professional team, and the federation's march to La Paz were all profound institutional upheavals.

While community commitment is central to a project's success, sometimes it can be counterproductive. El Ceibo's trucking fiasco, for instance, is an example of community tenacity gone overboard. For a while the El Ceibo community irrationally supported a costly transportation program that drained its leadership and morale and the federation's financial and economic resources. At times, a community eagerness can be a disadvantage because expectations may be long in being met; however, most often it is a critical factor in a development project's success.

6: Community Resource Mobilization

The nine projects featured here worked relatively well because the participating communities always channeled some of their own resources into the project activities. This in-kind support deepened commitment at the community level. Local participants contributed land, labor, local materials, and, in several of the self-managed organizations, occasionally made rare personal cash contributions as well. Many of the construction costs for training/meeting centers, weaving workshops, reforestation nurseries, fermentation and de-bittering plants, and alpaca fiber wholesale centers were borne by the local people themselves: local sweat equity and materials formed the scaffoldings of the buildings. Such community support gave the projects, as well as the buildings, much sturdier support structures. Without these supports, paternalistic and clientelistic behavior might very well have prevailed over practices of self-help and self-reliance.

7: Contributions of Social Research and Participatory Research

The historical background material presented in chapter 4 and in the various case study chapters illustrate the vital practical role social research may play in helping to revitalize cultural resources for grassroots development. The burgeoning Andean social sciences offered the Bolivian development community some new lenses for rediscovering the abundance of biological and cultural resources and technologies in the countryside. The activist social scientists described in these pages put their research skills and knowledge to work for recuperating technologies for native camelid raising, potato growing, and weaving, native languages for improved education, and practices for democratic organization. They also contributed in significant ways to broad-based ethnic movements in Bolivia and a deeper, more accurate understanding of the role of indigenous peoples in Bolivian and colonial history. Given the complexities of these depressed socioeconomic and environmentally degraded local settings for grassroots development, social research can be an important asset to local project organizers.

8: Outside Organizers as Key Actors

The selected project cases also point to the vital leadership provided by the outside organizers. The organizer is most often a professional from another geographic area such as a nearby city who, out of idealism and whatever mix of motives, opts to devote his or her career to empower communities and effect some social, economic, and even political change. Such a person can be a rural indigenous South American as was demonstrated with Luis Ticona and Max Paredes, the founders of AIGACAA. The organizers of the other projects included a Chilean, a Peruvian, and an Argentine, making Bolivia's cultural revitalization story truly a Latin American tale as well. In addition to grassroots leaders, these organizers were the individuals with whom I had the most contact in the course of my field work for the IAF. As the years passed, my admiration for their steadfast community service continued to grow. The personal drive these talented organizers applied toward their work with local communities made their careers seem to me more vocational callings than conventional jobs. Using ingenuity and innovation, they had to handle leadership and technical tasks ranging from capturing and brokering financial and economic resources to designing and implementing participatory training methodologies and local marketing strategies. In addition, they had to keep track of the many complications inherent to programs swimming against the tide of neo-colonialism and Western modernization. Good skill in cross-cultural communications and languages was essential, as was the ability to appraise the "people skills" and attitudes toward indigenous peoples of the development workers on their staffs.

Organizers often "stabilized" a project by overseeing at some level the management of economic and financial resources. In this role as stabilizer, each organizer provided a firm, steady hand for safeguarding proper uses of project funds when the inevitable temptations mounted. The scent of international funding brings an assortment of opportunists from all levels of society; this is no less true among indigenous leaders than in other social groups. The stabilizer's role often involved preventing the diversion of project resources to personal and private pockets. Such diversion, or the suspicion of diversion, can be the death knell to organizations striving for collective benefits.

Several projects gained organizational cohesiveness by having several family members working together under the same project roof. Husband-wife, mother-daughter teams seemed to provide added strengths to organizations such as CENDA, CIDAC, and ASUR. To some observers, these family patterns might seem to be signs of nepotism, yet these types of institutional arrangement exhibited high levels of trust, loyalty, effective teamwork, and creative energy—values treasured in grassroots development work.

All in all, these organizers, in addition to their diverse talents and relevant previous experiences, shared a special passion and analytical, self-examining approach to their work and a powerful moral vision of a just society for indigenous and non-indigenous peoples alike.

9: The Participation of Foreigners

A curious characteristic of many of these organizers was the fact that many of them were foreign nationals. To the reader familiar with the number and variety of people associated with the transfer of financial and economic resources to the Third World, this finding may not come as a surprise. Foreigners end up working at many development project outposts as volunteer development workers, technical consultants, and project evaluators, among other specialties. In a modest way, their work helps to offset the tremendous professional brain drain via emigration suffered by small Third World countries such as Bolivia. Sensitive foreigners, such as these, who had lived much of their lives outside of the neo-colonial Bolivian system of status hierarchy, viewed indigenous cultural resources with fresh and appreciative eyes. Their perceptiveness was useful to fledging community groups plunging headlong into the complex process of cultural revitalization.

Yet what sets the foreign organizers in these stories apart from many others is a commitment to micro-regional development over the long haul. With the exception of most of the German volunteers, who had fixed term assignments, the foreign organizers devoted many years of their lives and careers to the organizations and projects they founded. Despite foreign citizenship, these dedicated people were not about to abandon their chosen work and return home. Bolivia became home to many of them, and in a curious way they became "nationalized." Despite the fact that these projects were in an essential way grounded in the local culture, foreigners were sometimes the necessary catalysts for success. They became, using the term of renowned applied anthropologist Alan Holmberg, participant-interventionists.

10: The Role of the Church

Catholic Church workers wore assorted hats and contributed in different ways to projects scattered throughout rural and urban Bolivia. Sometimes their contributions were seminal, sometimes they were harmful; other times, they were small but significant nonetheless. The Belgian priests' quinoa development program in Nor Lipez in the 1970s is an example of the way that paternalistic church aid programs can cramp a people-centered development process. This kind of paternalism was writ large with the food aid programs of Cáritas Boliviano. On the other hand, the Franciscan priests provided engineering expertise for building roads along with environmental education to communities settled in the Alto Beni's tropical forest. The National Bishops' Conference conducted some of the country's pioneering work in bilingual and intercultural education beginning in the mid-1970s and then used its lobbying muscle to help secure the country's first education reform law to institutionalize such experiments on a broad national level. Antonio Sagrista's model public education center is another example of the Church's many highly relevant contributions to education in Bolivia. The indigenous march moved along briskly toward its goals thanks to alliance and support from the Church both at the local parish level in the Beni and at the national level of the Bishops' Conference in La Paz. The career of the foreign-born, Jesuit anthropologist, Xavier Albó, is testimony to the extraordinary contribution that a single person's religious vocation has made to indigenous-based development in Bolivia. Albó, an internationally renowned anthropologist, has been an omnipresent voice as an activist researcher, writer, advisor, facilitator, and public speaker on development, politics, education, and linguistics related to indigenous peoples.

11:The Role of the Outside Funder

Although officials from external funding agencies, such as myself, periodically swoop down and offer moral support to projects facing difficult problems, making timely grants to organizations and documenting the change process are, perhaps, our most important callings. In addition to arranging periodic field visits, my employer relied heavily on information gathered through monitoring and evaluation reports provided by resident Bolivians.

During six-week field trips to Bolivia, it was not uncommon for me to meet with representatives from over fifty ongoing projects. In some sense the field trips served as a conduit of information among projects, as opportunities to discuss and disseminate findings about educational methodologies, marketing strategies, and cultural revival that showed promise. There were also, of course, many days filled with dread and disappointment when encountering floundering projects.

It is important to mention a few things about IAF funding strategy for these projects. In the cases of ASUR, CIDAC, CENDA, CEMSE, and CIMCA, I renewed funding on a bi-annual basis in response to a growing participant population, whereas grants to El Ceibo and CECAOT were more sporadic. In the former examples, these organizations attracted funding from other donors and with our continuous support became sui generis experiences in "institution building" on Bolivia's varied social landscape of grassroots development.

As a Foundation representative, I had the freedom to select the people and organizations I believed the IAF could be convinced to fund. I imagine that my counterparts in the aid giants such as USAID or the World Bank were compelled to accept as colleagues the government functionaries assigned to them regardless of their true expertise or social commitment. Yet I was by no means a footloose social activist with a government checkbook. I had to make a convincing case for funding these Bolivian organizations and pushing their initiatives through layers of review committees, paperwork, and even Washington lawyers. Periodic evaluations were also carried out by Bolivians to provide an independent reading on project happenings. The cumulative amount of monies received by each organization from the IAF averaged about a half million dollars. Of course, they also received appreciable amounts from other foreign donors and the Bolivian government. The indigenous agro-exporters were also clients of local banks and other credit programs.

My methods for finding and funding social entrepreneurs included actively seeking recommendations from social activists, intellectuals, other funders, and grassroots leaders. Although IAF grants launched most of the organizations described in my case history section, the innovative project ideas were home grown. Without much if any organizational history to go on in judging their local development capacity, I had to examine their individual life stories and professional career tracks to form my views. A lesson here is that international and national donor agencies' financing of incipient organizations can allow new visionaries to surface and begin innovative small-scale projects that may eventually grow in importance and scope of impact.

12: Historical-Structural Economic Factors

Favorable historical-structural factors in the national economy were clearly important for project success. Often, the timely opening up of a pertinent economic niche greatly enhanced a project's success. Fortunately for El Ceibo and CECAOT, cacao beans and quinoa had never elicited much interest from Bolivia's economic and political elites. Again with regard to camelid development, Bolivia lacked a large commercial export sector such as Peru enjoyed, and so AIGACAA was able to take advantage of this void and surge to the top as the country's first exporter of alpaca TOPS. AIGACAA was also able to take advantage of Peru's policy of "whitening" its alpaca herds by breeding out alpacas with darker pelts and developing a complementary and contrasting export market for their natural darker shades.

In a different way, CEMSE found a tremendous advantage by choosing as its location the most densely populated school district in all of Bolivia.

13: Single-Minded Project Zeal

Success also seemed to come to projects that adhered to a single focus in their work over a substantial period of time.[2] The central all-encompassing focus, rather than a jumble of loosely connected, disparate activities, seemed to pay off in these stories of social change. Of course, the big caveat is that a focus, for example, on a single commercial crop or product for an indefinite time period may be highly vulnerable to commercial price swings. El Ceibo paid attention via research and marketing efforts to other tropical cash crops and to new approaches in order to add value to chocolate products. AIGA-CAA explored llama fiber markets to diversify. ASUR and CIDAC kept opening new product lines with the artisans and weavers as well. These are actions taken by organizations to minimize the commercial risk associated with too narrow a focus. Yet this branching out usually occurred after they had consolidated effective programs in support of the mentioned products.

14: Sustainable Development

Respect for the natural environment and developing plans that were eco-logically "sustainable" also characterize these successful development pro-jects. The farmers portrayed in these case histories tried to become better stewards of their natural environment. The project histories depict a wide range of environmental problems: deforestation, indiscriminate use of chemicals in production technologies, desertification of the landscape from overfarming, overgrazing, and tractor mechanization, and rampant erosion of genetic plant and animal biodiversity. Many of the projects were success-ful because they were committed to renewing an indigenous environmen-tal stewardship of the land and human environmental balance that had fallen on hard times, and combining it with emerging Western practices from the field of agro-ecology.

15: Interdependence among Andean Nations

For a small country like Bolivia finding its way within the international global order, these grassroots experiences show how historically rooted and culturally compatible interdependencies between neighboring Andean nations could work better for cultural resource utilization than dependence on a Western superpower. Perhaps herein lies a rationale for forging trading blocs among countries of comparable size (Castañeda 1994). Although Bolivian quinoa and alpaca fiber flowed to Peru as contraband in great quantities at low prices, as a commercial movement it helped build markets for these Bolivian products when consumer demands were weak at home. Now this leakage of these two increasingly important Andean commodities has become more problematic and detrimental. Yet Peru contributed to Bolivia's grassroots development by providing quinoa-processing technologies, advanced animal science training, camelid veterinary medicine, and university training and literature in the diverse fields within Andean studies.

Peruvian pro-indigenous activists are equally bent on importing aspects of cultural revitalization that flourish within Bolivia's now more markedly pro-indigenous political culture. For example, to tap international organic food markets, Peruvian NGO programs are striving to adapt the popular Bolivian variety of "quinoa real" to southern Peru's mountain conditions. Amazonian territorial rights struggles and bilingual/intercultural education are local phenomena in Peru while in Bolivia they have floated to the top of political discourse and are embraced by the highest levels of government, labor organizations, and political parties (Yashar 1998).

16: Replicability

Given their manageable human scale and modest funding, many projects were replicated in other microregions, and among different ethnic and peasant communities and organizations. This replicability is another strength of the organizations depicted here. For example, the ASUR textile revival methodology was replicated first among the Tarabucos and then in the neighboring Potosí region by an NGO working with the Calcha ethnic group (Giesel and Hernandez 1997). Former El Ceibo leaders hold key staff positions in a national organization devoted to connecting small organic farmer organizations, offering them advice on training, business management, and marketing practices. At the invitation of peasant sindicato federations, CENDA's staff and Yanapakuna promoters have exported their project methodology and agricultural and educational lessons for revitalizing potato diversity and creating intercultural, bilingual schooling to the province of Ayopaya with similar rugged Andean conditions. CECAOT's pioneering role in quinoa processing and marketing inspired another organization whose commercial export success has exceeded its own. CIMCA spun off other small-scale, like-minded educational entities after training them in rotafolios and other popular education methodologies. And finally, the social protest methodology of the long-distance march on the capital city became a staple practice of other militant peasant organizations in Bolivia and was even successfully deployed by an Ecuadorian ethnic federation in its quest for Amazonian territorial rights.

17: Luck and Synchronicity

The last, but perhaps not least, factors in the success of the nine develop-ment projects were luck and synchronicity. Even if a project had all sixteen above mentioned ingredients, it may not have achieved success without a sprinkling of luck and synchronicity. Sometimes the local system surround-ing a given set of crops and livestock is so locked in by macro-economic structures that successful economic development is next to impossible (de Janvry 1981). A number of the projects discussed in the book benefited greatly from a sudden chance happening or a seemingly random event, the timing of which made a big difference in the outcome of these small-scale initiatives. Binge-buying of llamas in Chile, for instance, triggered Bolivia to reappraise its depreciation of llamas which in turn set the stage to imple-ment the law that AIGACAA pushed through valuing Bolivia's herds. The appearance of organic food stores in Europe during the last half of the 1980s created a niche for El Ceibo's commercial ascent. While these bits of luck and synchronicity did play a part in project success, it must also be said that when the chance opportunities knocked on the doors of these projects, these organizations were able to seize the new opportunities, and be off and running.

All seventeen factors played critical roles in the set of projects described in this book. Some of these, such as the historical-structural factors, are per-haps more important than others and not surprisingly harder to find within a rapidly globalizing world order. Some factors may be less difficult to attain than others, yet various of them together tend to reinforce one another to push a process along the path of grassroots social change.

What helps tie all these factors together is the social capital they share. Social capital is currently a fashionable term within the social sciences and international development field. It refers to the dense social networks of family and community organization that reside within civil society and beyond the boundaries of the state. Social capital often embodies established norms of trust and reciprocity that underpin a societal fabric giving it legitimacy and staying power (Putnam 1993a, 1993b; Coleman 1988). The factors of community tenacity, resident skill, popular participation, and community resource mobilization perhaps are the most obvious expressions of social capital. Yet it was precisely the recognition of social capital that drew the interest of outside organizers—and funders—and helped account for the relative viability of these grassroots development strategies. Social capital viewed in this way becomes a subtext to our larger story and points again to the intricate knowledge systems and cultural practices of Bolivia's diverse indigenous peoples and the need to capitalize on them.

CONTINUING AND NEW CHALLENGES: GLOBALIZATION

Bolivia has been spinning ever faster in the international orbit of worldwide market integration since its structural adjustment reforms began over a decade ago. As in other Latin American countries, the advent of neoliberal policies has stabilized the national economy and led to higher economic growth rates and export earnings. Though economic stability has been appreciable, the social costs of structural adjustment in Bolivia have been exceedingly high. Even mainstream mass circulation magazines in the Western world such as the *Economist* bemoan the increasing socioeconomic inequalities arising with neo-liberalism across the hemisphere (*Economist* 1996). The World Bank and national governments themselves have acknowledged this social crisis by setting up "social emergency funds" throughout Latin America to bale poor people out of a worsening situation.

El Ceibo, CECAOT, and AIGACAA are among the rare but slowly increasing number of indigenous peasant enterprises making the most of international export opportunities without forsaking domestic markets. Meanwhile, the vast majority of Bolivian rural communities have been left behind. The trends are to unemployment and underemployment. Poverty and income distribution are either remaining the same or worsening (Kaimowitz, Thiele, and Pacheco 1987). Communities readily exceed their carrying capacity for subsistence and consequently are exporting entire families to the growing cities. The community's physical and socioeconomic limits have been exacerbated by trade liberalization policies which flood domestic markets with lower priced produce from foreign nations, benefiting urban consumers at the expense of poor rural producers. In the eastern lowlands, imports have driven down the price of rice, which is a key cash crop for tens of thousands of producers. Many indigenous communities have been invaded recently by foreign oil and gas companies scrambling for resources. The banking system has proceeded to place rural credit even further beyond the reach of small farmers, increasing their financial stress. Indeed, the great majority of Bolivian poor farmers have to swim against rather than with the tide of free market forces. Many are pushed all the way to urban centers and turn their back on farming, while still others strive to make a living combining work in both areas. Bolivia even exports workers to Argentina to bolster its neighbor's expanding agricultural and construction sectors. There is also a rapidly growing divide from the emergence of electronic information-based technologies both within Bolivia between social classes and ethnic groups and externally in relation to First World nations.

Yet the book's stories show how communities can be buoyed by effective strategies mounted by NGOs and grassroots federations to gain a better deal in the marketplace. The improved terms of trade altering the "free market" resulted from collectively organized transport and marketing programs supporting better quality and higher quantities. Cultural recuperation was augmented by the higher prices thus obtained for these rural products. Ironically, the fashion in wealthy societies for goods laboriously made by hand—as more prestigious and unique than manufactured sameness—has also contributed. Bolivia's cultural revitalization as a social force within civil society has also positioned the country to take advantage of one of the friendlier faces of globalization—small adventure travel or ecotourism companies—enabling First World tourists to co-mingle with Third World peoples, their cultures and natural settings, on a people-to-people basis. Since 1995, this type of tourism has been expanding at the rate of 20 percent per year. Neo-liberal economic policies, in summary, have contradictory impacts, many of which are negative. Yet there are exceptional cases such as those explored in this volume of rural communities finding a path to progress.

The effects of globalization on Bolivian culture and society are spreading rapidly, especially in major Bolivian cities. Western artifacts have accelerated cultural homogenization on a broad societal scale. There is evidence that the influence of Western neo-liberalism produces greater cultural

BLAZING A TRAIL OF MULTICULTURAL GRASSROOTS DEVELOPMENT

alienation in some sectors of the population. Many less-advantaged people have deep ambivalence about living in a globalizing, neo-colonial society which reinforces discrimination toward indigenous peoples.

The economic pressures fostering urban migration also alter native cultural identity, as indigenous peasants possessing expertise for protecting potato diversity and herding camelids on the high, windy Andean plains wind up peddling toothpaste and trinkets at curbside in La Paz or Cochabamba. Cultural identity also erodes when migrants adopt urban society's racist attitudes and reject their own identities and home communities.

While Westernization and globalization drive contemporary society in one direction, we have also seen throughout the book examples of initiatives to revitalize the "native" in Bolivia along with the cultural values, cultural expressions, and knowledge systems that underpin them. During this period, Bolivians have been redrawing old boundaries erased by neo-colonialism, re-labeling the new maps with Guaraní, Aymara, and Quechua names, reinstating traditional indigenous authorities, revitalizing flags symbolizing the reaffirmation of indigenous culture, and spreading bilingual/intercultural education through the public school system. Simultaneously the cases document examples of appropriating the artifacts and technology of globalization for greater cultural pluralism. The appearance of the Jalq'a and Tarabuco cosmovisions of weavings on a worldwide computer website page enhances marketing and the communication among indigenous leaders, sometimes even in native languages, over cellular telephones for business relations and during protest marches facilitate the struggle for cultural pluralism in Bolivia. CECAOT's interests were enhanced by the protests over the U.S. patenting of Bolivian quinoa communicated via the Internet. What is one to make of this seeming modus vivenda of these two contradictory impulses occupying the same national playing field?

A look at history informs us that nineteenth-century liberalism fueled not only imperialist European expansion throughout Africa, the Middle East, and parts of Asia, but the internal assault by the Bolivian oligarchic state on the Andean ayllu and other structures of the indigenous way of life. The liberal intent was to replace the collective forms of land tenancy and native political structures with privately owned haciendas, criollo political authorities, and land markets most convenient for amassing wealth via the exploitation of Indian labor.

Over a century later why is neo-liberalism compatible with the resurrection of the ayllu rather than reproducing the earlier liberal pattern of neo-colonial cultural repression? Cultural pluralism occupies new respect in public places such as the rural schoolhouse, and in important documents like the national constitution which radically redefines the formerly fictively "homogenous" Bolivian state as pluri-cultural and multi-ethnic and affirms state support for collective land rights for indigenous peoples. The unbridled capitalism of the global market undermines cultural identity when farms begin crumbling, forcing families to flee the countryside. Yet there have been important modifications in Bolivia that contrast with the workings of nineteenth-century free market forces and their encapsulating social Darwinian ideology of progress. The selection of an outspoken, culturally conscious Aymara vice-presidential running mate by the architect of the country's neo-liberal economic program is yet another sign of the curious neo-liberal–indigenous design (Albó 1994).

The differences in cultural outlook found between these two historic epochs can be attributed, at least in part, to the long indigenous activism culminating with the 1952 revolution, followed historically by the rise of Katarismo in the 1970s, and the subsequent social movement sponsored by CIDOB and Asamblea del Pueblo Guaraní among indigenous groups of the eastern lowland region. NGOs and grassroots economic federations charged forth waving the banner of cultural revitalization in their grassroots development schemes. They fit multiculturalism and biodiversity together into the same project box for mounting strategies for socioeconomic change. And the international environmental movement, the indigenous march, and the anti-quincentenary campaigns added fuel so this fire could spread and attain greater prominence.

The ambiguous stand-off between the forces validating the indigenous traditions and the forces for globalizing commerce was thrown into relief in a recent juxtaposition of two Bolivian events. The McDonald's Corporation of "Big Mac" fame, having established itself in 100 countries, recently opened its first franchises in Bolivian cities. The company imports its uniform and standardized french fried potatoes from North America. About the same time a colorful outdoor fair drew thousands of rural peasants, urban migrants, and local residents in a celebration of a wide variety of native potato dishes in the provincial town of Takipala in Cochabamba. These side-by-side events reveal the reality of neo-liberal consumer homogeneity and the élan of cultural pluralism functioning simultaneously at different levels of Bolivian society.

An anthropologist might be tempted to label this example as cultural hybridization writ large. Yet until McDonald's serves llama burgers with french fries drawing on Andean biodiversity or the people attending such popular fairs can afford McDonald's meals, "hybridization" will remain within the familiar terms of neo-colonial social and cultural hierarchy. Whereas the critics of globalization tend to focus on the impact of dominant societies like the United States on smaller, weaker countries and economies (A. Escobar 1995), a Bolivian perspective provides a reverse view of the globalization process. Indeed, North Americans have come full circle; nowadays cultural pluralism or multiculturalism is a catchword. Values and products native to the New World are viewed as holding valuable solutions to various "post-modern" needs in many parts of the U.S. During the 1990s, for example, there was an unprecedented interest among North Americans in consumption of indigenous foods from the native North American tribes such as "Blue Corn" of the Hopi (Soleri, Cleveland et al. 1994). Increasingly, private companies use native symbols to market products, and not always to the satisfaction or benefit of North American Native Americans. The appeal of "native" food products gains even greater ground when coupled with promotion of the values of food safety and enhanced nutrition.

Helped by these consumer trends, both quinoa real and organic chocolate products have become popular in organic and gourmet food stores throughout the United States, appealing to health-conscious consumers who wish to eliminate cancer-causing chemical residues from their food. The 20 percent annual growth rate in organic food sales in the United States during the 1990s (totaling $3 billion dollars in 1996 according to the *New York Times*) has transformed the corner health food store into the block-sized organic supermarket such as Fresh Fields and other chains. The chemically based agricultural technologies that the U.S. had so enthusiastically exported via its foreign aid programs eventually alienated a sector of its own consumers.

The llama-raising boom in the United States is another impressive example of an indigenous resource undervalued during Western modernization that has now gained its due recognition abroad as well as in Bolivia. Just outside of Washington, D.C., llamas are sold over the Internet via Llama.com. Llama owner associations have sprung up in Colorado and Montana, and trade magazines sharing information on camelid livestock circulate nationally. A rolling wave of similar enthusiasm for the alpaca is not far behind.

Steve Rolfing, the president of the Great Northern Llama Company from Montana, says that a llama population numbering 4,000 animals in 1978 has skyrocketed to 115,000 by the mid-1990s. This surge in llama rearing has raised the U.S. to fourth place among the world's llama producers. Bolivia is first, of course, followed by Peru and New Zealand. New Zealand, with technical savvy from a long historical experience with its own rangeland development, has even become a llama exporter.

In the western U.S. llamas carry supplies for trekkers along mountain trails and haul bags of golf clubs for outdoor sportsman. Wealthy yuppies pay as much as $20,000 for alpaca females. They use this "breeding stock" to obtain a tax write-off from the creation of "farm property," in effect disguising their home pets as livestock. The tremendous demand for llamas has spawned a lucrative breeding business among U.S. private investors and entrepreneurs. Rolfing predicts that nutritious, low cholesterol llama meat and soft alpaca fur will enjoy high-priced markets during the twenty-first century in the U.S. Camelids will have appeal among environmentalists as well because of the comparatively benign impact of their padded hoofs on rangelands.

Interesting ironies abound over the enthusiastic U.S. embrace of the Andean llama. Utah State University, which brought well-bred sheep to Bolivia for rural modernization, nowadays utilizes llamas as guard animals for—you guessed it—protecting the high-bred, super-productive sheep. Four-H clubs, an organization transplanted to Bolivia to modernize its agrarian institutional landscape, currently deploy llamas for trekking across mountain ranges of northern California.

Steve Rolfing's enthusiastic promotional brochure might just as easily have been written by Luis Ticona of AIGACAA. It reads, "They are wonderfully healthy and virtually disease-free; eat very little (about 3 bales of hay a month); nearly always have been problem-free, daylight births; are simple to fence, house and transport; and are easy for anyone—including children—to handle and train. Their natural curiosity and pasture antics are a source of endless enjoyment."

Although these are perhaps the most prominent indigenous cultural resources in the U.S., there are others making a hit in a similar process of reverse technology transfer from a "backward" to an "advanced" nation. Adele Cahlandar, a seventy-year-old weaver from Minnesota, studied weaving in Bolivian commentaries and published her findings in a "how-to" book for North American weavers called *The Art of Bolivian Highland Weaving* (Cahlander 1976). She then proceeded to travel by bus throughout the United States giving workshops on Andean designs and techniques to weavers' guilds. Her students marveled at the complexity and ingenuity of the many Bolivian or Andean techniques and imaginative patterns. Bolivian alpaca sweaters designed with the Jalq'a's stylized Andean bird motifs on black backgrounds are now popular items at some of the fanciest Western ski shops.

A North American medical doctor from Washington State leads student tours to the steep valleys of Charazani each year to hold workshops on ethno-medicine with the surviving Kallawayas. The book *8 Weeks to Optimum Health* by physician and ethno-musicologist Andrew Weil, advocating a mix of herbal medicine, nutrition, and lifestyle tips, became a best-selling book during 1997, a feat that no doubt would have made the Kallawayas stand up and cheer.

The list goes on. An Idaho commercial seed company markets purple Andean potatoes throughout the country by mail order catalogue. Five-hundred yards from my residence on the edge of the National Zoo property sits a recently constructed building presenting Amazonian wildlife, yet another symbol of increasing global consciousness of the interconnectedness of the ecosystems of the earth.

McDonald's french fries are not the only potatoes that are doing impressive globetrotting these days. Over the past ten years, the International Potato Center, together with agricultural scientists from Cornell University, has developed a new potato hybrid by mating a commercial variety of the "Irish" potato with the "hairy potato," a Bolivian wild species, so dubbed for its hairy gradular trichomes which emit sticky substances that trap and kill insects. The sticky substances can prevent the escape of the most clever predators. Although most Bolivians are unaware of their potential contribution to agricultural globalization, the genes of this hairy specimen are undergoing trials in countries as diverse as Poland, Turkey, Egypt, Morocco, Tunisia, Algeria, and Russia, as well as New York state, with the potential to benefit many poor farmers around the world. Use of the hairy potato could reduce the need of farmers to purchase expensive chemical pesticides, which, according to CIP, absorb $700 million annually and inflict incalculable damage on the health of human beings, livestock, and the environment. More recently pesticides have been increasingly ineffective in the face of growing natural resistance of insects and pests to the sprays and massive destruction of their natural predators. And from Canada and Italy even more good news about the Bolivian hairy potato's positive global reach. Scientists there claim that this new variety reduces late blight infection, the number one potato disease in the world, by 40 percent. According to CIP, "Late blight infection was responsible for the Irish potato famine of the 1850s when a million persons died and up to two million emigrated" (CIP 1992). My ancestors included.

THE APPROPRIATION OF INDIGENOUS KNOWLEDGE

Yet there is another side to the globalization of Bolivia's indigenous cultural resources that raises troubling questions about the imbalance in North-South power relations. This issue relates to the asymmetrical relations between a low-income struggling nation like Bolivia and a technological and economic superpower like the United States. A case in point is the patenting as intellectual property rights of quinoa hybrids made from Bolivian native varieties in the United States and Canada. Western law gives protective rights to individuals and corporations that are not accorded to indigenous peoples as collectivities. The new U.S. patent laws in recent decades have extended coverage to agricultural seeds which throughout human history in both Western and non-Western parts of the world had remained as public goods under the principle of "common heritage" (Brush and Stabinsky 1996). In a different yet related issue Colorado farmers may in the future successfully adapt the Nor Lipez "quinoa real" variety to the soils, climates, and growing seasons of the Rocky mountains and attain those unique marketing features. Will such trends result in the production of high-yielding hybrid quinoa seeds owned by U.S. agri-businesses and mechanized, large-scale quinoa farming in the United States and Canada, and displace these Andean Quechua and Aymara farmers from the global marketplace? This is not such a far-fetched proposition. Under NAFTA, Mexican indigenous corn farmers experienced this boomerang effect by having their production displaced by U.S. hybrid seeds engineered from their own native strains.

David Snorr, president of the Quinoa Corporation, the largest of its kind in the United States, sadly assesses the potential damage and injustice of such a future scenario. He told me in a phone interview, "North American investors have many choices about what row crops to grow for making business investments while the Quechua peoples dwelling near the salt flats of the southern altiplano have this ancestral grain for survival. Displacing them from the international markets they helped to open seems far from morally right to me." Yet if the production of quinoa in the U.S. cannot be halted, at least Andean quinoa producers in Nor Lipez should receive compensation from private corporations for their contributions.

The issue of losing control over such cultural resources is also relevant in relation to the U.S. llama boom. Camelids have traveled to the U.S. as both smuggled and legally imported livestock. Given the relatively rapid pace of adaptation of this livestock to varying conditions within the U.S. perhaps Bolivia is losing its comparative edge. Better veterinary care and advanced research in the U.S. on viruses affecting llama birthing and growth apparently has made a big difference. One glance at the hulking and heavily furred llama on the cover of the Great Northern Company brochure left me wondering about the lean, sleek physique and raw-boned rusticity of the llamas that grace the plains of the altiplano. Have the Bolivian government, civil society, and the private sector awakened too late to safeguard these precious cultural resources?

A related issue has to do with the appropriation of indigenous groups' cultural knowledge without giving either recognition or remuneration to the producer of such knowledge. Recently, I came across the course catalogue from a Latin American Studies Program of a prestigious North American university advertising a program of study on Latin American societies. The catalogue featured a Tarabuco stylized horse motif on its cover. Opening it, I discovered that the North American firm commissioned to design its cover took full credit for the image without acknowledging the Tarabucos.

Bio-prospecting for genetic resources in the Amazon by First World corporations is also picking up steam in Bolivia, which houses the world's sixth largest expanse of tropical rainforests and tropical dry and wet savannas. Bolivia's government for the first time passed national laws and established a regulatory office protecting the country's genetic resources from foreign appropriation. Grassroots organizations of the eastern lowlands such as CIDOB are also gearing up for campaigns around these hotly debated issues. The impetus for this concern over genetic resources originated not only with NGOs but also with the Environmental Summit in Brazil where the Latin American nations for the first time organized a common front to protect their genetic patrimonies for national development. This effort in Bolivia mirrors similar measures spearheaded by anthropologist Cristina Bubba to protect the cultural patrimony of weavings as well.

OTHER ENVIRONMENTAL CHALLENGES

Accompanying this process of globalization are various environmental challenges. Indiscriminate use of chemical fertilizers and pesticides which contaminate food and water supplies continues throughout many rural areas. In the highly commercialized vegetable production in Santa Cruz, these problems have become especially dangerous for products like the tomato. Despite the gains via cultural revitalization, plenty of public and private development organizations continue to peddle assorted technology packages. Since the advent of the 1986 structural adjustment policies, increased deforestation and environmental degradation has resulted from greatly expanded mechanized soybean production and timber extraction in Santa Cruz and the Beni (Kaimowitz, Theile, and Pacheco 1998). Unfortunately, the critics point out, this export-led development leaves degraded tropical soils, absolute losses of biodiversity, and carbon sequestration in its wake. The mining of land and resources enriches several hundred privileged families and leaves both current as well as future generations of the rural majority in these affected areas the same or worse off.

The critique made by these analysts argues, however, that this outcome was not pre-ordained by structural adjustment policies. The choice of the last three Bolivian governments since 1985 to support soybean growers and timber interests for export-led growth has as much to do with the political muscle of these elite constituencies as do the IMF prescriptions for market-led growth. These environmentally sensitive analysts point out that the same Bolivian resources could have been developed for export projects that involved community forestry initiatives employing animal traction and lighter machinery and using soil regeneration measures, with a far better distribution of social and economic benefits.

THE HOPE AND IMPORTANCE OF GRASSROOTS DEVELOPMENT

Although global social and economic trends driven by structural adjustment policies have brought little improvement for huge sectors of the world's poor, such modest success stories as found in this book give a glimmer of hope, a glimpse through a window of what is possible in grassroots development. The practice of multicultural grassroots development requires and implies faith in the power of people and their cultures to contribute in important ways to the reshaping of the contours of Third World development and democracy from the bottom up. Cultural revitalization strategies must be accompanied by genuine processes of collective empowerment and self-management among the participating communities. National governments need to open up space for initiatives emanating from civil society. They likewise need to take measures modifying the ubiquitous effects of an uncontrolled free market. As seen in this book's case studies, modest and timely funding can make a huge difference—bringing about changes that would not have happened without the initial financial impetus that permitted these organizations their start. The day may not be far away when nation-states and international donors come to recognize that "economic recovery" is not the only goal for development and that "cultural recovery" from neo-colonialism and Western modernization has a prominent place among the indexes for measuring the development process.

A BRIEF RETURN TO POTATOES

A recent experience shows how Bolivia's turn to cultural pluralism has penetrated the United States despite our long-term efforts to impose Western modernization on Bolivians both here and in their own country. At a recent Fourth of July parade along Constitution Avenue, a street lined with federal buildings and the Smithsonian museums, I stood watching from among a crowd of spectators as a jovial Irish-American group decked out in kelly green outfits danced by. Shortly thereafter, another dance troupe with towering, feathered headdresses in darker green costumes passed in front of me, swerving back and forth to the lively rhythms of Andean panpipes. These were Bolivian-Americans who were dancing along with Irish-Americans and many other representatives of our multicultural population. When I spotted the Bolivian-American group, I immediately recognized the stylized headgear, adapted from Aymara fertility dance rituals practiced during key moments of the potato-growing cycle near Lake Titicaca, across from the Peruvian community where I once served as a Peace Corps volunteer. I used to walk along those shores against the deep blues of Titicaca's waters and the big sky above on my way to visit farmers and convince them of the merits of "modern" potato-growing technologies. Little did I realize then that ancient Andean farmers first domesticated the potato for humankind in this same lake basin, and had been innovating for the past 5,000 years to extend the phenomenal biodiversity of the potato crop across the rugged mountain landscape. Now I knew better.

The simultaneous dancing of the two troupes made me think that our two societies, Bolivia and the United States, had grown closer together over the past fifty years as both countries have begun to recognize their cultural roots and publicly affirm them. The potatoes inspiring the Bolivians' colorful attire and vibrant music were not the Idaho whites fired up at McDonald's but rather the Andean varieties that come in all sizes, shapes, colors, and flavors.

Notes

1. There has been a voluminous outpouring of work by social and natural scientists over the past forty years on the achievements of Andean agriculture. For an excellent summary of the literature related to Andean agriculture see Karl Zimmerer's recent work (1996) on Paurcatambo, Peru. An important article written by an Aymara scholar on Andean agriculture is M. Mamani (1988). Works on historical developments would include Alan Kolata (1993) and John Murra's classic (1978). On Andean crops see Tapia et al. (1979). Also see Ravines (1978) on Andean technology and Brush and Taylor (1993) on potato biodiversity.

2. These insights I gained by sitting in on John Murra's class in Andean anthropology at Cornell University in 1974.

3. Indigenous cultural resources discussed in this book have Western, Spanish, and Native American cultural elements, which have been blending together in multiple ways over the past 500 years. A good example of the coming together of European and Andean traditions is the Andean costume for women. The bowler hat worn by Aymara and Quechua people in the altiplano was introduced by the British during the nineteenth century yet it became a mark of "indigenous identity."

4. Across the Andes an ethno-trans-culturation occurred throughout history that converted the distinct ethnicities with separate names into the broader ethnolinguistic categories of Aymara and Quechua. There are exceptions to this rule among the Quechuas such as the Jalq'as, Tarabucos, and Rayqaypampeños described in later chapters of this volume. Bouysse (1987) provides a spatial profile for the altiplano with corresponding ethnic names of these earlier Andean ethnic identities.

5. Silvia Rivera's phrase for conveying Bolivia's brand of internal colonialism is the "pigmentocracy of power," an expression of uneven distribution of resources, opportunities, legitimacy, and status among people of different ethnic background and skin color (1993). A chain of subtle forms of subordination and discrimination link the various layers of the country's multi-ethnic and mestizo social strata.

6. Also see Salmón (1997) and Cárdenas (1992; 1993).

7. A classic book in English on the impact of the agrarian reform is Heath, Erasmus, and Buechler (1969).

8. For important works on peasant sindicalism, see Jorge Dandler's work on Cochabamba (1982) and his co-edited book with Fernando Calderón (Calderón and Dandler 1984), especially the chapter with Juan Torrico on important antecedents to the rise of sindicalismo.

9. For details and background, see Gonzalo Flores (1984b).

10. In Jorge Casteñada's biography of Che Guevara, the author describes Che's revulsion upon observing the fumigation of peasant Indian leaders in the ministry he was visiting during the early years of the Bolivian revolution.

CHAPTER 2

1. A source for the extent of foreign aid financing from the U.S. can be found in James W. Wilkie (1982). Wilkie comments that overall "Given the fact of Bolivia's small population, the United States has undertaken a relatively large scale program to financially assist Bolivian regimes" (p. 83). Wilkie shows that after Milton Eisenhower visited Bolivia in 1953 and gave his blessing to the MNR and its revolution, U.S. aid increased considerably, averaging 22.8 percent of the central government's budget between 1957 and 1964. In 1962, these amounts approached the central government's entire budget and then exceeded it by 28 percent in 1964 (p. 92).

2. According to Castro Mantilla (1997) these indigenous groups included the Chácobo (contacted in 1955), Ignaciano (1961), Sirionó (1961), Tacana (1962), Itonama (1964), Esse-ejja, Guarayu (1961), Movima (1962), Aroana (1964), Baure, San Lorenza (1967), Pacahuara (1968), and Cavineño (1970).

3. A fuller discussion of this high-altitude agriculture is M. Mamani (1988). There was a small group of Bolivian agronomists and botanists focused on some native crops but their voices were low decibel in a context of Western rural modernization. For some positive assessments of the SAI program in terms of improved crop yields, see Wennergren and Whitaker (1975, 255) whose work is based on many of the classic Western modernization assumptions in viewing traditional agricultural as mostly unproductive, backward practices.

4. For an analysis of the PL-480 Program in the United States in terms of its origins and purpose, see Morgan (1979, 240-45) and more specifically in Bolivia, see Klein (1982). The wheat that was imported as donated food under PL-480 into Bolivia included bulgur, which is a variety of cracked wheat from the Dakotas. It should be pointed out that Bolivia had imported wheat from the United States since the 1920s and it had become a popular food item in Bolivian mining towns and some cities before greatly expanding its market through the assistance of PL-480. Beginning in 1956 the donated wheat from the United States eventually car-

ried this program to a larger scale of operation and helped to open markets for increased regular imports, having a significant impact on consumer food preferences. Within Latin America this was significant as well since, for example, Bolivia with 1.7 percent of the hemisphere's population received 14.4 percent of the total food aid available under PL-480 (Prudencio and Franqueville 1995, 19).

5. Klein points out that the U.S. also conditioned its economic aid on a reduction of the power of the left-leaning Central Obrero Boliviano, the national trade union confederation, and opening the economy for future U.S. investments which paved the way for the Gulf Oil Company until its nationalization in 1969 (Klein 1982, 240–45).

6. U.S. food aid came under three administratively separate "titles" or programs. The Title II program beginning in 1955 directly distributed the wheat and other items mostly through voluntary agencies. The Bolivian government had to cover transportation costs by ship to Arica, Chile, and then by railway to La Paz. In 1989, USAID's Title II program innovated with a "monetization program" to sell a portion of the wheat flour in Bolivia and use the earnings to purchase Bolivian agricultural products, most of which were processed and non-native such as rice and sugar. However, this new program covered only a small percentage of the food aid. Prudencio and Franqueville argue that despite some of the merits of this program, it does little to reduce the overall structural dependency on the United States for imported wheat and wheat flour. In 1978, the U.S. government began the Title III program in which the Bolivian government directly imports wheat for sale to Bolivian mills. These U.S. sales are made on concessional terms, giving a nine-month interest-free grace period for repayment. The income from this sale in turn is made available to the PL-480 program which channels investments in agriculture, health, and other activities. According to some analysts this program was a response to the critiques of U.S. paternalism and dependency inherent to these programs (Prudencio and Franqueville 1995). In this arrangement the Bolivian millers cover transportation costs from the Chilean coastal ports while the Bolivian government pays for shipping from the United States ports.

7. Private Bolivian millers in most cities coveted the food aid for the public subsidies it enjoyed and the ease and efficiency that standard U.S. wheat varieties could be processed by their industrial machines. The donated food products included milk, corn flour, oats, vegetable oils, lentils, dried milk, bulgur, wheat, wheat flour, canned products, and others. The United States supplied 86 percent of the food aid while official agencies of Canada, Spain, and the European Economic Community also made contributions.

8. Other evidence for this nutritious native food displacement can be found in an analysis of two nutritional/consumption surveys among middle-class groups in La Paz (Prudencio and Velasco 1988, 60–62). The first survey covered the period

1958−1962 and the second 1984. They found that while wheat and its derivatives gained greater ascendancy (from one product to five different ones such as macaroni noodles, cookies, bread, etc.), highly nutritious yet low-status native food such as quinoa, kañiwa, oca, and ulluco had disappeared from the diet of those surveyed. This change diminished urban markets for peasant production of these crops.

9. These observations were made by the NGO CIDAC whose work with indigenous women in Santa Cruz can be found in chapter 12.

10. The Inter-American Co-operative Education Service (SCIDE) also worked as an independent U.S. entity in rural education until 1955 at which time it broadened its material to include industrial and agricultural vocation programs. They worked directly with elementary schools and teachers' colleges to provide methods and techniques of instruction as well as programs in rural arts, agriculture, homelife, sanitation, and rural development (Point Four 1960, 23).

11. Antonio García (1970) offers a wide-ranging and penetrating critique of U.S. aid programs. He argues, for example, that SAI contributed directly to the dismemberment of government agencies and programs by having such a large budget and heavy presence in the countryside. García also criticizes the credit policy and institutional performance as disconnected from the needs of the Indian peasant beneficiaries emerging out of the agrarian reform. Instead of supporting these social groups, the credit favored the Japanese and commercial farmers of Santa Cruz (p. 355).

12. Xavier Albó related to me his personal conversation with Goni Sánchez de Lozada's father, the former Bolivian director who characterized the Andean base program as complete failures.

CHAPTER 3

1. However, the state-owned structure with respect to oil, the Yacimiento Petroleros Fiscales Bolivianos (YPFB), was interrupted by the Gulf Corporation's production operations and other private exploration. The U.S. economic assistance to the MNR came with the condition that Bolivia reform its petroleum investment code to foment foreign investment which it did in 1956. George Eder wrote that "U.S. policy at that time was opposed to financing government petroleum operations that could be undertaken by private capital" (Eder 1969, 60). Out of these changes, the Gulf Oil Company carried out oil production operations until its nationalization by the Ovando government in 1969. The YPFB resumed its oil monopoly yet began giving out exploration contracts to foreign oil companies under a new foreign investment code for hydrocarbons decreed by the Banzer government in 1972 (Dunkerley 1984, 204).

2. YPFB was created by the nationalization of the Standard Oil Companies holdings in Bolivia in 1936 when Bolivian government created a state monopoly.

3. The cattle ranchers and cotton producers were exclusively from the white and mestizo social sectors representing medium and large operators. For sugar cane production by 1980, the medium and large cañeros represented 37.3 percent of the production units yet controlled 81.7 percent of the area under production. The small-farm sector represented 43 percent of the production units while controlling 15.6 percent of the cultivated area (Arrieta et al. 1990, 232). There were better-off commercial groups producing rice during the MNR period and first few years of the military which switched to the more lucrative cotton. Subsequently, the rice producers in Bolivia were almost exclusively from the peasant class and the public policy supports for them began to greatly diminish.

4. The imported high-yielding variety of maize "Cubano Amarillo" primarily to be used as livestock feed also was greatly promoted under these agricultural modernization schemes under the Servicio Agrícola Interaméricano and was thus spread widely in tropical Santa Cruz (Arrieta et al. 1990, 188).

5. During the zenith of the Cold War period, United States government's economic and military aid to Bolivia between the mid-1950s through 1974 totaled $650 million while multilateral and third-country economic assistance through the same period amounted to $360 million. During the first period in the Banzer government (1972—1974) economic and military bilateral aid from the U.S. shot up to $150 million while international organizations provided $124 million and third countries at least $8 million (U.S. General Accounting Office 1975, 3). The grants of military aid for 1973 and 1974 were three times as great as any previously made to a Latin American government (Dunkerley 1984, 205). This was a period when military dictatorships pursuing a national security doctrine were the norm in the southern cone and Bolivia occupied a strategic geo-political position.

6. These mine-owners, representing twenty-five enterprises organized under the Asociación de Mineros Medianas (ANMM), received favorable government treatment and their members controlled a major part of the production of tungsten, antimony, and copper, in total approximately one-fifth of the country's total mineral production (Dunkerley 1984, 226).

7. Gill identifies multiple economic interests covering import houses, banks, automobile dealerships, retail stores, and money exchange houses (Gill 1987, 100—124). The pattern of land distribution by the 1980s had reverted to highly inegalitarian pre-revolutionary numbers. Now 93 percent of the landowners possessed 11 percent of the total land area for farming and ranching while 7 percent of the landowners possessed 89 percent of these total lands (Urioste 1987, 38).

8. During the Banzer period more agricultural and ranching lands were distributed through this public lands policy than during all the previous governments

combined since 1952 (Grupo de Estudios 1983; Albó 1979). Land grants went as high as 50,000 ha. for cattle enterprises and 2,000 ha. for agricultural enterprises. Medium-size holdings granted to individual operations were as high as 2,500 ha. for ranchers and 600 ha. in size for farms (Urioste 1987, 38). Also the military government's credit policies channeled 82.9 percent of the BAB's public credit for agriculture to non-indigenous commercial farmers with 3.5 percent destined for the peasant indigenous producers. Banzer raised the amount benefiting the peasant farming class to only 8.6 percent of the total which meant this policy, similar to the public land grants, was fueling social and economic inequalities in the countryside.

9. This pattern of production distribution changed when the military regime of Garcia Mesa, a notorious narcotics trafficker and repressive ruler, fell from power thereby opening the way for peasant producers to engage in the first stages of cocaine processing at the site where coca leaf was produced in Bolivia's tropical Chapare region. Santa Cruz and Beni economic elites subsequently shifted to higher levels of refining into pure cocaine and in trafficking to the Colombian processing centers.

10. The Banco Agrícola Boliviano (BAB) had to be bailed out of bankruptcy by the Bolivian government. The principal reasons under the military regimes especially Banzer were lax systems of internal control, rampant political cronyism, and improper loans for non-agricultural and speculative investments (including coca paste and cocaine base processing) as well as the participation of urban investors with little agricultural know-how for managing these farms when prices dropped (Dunkerley 1984; Malloy and Gamarra 1988).

11. However, over the 1980s oil sales under YPFB had dropped from 47,000 barrels per day in 1973 to 21,000 barrels in 1988, mostly from mismanagement. Some 75 percent of this oil production originated in Santa Cruz. Also it should be pointed out that in the late 1980s, YPFB was still exporting 90 percent of the country's natural gas.

12. The first part of YPFB sold to a private company in 1997 was its transport division and out of that effort a new company TRANSREDES emerged which absorbed a major part of the gas pipeline while another private company proceeded to acquire part of this infrastructure as well. The remaining installations including YPFB's oil refineries were slated to be privatized in 1998 and 1999.

13. Bolivia's capitalization program also generated considerable interest throughout Latin America. Under this arrangement 50 percent of the largest state enterprise ownership was sold off to investors. The remaining 50 percent ownership earnings were distributed as pension funds to 3.2 million Bolivians. The Bolivian government in effect was striking a balance between complete state ownership and private ownership and succeeded in capturing approximately $1.8 billion in foreign investments for these enterprises.

14. The production of soybeans in Bolivia originated with the Japanese colonists in Santa Cruz as it was a crop used by them traditionally for home con-

sumption (Arrieta et al. 1990, 254). Subsequently, better-off Bolivian farmers with access to agricultural machinery for cotton production were able to utilize the same agricultural technology for soybeans. The commercial production of soybeans began to attain importance in Bolivia during the agricultural year 1969–1970 when it reached 800 ha. Over the next ten years, the production area for soybeans increased to 41,000 ha. while the Japanese colonists' production percentage of the total diminished.

15. The World Bank reported in 1990 that the price index of agricultural products declined by 29 percent from the stabilization to the end of 1988 relative to overall consumer prices (World Bank 1990).

16. Total production fell by 17 percent during this period which in volume terms in 1988 remained 15 percent below the 1980–1985 average. A World Bank report summing up this spectacle of declining food production and falling farmer incomes commented that "both the volume and value-added of the goods produced by the poor have decreased, indicating a fall in welfare. This has resulted in a decline in real prices and quantity of agricultural products" (World Bank 1990, 32).

17. For an excellent discussion of Bolivia's informal sector economy in La Paz, see Buechler et al. (1998).

18. Bolivian tin mining industry was losing money with the highest cost underground mines and smelters in the world (Seyler 1989, 136) and was becoming increasingly obsolete given the types of technology and production practices being developed in Malaysia and China, other major world producers. The job exodus of so many mineworkers from these state enterprises also had a tremendous impact on Bolivia's labor movements. The Federation of Bolivian Mineworkers had always been the most combative and politicized sector of the national trade union movement under the COB and now its effectiveness had been greatly reduced by this loss of its membership.

19. The Social Emergency Fund concept caught on and by the end of the 1990s it had been created in thirty-four countries absorbing $3.5 billion from the World Bank and Inter-American Development Bank and half that amount from European governments (Tendler 1999). Graham (1998) and Bigo (1998) highlight some of the achievements of the SF experience in Bolivia. Tendler (1999) casts a more critical, pan-Latin American eye on the SFs arguing that their impact on employment, income, popular participation, and creation of a competitive environment was negligible and they were not the alternatives they were designed to be.

20. For an analysis of the Fondo del Medio Ambiente (FONAMA) which existed between 1990 and 1993, see Raza (1999, 19). This article argues that FONAMA played a positive role in various ways but lost its effectiveness when absorbed into the new Ministerio de Desarrollo Sostenible y Medio Ambiente in 1993 created by the Sánchez de Lozada government whose environmental record

left much to be desired. Raza argues that the country's environmental interests during the Sánchez de Lozada period were held hostage to the interests of private sector groups interested in minimizing any regulation of their exploitation of the country's natural resources (timber, minerals, hydrocarbons, etc.). The Fondo de Desarrollo Campesino while opening perhaps the only public channel of agricultural credit for the peasantry was rendered less effective by widely known financially corrupt practices among its managers.

21. Goni Sánchez de Lozada, as Bolivia's principal free market architect, was an intriguing figure. His family's mining interests placed him among Bolivia's wealthiest citizens, giving him the economic might to go with his talent to make a career climb to the top of the MNR Party. Interestingly, he had done his undergraduate studies at the University of Chicago, whose economics department is the citadel of neo-classical free-market thinking, yet Lozada majored in philosophy. He was the key technocrat among Paz Estenssoro's advisors in shaping the decree 21060 that instituted the NEP in 1985. However, when elected to office in 1992, he apparently set out to ameliorate Bolivia's social crisis that his own earlier advisory role had shaped under the NEP (see Grebe 1998).

22. For a critical social analysis of the discrepancies and difficulties with these gender-based programs instituted by the second generation on neo-liberal reforms, see Paulson and Calla (2000).

23. Banzer was elected president with the lowest voting percentage of any president in Bolivian history and according to opinion polls at the end of 1999 his popularity has declined significantly since taking office.

24. Kazan points out that the growth in cultivated area of soybeans has been at the annual rate of 23 percent between 1989 and 1996. He adds that the rapid increase in soybean production represents an expansion in land cultivated rather than improved technology and productivity (Kazan 1999, 50). Soybean exports in 1996 were sent as soybean grain, soybean cakes, and crude soybean oil, all of which require very little processing.

25. Rural credit for the peasant indigenous producers had become more inaccessible under the NEP with the closure of the national agricultural development bank. Since private banks typically made urban property a prerequisite form of collateral to qualify for loans, they were in effect excluding the low-income rural producer. Another problem with agricultural credit was the exorbitantly high interest rates charged for agricultural investments.

26. The debt relief program orchestrated by the World Bank for select countries grew out of the Jubilee 2000 Campaign of public education/advocacy efforts organized by faith-based organizations of the Catholic Church, OXFAM, and other voluntary agencies beginning in 1995 which focused on this important issue for combating Third World poverty. For more detail on the World Bank fundraising effort through a consortium see the *Bolivian Times* (1999f).

CHAPTER 4

1. Various indigenous movements focusing on indigenous cultural identity emerged in Latin America during the 1970s. The Kataristas focused on prevailing political economy issues, inappropriate rural development programs, monolingual Spanish schooling, and the political participation for the rural citizenry via cultural revitalization. This approach challenged aspects of Western modernization approaches being utilized in rural development and the re-concentration of landholdings within a small minority of ranchers, agri-business groups, and speculators in the eastern lowlands. This upsurge in indigenous social mobilization around indigenous cultural identity was encouraged throughout many parts of Latin America by the spread of Liberation Theology, de-colonization, and the impact of the worldwide student rebellions of 1968. The World Council of Churches and the United Nations Working Group also brought indigenous leaders together to share experiences and build common agendas and alliances. See Alison Brysk (1994) and Van Cott (1994). See also Yashar (1998) for a comparative analysis of indigenous movements in the hemisphere.

2. In his doctoral dissertation, historian Sinclair Thomson examined the shift in the Bolivian Andean communities toward democratic forms of rotation during the eighteenth century and found that the replacement of hereditary rule with more democratic practices reflected a blending of both Andean and Spanish political traditions into new forms. The new democratic communities emerged from this dialectical process of colonial imposition and Andean response. Some Andean service forms such as the mita (rotating turns) at the lower levels of community authority showed resilience while Iberian practices of rotation related to the town *cabildo* also came into play (personal interview 1999). Also see Thomson (1996).

3. The Katarista political bible during the first half of the 1970s was *Cinco Siglos de Guerra contra los de Tawantinsuyo* written by a polemicist, Fausto Reynaga, a Bolivian lawyer and former parliamentarian who founded a tiny altiplano group to agitate for indigenous rights in the early 1960s.

4. Another member of this activist team was Luis Rojas, an educator from Cochabamba who subsequently organized one of Bolivia's first cultural revitalization development projects with Quechua-speaking peoples in the Cochabamba Valley under the organization Ayni Ruway (Rojas et al. 1978; Healy 1981). The Argentine R. Kusch himself wrote an influential book for these intellectuals during the early 1970s entitled *America Profundo*.

5. The Bolivian Central Obrero Boliviano (COB) spearheaded by the federation of mineworkers was among the labor organizations most widely admired by the Latin American left for their revolutionary militancy and unity. Yet according to recent writings by Bolivian analysts they too were guilty of cultural

discrimination toward Aymara and Quechua leaders within the upper echelons of the COB. See references to this problem in Ticona, Rojas, and Albó (1995).

6. In the late 1970s, I wrote several chapters in my doctoral dissertation (later published as Healy 1981) about those living in haciendas in Chuquisaca as one of the country's most defeated, downtrodden ethnic groups at that time in the countryside, some twenty years after the 1952 land reform.

7. An additional tension between highland (*collas*) and lowland (*cambas*) ethnic groups stems from the aggressive and successful small retail businesses of the collas which predominate in lowland indigenous villages and communities. Shopkeepers, traders, and truck-owners of highland ethnic origins also tend to exercise commercial power over lowland ethnic groups and thus add to prevailing social and ethnic resentment and organizational cleavages.

8. Overviews of Andean studies by Frank Salomon (1982; 1985) present these works along with Larson (1995).

9. Brooke Larson provides a comprehensive and penetrating overview of this Andean intellectual production since the late 1970s in her reflections about working as a Bolivian Andeanist during this period of intellectual ferment and pathbreaking scholarship (Larson 1998). Although not discussed in this chapter, these efforts between foreign and Bolivian scholars were not always free from deep tensions and even acrimonious attacks by the latter group on the former's underlying motives and ostensible hegemony as Andeanists.

10. There were important exceptions to this characterization. Two shining examples of Bolivian scholars who pursued their work with great rigor and international esteem were Gunnar Mendoza of the Biblioteca Nacional and Alberto Crespo.

11. Some of the important works produced by Aymara scholars at THOA would include Choque (1996), Choque et al. (1992), and Mamani Condori (1991).

12. During the 1990s, the Inter-American Development Bank also created its first oversight office for indigenous interests where staff examine the impact of proposed IDB loan projects on indigenous communities and recommend ways to take indigenous interests into account. An example of the IDB's positive use of its power in such matters was the $1.7 million compensation given to indigenous organizations by private corporation loan recipients for environmental damage from a pipeline transporting natural gas to Brazil crossing their indigenous territories. This office also has a pro-active program in sponsoring educational events at the Bank involving indigenous peoples, scholars, and other development practitioners.

13. The Bank had learned that designing projects with Bolivian indigenous participation was not always easy given the competing claims and relatively greater political power of dominant economic and political interest groups. For example, in CIDOB's publicized foray into a $70 million World Bank project to expand soybean production under the NEP program, CIDOB was quickly marginalized from any major decision-making role in the project. This was ironic since Bank President

Barber Conable had earlier visited Bolivia, met with CIDOB representatives, and publicly hailed them as the first indigenous partner in a large Bank loan project anywhere in the world. Once the project management team excluded them, CIDOB leaders found difficulty in enlisting Bank support. A Bank Mission visited Bolivia to investigate the matter and at the end of their assignment only Shelton Davis, the activist anthropologist, was willing to defend CIDOB's role in the project. The remaining staffers sided with the regional elites to please their counterparts from the Bolivian government and contributed to removing CIDOB from the project. For a detailed analysis of CIDOB's struggle to participate in this Bank project, see Heijdra (1997).

CHAPTER 5

1. This group also included an emergent neo-populist party, CONDEPA, a political movement built around a television personality, Carlos Palenque, known affectionately in Bolivia as "Compadre Palenque," who effectively used ethnic symbols such as native language, popular music, artesanry, and lifestyle and made references to ancestors as ways to identify with his audience and political constituency. See Saravia and Sandoval (1991).

2. USAID's effort to improve grain production in the Bolivian Andes aimed at modernizing wheat production through a program conducted by Utah State University. After many frustrations, in an end of mission report, Utah State scientists suggested providing farmers with loans to finance quinoa production (USAID 1976). Unfortunately the recommendation fell on deaf ears. According to Nancy Ruther, a USAID official, "The rural development people within the USAID mission found there were too many production constraints on the peasant farms to build a food industry around quinoa or to justify investment in a major program. You have to remember that there were no health food stores in the U.S. in those days to jack up the prices for Bolivian producers. The Bolivian military government once passed a decree ordering flour millers to incorporate quinoa in their formula but it never followed up to enforce these measures."

3. This is not to say that quackery and incompetence do not exist in traditional medicine as they do in Western medicine. However, activist Jimmy Salles insists that the traditional healers are much more open to joint medical practices than are Western-trained, Bolivian physicians.

4. Bastien (1992) along with Crandon Malamud (1991) are among the best works in English regarding traditional or ethnomedicine in Bolivia. Of particular interest is a recently published biography of a traditional healer (Flores Apaza et al. 1999).

5. There have been major advances in research on Andean weaving traditions within Bolivia. Elayne Zorn's work on Sacaca in Norte de Potosí (1997) is a

fine example of foreign research on this topic. Bolivian historians have made major contributions, see Gisbert, Arze, and Cajías (1986); Arnold and Yapita (1996, 1998); Arnold, Jiménez, and Yapita (1992). Cristina Bubba (1997) on the Coroma textile traditions in addition to her activism is also noteworthy. Verónica Cereceda whose project with the Jalq'a is discussed in chapter 11 has been a pioneer scholar on this topic, see Cereceda, Dávalos, and Mejía (1993) and Dávalos, Cereceda, and Martínez (1992).

6. Bubba's indefatigable efforts led to Supreme Decree No. 22546 in 1988 prohibiting the removal from Bolivia of weavings made prior to 1950.

CHAPTER 6

1. Rochdale cooperativism refers to the nineteenth-century movement in England which generated the first organizational principles and bylaws that became influential in the development of agricultural co-operatives in the United States and subsequently in Latin America and other parts of the Third World through foreign aid programs.

2. Mirtembaum's analysis of the Alto Beni's colonization programs emphasizes the use of foreign models and advisors for establishing a program for "yeoman farmers" that was widespread in Latin America (Mirtembaum 1986). Perhaps the most important early book documenting colonization programs in the eastern Bolivian tropics which includes the Alto Beni is Nelson (1973). The model of rectilinear fields with stands of a single crop was commonplace throughout Africa as well as Latin America (see J. Scott 1998).

3. Anthony Bebbington together with El Ceibo staff members has produced several articles examining El Ceibo's agricultural development program. See Bebbington and Trujillo (1993) and Bebbington, Quisbert, and Trujillo (1996).

4. Judith Tendler perceptively discussed the spillover benefits to community members not belonging to El Ceibo (free riders) in her classic work analyzing the performance of Bolivian co-operatives (1983a).

5. The cocoa powder failed to pass the European environmental inspection of a count of micro-organisms. El Ceibo was able to lower this number after making adjustments in processing technologies yet fell short of the minimum requirement of these increasingly stringent regulations.

CHAPTER 7

1. For a fascinating glimpse of the economy of Nor Lipez in the nineteenth century, see Tristan Platt (1995). He follows the marketing relationships of ayllus in

Lipez and discusses an economy where hunting of vicunas, viscachas, chinchillas, and guanacos predominated.

2. Some of the early social science articles on quinoa in English are Cusack (1983) and McCamant (1992). See Tapia et al. (1979) for the work led by Mario Tapia and a group of Andean scientists on quinoa and kañiwa. Also see Wood (1989) for greater detail about the quinoa pioneers in the United States and numerous quinoa recipes.

3. In Nor Lipez, the soils on the mountain slopes retain more moisture and enjoy higher rainfall levels than on the pampas. Also a type of mulch mixture with small stones forms along the former and acts as a natural barrier, impeding insects from penetrating the soil. Moreover, frost tends to form in the pampa areas rather than on the mountain slopes, sparing the quinoa plants in the latter area from severe damage.

4. Tractor disking of the soil mixes together different stratum, consequently loosening the soil considerably and creating a habitat for insects harmful to plant growth. This soil condition contrasts with that on mountainsides where land preparation for quinoa planting is often done by hand. Quinoa growing on the pampas also contributed to the removal of large swaths of natural vegetation especially thola upsetting the ecological balance of the area and increasing agricultural risks (Augstburger 1992).

5. These soil conservation measures for the harvest included cutting the quinoa plant at ground level with a sickle instead of pulling its roots out of the ground. For land preparations, the recommendation was not to use disk plowing as it was more prone to cause soil erosion.

CHAPTER 8

1. Hale analyzes the marketing role of the Comité Boliviano de Fomento Lanero and its successor, the Institute for Wool Production (INFOL) (Hale 1981, 50–54). He indicates that alpaca fiber had been exported to Europe for women's garments, sports jackets, and traveling blankets and during both World Wars was used to line military uniforms.

2. Hale (1981, 22) explains how the ayllus assigned political posts to mostly male members as *cargos* which were rotated annually to other ayllu members. The federation of AIGACCA also distributes tasks and responsibilities, this time to members of different ayllus who also rotate. However, according to Hale, by the 1980s the important traditional ayllu leadership role of the *jiliqata* had disappeared in some of these communities as a consequence of the rise of evangelical sects there.

3. For more details and a critical analysis of AIGACCA's formative years, see Hale (1981).

4. The first income figures were taken from the United Nations' project proposal assessment document prior to funding and the second from an evaluation commissioned by ATI of the project's socioeconomic impact in the communities (Olívares, Budinich, and Hyman 1996).

5. Clare Sammells and Lisa Markowitz give an excellent analysis of the situation of discrimination faced by llama meat in altiplano cities and its potential for future use (Sammells and Markowitz 1995).

6. Lisa Markowitz provided this information in a telephone conversation in 1999. Hale also pointed out the wide price fluctuations that had historically characterized the international market for alpaca fiber (Hale 1981, 53).

CHAPTER 9

1. Paolo Friere's work reflects the influence of Liberation Theology and its spread via Catholic Church into educational and NGO development networks during the 1970s and 1980s (see his principal work, Friere 1970).

CHAPTER 10

1. This student organization, although using MINKA in its name, is different from the Aymara NGO known as MINKA in chapter 8 and mentioned in the original signing of the Manifesto de Tihuanaco.

2. This methodology of using the generative word and its relationship to naming was also part of the popular education process outlined in the preceding CIMCA chapter.

CHAPTER 11

1. Anne Rowe, the curator of Andean textiles at the Textile Museum in Washington, D.C., had an opportunity to observe the Jalq'a weaving techniques when they participated on the National Mall in the 1994 Festival of American Folklife. Through that encounter, she was able to determine that their weaving techniques are unique or at least not documented elsewhere.

2. According to ASUR's records approximately 60 percent of the final retail price in the Sucre store represents the labor cost of producing an axsu and the share of the earnings received by the individual weaver for her efforts.

3. A July 1993 income study conducted by ASUR found that most of the Jalq'a families were at least doubling their annual agricultural incomes with income from weaving sales (Fundación ASUR 1993).

4. The 1993 survey also showed that weavers are increasingly finding other family members or relatives to assume their traditional tasks of pasturing their livestock.

5. The forementioned income survey in 1993 examined fifty weavers both Jalq'a and Tarabuco to document their weaving production, quality, and sales income during a period of rapid growth in weaving workshops. The weaver population was stratified into three groups according to annual production and income figures from weavings (both large and small pieces). The highest income earned by an individual producer was $719. Some 75 percent of the sampled population in the two zones were earning annually above $260 per person (the top of the three stratified groups earned $340 from weaving sales per person) in a context where families' annual agricultural earnings were $266. However, much of the agricultural income represented production consumed rather than sold so in terms of cash earnings textile production was the more important source of earnings. The income figures did not account for more than one weaver per family. ASUR calculated that the most productive and highest earning weavers still have to spend half their time completing agricultural and domestic tasks (Fundación ASUR 1993). One would expect the weaving income to have increased over the past five years through increased practice, training, and strong monetary incentives for higher quality work.

CHAPTER 12

1. An excellent historical overview of the changing economic and political conditions and contemporary picture of the Guarayos can be found in Zulema Lehm (1996).

2. This study indicates that the income earned by the sale of hammocks is superior to that generated from products and wage payments for labor upon which the Guarayo local economy revolves. By weaving one hammock a month, a woman would receive $400 over the course of a year. Lehm writes, "The experience of production and marketing of hammocks within the framework of producer organizations, achieved a general increase in prices paid by middlemen and a more just remuneration for one's labor." (Lehm 1996, 57). This study also indicates that in addition to the 120 Guarayo weavers belonging to ARTECAMPO, 320 non-member hammock makers receive higher prices for their weaving thanks to ARTECAMPO's role in regulating the local market for this product.

3. By the end of 1998, CIDAC's total annual sales had reached $260,000, and 950 artisans were participating.

4. The source of this remark was based upon an evaluation of the CIDAC project conducted by Bolivian anthropologist Cristina Bubba for the Inter-American Foundation.

CHAPTER 13

1. AGRUCO is the NGO from Cochabamba specializing in organic agriculture and the recuperation of indigenous knowledge briefly discussed in chapter 5.

2. Orlove et al. (2000) conducted a study combining satellite imagery technology and ethnographic field work to affirm the accuracy of weather forecasting by Andean altiplano farmers. The researchers showed that indigenous farmers making their potato planting decisions in relation to the brightness of the stars proved to be quite accurate and were able to forecast the El Niño phenomenon which was linked to reduced rainfall.

3. Warisata is discussed in chapters 4 and 10.

CHAPTER 14

1. The cabildo is the form of local organization most prevalent among ethnic groups in eastern Bolivia which, although of Spanish origin from the mission experience, became fully indigenized. The cabildos comprise a rotating hierarchical system of formal work assignments which provide functions for the local government as well as for ceremonial and religious affairs in the communities (Ticona, Rojas, and Albó 1995, 73).

2. See the discussion of these public land grant programs under the military in chapter 3.

3. Fabricano was born in 1953 in San Lorenzo de Moxos and spoke only Trinitario prior to entering primary school. Similar to many other indigenous families, his father had lost the family ranch to "whites" who obtained titles under the new agrarian reform. The family subsequently moved into the Isiboro-Sécure National Park where he lived in a Mojeño community.

4. CIDOB was the first and largest federation of lowland ethnic groups in Bolivia from the regions of Santa Cruz and the Beni as well as the southern areas of Chuquisaca and Tarija. CIDOB began its congress with the return of Bolivian democracy in 1982 and also belongs to COICA, the trans-Amazonian political coordinating body for indigenous peoples from seven South American countries. For more detail on CIDOB, see chapter 4.

5. THOA is the oral history workshop created by Aymara activists in La Paz; see chapter 4.

6. The Ley INRA stipulated the incorporation of twenty-four territories to be titled under different time tables. The first to benefit were the indigenous peoples from the 1990 march and then in 1992 the Cirabo, Yuqui, and Weenhayek ethnic groups added their demands to the original set accepted by the Bolivian government. Their eight territories were fully titled shortly after the Ley INRA

passed. At the time of this passage, another sixteen demands from other ethnic groups also gained recognition yet were required to be "sanitized," which turned out to be an arduous technical and bureaucratic process with plenty of political obstacles. Although these groups were to be granted titles within ten months, as of 1999 they were still waiting. Subsequent to the passage of the Ley INRA, another sixteen demands were also incorporated into the law and also bogged down in the process of "saneamiento." The Banzer Administration and all its political ties to the land-owning elite became a major obstacle to the Ley INRA.

CHAPTER 15

1. The Inter-American Foundation led by Marion Ritchey-Vance created a grassroots development framework for measuring project results by creating the household, the community, and larger socioeconomic and political system as units of analysis. Some of the more innovative of these socioeconomic indicators of developmental change include cultural pride which had previously been ignored by mainstream donors such as the World Bank and the United Nations programs (Ritchey-Vance 1996).

2. Judith Tendler's comparative co-op studies in Bolivia (1983a, 1983b, 1984), which included the El Ceibo case together with three others, offered this insight as an explanation for their relative success.

Bibliography

Abercrombie, Thomas. 1998. *Pathways of Memory and Power: Ethnography and History among an Andean People.* Madison, Wisc.: University of Wisconsin Press.

AIGACAA (Asociación Integral de Ganaderos en Camélidos de los Andes Altos). 1991a. "Para Conferencia de Prensa." La Paz, July 23.

——. 1991b. "Aclaración a la Opinión Pública sobre la Exportación de Camélidos." La Paz, July 30.

Alba, Juan José, and Lila Tarifa. 1993. *Los Jampiris de Rayqaypampa.* Cochabamba: CENDA.

Albó, Xavier. 1977a. *El Futuro de los Idiomas Oprimidos.* Cuadernos de Investigación. La Paz: CIPCA.

——.1977b. *Idiomas, Escuelas y Radios en Bolivia.* 2nd ed. Cuadernos de Investigación. La Paz: CIPCA.

——. 1977c. *La Paradoja Aymara: Solidaridad y Faccionalismo.* La Paz: CIPCA.

——. 1979. *¿Bodas de Plata? O Réquiem por una Reforma Agraria.* Cuadernos de Investigación 17. La Paz: CIPCA.

——. 1984a. "Bases Étnicas y Sociales para la Participación Aymara." In *Bolivia: La Fuerza Histórica del Campesinado,* ed. Fernando Calderón and Jorge Dandler. Cochabamba: UN Research Institute for Social Development (UNRISD) and CERES.

——. 1984b. "Etnicidad y Clase en la Gran Rebelión Aymara/Quechua: Kataris, Amarus y Bases 1780–1781." In *Bolivia: La Fuerza Histórica del Campesinado,* ed. Fernando Calderón and Jorge Dandler. Cochabamba: UN Research Institute for Social Development (UNRISD) and CERES.

——1987. "From MNRistas to Kataristas to Katari." In *Resistance, Rebellion, and Consciousness in the Andean Peasant World, 18th to 20th Centuries,* ed. Steve J. Stern. Madison, Wisc.: University of Wisconsin Press.

——. Ed. 1988. *Raíces de América: El Mundo Aymara.* Madrid: UNESCO.

——. 1990a. "Lo Andino en Bolivia: Balance y Prioridades." *Revista Andina* 8 (no. 2): 411–63. [Centro de Estudios Regionales Andinos Bartolomé de las Casas, Cusco.]

————. 1990b. *Los Guaraní-Chiriguano: La Comunidad Hoy.* Cuadernos de Investigación 32. La Paz: CIPCA.

————. 1991a. "Introducción." In *Etapa de una Larga Marcha,* ed. A. Baspiniero Contreras. La Paz: Asociación Aquí Avance, Educación Radiofónica de Bolivia.

————. 1991b. "El Retorno del Indio." *Revista Andina* 9 (no. 2): 299–366 [Centro de Estudios Regionales Andinos Bartolomé de las Casas, Cusco.]

————. 1994. "And from Kataristas to MNRistas? The Surprising and Bold Alliance between Aymaras and Neoliberals in Boliva." In *Indigenous Peoples and Democracy in Latin America,* ed. Donna Lee Van Cott. New York: St. Martin's Press.

————. 1995. "Our Identity Starting from Pluralism in the Base." In *The Postmodern Debate in Latin America,* ed. John Beverly, Z. Oviedo, and M. Aronma. Durham, N.C.: Duke University Press.

————. 1996a. "La Búsqueda desde Adentro: Calidoscopio de Auto-Imágenes en el Debate Étnico Boliviano." In *Artículo Primero: Revista de Debate Social y Jurídico.* Santa Cruz: Centro de Estudios Jurídicos e Investigación Social.

————. 1996b. "Pobreza, Desarrollo e Identidad Indígena." In *Desarrollo Indígena: Pobreza, Democracia y Sustentabilidad,* ed. Diego Ituralde and Estevan Krotz. Serie Documentos No. 12. La Paz: Fondo Para el Desarrollo de los Pueblos Indígenas de Latinoamérica y el Caribe. November.

————. 1999. "Diversidad Étnica, Cultural y Linguistica." In *Bolivia: Etnias y Pueblos Originarios,* ed. Carlos Torranzo. La Paz: Harvard Club of Bolivia.

Albó, Xavier, and Joseph M. Barnadas. 1984. *La Cara Campesina de Nuestra Historia.* La Paz: UNITAS.

Alcoreza, Carmen, and Xavier Albó. 1979. "1978: El Nuevo Campesinado ante el Fraude." Cuadernos de Investigación 18. La Paz: CIPCA.

Alzérreca Angelo, H. 1982. "Recursos Forrajeros Nativos y la Desertificación de las Tierras Altas de Bolivia." In *Ecología y Recursos Naturales en Bolivia.* Cochabamba: Centro Pedagógico y Cultural de Portales. La Paz: Instituto de Ecología.

Antezana Ergueta, Luis. 1966. *El Movimiento Obrero Boliviano (1935–1943).* La Paz.

————. 1982. "La Revolución Campesina en Bolivia." La Paz: Cuadernos Hoy.

Apaza, Julio Tumiri. 1978. "The Indian Liberation and Social Rights Movement in Kollasuyu (Bolivia)." IWGIA Document.

Arias, Juan Felix. 1994. *Historia de una Esperanza: Los Apoderados Espiritualistas de Chuquisaca 1936–1964.* La Paz: Aruwiyiri.

Arnold, Denise Y., Domingo Jiménez, and Juan de Dios Yapita. 1992. *Hacia un Orden Andino de las Cosas.* La Paz: HISBOL/ILCA.

Arnold, Denise Y., and Juan de Dios Yapita. 1996. *Madre Melliza y sus Crías: Ispall Mama Wawampi, Antología de la Papa.* La Paz: HISBOL/ILCA.

————. 1998. *Río de Vellón, Río de Canto, Cantar a los Animales, Una Poética Andina de la Creación.* La Paz: HISBOL.

Arrieta, Mario. 1996. "Desarrollo Rural y Económico Campesino." In *Aspectos Sociales de Diez Años de Ajuste*. La Paz: ILDIS-UCB.

Arrieta, Mario, Briego Guadalupe, Castillo Abel, and Manuel De La Fuente. 1990. *Agricultura en Santa Cruz: de la Encomienda Colonial a la Empresa Modernizada*. La Paz: ILDIS.

Arze Aguirre, René Danilo. 1987. *Guerra y Conflictos Sociales: El Caso Rural Boliviano durante la Campaña del Chaco*. La Paz: CERES.

Augstburger, Franz. 1990. "Agroecologíe Andina: El Concepto y las Experiencias de AGRUCO." In *Agroecología y Saber Andino*. Cochabamba: AGRUCO-PRATEC.

————. 1992. "Informe de Inspección de Quinua Biológica Producida por ANAPQUI en el Altiplano sur de Bolivia." Asociación Nacional de Productores de Quinua (ANAPQUI). Unpublished report.

Avirgan, Tony, Laura Parsons, and Ross Hammond. 1995. "Structural Adjustment in Bolivia: Inducing Illegal Drug Production." In *Structual Adjustment and the Spreading Crisis in Latin America*. Washington, D.C.: Development Gap.

Badani Aguirre, Alvaro, José Luis Perez Ramirez, and Carlos Villegas Quiroga. 1990. *NPE: Recesión Económica*. La Paz: CEDLA.

Barnadas, Josep. 1987. *Introducción a los Estudios Bolivianos Contemporáneos 1960–1984*. Cusco: Centro de Estudios Regionales Andinos Bartolomé de las Casas.

Barragan Romano, Rossana. 1994. *¿Indios de Arco y Flecha? Entre la Historia y la Arqueología de las Poblaciones del Norte de Chuquisaca (Siglos XV–XVI)*. Sucre: Ediciones ASUR 3.

Bastien, Joseph. 1978. *Mountain of the Condor: Metaphor and Ritual in an Andean Ayllu*. St. Paul, Minn.: West.

————. 1992. *Drum and Stethoscope: Integrating Ethno-Medicine and Bio-medicine in Bolivia*. Salt Lake City: University of Utah Press.

Bebbington, A., J. Quisbert, and G. Trujillo. 1996. "Technology and Rural Development Strategies in a Small Farmers' Organization: Lessons from Bolivia for Rural Policy and Practice." *Public Administration and Development* 16 (no. 879): 1–19.

Bebbington, Anthony, and Graham Thiele, with Penelope Davies, Martin Prager, and Hernando Rivers. 1993. *Non-governmental Organizations and the State in Latin America: Rethinking Roles in Sustainable Agricultural Development*. New York: Routledge.

Bebbington, A., and G. Trujillo. 1993. "El Ceibo." In *Non-Governmental Organizations and the State in Latin America: Rethinking Roles in Sustainable Agricultural Development,* ed. Anthony Bebbington and Graham Thiele. New York: Routledge.

Bigo, Anthony. Ed. 1998. *Social Funds and Reaching the Poor: Experiences and Future Directions*. Washington, D.C.: World Bank.

Block, David. 1994. *Mission Culture on the Upper Amazon: Native Tradition, Jesuit Enterprise, and Secular Policy Moxos, 1660–1880*. Lincoln: University of Nebraska Press.

Bohan, Merwin. 1942. *A Report of the Economic Mission of the United States to Bolivia*. Washington, D.C.: U.S. State Department.

Bolivian Times. [La Paz.] 1998a. "Bolivia's Quiet Stock Market Revolutions." November 12.

———. 1998b. "When You Can Surf the Net à la Boliviana." December 3.

———. 1998c. "Mining, the Rocky Road Ahead." December 10.

———. 1998d. "Report: Neo-liberalism Helped Produce Street Children Problem." December 10.

———. 1999a. "The Challenges of an Emerging Market." April 15.

———. 1999b. "Legal Reforms to Sweep Nation." May 13.

———. 1999c. "The Pizza Revolution Takes Miraflores." May 27.

———. 1999d "Ericsson Poised to be Market Leader in Bolivia." June 10.

———. 1999e. "Dressing Down the Textile Market."

———. 1999f. "980 Million in Foreign Aid for Bolivia." July 1.

Bouysse-Cassagne, Thérèse. 1987. *La Identidad Aymara*. La Paz: HISBOL-IFEA.

Brush, Stephen B. 1994. "A Non-Market Approach to Protecting Biological Resources." In *Intellectual Property Rights for Indigenous People: A Source Book*, ed. Tom Greaves. Oklahoma City: Society for Applied Anthropology.

Brush, Stephen B., and Doreen Stabinsky. 1996. *Valuing Local Knowledge: Indigenous People and Intellectual Property Rights*. Washington, D.C.: Island Press.

Brush, Stephen B., and E. Taylor. 1993. "Diversidad Biológica en el Cultivo de la Papa." In *Chacra de Papa, Economía y Ecología*, ed. E. Mayer, M. Glave, S. Brush, and E. Taylor. Lima: CEPES.

Brysk, Alison. 1994. "Acting Globally: Indian Rights and International Politics in Latin America." In *Indigenous Peoples and Democracy in Latin America*, ed. Donna Lee Van Cott. New York: St. Martin's Press.

Bubba, Cristina. 1997. "Los Rituales a los Vestidos de María Titiqhawari, Juna Palla y Otros Fundadores de los Ayllus de Coroma." In *Saberes y Memorias en los Andes in Memoriam a Thierry Saignes*, ed. Thérèse Bouysse-Cassagne. La Paz: Institute Français d'Études Andines.

Buechler, H. C., and J. M. Buechler. 1971. *The Bolivian Aymara*. New York: Holt, Rinehart and Winston.

Buechler, Hans, Judith-Marie Buechler, Simon Buechler, and Stephanie Buechler. 1998. "Financing Small-Scale Enterprises in Bolivia." In *The Third Wave of Modernization in Latin America: Cultural Perspectives of Neo-liberalism*, ed. Lynne Phillips. Wilmington, Del.: Jaguar Books.

Buford, Bill. 1996. "The Seductions of Storytelling," *The New Yorker*, pp. 11–12. June 24 and July 1.

Burke, Melvin. 1971a. "Does Food for Peace Assistance Damage the Bolivian Economy?" *Inter-American Economic Affairs* 25: 3−26.

―――. 1971b. "Land Reform in the Lake Titicaca Region." In *Beyond the Revolution: Bolivia since 1952,* ed. James M. Malloy and Richard S. Thorn. Pittsburgh: University of Pittsburgh Press.

Cahlander, Adele Marjorie Cason. 1976. *The Art of Bolivian Highland Weaving.* New York: Watson-Gupstill.

Calderón, Fernando, and Jorge Dandler. Eds. 1984. *Bolivia: La Fuerza Histórica del Campesinado.* Cochabamba: UN Research Institute for Social Development / CERES.

Calla Ortega, Ricardo. 1993. "Identificación Étnica y Procesos Políticos en Bolivia 1973−1991." In *Democracia, Etnicidad, y Violencia Política en Los Países Andinos.* Instituto Francés de Estudios Andinos; Instituto de Estudios Peruanos.

―――. 1994. "Mapa de Ayllus y Comunidades de Potosí." *ProCampo: Revista del Desarrollo Rural,* no. 53 (June/July): 4−8.

―――. 1995. "Aproximaciones Etnográficas a la Cubierta Vegetal en Potosí." Potosí: Proyecto FAO/HOLANDA/CDF.

Calla Ortega, Ricardo, José Enrique Pinelo, and Miguel Urioste. 1989. *CSUTCB: Debate sobre Documentos Políticos y Asamblea de Nacionalidades.* La Paz: CEDLA.

Calvo, Luz María, Carlos Espinoza, Teresa Hosse, and Pablo Regalsky. 1994. *Raqaypampa: Los Complejos Caminos de una Comunidad Andina.* CENDA.

Cárdenas, Víctor Hugo. 1988. "La Lucha de un Pueblo." In *Raíces de América: El Mundo Aymara,* ed. Xavier Albó. Madrid: UNESCO.

―――. 1991. "Bolivia: Hacia una Educación Intercultural." In *Etnias, Educación y Cultura: Defendemos lo Nuestro,* ed. ILDIS-Bolivia. La Paz: Editorial Nueva Sociedad.

―――. 1992. "Prologo." In *Educación Indígena: ¿Ciudadanía o Colonización?* ed. R. Choque, V. Soria, H. Mamani, E. Ticona, and R. Conde. La Paz: Aruwiyiri.

―――. 1993. "Inaugural Address to the National Congress." La Paz, August 6.

Cardozo, Armando G. 1986. "Ganaderos en Justa Defensa de sus Llamas y sus Alpacas." *Presencia,* January 23.

Cardozo, Armando, and Irma Aliaga de Vizcarra. 1967. *Bibliografía sobre la Quinua.* Boletín Bibliográfico No. 4. La Paz: Sociedad de Ingenieros Agrónomos de Bolivia.

Cariaga, Juan L. 1982. "The Economic Structure of Bolivia after 1964." In *Modern-Day Bolivia: Legacy of the Revolution and Prospects for the Future,* ed. Jerry R. Ladman. Tempe, Ariz.: Center for Latin American Studies, Arizona State University.

Caro, Deborah. 1992. "The Socio-economic and Cultural Context of Andean Pastoralism: Constraints and Potential for Biological Research and Interventions."

In *Sustainable Crop-Livestock Systems for the Bolivian Highlands*, Proceedings of the SR-CRSP Workshop, ed. Corinne Valdivia. Columbia, Mo.: University of Missouri.

Carroll, Thomas F. 1992. *Intermediary NGOs: The Supporting Link in Grassroots Development*. West Hartford, Conn.: Kumarian Press.

Carter, William E. 1964. *Aymara Communities and the Bolivian Agrarian Reform*. Gainesville: University of Florida Press.

————. 1971. *Bolivia: A Profile*. New York: Praeger.

Carter, William, and Xavier Albó. 1988. "La Comunidad Aymara: Un Mini-estado en Conflicto." In *Raíces de América: El Mundo Aymara*, ed. Xavier Albó. Madrid: UNESCO.

Castañeda, Jorge. 1994. *Utopia Unarmed: The Latin American Left after the Cold War*. New York: Vintage Books.

————. 1997. *Compañero: The Life and the Death of Che Guevara*. New York: Knopf.

Castro Mantilla, María Dolores. 1997. *La Viva de las Tribus, El Trabajo del ILV en Bolivia, 1954–1980*. La Paz: Ministerio de Desarrollo Sostenible y Planificación, Viceministerio de Asuntos Indígenas y Pueblos Originarios.

CEE (Comisión Episcopal de Educación). 1988. *Educación y Transformación Social*. La Paz: Comisión Episcopal.

Centro Pedagógico y Cultural de Portales and Instituto de Ecología. 1982. *Ecología y Recursos Naturales en Bolivia*. Cochabamba: Centro Portales. May 3–8.

CEPA (Centro de Ecología y Pueblos Andinos). 1996. *Eco Andino* 1 (no. 1).

CEPAL-ONU. 1958. *El Desarrollo Económico de Bolivia*. Mexico.

Cereceda, Verónica, Jhonny Dávalos, and Jaime Mejía. 1993. *Una Diferencia, Un Sentido: Los Diseños de los Textiles Tarabuco y Jalq'a*. Sucre: Antropólogos del Sur Andino (ASUR).

Chambers, Robert. 1992. "Rural Appraisal: Rapid, Relaxed, and Participatory." Institute of Development Studies, Discussion Paper 311. Brighton, England. October.

Chapin, Mac. 1997. "Mapping in the Izozog of Bolivia." Unpublished report of Native Lands. January.

Chirif, Alberto, Pedro García, and Richard Chase Smith. 1991. *El Indígena y Su Territorio*. Lima: OXFAM-America-COICA.

Choque, Roberto. 1996. *La Sublevación de Jesús de Machaqa*. La Paz: Ediciones Chitakolla.

Choque, Roberto, Vitaliano Soria, Humberto Mamani, Esteban Ticona, and Ramón Conde. 1992. *Educación Indígena: Ciudadanía o Colonización*. La Paz: Ediciones Aruwiyiri.

Choque, Roberto, and Esteban Ticona with Felix Layme Pairumani and Xavier Albó Corrons. 1996. *Jesús de Machaqa: La Marka Rebelde 2: Sublevación y Masacre de 1921*. La Paz: CIPCA & CEDOIN (Colección Historia y Documento).

Chumiray, G. 1992. "La Experiencia de la Asamblea del Pueblo Guaraní." In *Futuro de la Comunidad Campesina*. Cuadernos de Investigación 35. La Paz: CIPCA.

CIEP (Centro de Investigación de Energía y Población). 1990. "Primer Encuentro Interdepartamental del Amaranto." La Paz: Unidad de Tecnología Alimentaria Boliviana del CIEP.

CIEP-UTAB (Centro de Investigación de Energía y Población and Unidad de Tecnología Alimentaria Boliviana del CIEP). 1991. "Primer Encuentro de Productores Campesinos de Amaranto." La Paz.

CIP (Centro Internacional de la Papa). 1992. "CIP to Launch Global Assault on Potato Pests Using Environmentally-Friendly Methods." CIP Working Paper. Lima, Peru.

CIPCA. 1991. *Por una Bolivia Diferente: Aportes para un Proyecto Histórico Popular*. Cuadernos de Investigación 34. La Paz.

————. 1992. *Futuro de la Comunidad Campesina*. Cuadernos de Investigación 35. La Paz.

COICA—OXFAM-America. 1996. *Amazonia: Economía Indígena y Mercado: Los Desafíos del Desarrollo Autónomo*. Quito: FIDA.

Coleman, J. 1988. "Social Capital in the Creation of Human Capital." *American Journal of Sociology* 94 (supplement): 5.95–120.

Conaghan, Catherine, and James M. Malloy. 1994. *Unsettling Statecraft, Democracy, and Neoliberalism in the Central Andes*. Pittsburgh: University of Pittsburgh Press.

Conaghan, Catherine, James M. Malloy, and Luis A. Abugattas. 1990. "Business and the Boys: The Politics of Neoliberalism in the Central Andes." *Latin American Research Review* 2 (no. 25): 3–30.

Condarco Morales, Ramiro. 1965. *Zarate, El "Temible" Willka: Historia de la Rebelión Indígena de 1899*. La Paz: Talleres Gráficos Bolivianos.

Condori, A. M. 1988. *Nayan Uñatatawi: Mí Despertar*. La Paz: HISBOL.

Contreras, Baspineiro. 1991. *Etapa de una Larga Marcha*. La Paz: Asociación Aquí Avance, Educación Radiofónica de Bolivia.

CORDECH-COTESU (Corporación de Desarrollo de Chuquisaca and Corporación Técnica Suiza). 1992. *Plan Agroforestal de Chuquisaca, Informe Annual*. Sucre: CORDECH.

Crandon Malamud, Libbet. 1991. *From the Fat of Our Souls: Social Change, Political Process, and Medical Pluralism in Bolivia*. Berkeley: University of California Press.

CSUTCB (Confederación Sindical Única de Trabajadores Campesinos de Bolivia). 1983. *Bolivia, Plataforma de Lucha de los Explotados del Campo en su Segundo Congreso de Unidad Campesino*. La Paz.

————.1984a. *Después de Cuatro Siglos de Opresión*. La Paz.

————. 1984b. "Ley Agraria Fundamental." Presented at Congreso Nacional de Cochabamba, Cochabamba, January 16–20.

————. 1988. *I Congreso Extraordinario: Informes y Conclusiones.* Potosí, July 11–17.

————. 1989. *Debate sobre Documentos Políticos y Asamblea de Nacionalidades.* La Paz: CEDLA.

Cuadernos de Justicia y Paz. 1975. *La Masacre del Valle Enero 1974.* La Paz.

Cuadros, Diego. Ed. 1991. *La Revuelta de las Nacionalidades.* La Paz: UNITAS.

Cultural Survival Quarterly. 1987. "Grassroots Economic Development." Vol. 11 (no. 1).

Cusack, David F. 1983. "Quinoa: Grain of the Incas." Presentation to the 1983 Annual Meeting of the American Association for the Advancement of Science, Detroit, Michigan, May 26–31.

Dandler, Jorge. 1982. *El Sindicalismo Campesino en Bolivia, Cambios Estructurales en Ucurena, 1935–1952.* Cochabamba: CERES.

————. 1984. "Campesinado y Reforma Agraria en Cochabamba (1952–1953): Dinámica de un Movimiento Campesino en Bolivia." In *Bolivia: La Fuerza Histórica del Campesinado,* ed. Fernando Calderón and Jorge Dandler. Cochabamba: UN Research Institute for Social Development/CERES.

Dandler, Jorge, José Blanes, Julio Prudencio, and Jorge Muñoz. 1987. *El Sistema Agro-Alimentario en Bolivia.* La Paz: CERES.

Dandler, Jorge, and C. Sage. 1985. "What is Happening to Andean Potatoes?" *Development Dialogue* 1: 125–138.

Dávalos, Jhonny, Verónica Cereceda, and Gabriel Martínez. 1992. *Textiles Tarabuco, Proyecto Norte Chuquisaca CORDECH.* Sucre: La Madona.

de Janvry, Alain. 1981. *The Agrarian Question and Reformism in Latin America.* Baltimore, Md.: Johns Hopkins University Press.

Delgado, Freddy. 1990. *Agroecología y Saber Andino.* Cochabamba: AGRUCO-PRATEC.

D'Emilio, L. 1991a. "Bolivia: La Conquista de la Escuela. El Proyecto Educativo de los Guaraní-Chiriguanos." In *Etnias, Educación y Cultura: Defendemos lo Nuestro,* ed. ILDIS-Bolivia. La Paz: Editorial Nueva Sociedad.

————. 1991b. "Educación Bilingüe: Estrategia, Conquista, o Derecho." *Revista Unitas* 3: 21–27. [La Paz]

De Moya, Viviana Ortiz, and Marcos Van Rijckeghem. 1993. *En Defensa de la Carne de Llama/Alpaca.* Oruro, Bolivia: Centro Diocesano de Pastoral Social.

Dennis, Marie. 1997. "Bolivia: The Social Consequences of Debt." *NACLA Report on the Americas* 31 (no. 3, November/December): 37–41.

de Papic, Bonnie Lynn. 1988. *Curaciones Simples y Eficientes.* 6 vols. La Paz: CALA.

De Vries, Albert. 1998. *Territorios Indígenas en las Tierras Bajas de Bolivia: Un Análisis de su Estado a 1998.* Santa Cruz: CIDOB, SNV, and CPTI.

Diario. [La Paz.] 1987. "Se Dispuso Prohibir Exportación del Patrimonio Camélido del País." August 19.

Dunkerley, James 1984. *Rebellion in the Veins: Political Struggle in Bolivia 1952–1982.* London: Verso.

Earls, John. 1991. *Ecología y Agronomía en los Andes.* La Paz: HISBOL.

Economist. 1996. "The Poor and the Rich." Pp. 23–25. May 25.

Eder, George Jackson. 1969. *Inflation and Development in Latin America: A Case Study of Bolivia.* Ann Arbor: University of Michigan Press.

Ellison, Katherine. 1997. "The Seeds of Biopiracy?" *Miami Herald,* Section F. November 19.

Erickson, Clark. 1995. "Archaeological Methods for the Study of Ancient Landscapes of the Llanos de Mojos in the Bolivian Amazon." In *Archaeology in the Lowland American Tropics: Current Analytical Methods and Applications,* ed. Peter W. Stahl. Cambridge: Cambridge University Press.

———. 1996. *Investigación Arqueológica del Sistema Agrícola de los Camellones en la Cuenca del Lago Titicaca del Perú.* La Paz: PIWA.

Escobar, Arturo. 1991. "Anthropology and the Development Encounter: The Making and Marketing of Development Anthropology." *American Ethnologist* 18 (no. 4).

———. 1992. "Planning." In *The Development Dictionary: A Guide to Knowledge as Power,* ed. Wolfgang Sachs. New Jersey: Zed Books.

———. 1995. *Encountering Development: The Making and Unmaking of the Third World.* Princeton, N.J.: Princeton University Press.

Escobar, Gabriel. 1996. "Andean Heirlooms: Is There a Global Future for Peru's Weird Tubers?" *Washington Post,* p. E 1. January 10.

Esman, Milton, Royal Colle, Norman Uphoff, and Ellen Taylor with Forest Colburn, Douglas Gritzinger, Robert Hall, and Cynthia Moore. 1980. *Paraprofessionals in Rural Development.* Special Series on Paraprofessionals, no. 1. Rural Development Committee, Cornell University.

Esman, Milton J., and Norman T. Uphoff. 1984. *Local Organizations: Intermediaries in Rural Development.* Ithaca, N.Y.: Cornell University Press.

Feraudy, Fabián II Yaksic, and Luis Tapia Meallas. 1997. *Bolivia, Modernizaciones Empobrecidas desde su Fundación a la Desrevolución.* La Paz: Muela de Diablo.

Ferguson, James. 1990. *Anti-Politics Machine: Development, Depoliticization and Bureaucratic Power in Lesotho.* Cambridge: Cambridge University Press.

FIDA (Fondo Internacional de Desarrollo Agrícola). 1985. *Propuesta para una Estrategia de Desarrollo Rural de Base Campesina, Informe de la Misión Especial de Programación a la República de Bolivia, 1985.* 2 vols. La Paz: CEDLA and FIDA.

Fischer, Edward F., and R. McKenna Brown. Ed. 1996. *Maya Cultural Activism in Guatemala.* Austin: University of Texas Press.

Flores, Gonzalo. 1984a. "Estado, Políticas Agrarias y Luchas Campesinas: Revisión de una Década en Bolivia." In *Bolivia: La Fuerza Histórica del Campesinado,* ed.

Fernando Calderón and Jorge Dandler. Cochabamba: UN Research Institute for Social Development/CERES.

———. 1984b. "Levantamientos Campesinos durante el Período Liberal (1900–1920)." In *Bolivia: La Fuerza Histórica del Campesinado,* ed. Fernando Calderón and Jorge Dandler. Cochabamba: UN Research Institute for Social Development/ CERES.

Flores Apaza, Policarpio, Fernando Montes, Elizabeth Andía, and Fernando Huanacuni. 1999. *El Hombre que Volvió a Nacer, Vida, Saberes, de una Amawt'a de Tiwanaku.* La Paz: Plural.

Fortun, Julia Elena. 1968. "Indigenismo en Bolivia." *América Indígena* 28 (no. 4).

———. 1972. "Tecnificación del Campesinado." *América Indígena* 32 (no. 3, July-September).

Frank, André Gunder. 1969. *Capitalism and Underdevelopment in Latin America.* New York: Modern Reader.

Fredrick, R. G. 1977. "The United States Aid to Bolivia 1953–1972." Doctoral dissertation, University of Maryland.

Freire, Paulo. 1970. *Pedagogía del Oprimido.* Montevideo: Siglo XXI.

Friedman, Thomas, L. 1999. *The Lexus and the Olive Tree: Understanding Globalization.* New York: Farrar Straus Giroux.

Fundación ASUR. 1993. "Evaluación del Proyecto Textil." Unpublished document.

Gandarillas, Humberto. 1971. *Los Cultivos Andinos en el Altiplano de Bolivia.* Boletín Técnico No. 3. La Paz: Sociedad de Ingenieros Agrónomos de Bolivia. February.

García, Antonio. 1970. "Agrarian Reform and Social Development in Bolivia." In *Agrarian Problems and Peasant Movements in Latin America,* ed. Rodolfo Stavenhagen. Garden City, N.J.: Anchor Books, Doubleday.

García-Rodríguez, L. Enrique. 1982. "Structural Change and Development Policy in Bolivia." In *Modern-Day Bolivia: Legacy of the Revolution and Prospects for the Future,* ed. Jerry R. Ladman. Tempe, Ariz.: Center for Latin American Studies, Arizona State University.

Giesel, Elizabeth, and Claudia Hernandez. 1997. "De Apéndice a Línea Transversal: Una Experiencia de Trabajo con Género en los Ayllus Calcheños." In *Teorías y Prácticas de Género, una Conversación Dialéctica,* ed. Susan Paulson and Monica Crespo. La Paz.: Embajada de los Países Bajos.

Gill, Leslie. 1987. *Peasants, Entrepreneurs, and Social Change: Frontier Development in Lowland Bolivia.* Boulder: Westview Press.

———. 1994. *Precarious Dependencies: Gender, Class, and Domestic Service in Bolivia.* New York: Columbia University Press.

Gisbert, Teresa, Silvia Arze, and Martha Cajías. 1986. *Arte Textil y Mundo Andino.* La Paz: Gisbert.

Godoy, R. A. 1984. "Ecological Degradation and Agricultural Intensification in the Andean Highlands." *Human Ecology* 12 (no. 4).

Godoy, R. A., and M. Franco. 1992. "Small Potatoes and Big Ears: Neglect and Biases in Bolivia's Agricultural Research." Copy of manuscript on file, Harvard Institute of International Development.

Goldstein, Daniel M. 1996. "The Local (Re)Production of National Culture: Performing the Nation's Folklore in Villa Sebastián Pagador (Cochabamba, Bolivia)." Paper presented at the 95th Annual Meeting of the American Anthropological Association, San Francisco, November 20–24.

Goulet, Denis. 1981. "In Defense of Cultural Rights: Technology, Tradition, and Conflicting Models of Rationality." *Human Rights Quarterly* [Johns Hopkins University Press].

———. 1992. "Development: Creator and Destroyer of Values." *World Development* 20 (no. 3): 467–75.

———. 1994. "Development and Cultural Resistance in Latin America: Prospects." In *Futures of Culture*. Paris: UNESCO.

Graham, Carol. 1998. "The Capitalization and Popular Participation Program in Bolivia." In *Private Markets for Public Goods: Raising the Stakes in Economic Reform*. Washington, D.C.: Brookings Institution.

Grebe Horst, López. 1998. "La Crisis del Patrón del Desarrollo y la Reforma del Estado." In *Las Reformas Estructurales en Bolivia*, ed. Juan Carlos Chávez Corrales. La Paz: Fundación Milenio.

Grupo de Estudios Andrés Ibañez. 1983. *Tierra, Estructura Productiva y Poder en Santa Cruz*. Santa Cruz.

Hahn, Dwight R. 1996. "The Use and Abuse of Ethnicity: The Case of the Bolivian CSUTCB." *Latin American Perspectives* 23 (no. 2, Spring): 91–106.

Hale, Charles Rice. 1981. "Subsistence Production, Capitalist Exchange, and Indigenous Self-determination: A Study of a Bolivian Herding Community." Bachelor of Arts Thesis, Harvard University.

Harvey, David. 1990. *The Condition of Postmodernity. An Enquiry into the Origins of Cultural Change*. Oxford: Blackwell Press.

Hatch, J. 1983. "Nuestros Conocimientos: Prácticas Agropecuarias Tradicionales en Bolivia, vol. 1: Región Altiplano." La Paz: Ministerio de Agricultura y Asuntos Campesinos (MACA), Agencia Internacional de Desarrollo (AID), and Rural Development Services (RDS).

Healy, Kevin. 1981. "Old Traditions and New Practices: Ayni Ruway of Bolivia." *Journal of the Inter-American Foundation* (no. 1).

———. 1982. *Caciques y Patrones: Una Experiencia de Desarrollo Rural en el Sud de Bolivia*. Cochabamba: CERES.

———. 1985. "On the Road in Rural Bolivia: In Search of the Small, the Brave, and the Beautiful." *Grassroots Development* 9 (no. 1).

————. 1986a. "The Boom within the Crisis: Some Recent Effects of Foreign Cocaine Markets on Bolivian Rural Society and Economy." In *Coca and Cocaine: Effects of People and Policy in Latin America,* ed. Deborah Pacini and Christine Franqemont. Cambridge, Mass.: Cultural Survival.

————. 1986b. *Desarrollo Rural y Sindicalismo Campesino.* La Paz: HISBOL.

————. 1987. "From Field to Factory: Vertical Integration in Bolivia." *Grassroots Development* 11 (no. 2).

————. 1988. "A Recipe for Sweet Success: Consensus and Self-Reliance in the Alto Beni." *Grassroots Development* 12 (no. 1).

————. 1991. "Animating Grassroots Development: Women's Popular Education in Bolivia." *Grassroots Development* 15 (no. 1).

————. 1992. "Back to the Future: Ethno-Development among the Jalq'a." *Grassroots Development* 16 (no. 2).

————. 1994a. "Recovery of Cultural Resources for Development in Latin America." In *1994 Festival of American Folklife.* Washington, D.C.: Smithsonian Institution. July.

————. 1994b. "The Shape of Things to Come: CEMSE and the Reinvention of Bolivian Public Education." *Grassroots Development* 18 (no. 2).

————. 1996. "Ethnodevelopment of Indigenous Bolivian Communities, Emerging Paradigms." In *Tiwanaku and Its Hinterland: Archaeology and Paleoecology of an Andean Civilization,* ed. Alan Kolata. Washington, D.C.: Smithsonian Institution Press.

Healy, Kevin, and Susan Paulson. 2000. "Political Economies of Identity in Bolivia, 1952–1998." *Journal of Latin American Anthropology* (spring).

Healy, Kevin, and Elayn Zorn. 1994. "Taquile's Homespun Tourism." In *Cultural Expression and Grassroots Development: Cases from Latin America and the Caribbean,* ed. Charles David Kleymeyer.

Heath, Dwight B. 1959. "Commercial Agriculture and Land Reform in the Bolivian Oriente." *Inter-American Economic Affairs* 13 (no. 2, autumn).

————. 1960. "Land Tenure and Social Organization: An Ethnohistorical Study of the Bolivian Oriente." *Inter-American Affairs* 13 (no. 4, spring).

Heath, Dwight B., Charles J. Erasmus, and Hans C. Buechler. 1959. "Land Reform in Bolivia." *Inter-American Affairs* 12 (no. 4): 5–26.

————. 1969. *Land Reform and Social Revolution in Bolivia.* New York: Praeger.

Heijdra, Hans. 1997. *Participación y Exclusión Indígena en al Desarrollo, Banco Mundial, CIDOB y al Pueblo Ayoreo en el Proyecto Tierras Bajas del Este de Bolivia.* Pueblos Indígenas de las Tierras Bajas de Bolivia, vol. 6. Santa Cruz de la Sierra.

Heilman, Lawrence C. 1982. "U.S. Development Assistance to Rural Bolivia, 1941–1974: The Search for a Development Strategy." Doctoral dissertation, American University, Washington, D.C.

Henkel, Ray. 1982. "The Move to the Oriente: Colonization and Environmental Impact." In *Modern-Day Bolivia: Legacy of the Revolution and Prospects for the Future,* ed. Jerry R. Ladman. Tempe, Ariz.: Center for Latin American Studies, Arizona State University.

Hirsch, Silvia María. 1995. "The Emergence of Indigenous Political Organizations among the Guaraní Indians of Bolivia and Argentina: A Transnational and Comparative Perspective." Presented at the 94th Annual Meeting of the American Anthropological Association, Washington, D.C., November 15–19.

Hoopes, R.W., and C. Sage. 1982. "Limiting Factors in Bolivian Potato Production and Prospects for Improvement." Working Paper No. 005/82. La Paz: Consortium for International Development.

Hoy. 1998. "VR-9 Pide Informe Oficial sobre Política para Ganadería Camélida." La Paz, November 30.

Huanca, Tomas. 1989. *El Yatiri en la Comunidad Aymara.* La Paz: Ediciones CADA.

———. 1991a. "Bolivia: Bilingüalismo y Enseñanza Bilingüe." In *Etnias, Educación y Cultura: Defendemos lo Nuestro,* ed. ILDIS. La Paz: Editorial Nueva Sociedad.

———. 1991b. *Jilirinaksan Arsuwipa: Testimonios de Nuestros Mayores.* La Paz: Taller de Historia Oral Andina.

Huizer, Gerrit. 1972. *The Revolutionary Potential of Peasants in Latin America.* Lexington, Ky.: Lexington Books.

Huntington, Samuel P. 1996. *The Clash of Civilizations and the Remaking of World Order.* New York: Simon and Schuster.

Hurtado, Javier. 1986. *El Katarismo.* La Paz: HISBOL.

IAF (Inter-American Foundation). 1977. *They Know How . . . : An Experiment in Development Assistance* Washington, D.C.

IBTA (Instituto Boliviano de Tecnología Agropecuaria). 1994. "Primera Reunión Internacional de Recursos Genéticos de Papa, Raíces, y Tubérculos Andinos, 7–10 de febrero 1994 Cochabamba, Bolivia: Memorias." Programa de Investigación de la Papa (PROINPA), Convenio IBTA-CIP-COTESU. Cochabamba: PROINPA.

ILDIS (Instituto Latinoamericano de Investigaciones Sociales). Ed. 1995. *Árboles y Alimentos en Comunidades Indígenas.* La Paz: Publicidad Arte Producciones (PAP).

ILDIS-UCB. 1996. *Aspectos Sociales de Diez Años de Ajuste* La Paz.

International Labor Review. 1962. "The Use of Social Promoters at the Puno Base of the Andean Indian Program." Vol. 86 (no. 3, September).

Iriarte, P. Gregorio. 1989. *Análisis Crítico de la Realidad: Esquemas de Interpretación.* La Paz: Secretariado Nacional de Pastoral Local (SENPAS).

Izko, Xavier. 1992. *La Doble Frontera: Ecología, Política y Ritual en el Altiplano Central.* La Paz: HISBOL, CERES.

Jelin, Elizabeth. 1987. "Ciudadanía e Identidad: Una Reflexion Final." In *Ciudadanía e Identidad: Las mujeres en los Movimientos Sociales Latino-americanos.* Geneva: UNRISD.

Jones, James. 1980. "Conflict between Whites and Indians on the Llanos de Moxos, Beni Department: A Case Study of Development from the Cattle Regions of the Bolivian Oriente." Doctoral dissertation, University of Florida, Gainesville.

————. 1984. "Native Peoples of Lowland Bolivia." In *Frontier Expansion in Amazonia,* ed. Marianne Schmink and Charles H. Wood. Gainesville: University of Florida Press.

————. 1990. "A Native Movement and March in Eastern Bolivia: Rationale and Response." *Bulletin of the Institute for Development Anthropology* 8 (no. 2).

————. 1997. "Development: Reflections from Bolivia." *Human Organizations* 56 (no. 11, spring): 111–20.

Kaimowitz, David, Graham Thiele, and Pablo Pacheco. 1987. "The Effects of Structural Adjustment on Deforestation and Forest Degradation in Lowland Bolivia." Unpublished manuscript.

Kazan, Alexander Philip. 1999. "Neo-liberalism, Export Booms, and Rural Poverty in Santa Cruz, Bolivia." Master's thesis, Georgetown University, Washington, D.C.

Kietz, Renate. 1992. *Compendio del Amaranto: Rescate y Revitalización en Bolivia.* La Paz: ILDIS.

Klein, Herbert S. 1982. *Bolivia: The Evolution of a Multi-Ethnic Society.* New York: Oxford University Press.

Kleymeyer, David. Ed. 1994. *Cultural Expression in Grassroots Development.* Boulder, Colo.: Lynne Reinner.

Kolata, Alan L. 1993. *The Tiwanaku: Portrait of an Andean Civilization.* Cambridge: Blackwell.

————. Ed. 1996. *Tiwanaku and Its Hinterland: Archaeology and Paleoecology of an Andean Civilization.* Washington, D.C.: Smithsonian Institution Press.

Korten, David C. 1990. *Getting to the 21st Century: Voluntary Action and the Global Agenda.* West Hartford, Conn.: Kumarian Press.

Krishna, Anirudh, Norman Uphoff, and Milton J. Esman. Eds. 1996. *Reasons for Hope: Instructive Experiences in Rural Development.* West Hartford, Conn.: Kumarian Press.

Ladman, Jerry R. 1982. "The Political Economy of the Economic Miracle of the Banzer Regime." In *Modern-Day Bolivia: Legacy of the Revolution and Prospects for the Future,* ed. Jerry R. Ladman. Tempe, Ariz.: Center for Latin American Studies, Arizona State University.

Lagos, María Laura. 1994. *Autonomy and Power: The Tyranny of Class and Culture in Rural Bolivia.* Philadelphia: University of Pennsylvania Press.

Langer, Erick D. 1988. "El Liberalismo y la Abolición de la Comunidad Indígena en el Siglo XIX." *Historia y Cultura* 14 (October). [La Paz]

———. 1989. *Economic Change and Rural Resistance in Southern Bolivia, 1880–1930.* Stanford, Calif.: Stanford University Press.

———. 1990. "Taking Pears from the Elm Trees: A History of Franciscan Mission among Chiriguano Indians 1840–1949." Unpublished manuscript.

Larrazábal, Hernando. 1996. "La Pequeña y Microempresa en Diez Años de Ajuste." In *Aspectos Sociales de Diez Años de Ajuste.* La Paz: ILDIS-UCB.

Larson, Brooke. 1995. "Andean Communities, Political Cultures, and Markets: The Changing Contours of a Field." In *Ethnicity, Markets, and Migration in the Andes: At the Crossroads of History and Anthropology,* ed. Brooke Larson and Olivia Harris with Enrique Tandeter. Durham, N.C.: Duke University Press.

———. 1998. *Cochabamba, 1550–1900: Colonialism and Agrarian Transformation in Bolivia.* Durham, N.C.: Duke University Press.

Larson, Brooke, and Olivia Harris. 1995. *Ethnicity, Markets, and Migration in the Andes: At the Crossroads of History and Anthropology,* with Enrique Tandeter. Durham. N.C.: Duke Unversity Press.

Lazarte, Jorge Mario, and Napoleón Pacheco. 1992. *Bolivia: Economía y Sociedad, 1982–1985.* La Paz: CEDLA.

Lehm Ardaya, Zulema. 1996. *Bolivia: El Pueblo Guarayo in Amazonia: Economía Indigena y Mercado los Desafios del Desarrollo Autónomo Quito.* Santa Cruz: CIDOB, COICA, and OXFAM-America.

———. 1999. *Milenarismo y Movimientos Sociales en la Amazonia Boliviana, La Búsqueda de la Loma Santa y la Marcha Indígena por el Territorio y la Dignidad.* Santa Cruz: APCOB, CIDDEBENI, and OXFAM-America.

Leonard, Olen. 1966. *El Cambio Económico y Social en Cuatro Comunidades del Altiplano de Bolivia.* Mexico: Instituto Indigenista Interamericano.

López, Jaime, Willer Flores, and Catherine Letourneux. 1992. *Lliqllas Chayantakas, Programa de Autodesarrollo Campesino (PAC).* La Paz: Potosí/Ruralter.

———.1993. *Laymi Salta, Programa de Autodesarrollo Campesino (PAC).* La Paz: Potosí/Ruralter.

Luykx, Aurolyn. 1999. *The Citizen Factory: Schooling and Cultural Production in Bolivia.* Albany: University of New York Press.

MACA (Ministerio de Asuntos Campesinos y Agropecuario). 1974. *Diagnóstico del Sector Agropecuario.* 2 vols. La Paz: MACA, Oficina de Planeamiento Sectorial.

———. 1985. *Encuesta de Pronóstico del Sector Agropecuario.* La Paz: MACA, Oficina de Planeamiento Sectorial.

Malloy, James. 1970. *Bolivia: The Uncompleted Revolution.* Pittsburgh: University of Pittsburgh Press.

Malloy, James, and Eduardo Gamarra. 1988. *Revolution and Reaction: Bolivia 1964–1985.* New Brunswick: Transaction Books.

Mamani, Mauricio. 1988. "Agricultura a los 4 mil metros." In *Raíces de América: El Mundo Aymará,* ed. Xavier Albó. Madrid: UNESCO.

Mamani Condori, Carlos B. 1991. *Taraqu: 1866–1935, Masacre, Guerra y "Renovación" en La Biografía de Eduardo L. Nina Qhispi.* La Paz: Ediciones Aruwiyiri.

Martínez P., Juan Luis. 1990. *Contribuciones sobre Educación Intercultural Bilingüe en Bolivia.* La Paz: CEBIAE.

Maybury-Lewis, David, and Theodore Macdonald, Jr. 1997. "25 Years of the Indigenous Movement: The Americas and Australia." *Cultural Survival Quarterly* 21 (no. 2, summer).

Mayer, Enrique, Manual Glave, Stephen S. Brush, and Edward Taylor. 1992. *La Chacra de Papas, Economía and Ecología.* Lima: Centro Peruano de Investigación Social (CEPES).

Mayorga, René Antonio. 1994. "Outsiders y Kataristas en el Sistema de Partidos: La Política de Pactos y la Gobernabilidad en Bolivia." In *Los Partidos en América Latina en la Década de los 90,* ed. Carina Perelli. San José.

McCamant, John F. 1992. "Quinoa's Roundabout Journey to World Use." In *Chilies to Chocolate: Food the Americas Gave the World,* ed. Nelson Foster and Linda S. Cordell. Tucson: University of Arizona Press.

Menchú, Rigoberta. 1998. *Crossing Borders.* New York: Verso.

Mendes Morales, Armando. 1996. "Financiamiento Externo, Deuda, Exportaciones y Sostenibilidad Financiera del Ajuste." In *Aspectos Sociales de Diez Años de Ajuste.* ILDIS-UCB.

Ministerio de Asuntos Campesinos y Agropecuarios. 1987. *Resolución Ministerial No. 251.* La Paz. August.

Mink'a (Revista Trimestral de Collasuyo). 1977. "Collasuyo: No." *Invasión Racista* (no. 7).

Miranda, L., and D. Moricio. 1992. "Memorias de un Olvido: Testimonios de Vida Urus-Muratos." La Paz: HISBOL.

Mirtenbaum, Chil Zenamon. 1986. "The Administration of Resettlement in Bolivia." Doctoral thesis, Cornell University.

Morales, Anaya Ramiro. 1984. *Desarrollo y Pobreza en Bolivia: Análisis de la Situación del Niño y la Mujer.* La Paz: UNICEF.

———. 1996. "La Evolución de la Pobreza y de la Distribución del Ingreso durante el Ajuste." In *Aspectos Sociales de Diez Años de Ajuste.* La Paz: ILDIS-UCB.

Moreno, Claribel Catoira. 1994. *Nuestra Casa Grande.* Santa Cruz, Bolivia: Confederación Indígena del Oriente, Chaco y Amazonia de Bolivia (CIDOB) and Fondo de las Naciones para la Infancia (UNICEF).

Morgan, Dan. 1979. *Merchants of Grain.* New York: Penguin Press.

Murra, John V. 1975. *Formaciones Económicas y Políticas del Mundo Andino.* Lima: Instituto de Estudios Peruanos.

———. 1978. *La Organización Económica del Estado Inca.* Mexico: Siglo XXI.

———. 1988. "El Aymara Libre de Ayer." In *Raíces de América: El Mundo Aymara,* ed. Xavier Albó. Madrid: UNESCO.

National Research Council. 1989. *Lost Crops of the Incas: Little-Known Plants of the Andes with Promise for Worldwide Cultivation.* Washington, D.C.: National Academy Press.

Nelson, Michael. 1973. *The Development of Tropical Lands.* Baltimore, Md.: Johns Hopkins University Press.

Niekerk, Niko van. 1992. *La Cooperación Internacional y la Persistencia de la Pobreza en los Andes Bolivianos.* La Paz: UNITAS.

OIT (Organización Internacional de Trabajo). 1989. *Convenio No. 169 sobre Pueblos Indígenas y Tribales en Países Independientes.* Lima: Oficina Regional de la OIT para América Latina y el Caribe.

Olívares, Mirtha, Valeria Budinich, and Eric Hyman. 1996. "Evaluación de Impacto del Proyecto 'Producción y Procesamiento de Fibra de Alpaca.'" Washington, D.C.: Appropriate Technology International.

Oliver, Gregorio Machicado. 1993. *El Mercado y el Comercio de la Carne de Llama en las Ciudades de La Paz y El Alto.* La Paz: CIPCA. May.

Orlove, Benjamin, S. John, C. H. Chiang, and Mark A. Cane. 2000. "Forecasting Andean Rainfall and Crop Yield from the Influence of El Niño on Pleiades Visibility." *Nature* (January).

Ortíz de Moya, Viviana, and Marcos Van Rijckeghem. 1993. *En Defensa de la Carne de Llama / Alpaca.* Oruro, Bolivia: EDIPAS.

Otra, Andrew. 1995. "From Theologies of Liberation to Theologies of Inculturation: Aymara Catechists and the Second Evangelization in Highland Bolivia." In *Organized Religion in the Political Transformation of Latin America.* Lanham, Md.: New York University Press of America.

Pacheco, Diego. 1992. *El Indianismo y los Indios Contemporáneos en Bolivia.* La Paz: HISBOL/MUSEF.

Pacheco, Mario Napoleón. 1998. "Apuntes sobre las Transformaciones de la Economía Boliviana, 1986–1997." In *Reflexiones sobre el Crecimiento Económico,* ed. Baldivia, José Urdininea, Jordán Rolando Pozo, Mercado Alejandro F. Salazar, and Mario Napoleón Pacheco Torrico. La Paz: Fundación Milenio.

Paige, Jeffrey. 1996. "Land Reform and Agrarian Revolution in El Salvador: Comment on Selipar and Fisher." *Latin American Research Review* 31 (no. 2):127–39.

Painter, Michael. 1995. "Upland-Lowland Production Linkages and Land Degradation in Bolivia." In *The Social Causes of Environmental Destruction in Latin America,* ed. Michael Painter and William H. Durham. Ann Arbor: University of Michigan Press.

———. 1998. "Economic Development and the Origins of the Bolivian Cocaine Industry." In *The Third Wave of Modernization in Latin America: Cultural Perspectives on Neoliberalism,* ed. Lynne Phillips. Wilmington, Del.: Jaguar Books.

Palacios, Félix. 1988. "Pastores de Llamas y Alpacas." In *Raíces de América: El Mundo Aymara,* ed. Xavier Albó. Madrid: UNESCO.

Paladines, Osvaldo, and Jorge Delgadillo. 1989. "Seminario Pastizales Andinos: Importancia, Producción y Mejoramiento." Centro de Investigación en Forrajes La Violeta, CIF, UMSS. Cochabamba, Bolivia, July 4–7.

Patch, Richard. 1960. "U.S. Assistance in a Revolutionary Setting." In *Social Change in Latin American Today.* Council of Foreign Relations. New York: Vintage Books.

Paulson, Susan, and Pamela Calla. 2000. "Gender and Ethnicity in Bolivian Politics: Transformation or Paternalism?" *Journal of Latin American Anthropology* (spring).

Pearse, Andrew. 1975. *The Latin American Peasant.* London: Frank Cass.

———. 1984. "Campesinado y Revolución: El Caso de Bolivia." In *Bolivia: La Fuerza Histórica del Campesinado,* ed. Fernando Calderón and Jorge Dandler. Cochabamba: UN Research Institute for Social Development and CERES.

Pérez, Elizardo. 1992. *Warisata: La Escuela—Allyu.* La Paz: CERES/HISBOL.

Pérez, Juan Antonio. 1996. "Commentary on 'Financiamiento Externo, Deuda, Exportaciones y Sostenibilidad Financiera del Ajuste.'" In *Aspectos Sociales de Diez Anos de Ajuste.* La Paz: ILDIS-UCB.

Pifarre, Francisco. 1989. *Historia de un Pueblo.* Cuadernos de Investigación 31. La Paz: CIPCA.

Platt, Tristan. 1982. *Estado Boliviano y Ayllu Andino: Tierra y Tributo en el Norte de Potosí.* Lima: Instituto de Estudios Peruanos.

———.1995. "Ethnic Calendars and Market Interventions among the Ayllus of Lipez during the 19th Century." In *Ethnicity, Markets, and Migrations in the Andes: At the Crossroads of History and Anthropology,* ed. Brooke Larson and Olivia Harris with Enrique Tandetar. Durham, N.C.: Duke University Press.

Point Four. 1960. *Point Four in Bolivia 1942–1960: Programs of Technical Cooperation and Economic Assistance of the United States of America and Bolivia.* U.S. Operations Mission to Bolivia. December.

Presencia. [La Paz.] 1991a. "Material Genético de Llamas y Alpacas Debe ser Protegido." July 10.

———. 1991b. "Diferentes Sectores Coinciden en que No Se Debe Exportar Llamas." September 13.

Preston, Pattie, and Albert Brown. 1988. *Agriculture Sector Assessment for Bolivia: Prepared for Agriculture and Rural Development Office USAID/ Bolivia Mission.* Chemonics International Consulting Division. January.

Programa Indígena (PNMD). 1994. *Primer Centro Indígena Rural de las Tierras Bajas Bolivianas.* La Paz.

Prudencio, Julio, and André Franqueville. 1995. *La Incidencia de la Ayuda Alimentaria en Bolivia.* UNITAS.

Prudencio, Julio, and Mónica Velasco. 1988. *La Defensa del Consumo, Crisis de Abastecimiento Alimentaria y Estrategias de Sobrevivencia.* La Paz: CERES.

Putnam, R. 1993a. "The Prosperous Community—Social Capital and Public Life." *American Prospect* 13: 35–42.

———. 1993b. *Making Democracy Work: Civic Traditions in Modern Italy.* Princeton, N.J.: Princeton University Press.

Ranaboldo, Claudia. 1986. *Los Campesinos Herbolarios Kallawayas.* La Paz: SEMTA.

———. 1987. *El Camino Perdido: Biografía del Líder Kallawaya Antonio Alvarez Mamani.* La Paz: Unidad de Investigación SEMTA.

Rasnake, Roger. 1988. *Domination and Cultural Resistance, Authority and Power among Andean People.* Durham, N.C.: Duke University Press.

Ravines, R. Ed. 1978. *Tecnología Andina.* Lima: Instituto de Estudios Peruanos and the Instituto de Investigación Tecnológica Industrial y de Normas Técnicas.

Raza, Werner. 1999. "La Experiencia Boliviana en Políticas de Sostenibilidad." *Procampo CID* (no. 83): 18–20.

Rea, J. 1985. "Recursos Fitogenéticos Agrícolas de Bolivia: Bases para Establecer el Sistema." Paper presented to the Comité Internacional de Recursos Fitogenéticos, La Paz.

———. 1991. "La Papa Amarga." Paper presented at the Primera Mesa Redonda sobre la Papa Amarga, La Paz.

Red Boliviana de Producción de Camélidos, PRODENA, and CERENA. 1995. "Lineamientos de Políticas para el Desarrollo Sostenible del Recurso Camélido." In *Documentos del Seminario Taller Nacional Realizado en La Paz, Bolivia, del 21 al 22 de Octubre de 1993.* La Paz.

Reed, Richard K. 1995. *Prophets of Agroforestry: Guaraní Communities and Commercial Gathering.* Austin: University of Texas Press.

Rens, Jeff. 1961. "Andean Program." *International Labour Review* 84 (no. 6, December): 423–61.

———. 1963. "The Development of the Andean Program and Its Future." *International Labour Review* 87 (no. 6, December): 547–64.

REPAAN. 1990. *Pastizales Andinos: Importancia, Producción y Mejoramiento.* Cochabamba: REPAAN.

Rice, Edward B. 1974. *Extension in the Andes: An Evaluation of Official U.S. Assistance to Agricultural Extension Services in Central and South America.* Cambridge, Mass.: MIT Press.

Rich, Bruce. 1994. *Mortgaging the Earth: The World Bank, the Environmental Impoverishment, and the Crisis of Development.* Boston: Beacon Press.

Riester, Juergen. 1976. *En Busca de la Loma Santa.* La Paz: Los Amigos del Libro.

———. 1984. "Textos Sagrados de los Guaraníes en Bolivia." La Paz: Los Amigos del Libro.

Ritchey-Vance, Marion. 1996. "Social Capital, Sustainability, and Working Democracy: New Yardsticks for Grassroots Development." *Grassroots Development* 20 (no. 1).

Rivera, J. 1991. "Bolivia: El SENALEP, Importancia y Limitaciones." In *Etnias, Educación y Cultura: Defendemos lo Nuestro,* ed. ILDIS. La Paz: Editorial Nueva Sociedad.

Rivera Cusicanqui, Silvia. 1984. *Oprimidos Pero no Vencidos, Luchas del Campesinado Aymara y Quechua, 1900–1980.* La Paz: Confederación Sindical Única de Trabajadores y Campesinos de Bolivia, HISBOL.

————. 1990. "Democracia liberal y democracia de ayllu, El caso del Norte de Potosí, Bolivia." In *El Difícil Camino Hacia la Democracia.* La Paz: ILDIS.

————. 1992. *Ayllus y Proyectos de Desarrollo en el Norte de Potosí.* La Paz: Taller de Historia Oral Andina, Aruwiyiri.

————. 1993. "La Raíz: Colonizadores y Colonizados." In *Violencias Encubiertas en Bolivia: Cultura y Política,* ed. Xavier Albó and Raúl Barrios Morón. La Paz: CIPCA-Aruwiyiri.

Rojas, Luis, H. Romero, R. Kusch, O. Onanativa, and O. Maidana. 1978. *Ayni Ruway.* Cochabamba: Ediciones América Profunda.

Rojas Ortuste, Gonzalo. 1989. "La Homogenización desde Arriba: El Problema Criollo-Europeo en América Latina." *América Indígena 49.*

————. 1994. *Democracia en Bolivia Hoy y Mañana: Enraizando la Democracia con las Experiencias de los Pueblos Indígenas.* La Paz: CIPCA.

Ruddell, Edward. 1995. "Growing Food for Thought: A New Model of Site-Specific Research from Bolivia." *Grassroots Development* 19 (no. 1): 18–26.

Ruddell, Edward D., and Robert C. Ainslie. 1996. "Building Linkages for Future Protection of the Environment: The Role of Participatory Technology Development." Santiago, Chile: World Neighbors.

Ruderfer, Isidor F. 1995a. "Preserving Native Andean Crops." La Paz: SEMTA.

————. 1995b. "Soil Conservation and Pasture Restoration in Bolivia's Central Andean Highlands: The SEMTA Initiatives." Unpublished manuscript.

————. 1995c. "Stables and Credit: SEMTA's Livestock Project in Bolivia's Central Andean Highlands." Unpublished manuscript.

————. 1996. "Greenhouses in Bolivia's Central Andean Highlands: Lessons from the SEMTA Experience." Unpublished manuscript.

Saignes, Thierry. 1983. "¿Quiénes son los Kallawaya? Nota sobre un Enigma Etnohistórico." *Revista Andina* (no. 2, December): 357–84.

Salmón, Josefa. 1997. *El Espejo Indígena: El Discurso Indigenista en Bolivia 1900–1956.* Colección Academia 5. La Paz: Plural.

Salomon, Frank. 1982. "Andean Ethnology in the 1970s: A Retrospective." *Latin American Research Review* 17 (no. 2): 75–128.

————. 1985. "The Historical Development of Andean Ethnology." *Mountain Research and Development* 5 (no. 1): 79–98.

Sammells, Clare. 1995. "The Negotiation of Ethnic Identity: Multifaceted Images of Llama Meat in La Paz, Bolivia." Unpublished honors thesis, Harvard University.

Sammells, Clare, and Lisa Markowitz. 1995. "Carne de Llama: Alta Viabilidad, Baja Visibilidad." In *Waira Pampa, un Sistema Pastoril Camélidos-Ovinos del Altiplano árido Boliviano,* ed. Didier Genin, Hans-Jachim Picht, Rudolfo Lizarazu, and Tito Rodríguez. La Paz: OSTOM, CONPAC, and IBTA.

Saravia C., Joaquín, and Godofredo Sandoval. 1991. *Jach'a Uru: ¿La Esperanza de un Pueblo?* La Paz: CEP and ILDIS.

Schwend, Lorand D. 1962. "An Indian Community Development Project in Bolivia." *América Indígena* 22 (no. 2, April).

Scott, Catherine V. 1995. *Gender and Development: Rethinking Modernization and Dependency Theory.* Boulder, Colo.: Lynne Rienner.

Scott, James. 1998. *Seeing Like a State: How Certain Schemes to Improve the Human Condition Have Failed.* New Haven, Conn.: Yale University Press.

Seyler, Dan. 1989. "The Economy." In *Bolivia: A Country Study,* ed. Rex. H. Hudson. Washington, D.C.: Library of Congress.

Smith, Richard Chase. 1993. "Indians, Forest Rights, and Lumber Mills." *Cultural Survival Quarterly* (spring).

SOBOMETRA (Sociedad Boliviana de Medicina Tradicional). 1986. *Congreso Nacional de Medicina Tradicional, El Kallawaya.* Vol. 1, no. 1. La Paz.

Soleri, Daniela, and David Cleveland with Donald Eriacho, Fred Bowannie, Jr., Andrew Laghty, and Zuni Community Members. 1994. "Gifts from the Creator: Intellectual Property Rights and Folk Crop Varieties." In *Intellectual Property Rights for Indigenous People: A Source Book,* ed. Tom Greaves. Oklahoma City: Society for Applied Anthropology.

Soria Choque, Vitaliano. 1992. "Los Caciques-Apoderados y la Lucha por la Escuela (1900–1952)." In *Educación Indígena: ¿Ciudadanía o Colonización?* ed. R. Choque, V. Soria, H. Mamami, E. Ticona, and R. Conde. La Paz: Ediciones Aruwiyiri.

Stavenhagen, Rodolfo. 1992. "Challenging the Nation-State in Latin America." *Journal of International Affairs* 34 (no. 2, winter).

Stearman, Allyn MacLean. 1985. *Camba and Kolla: Migration and Development in Santa Cruz, Bolivia.* Orlando: University of Central Florida Press.

Stephenson, Marcia. 1999. *Gender and Modernity in Andean Bolivia.* Austin: University of Texas Press.

Strobele-Gregor, Juliana. 1996. "Culture and Political Practice of the Aymara and Quechua in Bolivia: Autonomous Forms of Modernity in the Andes." *Latin American Perspectives* 23 (no. 2, Spring): 72–90.

Szkeley, Miguel. 1997. "La Pérdida y la Recuperación del Concepto de la Milpa Tradicional Frente a los Retos de la Globalización." Paper presented at the Latin American Studies Congress.

Tapia, Luciano (Lusiku Qhispi Mamani). 1995. *Ukhamawa Jakawisaxa (Así es Nuestra Vida): Autobiografía de un Aymara.* La Paz: HISBOL.

Tapia, Mario. 1990. "Cultivos Andinos Subexplotados y su Aporte a la Alimentación." Lima: Organización de las Naciones Unidas para la Agricultura y la Alimentación, Oficina Regional para América Latina.

Tapia, Mario, Humberto Gandarillas, Segundo Alandia, Armando Cardozo, Angel Mujica, René Ortiz, Víctor Otazu, Julio Rea, Basilio Salas, and Eulogio Zanabria. 1979. *La Quinua y la Kañiwa: Cultivos Andinos.* Bogota: CIID and IICA.

Televisión Universitaria Trinidad, Beni. "Por el Territorio y la Dignidad." (video)

Tendler, Judith. 1983a. *What to Think about Co-operatives: A Guide from Bolivia.* In collaboration with Kevin Healy and Carol Michaels O'Laughlin. Washington, D.C.: Inter-American Foundation.

————. 1983b. "What to Think about Co-operatives: A Guide from Bolivia." *Grassroots Development* 7 (no. 2): 19.

————. 1984. "The Well-Tempered Capitalist: Profiles from Some Bolivian Co-ops." *Grassroots Development* 8 (no. 2): 37.

————. 1999. "The Rise of Social Funds: What Are They a Model of?" With Rodrigo Serrano, for the MIT/UNDP Decentralization Project, Management and Governance Division. New York: United Nations Development Program. January.

THOA (Taller de Historia Oral Andina). 1988. "El Indio Santos Marka T'ula, Cacique Principal de Los Ayllus de Qallapa y Apoderado General de Las Comunidades Originarias de la República." La Paz.

————. 1993. *Federación de Ayllus—Provincia Ingavi, Estructura Orgánica.* La Paz: Ediciones Aruwiyiri.

Thomson, Sinclair Stephen. 1996. "Colonial Crisis, Community, and Andean Self-Rule: Aymara Politics in the Age of Insurgency (Eighteenth-Century La Paz)." Doctoral dissertation, University of Wisconsin, Madison.

Tichit, Muriel. 1991. *Los Camélidos en Bolivia.* La Paz: FADES.

Ticona, Esteban, Gonzalo Rojas Ortuste, and Xavier Albó. 1995. *Votos y Wiphalas: Campesinos y Pueblos Originarios en Democracia.* Cuadernos de Investigación 43. La Paz: CIPCA.

Torrico, Cassandra. 1995. "Evaluación del Proyecto Textil Jalq'a." La Fundación Interamericana. Unpublished document.

Torrico, José Isaac. 1982. "The Public Sector in Bolivian Agricultural Development." In *Modern-Day Bolivia: Legacy of the Revolution and Prospects for the Future,* ed. Jerry R. Ladman. Tempe, Ariz.: Center for Latin American Studies, Arizona State University.

Troll, C. 1968. "The Cordilleras of the Tropical Americas: Aspects of the Climatic, Phytogeographical and Agrarian Ecology." In *Geo-Ecology of the Mountainous Regions of the Tropical Americas,* ed. C. Troll. Colloquium Geographicum, Band 9. Bonn: Ferd. Dummlers Verlag.

UNITAS (Unión Nacional de Instituciones para el Trabajo de Acción Social). 1989. *Realidad pluricultural en el Oriente y Chaco Bolivianos.* La Paz: UNITAS-CEJIS.

———. 1991. *La revuelta de las Nacionalidades.* La Paz: UNITAS.

United Nations. 1951. "Report of the United Nations of Technical Assistance to Bolivia." New York.

Uphoff, Norman, and Milton J. Esman. 1984. *Local Organizations: Intermediaries in Rural Development.* Ithaca, N.Y.: Cornell University Press.

Uphoff, Norman, Milton J. Esman, and Anirudh Krishna. 1998. *Reasons for Success: Learning from Institutional Experiences in Rural Development.* West Hartford, Conn.: Kumarian Press.

Urioste, Miguel. 1987. *Segunda Reforma Agraria: Campesinos, Tierra y Educación Popular.* La Paz: CEDLA.

———. 1991. *Proyecto: Ley de Comunidades Campesinas e Indígenas.* La Paz: Ediciones MBL.

———. 1992. *Fortalecer las comunidades: Una Utopía Subversiva, Democrática y posible.* La Paz: AIPE.

USAID (United States Agency for International Development). 1974. *Agricultural Development in Bolivia, a Sector Assessment, Report of the United States AID Mission to Bolivia.* La Paz.

———. 1975. "Evaluation of the Training Component of the Servicio Nacional de Desarrollo de la Comunidad." Unpublished evaluation by Mel Buschman and Manfred Thullen. June.

———. 1976. "Cereals Development." Project Appraisal Report by Utah State University.

———. 1978. "End of Tour Report." Boyd Wennergren, Utah State University Mission in Bolivia.

USAID and Instituto Internacional para el Desarrollo y Medio Ambiente (IIPDMA). 1986. "Perfil Ambiental de Bolivia." Ed. C. E. Brockmann. Washington, D.C., and La Paz. July.

U.S. Congress. 1960. "Report of the Committee on Government Operations." Administration of United States Foreign Aid Programs in Bolivia. Washington, D.C.: United States Government Printing Office.

U.S. General Accounting Office. 1975. *Bolivia—An Assessment of U.S. Policies and Programs, Report to the Congress.* January 30.

Vacaflor Gonzalez, Jorge. 1997. "Legislación Indígena en Bolivia." In *Legislación Indígena,* ed. Jorge Luis Vacaflor Gonzalez, Asesor Jurídico en Asuntos Agrarios e Indígenas de la Vicepresidencia de la República. La Paz.

Valenzuela, Samuel, and Arturo Valenzuela. 1978. "Modernization and Dependency: Alternative Perspectives in the Study of Latin American Underdevelopment." *Comparative Politics* 10 (July): 543–57.

Vallejos, Fermín. 1995. *Tata Fermín: Llama Viva de un Yachaq*. Cochabamba: CENDA.

Van Cott, Donna Lee. 1994. "Indigenous Peoples and Democracy for Policymakers." In *Indigenous Peoples and Democracy in Latin America*, ed. Donna Lee Van Cott. New York: St. Martin's Press.

———. 1998. "Constitution-Making and Democratic Transformation: The Bolivian and Colombian Constitutional Reforms." Doctoral dissertation, Georgetown University.

Vargas, Jorge Caballero. 1993. "Los Eucaliptos Están de Luto." *ProCampo* (April).

Verhelst, Terry. 1990. *No Life without Roots: Culture and Development*. New Jersey: Zed Books.

Villa, Rojas. 1968. "Sobre la Orientación Antropológica de Expertos en Desarrollo de la Comunidad." *América Indígena* 23 (no. 3).

Wankar (Ramiro Reynaga Burgoa). 1978. *Tawantinsuyu: Cinco Siglos de Guerra Qheswaymara contra España*. La Paz: Centro de Coordinación y Promoción Campesina MINKA, Chukiapu-Kollasuya.

Warren, Michael, Jan Slikkerveer, and David Brokensha. 1995. "Introduction." In *The Cultural Dimension of Development*. London: Intermediate Technology Publications.

Weinstein, Barbara. 1983. *The Amazon Rubber Boom, 1850–1920*. Stanford, Calif.: Stanford University Press.

Wennergren, E. Boyd, and Morris D. Whitaker. 1975. *The Status of Bolivian Agriculture*. New York: Praeger.

Weschler, Lawrence. 1990. "A Reporter At Large." *The New Yorker*, December 10, pp. 86–136.

Whitaker, Morris D., and E. Boyd Wennergren. 1982. "Bolivia's Agriculture since 1960: Assessment and Prognosis." In *Modern-Day Bolivia: Legacy of the Revolution and Prospects for the Future*, ed. Jerry R. Ladman. Tempe, Ariz.: Center for Latin American Studies, Arizona State University.

Wilkie, James W. 1982. "U.S. Foreign Policy and Economic Assistance in Bolivia, 1948–1976." In *Modern-Day Bolivia: Legacy of the Revolution and Prospects for the Future*, ed. Jerry R. Ladman. Tempe, Ariz.: Center for Latin American Studies, Arizona State University.

Wolf, Eric. 1982. *Europe and the People without History*. Berkeley: University of California Press.

Wood, Rebecca. 1989. *Quinoa, the Supergrain: Ancient Food for Today*. New York: Harper and Row, Japan Publications.

World Bank. 1976. "Appraisal of Ingavi Rural Development Project in Bolivia." Report #936—BO. Projects Department—Latin America and the Caribbean Regional Office, International Bank for Reconstruction and Development, International Development Association. February 5.

————. 1984. *Bolivia:Agricultural Pricing and Investment Policies.* World Bank Country Study.

————. 1990. "Bolivia Poverty Report." Internal document, Report #8646.

————. 1993a. "National Resource Management in Bolivia: Thirty Years of Experience." Report #11-891. Operations Evaluation Department. May 19.

————. 1993b. "Pueblos Indígenas y Desarrollo en América Latina: Memorias del Segundo Taller Inter-Institucional." La Paz: División del Medio Ambiente Departamento Técnico. December.

————. 1996. "Bolivia, Poverty, Equity, and Income: Selected Policies for Expanding Earning Opportunities for the Poor." Report #15272-BO. Washington, D.C.: World Bank Latin American and the Caribbean Region.

————. 1998. "Memorandum of the President of the International Development Association and the International Finance Corporation to the Executive Directors on a Country Assistance Strategy of World Bank Group for the Republic of Bolivia." Report #17890-BO. May 21.

Worster, Donald. 1979. *Dust Bowl, The Southern Plains in the 1930s.* Oxford: Oxford University Press.

Yampara Huarachi, Símon. 1993. *Naciones Autóctonas Originarias: Vivir-Convivir en Tolerancia y Diferencia.* 3er. Seminario Amáutico del Área Andina Pre y Post V Centenario. La Paz: Ediciones CACA.

Yashar, Deborah J. 1998 "Contesting Citizenship: Indigenous Movements and Democracy in Latin America." *Comparative Politics* (October).

Zimmerer, Karl S. 1996. *Changing Fortunes: Bio-diversity and Peasant Livelihood in the Peruvian Andes.* Berkeley: University of California Press.

Zondag, Cornelius. 1982. "Bolivia's 1952 Revolution: Initial Impact and U.S. Involvement." In *Modern-Day Bolivia: Legacy of the Revolution and Prospects for the Future,* ed. Jerry R. Ladman. Tempe, Ariz.: Center for Latin American Studies, Arizona State University.

Zorn, Elayne. 1997. "Marketing Diversity: Global Transformation in Cloth and Identity in Highland Bolivia." Doctoral dissertation, Cornell University.

Zuniga, Edgar Apaza. 1980. "Conversatorio sobre la Problemática de los Criadores de Camélidos Sudamericanos en Bolivia." La Paz: Fomento de la Ganadería Camélida, Oficina de Apoyo Técnico. December.

Index